Interdisciplinary Studies in Human Rights

Volume 3

Editor-in-chief

Markus Krajewski
Faculty of Law, Friedrich-Alexander-University Erlangen-Nürnberg,
Erlangen, Germany

Series editors

Petra Bendel
Center for Area Studies, Friedrich-Alexander-University Erlangen-Nürnberg,
Erlangen, Germany

Heiner Bielefeldt
Institute of Political Science, Friedrich-Alexander-University
Erlangen-Nürnberg, Erlangen, Germany

Andreas Frewer
Institute for History and Ethics of Medicine, Friedrich-Alexander-University
Erlangen-Nürnberg, Erlangen, Germany

Manfred L. Pirner
Religious Education, Friedrich-Alexander-University Erlangen-Nürnberg,
Nürnberg, Germany

Human rights are one of the normative cornerstones of contemporary international law and global governance. Due to the complexities of actual or potential violations of human rights and in light of current crises, new and interdisciplinary research is urgently needed. The series Interdisciplinary Studies in Human Rights recognizes the growing importance and necessity of interdisciplinary research in human rights. The series consists of monographs and collected volumes addressing human rights research from different disciplinary and interdisciplinary perspectives, including but not limited to philosophy, law, political science, education, and medical ethics. Its goal is to explore new and contested questions such as the extraterritorial application of human rights and their relevance for non-state actors, as well as the philosophical and theoretical foundations of human rights. The series also addresses policy questions of current interest including the human rights of migrants and refugees, LGBTI rights, and bioethics, as well as business and human rights.

The series editors are Members of the Centre for Human Rights Erlangen-Nürnberg (CHREN), an interdisciplinary research center at Friedrich-Alexander-University Erlangen-Nürnberg. The Advisory Board brings together human rights scholars from a wide range of academic disciplines and regional backgrounds. The series welcomes suggestions for publications of academic research falling into the series subject matter.

More information about this series at http://www.springer.com/series/15339

Isabel Feichtner • Markus Krajewski •
Ricarda Roesch

Editors

Human Rights
in the Extractive Industries

Transparency, Participation, Resistance

 Springer

Editors
Isabel Feichtner
School of Law
University of Würzburg
Würzburg, Germany

Markus Krajewski
Faculty of Law
University of Erlangen-Nuremberg
Erlangen, Germany

Ricarda Roesch
School of Law
University of Erlangen-Nuremberg
Erlangen, Germany

ISSN 2509-2960   ISSN 2509-2979   (electronic)
Interdisciplinary Studies in Human Rights
ISBN 978-3-030-11381-0   ISBN 978-3-030-11382-7   (eBook)
https://doi.org/10.1007/978-3-030-11382-7

This Springer imprint is published by the registered company Springer Nature Switzerland AG.
The registered company address is: Gewerbestrasse 11, 6330 Cham, Switzerland

Preface

The idea of this book was first developed in the context of the research project "Human rights as standards for transnational economic law" funded by the German Research Foundation (Deutsche Forschungsgemeinschaft, DFG) at the Centre for Human Rights Erlangen-Nürnberg (CHREN) of Friedrich-Alexander-University Erlangen-Nürnberg. Later, the topic of this volume became the theme of an international conference entitled "Human Rights in the Extractive Industries" organised in Frankfurt by the Graduate Programme Law and Economics of Money and Finance (LEMF) of Goethe University Frankfurt am Main and CHREN in July 2016. This conference was generously supported by LEMF and the Wilhelm Merton Centre for European Integration and International Economic Order, both at Goethe University Frankfurt, the German Branch of the International Law Association (ILA) and the Dr. Alfred Vinzl-Stiftung Erlangen.

Many of the papers delivered and debated at the conference were the basis of the chapters of this book. As a result of the conference, papers were revised and partly rewritten and reviewed by the editors. A long process came finally to an end in the fall of 2018 when the final versions of the contributions to this volume were delivered and submitted to the publisher.

We would like to thank all those who helped in the long process from the first idea to the final book. Franziska Wohltmann, research fellow at the project "Human rights as standards for transnational economic law", provided enormous input and many invaluable suggestions in the conceptual phase leading to the conference. Ronja Hess and Pia Zecca took care of the tedious tasks of copy-editing the manuscripts according to the publishing guidelines. In addition, Franziska Oehm, Selina Roßgardt and Monika Wehrhahn were of extraordinary help during the Frankfurt conference. We hope that they as well as all readers of this book will feel that their efforts were worthwhile.

Würzburg, Germany
Erlangen, Germany
Erlangen, Germany
November 2018

Isabel Feichtner
Markus Krajewski
Ricarda Roesch

Contents

Introduction.. 1
Isabel Feichtner, Markus Krajewski, and Ricarda Roesch

Part I Transparency

**The Extractive Industries Transparency Initiative (EITI)
as a Human Rights Instrument: Potentials and Shortcomings**.......... 11
Heidi Feldt

United States Law and Conflict Minerals.......................... 27
Patrick J. Keenan

**The 2017 EU Conflict Minerals Regulation: A Promising European
Rite to Remove the Natural Resource Curse?**...................... 51
Karsten Nowrot

**Community Development Agreements as Tools for Local Participation
in Natural Resource Projects in Africa**............................ 77
Evaristus Oshionebo

**Stabilization Clauses and Human Rights: The Role of Transparency
Initiatives**.. 111
Sotonye Frank

**Improving Tax Strategy Transparency in the Extractive Industries
Sector for the Advancement of Human Rights**...................... 141
Wasima Khan

Part II Participation

**The Evolving Duty to Consult and Obtain Free Prior and Informed
Consent of Indigenous Peoples for Extractive Projects in the
United States and Canada**....................................... 169
Cathal M. Doyle

**Asserting the Principle of Free, Prior and Informed Consent (FPIC)
in Sub-Saharan Africa in the Extractive Industry Sector** 219
Pacifique Manirakiza

**The Corporate Responsibility to Respect Consultation Rights
in the Americas: How the Inter-American System Can Better
Promote Free, Prior, and Informed Consent** 247
C. Ignacio de Casas

**Free, Prior, and Informed Consent in the Philippines: A Fourth World
Critique** 281
Armi Beatriz E. Bayot

**Norm Contestation and (Non-)Compliance: The Right to Prior
Consultation and FPIC in the Extractive Industries** 311
Almut Schilling-Vacaflor

**State-Investor Contracts and Human Rights: Taking a Critical Look
at Transparency and Participation** 339
Nora Götzmann

**Disruption and Institutional Development: Corporate Standards
and Practices on Responsible Mining** 375
Radu Mares

Part III   Resistance

**Taking Sides in Scientific Research? The Struggle for the Right
to Participate in Public Decision-Making Related to a Mining
Project in Brazil** 415
Aline Rose Barbosa Pereira

**Building the Case for a Home-State Grievance Mechanism:
Law Reform Strategies in the Canadian Resource Justice Movement** . . . 455
Charis Kamphuis

**Transnational Human Rights and Environmental Litigation:
A Study of Case Law Relating to Shell in Nigeria** 511
Liesbeth F. H. Enneking

Editors and Contributors

About the Editors

Isabel Feichtner is professor of public law and international economic law at Würzburg University. Before moving to Würzburg, she worked as researcher at the Max-Planck-Institute for Comparative Public Law and International Law and was associate professor at Goethe University. She is a member of the *European Journal of International Law*'s editorial board and of the ILA Committee on the Role of International Law in Sustainable Resource Management. Her main research interests lie in the field of international economic law, transnational resource law and the legal design of money.

Markus Krajewski is professor of public law and public international law at Friedrich-Alexander-University Erlangen-Nürnberg. He is one of the directors of the Master programme Human Rights and coordinator of the Center for Human Rights Erlangen-Nürnberg (CHREN). He also chairs the Board of Trustees of the German Institute for Human Rights. Before taking up his current position he taught at King's College London and the University of Potsdam. He holds a PhD and post-doctoral qualification from the University of Hamburg.

Ricarda Roesch is PhD candidate at Friedrich-Alexander-University of Erlangen-Nuremberg. From 2014 to 2017, she worked in the research project "Human Rights as Standards for Transnational Economic Law". She holds law degrees from Hanse Law School, Universities of Bremen and Oldenburg and the School of Oriental and African Studies (SOAS), University of London. The focus of her research is on the right to free, prior and informed consent (FPIC) in sub-Saharan Africa.

Contributors

Armi Beatriz E. Bayot Commission on Human Rights of the Republic of the Philippines, University of the Philippines Diliman, Quezon City, Philippines

C. Ignacio de Casas Universidad Austral, Buenos Aires, Argentina

Cathal M. Doyle Middlesex University School of Law, London, UK

Liesbeth F. H. Enneking Erasmus School of Law, Erasmus University Rotterdam, Rotterdam, The Netherlands

Isabel Feichtner School of Law, University of Würzburg, Würzburg, Germany

Heidi Feldt Beratung entwicklungspolitischer Prozesse, Berlin, Germany

Sotonye Frank Rivers State University, Port Harcourt, Nigeria

Nora Götzmann Human Rights and Business, The Danish Institute for Human Rights, Copenhagen, Denmark

Centre for Social Responsibility in Mining, Sustainable Minerals Institute, The University of Queensland, Brisbane, QLD, Australia

Charis Kamphuis Thompson Rivers University, Kamloops, BC, Canada

Patrick J. Keenan University of Illinois College of Law, Champaign, IL, USA

Wasima Khan Erasmus University Rotterdam, Erasmus School of Law, Rotterdam, The Netherlands

Markus Krajewski Faculty of Law, University of Erlangen-Nürnberg, Erlangen, Germany

Pacifique Manirakiza University of Ottawa, Faculty of Law, Ottawa, ON, Canada

Radu Mares Dr. Docent Raoul Wallenberg Institute of Human Rights and Humanitarian Law, Lund, Sweden

Karsten Nowrot University of Hamburg, Hamburg, Germany

Evaristus Oshionebo Faculty of Law, University of Calgary, Calgary, AB, Canada

Osgoode Hall Law School, York University, Toronto, ON, Canada

Aline Rose Barbosa Pereira Center for Development Research (ZEF), University of Bonn, Bonn, Germany

Ricarda Roesch School of Law, University of Erlangen-Nürnberg, Erlangen, Germany

Almut Schilling-Vacaflor Osnabrück University, Institute for Social Sciences, Osnabrück, Germany

Introduction

Isabel Feichtner, Markus Krajewski, and Ricarda Roesch

Contents

Reference 8

Environmental pollution through oil leakages in the Niger delta, forced evictions of Indigenous peoples from their ancestral lands and the exploitation of children in gold and diamond mines are among the most prominent cases of human rights violations caused by or directly associated with extractive industries. However, they are by far not the only examples. In one of his first interim reports, the then newly appointed Special Representative of the Secretary-General on the issue of human rights and transnational corporations and other business enterprises, *John Ruggie* noted in 2006:

> The extractive industries (…) account for most allegations of the worst abuses, up to and including complicity in crimes against humanity. These are typically for acts committed by public and private security forces protecting company assets and property; large-scale corruption; violations of labour rights; and a broad array of abuses in relation to local communities, especially Indigenous people[1]

The Special Representative based his findings on a survey of 65 instances of alleged corporate human rights abuses reported by NGOs in the 2000s. Even though

---

[1] Commission on Human Rights. Interim Report of UN Special Representative on Business and Human Rights, E/CN.4/2006/97, 22 February 2006, para. 25.

I. Feichtner
School of Law, University of Würzburg, Würzburg, Germany
e-mail: feichtner@jura.uni-wuerzburg.de

M. Krajewski (✉)
Faculty of Law, University of Erlangen-Nürnberg, Erlangen, Germany
e-mail: markus.krajewski@fau.de

R. Roesch
School of Law, University of Erlangen-Nürnberg, Erlangen, Germany
e-mail: ricarda.roesch@fau.de

© Springer Nature Switzerland AG 2019
I. Feichtner et al. (eds.), *Human Rights in the Extractive Industries*,
Interdisciplinary Studies in Human Rights 3,
https://doi.org/10.1007/978-3-030-11382-7_1

1

this survey is more of an illustration and not a representative sample, its findings coincide with the observations of many human rights activists and scholars.[2] Indeed, the pervasiveness of human rights violations in the extractive industries is so widely acknowledged that the Committee on Social, Economic and Cultural Rights merely referred to "the well-documented risks associated with the extractive industry" in its 2017 General Comment No. 24 on business and human rights noting that "particular due diligence is required with respect to mining-related projects and oil development projects."[3]

In light of the human rights violations and risks associated with the extractive industries, states, international organisations and non-state actors have developed a variety of different national and international legal instruments and initiatives aimed at mitigating, preventing and remedying human rights violations in this field. These instruments do not amount to a uniform area of law, but form multilevel, pluralistic and transnational responses to human rights challenges in the extractive industries. Despite its diversity, the transnational law of protecting human rights in the extractive industries is based on general principles that inform and shape the application and development of existing norms and legal instruments.

Key principles informing the transnational law of protecting human rights in the extractive industries are the general principles of transparency and participation. Both, transparency and participation, bear the promise of enhancing collective self-determination as concerns questions of whether to exploit natural resources as well as the distribution of costs and benefits once extraction is taking place. It should be cautioned, however, that while participation and transparency may help to bring the extractive industries in line with the promise of self-determination and human rights, transparency and consultation may also serve to legitimize extractive industry projects with dubious human rights records. In order to assess the human rights record of the extractive industries it is therefore also important to take account of resistance. Participation and transparency may facilitate effective resistance to particular extraction projects; yet, resistance may also be a reaction to transparency and participation initiatives that do not afford real opportunities for populations to actively shape and benefit from political economies of extraction; and, finally, rights of participation and transparency, as do human rights more generally, provide a vocabulary to affected communities in which to voice their grievances concerning extraction projects. Transparency, participation and resistance therefore emerge as three distinct, but interrelated categories of responses to the challenges and violations of human rights in the extractive industries. They form the three main themes of this volume.

Transparency is an important part of many attempts to prevent, reduce and mitigate human rights violations in the extractive industries. Legal instruments that enhance transparency in the extractive sector may enable affected communities,

---

[2] Francioni (2016), pp. 66–67.

[3] Committee on Economic, Social and Cultural Rights, General comment No. 24 (2017) on State obligations under the International Covenant on Economic, Social and Cultural Rights in the context of business activities, E/C.12/GC/24, 10 August 2017, para 32.

populations of resource states, shareholders and consumers to shape the political economy of extraction through political and economic action. Transparency is a key element of legal initiatives at the international level—including most prominently the Extractive Industries Transparency Initiative (EITI). Its effectiveness in making revenue flows transparent for public scrutiny is enhanced by national and regional legislation mandating corporations to report on payments to governments. Furthermore, legislation on conflict minerals and non-financial reporting seeks to complement transparency of financial flows with transparency regarding the origin of raw materials used in the production of consumer goods. Transparency does not function as a direct instrument of change. Yet, by allowing the public, stakeholders, shareholders, and consumers to access information regarding revenue flows and the origin of products it meets a necessary condition for actions for change—as for example the exercise of consumer choice or the implementation of accountability mechanisms. Transparency, moreover, is central to meaningful consultation and participation, the subject of the second part of the book.

The volume's second chapter addresses the development, impact and reform options of the EITI. *Heidi Feldt* discusses how the EITI seeks to enhance account-ability of governments and the sharing of financial benefits from extraction with affected stakeholders. While the EITI has contributed to greater disclosure of infor-mation about the extractive sector, Feldt argues that there is little progress towards greater accountability. She suggests that in the absence of freedom of expression and political rights, the impact of the EITI is minimal. Therefore, protection and respect of these human rights are key if the EITI is to achieve its goal.

While EITI remains a voluntary framework at the international level, some states have adopted and implemented binding transparency obligations for the extractive industries. They are part of a broader movement to address the human rights impacts of corporate activity through disclosure-based rules. Disclosure shall allow consum-ers through their consumption choices to express their human rights concerns and thus to ultimately influence production processes. Disclosure legislation requires companies to gather and disclose to regulators information about their own supply chains and the materials used to make their products. A prominent example of such regulation are the conflict minerals and disclosure of payments provisions of the U.S. Dodd-Frank Act, discussed by *Patrick Keenan* in the third chapter. These provisions would require thousands of companies to investigate their supply chains, report their findings, and disclose payments to foreign officials. *Keenan* also notes the Trump Administration's steps to dismantle these rules and abandon the U.S. leader-ship role in the human rights movement. Based on analyses of recent cases, *Keenan* argues that in the absence of U.S. rules less transparency can create the conditions for more corruption and diminished respect for human rights.

Following the model of the U.S., but also deviating from it, the EU adopted its own transparency regulation. *Karsten Nowrot,* in the fourth chapter, takes account of the EU Conflict Minerals Regulation that was adopted by the European Parliament and the Council in spring 2017 and entered into force in June 2017. *Nowrot* takes a closer look at this recent and rather ambitious regulatory regime in the field of raw materials governance aimed at promoting responsible business in the context of so-called conflict minerals. The analysis shows that the regulatory features of the 2017 EU Conflict Minerals Regulation transcend the distinction between traditional law enforcement and law-realisation approaches by combining command and control elements in the form of legally binding supply chain due diligence obligations with more indirect steering tools aimed at improving transparency.

The next chapters take perspectives of the Global South: *Evaristus Oshionebo* examines the nature, scope and content of Community Development Agreements (CDAs) in Africa's extractive industries and assesses the degree to which CDAs enable host communities to participate in project implementation and resource revenue-sharing. He identifies certain factors inhibiting the utility of CDAs in Africa including the power imbalance between extractive companies and host communities. While extractive companies have enormous financial resources that allow them to retain the services of highly trained experts, including lawyers, local communities in Africa often lack the requisite capacity and expertise to negotiate and implement CDAs. As a result, in some cases extractive companies dictate the terms of CDAs. Given this reality, the article suggests that African countries should enact legislative provisions mandating certain contents of CDAs in the extractive sector. Such legislative provisions could ameliorate the power imbalance and ensure that extractive companies do not take advantage of their superior power in the course of negotiating CDAs with host communities in Africa.

Sotonye Frank, in the chapter "Stabilization Clauses and Human Rights: The Role of Transparency Initiatives", shows how the use of stabilization clauses in state-investor-contracts declines as transparency increases. On the basis of case studies of Tanzania, Liberia, Sierra Leone and Zambia, Frank argues that a lack of transparency in the extractive industry contractual process correlates with a wide scope of stabilization clauses. This has implications for human rights as stabilization clauses either freeze the law regulating the extraction project or make legislative changes subject to compensation payments by the state to the investor and thus limit the scope of the state to adopt and implement legislation protecting populations and environment from harm caused by extraction projects. Conversely, the increases in transparency, including the publication of contracts, that have resulted from resource states' involvement with the EITI contributed to a reduced scope or even an abolition of stabilization clauses.

In the final chapter of this volume's first part, *Wasima Khan* addresses the link between taxation and human rights. Many of the world's resource-rich countries are developing countries and dependent on their natural resource wealth. Yet, they systematically fail to translate this wealth into economic stability and growth and an enjoyment of basic human rights—such as access to health, education, and sanitation—for their citizens *inter alia* due to tax avoidance and evasion by multinational companies. While wealthy resource importing states have contributed to an international tax law that impedes resource states' capacity to effectively tax and share in the revenues from extraction, *Khan* focusses on multinational companies. In her chapter *Khan* proposes a legal obligation for multinational companies to establish and publish a tax strategy as a pragmatic means building on a strategy of "naming and faming" to counter tax avoidance.

The second part of the book focusses on the participation of affected communities throughout the mining cycle. The right to free, prior and informed consent (FPIC) increasingly is being understood as a continuous process of participation and thus as a way of preventing and mitigating human rights violations in the course of extraction projects. FPIC originated in the context of international indigenous rights and is seen as an expression or derivate of the indigenous right to self-determination. By drawing on examples from different regions of the world, the chapters in this part show how contested the legal status and scope of FPIC still are, as well as the potential and limits of participation in realizing self-determination and human rights.

The part begins with *Cathal Doyle's* comparison of FPIC in Canada and the United States. In both jurisdictions, ambiguity persists regarding the nature of the duty to consult. While Canadian and US Courts have interpreted the governments' responsibilities and duties under international law, their jurisprudence is still informed by historical international law principles. These tend to be blind to the role that indigenous sovereignty and consent of Indigenous peoples play and should be playing. Doyle argues that in both jurisdictions legislation could be brought in line with the human rights of Indigenous peoples. Despite recent judicial setbacks effective protection of indigenous rights seems more likely in Canada than in the US given the Trump administration's endeavours to facilitate resource extraction, including in Native American territories. As Indigenous peoples in Canada have repeatedly and effectively pressed their government to implement the UN Declaration on the Rights of Indigenous Peoples, Canada could set an important precedent that would help Indigenous peoples throughout the world.

Pacifique Manirakiza sheds light on the re-negotiation of FPIC in sub-Saharan Africa. FPIC is even more controversial in sub-Saharan Africa than in other regions of the world, as the traditional concept of indigeneity does not take African experiences into consideration and is subject to contestation by many African governments. Taking a resistance theory perspective on human rights, *Manirakiza* argues that FPIC needs to be detached from indigeneity in sub-Saharan Africa, extending its scope to non-indigenous local communities. The chapter posits that, in the African human rights context, the right to FPIC does not entail the right to veto extraction projects. Rather, it has to be exercised in relation to other compelling interests, meaning that the rights and interests of affected communities are balanced against the legitimate interests of the rest of the population to benefit from the economic exploitation of the national natural wealth.

Ignacio de Casas moves the discussion on FPIC to Latin America and the corporate responsibility to respect consultation rights. While he finds that the Inter-American Human Rights System (IAHRS) does not give rise to direct obligations of corporations, he argues that it includes implicit corporate responsibilities that arise from the state due diligence standard. He proposes a way to construe direct corporate responsibilities on the basis of the existing Inter-American human rights framework and suggests how the organs of the IAHRS may promote these responsibilities.

The Philippines are often portrayed as one of the role models in Asia with regard to the recognition of the rights of Indigenous peoples. In her chapter entitled "Free,

Prior, and Informed Consent in the Philippines: A Fourth World Critique", *Armi Beatriz Bayot* explores the limits of FPIC in the Philippines from a Fourth World perspective to international law. She argues that due to the state-centrism of international and domestic law, state prerogatives trump Indigenous peoples' rights over natural resources. FPIC continues to be qualified by the Regalian doctrine, according to which natural resources belong to the state as well as the international law principle of Permanent Sovereignty over Natural Resources. Consequently, FPIC remains a regime of unfulfilled promises in a framework based on a Western conception of state sovereignty and characterized by the denial of the (pre-)existence and validity of indigenous polities and their sovereignty. The way forward, according to *Bayot*, is to assert Indigenous peoples' participation in international lawmaking, based on their right to self-determination and historical sovereignty, and to empower them to influence the content of international law norms that affect them—not just those that exist specifically for the protection of Indigenous peoples.

Almut Schilling-Vacaflor in her chapter on "Norm Contestation and (Non-) Compliance: The Right to Prior Consultation and FPIC in the Extractive Industries" looks at FPIC in Latin America, in particular Bolivia, Columbia and Chile who have adopted and implemented prior consultation legislation from a legal anthropological perspective. She finds, based on empirical data, that divergent claims of authority, territorial control and decision-making coexist within the analysed domestic contexts and that these divergences lie at the root of the fierce contestations over indigenous participatory rights. In addition, such claims and competing resource sovereignties are embedded within power asymmetries that advantage strategic economic interests in extraction over strong indigenous and participatory rights. *Schilling-Vacaflor* concludes that as long as these contestations persist, the emergence of a shared understanding remains improbable.

The contributions on FPIC are complemented by two chapters of which one focusses on the potential of state-investor-contracts to promote participation and the other on corporations' changing perspectives on corporate social responsibility and in particular their engagement with affected communities.

Nora Götzmann, in her chapter on "State-Investor Contracts and Human Rights: Taking a Critical Look at Transparency and Participation", analyses the potential of state-investor-contracts for strengthening participation rights and improving transparency. While state-investor-contracts are globally on the decline, they are still common in some regions, in particular in Africa. *Götzmann* notes that they, generally, make little reference to human rights. They may further limit the realization and protection of human rights as corporations frequently have greater negotiating capacity than the governments of resource states and contract negotiations often are conducted secretively and without participation of civil society actors. Stabilisation clauses, for instance, may impair the host government's ability to adopt human rights-related laws. Moreover, the classification of investor-state-contracts as purely commercial is problematic as is the possibility that bilateral investment treaties offer to investors for enforcing contractual claims through investor-state arbitration. *Götzmann*, consequently, supports reforms to remedy this situation. These include the promotion of human rights expertise and training of negotiators, greater contractual transparency and the implementation of mining frameworks that provide investors with legal certainty and thus render stabilization clauses unnecessary.

Radu Mares examines, in his chapter "Disruption and Institutional Development: Corporate Standards and Practices on Responsible Mining", how corporations in the extractive industry sector understand and implement their corporate duty to respect human rights with a particular focus on participation. From an institutional development perspective, he examines reports of mining companies and international development organisations. He observes a growing commitment of companies and industry associations to local capacity building and institutional development, while cautioning that these new commitments might remain of a declaratory character. As concerns the operational level, *Mares* notes that some companies and multi-stakeholder processes seek to move beyond the rhetoric of institutional development and put their commitments into practice. He concludes that institutional development as a cross-cutting dimension creates an opportunity for more transparency and participation.

Human Rights not only provide guidance and content for the (self-)regulation of extractive industries. Human Rights also provide important references, narratives and instruments to resist extractivism. Civil society actors and parliamentarians invoke human rights to advocate for legal change; persons adversely affected by extraction bring their grievances formulated as human rights claims to the courts—often aided by institutions that support these cases for strategic litigation purposes to achieve legal change beyond the individual case; and affected local populations, workers, and farmers use human rights as a powerful language to express their protest against extraction projects that threaten to unsettle and hurt them and their habitat. Researchers in the contentious field of extraction not seldom become themselves part of a human rights activism resisting expulsions resulting from extraction. The third part of the book explores these links between human rights and resistance.

In her chapter entitled "Taking Sides in Scientific Research? The Struggle for the Right to Participate in Public Decision-Making Related to a Mining Project in Brazil", *Aline Pereira* not only presents the struggle of local communities affected by the Minas-Rio iron-ore mining project in Minas Gerais in Brazil, but also reflects on her role as a researcher engaging in action research. *Pereira* conceptualizes the rights to information and participation in decision-making on extraction projects as empowering individuals and communities and as important elements of democratic self-determination. She shows, on the basis of her field work, how during the environmental licensing process these rights were being continuously undermined, and a merely functional value was accorded to participation. She acknowledges her positionality and subjectivity as a researcher and stets out the ethical and methodological challenges of action research in general and of her own interactions with the affected communities in Conceição do Mato Dentro engaging in resistance against the Minas-Rio iron-ore mine in particular.

Charis Kamphuis in her chapter entitled "Building the Case for a Home-State Grievance Mechanism: Law Reform Strategies in the Canadian Resource Justice Movement", offers a detailed account of the strategies that social justice advocates in Canada between 2000 and 2017 employed in their endeavour to make the Canadian government address Canadian corporate conduct in the extractive sector abroad. According to *Kamphuis* these strategies eventually led to a breakthrough in 2018 when the Canadian government announced that it would establish the Canadian Ombudsman for Responsible Enterprise as a new grievance mechanism. Steps in this struggle for resources justice included the empirical documentation not only of human rights violations by Canadian extractive industry corporations abroad but also the support provided to these companies by the Canadian government; sustained debate with policy makers, industry leaders and international human rights bodies over appropriate regulatory responses by the Canadian government, as well as the civil society proposal in 2016 of a draft Business & Human Rights Act.

In this volume's last chapter *Liesbeth Enneking* presents an analysis of a number of transnational human rights and environmental litigations in the US, the UK and the Netherlands, all relating to operations of Shell in Nigeria. She holds these cases to be indicative of a trend towards increased foreign liability litigation to hold companies engaging in resource extraction accountable in their home states. Through an assessment of rules on jurisdiction, the applicable law, the legal basis of claims as well as procedural rules and practices, *Enneking* identifies the hurdles which litigants have to take in different jurisdictions in order to succeed with their claims.

Reference

Francioni F (2016) Natural resources and human rights. In: Morgera E, Kulovesi K (eds) Research handbook on international law and natural resources. Edward Elgar, Cheltenham, pp 66–67

Isabel Feichtner is Professor for Public Law and International Economic Law at Würzburg University. Before moving to Würzburg, she worked as researcher the Max-Planck-Institute for Comparative Public Law and International Law and was associate professor at Goethe University. She is a member of the European Journal of International Law's editorial board and of the ILA Committee on the Role of International Law in Sustainable Resource Management. Her main research interests lie in the field of international economic law, transnational resource law and the legal design of money.

Markus Krajewski is professor of public law and public international law at Friedrich-Alexander-University Erlangen-Nürnberg. He is one of the directors of the Master programme Human Rights and coordinator of the Center for Human Rights Erlangen-Nürnberg (CHREN). He also chairs the Board of Trustees of the German Institute for Human Rights. Before taking up his current position he taught at King's College London and the University of Potsdam. He holds a PhD and postdoctoral qualification from the University of Hamburg.

Ricarda Roesch is PhD candidate at Friedrich-Alexander-University of Erlangen-Nuremberg. From 2014 to 2017, she worked in the research project "Human Rights as Standards for Transnational Economic Law". She holds law degrees from Hanse Law School, Universities of Bremen and Oldenburg, and the School of Oriental and African Studies (SOAS), University of London. The focus of her research is on the right to free, prior and informed consent (FPIC) in sub-Saharan Africa.

Part I
Transparency

The Extractive Industries Transparency Initiative (EITI) as a Human Rights Instrument: Potentials and Shortcomings

Heidi Feldt

Contents

1 Extractive Industries Transparency Initiative (EITI) 11
   1.1 Brief History of EITI 13
   1.2 Requirements 14
   1.3 Development of the EITI Standard 15
   1.4 Structure of EITI 18
2 EITI and Human Rights Challenges 19
   2.1 Civil Society Organisations' Participation in EITI 20
   2.2 Enabling Environment for Civil Society Participation in Repressive States 21
   2.3 Reporting on Social and Environmental Impacts 23
   2.4 Integrating Artisanal and Small-Scale Mining 23
3 Conclusion 25
Reference 25

1 Extractive Industries Transparency Initiative (EITI)

While there is an on-going discussion about whether living free of corruption should be enshrined as a human right,[1] the Human Rights Council has already recognised the negative impact of corruption on the enjoyment of human rights. Navi Pillay, former United Nations High Commissioner for Human Rights, stated 2013: "*Let us be clear. Corruption kills. The money stolen through corruption every year is enough to feed the world's hungry 80 times over. Nearly 870 million people go to bed hungry*

---

[1] Bantekas and Oette (2016); Peters A, Corruption and Human Rights. Basel Institute on Governance, Working paper series No. 20, September 2015, http://www.mpil.de/files/pdf4/Peters_Corruption_and_Human_Rights20151.pdf (last accessed 12 June 2018); Murray M and Spalding A, Freedom from Official Corruption as a Human Right. Governance Studies at Brookings, January 2015, https://www.brookings.edu/wp-content/uploads/2016/06/Murray-and-Spalding_v06.pdf (last accessed 12 June 2018).

H. Feldt (✉)
Beratung entwicklungspolitischer Prozesse, Berlin, Germany

© Springer Nature Switzerland AG 2019
I. Feichtner et al. (eds.), *Human Rights in the Extractive Industries*,
Interdisciplinary Studies in Human Rights 3,
https://doi.org/10.1007/978-3-030-11382-7_2

every night, many of them children; corruption denies them their right to food, and,
in some cases, their right to life. A human rights-based approach to anti-corruption
responds to the people's resounding call for a social, political and economic order
that delivers on the promises of freedom from fear and want."[2]

This is the underlying assumption of the EITI: As billions of US dollars slip past
the national budgets of resource-rich countries each year, those countries lack the
revenue they need to build schools, maintain health systems or undertake infrastructure programmes. And yet in almost every country of the world, mineral resources
are the property of the state or its population. It follows that the population has the
right that the revenue from extracting such resources should benefit it and that governments can be held accountable. A precondition to citizens demanding accountability is that there is transparency with relation to the level of revenue and the
prices and terms under which resources are extracted in their countries. Transparency
of payments, disclosure of extraction contracts and disclosure of the true owners
("beneficial owners" in EITI terminology[3]) of the mining, oil and gas companies, as
required by EITI, are essential if it is to be at all possible to curb corruption and hold
governments accountable. This is vital to ensure that the revenue can be used to
realise social human rights such as the right to education and the right to
healthcare.

The extractive industries are considered one of the most corrupt business sectors.
It is difficult to assess the corruption of different sectors due to the obfuscating
nature of corruption itself. Most of the information concerning corruption is anecdotal, whether in the mining and the oil/gas sector or any other sector. Nevertheless,
the Bribe Payers Index of Transparency International indicates mining and oil and
gas industry as bribe payers, listed after construction, utilities and real estate.[4]

EITI focuses on the transparency of payments made by gas, oil and mining companies to the governments of the countries in which they operate and on disclosure
of the relevant revenue by these governments. The aim is to enable a public debate
on the economic use of raw materials and the use of revenue, as well as empower
the populations to hold their governments accountable. The initiative brings together
governments, companies, NGOs and banks seeking to create an international framework for transparency of payments to governments by the extractive industry.

---

[2] Office of the United Nations High Commissioner for Human Rights (2013) The human rights
case against corruption. 22nd session of the Human Rights Council, https://www.ohchr.org/
Documents/Issues/Development/GoodGovernance/Corruption/HRCaseAgainstCorruption.pdf
(last accessed 12 August 2017), p. 3.

[3] Extractive Industries Transparency Initiative, Beneficial ownership, Revealing who stands behind
the companies, https://eiti.org/beneficial-ownership (last accessed 24 May 2018).

[4] Hardoon D and Heinrich F, Bribe Prayers Index 2011. Transparency International, 2011, http://
issuu.com/transparencyinternational/docs/bribe_payers_index_2011?mode=window&backgroun
dColor=%23222222 (last accessed 12 June 2018), p. 15.

1.1 Brief History of EITI

In the 1990s, studies by Global Witness, Christian Aid, Save the Children and various other organisations revealed that public budgets in many resource-rich countries in Africa, Asia and Latin America were losing out on billions of dollars of revenue as a result of bribery and corruption in the extractive industries. Pressure on governments to take action against corruption had yielded little success. As a result, NGOs adopted a different tactic, urging the extractive industries—the mining, oil and gas companies—to publish the payments they were making to governments. This gave the campaign its name—"Publish What You Pay" (PWYP). PWYP found important advocates and supporters elsewhere, notably in George Soros, whose Open Society Institute and Revenue Watch Institute provided vital financial and political support and played a key role in opening doors for the campaign.

When Global Witness launched its report, "A Crude Awakening", on the mismanagement of oil revenues of the Angolan government in 1999, they challenged the oil industry, lending banks and the national governments involved to change their policy and adopt one of "full transparency".[5] Responding to the demand, British Petroleum (BP) announced the publication of payments it made to the Angolan government for an offshore licence in 2001.[6] In response, the Angolan Government threatened the company with losing its licence to less scrupulous competitors.[7] According to the former chair of EITI, Clare Short, as a reaction the oil companies argued for a shift away from company reporting, as demanded by PWYP, to reporting by governments, in order to reduce conflict with host governments. If company reporting was to be required, they wanted a global effort to level the playing field that required all companies operating in a country to disclose, so that those, which embraced transparency would not be at a competitive disadvantage.[8]

These demands were taken up by the UK government, which presented the idea of the Extractive Industries Transparency Initiative in 2002. EITI was officially launched in June 2003, when representatives of governments, industries, and civil society groups met in London and agreed upon a common set of EITI Principles. Four countries started piloting national EITI implementation: Azerbaijan, Ghana, Nigeria and the Kyrgyz Republic.

---

[5] Global Witness, A crude awakening. Report, 1 December 1999, https://www.globalwitness.org/en/archive/crude-awakening/ (last accessed 1 October 2018), p. 21.

[6] Global Witness, Campaign success: BP makes move for transparency in Angola. Press release, 12 February 2001, https://www.globalwitness.org/en/archive/campaign-success-bp-makes-move-transparency-angola/ (last accessed 1 October 2018).

[7] Global Witness, Time for transparency: Coming clean on oil, mining and gas revenues, Report, 26 March 2004, https://reliefweb.int/report/angola/time-transparency-coming-clean-oil-mining-and-gas-revenues (last accessed 12 August 2017), p. 6.

[8] Short C The development of the Extractive Industries Transparency Initiative. Journal of World Energy Law & Business, 16 January 2014, https://eiti.org/sites/default/files/documents/The-development-of-the-EITI-Clare-Short.pdf (last accessed 1 October 2018), p. 2.

The EITI Principles of 2003 set out the shared basis of the initiative. The basic principle is that "the prudent use of natural resource wealth should be an important engine for sustainable economic growth that contributes to sustainable development and poverty reduction, but if not managed properly, can create negative economic and social impacts."[9] The approach is that a public understanding of government revenues and expenditure over time could help public debate and inform choice of appropriate and realistic options for sustainable development. The principles reaffirm the importance of all stakeholders to contribute—including governments and their agencies, extractive industry companies, service companies, multilateral organisations, financial organisations, investors and non-governmental organisations. The mechanism to bring the principles to fruition is the EITI Standard.

This standard has evolved over time. In 2006, the standard only reflected a minimum requirement of transparency, allowing for aggregated data. Information on project base was recommended but not obligatory. There was a danger that EITI reporting would be reduced to a tick box assessment of compliance with the rules but not provide meaningful information for the population of resource extracting countries. With adoption of the 2013 standard and its update in 2016, implementing countries now have to go beyond the minimum requirements.

1.2 Requirements

To join EITI, the government must appoint an EITI coordinator to oversee implementation, inter alia of the work plan agreed by the Multi-Stakeholder Group (MSG). The government must undertake work with civil society organisations and the private sector. The national MSG is the backbone of the implementation process.[10]

If these requirements are met, an application for membership can be submitted to the EITI Board. At that point the country has candidate status and must publish its first EITI report within 18 months, publishing further reports annually thereafter. The reporting standards cover publication of all relevant payments and revenues and extractive industry production data; however, it is left to the MSG to define the materiality of the payments and revenues in its country.[11]

The typical process of producing an EITI report comprises the following stages (Fig. 1):

---

[9] Extractive Industries Transparency Initiative International Secretary, The EITI Standard 2016. Extractive Industries Transparency Initiative, 24 May 2017, https://eiti.org/sites/default/files/documents/the_eiti_standard_2016_-_english.pdf (last accessed 1 October 2018), p. 10.

[10] Extractive Industries Transparency Initiative International Secretary, The EITI Standard 2016. Extractive Industries Transparency Initiative, 24 May 2017, https://eiti.org/sites/default/files/documents/the_eiti_standard_2016_-_english.pdf (last accessed 1 October 2018), pp. 13–16.

[11] Extractive Industries Transparency Initiative International Secretary, The EITI Standard 2016. Extractive Industries Transparency Initiative, 24 May 2017, https://eiti.org/sites/default/files/documents/the_eiti_standard_2016_-_english.pdf (last accessed 1 October 2018), p. 22.

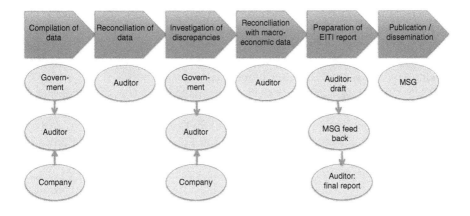

Fig. 1 Stages in the production of an EITI report. Source: author based on EITI

An external auditor collates and reconciles the details provided by companies and the government. The external auditor is appointed by the MSG, which ultimately adopts the final report and releases it for publication.

1.3   Development of the EITI Standard

The EITI Standard was revised at the 2013 EITI Conference in Sydney. Ten years after the official founding of EITI and an external evaluation, it was necessary to improve reporting obligations and processes. The survey team found that *"there is not any solid theory of change behind some of the EITI aspirations, nor do data show any links at this aggregate level."* The team concluded that *"the lack of societal change is also a function of the narrow focus of EITI activities. If the Standard were more in line with its own Principles and if it had more focus on strategic partnerships beyond the sector, EITI would be more likely to reach its objectives. The main Recommendation is thus for EITI to consider a Standard that covers a greater part of the value chain in the sector, combined with a flexible rating scheme that would grade actual performance rather than giving a Yes/No value."*[12]

While transparency has improved, accountability does not appear to have changed greatly. One reason is that most EITI activities were dissemination activities and were not designed for supporting social actors to empower them to use the data, which is difficult if the government of a given country is the owner of the process.

---

[12] Reite et al., Achievements and Strategic Options: Evaluation of the Extractive Industries Transparency Initiative. Scanteam, Final Report, May 2011, https://eiti.org/sites/default/files/migrated_files/2011-EITI-evaluation-report.pdf (last accessed 1 October 2018), p. 1.

The reporting standards were therefore expanded and further substantiated at the 2016 EITI Conference in Lima. To make national EITI reports clearer, they must now include contextual information including information about the legal basis, the contribution of extractive industries to the country's economy, state holdings in the resource industry and the allocation of revenue.

Disclosure of beneficial ownership has been included as a new requirement. A pilot project in 12 countries explored how the publication of the names of the real owners of companies can be achieved in the EITI context.[13] At the 2016 EITI Conference in Lima, Peru, the disclosure of beneficial ownership was included in the EITI list of information that must be published. By 1 January 2020, all countries have to ensure that privately held companies disclose their beneficial owners as part of their EITI reports. This information must include the identity of the beneficial owner, the level of ownership and details about how control and ownership is exerted. It is also recommended that this information be maintained in a public beneficial ownership register. Furthermore, the reporting obligations of state-owned enterprises have been extended. All transfers of funds between state-owned enterprises and state institutions must be disclosed including volumes sold and received, retained earnings, reinvestments and third party financing.[14]

Another addition is the requirement for member states to maintain a publicly accessible register containing the names of licence or concession holders and geographical and resource-related information.[15] Experience with recommendations showed that relatively few recommendations based on EITI reporting have been implemented. The new standard requires plans for implementing recommendations to be outlined in the national EITI work plans. Furthermore, publication of project-specific data is called for. However, it is the responsibility of the MSG to define the level of disaggregation required. Encouraged but not obligatory is the publication of contracts.[16]

Overall, the aim is to make EITI reports easier to read, comprehensible to a wider audience and therefore more useful. EITI hopes that clear and contextual reports will help it to achieve its goal of enabling an informed public to hold its government accountable. One of the biggest changes was the inclusion of beneficial ownership as a reporting requirement. It was launched in 2013 as a pilot process, until it became mandatory in Lima.

---

[13] Extractive Industries Transparency Initiative, Beneficial ownership, Revealing who stands behind the companies, https://eiti.org/beneficial-ownership (last accessed 1 October 2018).

[14] Extractive Industries Transparency Initiative International Secretary, The EITI Standard 2016. Extractive Industries Transparency Initiative, 24 May 2017, https://eiti.org/sites/default/files/documents/the_eiti_standard_2016_-_english.pdf (last accessed 1 October 2018), p. 21.

[15] Extractive Industries Transparency Initiative International Secretary, The EITI Standard 2016. Extractive Industries Transparency Initiative, 24 May 2017, https://eiti.org/sites/default/files/documents/the_eiti_standard_2016_-_english.pdf (last accessed 1 October 2018), p. 18.

[16] Extractive Industries Transparency Initiative International Secretary, The EITI Standard 2016. Extractive Industries Transparency Initiative, 24 May 2017, https://eiti.org/sites/default/files/documents/the_eiti_standard_2016_-_english.pdf (last accessed 1 October 2018), p. 19.

Enforcement mechanisms are weak, as in any other organisations based on voluntary membership. The first step to assess compliance with EITI rules is the validation process. EITI implementation is verified in each country through a validation process headed by the secretariat of EITI. The secretariat prepares the validation and visits the country concerned, talking to the different stakeholders. The findings are then verified by an independent validator, who performs a risk-based analysis and proposes an overall rating of the country's performance. The first validation is due two and a half years after the country has been accepted as a candidate. If the outcome of the validation is positive, the country is recognised as a full member. Full members are required to repeat the validation process every 3 years.

The Board rates the country as (a) having made satisfactory progress (being "compliant"), (b) having made meaningful progress, (c) having made inadequate progress or no progress. If the country does not improve its performance, a compliant country can be downgraded to candidate status. If progress continues to be inadequate or if there has been no progress, a country can be suspended or finally delisted (Fig. 2).

Hence, sanction mechanisms are internal to the organisation. There are no further sanction mechanisms such as conditions to access credit. This set-up is entirely inherent to the kind of initiative based on self-regulation.

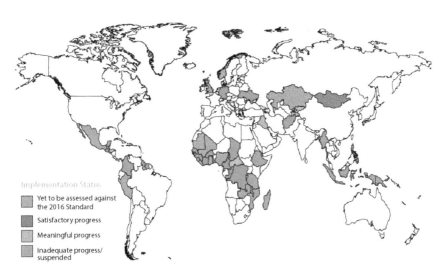

Fig. 2 EITI member countries and implementation status. Source: EITI Factsheet, February 2018 (https://eiti.org/sites/default/files/documents/data_eiti_2_0.pdf) accessed: 24.05.2018

1.4   Structure of EITI

The initiative is coordinated internationally by a multi-stakeholder board consisting of representatives of implementing and supporting countries, companies, non-governmental organisations and investors. EITI International lays down the framework; implementation is the responsibility of member countries. Formally, EITI is a non-profit association organised under Norwegian law. The permanent institutional bodies are the EITI Members' Meeting alongside the EITI Global Conference, which must be organised at least every 3 years, the EITI Board led by the EITI Chair and the EITI Secretariat in Oslo which supports the work of the EITI Board as well as of the members. The constituency groups of EITI are implementing and supporting countries and companies, including institutional investors, and civil society organisations. The Members' Meeting aims to adopt all decisions by consensus. If a vote is necessary, the votes of the three constituencies are equally balanced. The main task of the Members' Meeting is to appoint the EITI Board, the constituencies determine amongst themselves whom they wish to nominate to the EITI Board. Between the Members' Meetings, the EITI Board is the decision making body of the EITI International. The EITI Board has 21 members, with each constituency being entitled to representation. The EITI Board is represented by the EITI Chair.[17]

EITI is a government-led initiative. Governments are members and are ultimately responsible for national implementation: they have to ensure the implementation of the work plan, finance the coordinator of the national process and provide the enabling political framework for EITI. From four piloting countries in 2003, membership has grown to currently 51 implementing countries, of which just 23 have been assessed according to the new 2016 standard.[18] Only three countries (Mongolia, the Philippines and Timor Leste) made satisfactory progress and complied with all the requirements of the standard. Fourteen countries made meaningful progress. One country (Central African Republic) is currently suspended for political reasons, as the state is almost non-existent. Five more countries (Honduras, Iraq, the Kyrgyz Republic, Solomon Islands and Tajikistan) are suspended for failure to comply with the requirements of the EITI Standard. Since 2015, more industrialised countries joined EITI: the UK and Germany have been among the member countries required to publish their reports during 2017.[19]

The reasons for countries to join EITI diverge largely. Some most likely expected to receive better credit conditions, while others wanted to curb corruption in the

---

[17] Extractive Industries Transparency Initiative International Secretary, The EITI Standard 2016. Extractive Industries Transparency Initiative, 24 May 2017, https://eiti.org/sites/default/files/documents/the_eiti_standard_2016_-_english.pdf (last accessed 1 October 2018), pp. 47 et seq.

[18] Extractive Industries Transparency Initiative, https://eiti.org/countries (last accessed 26 March 2018).

[19] The USA joined Extractive Industries Transparency Initiative in 2014, when the Extractive Industries Transparency Initiative board excepted the country as a candidate. In November 2017, the U.S. announced its withdrawal from EITI—a serious setback for Extractive Industries Transparency Initiative trying to integrate resource rich industrialized countries.

sector (Liberia, Nigeria). Others wanted to contribute to setting a transparency standard (Norway, Germany).

A shortcoming is that EITI cannot oblige extractive companies to disclose. Although some do so voluntarily, the majority do not. Another shortcoming of EITI is that as a membership-based organisation, non-member states are not bound to adhere to its transparency standards—for instance, the major economies based on resource extraction like Australia, Brazil, Canada, China, India, Russia and South Africa as well as Angola, Equatorial Guinea and Venezuela. In other words, a large percentage of payment flows is not covered by EITI.

As a consequence, civil society organisations organised in PWYP have successfully lobbied for mandatory disclosure for mining, oil and gas companies in host jurisdictions of companies such as the USA,[20] Canada and Europe.[21] It is still too early to assess how EITI and mandatory disclosure are connected to one another and what impacts the combination of both approaches will have. Some companies are lobbying against mandatory disclosure rules and have been successfully doing so in the USA where the American Petroleum Institute (API) in the name of its members, like ExxonMobile, have opposed the Dodd Frank Act Section 1504 since the very beginning. Nevertheless, in conjunction with the European Union's Accounting Directive and similar provisions in Norway, Canada and Switzerland, EITI bears the potential to become an international reporting standard for the resource sector.

2   EITI and Human Rights Challenges

Human rights violations seriously endanger the success and the implementation of EITI. The initiative itself in its 2013 version lists reported violations of human rights of its civil society members. According to the EITI Board, civil society representatives participating in the implementation of the EITI have been harassed and intimidated and, in several cases, travel permits sought by civil society representative to attend related meetings have been denied. Furthermore, governments interfered in the autonomy of civil society representation in the EITI process mounting legal, administrative, procedural and other obstacles to the registration and

---

[20] The Dodd-Frank Wall Street Reform and Consumer Protection Act, otherwise known as the Dodd-Frank Act, was signed in the USA in July 2010. It is designed to promote transparency and stability in the financial system and includes new provisions on corporate accountability. Section 1504 requires all resource extraction companies listed on the US stock exchange to disclose payments made to governments anywhere in the world on a project-by-project basis. One of the first actions of the Trump government on coming into office was to suspend Section 1504. See on this the contribution by *Keenan* in this volume.

[21] Directive 2013/34/EU of the European Parliament and of the Council of 26 June 2013 on the annual financial statements, consolidated financial statements and related reports of certain types of undertakings, amending Directive 2006/43/EC of the European Parliament and of the Council and repealing Council Directives 78/660/EEC and 83/349/EEC. The Directive has now been transposed into the national law of EU member states. See the contribution by *Nowrot* in this volume.

operation of independent civil society organisations or impeding the free selection of civil society representation for the Multi-Stakeholder Group.[22]

2.1 Civil Society Organisations' Participation in EITI

Civil society organisations' participation in EITI is a key factor and has been at the centre of EITI right from the outset as it is civil society, which gives—inter alia— credibility to the EITI system. For EITI to attain its goal of accountability and public debate, civil society organisations must be able to organise themselves without interference from government, to speak out freely and to have access to public policy. There is no strict definition of civil society organisations (CSO) in EITI. NGOs, unions, journalists, representatives of religious organisations and in some cases even parliamentarians are all considered representatives of civil society.

The importance of civil society organisations is underlined by the fact that a specific Civil Society Protocol (CSP)[23] is an integral part of the EITI Standard and that in the validation process a country's compliance with this Protocol is the single most relevant issue. The Civil Society Protocol evolved from a set of principles intended to allow civil society representatives to express their opinion without any restraint, coercion or reprisal. The CSP states that civil society must be able to fully, actively and effectively engage in the EITI process. The government must ensure that there is an enabling environment for civil society participation with regard to relevant laws, regulations, and administrative rules as well as actual practice in implementation of the EITI. According to the CSP the fundamental rights of civil society substantively engaged in the EITI, including but not restricted to members of the Multi-Stakeholder Group, must be respected.

Furthermore, EITI introduced a safeguard policy under its validation provisions. A country will be suspended if it infringes the requirements. In practice, this has already been done in two cases, Azerbaijan and Tajikistan, where the validation process found severe shortcomings when it came to the possibilities for civil society to participate.

While the CSP and the validation process address human rights as structural issues, a Rapid Response Committee addresses human rights violations against individuals.[24] The members of the committee are EITI Board members. They have

---

[22] Extractive Industries Transparency Initiative International Secretary, The EITI Standard. Extractive Industries Transparency Initiative, 1 January 2015, https://eiti.org/sites/default/files/documents/english_eiti_standard.pdf (last accessed 1 October 2018), pp. 40–41.

[23] Extractive Industries Transparency Initiative, EITI Protocol: Participation of Civil Society, February 2016, https://eiti.org/document/eiti-protocol-participation-of-civil-society (last accessed 1 October 2018).

[24] Extractive Industries Transparency Initiative, EITI Board Committees, https://eiti.org/board-committees#rapid-response-committee (last accessed 1 October 2018).

to react in cases where detention or other forms of intimidation against civil society members of national EITI MSGs or representatives of organisations engaged in EITI occur—if the repression is somehow related to EITI. This last point often gives rise to debate between CSO representatives in the Committee and the other members as it is not easy to determine if one suffers harassment because of his or her engagement in general or because of his or her engagement in EITI. A case in point is the example of Gabon, where the CSO representative in EITI was detained and the government denied any relation with EITI and justified the detention with "treason".[25] The Rapid Response Committee was at odds whether this was a case for the Committee or not. The Committee ultimately decided to call for release, but the case illustrates how difficult it is to demonstrate unequivocally whether a matter is linked to EITI or not.

2.2   Enabling Environment for Civil Society Participation in Repressive States

In recent years, structural restrictions upon freedom to operate, such as those imposed by laws on NGOs, e.g. in Ethiopia and Azerbaijan, have fundamentally curtailed the activities of civil society organisations in EITI.

But the case of Ethiopia shows how fractured the debate is and how divergent the positions adopted by different civil society organisations can be.[26] In 2012, the EITI Board rejected Ethiopia's application for membership. The reasons stated included a law designed to control non-governmental organisations, and the generally repressive response of the government to dissent. Although the human rights situation in the country had not improved, in 2014 Ethiopia was accepted as candidate. Both decisions were preceded by internal discussions within Ethiopia's civil society about whether joining EITI would expand the scope for activity by the organisations or not. A further question was whether EITI would lose credibility through Ethiopia's accession, given that NGOs cannot operate freely in the country and there was therefore serious doubt as to whether the members of the national MSG could work freely. In the meantime, Ethiopia's membership was suspended because the country did not meet the deadlines for reporting.

---

[25] Publish What You Pay International, Gabon: Anti-Corruption advocates imprisoned on trumped-up charges. Press release, 9 January 2009, https://webcache.googleusercontent.com/search?q=cac he:BlDkgxrv70UJ:https://www.globalwitness.org/documents/15088/microsoft_word_gabon_ pr_9janeng.pdf+&cd=14&hl=de&ct=clnk&gl=de (last accessed 1 October 2018); Kråkenes A, EITI Chairman expresses concern about arrests of Civil Society representatives in Gabon. Extractive Industries Transparency Initiative, 8 January 2009, https://eiti.org/news/eiti-chairman-expresses-concern-about-arrests-of-civil-society-representatives-in-gabon (last accessed 1 October 2018).

[26] Human Rights Watch, Extractive Industries: A New Accountability Agenda. 21 May 2013, https://www.hrw.org/news/2013/05/21/extractive-industries-new-accountability-agenda (last accessed 1 October 2018), pp. 50 et seq.

Another case in point is Azerbaijan.[27] Azerbaijan was one of the piloting countries of EITI implementation and was granted compliant status in 2009. This status
was given only on a conditional basis as it failed to fully install a Multi-Stakeholder
Group; it only did so in the following year. Nevertheless, the country received the
"EITI Chairman's Award" in 2009. Azerbaijan is a striking example of the gap
between complying with the minimum standards of transparency of the early EITI
standard and providing for an enabling environment for civil society participation.
Human Rights Watch reports that the country's human rights record has declined
since it received the award in 2009.[28]

A law repressing NGOs signed by President Aliyev 2013 prevented meaningful
EITI participation by civil society. Civil society representatives in the EITI Multi-
Stakeholder Group complained that the new legal and administrative requirements
imposed on them severely restrict their ability to undertake NGO work. These measures have been accompanied by the arrest of human rights activists, prosecution
and the freezing of NGO bank accounts. PWYP called repeatedly for a re-validation
of Azerbaijan as problems related to civil society participation and their possibilities
to act freely persisted.[29] After years of discussion in the EITI Board, in 2016 the
Board decided to suspend the country. In response, Azerbaijan decided to withdraw
from the initiative in March 2017.

The examples reveal a dilemma of the initiative: since it does not commit its members to realise human rights, it has little leverage to demand observation of fundamental human rights, such as freedom of speech. Yet EITI needs human rights to be
observed if it is to be effective. In addition to civil society participation and the provision of an enabling environment, there are more approaches to human rights in the
context of EITI.

---

[27] Human Rights Watch, Extractive Industries: A New Accountability Agenda. 21 May 2013,
https://www.hrw.org/news/2013/05/21/extractive-industries-new-accountability-agenda   (last
accessed 1 October 2018), pp. 32 et seq.

[28] Human Rights Watch, Extractive Industries: A New Accountability Agenda. 21 May 2013,
https://www.hrw.org/news/2013/05/21/extractive-industries-new-accountability-agenda   (last
accessed 1 October 2018), p. 32.

[29] Human Rights Watch, Azerbaijan – no progress on key reforms. 2 March 2017, https://www.hrw.
org/news/2017/03/02/azerbaijan-no-progress-key-reforms (last accessed 12 August 2017); Publish
What You Pay, News: Extractive Industries Transparency Initiative (EITI) passes credibility test by
placing accountability squarely at the heart of the initiative. 9 March 2017, http://www.publish-
whatyoupay.org/pwyp-news/eiti-places-accountability-squarely-at-its-heart/ (last accessed 1
October 2018).

2.3 Reporting on Social and Environmental Impacts

Human rights abuses frequently associated with the extractive industry on the local level include forced resettlement, environmental pollution (including adverse impacts on the health of local communities), a lack of community consultation and repression of opponents of mining and oil/gas exploration. Although EITI does not question the legitimacy of oil and gas explorations and mining projects, it can contribute to minimising human rights abuses committed by companies and/or the state in connection with mining projects, by integrating transparency on environmental and social impacts in its reporting requirements. Some EITI member countries already integrate environmental concerns in one way or the other in their reports. However, none integrates environmental issues in a systematic manner providing reliable information on which local communities could build. That's why Publish What You Pay demands comprehensive environmental reporting as an integral part of EITI context information included in the national report.[30]

Some EITI Multi-Stakeholder Groups, such as the one in the Philippines, go beyond the mere transparency agenda and include Free Prior Informed Consent as a component of EITI reporting.[31]

2.4 Integrating Artisanal and Small-Scale Mining

EITI mainly addresses large scale projects, although Artisanal and Small-scale Mining (ASM) is in many countries an important area for income generation. The ASM sector creates significantly more employment opportunities than large-scale mining and provides alternative livelihoods for rural populations. But the sector does not typically generate material revenues at national level and is thus often excluded from EITI reporting.

However, there are many problems associated with ASM, including serious environmental pollution, e.g. as a result of the use of mercury in gold mining, poor working conditions and child labour. In addition, in countries characterised by conflict and/or with weak state structures, armed or criminal groups target the ASM sector in order to extort money from miners through blackmail, or to fill their war

---

[30] Sierra TA, Towards socio-environmental Transparency, Analysis of EITI processes in Latin America and the Caribbean: lessons and proposals. Latin American Civil Society Network of Extractive Industries, February 2016, http://propuestaciudadana.org.pe/wp-content/uploads/2016/02/Estudio-2-Socio-ambiental-INGL%C3%89S-web.pdf (last accessed 1 October 2018), pp. 18 et seq.

[31] Philippine Extractive Industries Transparency Initiative, Moving beyond Transparency. Extractive Industries Transparency Initiative, The forth PH-EITI Report (FY2015-2016), 30 December 2017, https://eiti.org/sites/default/files/documents/the-fourth-ph-eiti-report.pdf (last accessed 1 October 2018).

chests by controlling illegal trade in conflict minerals, as is the case in the Democratic Republic of Congo.

ASM plays an important role in the Congolese economy. Precise details are unavailable, but according to the Federal Institute for Geoscience and Natural Resources (BGR) around two million people are working in the sector and a total of ten million people in the country are dependent on it.[32] Between 300,000 and 400,000 people are involved in mining gold, tungsten, tantalum and tin in the East of the country. Much artisanal mining takes place on an informal basis, with no record of trade and payment flows.

The illegal trade in resources is an important source of income for armed groups in the East of the DRC. Halting trade in these conflict-financing minerals and applying due diligence throughout the supply chain would deprive various armed groups of an important source of funding. The last report of the Group of Experts on the DRC to the UN Security Council (2017)[33] established that this has to some extent been achieved. It states that in 2015, 26% of the tin, tungsten and tantalum (3T) mines were still controlled by armed groups. While the number of militarised 3T mines is falling, the focus of the illegal resource trade is shifting to other commodities. Gold, other minerals, timber and ivory worth USD 0.7–1.3 billion are smuggled out of the eastern DRC and surrounding areas every year. The 2012 EITI report suggested that mineral smuggling from artisanal mining was costing the government to lose significant revenue. Lost revenue due to mineral smuggling was estimated at USD 8 million per year for gold alone.

Several countries, including Afghanistan, Colombia, Myanmar and the Philippines, have included ASM in their EITI reports. The extent of ASM activities must usually be estimated as much of the mining is informal or illegal, and there are no accurate fiscal records of the sector's output.

No single initiative will improve conditions in the ASM sector, and greater data transparency will not automatically lead to reform of a country's resource policy in relation to this sector. But combined with other initiatives, the recording and publication of data through EITI can help to improve the situation. For example, to curb the financing of armed groups through the illegal resource trade, the EU and the USA have drawn up rules on due diligence in processing industries. By improving fiscal recording of the ASM sector and addressing environmental and social issues in the reporting scheme, EITI could do much to improve transparency in this area and might indirectly contribute to an improved human rights situation of mine workers and surrounding communities.

---

[32] Bundesanstalt für Geowissenschaften und Rohstoffe, DR Congo, https://www.bgr.bund.de/EN/Themen/Min_rohstoffe/CTC/Mineral-Certification-DRC/CTC_DRC_inhalt_en.html   (last accessed 1 October 2018).

[33] UN Security Council, Final report of the Group of Experts on the Democratic Republic of Congo, S/2017/672, 10 August 2017.

3   Conclusion

EITI has significantly contributed to the transparency of the extractive industries sector and financial streams, and has helped to set up dialogue platforms in several countries. Its standards and procedures are involved in an ever-evolving process. While at the beginning the initiative focused only on revenue transparency in an aggregated manner, it gradually extended to other segments of the value chain, such as contract transparency and, ultimately, to beneficial ownership of involved companies. EITI embraces a wide variety of countries with different political and social systems and situations, which makes it difficult to assess the real impact of EITI on the ground. However, various examples show that EITI has not yet moved much closer to its goal of improving accountability. EITI was designed for resource-rich countries and to support their improvement of resource governance. Achieving this aim requires the will to engage in reform and to guarantee fundamental democratic ground rules and human rights. Without freedom of speech and assembly, civil society cannot make effective calls for accountability.

If transparency is not an end in itself but is intended to help ensure that resource wealth benefits the people of the countries in which mining, oil and gas extraction takes place, then it is important that EITI is linked to the protection and respect of human rights. EITI is not a human rights organisation nor is it expected to become one. Nevertheless, neglecting human rights jeopardises the impact and success of EITI's own aim of improving transparency and accountability in the extractive industries.

Reference

Bantekas I, Oette L (2016) International human rights law and practice, 2nd edn. Cambridge University Press, Cambridge

Heidi Feldt   works as an independent consultant with longstanding experience on natural resource governance, transparency and accountability in the extractive sector and in development cooperation. She is a geologist by training and holds an MSc in rural development from London University and an PhD from Kassel University.

United States Law and Conflict Minerals

Patrick J. Keenan

Contents

1 Introduction 27
2 Conflicts and Conflict Minerals 29
3 Transparency Regimes 32
   3.1 Examples of Transparency Regimes 32
      3.1.1 Dodd-Frank: Conflict Minerals 32
      3.1.2 Dodd Frank: Disclosure of Payments Provisions 35
      3.1.3 California Transparency in Supply Chains Act 36
      3.1.4 European Union Conflict Minerals Regulations 36
   3.2 What Does Transparency Do, and How? 37
   3.3 Early Results of Disclosure-Based Regulations 40
4 The Future of Transparency-Based Regulations 45
   4.1 Less Transparency, Higher Risk of Corruption 45
   4.2 Prospects for Reform 47
      4.2.1 Increasing Compliance: More Guidance and Predictability 47
      4.2.2 Increasing Impact: Leverage Consumer Attention 48
5 Conclusion 48
References 49

1 Introduction

One of the most important trends in business and human rights is the increasing prominence of transparency-based regulation. This kind of regulation has as its goal to reduce unwanted practices or promote salutary practices by forcing companies to assemble and release information about their activities. A prominent example of such regulation was the conflict minerals disclosure requirements in the

P. J. Keenan (✉)
University of Illinois College of Law, Champaign, IL, USA
e-mail: pjkeenan@illinois.edu

© Springer Nature Switzerland AG 2019   27
I. Feichtner et al. (eds.), *Human Rights in the Extractive Industries*,
Interdisciplinary Studies in Human Rights 3,
https://doi.org/10.1007/978-3-030-11382-7_3

Dodd-Frank Wall Street Reform and Consumer Protection Act (Dodd-Frank).[1] These provisions were designed to force companies to investigate their own supply chains and make public a range of information that might be useful to consumers, investors, and other stakeholders. In one of its first series of actions, the Trump Administration has indicated that it intends to dismantle these regulations, effectively abdicating the leadership role the United States had played in the advent of such regulations. In February 2017, soon after taking office, the Trump Administration had drafted an executive order that would have effectively killed the Dodd-Frank conflict minerals requirements. According to a leaked version of the order,[2] the companies would no longer be required to comply with conflict minerals regulations and would be free to use conflict minerals without disclosing that fact to consumers. With the U.S. and the European Union on seemingly divergent paths with respect to transparency, now is an opportune time to look back at transparency-based regulations to analyse their effectiveness and their weaknesses, and to look forward to ask what might look different in the absence of such regulations.

The Dodd-Frank provisions are an example of an important type of regulation for human rights-related issues: regulation by transparency. Increasingly scholars and policymakers have pointed to transparency as an important part of the solution to these problems.[3] The core of the argument is that exposing as much of the process as possible to the sunlight of public and market scrutiny will deter bad behaviour by politicians and corporations, promote better decision making, and increase community satisfaction with how resources are exploited and the revenue is put to work.

Transparency and disclosure rules come in many forms and from many sources, but in the context of the extractive industries, they share important features. Some disclosure and transparency requirements pertain mostly to the financial relationship between companies and governments. These requirements make public information that would otherwise be private. Citizens can find out how much an oil company has paid in royalties to the government and then compare that to what the government reported it received or booked into the national treasury. Armed with this information, citizens would be in a position to hold accountable public officials if their actions deviate from the citizens' desires, or so the theory goes. Proponents argue that the same information reduces the incentives to give or receive bribes because it increases the likelihood of detection and of political or legal penalties for such behaviour. Other transparency or disclosure requirements require governments to document the full extent of the costs associated with resource extraction projects. For example, such a requirement might require a company to determine and then reveal the extent of environmental or social impacts the project would cause. This information would permit citizens to make better decisions as to the desirability of a new project and enable governments to negotiate better terms with a company

---

[1] Dodd-Frank Wall Street Reform and Consumer Protection Act (2010), Pub. L. No. 111-203, § 1502, 124 Stat. 1376, 2213-18.

[2] Fang L., Leaked Trump Presidential Memo Would Free U.S. Companies to Buy Conflict Minerals from Central African Warlords, The Intercept, February 8, 2017. The leaked version of the order is available here: https://perma.cc/8NAL-Y5YU (last accessed 1 October 2018).

[3] Gupta and Mason (2014), p. 3.

undertaking a project. Finally, some transparency or disclosure requirements require companies to document the conditions under which their products are extracted or manufactured. Disclosures of this type might require a company to show that its supply chain was free from the use of child labour or other violations of human rights.

In this chapter, I argue that transparency-based regulation is an important tool to address human rights violations. In Part II, I trace the origins of the Dodd-Frank conflict minerals provisions and examine the problems they were designed to address. In Part III, I examine four prominent transparency-based regimes to show how such regimes operate. Taken together, the four examples—including the conflict minerals provisions of Dodd-Frank, a separate disclosure of payments provision of Dodd-Frank, the California Transparency in Supply Chains Act, and the European Union's recent conflict minerals regulations—show the limits of regulation by transparency. I also argue that the theories underlying regulation by transparency are surprisingly thin and are not perfectly suited to the human rights context. Regulation by transparency is likely to be effective, if at all, only under conditions that are unlike those of human rights violations. I conclude Part III by examining empirical studies of the first series of reports filed pursuant to Dodd-Frank. These reports show that companies are learning how to implement the provisions and that they were beginning to have some impact, albeit one that it difficult to measure with any precision. In Part IV, I conclude by looking forward to two possible futures. First, I examine past problems and argue that such issues are likely to recur without disclosure-based regulations. Second, I argue that if disclosure-based regulations are to make a comeback in the U.S., they should be reformed in specific ways to make them more effective. I show that, despite their shortcomings, transparency regimes can be a useful, if limited, component of a regulatory response to human rights violations. They are not a substitute for more substantive regulation, but they can be an effective tool to force the disclosure of information from corporations and to create incentives to adopt soft law standards.

2   Conflicts and Conflict Minerals

By 2010, when Dodd-Frank was signed into law in the United States, the war in the Eastern Democratic Republic of Congo had been underway for more than a decade and a half. The conflict in Eastern DRC began in earnest after the 1994 genocide in Rwanda.[4] During 100 days in April of that year, thousands of mainly Hutu perpetrators killed approximately 800,000 Tutsis and moderate Hutus while most of the world did nothing.[5] As the Rwandan Patriotic Front swept into Rwanda and brought

---

[4] Stearns (2011), p. 113.

[5] Stearns (2011), p. 15; Des Forges (1999) Leave none to tell the story: genocide in Rwanda. Human Rights Watch, New York, https://www1.essex.ac.uk/armedcon/story_id/Leave%20 None%20to%20tell%20the%20story-%20Genocide%20in%20Rwanda.pdf (last accessed 1 October 2018), pp. 899–900.

an end to the genocide, many of the perpetrators of the genocide streamed across the border from Rwanda into the DRC. The DRC was suffering from its own problems at the time, and the presence in DRC of foreign militias exacerbated existing conflicts over land and resources. As the conflict intensified throughout the 1990s and into the 2000s, the various combatants—through the auspices of the United Nations—signed (and violated) a series of ceasefires and peace accords, none of which brought an end to the violence.[6] By the mid-2000s, journalists and advocates were calling the conflict in Eastern DRC the deadliest conflict the world had seen since the Second World War.[7]

At the same time, devices such as smartphones and iPads exploded in popularity. With the introduction of Apple's iPhone in 2006, the iPad in 2010,[8] and hundreds of similar devices from other companies near the same time, there was a significant increase in the demand for a handful of minerals used to make some of the essential components of these devices. It turned out that columbine-tantalite, wolframite, and other essential minerals were found in relative abundance in the Eastern DRC.[9] Large Western companies increased their demand for these so-called "conflict minerals" in order to meet consumer demand for smartphones and similar products.

The problem was that access to these minerals was controlled by a fluid roster of militias and government forces who fought deadly battles for control of the mines and abused the local population along the way. As attempts to end the conflict or even mitigate its effect on civilians had little effect, advocates began to look for more creative ways to curb the violence. Beginning in 2009, advocates were arguing in favour of some kind of regulatory response in an attempt to curb the violence in the DRC.[10] Representative Jim McDermott attempted several times to pass the Conflict Minerals Trade Act. Senators Sam Brownback, Dick Durbin, and Russ Feingold attempted to pass the Congo Conflict Minerals Act with the same goal. None of these efforts succeeded. After the financial crisis of 2008, the U.S. Congress began debating reforms that would eventually become the Dodd-Frank Act. Senators Brownback and Feingold inserted the conflict minerals provisions into Dodd-Frank during negotiations, and the Act was signed into law on July 21, 2010.[11] The conflict

---

[6] International Crisis Group, Africa Briefing No. 91, Eastern Congo: Why Stabilisation Failed (2012).

[7] Gettleman J, The World's Worst War, New York Times, 15 December 2012, https://www.nytimes.com/2012/12/16/sunday-review/congos-never-ending-war.html (last accessed 1 October 2018).

[8] Allison K, Palmer M (2007) Into the Pack: Apple Takes Risks in its Bid to Shake Up the Mobile Market. Financial Times, 26 June 2007; Waters R, Apple Adds to Firepower with Launch of the iPad. Financial Times, 28 January 2010.

[9] Business and Social Responsibility, Conflict Minerals and the Democratic Republic of Congo, May 2010, https://www.bsr.org/reports/BSR_Conflict_Minerals_and_the_DRC.pdf (last 1 October 2018), pp. 6–7.

[10] Taylor (2015), pp. 203–204.

[11] Protess B, Unearthing Exotic Provisions Buried in Dodd-Frank, New York Times, 13 July 2011, https://dealbook.nytimes.com/2011/07/13/unearthing-exotic-provisions-buried-in-dodd-frank/?action=click&contentCollection=Opinion&module=RelatedCoverage&region=EndOfArticle&pgtype=article (last accessed 1 October 2018).

minerals provisions of Dodd-Frank were inserted in an explicit attempt to address the seemingly intractable violence in the Eastern Democratic Republic of Congo.

The problem of conflict minerals combines two well-known maladies: parties to conflicts often steal natural resources to fund their war efforts, and countries with exploitable natural resources find that their new wealth can make the country worse off in many ways. The first issue—the association between conflict and natural resources—is a crude solution to a practical problem. Governments involved in conflicts can fund their war efforts through taxes or other legitimate (or quasi-legitimate) means.[12] Non-state combatants have similar needs but fewer legitimate options and often end up funding their operations through what amounts to pillage. In Sierra Leone, for example, the fighting forces funded many of their operations through the sale of illegally-harvested timber and diamonds. In Colombia, the main rebel group has long relied on the sale of cocaine or its antecedents to fund its activities. To be clear: I do not take a position in the debate about whether the presence of exploitable resources causes armed conflict. Instead, I observe that armed groups have, with disturbing frequency, used revenue from exploitable resources to fund their war efforts.

The second issue is an apparent conundrum. The discovery of minerals, gold, oil or some other valuable natural resource should be a moment to celebrate, especially in a poor country with few other sources of revenue. The formula seems simple: extract the resource, sell it, and use the revenue to improve the country's prospects. But scholars and policymakers have long observed that countries rich in natural resources have been apt to grow more slowly than countries without such resources. Scholars have documented an association between resource wealth and slower growth, a higher likelihood of conflict, more official corruption, and worse governance.

Conflict minerals can combine the worst strands of these already difficult stories. Conflict minerals are exploitable natural resources such as columbite-tantalum, gold, tin, and tungsten found in places plagued by violent conflict. Perhaps the most prominent example is in the Eastern DRC, where there are rich deposits of such minerals that have been associated with some of the most violent conflicts in the world for more than a decade. Exploitable natural resources thus present two problems: how to use the revenue to transform the country for the better, and how to curb the negative outcomes that often accompany resource wealth.

The conflict minerals provisions of Dodd-Frank were an attempt to address both components of the problem. Dodd-Frank was a response to the 2008 financial crisis and attendant complications in the banking industry. The primary objective of Dodd-Frank was to identify large-scale risks in the financial markets and improve government oversight and regulation of banks. But included in Dodd-Frank, at the urging of Senators Sam Brownback and Russ Feingold, was a provision designed to address the conflict in the Eastern Democratic Republic of Congo. This provision, Section 1502, required companies to disclose if their products contain minerals originating in the Democratic Republic of Congo or one of the surrounding states.

---

[12] Ochoa and Keenan (2011), pp. 131–132.

Since then, the Securities and Exchange Commission has promulgated regulations to implement the statute and companies have begun to file the required disclosures. Importantly, the conflict minerals provisions of Dodd-Frank do not prohibit the use of minerals from conflict zones or even penalize companies that use them; the regulations merely require companies to disclose if they use them.

3 Transparency Regimes

Since the 2008 financial crisis, there have been several attempts to institute transparency-based regulations in the U.S. In this part, I first examine four examples of disclosure-based regulations. The two most prominent examples were part of the Dodd-Frank act, which came into law in 2010. One section required companies to monitor and disclose the origins of the minerals used in many personal electronic devices. A second provision required energy companies to disclose payments made to foreign governments when pursuing energy contracts. A third example is a statute from the State of California regulating supply chains more broadly. Finally, the E.U. has recently instituted regulations that require companies to monitor conflict minerals.

I then analyse the theories underlying disclosure-based regulations. Scholars and advocates have long argued that disclosure has the potential to change the substantive behaviour of companies and reduce unwanted behaviour. I examine the conditions under which this is likely to be effective. Finally, I examine some early empirical results of disclosure-based regulations, drawing on reports filed pursuant to the conflict minerals provisions of Dodd-Frank.

3.1 Examples of Transparency Regimes

3.1.1 Dodd-Frank: Conflict Minerals

The conflict minerals provisions of Dodd-Frank were the most prominent recent attempt to address human rights violations through transparency. The Dodd-Frank Act imposed substantive reporting requirements on companies—described below—and it required the Securities and Exchange Commission to issue rules implementing the Act. The history of Section 1502—and the regulations designed to implement it—is convoluted,[13] but a general understanding of the structure of the statute and its necessary to assess whether it functions as promised and how to improve it should the political will exist in the future. In general, companies were required to answer a series of questions. First, companies would determine if any of the specified minerals are necessary to their products. If not, no disclosure was required. If so, the

---

[13] Whitney (2015).

company would make a preliminary determination as to whether the minerals came from the DRC or its neighbours. If they came from outside the DRC (or its neighbours), the company reported that fact and how it came to this determination. If the minerals came from the DRC or one of its neighbours, or if the company could not be certain, the company would undertake a much more detailed determination as to the origin of the minerals. Again, if the minerals came from outside the DRC or its neighbours, the company would report that fact and describe its process for determining the minerals' origins. A company was permitted to choose to describe its products as DRC conflict free, in which case the company was required to submit an audited report on their conflict minerals.

Section 1502 applied to companies required to file specified reports with the SEC pursuant to Section 13 or 15(d) of the Exchange Act. The statute had three basic requirements. First, covered companies were required to disclose annually to the SEC and make available on their websites whether conflict minerals that were necessary to the "functionality or production of a product" they manufactured originated in the DRC or in any country with which it shares a border (Angola, Burundi, Central African Republic, Republic of Congo, Rwanda, Sudan, Tanzania, Uganda, and Zambia). Companies were also required to disclose the steps they had taken to "exercise due diligence on the source and chain of custody" of conflict minerals, and a description of their products that are not DRC conflict free.

Pursuant to Section 1502, the SEC was required to promulgate regulations to implement the law, which it did in 2012. The first iteration of SEC regulations provided for a three-step process for companies to follow. Companies first had to determine if they were covered by the rule. Under this requirement, the company had to determine if it was required to file reports with the SEC (a simple task) pursuant to the Exchange Act *and* whether any of the specified minerals were necessary to the functionality or production of any of its products. If such minerals were not used or were not necessary to the functionality or production of a product, the company was not required to make any disclosure. If the specified minerals were necessary to the functionality or production of a product, the company was subject to the Section 1502.

The second step was for companies to make a "reasonable country of origin inquiry" into the source of the covered minerals. If the company determined that the minerals did not originate in the DRC or one of its neighbours, the company was required to report this fact in its annual report and explain how it conducted the country of origin inquiry, and publish the same information on its website.

Third, if the company determined that it was covered and determined either that conflict minerals from a covered company were used or that it could not determine with certainty where the minerals originated, the company was required to investigate the source of the minerals. The company was required to exercise due diligence on the source and chain of custody of the minerals. If the due diligence process revealed that the conflict minerals did not originate in the DRC or its neighbours or that its conflict minerals came from recycled or scrap sources, the company was not required to file a separate Conflict Minerals Report. Such companies were required to indicate in their disclosure reports how they reached their determination. If a company exercised due diligence and determined that its conflict minerals did originate in the DRC or its neighbours, or it was unable to determine where the minerals originated, then the company was required to file a separate Conflict Minerals Report as an exhibit to its disclosure report. The Conflict Minerals Report must provide information about the origins of the minerals in the product and the steps the company took to determine those origins.[14]

Before moving on, it is important to note three distinctive characteristics about conflict minerals and attempts to address the violence through Section 1502. First, Section 1502 defined "conflict minerals" as cassiterite (the ore that is used to make tin), columbite-tantalite (also known as coltan), wolframite (tungsten ore) and gold.[15] These minerals are found in many countries, most of which are not affected by violence or conflict. Any attempt to regulate the use of conflict minerals required at least a two-step process: determining whether the specified minerals are present in a company's products, and determining where those minerals came from. Complicating this is the fact that the specified minerals are combined with the same minerals from other sources in the manufacture of most products. An end-user company that purchases a component from a manufacturer that purchased refined metals from a smelter might have no information about the origin of all of the raw materials used in the manufacturing process. Thus Section 1502 was more than simply a disclosure-based regulation; it required companies to acquire information they do not possess, verify it, and then disclose it.

A second important characteristic of conflict minerals regulation is the nature of the minerals themselves. Conflict minerals are useless to people in their raw form.[16] They must be refined and processed many times before they can be turned into valuable products. The supply chain originates in a largely unregulated, informal environment in which armed groups, small companies, and so-called artisanal miners—often local people digging with hand tools—bring the minerals out of the ground. The minerals are sold along in a series of transactions before they end up in consumer products. The beginning of the supply chain is the least transparent and most difficult to regulate. The end of the supply chain, because it involves companies subject to SEC rules, was the most amenable to regulation but the most removed from the conflict and the information targeted by the rules.

Finally, regulators and consumers of the information disclosed by companies have no way to verify the information. Conflict minerals originate in conflict zones: areas that are inaccessible, prone to violence, and rarely visited by journalists or activist investors. There is no reasonably efficient way to determine whether companies are making accurate disclosures or how much they actually spend to investigate their own supply chains.

---

[14] U.S. Securities and Exchange Commission, Fact Sheet: Disclosing the Use of Conflict Minerals, 14 March 2017, https://www.sec.gov/opa/Article/2012-2012-163htm%2D%2D-related-materials.html (last accessed 1 October 2018).

[15] Dodd-Frank Wall Street Reform and Consumer Protection Act (2010), Pub. L. No. 111-203, § 1502, 124 Stat. 1376, 2213-18, §1502(e)(4).

[16] Ochoa and Keenan (2011), pp. 132–133 (201).

3.1.2   Dodd Frank: Disclosure of Payments Provisions

There is a separate provision in Dodd-Frank that has received much less attention so far because the SEC was slow to promulgate the regulations to implement it. This provision, Section 1504 of Dodd-Frank and known as the Lugar-Cardin Amendment, required the SEC to create regulations to require companies to disclose what they pay to foreign governments (or the U.S. government) for the purpose of developing mineral, natural gas, or oil projects. Because of delays in the SEC rule-making process and litigation, the SEC issued its proposed rules in 2016, 6 years after the passage of Dodd-Frank. As with the conflict minerals provisions, the proposed payment transparency rules did not prohibit payments to foreign governments.[17] Instead, they required companies to disclose any payments they make.

The rules required the disclosure of all payments made by a covered company— one that meets the definition of an issuer pursuant to the Exchange Act—or any of its agents or subsidiaries to foreign governments or the U.S. government to advance the commercial development of an oil, natural gas, or minerals project. The rules covered payments to subnational levels of government, including state, province, and local governments. Covered payments include taxes, royalties, license fees, bonuses, and payments for infrastructure improvements. In addition, if the resource development contract requires the company to make payments for community development or other corporate social responsibility endeavours, those payments were also to be disclosed.

The rules permitted companies engaging in exploratory activities to delay making their required disclosures by 1 year. The rules also provided a 2-year phase-in, and permitted the SEC to grant exemptions to the rule if the disclosure of otherwise covered payments was illegal in the country in which the project took place. Importantly, the rules required disclosure of payments that are "not de minimis," which means payments that individually or in total equal or exceed $100,000. The rules would have required that disclosures be made at the "project level," which covers operational activities governed by a single contract or license. That approach would have made it difficult for companies to avoid their reporting responsibilities by making a series of smaller payments through subsidiaries to different levels of government.

---

[17] To be sure, the payment of bribes is prohibited under U.S. law. The Foreign Corrupt Practices Act prohibits U.S. companies from paying bribes to foreign governments or their agents. But the FCPA carves out exceptions for payments for "facilitating or expediting" government actions. Section 1504 would cover both payments that would violate the FCPA and payments that would fall within one of the exceptions.

3.1.3 California Transparency in Supply Chains Act

Dodd-Frank's disclosure requirements were not the only requirements that companies operating in the U.S. face. Another prominent example is the California Transparency in Supply Chains Act, which went into force in 2010. The economy of the State of California is larger than the economies of all but seven countries in the world.[18] This means that state-level regulation in California can have as powerful an effect as national regulation in most countries. The stated purpose of the CTSCA was to provide more, and more accurate, information to consumers as a way to enable them to make more careful consumption decisions. The CTSCA states that its purpose is to provide the information necessary to permit consumers "to force the eradication of slavery and trafficking by way of their purchasing decisions."[19] The CTSCA requires companies with worldwide gross receipts of $100 million or more that do business in California to disclose their efforts to eradicate slavery and human trafficking from their supply chains. Companies must disclose if they verify the supply chains for their products, audit suppliers, provide training for their employees to fight trafficking and forced labour, and require suppliers to comply with laws prohibiting trafficking and forced labour. As with the Dodd-Frank provisions, the CTSCA requires companies to disclose what they do; it does not directly require companies to change what they do. As with Dodd-Frank, the impetus to change would come from consumer pressure once consumers are armed with accurate information.

3.1.4 European Union Conflict Minerals Regulations

In 2016, after years of negotiation, the institutions of the European Union reached an agreement on a new regulation designed to address conflict minerals and their effect on human rights violations.[20] The regulation requires minerals processed in smelters or refiners in the EU to go through a due diligence process. All but the smallest importers will be required to undertake due diligence checks in accordance with the OECD *Due Diligence Guidance for Responsible Supply Chains of Minerals from Conflict-Affected and High-Risk Areas.*[21] The OECD's due diligence requirements impose obligations on companies to improve their management systems and assess and manage supply chain risks. The OECD guidelines also require

---

[18] Sisney J and Garosi J, California Legislative Analyst's Office, 2014 GDP: California Ranks 7th or 8th in the World, 1st July 2015, http://www.lao.ca.gov/LAOEconTax/Article/Detail/90 (last accessed 1 October 2018).

[19] California Transparency in Supply Chains Act of 2010, https://leginfo.legislature.ca.gov/faces/billNavClient.xhtml?bill_id=200920100SB657 (last accessed 1 October 2018).

[20] See the contribution by *Nowrot* in this volume.

[21] OECD Due Diligence Guidance for Responsible supply Chains of Minerals from Conflict-Affected and High-Risk Areas, 3rd edition, 2016, http://www.oecd.org/daf/inv/mne/OECD-Due-Diligence-Guidance-Minerals-Edition3.pdf (last accessed 1 October 2018).

third-party audits and reporting on supply chain due diligence. The EU regulation avoids one critique of the Dodd-Frank provisions by focusing on minerals from any conflict-affected or high-risk area instead of focusing solely on minerals from Central Africa.

3.2   What Does Transparency Do, and How?

The natural resources supply chain is a complex series of transactions, with minerals often originating in a developing country and passing through a series of other countries as they are refined and made into consumer products. At every stage in the process there is the potential for corruption, abuse, or other problematic behaviour. When a country finds itself with an exploitable natural resource, the discovery sets in motion a chain of decisions and transactions that can determine how the new wealth will affect the country. This series of transactions has two distinct parts, one centred mainly around government processes and the other around commercial processes, though they are inextricably interlinked. When natural resources are discovered, the government must first determine who will conduct the exploration and extraction of the resource.[22] This typically involves awarding contracts and licenses to one or more companies to determine how much of the resource exists and then to extract it. The next significant part of the process involves the government setting and enforcing the conditions under which the project will operate. This can include setting labour policies, environmental protection standards, and similar issues. A third part of the process is to determine how much of the revenue will flow directly to the government through taxes and royalties or other payments.[23] Fourth, the government must manage the revenue on behalf of the country, including determining how to distribute the benefits to various domestic constituencies and how to allocate the revenue over time.

The second part centres around supply chain that takes a natural resource from the ground to market in consumer products. This process is as complex as the government-centred process described above, and can be shaped in large part by government regulation, but it is helpful to analyse it as a separate process. Even for conflict minerals, the supply chain takes a predictable form, even when it is not transparent or well managed. Minerals are mined by local people, sold to traders who bundle them with other minerals, transported out of the country of origin and on to the international market. They are then smelted, made into components,

---

[22] The government section draws on Eleodoro Mayorga Alba, Extractive Industries Value Chain: A Comprehensive Integrated Approach to Developing Extractive Industries. Working Paper, World Bank Division of Oil, Gas and Mining Policy, March 2009, http://siteresources.worldbank.org/INTOGMC/Resources/ei_for_development_3.pdf (l last accessed 1 October 2018).

[23] It is, of course, possible that governments will utilize what is often called the Angola Model of financing, in which the government receives infrastructure or other in-kind assistance from the company.

assembled into consumer products, then sold to consumers. Every step in this process is a transaction; it is a series of sales that takes a mineral from its raw state and transforms it into a valuable consumer product. The process is also a journey that takes place over time and across great distances and each step in the process presents an opportunity to preserve or lose information about the origin and history of the product. The seller might sell the product with full and accurate information about its history. The seller might provide incomplete or inaccurate information or deliberately attempt to mislead the buyer. Or the seller may not have much information about the product's history to that point and may simply transfer the product.

Disclosure and transparency regimes have as their goal the revelation of information about the interactions between the government and industry that set in motion the extraction process, or about a product's history. Such regulations target specific and unwanted activity, such as the use of conflict minerals, employing children in manufacturing, or the payment or receipt of bribes by government officials. What is noteworthy about this style of regulation is that it typically does not proscribe the unwanted activity. Instead, the regulation forces those involved in the process to gather and make public information about the transaction.[24] To be sure, there are regulations that prohibit much of the unwanted activity, especially bribery or the misuse of official authority. But disclosure-based regimes operate differently, by making public information that would either never be recorded or that would otherwise remain in the hands of those engaging in the unwanted activity.

Because the regulation does not directly proscribe the unwanted activity, there are several closely-linked considerations that are implicit in understanding how such regulation might actually achieve its goals. The information that is made public must be salient to someone outside the transaction or supply chain. Proponents of disclosure believe or assume that some actor will change its behaviour when it learns of the new information. For example, if a disclosure regime requires apparel manufacturers to disclose if there was child labour anywhere in the supply chain, regulators must believe that consumers would be less likely to buy the apparel if they knew that it was or might have been made by children. Connected to this assumption—that of an interested recipient of the information—is the assumption that the recipient has the power to take some action that would either reward a company operating appropriately or punish a company engaging in the unwanted activity. This logic applies in the official corruption context as well, with engaged constituents standing in for engaged consumers or other market participants and politicians standing in for companies.

A second cluster of considerations has to do with the information itself. Disclosure-based regulations assume that the targeted information is readily available and can be disclosed. With respect to official corruption, this assumption is eminently reasonable. It will always be the case that those in power know who is involved in a resource extraction transaction, what each person's role was, and how each person is rewarded or compensated. This information may be embarrassing or known only to a very few, or it may be available only in bits and pieces, but it exists

---

[24] For an analysis of such regulations, Ochoa and Keenan (2011), pp. 136–137.

and can be disclosed. With respect to the conflict minerals supply chain, the story might be more complex. Consider again a simplified model of the supply chain (Fig. 1).

If the target of the regulation is to ensure that minerals from conflict areas or from areas controlled by illegal armed groups are not used in the manufacture of consumer products, the best information is closest to the mine. Each step in the process from left to right reduces the reliability of the most important information; traders know less than miners about the mine conditions, exporters know less than traders, and so on. The problem is that for practical and pragmatic reasons, most such regulation targets companies on the right end of the supply chain: companies that sell consumer products or manufacture components. These companies are the easiest to regulate because they typically have some connection to the United States or other industrialized countries, and because they are the closest to consumers who may change their consumptive behaviour if their favoured product is connected to the unwanted activity.

This creates several challenges for disclosure-based regulations in this area to be effective. First, the regulated company must somehow acquire the necessary information from other actors in the supply chain, even if those actors are a continent away and separated from the regulated company by several transactions. This is especially difficult when, as with the conflict minerals supply chain, there are multiple points along the chain in which products from multiple sources are aggregated and transformed into something new. For example, smelters combine ore from multiple sites to create the refined raw material that component manufacturers use. After smelting, it is impossible to state that the refined material came from any particular site because it came from many sites. When there is a series of arms-length transactions, there is little likelihood that a consumer products company would have any idea where the raw materials were mined.

A second challenge is that changing the unwanted primary behaviour requires each participant in the supply chain to exert pressure on the participants that come before it. Manufacturers must pressure smelters, who must pressure exporters, and so forth. What makes this difficult is that some participants, especially those that are at the far left end of the supply chain, may have little incentive or capacity to gather or maintain the kind of information that the end user will require. If the end user wishes to avoid having to state that it used tainted materials, the end user might set up a system to enable it to avoid the use of possibly tainted materials, or it might create a system to force other participants to change their behaviour. Either way, the end user faces a significant challenge. The situation is similar but not identical with respect to the misuse of public office. In that context, the challenge is that each

Fig. 1 Mineral supply chain

participant has a better chance to extract rents from the secret information if all of the other participants remain silent.

Proponents of transparency and disclosure as tools for better governance point to three principal mechanisms by which transparency might produce results.[25] Transparency can bolster attempts to improve governance by shifting the incentives faced by potentially corrupt officials. When a public official must make a decision regarding a resource extraction contract, the official may decide to demand a bribe from the company. Proponents of transparency argue that the more transparent the transaction, the more difficult it is for a potentially corrupt official to "distort information" and demand a bribe.[26] When the transaction is completely transparent—the terms of the contract are available to the public, the official's role in the transaction is apparent to all—official misbehaviour is more likely to be detected and therefore less likely to occur in the first place. On this account, transparency deters official rent-seeking by making it more difficult to leverage secret information and by increasing the likelihood of detection. Another argument in favour of transparency is that it can empower political actors and citizens. Proponents of this theory argue that citizens have the power to affect the behaviour of politicians by voting them out of office. Armed with accurate information about their role in important transactions, citizens can reward honest politicians and punish dishonest politicians. A third argument in favour of transparency is that it enables market actors to discipline companies and governments. For example, engaged consumers might refuse to purchase products made under undesirable conditions or purchased from corrupt or abusive regimes.

3.3 Early Results of Disclosure-Based Regulations

When evaluating the success of disclosure-based regulations there are two relevant concerns: whether companies comply with the rules and whether the behavioural changes compelled by the rules affect the underlying problem. Disclosure-based regulations do not directly prohibit the underlying conduct. Companies are still free to use conflict minerals, even those mined in the midst of the violence in Congo, and they are still free to provide payments to governments in exchange for the commercial development of oil, gas, or minerals projects. Disclosure-based rules only affect the underlying problem if they induce sufficient behavioural change from companies. One of the complications with disclosure-based rules, particularly in the area of human rights in conflict zones, is that it is almost impossible to determine with any certainty that a reduction in conflict or an improvement in the respect for human rights was caused by the rule. Any analysis of conflict minerals disclosures and their effects on the ground must acknowledge that it is impossible to prove a causal connection between the rules and the situation on the ground. The best available

---

[25] Kolstad and Wiig (2008), pp. 522–525.
[26] Kolstad and Wiig (2008), pp. 522–525.

evidence therefore takes two forms: studies that show the extent of compliance with the disclosure rules and investigations into the human rights situation on the ground in the relevant locations at the relevant time.

Disclosure-based regulatory regimes are sometimes called "name and shame" efforts, designed to change behaviour by using the disapprobation of an audience toward a wrongdoer to prompt the wrongdoer to change its behaviour.[27] Such efforts can provide some insight into the conditions under which a disclosure-based regime is likely to work. Shaming is essentially the use of some expression of disapproval as a way to reduce unwanted behaviour.[28] Under what conditions is this kind of mechanism likely to be effective? A useful schema comes from the norms literature. Some norms scholars argue that for norms to be effectively enforced, there must be "an actor," "an enforcer," and "member[s] of the audience."[29] Most important in the context of human rights-focused disclosure regimes is the idea of the enforcer: the entity that invokes and imposes the penalty.

For transparency to affect governance, the appropriate conditions must be present.[30] One important consideration is the presence of an entity to monitor and disseminate information so that it can be used by others to further the goals of the regulation. For example, the media might report on the disclosures, or members of civil society might obtain the information and put it into a form that citizens or activists could use.[31] Transparency-based regimes are unlikely to be effective when there is a disconnect between those who obtain the information and would use it (the "enforcers") and those whose actions are causing the underlying problem. In the context of human rights violations, those engaging in the violations typically have more power than the victims and have few incentives to respond to the victims. If the enforcers are consumers in another country, who impose their penalty through diffuse purchasing decisions, the penalty might be felt by a company, but it is unlikely to be felt by the primary violator.

Most disclosure regimes give too little attention to identifying why and how the enforcer will impose a penalty.[32] Disclosure-based regimes will only be effective if recipients of the information actually act on it. They must be able to obtain the information, perceive it to be salient, and then have some avenue for action. In the context of human rights regimes, the incentives to obtain information or act on it are very weak. For example, if consumers are the "enforcers," their decisions are

---

[27] Hafner-Burton (2008); Ron J et al. (2005) Transnational Information Politics: NGO Human Rights Reporting. 1986–2000, https://onlinelibrary.wiley.com/doi/abs/10.1111/j.1468-2478.2005.00377.x (last accessed 1 October 2018).

[28] Skeel (2001), p. 1816.

[29] Ellickson R (1991) The evolution of social norms: a perspective from the legal academy. Yale Law School, Program for Studies in Law, Economics and Public Policy, Working Paper No. 230, https://papers.ssrn.com/sol3/papers.cfm?abstract_id=191392 (last accessed 1 October 2018), p. 37.

[30] Frynas (2010), p. 169.

[31] Frynas (2010), pp. 169–170.

[32] Skeel (2001), p. 1816.

inevitably the product of a long list of reasons. What is more, the information disclosed makes it difficult for companies to distinguish themselves. In the context of conflict minerals, for example, most companies disclose the same information, making it difficult for any company to gain an advantage in the market touting its clean supply chain.

Companies were first required to file reports on their use of conflict minerals in 2014; the disclosures pertained to minerals used during 2013. Because the disclosure of payments rules went into effect only in 2016, no reports have been filed at the time of writing. Recall that the conflict minerals disclosures follow a three-step process: determining if the rules apply in the first place, conducting a country of origin inquiry regarding any conflict minerals, and exercising due diligence to determine the source and chain of custody of the conflict minerals used.

In August 2015, the U.S. Government Accountability Office (GAO), issued a report on the first cycle of company disclosures covering reporting year 2013.[33] The GAO's findings were based on a representative sample of the disclosures filed by a total of 1321 companies. The GAO found that 99% of companies that filed reports conducted a country-of-origin inquiry.[34] Of these, 67% were unable to determine the country of origin of the conflict minerals contained in their products.[35] Only 4% of companies reported that the conflict minerals came from one of the covered countries (the DRC or its neighbours), and 24% reported that the conflict minerals originated in a place other than a covered country.

Beyond the raw numbers, the GAO report is noteworthy for two additional reasons. First, the GAO found that the number of companies filing reports was much lower than the number the SEC estimated would be affected by the rule. Before reports were filed, the SEC estimated that 6000 companies would be affected by the rule.[36] Only 1321 companies actually filed reports covering reporting year 2013. The difference might be explained at least in part on the complexity and novelty of the rule, of course. But it might also reflect the relative absence of enforcement mechanisms in the rule. Companies determine for themselves if they are required to file the disclosure, and there is no effective way to look behind a company's decision.

---

[33] The U.S. GAO is an independent, non-partisan agency that reports to the U.S. Congress on the ways that public funds are spent, https://www.gao.gov/about/index.html (last accessed 1 October 2018).

[34] United States Government Accountability Office, SEC Conflict Minerals Rule: Initial Disclosures Most Companies Were Unable to Determine the Source of Their Conflict Minerals 14. GAO-15-561, August 2015, https://www.gao.gov/assets/680/672051.pdf (last accessed 1 October 2018).

[35] United States Government Accountability Office, SEC Conflict Minerals Rule: Initial Disclosures Most Companies Were Unable to Determine the Source of Their Conflict Minerals 15, GAO-15-561, August 2015, https://www.gao.gov/assets/680/672051.pdf (last accessed 1 October 2018).

[36] It is important to note that the SEC itself acknowledged that its estimate was "intentionally overly inclusive.", United States Government Accountability Office, SEC Conflict Minerals Rule: Initial Disclosures Most Companies Were Unable to Determine the Source of Their Conflict Minerals 13, GAO-15-561, August 2015, https://www.gao.gov/assets/680/672051.pdf (last accessed 1 October 2018).

Second, the GAO found that 96% of companies that undertook a country-of-origin inquiry did so by surveying their suppliers. They conducted the surveys in a variety of ways, some more rigorous than others, but the rule appears to have created a strong incentive for companies to engage directly with their suppliers. If disclosure-based regulations are to have an effect on the underlying behaviour, proponents suggest that one of the most promising pathways is for companies to impose more and more control on their suppliers. One year of reports does not prove that this is happening, but it is at least promising that the rule appears to have increased company engagement with suppliers.

A separate academic study of the same pool of filings went somewhat further.[37] That study combined quantitative analysis of the filings with qualitative research. The first finding was that many companies are not at all good at due diligence. Many companies have little detailed information about their supply chains and have done little to mitigate the risk that suppliers will use conflict minerals or permit exploitive practices. A separate finding is that companies that previously had worked with voluntary supply chain initiatives do a better job than do companies without such experience.

There is some data regarding reporting year 2014 (reports filed in 2015). According to an academic analysis of filings, 1271 companies filed reports on their use of conflict minerals in 2014.[38] Researchers found that 65% of companies could not determine the origin of their conflict minerals.

The evidence regarding the California Supply Chains Transparency Act is similarly limited. In a recent academic analysis of compliance with the act, researchers found that approximately 2126 companies "potentially" fit the criteria that would require a disclosure, and identified 1325 such disclosures on company websites.[39] The same study found that while "many companies are fully compliant," "others still have homework to do" to improve the quality and accuracy of their disclosures.[40]

It should come as no surprise that Section 1502 has had relatively little demonstrable impact on the violence in DRC, and the reasons for this point to general problems with transparency as regulation. There have been two reporting cycles since the SEC regulations went into effect, and recent scholarly analyses of these reports show that companies comply with the regulations in a way that is superficial and uninformative.[41] There are several reasons for this. Companies appear to fulfil

---

[37] Sarfaty (2015).

[38] Bayer C, Corporate compliance with the California Transparency in Supply Chains Act of 2010. Dodd-Frank 1502 – RY 2014 Filing Evaluation, 16 November 2015, http://media.wix.com/ugd/f0f801_f1950a1d7a0741e7bc878f38964dd7bf.pdf (last accessed 1 October 2018).

[39] Bayer C, Corporate compliance with the California Transparency in Supply Chains Act of 2010. Dodd-Frank 1502 – RY 2014 Filing Evaluation, 16 November 2015, http://media.wix.com/ugd/f0f801_f1950a1d7a0741e7bc878f38964dd7bf.pdf (last accessed 1 October 2018).

[40] Bayer C, Corporate compliance with the California Transparency in Supply Chains Act of 2010. Dodd-Frank 1502 – RY 2014 Filing Evaluation, 16 November 2015, http://media.wix.com/ugd/f0f801_f1950a1d7a0741e7bc878f38964dd7bf.pdf (last accessed 1 October 2018).

[41] Schwartz (2016).

their regulatory obligations as inexpensively as possible. This is likely true of all regulations, but it is a particular problem with conflict minerals disclosures for at least two reasons. First, information about each company's supply chain is best known to the company. It is virtually impossible for regulators, journalists, or anyone else to assemble the required information. Therefore companies run little risk of exposure if their disclosures are incomplete or inaccurate. Compounding this problem are the weak penalties that attach to non-compliance. Companies face little more than a fine of $100 per day for non-compliance, and that penalty only comes if the SEC decides to actually investigate, which itself is unlikely.

Another explanation for the underwhelming compliance with the disclosure requirements is that the statute and rules are poorly designed.[42] Companies are not required to describe their products with any specificity. Consumers have no way to know which products contain conflict minerals without this information. Similarly, companies are permitted to provide information about the processing facility and country of origin only if they could link minerals from specific countries or facilities to their products. If a company is unable to do this, they could omit the information.

This points to a larger problem with disclosure-based regulation. The type and amount of information required to be disclosed is likely to determine whether the regulations are effective. When most companies report no conclusion with respect to their products' conflict status,[43] consumers have little useful information. Faced with this, even the most diligent consumer would know little more than that one product in their favourite brand's product line might contain a component made with minerals that might have come from a conflict mine.

The problems that affect other human rights-focused disclosure regimes are also relevant to the disclosure of payments provisions. One obvious model for Dodd-Frank Section 1504 was the Extractive Industries Transparency Initiative (EITI).[44] The EITI was at first an initiative of the United Kingdom designed to require governments and companies to make public the payments companies made to governments for extractive activities.[45] Proponents of the EITI argued that transparency with respect to payments would produce two types of benefits. The first benefits would be substantive: "better management of … natural resource[s,] less corruption, more equitable distribution of the revenues, less waste and fraud, more economic development, and less violent conflict."[46] The second type of benefits would be more process-based: "the mobilization and empowerment of civil society … to hold both governments and corporations accountable."[47] Despite some progress, however, the results have not been consistent with the theory.[48]

---

[42] Schwartz (2016), pp. 163–164.

[43] Schwartz (2016), pp. 152–153.

[44] See the chapter by Feldt in this volume.

[45] David-Barrett and Okamura (2016), pp. 229–230.

[46] Haufler (2010), p. 59.

[47] Haufler (2010), p. 59.

[48] Haufler (2010), p. 55.

As with the EITI, Dodd-Frank Section 1504 required the disclosure of payments to governments from companies working in the extractive industries. Because it does so in a context similar to the EITI, the same problems are likely. One of the problems with the EITI is that the causal mechanism—the process by which the revelation of information is supposed to lead to change—is weak. Unless the information disclosed reveals evidence of a crime or a civil fraud, there are no legal or political mechanisms by which to hold accountable the entity engaged in undesirable conduct. Put differently, there is little that the recipients of information can do to discipline anyone engaging in unwanted but not illegal conduct.

4 The Future of Transparency-Based Regulations

Before reversing course, the US had been at the forefront of a growing trend toward more transparency, not less. Indeed, Canada, France, Norway, and the United Kingdom have all adopted similar rules in the years since the US law was first passed in 2010. The corporations that argued against the rule—led by ExxonMobil, which was led by Rex Tillerson until he became Secretary of State in the new administration—argued that the rules put them at a competitive disadvantage. By abandoning its leadership role, the US may contribute to harms in resource-rich developing countries without providing any benefit to corporations. With the US removed from the states to which companies must report, Congress and the Trump Administration have done little to ease any regulatory burden on companies (light though the burden was in the first place). The same is true with respect to the conflict minerals supply chain rules. Although the regulations are still in flux, it appears inevitable that the Trump Administration will suspend the rules for at least 2 years and may well eliminate them entirely. Initial reaction to the proposed changes in the rules from consumer-facing companies has been largely negative. Now that they have invested in the infrastructure necessary to better control their supply chains, corporations such as Apple have argued against abandoning the rules.

4.1 *Less Transparency, Higher Risk of Corruption*

With the Trump Administration's apparent abandonment of transparency-based regulations, the problems associated with businesses and payments to governments are likely to recur. For example, for many years Nigeria has been plagued with corruption scandals surrounding the oil industry.[49] One important component of this problem has been the practice of Nigerian officials of selling oil and gas at below-market rates using contracts that appear not to violate domestic law but are nonetheless irregular and have the effect of enriching officials at the expense of the country.

---

[49] Keenan (2014), pp. 237–239, 219–220, 232–242.

A report produced by a task force assigned to investigate the oil and gas industry showed that officials had awarded contracts at far lower rates than they would have realized if they had been sold on the open market.[50] The report showed that officials, in transactions completely shielded from public scrutiny, had deprived the national treasury of approximately $35 billion dollars over 10 years.[51] Officials profited from the non-transparent nature of these transactions in a number of ways. Some officials awarded discretionary contracts and received, cumulatively, more than $180 million in signature bonuses that were not accounted for.[52] Another arrangement involved the use of a joint venture as an intermediary between the government and the international markets. Government officials sold gas at far below market rates to the joint venture, which then sold the gas onto the international market at market rates.[53] What unites these schemes is that they thrived in the dark. Citizens, other bidders, and legitimate regulators had no way to acquire information about the deals or who was profiting from them.

The situation in Angola illustrates another facet of the problem.[54] There the Angolan national oil company, Sonangol, manages oil concessions and has the power to award contracts to exploit oil and gas resources.[55] By setting up a complex web of joint ventures and co-owed blocks, Sonangol has made it possible for officials to personally profit from the sale of national resources and costing the country nearly $1 billion.[56] As with below-market rate sales, this problem thrives only in the darkness.

The US disclosure of payments rules, if enforced effectively, could have addressed at least part of the problem. Under the recently-abandoned disclosure of payments rules, any company that was covered by the rules would have been required to disclose in detail any payments made to government officials. Many of the companies most active in the Angolan oil industry are listed in the US (that is, they would have been covered by the disclosure rules), including BP, Chevron, Cobalt, Eni, ExxonMobil, Petrobras, Total, and Vaalco.

---

[50] Wallis W, Ribadu Report: Inquiry Shines Light on Murky Mechanics of the Oil Industry. Financial Times, 12 November 2012, https://www.ft.com/content/9968e666-34b1-11e2-8b86-00144feabdc0 (last accessed 1 October 2018).

[51] Allison S, Nigeria: How to Lose $35 Bn. The Guardian, 13 November 2012, https://www.the-guardian.com/world/2012/nov/13/nigeria-oil-corruption-ridabu (last accessed 1 October 2018).

[52] Brock J, Exclusive: Nigeria Loses Billions in Cut Price Oil Deals. Reuters, 24 October 2012, https://www.reuters.com/article/us-nigeria-oil/exclusive-nigeria-loses-billions-in-cut-price-oil-deals-report-idUSBRE89N0VV20121024 (last accessed 1 October 2018).

[53] Brock J, Exclusive: Nigeria Loses Billions in Cut Price Oil Deals. Reuters, 24 October 2012, https://www.reuters.com/article/us-nigeria-oil/exclusive-nigeria-loses-billions-in-cut-price-oil-deals-report-idUSBRE89N0VV20121024 (last accessed 1 October 2018).

[54] Keenan (2014), pp. 235–236.

[55] Petroleum Activities Law, No. 10/04 (2004) (Rep. of Angola), http://www.eisourcebook.org/cms/files/attachments/other/Angola%20Petroleum%20Activities%20Law,%202004.pdf (last accessed 1 October 2018).

[56] Pearce J, IMF: Angola's "Missing Millions". BBC, 18 October 2002, http://news.bbc.co.uk/2/hi/africa/2338669.stm (last accessed 1 October 2018).

4.2   Prospects for Reform

When the conflict minerals provisions of Dodd-Frank were being debated, many scholars were optimistic about the potential of disclosure-based regulation.[57] Scholars and advocates made a range of claims about such regulation, many of which were much too ambitious. Before moving on, it is important to put any recommendations in context. It was never true that the conflict in Eastern Congo was principally due to the presence of valuable minerals, or that the eradication of the minerals trade would halt the violence. That conflict had many causes and has had many consequences. Conversely, it is not accurate to say that the minerals trade is irrelevant to the conflict. The fighting forces derive the funds to buy weapons at least in part from their control of minerals. The most that can be said is that the minerals trade is connected to the conflict and likely exacerbates it. A second strand of argument maintained that the imposition of conflict minerals disclosure requirements would bring an end to the minerals trade in Eastern Congo and would cause great harm to local people who already struggled to find a way to survive. Again, the minerals trade was an important source of work for many people in a terribly impoverished region, but minerals disclosure regulations did not cause it to collapse or come to an end. Finally, the underlying premise of most disclosure-based regulations is that there is a pool of engaged consumers (or other market actors) eager for more information to guide their consumption decisions. There is little evidence that this is true. With these observations as a backdrop, my recommendations are appropriately modest. Disclosure-based regulations should not be the only approach to addressing the underlying problem, but they can be a part of a comprehensive strategy to address a problem.

4.2.1   Increasing Compliance: More Guidance and Predictability

One of the findings of Galit Sarfaty's careful study of compliance with the Dodd-Frank conflict minerals rules is that companies do a better job of compliance when it is easier for them. The first half-decade of the conflict minerals rules was rocky, partly because the SEC was unsure how it wanted to implement the statutory requirements, and partly because the rules and the statute were the subject of litigation. Now that there is a body of rules that appear likely (at least so far) to withstand legal challenges, companies will likely find ways to increase their compliance. Regulators could facilitate this in two ways. First, even as the rules have become more certain, they remain complex. Simplifying the rules would go a long way toward increasing compliance. One way to accomplish this would be to create a single set of due diligence requirements for companies to follow. As things now stand, companies approach due diligence in a wide variety of ways. If there were one set of rules, companies—and the accountants, lawyers, and consultants who

---

[57] Ochoa and Keenan (2011), pp. 136–137.

help implement the rules—would become more efficient and effective. Second, regulators could permit companies to comply with one or more of the industry association approaches to due diligence. This would mean that there was not a single way to conduct due diligence but a handful of different approaches tailored to each industry sector.

4.2.2   Increasing Impact: Leverage Consumer Attention

Disclosure-based regimes rely on consumers and other market actors to change their behaviour, thereby affecting the underlying activity. The existing regimes require companies to produce substantial amounts of information and put it on their websites, but there is little reason to expect that substantial numbers of consumers will ever acquire the information. When most consumers make decisions about what products to buy, they do not go to a company's corporate website, which might be different from its consumer-oriented website, to read a long, complicated report about compliance with an obscure set of regulations. Disclosure-based regimes would be more effective if they required companies to publish the relevant information as close to consumers as possible. For example, mobile phone manufacturers could be required to put a label on the product or its packaging indicating whether the product was conflict free. Apparel manufacturers could engage in similar labelling.

5   Conclusion

In this Chapter I have argued that the use of disclosure regimes to address the harms associated with conflict minerals is unlikely to effectively address the underlying harms in the near term. The future is difficult to predict. The reforms suggested herein are unlikely to be adopted by the Trump Administration. The Trump Administration appears unlikely to expand requirements for companies and, as stated, has indicated that it wishes to reduce regulations. There are some reasons for optimism, however. First, the procurement rules for the U.S. government now require disclosures about the use of conflict minerals and the steps computer manufacturers have taken to investigate their own supply chains.[58] Second, states in the U.S. have passed their own regulations designed to address conflict minerals,[59] and there have been no indications to date that states are likely to abdicate their responsibilities in the way the federal government has.

---

[58] Callaway A and Lezhnev S (2018) An import signal to companies: new federal procurement requirements for computers include conflict minerals criteria. Enough Project, 17 April 2018, https://enoughproject.org/blog/important-signal-companies-new-federal-procurement-requirements-computers-include-conflict-minerals-criteria (last accessed 1 October 2018).

[59] Prenkert and Shackelford (2014), pp. 482–483.

References

David-Barrett E, Okamura K (2016) Norm diffusion and reputation: the rise of the extractive industries transparency initiative. Governance 29:227–246

Frynas J (2010) Corporate social responsibility and societal governance: lessons from transparency in the oil and gas sector. J Bus Ethics 93:163–179

Gupta A, Mason M (2014) A transparency turn in global environmental governance. In: Gupta A, Mason M (eds) Transparency in global environmental governance. MIT Press, Cambridge, pp 3–38

Hafner-Burton E (2008) Sticks and stones: naming and shaming the human rights enforcement problem. Int Organ 62:689–716

Haufler V (2010) Disclosure as governance: the extractive industries transparency initiative and resource management in the developing world. Global Environ Polit 10:53–73

Keenan P (2014) International institutions and the resource curse. Penn State J Law Int Aff 3:216–260

Kolstad I, Wiig A (2008) Is transparency the key to reducing corruption in resource-rich countries? World Dev 37:521–532

Ochoa C, Keenan P (2011) Regulating information flows, regulating conflict: an analysis of United States conflict minerals legislation. Goettingen J Int Law 3:129–154

Prenkert JD, Shackelford S (2014) Business, human rights, and the promise of polycentricity. Vanderbilt J Transnatl Law 47:451–500

Sarfaty G (2015) Shining light on global supply chains. Harv J Int Law 56:419–463

Schwartz J (2016) The conflict minerals experiment. Harv Bus Law Rev 6:129–183

Skeel D (2001) Shaming in corporate law. Pa Law Rev 149:1811–1868

Stearns J (2011) Dancing in the glory of monsters: the collapse of the Congo and the great war of Africa. Public Affairs, New York

Taylor C (2015) Using securities disclosures to advance human rights: a consideration of Dodd-Frank section 1502 and the Securities and Exchange Commission conflict minerals rule. J Hum Rights 14:201–217

Whitney T (2015) Conflict minerals, black markets, and transparency: the legislative background of Dodd-Frank section 1502 and its historical lessons. J Hum Rights 14(2):183–200

Patrick J. Keenan is professor of law at Illinois College of Law. Before that, he litigated death penalty cases in Georgia and Alabama as an attorney with the Southern Center for Human Rights. He graduated from Yale Law School and Tufts University and clerked at the U.S. District Court for the Middle District of Alabama. His research and scholarship focus on the connection between human rights, economic development, and business.

The 2017 EU Conflict Minerals Regulation: A Promising European Rite to Remove the Natural Resource Curse?

Karsten Nowrot

Contents

1 Introduction: Of "Natural Resource Curses" Resulting from "Conflict Minerals"—and
   Enhanced Transparency as a Possible Cure 51
2 Translating Foreign Policy Objectives into Practice: EU Constitutional Underpinnings
   of the 2017 Conflict Minerals Regulation 55
3 It's a Long Way to ...: On the Legislative History of the Regulation 58
4 Between "Dodd-Frank Act Plus" and "Dodd-Frank Act Minus": Some Thoughts on
   the Regulatory Features of the Final Normative Outcome 62
   4.1 Material Scope of Application: "Dodd-Frank Act Reloaded" 63
   4.2 Personal Scope of Application: "Union Importers Only" 63
   4.3 Territorial Scope of Application: "Only the World Is Enough" 65
   4.4 Regulatory Approach: Stipulating Legally Binding Due Diligence Obligations 66
   4.5 Enforcement Mechanisms: The Perceived Virtue of (Temporary) Modesty 68
5 (By Way of an) Outlook: Let There Be (also) Light and Information—On the More
   Limited Role of Transparency in the Steering Approaches of the 2017 EU Conflict
   Minerals Regulation 70
References 72

1 Introduction: Of "Natural Resource Curses" Resulting from "Conflict Minerals"—and Enhanced Transparency as a Possible Cure

It would probably amount only to a minor exaggeration to consider the continuous supply of mineral raw materials as the central lifeblood of the technological and computerized societies of our time. Metals and other minerals are of essential

---

The introductory section as well as the first two parts of this contribution substantially borrow from Nowrot (2017).

K. Nowrot (✉)
University of Hamburg, Hamburg, Germany
e-mail: Karsten.Nowrot@wiso.uni-hamburg.de

© Springer Nature Switzerland AG 2019
I. Feichtner et al. (eds.), *Human Rights in the Extractive Industries*,
Interdisciplinary Studies in Human Rights 3,
https://doi.org/10.1007/978-3-030-11382-7_4

importance for the industrial production of countless manufactured goods, most certainly including products in the realm of modern environmental, entertainment and information technology such as wind power plants, laptops, digital cameras, video game consoles and smartphones. At least equally well-known, these indispensable raw materials are usually far from evenly distributed around the globe but rather often concentrated in certain geographic areas. Consequently, most manufacturing countries, including the European Union (EU) member states, are heavily dependent on the import of the respective minerals. Since many of the natural-resource-exporting states happen to be developing countries, this demand situation would at first sight most naturally be regarded as offering a considerable potential for their economic and social development.

Nevertheless, and quite to the contrary, it is sadly well-known that the "natural resource wealth" of many of these exporting countries has from the perspective of societal and economic development as a whole frequently rather turned out to be a kind of "natural resource curse" for the political communities in question. The often obvious focus on the extraction, production and exportation of certain minerals or other raw materials results in practice not infrequently in neglecting to establish an own raw materials processing industry, and visibly contributes to the creation or perpetuation of authoritarian regimes, widespread corruption, severe damages to the natural environment as well as last, but surely and unfortunately not least, serious and often systematic violations of fundamental human rights and labour standards, to mention only a few quite negative effects.[1] In light of these findings and in order to remedy—or at least to mitigate—these undesirable consequences, the transnational regulatory regimes dealing with commodity markets have undergone in recent decades notable modifications. Many of the new transboundary steering mechanisms, established on the basis of "hard law" as well as—more frequently—of "soft law", now aim more broadly at promoting changes in the general societal, economic and political conditions of the resource producing and exporting countries.[2]

In order to effectively achieve these broader purposes, the respective normative regimes are often relying on more indirect steering approaches such as for example incentive-based mechanisms and cooperative implementation structures. Quite prominently among these regulatory techniques is also the stipulation of disclosure and reporting requirements aimed at enhancing transparency. In this connection, transparency serves a dual purpose—first and directly, allowing the public, including stakeholders and consumers, to access information for example on the (due diligence) activities of respective economic actors, but, second and more indirectly, thereby in particular also inducing and influencing a behaviour change of these actors in the interest of protecting and promoting human rights and other community interests.[3] An illustrative example is the Extractive Industries Transparency

---

[1] Generally on the phenomenon of the so-called "natural resource curse" see for example WTO, World Trade Report 2010: Trade in Natural Resources. 2010, pp. 91 et seq.; DeKoninck (2015), pp. 134 et seq., each with numerous further references.

[2] See also already Schorkopf (2008), pp. 252 et seq.; Nowrot (2013), pp. 21 et seq.

[3] See generally thereto more recently for example Chilton and Sarfaty (2017), pp. 20 et seq.

Initiative (EITI), a coalition of governments, companies, NGOs, investors and international governmental organisations launched in 2002 at the initiative of the former UK Prime Minister Tony Blair. The central purpose of this transnational good governance regime is promoting improved governance structures and activities in resource-rich countries through the full disclosure and verification of company and investor payments as well as government revenues from the extractive industries sectors of oil, gas and mining.[4] In a broader sense, EITI thereby serves as a clear indication that the international community as a whole more recently approaches the economic and societal challenges connected with the international trade in raw materials in a more holistic manner.

The same underlying considerations also strongly influence the regulatory approaches towards the political and societal implications arising from the phenomenon of so-called "conflict raw materials" in general and "conflict minerals" in particular. Disputes over natural resources are seldom the primary reason for the outbreak of civil wars and the accompanying formation of armed rebel groups. However, it is generally recognised that resource-rich countries, in particular those that rely heavily on the export of primary commodities, face an overall higher risk of prolonged and even increasingly intensified non-international armed conflicts precisely due to the fact that the production of and international trade in raw materials such as diamonds and other gemstones, gold, timber, rare minerals, oil or illegal narcotics often presents itself as one of the primary sources of funding for insurgents and other organised armed groups. In order to illustrate and substantiate the proposition that natural recourses have thus a clear potential to "fuel" ongoing civil wars, one only needs to refer to the respective conditions prevailing in the armed conflicts in Angola, Colombia, Myanmar, Sierra Leone, Peru, Cambodia, Iraq, Libya and—last but unfortunately surely not least—in the Democratic Republic of Congo.[5] Especially in the last two decades a number of international steering mechanisms have been created with the aim to suppress or at least limit this funding of parties to internal armed conflicts by means of transboundary trade in natural resources and to prevent in particular also the accompanying human rights violations in the interest of good global governance. The probably still most well-known example is the Kimberley Process Certification Scheme, a joint initiative of governments, NGOs as well as representatives from the diamond industry formally launched in 2003. This regime portrays itself as an attempt to curb the transboundary trade in so-called "rough" or "blood" diamonds that are used by armed insurgent groups to finance the continuation of civil wars, in particular in Africa.[6]

---

[4] On this steering regime see the contribution by Heidi Feldt in this volume. For an overview and evaluation of other related normative instruments see for example Al Faruque (2006), pp. 72 et seq.

[5] See thereto as well as generally on the correlation between natural resources and civil wars Ross (2004), pp. 35 et seq.; Smillie (2013), pp. 1003 et seq.; as well as specifically with regard to the violent conflict in the Democratic Republic of Congo more recently Final Report of the Group of Experts on the Democratic Republic of the Congo of 26 November 2014, UN Doc. S/2015/19, 12 January 2015, paras. 73 et seq., 156 et seq.

[6] Generally on the Kimberley Process Certification Scheme see, e.g., Brouder (2009), pp. 969 et seq.; Meessen (2015), pp. 173 et seq.; Vidal (2012), pp. 505 et seq. On the role of the EU in this

The fact that the respective steering instruments, in the interest of effectiveness most certainly rightly, first and foremost also include and directly or at least indirectly address the activities of non-state business enterprises as the primary actors in the international trade in (conflict) raw materials and thereby emphasise the importance of transparency is specifically in the context of the ongoing conflict in the Eastern Democratic Republic of Congo, *inter alia*, also illustrated by the respective UN Security Council resolutions. In resolution 1952 (2010), for example, the members of this primary organ of the UN call upon "all States to take appropriate steps to raise awareness of the due diligence guidelines referred to above, and to urge importers, processing industries and consumers of Congolese mineral products to exercise due diligence by applying the aforementioned guidelines, or equivalent guidelines, containing the following steps [...]: strengthening company management systems, identifying and assessing supply chain risks, designing and implementing strategies to respond to identified risks, conducting independent audits, and publicly disclosing supply chain due diligence and findings".[7] In addition, and already with a view to the main focus of this contribution, reference can be made in the present context to the Organisation for Economic Co-operation and Development (OECD) Due Diligence Guidance for Responsible Supply Chains of Minerals from Conflict-Affected and High-Risk Areas, adopted by the OECD Council at Ministerial level on 25 May 2011 and subsequently amended on 17 July 2012 as well as on 25 September 2015. The central purpose of this soft law steering instrument is "to help companies respect human rights and avoid contributing to conflict through their mineral sourcing practices"[8] and, in this regard, it foresees in particular also on the implementation of measures aimed at enhancing transparency.

Against this background and in light of the importance of the respective steering instruments for the protection of human rights in the realm of the extractive industries, the present contribution is aimed at taking a closer look at another quite recent regulatory approach in the field of good raw materials governance intended to promote responsible business practices in the context of so-called "conflict minerals", namely the EU Regulation 2017/821 laying down supply chain due diligence obligations for Union importers of tin, tantalum and tungsten, their ores, and gold originating from conflict-affected and high-risk areas of 17 May 2017 (EU Conflict

---

regime see, e.g., Council Regulation (EC) No 2368/2002 of 20 December 2002 implementing the Kimberley Process certification scheme for the international trade in rough diamonds, OJ EC L 358/28, 31 December 2002; and Fernandez Arribas (2014) The European Union and the Kimberley process. CLEER Working Papers, 2014/3, http://www.asser.nl/media/1645/cleer14-3_web.pdf (last accessed 30 September 2017), pp. 7 et seq.

[7] UN Security Council Resolution 1952 (2010), UN Doc. S/RES/1952 (2010), 29 November 2010, para. 8, with reference to the Final Report of the Group of Experts on the Democratic Republic of the Congo of 26 October 2010, UN Doc. S/2010/596, 29 November 2010, paras. 356 et seq. See also subsequently for example UN Security Council Resolution 2198 (2015), UN Doc. S/RES/2198 (2015), 29 January 2015, paras. 20 et seq.

[8] OECD, Due Diligence Guidance for Responsible Supply Chains of Minerals from Conflict-Affected and High-Risk Areas, 3rd Edition, 2016, http://www.oecd.org/daf/inv/mne/OECD-Due-Diligence-Guidance-Minerals-Edition3.pdf (last accessed 1 October 2018), p. 3.

Minerals Regulation).[9] For this purpose, the following assessment is divided into four main parts. The first section addresses the legal basis as well as in particular the EU primary law background of the newly adopted regulation (Sect. 2). The following second part outlines and evaluates the comparatively long and complex legislative history of this steering instrument (Sect. 3). Subsequently, the third part is intended to provide some thoughts on the regulatory structure and primary steering mechanisms stipulated in the 2017 EU Conflict Minerals Regulation (Sect. 4). Based on the findings made in this section, in the fourth and final part of this contribution an attempt will be made to specifically assess the importance of the concept of transparency in the present context (Sect. 5).

2   Translating Foreign Policy Objectives into Practice: EU Constitutional Underpinnings of the 2017 Conflict Minerals Regulation

At first sight and viewed from a more formal perspective, the EU Conflict Minerals Regulation presents itself as a rather "ordinary" supranational steering instrument under EU secondary law in the realm of the autonomous common commercial policy on the basis of Article 207 of the Treaty on the Functioning of the European Union (TFEU).[10] Although such a perception is undoubtedly not mistaken, it seems appropriate in particular in the present context of human rights in the extractive industries to also briefly draw attention to the underlying foreign policy objectives enshrined in EU primary law. The implementation of these provisions stipulating objectives to be achieved by the design of EU external relations can very well be regarded as the overarching purpose pursued by this recently adopted regulation in the sense of Article 288 (2) TFEU.[11]

Contrary to the traditional understanding of foreign policy as an almost exclusive prerogative of the executive branch largely unconstrained by substantive constitutional requirements,[12] the stipulation of legally binding foreign policy objectives is today no longer an unusual phenomenon in national constitutional law. Quite to the contrary, an increasing number of states, among them EU member states as well as

---

[9] Regulation (EU) 2017/821 of the European Parliament and of the Council of 17 May 2017 laying down supply chain due diligence obligations for Union importers of tin, tantalum and tungsten, their ores, and gold originating from conflict-affected and high-risk areas, OJ EU L 130/1 of 19 May 2017. Generally on EU regulations in the sense of Article 288 (2) TFEU see, e.g., Schütze (2015), pp. 89 et seq.; Bradley (2017), pp. 99 et seq.

[10] The Treaty on the Functioning of the European Union is for example reprinted in Foster (2017), pp. 21 et seq. Generally on the distinction between the autonomous and the contractual trade policy in the field of the common commercial policy see, e.g., Khan (2015), paras. 17 et seq.; Lenaerts and Van Nuffel (2011), pp. 963 et seq.

[11] On this perception see also for example already van der Velde (2017).

[12] See thereto, e.g., Krajewski (2013), pp. 68 et seq.; Tietje and Nowrot (2016), pp. 1469 et seq.; Larik (2016), pp. 55 et seq., each with further references.

several third countries, provide at the top level of their domestic hierarchy of norms a range of objectives pertaining to their external action.[13] In particular also with regard to the realm of international economic relations, this trend is obviously supported and further strengthened by the substantive constitutionalisation of the EU external action on the basis of the foreign policy objectives stipulated in Article 21 of the Treaty on European Union (TEU).[14] The scope of application of this provision also includes the common commercial policy and thus encompasses what has already been qualified as the "external economic constitution of the Union".[15] Stipulating a common set of overarching principles and objectives governing all EU external action, and thus first and foremost also including the, in practical and doctrinal terms, still most important area of EU external relations, the common commercial policy,[16] on the basis of Article 21 (3) TEU as well as the Articles 205 and 207 (1) 2nd sentence TFEU, has been and continues to be—at least from the perspective of foreign trade and investment policy—one of the principal innovations of the Treaty of Lisbon.[17] Among the foreign policy objectives of relevance in the present context are the protection of human rights under Article 21 (1) and (2) (b) TEU, the prevention of conflicts under Article 21 (2) (c) TEU, the sustainable social and economic development of developing countries under Article 21 (2) (d) TEU as well as the sustainable management of global natural resources in accordance with Article 21 (2) (f) TEU.

It hardly needs to be recalled that in practice the incorporation of non-economic concerns like the promotion of democracy, the protection of human rights, issues of supra- and international security as well as the protection of the environment into the law-making processes of the Union's contractual as well as autonomous foreign commercial policy has been, already prior to the entry into force of the Reform Treaty in December 2009, not without precedents.[18] Nevertheless, it is equally well-known that among legal scholars the now—for the first time in the process of European integration—explicit and EU primary law based self-commitment[19] of this supranational organisation to pursue the principles and objectives enshrined in Article 21 (1) and (2) TEU also within the context of implementing the common commercial policy was and still is not only met with approval. This stipulated list of external policy goals has occasionally been perceived as "lengthy and

---

[13] Larik (2016), pp. 88 et seq.; see in particular *id.*, 88 ("This chapter shows that foreign policy objectives abound in contemporary constitutional law. They are not the exception, but rather the rule, both within and outside the EU.").

[14] The Treaty on European Union is for example reprinted in Foster (2017), pp. 1 et seq. Generally on the idea of a constitutionalisation of the EU foreign (trade) policy on the basis of constitutional-like foreign policy objectives see also for example von Arnauld (2014), p. 54; Krajewski (2016), p. 248; Larik (2016), pp. 125 et seq.

[15] Vedder (2013), pp. 143 et seq.

[16] See also already, e.g., Krajewski (2005), p. 92 ("the common commercial policy was and still is the most important constitutional battleground for European external relations").

[17] On this perception see for example also Cottier and Trinberg (2015), para. 7.

[18] See thereto, e.g., Vedder (2013), pp. 127 et seq.; Weiß (2014), p. 527.

[19] Vedder (2013), p. 137, with further references.

wide-ranging",[20] as a mere "wish list for a better world" or even as "redolent of motherhood and apple pie".[21] Furthermore, it is in particular the alleged dangers of, first, an increasing "politicisation" of the EU trade and investment policy as well as, second and closely related, of a notable (and thus undesirable) "downgrading" of the specific trade policy objectives aimed at a gradual trade and investment liberalisation as enshrined in Article 206 TFEU that have at times given cause to serious concern and criticism.[22]

Since this is not the appropriate place for a detailed engagement with that debate and the individual arguments brought forward in this connection, I will confine myself to two more general remarks intended to at least relativize the respective reservations and objections voiced in the legal literature. On the one hand we should not forget that just as transboundary economic relations never develop—and as a consequence should never be considered—in isolation from, and thus uninfluenced by, the respective political relationship between the states concerned,[23] foreign trade policy measures and regulations have not infrequently been, and continue to be, used also as governmental means to promote and protect non-economic interests and objectives.[24] On the other hand it seems worth recalling the quite broad consensus in the scholarly literature—confirmed by the case law of EU courts[25]—on the, for a number of reasons rightly assumed, existence of a wide margin of appreciation enjoyed by EU institutions with regard to the practical means and feasibility of implementation as well as the prioritisation of the principles and objectives stipulated in Article 21 (1) and (2) TEU.[26] Despite this last-mentioned observation, however, the legally binding character of this provision—as well as of Article 205 and Article 207 (1) 2nd sentence TFEU—as normative guidelines for the EU common commercial policy is in principle clearly beyond reasonable doubt.[27] The same applies to their judiciability and thus to the possibility of judicial review by EU courts, since Article 275 TFEU limiting the jurisdiction of the Court of Justice of the

---

[20] Cremona (2003), "the lengthy and wide-ranging list of external policy objectives [...] is unlikely to bring about a greater policy focus", p. 568.

[21] See the references provided by Larik (2016), p. 168.

[22] See thereto for example also Tietje (2009), pp. 19 et seq.; Hahn (2016), paras. 5 et seq.; Bungenberg (2010), p. 128; Terhechte (2012), para. 7.

[23] Meng (1997), pp. 271 et seq.; Boor and Nowrot (2014), p. 241.

[24] See also, e.g., Krajewski (2012), p. 297; Boysen (2014), pp. 468 et seq.; Nettesheim and Duvigneau (2012), paras. 37 et seq.

[25] See for example General Court, Case T-512/12, *Front Polisario/Council*, 10 December 2015, paras. 164 et seq. This judgment was on appeal subsequently—albeit for reasons unrelated to the present issue—set aside by European Court of Justice, Case C-104/16 P, *Council/Front Polisario*, 21 December 2016. See in the present context also the Opinion of Advocate General Melchior Wathelet of 13 September 2016, Case C-104/16 P, *Council/Front Polisario*, paras. 220 et seq.

[26] See also, e.g., Dimopoulos (2010), p. 165; Herrmann and Müller-Ibold (2016), p. 647; Hahn (2016), para. 4; Tietje (2015), p. 802; Krajewski (2016), p. 243.

[27] See also for example Heintschel von Heinegg (2017), para. 11; Larik (2016), pp. 154 et seq.; Dimopoulos (2010), p. 165; Krajewski (2016), p. 242; Nettesheim and Duvigneau (2012), para. 24; Cremer (2016), para. 2.

EU does only cover the provisions relating to the common foreign and security policy. Consequently, the scope of application of this provision cannot be extended to the supranational policies dealing with the Union's external actions as regulated in Part Five of the TFEU, prominently among them the common commercial policy.[28]

3   It's a Long Way to …: On the Legislative History of the Regulation

The main external regulatory impulse and initial general role model for the 2017 EU Conflict Minerals Regulation came from the other side of the Atlantic Ocean in the form of section 1502 of the Dodd-Frank Wall Street Reform and Consumer Protection Act (Dodd-Frank Act) that became effective on 21 July 2010 following its approval by the United States Congress[29] and is currently subject to legal as well as political challenges.[30] Section 1502 (b) Dodd-Frank Act stipulates that all companies are required to file periodic reports with the United States Securities and Exchange Commission (SEC), among them in particular publicly traded companies including foreign issuers with securities registered in the United States,[31] have to make annual disclosures to the SEC regarding the origins of covered conflict minerals as well as the respective measures and precautions taken by the corporation to exercise due diligence on the source and chain of custody of such minerals. In addition, respective enterprises are also obliged to make this reported information available to the public on their internet website (section 1502 (b) (1) E Dodd-Frank Act).[32] The personal scope of application of the reporting requirements thus covers all corporations—to which the other stipulations of section 1502 Dodd-Frank Act apply—involved in the entire supply chain for conflict minerals in all industrial sectors (e.g. automotive, electronics, packaging, aerospace, construction, lighting, industrial machinery and tooling as well as jewellery). It therefore potentially

---

[28] Thereto among others also for example Bungenberg (2017), para. 10; Terhechte (2012), para. 8; Lachmayer (2015), para. 11; Nettesheim and Duvigneau (2012), para. 24; Krajewski (2016), p. 242.

[29] Dodd-Frank Wall Street Reform and Consumer Protection Act, Public Law 111–203—July 21, 2010, 124 Stat. 1375 (2010), https://www.congress.gov/111/plaws/publ203/PLAW-111publ203. pdf (last accessed 1 October 2018). The steering influence exercised by this legislation on the current EU initiative is for example illustrated by European Commission, Commission Staff Working Document—Impact Assessment, SWD(2014) 53 final, 5 March 2014, p. 8, 13 and *passim*; European Commission, Assessment of Due Diligence Compliance Cost, Benefit and Related Effects on Selected Operators in Relation to the Responsible Sourcing of Selected Minerals, Final Report by Katie Böhme, Paulina Bugajski-Hochriegl and Maria Dos Santos, September 2013, p. 9.

[30] See thereto, e.g., Taylor (2017); as well as the contribution by Patrick Keenan in this volume.

[31] For a more detailed description of the personal scope of application of this provision see, e.g., Nelson (2014), pp. 227 et seq.; and the contribution by Patrick Keenan in this volume.

[32] On section 1502 Dodd-Frank Act see also the contribution by Patrick Keenan in this volume.

includes the so-called "upstream" activities of miners, traders and smelters/refiners as well as the "downstream" activities of traders, component producers, manufacturers and end-users.[33]

Almost immediately after the adoption of the Dodd-Frank Act in the summer of 2010, the European Parliament in a resolution of 7 October 2010 not only welcomed this legislative act but also asked the Commission and the Council "to examine a legislative initiative along these lines".[34] This request for a suitable legislative proposal by the Commission, supported by numerous representatives of civil society, was subsequently reiterated on a number of occasions.[35] Nevertheless, it was only on 5 March 2014 that the Commission finally presented its proposal for an EU regulation setting up a Union system for supply chain due diligence self-certification of responsible importers of tin, tantalum and tungsten, their ores, and gold originating in conflict-affected and high-risk areas.[36] This legislative proposal's material scope of application was virtually identical to section 1502 Dodd-Frank Act, covering with tin, tantalum, tungsten and the respective ores as well as gold in accordance with its Article 1 and Article 2 lit. a and b basically the same conflict minerals. For the rest, however, many of the regulatory approaches foreseen in the 2014 Commission's draft regulation differed considerably from its previously adopted US counterpart. Three aspects seem to be particularly worth drawing attention to in this regard.[37]

First, the territorial scope of application of the proposed EU regulation was not confined to the Democratic Republic of Congo and nine adjoining countries but intended to extend to respective minerals from all "conflict affected and high-risk areas" in the world. This regulatory approach aiming not at any specific region of

---

[33] For a vivid description of the supply chain for conflict minerals see for example European Commission/High Representative of the European Union for Foreign Affairs and Security Policy, Joint Communication to the European Parliament and the Council: Responsible Sourcing of Minerals Originating in Conflict-Affected and High-Risk Areas—Towards an Integrated EU Approach, JOIN(2014) 8 final, 5 March 2014, p. 6.

[34] European Parliament, Resolution of 7 October 2010 on failures in protection of human rights and justice in the Democratic Republic of Congo, P7_TA(2010)0350, para. 14.

[35] See for example European Parliament, Resolution of 5 July 2011 on increasing the impact of EU development policy, P7_TA(2011)0320, para. 60 ("Calls on the Commission to make a legislative proposal with a similar objective to the new US 'Conflict Minerals Law', namely to combat the illegal exploitation of minerals in developing countries, in particular in Africa, which fuels civil war and conflicts, and to ensure traceability of imported minerals in the EU market;"); European Parliament, Resolution of 26 February 2014 on promoting development through responsible business practices, including the role of extractive industries in developing countries, P7_TA(2014)0163, paras. 45 et seq.

[36] European Commission, Proposal for a Regulation of the European Parliament and of the Council setting up a Union system for supply chain due diligence self-certification of responsible importers of tin, tantalum and tungsten, their ores, and gold originating in conflict-affected and high-risk areas, COM(2014) 111 final, 5 March 2014.

[37] For a more in-depth evaluation of the 2014 Commission's draft regulation see also already for example Brackett et al. (2015), pp. 80 et seq.; Vyboldina (2015), pp. 341 et seq.; Nowrot (2016), pp. 240 et seq.

the world but establishing potentially a global geographical applicability should first and foremost be seen as an attempt to avoid one of the major regulatory challenges arising in connection with section 1502 Dodd-Frank Act. This applies in particular to the—indeed at least partially materialized—possibility that companies might altogether avoid conflict minerals from the targeted region thereby creating a kind of de facto embargo with often disastrous socio-economic consequences in particular for artisanal miners and their families.[38]

Second, and in contrast to the broad territorial coverage stipulated in the proposal, the personal scope of application was envisioned to be quite narrow in comparison to section 1502 Dodd-Frank Act. The draft regulation was not intended to apply to all companies in the whole supply chain but only to "importers" of respective conflict minerals. These actors were defined—pursuant to Article 2 lit. g of the proposal—as "any natural or legal person declaring minerals or metals within the scope of this Regulation for release for free circulation within the meaning of Article 79 of Council Regulation (EEC) No 2913/1992". The Commission estimated in 2014 that, while there were some 880,000 companies in the EU trading or processing tin, tantalum, tungsten or gold, only "about 300 EU traders and around 20 smelters/refiners importing ores and metals derived from the four minerals and more than 100 EU component manufacturers importing derived metals" existed at that time.[39]

Third, and at least equally noteworthy, the 2014 Commission's proposal differed from its US counterpart also insofar as it did not stipulate mandatory disclosure obligations for respective EU companies. Rather, its Article 3 only foresaw for the quite limited number of covered enterprises—and exclusively for them[40]—the option of a voluntary self-certification as "responsible importer". As proscribed by Article 3 of the 2014 proposal, interested companies were for that purpose envisioned to declare to a member state competent authority that they adhere to the supply chain due diligence obligations as set out in the Articles 4–6 that were closely modelled after and in part even explicitly referring to the above mentioned OECD Due Diligence Guidance for Responsible Supply Chains of Minerals from Conflict-Affected and High-Risk Areas. Finally, it were only these "responsible investors"

---

[38] See thereto, e.g., Commission/High Representative of the European Union for Foreign Affairs and Security Policy, Joint Communication to the European Parliament and the Council: Responsible Sourcing of Minerals Originating in Conflict-Affected and High-Risk Areas—Towards an Integrated EU Approach, JOIN(2014) 8 final, 5 March 2014, p. 7; European Commission, Commission Staff Working Document—Executive Summary of the Impact Assessment, SWD(2014) 52 final, 5 March 2014, p. 3; Conflict Minerals—An Evaluation of the Dodd-Frank Act and other Resource-Related Measures, Öko-Institut e.V., August 2013, p. 27; Centre for Research on Multinational Corporations (SOMO), Conflict Due Diligence by European Companies, SOMO Paper, October 2013, p. 3; Veale (2013), pp. 533 et seq.; Brackett et al. (2015), pp. 74 et seq.; for a more optimistic perception see, however, also Schwartz (2016), pp. 171 et seq.

[39] European Commission/High Representative of the European Union for Foreign Affairs and Security Policy, Joint Communication to the European Parliament and the Council: Responsible Sourcing of Minerals Originating in Conflict-Affected and High-Risk Areas—Towards an Integrated EU Approach, JOIN(2014) 8 final, 5 March 2014, p. 6.

[40] See thereto already my critical evaluation in Nowrot (2016), p. 243.

that were subjected to respective disclosure obligations in accordance with Article 7 of the draft regulation.[41]

Since an EU regulation on conflict minerals as part of the Union's autonomous common commercial policy is subject to the ordinary legislative procedure with the European Parliament and the Council acting as co-legislators, the 2014 Commission's proposal was submitted to these two EU institutions in accordance with Articles 207 (2), 294 (2) TFEU.[42] Bearing in mind that many members of the European Parliament originally envisioned and also explicitly asked for a regulation creating legally binding due diligence obligations for a large number of companies involved in the trading or processing of respective raw materials,[43] it is hardly surprising that not only for example numerous civil society groups but also the representatives of this EU institution were in their majority considerably less than entirely pleased with the draft presented by the Commission. On 20 May 2015, the European Parliament during the first reading of the proposal under Article 294 (3) TFEU favourably considered and approved a significant number of, in part quite fundamental, amendments. Among them was the regulatory approach of imposing on all EU importers of covered conflict minerals legally binding supply chain due diligence obligations (amendment 154: new version of Article 1 (2) of the EU regulation). Furthermore, and inspired by section 1502 Dodd-Frank Act, all other "downstream" companies would have been asked to take "all reasonable steps to identify and address any risks arising in their supply chains for [covered] minerals and metals" and, in this connection, would have been legally required to "provide information on the due diligence practices they employ for responsible sourcing" (amendment 155: new Article 1 (2) lit. d of the regulation).[44] In light of these substantial "modifications", which in fact amounted to fundamentally changing the proposed regulation's underlying regulatory approach from "voluntary" to "mandatory", the European Parliament ultimately decided on the same day by a vote of 343–331, with nine abstentions, to postpone the final vote on the draft legislative resolution in accordance with Article 61 (2) of the Rules of Procedure of the European Parliament (RoP EP) and thus not to close the first read-

---

[41] For a more detailed evaluation, also on the envisioned incentives for as well as control mechanisms in case of participation in this self-certification process, see for example Brackett et al. (2015), pp. 80 et seq.; Nowrot (2016), pp. 243 et seq.; Schuele (2015), pp. 772 et seq.

[42] Generally on the Union's ordinary legislative procedure see, e.g., Schütze (2015), pp. 243 et seq.; Bradley (2017), pp. 120 et seq.

[43] See for example European Parliament, Resolution of 26 February 2014 on promoting development through responsible business practices, including the role of extractive industries in developing countries, P7_TA(2014)0163, "create a legally binding obligation for all upstream companies operating in the EU that use and trade natural resources sourced from conflict-affected and high-risk areas and all downstream companies that act as the first placer on the European market to undertake supply chain due diligence to identify and mitigate the risk of conflict financing and human rights abuse" para. 46 (a).

[44] Thereto as well as with regard to all other amendments see European Parliament, Amendments adopted on 20 May 2015 on the proposal for a regulation of the European Parliament and of the Council setting up a Union system for supply chain due diligence self-certification of responsible importers of tin, tantalum and tungsten, their ores, and gold originating in conflict-affected and high-risk areas, P8_TA(2015)0204.

ing position under Article 294 (3) TFEU.[45] Officially, the matter was thus under Article 61 (2) RoP EP deemed to be referred back to the committee responsible, in the present case the EP Committee for International Trade (INTA Committee).

Less officially, but surely no less important, this course of action was intended to open the way for informal tripartite meetings between representatives of the Parliament, the Council and the Commission ("trilogues") aimed at seeking a political understanding on the regulatory approach and content of an EU regulation on conflict minerals.[46] After the Council clarified its own position on the draft legislation, the trilogue process commenced in early 2016. On 16 June 2016 the three institutions announced that they had reached an agreement with regard to the broad framework and regulatory design of a future conflict minerals regulation.[47] Following a consensus on the technical details of the legislative instrument on 22 November 2016,[48] the EU Conflict Minerals Regulation was adopted by the European Parliament and the Council on 16 March 2017 as well as 3 April 2017 respectively and, in accordance with its Article 20 (1), ultimately entered into force in June 2017.

4 Between "Dodd-Frank Act Plus" and "Dodd-Frank Act Minus": Some Thoughts on the Regulatory Features of the Final Normative Outcome

With one quite notable exception, the 2017 EU Conflict Minerals Regulation is in principle very much in line with the 2014 Commission's draft. This finding is likely to be at first sight, at least to a number of observers and readers, somewhat surprising, in particular considering the rather fundamental opposition voiced by the Parliament with regard to this proposal. Nevertheless, this outcome can ultimately be to a certain extent explained on the basis of the quite strong institutional and

---

[45] On the respective voting at the initiative of the Chair of the INTA Committee, Bernd Lange, see PV 20/05/2015—10.7.

[46] On the approach of institutional trilogues in the EU legislative procedures see European Parliament/Council/Commission, Joint Declaration on Practical Arrangements for the Codecision Procedure, OJ EU C 145/5 of 30 June 2007; as well as, e.g., Schütze (2015), pp. 249 et seq.; Chalmers (2015), pp. 322 et seq., with further references.

[47] See European Parliament, Conflict Minerals: MEPs Secure Mandatory Due Diligence for Importers, Press Release of 16 June 2016, http://www.europarl.europa.eu/pdfs/news/expert/infopr ess/20160615IPR32320/20160615IPR32320_en.pdf (last accessed 1 October 2018) European Council/Council of the EU, EU Political Deal to Curb Trade in Conflict Minerals, Press Release 342/16 of 16 June 2016, http://www.consilium.europa.eu/de/press/press-releases/2016/06/16-conflict-minerals/ (last accessed 1 October 2018); European Commission, EU Political Deal to Curb Trade in Conflict Minerals, Press Release of 16 June 2016, http://europa.eu/rapid/press-release_ IP-16-2231_en.htm (last accessed 1 October 2018).

[48] See European Commission, EU Reaches Landmark Agreement on Conflict Minerals Regulation, Press Release of 22 November 2016, http://europa.eu/rapid/press-release_IP-16-3931_en.htm (last accessed 1 October 2018).

procedural orientation towards compromise solutions as being an inherent characteristic of the ordinary legislative procedure involving the Parliament and the Council. When attempting to systemize the regulatory content and to identify the main steering features of this recently adopted instrument, it seems useful to draw attention to five issues that are particularly worth highlighting in this regard.

4.1 Material Scope of Application: "Dodd-Frank Act Reloaded"

First, despite earlier intentions expressed by the Parliament to extend the material scope of application of the regulation to literally "all natural resources, without exception",[49] Article 1 (1) and (2) as well as Article 2 (a) and (b) in connection with Annex I of the Conflict Minerals Regulation all stipulate that the regime only covers minerals and metals containing or consisting of tin, tantalum, tungsten, their ores and gold as already foreseen in the 2014 Commission's proposal and in line with section 1502 Dodd-Frank Act. Following the adoption of this steering instrument, it's quite narrow substantive focus on a very limited number of minerals has most certainly given rise to—renewed—criticism.[50] Nevertheless, it seems not entirely unreasonable to start this regulatory experiment on the basis of a rather small number of raw materials that appear to be—according to the European Commission—the "most mined in areas affected by conflict or in mines that rely on forced labour".[51] Such an approach surely does not foreclose the possibility of subsequently—based on a re-evaluation of the regulation as foreseen in its Article 17 (2)—enlarging the substantive scope of application by including in the future also other "notorious" conflict raw materials like jade and cobalt.

4.2 Personal Scope of Application: "Union Importers Only"

Second, and again quite contrary to the previous majority opinion of the Parliament[52] as well as—at least equally noteworthy—to the expectations raised by the political understanding reached in June 2016,[53] the EU Conflict Minerals Regulation does

---

[49] European Parliament, Resolution of 26 February 2014 on promoting development through responsible business practices, including the role of extractive industries in developing countries, P7_TA(2014)0163, para. 46 (c).

[50] See thereto, e.g., van der Velde (2017); Heße and Klimke (2017), p. 450.

[51] See the information provided by the European Commission under http://ec.europa.eu/trade/policy/in-focus/conflict-minerals-regulation/regulation-explained/ (last accessed 1 October 2018).

[52] See, e.g., European Parliament, Resolution of 26 February 2014 on promoting development through responsible business practices, including the role of extractive industries in developing countries, P7_TA(2014)0163, para. 46 (a).

[53] On the respective content of the political understanding see European Parliament, Conflict Minerals: MEPs Secure Mandatory Due Diligence for Importers, Press Release of 16 June 2016,

not extend its personal scope of application to in principle all corporate actors in the whole supply chain of conflict minerals. Rather, it retains on the basis of its Article 1 (2) the comparatively narrow focus on "Union importers" in accordance with the definition stipulated in Article 2 lit. I.[54] Consequently, as already envisioned in the 2014 Commission's draft, the clear distinction between direct EU importers of the respective raw materials on the one hand and the "downstream" activities of other traders, component producers, manufacturers and sellers on the other hand is maintained as far as the respective obligations enshrined in this steering instrument are concerned.

This regulatory approach of focusing first and foremost on European "upstream" businesses in the form of smelters and refiners situated in the EU[55] as well as those "downstream" businesses like traders that act as the first placers on the EU market, now estimated by the Commission to comprise of a combined number of 600–1000 EU importers,[56] seems in principle not implausible. Attention might be drawn in this regard to the well-known fact that—as for example also emphasized in recital 16 of Regulation 2017/821—this part of the conflict minerals supply chain is of critical importance since in particular smelters and refiners are normally the last stage where it is still technically feasible to identify the origin and chain of custody of minerals and thus to effectively assure due diligence. However, it appears considerably less plausible why other "downstream" EU companies continue to be[57] entirely excluded from the personal scope of application of the Conflict Mineral Regulation and are thus not, inter alia, granted the possibility of a kind of voluntary self-certification as "responsible manufacturers" or "responsible sellers"; an option apparently, if only for a while, also foreseen in the political understanding reached in June 2016.

---

http://www.europarl.europa.eu/pdfs/news/expert/infopress/20160615IPR32320/20160615 IPR32320_en.pdf (last accessed 1 October 2018); as well as Nowrot (2017), pp. 398 et seq.

[54] Article 2 lit. I EU Conflict Minerals Regulations states that Union importer refers to "any natural or legal person declaring minerals or metals for release for free circulation within the meaning of Article 201 of Regulation (EU) No 952/2013 of the European Parliament and of the Council or any natural or legal person on whose behalf such declaration is made, as indicated in data elements 3/15 and 3/16 in accordance with Annex B to Commission Delegated Regulation (EU) 2015/2446".

[55] In accordance with Article 2 lit. j and k of the EU Conflict Minerals Regulation, "upstream" refers to "the mineral supply chain from the extraction sites to the smelters and refiners, inclusive", whereas "downstream" means "the metal supply chain from the stage following the smelters and refiners to the final product".

[56] See the information provided by the European Commission under http://ec.europa.eu/trade/policy/in-focus/conflict-minerals-regulation/regulation-explained/ (last accessed 1 October 2018). See also, e.g., European Commission/High Representative of the European Union for Foreign Affairs and Security Policy, Joint Communication to the European Parliament and the Council: Responsible Sourcing of Minerals Originating in Conflict-Affected and High-Risk Areas—Towards an Integrated EU Approach, JOIN(2014) 8 final of 5 March 2014, p. 6.

[57] See also already the respective regulatory approach foreseen in the 2014 Commission's draft, see Sect. 4.3.

4.3 Territorial Scope of Application: "Only the World Is Enough"

Third, Regulation 2017/821 stipulates with regard to the territorial application that this steering instrument retains—in deviation from section 1502 Dodd-Frank Act being applicable only to the Democratic Republic of Congo and nine adjoining countries—the broad territorial coverage as already suggested in the 2014 Commission's draft. It thus has a potentially global reach by applying to respective minerals and metals from all conflict-affected and high-risk areas around the world. In accordance with the definition provided in Article 2 lit. f of the regulation, this term covers all "areas in a state of armed conflict or fragile post-conflict as well as areas witnessing weak or non-existent governance and security, such as failed states, and widespread and systematic violations of international law, including human rights abuses".[58]

In order to assist EU importers in their task to employ these rather abstract criteria in practice, and thereby also to facilitate consistency in the identification of conflict-affected and high-risk areas, Article 14 of the Conflict Minerals Regulation provides for two approaches. Article 14 (1) stipulates that the European Commission is entrusted with the task of preparing—in consultation with the European External Action Service and the OECD—a handbook for economic operators containing non-binding guidelines on how to apply the criteria for respective areas as stated in Article 2 lit. f. In addition, and on the basis of these guidelines, Article 14 (2) foresees that this supranational organ also calls upon "external expertise that will provide an indicative, non-exhaustive, regularly updated list of conflict-affected and high-risk areas".[59] Already in the interest of legal certainty and practicability, these measures in principle surely deserve applause. Nonetheless, it should not be left unmentioned here that the last-mentioned approach potentially entails the danger—already partially realised in connection with section 1502 Dodd-Frank Act—that such a list, even if only indicative and not necessarily exhaustive, will nevertheless with regard to the covered countries be interpreted and somewhat "misapplied" by the respective EU importers as constituting something like current de facto "no-trade areas" for the minerals and metals in question,[60] with undoubtedly severe consequences for affected artisanal miners and their dependents.

---

[58] On this definition see in principle also OECD, Due Diligence Guidance for Responsible Supply Chains of Minerals from Conflict-Affected and High-Risk Areas, 3rd Edition, 2016, p. 13, http://www.oecd.org/daf/inv/mne/OECD-Due-Diligence-Guidance-Minerals-Edition3.pdf   (last accessed 1 October 2018).

[59] See in this connection also for example already Directorate-General for External Policies, Briefing—EU Initiative on Responsibly Importing Minerals from Conflict-Affected Regions, December 2014, DG EXPO/B/PolDep/Note/2014_195, "To help 'responsible importers' determine whether their sources are in conflict-affected or high-risk areas, the European Commission will establish an expert group.", p. 6.

[60] See also already Brackett et al. (2015), pp. 83 et seq.; Nowrot (2016), pp. 241 et seq.; Heße and Klimke (2017), pp. 449 et seq.

4.4 Regulatory Approach: Stipulating Legally Binding Due Diligence Obligations

And this danger of ultimately turning the intended socio-economic effects of an EU conflict minerals regulation quasi "on their head"[61] is in fact quite real, even more so because—and this is the fourth quite notable aspect—the recently adopted Regulation 2017/821 profoundly changes the quality of the normative expectations of the covered economic actors in line with the demands voiced by the European Parliament. Contrary to the regulatory approach envisioned by the Commission's 2014 draft, EU importers at the upper segments of the conflict minerals supply chain no longer find themselves merely encouraged to undertake a voluntary self-certification. Rather, they are under Article 3 (1) now in fact legally required to comply with the due diligence obligations stipulated in the EU regulation and are obliged to keep documentation demonstrating this compliance. The respective supply chain due diligence obligations in relation to management systems, risk management, independent third-party audits as well as the disclosure of information are set out in detail in the Articles 4–7 of this steering instrument and are closely modelled after and frequently even explicitly referring to—and thus in effect partly incorporating[62]—the non-binding OECD Due Diligence Guidance for Responsible Supply Chains of Minerals from Conflict-Affected and High-Risk Areas, in particular the OECD Model Supply Chain Policy as laid down in its Annex II.

Articles 4 and 5 of the EU regulation provide for what might be regarded as the core set of substantive obligations incumbent upon covered economic actors. Article 4 stipulates various organizational, institutional and procedural requirements in relation to the importer's management system. Among them are the obligation to adopt and publicly communicate a supply chain policy in line with the model included in Annex II of the OECD Due Diligence Guidance and to incorporate these standards into contracts with suppliers (Article 4 lit. a, b and d), the duty to establish a—or provide for access to an external—grievance mechanism in the sense of Article 2 lit. p (Article 4 lit. e) as well as the need to operate a chain of custody traceability system for minerals and metals that generates and thus provides for quite detailed information on such aspects like the country of origin, the supplier and, if applicable, the smelters and refiners (Article 4 lit. f and g). Within the framework of a management system so designed and maintained and on the basis of the information retrieved in accordance with Article 4, Article 5 subsequently sets out

---

[61] For a vivid description with regard to the potentially adverse effects of section 1502 Dodd-Frank Act, see Brackett et al. (2015), "The result could in fact exacerbate the harm the Conflict Minerals Rule is seeking to address by increasing smuggling, weakening governance, and depressing prices for ore. Together, these factors make the violation of human rights even more likely.", p. 76; Abelardo (2017), pp. 609–610.

[62] On this aspect see also Partiti and van der Velde (2017) Curbing supply-chain human rights violations through trade and due diligence. Possible WTO concerns raised by the EU conflict minerals regulation. ASSER Research Paper 2017-02, June 2017, https://papers.ssrn.com/sol3/papers.cfm?abstract_id=2983039 (last accessed 1 October 2018).

generally phrased risk management obligations to be fulfilled by covered economic actors. Article 5 requires Union importers to respond to identified risks of adverse impacts in their supply chain by making risk mitigation efforts like, inter alia, reporting respective findings to senior management, exerting pressure on suppliers, engaging in consultations with the stakeholders concerned, as well as temporarily suspending or permanently terminating the trade relationships in question.

Supplementing these two provisions, Articles 6 and 7 of the Conflict Minerals Regulation stipulate measures first and foremost intended to foster the observance and implementation of the obligations enshrined in Articles 4 and 5. Clearly compliance-oriented in character, Article 6 (1) requires in principle all Union importers—again in conformity with recommendations included in the OECD Due Diligence Guidance[63]—to carry out independent third-party audits intended to assess and determine the conformity of applied supply chain due diligence practices with the obligations laid down in the EU regulation in accordance with Article 6 (1) lit. b as well as to make recommendations on how to further improve these practices (lit. c). The respective economic actors are, however, under Article 6 (2) exempted from this procedural obligation if they can provide "substantive evidence [...] demonstrating that all smelters and refiners" in the sense of Article 2 lit. h in their whole supply chain (and thus first and foremost those that are based in third countries) comply with the requirements stipulated in the 2017 Conflict Minerals Regulation. In this connection, a support measure by the European Commission as foreseen in Article 9 of this EU instrument comes into play. This provision entrusts the Commission with the task of drawing up—and of subsequently updating on a regular basis—a list of "global responsible smelters and refiners". The link between this measure and third-party audit obligations is established by Article 6 (2), stipulating that Union importers of metals are exempted from the duty to carry out third-party audits if they are able to "demonstrate that they are sourcing exclusively from smelters and refiners listed by the Commission pursuant to Article 9". Aside from this exception under Article 6 (2) that is for a variety of reasons likely to be of rather limited relevance in practice for quite some time to come, the equally noteworthy provision of Article 7, being at least in part also aimed at further strengthening the importance and impact of these third-party audits as generally foreseen in Article 6 (1), includes in its first three paragraphs a number of disclosure obligations of Union importers, namely vis-à-vis the competent authorities of the EU member state at issue, towards the "immediate downstream purchasers" as well as—on an annual basis and including the internet—with regard to the general public.

While in principle all Union importers—irrespective of their size and economic importance—are subjected to these supply chain due diligence obligations as just outlined and as set out in detail in the Articles 4–7, the 2017 EU Conflict Minerals Regulation also provides for three general exceptions. Among the respective provi-

---

[63] OECD, Due Diligence Guidance for Responsible Supply Chains of Minerals from Conflict-Affected and High-Risk Areas, 3rd Edition, 2016, pp. 19, 47 et seq., 106 et seq., http://www.oecd.org/daf/inv/mne/OECD-Due-Diligence-Guidance-Minerals-Edition3.pdf (last accessed 1 October 2018).

sions, Article 1 (6) stipulates that recycled metals are, with the exception of a specific disclosure obligation enshrined in Article 7 (4), excluded from the scope of
application of the EU regulation. In addition, small volume Union importers are
exempted from these obligations. According to Article 1 (3), the Conflict Minerals
Regulation does not apply to those importers whose annual import volume of the
respective mineral or metal is below the volume threshold stipulated in Annex I. In
order to provide for the flexibility, but also effectiveness, of this regulation, Articles
1 (4), (5) and 18 empower the Commission to amend the applicable thresholds
every 3 years, thereby continuously ensuring that—as stated in the second sentence
of Article 1 (3)—"the vast majority, but no less than 95 %, of the total volumes
imported into the Union of each mineral and metal" is indeed subject to the due diligence obligations set out in the Articles 4–7. Moreover, Article 3 (3) in connection
with Article 8 provides for the possibility of governments, industry associations and
other groupings to apply to the Commission, subject to certain criteria to be developed and laid down by this supranational organ in a delegated act under Article 8
(2), for recognition of their own due diligence schemes as being equivalent to the
requirements set out in the EU Conflict Minerals Regulation. Thereby, these last-
mentioned provisions do not exactly stipulate an exception from the observance of
the supply chain due diligence requirements of the EU regulation but rather allow
for recourse to external equivalent alternatives in order to facilitate the compliance
of Union importers with these obligations. Possible candidates for this recognition
procedure are currently, among others, the Conflict-Free Smelter Program developed by the Conflict-Free Sourcing Initiative (CFSI)[64] and the International Tin
Supply Chain Initiative (iTSCi) Programme.[65]

4.5   Enforcement Mechanisms: The Perceived Virtue of (Temporary) Modesty

In particular in light of all of these comparatively impressive normative obligations
imposed on Union importers, a fifth and final notable aspect of the regulatory features as manifested in the newly adopted EU Regulation 2017/821 obviously concerns the question how to effectively as well as adequately ensure the enforcement
of, and thus compliance by covered economic actors with, the legally binding
requirements as first and foremost set out in the Articles 4–7. Considering the
importance of this issue for the integrity and the overall functioning of the regulatory framework established by this EU regulation, it is hardly surprising that this
steering instrument devotes considerable space in the Articles 3 (2), 10–13, 16 and
17 (1) to the stipulation of enforcement measures.

---

[64] For additional information see http://www.conflictfreesourcing.org/conflict-free-smelter-pro-
gram/ (last accessed 1 October 2018).

[65] For respective information on this initiative see https://www.itri.co.uk/itsci/frontpage (last
accessed 1 October 2018).

In accordance with Article 10, each EU member state designates one or more competent domestic authorities responsible for ensuring the effective implementation of the Conflict Minerals Regulation. Among the compliance measures to be taken recourse to in this regard, Article 11 emphasises the importance of "appropriate ex-post checks", including on-the-spot inspections at the premises of the Union importers, in order to examine the implementation of supply chain due diligence obligations as well as the documentation and audit duties incumbent upon covered economic actors. Furthermore, in addition to various measures aimed at the exchange of information among member states (Article 13) and the stipulation of reporting obligations by member states towards the Commission (e.g. Articles 16 (2) and 17 (1)), Article 16 foresees in its first paragraph that each member state shall lay down the rules applicable to cases of infringements by Union importers of their obligations under this EU regulation. More specifically, the competent authorities under Article 16 (3) are required to issue a notice of remedial action to be taken by the economic actor in question in case of an infringement. Nevertheless, it can be inferred from Article 17 (2) and (3), stating in their relevant parts that the Commission shall assess by 1 January 2023 and every 3 years thereafter "whether Member State competent authorities should have competence to impose penalties upon Union importers in the event of persistent failure to comply with the obligations set out in this Regulation", that for the time being the EU member states are not expected—or even entitled—to adopt sanctions in cases of non-compliance; a quite notable, albeit potentially only temporary, limitation on the arsenal of enforcement instruments usually available to governmental actors in order to secure the observance of legal obligations.

Aside from this last mentioned and a number of other debatable features, however, the normative steering framework established by the 2017 Conflict Minerals Regulation as a whole seems to present itself, if viewed from an overarching perspective, as a rather promising—and thus laudable—regulatory approach to adequately address, and hopefully to constructively contribute to overcome and remove, one of the worst manifestations of the natural resource curse. When assessed from a comparative perspective in light of its initial role model, the mechanism established by section 1502 of the Dodd-Frank Act, the recently adopted EU Regulation 2017/821 can ultimately be positioned somewhere between a kind of "super Dodd-Frank Act" or "Dodd-Frank Act plus" piece of legislation on the one side and a "Dodd-Frank Act minus" instrument on the other side. In order to support, on the one hand, the perception of a "Dodd Frank Act plus" regulatory measure, one only needs to refer to the considerably broader territorial scope of application as well as in particular also to the fact that section 1502 Dodd-Frank Act only foresees mandatory annual disclosures but does not stipulate any specific due diligence obligations that covered businesses are legally bound to fulfil. On the other hand, the 2017 Conflict Minerals Regulation, contrary to its US counterpart, falls short of applying to economic actors in the whole supply chain of conflict minerals.

Taking into account that the EU regulation has been adopted only recently and in particular that most of its operational provisions, including the supply chain due diligence obligations set out in its Articles 4–7, will only apply from 1 January 2021 onwards in accordance with Article 20 (3), it goes without saying that is too early to make a definitive finding on the wisdom of introducing these and other regulatory deviations from the section 1502 Dodd-Frank Act role model. Ultimately, as it is not infrequently the case, only time will tell whether the in part quite far-reaching and ambitious normative scheme recently created by EU Regulation 2017/821 is able to successfully establish itself in practice as an effective European "rite" to remove the natural resource curse by adequately coping with the complex and multi-faceted challenges arising in connection with the conflict minerals "dilemma".

5   (By Way of an) Outlook: Let There Be (also) Light and Information—On the More Limited Role of Transparency in the Steering Approaches of the 2017 EU Conflict Minerals Regulation

When finally, against the background of the findings made so far, turning again more specifically to the importance of transparency in transnational steering regimes dealing with extractive industries in general as well as in the regulatory framework of the EU Regulation 2017/821 in particular, it seems appropriate to start with the observation that this normative principle does in the present context not play *the* dominant role that it frequently occupies in other steering regimes aimed at preventing human rights violations in this business sector. In order to illustrate and substantiate this initially probably somewhat surprising remark, attention needs to be drawn to the distinct regulatory approaches that characterise this EU regulation in the broader realm of these steering regimes.

Most hard law instruments, including section 1502 of the Dodd-Frank Act, as well as obviously all soft law regimes addressing the issue of human rights in the extractive industries are with regard to their implementation approaches primarily shaped by the wider concept of law-realisation.[66] In contrast to the traditional "command and control style of legislation",[67] the approach of law-realisation is characterized by more indirect steering mechanisms such as cooperative implementation structures, a recourse to economic steering models that rely on incentives and positive as well as adverse reputational effects and, last but not least, the provision of disclosure and reporting requirements intended to promote transparency[68]; a regulatory approach that finds its manifestation in the EU legal order for example in the so-called "Corporate Social Responsibility (CSR)" or "Non-Financial Reporting"

---

[66] Generally on the notion of "law-realisation" as being distinct from the considerably narrower concept of "law enforcement" see Tietje (1998), pp. 132 et seq.

[67] Zerk (2006), p. 36.

[68] Specifically with regard to section 1502 Dodd-Frank Act see thereto also, e.g., Ochoa and Keenan (2011), pp. 138 et seq.

Directive 2014/95/EU of October 2014.[69] As already indicated above,[70] transparency serves in this connection essentially a dual purpose by, first, allowing the public, among them in particular consumers and other stakeholders, to access information for example on the due diligence activities of the respective business actors, as well as, second, by inducing and thus influencing a change of behaviour on the side of these actors with the aim of protecting and promoting human rights as well as other transnational community interest concerns.[71]

In comparison, the 2017 Conflict Minerals Regulation is—primarily on the insistence of the European Parliament, thereby further indicating the important role played by this EU institution in the effective realisation of the EU (non-economic) foreign policy objectives laid down in Article 21 TEU[72]—first and foremost stipulating, especially in its Articles 4 and 5, direct and legally binding obligations of conduct for covered economic actors with regard to the exercise of supply chain due diligence. Against this background and bearing in mind the enforcement mechanisms as outlined above,[73] this regulatory regime is not to the same extent as other respective steering instruments relying on, and dependent on, disclosure obligations and other means of facilitating transparency for the purposes of ensuring effective compliance.

This necessary relativisation should nevertheless not give rise to the perception that the principle of transparency is assigned only a minor role in the regulatory framework of EU Regulation 2017/821. Already its Article 1 (1) states quite prominently that providing transparency and certainty as regards the supply practices of Union importers are the central purposes pursued by this steering instrument. In implementation of these legislative goals, the regulation is—on an intergovernmental level—obviously aimed at promoting information exchange, and thus conditions of transparency, between the various competent authorities of the member states (Article 13) as well as between the member states and the Commission (e.g. Article 16 (1) and 17 (1)). Moreover, also with regard to the inter-business level various provisions—among them Article 4 lit. a and Article 7 (2)—are intended to

---

[69] European Parliament and Council, Directive 2014/95/EU of 22 October 2014 amending Directive 2013/34/EU as regards disclosure of non-financial and diversity information by certain large undertakings and groups, OJ EU L 330/1, 15 November 2014.

[70] See Sect. 4.1.

[71] See thereto, specifically with regard to section 1502 Dodd-Frank Act, for example also Moncel (2016), "The U.S. Congress thus embraced a transparency-based regulatory theory, according to which exposing a problem to the public can foster public action against it. The result may be the same: several technology companies subject to the rule, including Apple, HP, Intel, and SanDisk, have already committed to removing all conflict minerals from their supply chains.", pp. 225–226; as well as more generally Chilton and Sarfaty (2017), pp. 20 et seq.

[72] Generally on the correlation between the considerably increased parliamentarisation of the EU common commercial policy on the basis of the Lisbon Treaty on the one hand and the effective realisation of the EU (non-economic) foreign policy goals see, e.g., Krajewski (2013), pp. 83 et seq.; Bungenberg (2010), pp. 129 et seq.; Tietje (2009), p. 21.

[73] See Sect. 4.4.5.

facilitate an increased flow of information between Union importers and their suppliers as well as downstream purchasers.

Finally and presumably most notable in the present context, the fact that various disclosure obligations incumbent upon covered economic actors are also concerned with providing access to information for the wider public, including consumers and other stakeholders, can be regarded as a clear indication that these procedural duties are not merely supplementary means aimed at facilitating the enforcement of substantive due diligence obligations by the competent authorities of the member states, but are actually envisioned as a compliance mechanism in its own right by allowing for public action like the exercise of consumer choices based on the information received.[74] This applies for example to the disclosure obligations of Union importers stipulated in Article 4 lit. a and Article 7 (3), but also to the publication requirements bestowed upon the Commission, inter alia, under Article 9 (5) and Article 10 (2).

In sum, the regulatory features of the 2017 EU Conflict Minerals Regulation transcend the distinction between traditional law enforcement mechanisms and law-realisation approaches by combining "command and control" elements in the form of legally binding supply chain due diligence obligations with more indirect steering tools aimed at improving transparency; a path so far less taken in the realm of international and domestic normative regimes aimed at promoting the observance of human rights in the extractive industries, but in principle undoubtedly promising and thus definitely worth exploring.

References

Abelardo J (2017) Who starved for that smartphone? Limitations of the SEC's approach to the Congolese conflict minerals trade problem and the need for the European Union to better address its associated human rights abuses. Fordham Int Law J 40:583–624

Al Faruque A (2006) Transparency in extractive revenues in developing countries and economies in transition: a review of emerging best practices. J Energy Nat Resour Law 24:66–103

Boor F, Nowrot K (2014) Von Wirtschaftssanktionen und Energieversorgungssicherheit: Völkerrechtliche Betrachtungen zu staatlichen Handlungsoptionen in der Ukraine-Krise. Die Friedens-Warte 89:211–248

Boysen S (2014) Das System des Europäischen Außenwirtschaftsrechts. In: von Arnauld A (ed) Europäische Außenbeziehungen. Nomos, Baden-Baden, pp 447–514

Brackett A, Levin E, Melin Y (2015) Revisiting the conflict minerals rule. Glob Trade Customs J 10:73–86

Bradley K (2017) Legislating in the European Union. In: Barnard C, Peers S (eds) European Union law, 2nd edn. Oxford University Press, Oxford, pp 97–142

Brouder A (2009) Kimberley Process Certification Scheme. In: Tietje C, Brouder A (eds) Handbook of transnational economic governance regimes. Martinus Nijhoff, Leiden, pp 969–987

---

[74] See in this regard also for example recital 13 of the EU Conflict Minerals Regulation: "Public reporting by an economic operator on its supply chain due diligence policies and practices provides the necessary transparency to generate public confidence in the measures economic operators are taking.".

Bungenberg M (2010) Going global? The EU common commercial policy after Lisbon. Eur Yearb Int Econ Law 1:123–151

Bungenberg M (2017) Artikel 205 AEUV. In: Pechstein M, Nowak C, Häde U (eds) Frankfurter Kommentar zu EUV, GRC und AEUV, vol III. Mohr Siebeck, Tübingen, pp 1521–1524

Chalmers D (2015) The democratic ambiguity of EU law making and its enemies. In: Arnull A, Chalmers D (eds) The Oxford handbook of European Union law. Oxford University Press, Oxford, pp 303–326

Chilton AS, Sarfaty GA (2017) The limitations of supply chain disclosure regimes. Stanf J Int Law 53:1–54

Cottier T, Trinberg L (2015) Artikel 207 AEUV. In: von der Groeben H, Schwarze J, Hatje A (eds) Europäisches Unionsrecht, Kommentar, vol 4, 7th edn. Nomos, Baden-Baden, pp 310–351

Cremer HJ (2016) Artikel 205 AEUV. In: Calliess C, Ruffert M (eds) EUV/AEUV, Kommentar, 5th edn. Beck, Munich, pp 1995–1996

Cremona M (2003) The Union as a global actor: roles, models and identity. Common Mark Law Rev 41:553–573

DeKoninck H (2015) Breaking the curse: a multilayered regulatory approach. Indiana J Glob Leg Stud 22:121–148

Dimopoulos A (2010) The effects of the Lisbon Treaty on the principles and objectives of the common commercial policy. Eur Foreign Aff Rev 15:153–170

Foster N (2017) Blackstone's EU Treaties & Legislation 2017–2018, 28th edn. Oxford University Press, Oxford

Hahn M (2016) Artikel 207 AEUV. In: Calliess C, Ruffert M (eds) EUV/AEUV, Kommentar, 5th edn. Beck, Munich, pp 2004–2070

Heintschel von Heinegg W (2017) Artikel 21 EUV. In: Pechstein M, Nowak C, Häde U (eds) Frankfurter Kommentar zu EUV, GRC und AEUV, vol I. Mohr Siebeck, Tübingen, pp 603–618

Herrmann C, Müller-Ibold T (2016) Die Entwicklung des europäischen Außenwirtschaftsrechts. Europäische Zeitschrift für Wirtschaftsrecht 27:646–653

Heße D, Klimke R (2017) Die EU-Verordnung zu Konfliktmineralien: Ein stumpfes Schwert? Europäische Zeitschrift für Wirtschaftsrecht 28:446–450

Khan DE (2015) Article 207 TFEU. In: Geiger R, Khan DE, Kotzur M (eds) European Union treaties – a commentary. Beck/Hart, Munich, pp 756–765

Krajewski M (2005) External trade law and the Constitution Treaty: towards a federal and more democratic common commercial policy? Common Mark Law Rev 42:91–127

Krajewski M (2012) The reform of the common commercial policy. In: Biondi A, Eeckhout P, Ripley S (eds) EU law after Lisbon. Oxford University Press, Oxford, pp 292–311

Krajewski M (2013) New functions and new powers for the European Parliament: assessing the changes of the common commercial policy from the perspective of democratic legitimacy. In: Bungenberg M, Herrmann C (eds) Common commercial policy after Lisbon. Springer, Heidelberg, pp 67–85

Krajewski M (2016) Normative Grundlagen der EU-Außenwirtschaftsbeziehungen: Verbindlich, umsetzbar und angewandt? Europarecht 51:235–255

Lachmayer K (2015) Artikel 205 AEUV. In: von der Groeben H, Schwarze J, Hatje A (eds) Europäisches Unionsrecht, Kommentar, vol 4, 7th edn. Nomos, Baden-Baden, pp 267–269

Larik J (2016) Foreign policy objectives in European constitutional law. Oxford University Press, Oxford

Lenaerts K, Van Nuffel P (2011) European Union law, 3rd edn. Sweet & Maxwell, London

Meessen KM (2015) Kimberley as a means of promoting good governance: the role of business. In: Bungenberg M, Hobe S (eds) Permanent sovereignty over natural resources. Springer, Heidelberg, pp 173–186

Meng W (1997) Wirtschaftssanktionen und staatliche Jurisdiktion – Grauzonen im Völkerrecht. Zeitschrift für ausländisches öffentliches Recht und Völkerrecht 57:269–327

Moncel R (2016) Cooperating alone: the global reach of U.S. regulations on conflict minerals. Berkeley J Int Law 34:216–244

Nelson AL (2014) The materiality of morality: conflict minerals. Utah Law Rev 2014:219–241

Nettesheim M, Duvigneau JL (2012) Artikel 207 AEUV. In: Streinz R (ed) EUV/AEUV, Kommentar, 2nd edn. Beck, Munich, pp 1933–1983

Nowrot K (2013) Bilaterale Rohstoffpartnerschaften: Betrachtungen zu einem neuen Steuerungsinstrument aus der Perspektive des Europa- und Völkerrechts. Beiträge zum Transnationalen Wirtschaftsrecht, vol 128. Institut für Wirtschaftsrecht, Halle (Saale)

Nowrot K (2016) Rohstoffhandel und Good Governance. In: Bungenberg M, Herrmann C (eds) Die gemeinsame Handelspolitik der Europäischen Union. Nomos, Baden-Baden, pp 214–250

Nowrot K (2017) Good raw materials governance – towards a European approach contributing to a constitutionalised international economic law. Eur Yearb Int Econ Law 8:381–407

Ochoa C, Keenan PJ (2011) Regulating information flows, regulating conflict: an analysis of United States conflict minerals legislation. Goettingen J Int Law 3:129–154

Ross ML (2004) How do natural resources influence civil war? Evidence from thirteen cases. Int Organ 58:35–67

Schorkopf F (2008) Internationale Rohstoffverwaltung zwischen Lenkung und Markt. Archiv des Völkerrechts 46:233–258

Schuele CK (2015) Healing the Congo's colonial scars: advocating for a hybrid approach to conflict minerals reporting regulations in the European Union. Wisconsin Int Law J 33:755–786

Schütze R (2015) European Union law. Cambridge University Press, Cambridge

Schwartz J (2016) The conflict minerals experiment. Harv Bus Law Rev 6:129–183

Smillie I (2013) Blood diamonds and non-state actors. Vanderbilt J Transnatl Law 46:1003–1023

Taylor CR (2017) The unsettled state of compelled corporate disclosure regulation after the conflict mineral rule cases. Lewis Clark Law Rev 21:427–452

Terhechte JP (2012) Artikel 205 AEUV. In: Schwarze J (ed) EU-Kommentar, 3rd edn. Nomos, Baden-Baden, pp 1894–1896

Tietje C (1998) Normative Grundstrukturen der Behandlung nichttarifärer Handelshemmnisse in der WTO/GATT-Rechtsordnung. Duncker & Humblot, Berlin

Tietje C (2009) Die Außenwirtschaftsverfassung der EU nach dem Vertrag von Lissabon. Beiträge zum Transnationalen Wirtschaftsrecht, vol 83. Institut für Wirtschaftsrecht, Halle (Saale)

Tietje C (2015) Außenwirtschaftsrecht. In: Tietje C (ed) Internationales Wirtschaftsrecht, 2nd edn. de Gruyter, Berlin, pp 792–862

Tietje C, Nowrot K (2016) Parlamentarische Steuerung und Kontrolle des internationalen Regierungshandelns und der Außenpolitik. In: Morlok M, Schliesky U, Wiefelspütz D (eds) Parlamentsrecht – Handbuch. Nomos, Baden-Baden, pp 1469–1505

van der Velde S (2017) The end of conflict minerals on the EU market? ASSER Policy Brief No. 3, 2017-03

Veale E (2013) Is there blood on your hands-free device? Examining legislative approaches to the conflict minerals problem in the Democratic Republic of Congo. Cardozo J Int Comp Law 21:503–544

Vedder C (2013) Linkage of the common commercial policy to the general objectives for the Union's external action. In: Bungenberg M, Herrmann C (eds) Common commercial policy after Lisbon. Springer, Heidelberg, pp 115–144

Vidal V (2012) Informal international lawmaking: the Kimberley process' mechanism of accountability. In: Berman A et al (eds) Informal international lawmaking: case studies. Torkel Opsahl Academic EPublisher, The Hague, pp 505–525

von Arnauld A (2014) Das System der Europäischen Außenbeziehungen. In: von Arnauld A (ed) Europäische Außenbeziehungen. Nomos, Baden-Baden, pp 41–101

Vyboldina E (2015) Solving the conflict minerals puzzle. Glob Trade Customs J 10:338–345

Weiß W (2014) Vertragliche Handelspolitik der EU. In: von Arnauld A (ed) Europäische Außenbeziehungen. Nomos, Baden-Baden, pp 515–586

Zerk JA (2006) Multinationals and corporate social responsibility. Cambridge University Press, Cambridge

Karsten Nowrot, LL.M. (Indiana) is Professor of Public Law, European Law and International Economic Law, Director of the Research Institute for Economic Law and Labour Law as well as the current Head of the Department of Law at the School of Socio-Economics of the Faculty of Business, Economics and Social Sciences at Hamburg University, Germany. He also serves as Deputy Director of the Master Programme "European and European Legal Studies" at the Institute for European Integration of the Europa-Kolleg in Hamburg.

Community Development Agreements as Tools for Local Participation in Natural Resource Projects in Africa

Evaristus Oshionebo

Contents

1	Introduction	77
2	Legal Regimes Governing CDAs in Africa	79
	2.1 Statutory CDAs	79
	2.2 CDAs as Tools for Providing Development Assistance	82
	2.3 Voluntary Systems of CDAs	83
	2.4 Challenges of Identifying the Affected "Local Community"	84
3	Contents of CDAs	86
4	CDAs as Tools for Local Participation in Natural Resource Projects	89
	4.1 Community Participation in Project Implementation	89
	4.2 Community Participation in Resource Benefit-Sharing	94
5	Factors Hindering the Utility of CDAs in Africa	97
	5.1 Power Imbalance and Lack of Capacity	97
	5.2 Non-disclosure	100
	5.3 Enforceability and Access to Justice	101
	5.4 Environmental Sustainability	102
	5.5 Representation of Host Communities	103
	5.6 Management of CDAs	105
6	Conclusion	107
	References	108

1 Introduction

Community Development Agreements (CDAs)[1] are usually negotiated between resource companies and local and indigenous host communities for the threefold purpose of promoting the participation of local communities in project execution,

---

[1] The term "Community Development Agreement" is used broadly to include Impact and Benefit Agreements, Community Benefit Agreements, Global Memoranda of Understanding and similar

---

E. Oshionebo (✉)
Faculty of Law, University of Calgary, Calgary, AB, Canada
e-mail: eoshione@ucalgary.ca

© Springer Nature Switzerland AG 2019
I. Feichtner et al. (eds.), *Human Rights in the Extractive Industries*,
Interdisciplinary Studies in Human Rights 3,
https://doi.org/10.1007/978-3-030-11382-7_5

ensuring that these communities derive material benefit from resource exploitation, and reducing the adverse impacts of resource development on host communities.[2] In essence, CDAs are instruments for ensuring not only the sharing of the benefits accruing from natural resource projects with host communities but also the minimization of the adverse impacts of resource projects through the mutual efforts of companies and communities.

CDAs have been described as "one of the most powerful tools that community groups have to shape development projects."[3] CDAs are not unique to the extractive industries as they have long been utilized in other sectors of the economy including urban development projects such as the world-famous Yankee Stadium in New York City and the Staples Centre in Los Angeles.[4] However, CDAs and similar agreements are widely used in the resource sector, particularly in countries such as Australia and Canada with a large population of Aboriginal and Indigenous peoples. In Canada, for example, mining and oil and gas companies are encouraged by the government to sign Impact and Benefit Agreements (IBAs) with Aboriginal communities. In some instances, IBAs are required under land claims agreements between federal and provincial governments and Aboriginal communities.[5] In other instances, the government may require resource companies to sign IBAs with Aboriginal communities in order to obtain regulatory approval for resource projects.[6]

While CDAs are, for the most part, voluntarily negotiated and signed by resource companies and host communities, some countries have enacted laws imposing an obligation on resource companies to provide financial and material benefits to host communities. In fact, as of 2014, 32 countries had enacted laws requiring companies in the resource sector to undertake socio-economic development projects in host communities.[7] Quite often, resource companies utilize CDAs as tools for discharging their obligation to provide development assistance to host communities.

This chapter focuses on CDAs as tools for local participation in resource projects in Africa. The chapter examines the nature, scope and contents of CDAs in Africa and assesses the degree to which CDAs enable host communities to participate in project implementation as well as how CDAs are being utilized to promote community participation in resource revenue sharing. It identifies certain factors hindering the utility of CDAs in Africa and notes that these factors arise primarily from the voluntary nature of CDAs in Africa. In view of the identified factors, the chapter

---

agreements between resource companies and local communities designed to aid the developmental goals of local communities.

[2] See Matiation (2002), p. 204.

[3] Musil (2012), p. 827.

[4] Musil (2012), p. 827.

[5] Matiation (2002), p. 210.

[6] Matiation (2002), p. 211.

[7] Dupuy (2014), p. 201.

concludes that Africa should statutorily require resource companies to negotiate and sign CDAs with host communities.

2 Legal Regimes Governing CDAs in Africa

CDAs in Africa's extractive industries arise in three distinct scenarios. In the first scenario, CDAs are mandated by statutes as exemplified by mining statutes in Nigeria,[8] Guinea,[9] Kenya,[10] Mozambique,[11] Sierra Leone,[12] and South Sudan.[13] The second scenario involves the utilization of CDAs by resource companies as tools for fulfilling a legal obligation to provide development assistance to host communities. The third scenario arises where, in the absence of statutory provisions requiring CDAs, CDAs are voluntarily negotiated by resource companies and local host communities.

2.1 Statutory CDAs

Under the first scenario, CDAs are required with regard to all industry participants or mandated only in specific circumstances such as a particular mining licence; production capacity; seriousness of the adverse impacts of a project; size of the workforce of mining companies; and the magnitude of a resource project. An example of a statute mandating all industry participants to have CDAs is the *Nigerian Minerals and Mining Act* which provides that:

.... The Holder of a Mining Lease, Small Scale Mining Lease or Quarry Lease shall prior to the commencement of any development activity within the lease area, conclude with the host community where the operations are to be conducted an agreement referred to as a Community Development Agreement or other such agreement that will ensure the transfer of social and economic benefits to the community.[14]

Similarly, Guinea requires holders of mining concessions to enter into Local Development Agreements with communities in the immediate vicinity of their mining operations.[15] In that country, Local Development Agreements are required for the express purpose of establishing "conditions that are conducive to the efficient

---

[8] Nigerian Minerals and Mining Act, 2007, section 116.

[9] Amended 2011 Mining Code, Articles 37 and Article 130.

[10] Mining Act, 2016, section 109.

[11] Mining Law No. 20/2014, 18 August 2014, Article 8.

[12] The Mines and Minerals Act, 2009, sections 138–141.

[13] Mining Act, 2012 (Act No. 36), section 68.

[14] Nigerian Minerals and Mining Act, 2007, section 116 (1).

[15] Amended 2011 Mining Code, Articles 37 and Article 130.

and transparent management of the contribution to local development paid by the holder of the Mining Operation Permit, and to strengthen the capacities of the local community in the planning and implementation of the community development program."[16]

Unlike Nigeria and Guinea where holders of mineral concessions and licences are statutorily obliged to have CDAs, Sierra Leone and South Sudan do not oblige all mining licence holders to enter into CDAs. Rather, in these countries this legal requirement is qualified by certain restrictions or limitations particularly with regard to the magnitude of a project and the adverse impacts of a project. For example, in Sierra Leone, mining licence holders are required to have CDAs with their "primary host community" only if the "approved mining operation will or does exceed any of the following limits –

(a) in the case of extraction of mineral from primary alluvial deposits, where annual throughput is more than one million cubic metres per year;
(b) in the case of underground mining operations, where annual combined run-of-mine ore and waste production is more than one hundred thousand tonnes per year (waste material not exiting mine mouth to be excluded);
(c) in the case of open-cast mining operations extracting minerals from primary non-alluvial deposits, where annual combined run-of-mine ore, rock, waste and overburden production is more than two hundred and fifty thousand tonnes per year; or
(d) where the licence holder employs or contracts more than one hundred employees or workers at the mine site on a typical working day (including all shifts)."[17]

In South Sudan, only large-scale mining licence holders are required to enter into CDAs under the *Mining Act* which provides that holders of Large-Scale Mining Licences "shall (a) assist in the development of communities near to or affected by its operations to promote the general welfare and enhance the quality of life of the inhabitants living there; and (b) enter into Community Development Agreements with such communities in cooperation with relevant government authorities."[18] Thus, in South Sudan holders of small-scale mining licences are not statutorily required to enter into CDAs.

The CDA regime in Kenya is unclear with regard to the companies required to enter into CDAs. While the *Mining Act* of Kenya appears to require all mining licence holders to "sign a community development agreement with the community where mining operations are to be carried out",[19] the Act defines a CDA as "an agreement entered into between a large-scale mining licence holder and a community".[20] Adding to the confusion is the fact that the Regulations made under the *Mining Act* do not restrict the CDA obligation to large-scale mining licence

---

[16] Amended 2011 Mining Code, Article 130.
[17] The Mines and Minerals Act, 2009, section 139.(1).
[18] Mining Act, 2012 (Act No. 36), section 68.(1).
[19] Mining Act, 2016, section 109(i).
[20] Mining Act, 2016, section 4.

holders.[21] Thus it is unclear at this time whether all mining licence holders are obliged to enter into CDAs in Kenya. However, because the *Mining Act* is superior to the Regulations it can be argued that only large-scale mining licence holders are required to enter into CDAs in Kenya.[22]

The mandatory nature of CDAs in some African countries including Nigeria, Kenya and Sierra Leone is underscored by statutory provisions requiring ministerial intervention where resource companies and host communities are unable to agree on the terms of a CDA. These provisions envisage that, in the event that a mining company is unable to conclude a CDA with host communities after several attempts to do so, the matter shall be referred to, and resolved by, the Minister responsible for solid minerals development.[23] While the Nigerian statute does not specify how the Minister is to resolve such impasse, in Sierra Leone the Minister shall make a determination in consultation with the local council.[24]

Most of the mandatory CDA regimes in Africa presuppose the acquisition of mineral rights prior to the negotiation and signing of CDAs. However, in some cases companies may be required to enter into CDAs with host communities prior to, or contemporaneously with, the execution of an investment contract with the government. For example, Mozambique's *Mining Law No. 20 of 2014* provides that the mining contract between the government and the holder of a Prospecting and Research Licence shall, amongst other things, contain a "memorandum of understanding between the Government, the company and the community(ies)" as well as "the way communities of the mining area are engaged and benefitted by the venture".[25] In Kenya, the government may sign a mineral development agreement with the holder of a mining licence and the terms of the agreement usually include community development plans which have been previously negotiated by the mining licence holder with the host communities and laid down in a CDA.[26] In extreme cases, however, CDAs must be concluded prior to the grant of mineral rights. For example, in Guinea an application for a mining concession must be accompanied by several documents including a community development plan annexed to the Local Development Agreement negotiated by the applicant with host communities.[27]

However, some of the mandatory CDA regimes in Africa appear confusing with regard to the scope of the regimes. It is unclear whether some of the statutory provisions requiring CDAs in Africa apply retroactively to extant mining projects or

---

[21] See section 2 of the Mining (Community Development Agreement) Regulations, 2017 which defines a CDA as "a legal agreement or commitment entered into by a holder and the affected mine community or communities".

[22] Nwapi (2017), p. 207.

[23] See Nigerian Minerals and Mining Act, 2007, section 116 (4); Kenya's Mining (Community Development Agreement) Regulations, 2017, section 9 (6); and Sierra Leone's The Mines and Minerals Act, 2009, section 141 (4).

[24] The Mines and Minerals Act, 2009, section 141 (4).

[25] Mining Law No. 20/2014, 18 August 2014, Article 8 (1), (2).

[26] The Mining Act, 2016, section 117 (1), (2).

[27] Amended 2011 Mining Code, Article 37.

whether they are designed to apply exclusively to new projects executed after the enactment of the statutes. In Nigeria, for example, CDAs are required "prior to the commencement of any development activity within the lease area", suggesting that the requirement applies to projects executed after the enactment of the Act.[28] Similarly, Kenya requires CDAs with regard to "the community where mining operations are to be carried out".[29] This presupposes that CDAs in Kenya must be concluded prior to the commencement of mining operations. However, the Regulations made under Kenya's *Mining Act* anticipate application of the CDA regime to existing projects. The Regulations require CDAs of holders of mining licences issued under the current *Mining Act* as well those issued under its predecessor statutes, provided that the licences are still valid and subsisting.[30]

The CDA regimes in Nigeria and Kenya are defective to the extent that they apply exclusively to new projects. It is preferable that the regimes apply equally to existing projects and new projects so as to avoid inequities in terms of community participation in resource projects. A limited application of the regimes would also be discriminatory and could lead to disaffection within host communities. By contrast, the CDA regime in South Sudan appears to apply to both existing projects and future projects because South Sudan's *Mining Act* requires companies to enter into CDAs with communities "affected by [their] operations".[31]

2.2   CDAs as Tools for Providing Development Assistance

A second instance in which CDAs commonly arise in Africa is when they are used by companies as tools for fulfilling their legal obligation to provide development assistance to host communities. Statutes governing mineral exploitation may impose an obligation on resource companies to assist host communities with infrastructural projects without, however, specifying the means by which this obligation shall be fulfilled, thus not mandating the conclusion of CDAs.[32] Resource statutes in this category may in fact require extractive companies to formally commit to providing development assistance to host communities prior to the acquisition of a mineral title. For example, in countries such as the Central African Republic,[33] Mali[34] and the Democratic Republic of Congo,[35] mining companies are required to submit a community development plan as part of their application for mineral rights. Thus, in

---

[28] Nigerian Minerals and Mining Act, 2007, section 116 (1).

[29] Mining Act, 2016, section 109 (i).

[30] Mining (Community Development Agreement) Regulations, 2017, section 4.

[31] Mining Act, 2012 (Act No. 36), section 68 (1).

[32] See, for example, Ethiopia's Mining Proclamation 678 of 2010, Article 60 and Mining Law for the Republic of Equatorial Guinea, Law No. 9/2006, Article 54.

[33] Mining Code of 2009, Law No. 09-005, Article 33.

[34] Law 2012-015 (Mining Code 2012); Decree No. 2012-311/P-RM.

[35] Mining Code, Law No. 007/2002 of July 11 2002, Article 33.

these countries a commitment to provide community development assistance is a condition to be met prior to the grant of mineral rights. Although these statutory provisions do not specifically compel companies to sign CDAs, they nonetheless create a statutory platform for CDAs given that CDAs are the primary instruments used by companies to fulfill their community development obligations.

CDAs can also arise where the government perceives that a particular project will have significant adverse impacts on local communities. The government can require the project proponent to undertake community development in the host communities so as to address and ameliorate such adverse impacts. In South Africa, for example, a proposed amendment to the *Mineral and Petroleum Resources Development Act* would empower the Minister of Minerals and Energy to direct the holder of a mining right to address the socio-economic challenges and needs of the host communities.[36] In such a case, CDAs can be employed as mechanisms for addressing the socio-economic challenges and needs of the host communities.

2.3   Voluntary Systems of CDAs

Most countries in Africa do not have statutory provisions requiring CDAs. Thus, the third scenario arises where resource companies voluntarily sign CDAs with local communities partly as a result of pressure exerted on the companies by civil society groups and partly in furtherance of the companies' desire to exploit natural resources in a sustainable manner. In Ghana, for example, CDAs are not mandated by statute but several CDAs have been voluntarily negotiated and signed by mining companies.[37] These CDAs include the Ahafo Social Responsibility Agreement[38] and the Newmont Ahafo Development Foundation Agreement,[39] both of which were signed by Newmont, a mining company, and local communities in and around Newmont's goldmine project. Similarly, while oil and gas companies in Nigeria are not statutorily obliged to have CDAs, many of these companies have voluntarily negotiated CDAs with local communities.[40] CDAs in the Nigerian oil and gas sector apparently were first concluded in 2005 when Chevron signed a Global Memorandum of Understanding (GMoU) with the Keffes and Dodo River communities in Bayelsa

---

[36] Mineral and Petroleum Resources Development Amendment Bill, B 15-2013, section 18 (c).

[37] World Bank Mining Community Development Agreements – Practical Experiences and Field Studies. June 2010 http://www.sdsg.org/wp-content/uploads/2011/06/CDA-Report-FINAL (last accessed 1 October 2018), p. 26.

[38] Ahafo Social Responsibility Agreement between the Ahafo Mine Local Community and Newmont Ghana Gold Limited. 2008, http://www.sdsg.org/wp-content/uploads/2011/06/Ahafo-Social-Responsibility-Agreement.pdf (last accessed 1 October 2018).

[39] Agreement between Newmont Ahafo Development Foundation and Newmont Ghana Gold Limited. 2008, http://www.sdsg.org/wp-content/uploads/2011/06/Newmont-Ahafo-Development-Agreement.pdf (last accessed 1 October 2018).

[40] See Odumosu-Ayanu (2014), p. 1.

State.[41] Since then, GMoU has "become the dominant model of corporate-community engagement in the [Niger Delta] region by almost all oil TNCs."[42] Following the Chevron example, Shell signed its first GMoU with local communities in 2006 and, as of the end of 2012, Shell had signed 33 GMoUs covering 349 communities in its areas of operation.[43]

2.4   Challenges of Identifying the Affected "Local Community"

Irrespective of the circumstances under which CDAs arise, a common problem facing the CDA regimes in Africa is the identification of the "local communities" with whom extractive companies sign CDAs. The problem of identification of communities can be particularly acute in countries lacking clear frameworks for delineating communities. The literature on community identification appears to focus on the geographical location of resource projects and the potential impacts of the projects.[44] However, the World Bank recommends three inter-connected processes for identifying "qualifying communities" for the purpose of CDAs. These are self-identification; assessment of risks and impacts; and an ongoing monitoring and adjustment program that caters to any changes and issues associated with identifying qualified communities.[45]

It is little surprising then that some CDA regimes in Africa identify communities on the basis of proximity to resource projects as well as the impacts of the projects. In this context, proximity to projects encompasses ownership and occupation of land in and around resource projects. In Kenya, for example, mining companies are required to enter into a CDA with "affected mine community", suggesting that the criteria for determining "community" in that country include the impact of the respective mining project.[46] Kenya also relies on the concept of proximity to mining projects to determine "community". Here, the phrase "affected mine community" means "(a) a group of people living around a mining operation; or (b) a group of people who may be displaced from land intended for exploration and mining operations."[47]

[41] See Oyadongha S, Nigeria: Chevron Signs Global MoU with Bayelsa's KEFFES Communities. Vanguard Newspaper, 2 November 2005, http://allafrica.com/stories/200511020101.html (last accessed 1 October 2018).

[42] Aaron (2012), p. 266.

[43] Shell, Shell in Nigeria: Global Memorandum of Understanding. April 2013, http://s08.static-shell.com/content/dam/shell-new/local/country/nga/downloads/pdf/2013bnotes/gmou.pdf   (last accessed 1 October 2018).

[44] See O'Faircheallaigh (2013), p. 222.

[45] World Bank, Mining Community Development Agreements: Source Book. March 2012, https://documents.worldbank.org/curated/en/522211468329663554/pdf/712990WP0minin00Box37006 5B00PUBLIC0.pdf (last accessed 1 October 2018), pp. 18–21.

[46] Mining (Community Development Agreement) Regulations, 2017, section 2.

[47] Mining (Community Development Agreement) Regulations, 2017, section 2.

The criterion of proximity or land ownership and occupation is also apparent in the statutory schemes in Guinea and South Sudan. Guinea requires mining companies to sign Local Development Agreements "with the local community residing on or in the immediate vicinity of " mining operations,[48] while South Sudan requires mining companies to sign CDAs with "communities near to or affected by [their] operations".[49] However, in some countries the "host community" is determined mutually by the mineral licence holder and the local government. This approach is adopted in Sierra Leone where mining companies are required to have CDAs with their "primary host community" and "primary host community" is defined as:

> ... the single community of persons mutually agreed by the holder of the small-scale or large-scale mining licence and the local council, but if there is no community of persons residing within thirty kilometres of any boundary defining the large-scale mining licence area, the primary host community shall be the local council."[50]

The criterion of impact could itself be problematic in situations where the adverse impacts of a resource project extend beyond the immediate vicinity of the project.[51] For example, gas flaring in Nigeria affects communities far removed from the location in which oil and gas facilities are located. In addition, the criterion of impact is less reliable in situations where the adverse impacts of extractive activities are not immediately apparent but are latent. This is particularly so in the oil and gas industry where the effects of oil operations only manifest after a latency period.[52] Injuries resulting from oil and gas operations "may not be immediately visible or may go undiscovered for a period of time."[53] In instances where the adverse impacts of a resource project extend beyond its immediate vicinity, a viable strategy may be to cluster the communities affected by the project and sign a CDA with the cluster of communities as a unit. This is the strategy adopted by oil and gas companies in Nigeria where Shell has signed thirty-three GMoUs covering 349 communities in its areas of operation.[54] The clustering of communities is also permitted in Kenya in situations where mining operations affect more than one community.[55]

The problem of community identification in Africa ought to be resolved by applying and utilizing local notions of community, particularly the customs and traditions of the peoples, tribes and ethnic nationalities inhabiting African countries. In much of Africa, communities self-define and self-identify along the lines of their

---

[48] Amended 2011 Mining Code, Article 130.

[49] Mining Act, 2012 (Act No. 36), section 68 (1).

[50] The Mines and Minerals Act, 2009, section 139 (2).

[51] See World Bank, Mining Community Development Agreements: Source Book. March 2012, https://documents.worldbank.org/curated/en/522211468329663554/pdf/712990WP0minin00Box 370065B00PUBLIC0.pdf (last accessed 1 October 2018), pp. 19–20.

[52] Frynas (1999), pp. 129–130.

[53] Frynas (1999), pp. 129–130.

[54] Shell, Shell in Nigeria: Global Memorandum of Understanding. April 2013, http://s08.static-shell.com/content/dam/shell-new/local/country/nga/downloads/pdf/2013bnotes/gmou.pdf (last accessed 1 October 2018).

[55] Mining (Community Development Agreement) Regulations, 2017, section 6 (1).

cultures, customs and traditions. Perhaps, this is what Yinka Omorogbe had in mind when she argued that "[i]n local parlance and ordinary meanings the local communities are those who are customarily resident or who are widely known as the owners of the land upon which the development is taking place."[56] And, quite often, the land occupied by communities in Africa was inhabited and passed onto them by their ancestors, thus leaving no room for doubt as to the identity of the communities. Today, communities in African countries are accepted and recognized by governments not only as the historical owners of the land they occupy but also as distinct and autonomous communities. Hence, in Ghana where CDAs are voluntary, land ownership and occupation were adopted as the basis for determining host communities with regard to Newmont's goldmine project. The three CDAs governing this project define "Ahafo Mine Local Communities" as "community towns that are physically located on the Mining Lease of Newmont Ghana Gold Limited [and] Community /traditional areas that have a significant amount of its traditional land covered by the Mining Lease of Newmont".[57]

3   Contents of CDAs

The contents of CDAs in Africa vary widely because, for the most part, CDAs are voluntarily negotiated by resource companies and local communities. As with any form of contractual arrangement, the contents of CDAs depend primarily on the interests of the contracting parties. Generally, the contents of CDAs in Africa mirror the recommendations of the International Bar Association[58] and the World Bank.[59] CDAs in Africa contain provisions on employment of local indigenes; training and education of local indigenes; the provision of social infrastructure such as schools, hospitals and roads; environmental protection; implementation procedures and mechanisms; and dispute resolution mechanisms.[60]

---

[56] Omorogbe (2002), p. 571.

[57] Ahafo Social Responsibility Agreement between the Ahafo Mine Local Community and Newmont Ghana Gold Limited. 2008, http://www.sdsg.org/wp-content/uploads/2011/06/Ahafo-Social-Responsibility-Agreement.pdf (last accessed 1 October 2018), Schedule 1. See also Agreement between Newmont Ghana Gold Limited and the Ahafo Mine Local Community on Local Employment. 2008, http://www.sdsg.org/wp-content/uploads/2011/06/Ahafo-Local-Employment-Agreement.pdf (last accessed 1 October 2018), Schedule 1.

[58] International Bar Association (April 2011) Model Mine Development Agreement. 4 April 2011, http://www.eisourcebook.org/cms/Dec%202012/Model%20Mine%20Development%20Agreement.pdf (last accessed 1 October 2018).

[59] Otto JM, Community Development Agreement: Model Regulations & Example Guidelines. World Bank, Report No. 61482, June 2010, http://documents.worldbank.org/curated/en/278161468009022969/Community-development-agreement-model-regulations-and-example-guidelines (last accessed 1 October 2018).

[60] See Nwapi (2017), p. 208.

However, in some African countries the contents of CDAs are dictated by statutes. For example, in Nigeria, CDAs in the mining sector must "contain undertakings with respect to the social and economic contributions that the project will make to the sustainability of [the host] community."[61] In addition, mining-related CDAs in Nigeria must "address all or some of the following issues when relevant to the host community –

(a) educational scholarship, apprenticeship, technical training and employment opportunities for indigenes of the communities;
(b) financial or other forms of contributory support for infrastructural development and maintenance such as education, health or other community services, roads, water and power;
(c) assistance with the creation, development and support to small scale and micro enterprises;
(d) agricultural product marketing; and
(e) methods and procedures of environment[al] and socio-economic management and local governance enhancement."[62]

Furthermore, mining-related CDAs in Nigeria are required to incorporate "appropriate consultative and monitoring frameworks" to ensure compliance with the CDAs.[63] In addition, CDAs must specify "the means by which the community may participate in the planning, implementation, management and monitoring of activities carried out under the agreement."[64]

Kenya has recently enacted CDA regulations which prescribe a broad scope regarding the contents of CDAs. Accordingly, CDAs must explain the goals, objectives, obligations and activities to be executed under the CDA and provide an organizational structure including the identity of the persons or body responsible for implementation of the CDA.[65] CDAs must also contain a community development programme specifying an implementation timetable, a schedule of anticipated expenditures, and metrics and indicators by which to measure progress; consultative and monitoring frameworks including the means by which the community shall participate in the planning, implementation, management, measurement and monitoring of the CDA; the means by which members of the community shall participate in the decision-making processes relating to the CDA; the means by which marginalized groups including women and youth will be represented in the decision-making processes; and the obligations and undertakings of the mineral right holder with regard to the social and economic benefits that the community will derive from the project, including assistance in creating income-generating activities for members of the community.[66] CDAs in Kenya must also specify the grievance and dispute

---

[61] Nigerian Minerals and Mining Act, 2007, section 116 (2).

[62] Nigerian Minerals and Mining Act, 2007, section 116 (3).

[63] Nigerian Minerals and Mining Act, 2007, section 117.

[64] Nigerian Minerals and Mining Act, 2007, section 117.

[65] Mining (Community Development Agreement) Regulations, 2017, section 11 (1-2)

[66] Mining (Community Development Agreement) Regulations, 2017, section 11 (3-7).

resolution mechanisms as well as the mechanism to be used when consultation between a mining company and the representatives of the community fails.[67]

Similarly, in Guinea, a Local Development Agreement covers issues such as environmental protection; the provision of social infrastructure including schools, hospitals, roads, water, electricity; and the training of indigenes of local communities.[68] In Sierra Leone, CDAs are required to contain provisions regarding specific matters including the person(s) or entities representing the primary host community for the purposes of the CDA; the objectives of the CDA; the obligations of the mining licence holder with regard to the host community including the undertakings of the licence holder regarding the social and economic contributions that the project will make to the sustainability of the community; assistance in creating jobs and other income-generating activities; and consultation with the host community with regard to mine closure measures.[69] In addition, CDAs in Sierra Leone's mining sector must specify the obligations of the host community in relation to the mining licence holder; the means by which the CDA shall be reviewed every five calendar years; a commitment to be bound by the agreement even in cases where the parties are unable to agree on a mutual modification of the agreement; the consultative and monitoring frameworks including "the means by which the community may participate in the planning, implementation, management and monitoring of activities carried out under the agreement"; and dispute resolution mechanisms.[70]

CDAs in Sierra Leone's mining sector must also identify the social and economic contributions to be made by the licence holder including educational scholarships, apprenticeships, technical training and employment opportunities; financial and material contributions towards infrastructural development; the creation and development of small-scale and micro enterprises; agricultural product marketing; methods and procedures of environmental and socio-economic management; and local governance enhancement.[71]

Irrespective of whether the contents of CDAs are voluntarily negotiated or mandated by statute, CDAs in Africa appear to focus primarily on the provision of social amenities to local host communities. This is hardly surprising given that a common grievance that local communities often hold against extractive companies is the economic neglect of these communities by governments and extractive companies. The provision of social amenities through CDAs not only acknowledges that such grievances are genuine but also recognizes that local communities ought to participate in sharing the enormous wealth generated from extractive projects on their land.

---

[67] Mining (Community Development Agreement) Regulations, 2017, section 11 (10).

[68] Amended 2011 Mining Code, Article 37 and Article 130.

[69] The Mines and Minerals Act, 2009, section 140 (1a-c).

[70] The Mines and Minerals Act, 2009, section 140 (1d-g).

[71] The Mines and Minerals Act, 2009, section 140 (2).

4   CDAs as Tools for Local Participation in Natural Resource Projects

The literature on public participation in natural resource development focuses primarily on statutory regulatory instruments and public administrative agencies.[72] How private instruments such as CDAs might facilitate public participation in natural resource development has yet to receive concerted attention. Although the extant literature focuses on public agencies, it holds important lessons for private participatory instruments such as CDAs. While this chapter focuses on CDAs as private instruments for local participation in resource development, it leans on, and draws lessons from, the literature on public participation particularly with regard to the scope and content of public participation.

Local participation in resource projects can assume various forms and occurs at several phases of a project. Local participation in resource projects may occur prior to the commencement of a project; during implementation and execution of a project; during post-project operations such as mine closure and land reclamation; and in the form of resource-benefit sharing. This section of the chapter examines the degree to which CDAs enable host communities to participate in project development in Africa, focusing in particular on the extent and scope of local participation in project implementation and benefit-sharing.

4.1   Community Participation in Project Implementation

There appears to be a broad consensus amongst legal scholars that public participation is an essential prerequisite for the sustainable management and exploitation of natural resources.[73] This consensus is supported by the *Convention on Access to Information, Public Participation in Decision-Making and Access to Justice in Environmental Matters* ("*Aarhus Convention*") which was adopted by the United Nations Economic Commission for Europe on 25 June 1998.[74] The *Aarhus Convention* provides for three key environmental rights: the right to receive environmental information from public authorities; the right to participate in environmental decision-making; and the right of access to justice in environmental matters.[75] With regard to public participation, the *Aarhus Convention* requires signatory countries to afford their citizens the right to participate in the decision-making process

---

[72] See, for example, Toomey (2012), Lee and Abbot (2003) and Zillman et al. (2002).

[73] See Fluker (2015) and Zillman et al. (2002).

[74] United Nations Economic Commission for Europe, Convention on Access to Information, Public Participation in Decision-Making and Access to Justice in Environmental Matters (Aarhus Convention). 25 June 1998, Aarhus (Denmark), entered into force on 30 October 2001.

[75] United Nations Economic Commission for Europe, Convention on Access to Information, Public Participation in Decision-Making and Access to Justice in Environmental Matters (Aarhus Convention). 25 June 1998, Aarhus (Denmark), entered into force on 30 October 2001, Article 1.

pertaining to specific activities listed in the convention including activities "which may have a significant effect on the environment."[76] The *Aarhus Convention* lists certain activities including the energy sector; production and processing of metals; and the mineral industry as activities which could have a detrimental effect on the environment, thus requiring the participation of the public.[77] Similarly, the African Union has adopted the position that, in order to exploit natural resources in a sustainable manner, African countries should "strengthen transparency, accountability and access to information, improve public participation and provide capacity building programmes for local communities" and civil society organizations.[78]

This consensus appears to be based on a concept of democracy which presupposes that citizens are collectively entitled to participate in decision-making processes in order to legitimize the decisions and outcomes arising from these processes.[79] Less clear, however, is the meaning, scope and content of public participation in resource decision making. Even the primary international instrument on the subject, the *Aarhus Convention*, does not define "public participation", although it defines "the public" as "one or more natural persons" including "their associations, organizations or groups".[80] That said, we can glean from international instruments and literature on the subject some of the vital components of public participation. For example, the *Aarhus Convention* envisions public participation to include access to environmental information[81]; actual participation by the public in the environmental decision-making process[82]; and access to justice, that is, access

---

[76] United Nations Economic Commission for Europe, Convention on Access to Information, Public Participation in Decision-Making and Access to Justice in Environmental Matters (Aarhus Convention). 25 June 1998, Aarhus (Denmark), entered into force on 30 October 2001, Article 6.

[77] United Nations Economic Commission for Europe, Convention on Access to Information, Public Participation in Decision-Making and Access to Justice in Environmental Matters (Aarhus Convention). 25 June 1998, Aarhus (Denmark), entered into force on 30 October 2001, Annex I.

[78] African Union, Addis Ababa Declaration on Building a Sustainable Future for Africa's Extractive Industry: From Vision to Action. October 2011, http://archive.au.int/collect/oaucounc/import/English/EX%20749%20(XXI)%20_E.pdf (last accessed 1 October 2018).

[79] See Razzaque and Kleingeld (2013), p. 227; Richardson and Razzaque (2006), p. 165.

[80] United Nations Economic Commission for Europe, Convention on Access to Information, Public Participation in Decision-Making and Access to Justice in Environmental Matters (Aarhus Convention). 25 June 1998, Aarhus (Denmark), entered into force on 30 October 2001, Article 2 (4).

[81] United Nations Economic Commission for Europe, Convention on Access to Information, Public Participation in Decision-Making and Access to Justice in Environmental Matters (Aarhus Convention). 25 June 1998, Aarhus (Denmark), entered into force on 30 October 2001, Articles 4–6.

[82] United Nations Economic Commission for Europe, Convention on Access to Information, Public Participation in Decision-Making and Access to Justice in Environmental Matters (Aarhus Convention). 25 June 1998, Aarhus (Denmark), entered into force on 30 October 2001, Articles 6–8.

by aggrieved members of the public "to a review procedure before a court of law or another independent and impartial body established by law."[83]

The *Aarhus Convention* may not be applicable to private non-governmental entities such as corporations but its provisions are instructive with regard to the utility of CDAs as tools for community participation in resource projects. The convention illustrates that, in the absence of requisite information, the public cannot be expected to participate meaningfully in resource-related decisions.[84] Participation is incomplete without disclosure of, and access to, information relating to natural resource projects. In the context of natural resources, public participation also encompasses participation in the monitoring and enforcement of compliance with legal and statutory requirements. Hence in many jurisdictions, private citizens are specifically empowered to institute public interest litigation to enforce environmental obligations. In Africa, for example, both South Africa and Zambia have enacted statutory provisions enabling individual citizens and groups of citizens to institute legal proceedings against extractive companies with regard to the breach or threatened breach of any statutory provisions governing the resource sector.[85]

CDAs provide a platform for African citizens to participate directly in project implementation. In Sierra Leone, for example, CDAs are specifically required to contain provisions on consultation with host communities with regard to mine closure measures.[86] Such consultation enables host communities to express their opinions and concerns regarding land reclamation and remediation. In addition, some CDAs in Africa promote community participation in environmental monitoring through the creation of environmental monitoring and compliance committees consisting of members of the host communities. This is exemplified by the CDA between Newmont and Ahafo community in Ghana which provides for an environmental monitoring committee consisting of representatives of the Ahafo community.[87] In fact, one of the primary objectives of the CDA between Newmont and the Ahafo community is to "provide the Community with the opportunity to participate in the Company's decisions and plans that may affect the Community and its environs."[88] To that end, this CDA empowers the Ahafo community to

---

[83] United Nations Economic Commission for Europe, Convention on Access to Information, Public Participation in Decision-Making and Access to Justice in Environmental Matters (Aarhus Convention). 25 June 1998, Aarhus (Denmark), entered into force on 30 October 2001, Article 9.

[84] See United Nations Economic Commission for Europe, Convention on Access to Information, Public Participation in Decision-Making and Access to Justice in Environmental Matters (Aarhus Convention). 25 June 1998, Aarhus (Denmark), entered into force on 30 October 2001, Article 6 (6).

[85] See South Africa's National Environmental Management Act 107 of 1998, section 32 (1); and Zambia's Mines and Minerals Development Act 2015, section 87 (7).

[86] The Mines and Minerals Act, 2009, section 140 (1a-c).

[87] Ahafo Social Responsibility Agreement between the Ahafo Mine Local Community and Newmont Ghana Gold Limited. 2008, http://www.sdsg.org/wp-content/uploads/2011/06/Ahafo-Social-Responsibility-Agreement.pdf (last accessed 1 October 2018), Article 25 and Annex 1.

[88] Ahafo Social Responsibility Agreement between the Ahafo Mine Local Community and Newmont Ghana Gold Limited. 2008, http://www.sdsg.org/wp-content/uploads/2011/06/Ahafo-Social-Responsibility-Agreement.pdf (last accessed 1 October 2018), Article 3(b).

participate in Newmont's environmental and social impact monitoring programmes, including water quality and blast vibrations.[89] In fact, at least three members of the committee responsible for monitoring the mining operations of Newmont are selected by the Ahafo community.[90] The direct participation of local communities in project implementation creates a sense of ownership amongst members of the community which not only builds trust between the community and project proponents but also secures a greater level of support for resource projects.[91]

That said, the extent to which CDAs in Africa have incorporated local participation in environmental monitoring is unclear given that many of these CDAs are confidential and undisclosed. However, examples abound in other countries of CDAs that have been successfully utilized as tools for local participation in environmental monitoring. For example, the IBA regarding the Musselwhite gold mine in the Province of Ontario, Canada, provides for an environmental working group consisting of representatives of both the mine owner and Aboriginal communities.[92] Similarly, the IBA regarding the Raglan Mine in Quebec, Canada, provides for an environmental protection committee with 50% Aboriginal representation.[93]

The CDA regimes in Africa also require local participation in the activities undertaken under the CDAs. In Nigeria and Sierra Leone, for example, CDAs in the mining sector must provide for appropriate consultative and monitoring frameworks including the means by which local communities are to participate in the planning, implementation, management and monitoring of activities carried out under the agreement.[94] In Kenya, a CDA committee consisting of representatives of affected mine communities is responsible for monitoring and evaluating compliance with the terms of the CDA.[95] The problem, however, is that while the CDA regimes in Africa require local participation in the activities undertaken under the CDAs, many of the regimes are silent on local participation in overall project implementation.

[89] Ahafo Social Responsibility Agreement between the Ahafo Mine Local Community and Newmont Ghana Gold Limited. 2008, http://www.sdsg.org/wp-content/uploads/2011/06/Ahafo-Social-Responsibility-Agreement.pdf (last accessed 1 October 2018), Article 25 and Annex 1.

[90] Ahafo Social Responsibility Agreement between the Ahafo Mine Local Community and Newmont Ghana Gold Limited. 2008, http://www.sdsg.org/wp-content/uploads/2011/06/Ahafo-Social-Responsibility-Agreement.pdf (last accessed 1 October 2018), Annex 1.

[91] World Bank Mining Community Development Agreements – Practical Experiences and Field Studies. June 2010 http://www.sdsg.org/wp-content/uploads/2011/06/CDA-Report-FINAL (last accessed 1 October 2018), p. 67.

[92] Natural Resources Canada, Musselwhite Mine - Ontario: Partnerships Agreements. 2015, http://www.nrcan.gc.ca/mining-materials/publications/aboriginal/bulletin/8818 (last accessed 1 October 2018).

[93] Natural Resources Canada, Raglan Mine – Quebec: Partnerships Agreements. 2007, http://www.nrcan.gc.ca/mining-materials/publications/aboriginal/bulletin/8814 (last accessed 1 October 2018).

[94] See the Nigerian Minerals and Mining Act, 2007, s. 117 and Sierra Leone's The Mines and Minerals Act, 2009, section 140 (1d-g).

[95] Mining (Community Development Agreement) Regulations, 2017, section 7 (6a).

This is quite unlike the situation in Canada and Australia where CDAs allow representatives of host communities to participate in project implementation.[96]

CDAs enable public participation in resource projects in another sense. CDAs promote the integration of local concerns into the planning, execution and regulation of extractive projects.[97] In this sense CDAs are potential mechanisms for extractive companies to obtain and retain a "social licence to operate" from local communities, thus ensuring a more positive working relationship between local communities and extractive companies.[98] The term "social licence" has been aptly described as engaging "with local communities that [are] directly affected [by extractive projects] to seek their approval for the establishment [and operation] of a mine in their vicinity."[99] A social licence is a risk management mechanism consisting of processes and procedures that enable companies and host communities to engage in consistent dialogue and consultation at every phase of project development. Thus, a social licence is not a one off tool but "an ongoing contract with society that allows a project to both start and continue in a community."[100] CDAs are often voluntarily executed by resource companies in an attempt to obtain a "social licence" from host local communities. This explains why CDAs contain provisions on sustainability including provisions on environmental stewardship, as discussed earlier.

Perhaps more significantly, CDAs enable host communities to participate directly in designing resource projects where the CDAs are agreed prior to the commencement of resource projects. In fact, in countries such as Nigeria, mining companies are required to negotiate and sign CDAs with host communities "prior to the commencement of any development activity within the lease area."[101] In the course of negotiating a CDA, members of the community can voice their concerns about the project and negotiate the manner and degree to which these concerns are to be addressed by the project proponent. Such negotiations may necessitate an amendment to the project design so as to assuage the concerns of the host community. In this sense then, CDAs potentially can serve a much larger purpose of cementing the free, prior and informed consent of local communities.

However, public participation is less effective in Africa where local communities lack the capacity, expertise and competence to understand complex aspects of resource projects. A cardinal component of the public participatory process is the competence of the participants in that process.[102] In this context competence means "the construction of the best possible understandings and agreements given what is reasonably knowable to the participants at the time the discourse takes place."[103]

---

[96] See Noble and Birk (2011), pp. 21–22; O'Faircheallaigh and Corbett (2005), p. 629.

[97] Shaffer et al. (2017), p. 71.

[98] Shaffer et al. (2017), p. 71.

[99] Cooney (2017), p. 3.

[100] Smith and Richards (2015), p. 89.

[101] Nigerian Minerals and Mining Act, 2007, section 116 (1).

[102] Webler (1995), p. 35.

[103] Webler and Tuler (2000), p. 571.

The participatory process is more effective where the participants possess the capacity to evaluate and interpret information and, if need be, assert, justify and validate their claims.[104] Thus, as discussed below, the capacity of host communities in Africa needs to be enhanced in order to ensure that these communities make the most of their opportunity to participate in resource projects.

The participation of local communities in project implementation could be enhanced by incorporating local and traditional knowledge into CDAs, thus legitimizing the participatory process from the perspective of local communities.[105] Some African countries appear to have recognized the utility of traditional knowledge, hence the requirement in Kenya that CDAs should recognize and incorporate traditional knowledge.[106] Tribal and ethnic communities in Africa possess certain traditional knowledge directly relevant to the extractive industries, including land and water conservation knowledge systems[107] and ecological knowledge systems.[108] These traditional knowledge systems are rich sources "of historical information about ecosystem change"[109] and they help to maintain the "sustainable utilization and protection of commonly shared natural resources."[110] The incorporation of traditional knowledge into CDAs enables project owners to capture "valuable information that might be missed by outside experts."[111]

4.2   Community Participation in Resource Benefit-Sharing

Host communities in Africa are often dissatisfied with resource projects primarily due to two factors: the lack of economic benefits from resource projects and the adverse impacts of resource projects on the environmental well-being of host communities. This general dissatisfaction has led to instances of violent resistance to

---

[104] Webler and Tuler (2000), p. 571.

[105] Economic Commission for Africa. Improving Public Participation in the Sustainable Development of Mineral Resources in Africa. December 2004, http://repository.uneca.org/bitstream/handle/10855/5560/bib.%2039823_I.pdf?sequence=1 (last accessed 1 October 2018).

[106] Mining (Community Development Agreement) Regulations, 2017, section 11 (1h).

[107] Ayaa and Waswa (2016), pp. 470–474.

[108] Lalonde A, African Indigenous Knowledge and its Relevance to Environment and Development Activities. September 1991, https://dlc.dlib.indiana.edu/dlc/bitstream/handle/10535/904/African_Indigenous_Knowledge_and_its_Relevance_to_Environment_and_Development_Activities.pdf?sequence=1 (last accessed 1 October 2018), p. 4.

[109] Fabricius (2004), p. 35.

[110] Lalonde A, African Indigenous Knowledge and its Relevance to Environment and Development Activities. September 1991, https://dlc.dlib.indiana.edu/dlc/bitstream/handle/10535/904/African_Indigenous_Knowledge_and_its_Relevance_to_Environment_and_Development_Activities.pdf?sequence=1 (last accessed 1 October 2018), p. 4.

[111] Economic Commission for Africa. Improving Public Participation in the Sustainable Development of Mineral Resources in Africa. December 2004, http://repository.uneca.org/bitstream/handle/10855/5560/bib.%2039823_I.pdf?sequence=1 (last accessed 1 October 2018).

resource projects by local indigenes in countries such as Nigeria.[112] Such resistance has occasionally led to the destruction of equipment and other assets belonging to resource companies.

In an apparent attempt to pacify host communities, some African countries have enacted statutory and constitutional provisions on the utilization and distribution of resource revenues. For example, the Constitution of Nigeria 1999 provides that at least 13% of the revenues accruing directly from natural resources shall be paid by the federal government of Nigeria to the states where the resources were exploited.[113] In addition, Nigeria has established the Niger Delta Development Commission for the primary purpose of implementing projects and programmes for the sustainable development of the oil producing communities.[114] Similarly, Ghana has established the Mineral Development Fund with the requirement that 20% of mining royalties received by the government of Ghana shall be paid into the Fund and subsequently distributed amongst host communities and mining-sector institutions.[115] However, these revenue-sharing arrangements have proved ineffective due to mismanagement and corruption.[116]

In addition to statutory provisions requiring African governments to share resource revenues with host communities, some African countries also require extractive companies to share the economic and financial benefits of resource exploitation directly with host communities. In fact, the express purpose of the mandatory CDA regimes in Africa is the sharing of resource benefits with local communities. In Kenya, for example, the purpose of the CDA regime is

... to provide a legal basis on which mining operations and mining-related activities are conducted in a manner that, for the life of the mine –

(a) benefits of the mining operations or activities are shared between the holder and affected community;
(b) mining operations are consistent with the continuing economic, social and cultural viability of the community; and
(c) mining operations significantly contribute to the improved economic, cultural social welfare of the community and its members.[117]

---

[112] See Iwilade (2014), pp. 571–595; Ikelegbe (2001), pp. 457–460.

[113] Constitution of the Federal Republic of Nigeria 1999, section 162 (2).

[114] Niger-Delta Development Commission (Establishment etc) Act, section 7 (1).

[115] World Bank, Project Performance Assessment Report: Ghana: Mining Sector Rehabilitation Project (Credit 1921-GH), Mining Sector Development and Environment Project (Credit 2743-GH). Report No. 26197 1 June 2003, http://documents.worldbank.org/curated/en/120891468749711502/pdf/multi0page.pdf (last accessed 1 October 2018), p. 20.

[116] See Duruigbo (2004), p. 138; World Bank, Project Performance Assessment Report: Ghana: Mining Sector Rehabilitation Project (Credit 1921-GH), Mining Sector Development and Environment Project (Credit 2743-GH). Report No. 26197 1 June 2003, http://documents.worldbank.org/curated/en/120891468749711502/pdf/multi0page.pdf (last accessed 1 October 2018), p. 21 (reporting how traditional leaders in Ghana misappropriated moneys allocated to their communities by the Mineral Development Fund).

[117] Mining (Community Development Agreement) Regulations, 2017, Reg. 3.

Even countries that do not legally mandate CDAs require extractive companies to engage in community development in their areas of operation. For example, Ghana, the Democratic Republic of Congo, Mozambique, South Africa, Equatorial Guinea, Niger, the Central African Republic, Ethiopia, and Zimbabwe have imposed a statutory obligation on mining companies to provide community development assistance to host communities.[118] In attempting to comply with the obligation to provide development assistance to host communities, extractive companies are increasingly negotiating and signing CDAs with host communities across Africa. Through these CDAs resource companies provide social amenities such as roads, hospitals and schools for their host communities.

Moreover, many resource companies have voluntarily executed CDAs which provide for profit-sharing with local communities in Africa. In Nigeria, for example, oil and gas companies are not statutorily obliged to have CDAs, but, as indicated earlier, most major oil and gas companies in Nigeria have voluntarily signed CDAs with their host communities. In fact, both Shell and Chevron's GMoUs are designed primarily to provide funding for development projects in host communities. For example, Shell reports that, as of April 2013, it had provided over US$117 million to fund projects and programmes in the oil-producing communities.[119]

Some of the statutory regimes in Africa specify the monetary value of development projects to be provided by extractive companies, while others are silent on the issue. For example, in Kenya, the minimum expenditure under a CDA is "one per cent of the gross revenue from the sale of minerals by the holder in the first calendar year and in every calendar year".[120] Similarly, the mining code of Guinea provides that holders of Mining Operations Title shall contribute "zero point five percent (0.5%) of the turnover of the company made on a Mining Title of a zone for category 1 mine substances and one percent (1%) for other mine substances."[121] Likewise, mining companies in Sierre Leone are required to "expend in every year that the [CDA] is in force no less than one percent of the gross revenue amount earned by the mining operations in the previous year to implement the agreement".[122]

The prescription of a minimum value of development assistance is not limited to mandatory CDA regimes. CDAs voluntarily negotiated by companies and host communities often contain provisions on the minimum amount of financial contributions to be made by resource companies to host communities. For example, one of the CDAs governing Newmont's goldmine in Ghana provides that Newmont shall pay to the Foundation established under the CDA

---

[118] Dupuy (2014), p. 201.

[119] Shell, Shell in Nigeria: Global Memorandum of Understanding. April 2013, http://s08.static-shell.com/content/dam/shell-new/local/country/nga/downloads/pdf/2013bnotes/gmou.pdf (last accessed 1 October 2018).

[120] Mining (Community Development Agreement) Regulations, 2017, section 11 (17).

[121] Amended 2011 Mining Code, Article 130.

[122] The Mines and Minerals Act, 2009, section 139 (4).

(i) One US dollar (US$1) for every ounce of gold sold by Newmont in its operations under the Ahafo Mining Lease as reported to the government of Ghana;

(ii) One per centum (1%) of Newmont's net pre-tax income after consideration of all inter-company transactions in each year derived from the Ahafo Mining Lease and computed pursuant to generally accepted accounting practice, any gains Newmont receives from the sale of assets when such gains are equal to or more than 100,000 United States Dollars in any such year....[123]

The Mining Law of Equatorial Guinea, by contrast, imposes a blanket obligation on mining companies to undertake social works in host communities without specifying the value of the required works.[124] Similarly, in Ethiopia mining companies owe a general obligation to provide community development assistance to their host communities.[125]

5 Factors Hindering the Utility of CDAs in Africa

5.1 Power Imbalance and Lack of Capacity

A number of factors impact negatively on the utility of CDAs in Africa, including the apparent inequality in bargaining power and the incapacity of host communities. A major obstacle faced by local host communities in the course of negotiating CDAs is the power imbalance between these communities and extractive companies.[126] Whereas extractive companies are, for the most part, financially powerful, highly capitalized and thus able to hire the services of the best experts and lawyers, host communities in Africa are poor, uneducated and ill-governed. Host communities in Africa lack the capacity to negotiate CDAs and they often negotiate CDAs with limited resources and limited knowledge of extractive projects.[127] In view of this power imbalance local host communities are often "in a position of inferiority in terms of negotiation power."[128] The enormity of the financial power of extractive companies also allows these companies to exert a considerable degree of leverage over host communities in developing countries.[129]

The ill effects of the power imbalance are more apparent in countries that do not statutorily mandate the contents of CDAs. In these countries the imbalance in

---

[123] Agreement between Newmont Ahafo Development Foundation and Newmont Ghana Gold Limited. 2008 http://www.sdsg.org/wp-content/uploads/2011/06/Newmont-Ahafo-Development-Agreement.pdf (last accessed 1 October 2018), section 11 (1).

[124] Mining Law for the Republic of Equatorial Guinea, Law No. 9/2006, Article 54.

[125] Mining Proclamation 678 of 2010, Article 60.

[126] Szablowski (2010), p. 125.

[127] St-Laurent and Le Billon (2015), p. 597.

[128] St-Laurent and Le Billon (2015), p. 597.

[129] Oshionebo (2009), p. 6.

bargaining power ensures that critical aspects of CDAs are skewed in favour of extractive companies. To give but one example, some CDAs in Africa exclude legal liability on the part of resource companies by stipulating that the CDAs are not legally enforceable. In this regard, the Ahafo Social Responsibility Agreement provides that:

> The parties further agree, acknowledge and confirm that this document does not create any legally enforceable rights to the benefit of either of them and that all disputes or grievances of any kind arising out of or related to this document or policies described herein, shall be settled through mediation and conciliation making use of the Dispute Resolution Committee provided for in this Agreement. The parties hereby renounce their rights to enter into any form of litigation or arbitration on any disputes or grievances arising out of this Agreement.[130]

A similar clause renouncing the right to litigate disputes or grievances is contained in the CDA between Newmont and the Ahafo community regarding employment of local indigenes.[131] These clauses are of little benefit to the Ahafo community, yet they signed the CDAs containing the clauses. Given the power imbalance between Newmont, a multinational mining company, and the Ahafo community, it is not unreasonable to speculate that these clauses were inserted into the CDAs at the behest of Newmont.

Recognizing that "a key determinant of the outcome of CDAs is the capacity of all actors involved" in the CDAs, the World Bank recommends that resource companies should help to build the capacity of host communities to negotiate and implement CDAs, including the provision of funds to host communities for capacity-building purposes.[132] In the opinion of the World Bank,

> Successful capacity building programs should strategically target specific groups, and should aim to develop skills in areas that will support the functioning of a CDA and the longer term sustainability of community development projects. This may involve building functional capacity such as the ability to negotiate or to engage effectively in participatory or multi-stakeholder processes, building technical capacity associated with specific tasks such as microfinance, education, health, or agriculture ….[133]

A number of resource companies in Africa are in fact engaged in capacity building in their host communities. In Nigeria, for example, Shell "provides access to development experts to oversee project implementation and build the capacity of the

---

[130] Ahafo Social Responsibility Agreement between the Ahafo Mine Local Community and Newmont Ghana Gold Limited. 2008, http://www.sdsg.org/wp-content/uploads/2011/06/Ahafo-Social-Responsibility-Agreement.pdf (last accessed 1 October 2018), section 4.2.

[131] Agreement between Newmont Ghana Gold Limited and the Ahafo Mine Local Community on Local Employment. 2008, http://www.sdsg.org/wp-content/uploads/2011/06/Ahafo-Local-Employment-Agreement.pdf (last accessed 1 October 2018), section 1.2.

[132] Otto JM, Community Development Agreement: Model Regulations & Example Guidelines. World Bank, Report No. 61482, June 2010, http://documents.worldbank.org/curated/en/278161468009022969/Community-development-agreement-model-regulations-and-example-guidelines (last accessed 1 October 2018), section 8.

[133] World Bank Mining Community Development Agreements – Practical Experiences and Field Studies. June 2010 http://www.sdsg.org/wp-content/uploads/2011/06/CDA-Report-FINAL (last accessed 1 October 2018), p. 77.

[Cluster Development Boards] to grow into functional community development foundations."[134] And, as part of its capacity building efforts in Nigeria, Shell has reportedly funded the training of 61 representatives of host communities in Bayelsa State regarding budget tracking and advocacy skills.[135] Similarly, in Ghana, Newmont provides capacity training for indigenes of the Ahafo community particularly with regard to environmental monitoring and conflict resolution.[136]

While it is desirable for companies to assist host communities to build their capacity to negotiate and implement CDAs, capacity building ought not to be placed exclusively on the shoulders of resource companies. Governments and civil society organizations should participate in the collective effort to build the capacity of host communities. For example, governments can identify specific indigenes of local communities and educate them on the process and procedure for negotiating a CDA. For their part, civil society organizations can lend their expertise, be it legal, financial or managerial, to host communities by representing these communities in the course of negotiating CDAs. Perhaps more significantly, there must be cooperation and sharing of experiences amongst local communities. Local communities should harmonize their negotiation strategies and draw appropriate lessons from the experiences of other communities that have successfully negotiated CDAs in the past.

Access to information is vital to the participation of local communities in resource projects particularly in terms of project planning and implementation. The *Aarhus Convention* underscores this fact by urging signatory states to encourage project proponents to provide information to the public regarding the objectives of their proposed projects even before they apply for a permit.[137] Access to information enables members of host communities to appreciate the scope and magnitude of a proposed project, including the potential risks and benefits arising from the project. In this sense, access to information is a pre-requisite to the free, prior and informed consent of host communities. Regrettably, host communities in Africa often do not have access to corporate information prior to negotiating CDAs with extractive companies. A more worrisome observation is that, the statutes mandating CDAs in Africa do not require companies to provide the requisite information to host communities. Thus, whether or not corporate information is disclosed to host communities depends wholly on the will of extractive companies.

---

[134] Shell, Shell in Nigeria: Global Memorandum of Understanding April 2013, http://s08.static-shell.com/content/dam/shell-new/local/country/nga/downloads/pdf/2013bnotes/gmou.pdf   (last accessed 1 October 2018).

[135] Shell, Shell in Nigeria: Global Memorandum of Understanding. April 2013, http://s08.static-shell.com/content/dam/shell-new/local/country/nga/downloads/pdf/2013bnotes/gmou.pdf   (last accessed 1 October 2018).

[136] Ahafo Social Responsibility Agreement between the Ahafo Mine Local Community and Newmont Ghana Gold Limited. 2008, http://www.sdsg.org/wp-content/uploads/2011/06/Ahafo-Social-Responsibility-Agreement.pdf (last accessed 1 October 2018), section 23 (2) and Annex 1.

[137] See United Nations Economic Commission for Europe, Convention on Access to Information, Public Participation in Decision-Making and Access to Justice in Environmental Matters (Aarhus Convention). 25 June, Article 6(5).

5.2   Non-disclosure

A further issue arising from CDAs in Africa and other parts of the developing world is that, in some instances, CDAs are shrouded in secrecy.[138] While some of the CDA regimes in Africa specify the contents of CDAs, in some instances the actual contents of CDAs in Africa are not disclosed to the public. In other instances, CDAs contain confidentiality clauses prohibiting the parties from disclosing the contents of the CDAs.[139] To be sure, CDAs are primarily private agreements between host communities and resource companies. Thus, the parties to a CDA have the right to include a confidentiality clause in their CDA. Even in Nigeria where mining companies are statutorily required to sign CDAs with host communities, the *Nigerian Minerals and Mining Act 2007* does not expressly prohibit the inclusion of confidentiality clauses in CDAs.

However, non-disclosure of the contents of CDAs is counter-productive to the primary goal of any CDA which is to obtain a "social licence" to operate by encouraging local participation in resource exploitation. It is implausible to expect a host community to grant a "social licence" to resource companies if members of the community are unaware of the details of their relationship with these companies. Non-disclosure of the contents of CDAs also diminishes the extent to which host communities can participate in monitoring compliance with the CDAs. Moreover, it is impossible to know whether or not a company is fulfilling its contractual commitments under a CDA if the contents of the CDA are undisclosed.

Non-disclosure of the contents of CDAs is equally counter-productive to the goals of transparency and accountability in the resource sector and it violates a cardinal tenet of participatory governance which requires that policy decisions be disclosed to the public at large. In order to ensure that the participatory process is effective, the contents of CDAs should be disclosed and explained to the public so that they can appreciate the breath and scope of the CDAs. Governments of African countries can assuage these concerns by legislating mandatory disclosure of the contents of CDAs. Guinea recently amended its mining code to provide expressly that the contents of Local Development Agreements shall "be published and made available to the local community."[140] Similarly, both Sierra Leone and South Sudan require all CDAs to be submitted to the Mining Cadastre Office which shall then make the CDAs accessible to the public.[141] In much the same manner, the CDA Regulations in Kenya require parties to a CDA to indicate in the agreement the location where the CDA may be accessed by members of the community.[142] While the CDA regimes in Guinea, Kenya and South Sudan appear to preempt confidentiality

---

[138] Bruckner (2016), p. 424.

[139] Bruckner (2016), p. 424.

[140] Amended 2011 Mining Code, Article 130.

[141] Sierra Leone's The Mines and Minerals Act, section 141 (6); South Sudan's Mining (Mineral Title) Regulations 2015, section 56 (3).

[142] Mining (Community Development Agreement) Regulations, 2017, section 11 (15).

clauses in CDAs by requiring the disclosure of CDAs, the CDA regime is Sierra Leone expressly prohibits confidentiality clauses in CDAs.[143]

5.3   Enforceability and Access to Justice

Although as indicated above CDAs often contain provisions on the implementation of CDAs, the question remains as to whether or not CDAs can be enforced in a court of law.[144] To put the question differently, do the parties to a CDA owe legal obligations under the CDA? This question is significant because, as recognized under the *Aarhus Convention*, access to justice including access to a court is an essential component of public participation is resource projects.[145] It is not my intention here to dwell on this question in detail but it suffices to say that the answer to the question lies in the nature of the particular CDA in question. If CDAs are viewed purely as contractual agreements, then CDAs may not be binding on the parties in at least two instances. The first instance is where the parties to a CDA expressly provide that the CDA shall not have legal consequences. As discussed above, this is the position adopted by the parties to the CDAs governing Newmont's goldmine in Ahafo, Ghana.[146] In the second instance, a CDA is not binding if it does not satisfy the legal requirements for a binding contract including, in the case of common law, the requirements of offer, acceptance, consideration, and intention to enter into legal relations.

However, CDAs ought not to be viewed exclusively in contractual terms in countries where CDAs are mandated by statutes. In such countries CDAs are statutory in nature and thus, the question of enforcement of CDAs must be determined on the basis of the statutory regime governing CDAs. The mandatory CDA regimes in Africa are premised on the notion that CDAs are binding and enforceable in court. For example, mining-related CDAs in Nigeria have legislative force and are binding on the parties,[147] while the CDA regime in Sierra Leone imposes a positive obligation on mining companies to implement and fulfill their commitments under the CDA.[148] Furthermore, Sierra Leone requires parties to a CDA to expressly stipulate

---

[143] The Mines and Minerals Act, section 141 (6).

[144] See Nwapi (2017), p. 210.

[145] See United Nations Economic Commission for Europe, Convention on Access to Information, Public Participation in Decision-Making and Access to Justice in Environmental Matters (Aarhus Convention). 25 June, Article 9.

[146] See Ahafo Social Responsibility Agreement between the Ahafo Mine Local Community and Newmont Ghana Gold Limited. 2008, http://www.sdsg.org/wp-content/uploads/2011/06/Ahafo-Social-Responsibility-Agreement.pdf (last accessed 1 October 2018), section 4.2; Agreement between Newmont Ghana Gold Limited and the Ahafo Mine Local Community on Local Employment. 2008, http://www.sdsg.org/wp-content/uploads/2011/06/Ahafo-Local-Employment-Agreement.pdf (last accessed 1 October 2018), section 1.2.

[147] Nigerian Minerals and Mining Act, 2007, section 116 (5).

[148] Mines and Minerals Act 2009, section 139 (1).

in the CDA a commitment to be bound by the CDA.[149] Likewise, in Kenya CDAs acquire the force of law once they are signed by the parties.[150] The binding nature of CDAs in South Sudan is underscored by the provision that non-compliance with the requirements of community development is grounds for suspending a large-scale mining licence.[151]

That said, the legal enforcement of CDAs may yet be problematic in common law countries in Africa because of the doctrine of privity of contract which prevents third party beneficiaries from suing to enforce a contract unless they come within any of the exceptions to the doctrine.[152] Thus, where the traditional rulers or other representatives who signed a CDA on behalf of an African community refuse or fail to sue to enforce the contract, individual members of the community may not be able to enforce the contract in a court of law. The representatives of host communities may not want to enforce a CDA for a variety of reasons including corruption which, as we all know, is rampant in Africa. In order to forestall this problem, African countries may want to formally recognize the third party beneficiary principle which allows third party beneficiaries under a contract to enforce the contract even though they are not parties to the contract.[153] The recognition of the third party beneficiary principle would enable aggrieved members of host communities in Africa to seek judicial enforcement of CDAs even though they are not parties to the CDAs.[154]

5.4 Environmental Sustainability

A more worrisome observation is that, although CDAs rightly attempt to advance the economic interests of local communities, many CDAs in Africa appear to pay very little attention to environmental sustainability. These CDAs appear to neglect the prevention or amelioration of the adverse environmental impacts of resource projects. This is particularly so in countries where the contents of CDAs are not prescribed by statute. In Nigeria, for example, the contents of CDAs in the oil and gas sector are not prescribed by statute. Thus, GMoUs in Nigeria's oil and gas sector, including Shell and Chevron's GMoUs, pay very little attention to the adverse

---

[149] The Mines and Minerals Act, 2009, section 140 (1e).

[150] Mining (Community Development Agreement) Regulations, 2017, section 23.

[151] Mining Act, 2012 (Act No. 36), section 68 (2).

[152] Although the doctrine of privity of contract has been relaxed in the United Kingdom through the Contracts (Rights of Third Parties) Act 1999, many common law African countries have retained the doctrine.

[153] See, for example, the United Kingdom's Contracts (Rights of Third Parties) Act 1999 which allows a person who is not a party to a contract to enforce the contract if the contract expressly provides that they may enforce the contract or if the contract confers a benefit on the third party.

[154] See Gathii (2014), p. 93; Marco (2011), p. 34.

environmental impacts of oil and gas operations in Nigeria.[155] This omission to address environmental impacts could jeopardize the success of the GMoUs given that the restiveness in the oil producing communities is due primarily to the adverse environmental impacts of oil and gas operations.

Relatedly, the CDA regimes in Africa do not require adoption of best environmental management practices. This is in sharp contrast with the situation in developed economies such as the United States where CDAs often contain clear provisions on environmental best practices. For example, the memorandum of understanding between the community of Erie, Colorado, USA and an oil and gas company requires the company to adopt best management practices that surpass statutory regulations in the state of Colorado.[156] The deficiency with regard to environmental sustainability may be due to a confluence of factors including the incapacity of host communities to negotiate CDAs.

CDAs in Africa ought to be broad and expansive in the sense that, in addition to the funding of infrastructure projects in host communities, CDAs should also take account of the adverse social and environmental impacts of resource projects. This is the position in developed countries such as Canada where IBAs between mining companies and Aboriginal communities usually contain express provisions on environmental protection. For example, as mentioned previously, the IBAs regarding the Musselwhite goldmine in Ontario and the Raglan mine in Quebec contain provisions on a broad range of issues including environmental protection.[157]

5.5　Representation of Host Communities

A further inhibiting factor is the issue of representation of host communities. As discussed above, some of the CDA regimes in Africa provide criteria for determining host communities. However, even where a community is identified, there is the ancillary issue as to how to determine or choose the representatives of the community for the purpose of negotiating and managing a CDA. The issue of representation is of vital significance because the success of a CDA depends in large part on whether members of the community buy into the aims and objectives of the CDA. It would be difficult for members of a community to buy into a CDA where the negotiators of the CDA do not enjoy the confidence and support of the community. The issue of representation also determines the legitimacy of a CDA and the legitimacy

---

[155] Aaron (2012), pp. 267–268 (arguing that "the environment has not been mainstreamed in [Chevron's] GMoU" and that there is "a lack of any indication of mainstreaming the environment" in Shell's GMoU).

[156] Shaffer et al. (2017), p. 70.

[157] Natural Resources Canada, Musselwhite Mine - Ontario: Partnerships Agreements, http://www. nrcan.gc.ca/mining-materials/publications/aboriginal/bulletin/8818 (last accessed 1 October 2018); Natural Resources Canada, Raglan Mine – Quebec: Partnerships Agreements, http://www. nrcan.gc.ca/mining-materials/publications/aboriginal/bulletin/8814 (last accessed 1 October 2018).

of a CDA requires that the CDA be negotiated by the authorized representatives of the host community. To be legitimate a CDA must be inclusive of all groups within the host community. The World Bank has noted, for example, that "[s]takeholder participation in the CDA process should focus on participatory and representative practices that are fully inclusive and sensitive to potentially marginalized groups, including those marginalized due to gender, ethno-linguistic group, religion, age, [and] disability".[158] Aside from the issue of diversity, the representatives of host communities must also be well informed in order to participate meaningfully in the negotiation process.

The question then is, how do we ensure that those who negotiate and manage CDAs on behalf of host communities in Africa are the true representatives of the communities? Various mechanisms could be adopted to determine the representatives of host communities including democratic elections and reliance on existing traditional institutions. The mandatory CDA regimes in Nigeria, Guinea, Mozambique, Sierra Leone, and South Sudan do not contain provisions regarding the selection of community representatives. The CDA regime in Kenya, however, contains an elaborate scheme for selecting the representatives of project-impacted communities for the dual purposes of negotiating and implementing CDAs.[159] The Kenyan regime provides for a CDA committee with membership consisting of diverse groups including representatives of NGOs and vulnerable groups.[160] While most members of the CDA committee are elected by "affected mine communities", others are chosen on the basis of their positions within the executive and legislative arms of government. Members of the CDA committee elected by the affected mine community include one representative of women; two community leaders or elders; two representatives of the youth at least one of whom is a woman; one representative of marginalized groups, ethnic and other minorities; and one representative of persons with disability.[161] One member of the CDA committee is elected by NGOs working in the community, while the remaining members represent local and state governments, the parliament, and the holder of the mining licence.[162]

Interestingly, the Kenyan regime appears to ignore traditional institutions such as kingships. While it provides for the election of two community leaders or elders, it does not create any special role for traditional rulers. Obviously, the traditional ruler of a community could be elected into the CDA committee as one of the two leaders or elders. However, the exclusion of traditional rulers from the CDA committee is ill-advised because it could alienate a large segment of the host community from the

---

[158] World Bank Mining Community Development Agreements – Practical Experiences and Field Studies. June 2010 http://www.sdsg.org/wp-content/uploads/2011/06/CDA-Report-FINAL (last accessed 1 October 2018), p. 75.

[159] Mining (Community Development Agreement) Regulations, 2017, sections 7, 9.

[160] Mining (Community Development Agreement) Regulations, 2017, section 7.

[161] Mining (Community Development Agreement) Regulations, 2017, section 7 (2).

[162] Mining (Community Development Agreement) Regulations, 2017, section 7 (2).

CDA process. In extreme cases, such alienation could "elicit strong opposition capable of disrupting the CDA process."[163]

5.6 Management of CDAs

With the notable exception of Kenya where CDAs are managed by CDA committees,[164] the mandatory CDA regimes in Africa do not prescribe mechanisms for managing CDAs. Thus, for the most part, the management mechanisms for CDAs in Africa are determined by the parties to the CDAs. However, because of the power imbalance between resource companies and host communities in Africa, the issue of management of CDAs ought to be the subject of statutory prescription. This is the more so because the degree to which CDAs promote local participation in resource projects depends in part on how well CDAs are managed and implemented.

In order to forestall managerial problems, CDA regimes in Africa should contain express provisions regarding the persons responsible for managing and supervising CDAs, as well as how the managers are chosen.[165] The managers of a CDA may be a person, board, committee, foundation, trust, forum, body or other entity registered or incorporated.[166] Whatever model of governance a CDA assumes, it is imperative for CDAs to have a governance structure that is diverse particularly in terms of representation of various stakeholders and constituencies. Diversification of the governance of CDAs could in fact legitimize the CDA as well as the decisions taken by the managers of the CDA. Thus, the governance of CDAs ought not to be confined exclusively to representatives of resource companies and local host communities. Successful implementation of CDAs requires the participation of independent third parties such as non-governmental organizations.[167] The participation of independent third parties in the governance of CDAs could help to ameliorate the problem of incapacity of host communities which, as argued above, impacts negatively on CDAs in Africa.

Oil and gas companies in Nigeria have in fact adopted a governance model that permits, in varying degrees, the participation of independent third parties in the implementation of GMoUs. The GMoUs between oil and gas companies and host

---

[163] Nwapi (2017), p. 213.

[164] Mining (Community Development Agreement) Regulations, 2017, section 7 (2), (6).

[165] International Bar Association, Model Mine Development Agreement. 4 April 2011, http://www.eisourcebook.org/cms/Dec%202012/Model%20Mine%20Development%20Agreement.pdf (last accessed 1 October 2018), p. 171.

[166] International Bar Association, Model Mine Development Agreement. 4 April 2011, http://www.eisourcebook.org/cms/Dec%202012/Model%20Mine%20Development%20Agreement.pdf (last accessed 1 October 2018), p. 171.

[167] World Bank, Mining Community Development Agreements: Source Book. March 2012, https://documents.worldbank.org/curated/en/522211468329663554/pdf/712990WP0minin00Box37006 5B00PUBLIC0.pdf (last accessed 1 October 2018), pp. 27–28.

communities in Nigeria are implemented by Cluster Development Boards or Regional Development Boards consisting of representatives of host communities, oil and gas companies, NGOs, and governments.[168] Shell explains the governance structure of its GMoUs as follows:

> The governing structures are well defined, with a 10-person Community Trust, a CBD [Cluster Development Board] and a Steering Committee chaired by the State Government. The CBD functions as the main supervisory and administrative organ, ensuring implementation of projects and setting out plans and programmes. It is the decision-making committee, and the GMOU enables representatives of state and local governments, SPDC [Shell Petroleum Development Company] non-profit organisations (such as development NGOs) to come together under the auspices of the CBD as the governing body.[169]

Similarly, Chevron's GMoUs in Nigeria are implemented by Regional Development Boards and Regional Development Councils consisting of representatives of non-governmental organizations.[170] Unlike the GMoUs in Nigeria's oil and gas industry, the CDAs governing Newmont's goldmine in Ahafo, Ghana do not allow third party participation. Rather, these CDAs are governed by a board of trustees consisting of representatives of Newmont and the Ahafo community.[171]

Finally, there is the problem of endemic corruption in Africa particularly with regard to public institutions. The rampant poverty and economic marginalization in the mineral producing areas of Africa create optimal conditions for corruption.[172] Thus, the negotiation and implementation of CDAs could be corrupted unless structures that dissuade corruption are institutionalized in Africa. In this regard, host communities must ensure that their representatives have impeccable character and are beyond reproach. Equally, the legal regimes governing CDAs in Africa must erect barriers and obstacles so as to forestall corrupt practices. This appears to be the case in both Kenya and Sierra Leone where mining companies are prohibited from making direct payments to members of the host communities including the representatives of host communities.[173] In addition, in both Kenya and Sierra Leone it is illegal for CDAs to impose an obligation on mining companies to pay any additional rent, fee or tax to the host community; or provide any material benefit to individuals and family units within the host community.[174]

---

[168] Shell, Shell in Nigeria: Global Memorandum of Understanding. April 2013, http://s08.static-shell.com/content/dam/shell-new/local/country/nga/downloads/pdf/2013bnotes/gmou.pdf   (last accessed 1 October 2018); Aaron (2012), p. 266.

[169] Shell, Shell in Nigeria: Global Memorandum of Understanding. April 2013, http://s08.static-shell.com/content/dam/shell-new/local/country/nga/downloads/pdf/2013bnotes/gmou.pdf   (last accessed 1 October 2018).

[170] Aaron (2012), p. 266.

[171] See Agreement between Newmont Ahafo Development Foundation and Newmont Ghana Gold Limited. 2008, http://www.sdsg.org/wp-content/uploads/2011/06/Newmont-Ahafo-Development-Agreement.pdf (last accessed 1 October 2018), section 5.

[172] See Eberlain (2006), p. 582.

[173] See Kenya's Mining (Community Development Agreement) Regulations, 2017, section 11 (18) and Sierra Leone's The Mines and Minerals Act, 2009, section 140 (3).

[174] See Kenya's Mining (Community Development Agreement) Regulations, 2017, section 13 and Sierra Leone's The Mines and Minerals Act, 2009, section 140.(3).

6   Conclusion

The participation of host communities in resource projects potentially creates a mutually beneficial and respectful environment in which companies and host communities can attain their economic and social objectives. Through CDAs companies may obtain and retain a social licence to operate, thus ensuring a peaceful environment in which investments can flourish. Local host communities could derive direct economic benefits from resource projects in the form of the provision of social amenities and infrastructure. However, successful outcomes depend on a number of factors including access to corporate information; the capacity of local communities to negotiate complex issues associated with resource projects; good faith implementation of the agreements reached by the parties and, of course, mutual settlement of any disputes that may arise from the agreements.

While CDAs have proved to be useful tools for local participation in resource projects, a number of factors inhibit the overall utility of CDAs in Africa. For the most part, CDAs in Africa are voluntary and, in some countries where CDAs are mandated by statute, there are no clear provisions dictating the contents of CDAs. The effect then is that parties to CDAs determine the contents of their CDAs. To be sure, there is nothing inherently wrong with voluntary CDAs. After all, contracts are freely negotiated by parties all the time. However, economic realities in Africa render voluntary CDA regimes unattractive options. For example, there is a glaring power disparity between extractive companies and local communities in Africa. While extractive companies have enormous financial resources that allow them to retain the services of highly trained experts including lawyers, local communities in Africa are predominantly poor and lacking the requisite capacity and expertise to negotiate CDAs. Thus, in the course of negotiations, these communities are often unable to extract favourable terms from extractive companies.

Given this reality, African countries should give serious consideration to the enactment of legislative provisions mandating and dictating the terms of CDAs in the extractive sector. The statutory prescription of the contents of CDAs is likely to diminish the ability of extractive companies to exert their influence and leverage over host communities. This is particularly so because extractive companies will not be able to opt out of such mandatory statutory provisions. While the ambit and scope of such mandatory regimes are not the focus of this chapter, a mandatory CDA regime must ensure that, prior to the commencement of a resource project, host communities are afforded an opportunity to voice their concerns and that such concerns are taken into account by project proponents. However, any mandatory regime must be flexible and adaptable to changing circumstances.

References

Aaron KK (2012) New corporate social responsibility models for oil companies in Nigeria's delta region: what challenges for sustainability? Prog Dev Stud 12(4):259–273

Ayaa DD, Waswa F (2016) Role of indigenous knowledge systems in the conservation of the bio-physical environment among the Teso Community in Busia County – Kenya. Afr J Environ Sci Technol 10(12):467–475

Bruckner KD (2016) Community development agreements in mining projects. Denver J Int Law Policy 44:413–427

Cooney J (2017) Reflections on the 20th anniversary of the term "social licence". J Energy Nat Resour Law 35(2):197–200

Dupuy KE (2014) Community development requirements in mining laws. Extr Ind Soc 1(2):200–215

Duruigbo E (2004) Managing oil revenues for socio-economic development in Nigeria: the case for community-based trust funds. N C J Int Law Commer Regul 30(1):121–196

Eberlain R (2006) On the road to the state's perdition? Authority and sovereignty in the Niger Delta, Nigeria. J Mod Afr Stud 44(4):573–596

Fabricius C (2004) The fundamentals of community-based natural resource management. In: Fabricius C, Koch E (eds) Rights, resources & rural development: community-based natural resource management in Southern Africa. Earthscan, London, pp 3–43

Fluker F (2015) The right to public participation in resources and environmental decision-making in Alberta. Alberta Law Rev 52:567–603

Frynas JG (1999) Legal change in Africa: evidence from oil-related litigation in Nigeria. J Afr Law 43(2):121–150

Gathii JT (2014) Incorporating the third party beneficiary principle in natural resource contracts. Georgia J Int Comp Law 43(1):93–139

Ikelegbe A (2001) Civil society, oil and conflict in the Niger Delta region of Nigeria: ramifications of civil society for a regional resource struggle. J Mod Afr Stud 39(3):437–469

Iwilade A (2014) Networks of violence and becoming: youth and the politics of patronage in Nigeria's oil-rich Delta. J Mod Afr Stud 52(4):571–595

Lee M, Abbot C (2003) The usual suspects? Public participation under the Aarhus Convention. Mod Law Rev 66(1):80–108

Marco M (2011) Accountability in international project finance: the equator principles and the creation of third-party-beneficiary status for project-affected communities. Fordham Int Law Rev 34(3):452–503

Matiation S (2002) Impact benefits agreements between mining companies and aboriginal com-munities in Canada: a model for natural resource developments affecting indigenous groups in Latin America? Great Plains Nat Resour J 7(1):204–232

Musil TA (2012) The sleeping giant: community benefit agreements and urban development. Urban Lawyer 44(4):827–851

Noble B, Birk J (2011) Comfort monitoring? Environmental assessment follow-up under community-industry negotiated environmental agreements. Environ Impact Assess Rev 31(1):17–24

Nwapi C (2017) Legal and institutional frameworks for community development agreements in the mining sector in Africa. Extr Ind Soc 4(1):202–215

O'Faircheallaigh C (2013) Community development agreements in the mining industry: an emerg-ing global phenomenon. Community Dev 44(2):222–238

O'Faircheallaigh C, Corbett T (2005) Indigenous participation in environmental management of mining projects: the role of negotiated agreements. Environ Polit 14(5):629–647

Odumosu-Ayanu I (2014) Governments, investors and local communities: analysis of a multi-actor investment contract framework. Melbourne J Int Law 15(2):1–42

Omorogbe Y (2002) The legal framework for public participation in decision-making on mining and energy development in Nigeria: giving voices to the voiceless. In: Zillman D, Lucas A,

Pring G (eds) Human rights in natural resource development: public participation in the sustainable development of mining and energy projects. Oxford University Press, Oxford, pp 549–587

Oshionebo E (2009) Regulating transnational corporations in domestic and international regimes: an African case study. University of Toronto Press, Toronto

Razzaque J, Kleingeld ES (2013) Integrated water resource management, public participation and the rainbow nation. Afr J Leg Stud 6(2–3):213–247

Richardson BJ, Razzaque J (2006) Public participation in environmental decision-making. In: Richardson BJ, Woods S (eds) Environmental law for sustainability. Hart, Oxford

Shaffer A, Zilliox S, Smith J (2017) Memoranda of understanding and the social licence to operate in Colorado's unconventional energy industry: a study of citizen complaints. J Energy Nat Resour Law 35(1):69–85

Smith DC, Richards JM (2015) Social licence to operate: hydraulic fracturing-related challenges facing the oil & gas industry. Oil Gas Nat Resour Energy J 1(2):81–163

St-Laurent GP, Le Billon P (2015) Staking claims and shaking hands: impact and benefit agreements as a technology of government in the mining sector. Extr Ind Soc 2(3):590–602

Szablowski D (2010) Operationalizing free, prior and informed consent in the extractive industry sector? Examining the challenges of a negotiated model of justice. Can J Dev Stud 30(1-2):111–130

Toomey E (2012) Public participation in resource management: the New Zealand experience. N Z J Environ Law 16:117–165

Webler T (1995) Right discourse in citizen participation: an evaluative yardstick. In: Renn O, Webler T, Wiedemann PM (eds) Fairness and competence in citizen participation: evaluating models for environmental discourse. Kluwer Academic Publishers, Dordrecht

Webler T, Tuler S (2000) Fairness and competence in citizen participation: theoretical reflections from a case study. Adm Soc 32(5):566–595

Zillman D, Lucas A, Pring G (eds) (2002) Human rights in natural resource development: public participation in the sustainable development of mining and energy projects. Oxford University Press, Oxford

Evaristus Oshionebo is Professor of Law at the University of Calgary. Prior to that, he was a tenured Associate Professor at the University of Manitoba and worked as a lawyer in Nigeria specializing in corporate and commercial litigation. He holds law degrees from the Obafemi Awolowo University, University of Alberta, as well as a PhD from Osgoode Hall Law School, York University. His research focuses primarily on the law and policy governing extraction and mining of natural resources.

Stabilization Clauses and Human Rights: The Role of Transparency Initiatives

Sotonye Frank

Contents

1 Introduction 111
2 Overview of Stabilization Clauses and Human Rights 113
3 Corruption, Transparency and Scope of Stabilisation Clauses 117
4 Transparency Initiatives and Stabilization Clauses: Some Case Studies 122
    4.1 Liberia 123
    4.2 Zambia 127
    4.3 Tanzania 130
    4.4 Sierra Leone 134
5 Concluding Remarks 137
References 139

1 Introduction

The lack of transparency and presence of corrupt practices (both real and perceived) in the contracting process of the extractive industries in many developing countries are well documented in the literature.[1] Corruption and lack of transparency manifest themselves not only during the receipt of revenues accruing from the extractive industry but also during the negotiation of contracts and licenses.[2] It is therefore not

Many thanks to the Centre for Human Rights Erlangen-Nürnberg (CHREN), Erlangen, Germany for their assistance and support.

[1] See, for example, Kolstad and Søreide (2009); Marshall IE, A Survey of Corruption Issues in the Mining and Mineral Sector. Report of Mining, Minerals and Sustainable Development Project, No. 15, November 2001, http://pubs.iied.org/pdfs/G00949.pdf? (last accessed 1 October 2018).

[2] Kolstad and Søreide (2009); Marshall IE, A Survey of Corruption Issues in the Mining and Mineral Sector. Report of Mining, Minerals and Sustainable Development Project, No. 15, November 2011 http://pubs.iied.org/pdfs/G00949.pdf? (last accessed 1 October 2018).

S. Frank (✉)
Rivers State University, Port Harcourt, Nigeria
e-mail: sotonye.frank@ust.edu.ng

© Springer Nature Switzerland AG 2019
I. Feichtner et al. (eds.), *Human Rights in the Extractive Industries*, Interdisciplinary Studies in Human Rights 3, https://doi.org/10.1007/978-3-030-11382-7_6

111

surprising that several studies containing legal and economic analyses of contracts granted under opaque circumstances reveal that these contracts contain terms that are particularly generous to the extractive companies.[3] These particularly generous terms are then locked in with stabilization clauses.

Stabilization clauses are clauses that protect investors from the adverse effect of changes in the laws and regulations applicable to their investment. This protection is achieved either by exempting the investors from the applicability of the changes or by entitling them to compensation for the cost of compliance. Stabilization clauses therefore limit the ability of host states to enact laws and regulations that might affect the economic position of investors in an adverse way.

When compared with other regions of the world, the extractive industry of sub-Saharan Africa exhibits the most extensive forms of stabilization clauses, protecting investors against changes in all types of laws.[4] The broad scope of these clauses gives investors a prima facie basis to seek exemption from all new laws including social and environmental laws. They therefore limit host states' ability to implement their human rights obligations under international law especially in the areas of health and safety, labor and employment, and the environment.

This chapter examines what role, if any, transparency initiatives play in minimizing the potential effect of stabilization clauses on human rights.[5] In particular, it examines how transparency initiatives introduced by sub-Saharan African countries as a result of their involvement with the Extractive Industries Transparency Initiative (EITI) have affected stabilization clauses' potential impact on human rights. Using case studies of Tanzania, Liberia, Sierra Leone and Zambia, the chapter argues that increased transparency and accountability by African countries following their involvement with the EITI has helped to significantly reduce the potential adverse effects that stabilization clauses might have had on human rights.

During the pre-EITI era characterized by a lack of transparency, many African countries included the broadest forms of stabilization clauses in the extractive industry contracts signed with foreign investors. These clauses make no distinction between fiscal and non-fiscal laws as they are drafted to protect investors against any change in law that adversely affects the economic position of the investor. They could therefore be used by investors to justify non-compliance with new laws

---

[3] See, for example, Global Witness, Heavy Mittal: A State within a State: The inequitable Mineral Development Agreement between the Government of Liberia and Mittal Steel Holdings NV. Report, October 2006, https://www.globalwitness.org/sites/default/files/pdfs/mittal_steel_en_oct_2006_low_res.pdf (last accessed 1 October 2018); Lay T and Minio-Paluello M (2010) A Lake of Oil Congo's contracts escalate conflict, pollution and poverty. Platform, http://platformlondon.org/carbonweb/documents/drc/A_Lake_of_Oil_Congo_DRC_Tullow_PLATFORM_May_2010.pdf (last accessed 19 June 2018); UN Security Council, Report of the Panel of Experts on the Illegal Exploitation of Natural Resources and Other Forms of Wealth of the Democratic Republic of Congo, UN Doc S/2003/1027, 23 October 2003.

[4] Shemberg A, Stabilization Clauses and Human Rights. International Finance Corporation. World Bank Group, Report, 27 May 2009, https://www.ifc.org/wps/wcm/connect/9feb5b00488555eab8c4fa6a6515bb18/Stabilization%2BPaper.pdf?MOD=AJPERES (last accessed 1 October 2018).

[5] Human right is used in this paper as a surrogate for social and environmental laws.

enacted to promote and protect human rights. However, following increased transparency and accountability in the extractive industries of these countries as a result of transparency initiatives which formed part of their implementation of the EITI, they no longer adopt stabilization clauses or more limited forms of the clause. In particular, stabilization clauses in these countries now exclude socially and environmentally desirable laws from their ambit.

The chapter begins with an overview of stabilization clauses and the debate on the impact of stabilization clauses on human rights. The chapter then examines the link between corruption/lack of transparency and the scope of stabilization clauses. The effects of transparency measures adopted to implement EITI on the scope of stabilization clauses is then discussed in the context of case studies from four African countries, namely Liberia, Zambia, Tanzania and Sierra Leone. The paper concludes with a summary of the key findings from these case studies.

2   Overview of Stabilization Clauses and Human Rights

Stabilization clauses are provisions that protect foreign investors from the adverse effects of changes in the laws and regulations that apply to their investment.[6] They may be found in investment contracts, international investment agreements, national laws or in 'stability agreements' between host states and investors. Whichever technique a host state chooses, the same objective is achieved, namely, to insulate the investor from the adverse effect of changes in the laws of the host state.

In practice, stabilization clauses may be drafted to ensure stability in different ways. For this reason, they are usually categorized according to the way in which they maintain stability, namely, freezing clauses, economic equilibrium clauses and hybrid clauses.[7]

Freezing clauses 'freeze' the laws of the host state as they stood at the time the contract was concluded.[8] They preserve the laws applicable to an investment for a specified period or for the duration of the project by exempting the investor from

---

[6] For a detailed examination of stabilisation clauses, see Shemberg A, Stabilization Clauses and Human Rights. International Finance Corporation. World Bank Group, Report, 27 May 2009, https://www.ifc.org/wps/wcm/connect/9feb5b00488555eab8c4fa6a6515bb18/ Stabilization%2BPaper.pdf?MOD=AJPERES (last accessed 1 October 2018); Cameron P (2005) Stabilisation in investment Contracts and Changes of Rules in Host Countries: Tools for Oil & Gas Investors. Association of International Petroleum Negotiators, Final Report, https://www.international-arbitration-attorney.com/wp-content/uploads/arbitrationlaw4-Stabilisation-Paper.pdf (last accessed 1 October 2018); Nassar (1995), Wälde and N'Di (1996), Bernardini (1998) and Maniruzzaman (2008).

[7] Shemberg A, Stabilization Clauses and Human Rights. International Finance Corporation. World Bank Group, Report, 27 May 2009, https://www.ifc.org/wps/wcm/connect/9feb5b00488555eab8c4fa6a6515bb18/Stabilization%2BPaper.pdf?MOD=AJPERES (last accessed 1 October 2018).

[8] Shemberg A, Stabilization Clauses and Human Rights. International Finance Corporation. World Bank Group, Report, 27 May 2009, https://www.ifc.org/wps/wcm/connect/9feb5b00488555eab8c4fa6a6515bb18/Stabilization%2BPaper.pdf?MOD=AJPERES (last accessed 1 October 2018).

complying with changes in the law made subsequently to the contract. Thus, while the host state may amend or modify its laws, the amended or modified laws cannot be applied to the investor.[9] An example of a freezing clause can be cited from a 2007 Production Sharing Agreement (PSA) from Mauritania which provides that any law that increases directly or by implication the expenses or obligations of the contractor more than the laws in effect at the date the contract was signed cannot be applied.[10]

On the other hand, economic equilibrium clauses do not exempt investors from complying with changes in the law. Rather, they entitle investors to receive compensation from host states to cover the additional financial costs incurred in complying with the change. In other words, while a freezing clause aims to stabilize the law, economic equilibrium clauses aim to stabilize the economic position of the investor.[11] An example of an economic equilibrium clause in a 2013 Petroleum Agreement from Morocco provides that in the event that a change in law has a significant adverse effect on the investor, the terms of this agreement will be adjusted "in order to compensate" the investor "for such adverse effect".[12]

Hybrid clauses combine features of freezing clauses and economic equilibrium clauses.[13] For example, a stabilization clause may provide that the investor shall be compensated for the cost of complying with changes in the law (economic equilibrium) but goes further to state that one of the ways to compensate investors is to exempt them from complying with the changes (freezing).[14]

The scope of a stabilization clause may be limited or full. A limited stabilization clause protects the investor against a limited range of legislative action by the host state as stipulated by the clause. In some cases, the scope is limited to changes made to specific laws or regimes applicable to the investment. For example, the scope of an economic equilibrium clause in a 2012 PSA from Uganda is limited to "any

---

[9] On the legal effect of freezing clauses, see ICSID, Case No. ARB/06/13, *Aguaytia Energy LLC v. Republic of Peru*, para. 95; ICSID, Case No. ARB/03/28, *Duke Energy International Peru Investments No 1 Ltd v. Peru*, paras. 227–228.

[10] Profit Sharing Agreement between Mauritania and Blue Chip Energy SA relating to Block. 25 February 2007, http://www.resourcecontracts.org/contract/ocds-591adf-8615350441/view#/pdf (last accessed 1 October 2018), Article 27(3).

[11] Note, however, that in practice the consequence of a breach of either freezing clause or economic equilibrium clauses is the same, i.e. payment of compensation by the host state to the investor.

[12] Petroleum Agreement between ONHYM and Kosmos Energy Ltd over Tarhazoute offshore. 10 October 2013, http://downloads.openoil.net/contracts/ma/ma_Tarhazoute_dd20131010_ Exploration-Exploitation_Kosmos-Energy.pdf, (last accessed 1 October 2018), Article 16.

[13] Shemberg A, Stabilization Clauses and Human Rights. International Finance Corporation. World Bank Group, Report, 27 May 2009, https://www.ifc.org/wps/wcm/connect/9feb5b00488555eab8c 4fa6a6515bb18/Stabilization%2BPaper.pdf?MOD=AJPERES (last accessed 1 October 2018), p. 8.

[14] See, for example, Baku-Tbilisi-Ceyhan (BTC) Host Government Agreement between Azerbaijan Republic and BP Exploration (Azerbaijan) Limited. February 2002, https://www.bp.com/content/ dam/bp-country/en_az/pdf/legalagreements/BTC_eng_agmt1_agmt1.pdf (last accessed 1 October 2018), Article 7(X).

change in any law in Uganda dealing with income tax."[15] In other cases, the scope of stabilization clauses is limited in order to exclude changes in specific aspects of the host state's laws from the ambit of the clause. In practice, health, safety, environmental and other socially desirable laws are usually excluded in a limited stabilization clause. For example, a limited freezing clause in a 2012 Exploration and PSC from Mauritania excludes the application of legislative and regulatory provisions which are generally applicable and enacted in the matter of safety of persons and of protection of the environment or employment law.[16]

Full stabilization clauses, by contrast, protect investors from all changes in the host state's laws and regulations regardless of whether such laws are fiscal (such as tax laws) or non-fiscal (such as social and environmental laws).[17] Full stabilization clauses are therefore the broadest and most stringent type of stabilization clauses as they may impose a constraint on the ability of a host state to enact and implement laws and measures to promote and protect human rights.

Concerns over the impact of stabilisation clauses on human rights were heightened in 2003 following the publication of the legal documents governing the Baku-Tbilisi-Ceyhan (hereafter 'BTC') pipeline project, a major cross-border project crossing Azerbaijan, Georgia, and Turkey.[18] Amnesty international published a report raising concerns over the potential human rights impact of the stabilisation clauses in the agreements.[19] In its report, the NGO argued that the freezing clauses may make new bona fide social and environmental laws inapplicable to investors while the economic equilibrium clauses may create a financial disincentive for the host state in applying such laws.[20] As a result, the clauses may limit host states' ability to implement their human rights obligations under international law especially in the areas of health and safety, labour and employment, and the environment.[21] This

[15] Profit Sharing Agreement between Uganda and Tullow Uganda Limited in respect of the Kanywataba Prospect Area. 3 February 2012, https://www.resourcecontracts.org/contract/ocds-591adf-1718452998/view?lang=fr#/ (last accessed 1 October 2018), Article 33.2.

[16] Exploration and Product Contract between Mauritania and Kosmos Energy Ltd for Bloc C12. 5 April 2012, https://www.sec.gov/Archives/edgar/data/1509991/000155837017001056/kos-20161231ex104251f39.htm (last accessed 1 October 2018), Article 26.

[17] See Profit Sharing Agreement between Mauritania and Blue Chip Energy SA relating to Block 25. February 2007, https://www.resourcecontracts.org/contract/ocds-591adf-8615350441/view#/ (last accessed 1 October 2018), Article 27(2).

[18] Shemberg A, Stabilization Clauses and Human Rights. International Finance Corporation. World Bank Group, Report, 27 May 2009, https://www.ifc.org/wps/wcm/connect/9feb5b00488555eab8c 4fa6a6515bb18/Stabilization%2BPaper.pdf?MOD=AJPERES (last accessed 1 October 2018); BP Caspian, Legal Agreements, https://www.bp.com/en_az/caspian/aboutus/legalagreements.html (c).

[19] Amnesty International UK, Human Rights on the Line: The Baku-Tbilisi-Ceyhan Pipeline Project. 20 May 2003, https://www.amnesty.org.uk/press-releases/baku-tbilisi-ceyhan-pipeline-project-puts-human-rights-line (last accessed 1 October 2018).

[20] Amnesty International UK, Human Rights on the Line: The Baku-Tbilisi-Ceyhan Pipeline Project. 20 May 2003, https://www.amnesty.org.uk/press-releases/baku-tbilisi-ceyhan-pipeline-project-puts-human-rights-line (last accessed 1 October 2018).

[21] Amnesty International UK, Human Rights on the Line: The Baku-Tbilisi-Ceyhan Pipeline Project. 20 May 2003, https://www.amnesty.org.uk/press-releases/baku-tbilisi-ceyhan-pipeline-project-puts-human-rights-line (last accessed 1 October 2018).

is all the more so because the situation in many developing countries requires rapid enactment and implementation of new human rights laws rather than obstacles to their enactment.[22]

The report by Amnesty International generated substantial interest and resulted in several academic articles on the potential impacts of stabilisation clauses on host states' regulatory ability, all of which arrived at similar conclusions.[23] In response to these claims, the United Nations Representative to the Secretary-General for Business and Human Rights commissioned a study to examine whether stabilisation clauses may affect a state's ability to implement its international human rights obligations.[24] In particular, the study examined the impact of stabilisation clauses on the ability of host states to apply new social and environmental regulations to investment activities. The findings from the study supported earlier claims that stabilisation clauses can be used to limit host states' abilities to implement new social and environmental legislation to long-term investments.[25] In particular, it found that investors could rely on some stabilisation clauses to not comply with new laws enacted to protect human rights or to receive compensation from the state for the cost of compliance.[26] This could discourage host states' ability or willingness to apply new social and environmental laws to investors.[27] Where host states press

---

[22] Amnesty International UK, Human Rights on the Line: The Baku-Tbilisi-Ceyhan Pipeline Project. 20 March 2003, https://www.amnesty.org.uk/press-releases/baku-tbilisi-ceyhan-pipeline-project-puts-human-rights-line (last accessed 1 October 2018).

[23] See, for example, Cotula (2008); Letnar Cernic (2010); Tienhaara (2007); Oshionebo (2010); Sheppard and Crockett (2011); Howse R, Freezing government policy: Stabilization clauses in investment contracts. Investment Treaty News, 4 April 2011, https://www.iisd.org/itn/2011/04/04/freezing-government-policy-stabilization-clauses-in-investment-contracts-2/ (last accessed 1 October 2018); Mann H, Stabilization in investment contracts: Rethinking the context, reformulating the result. Investment Treaty News, 7 October 2011, https://www.iisd.org/itn/2011/10/07/stabilization-in-investment-contracts-rethinking-the-context-reformulating-the-result/ (last accessed 1 October 2018); Sikka (2011); Hirsch (2011); Gehne and Brillo, Stabilization Clauses in International Investment Law: Beyond Balancing and Fair and Equitable Treatment. Swiss National Centre of Competence in Research, Working Paper No 2013/46, January 2014, www.nccr-trade.org/fileadmin/user_upload/nccr-trade.ch/wp2/Stab_clauses_final_final.pdf (last accessed 1 October 2018).

[24] The study resulted in Shemberg A, Stabilization Clauses and Human Rights. International Finance Corporation. World Bank Group, Report, 27 May 2009, https://www.ifc.org/wps/wcm/connect/9feb5b00488555eab8c4fa6a6515bb18/Stabilization%2BPaper.pdf?MOD=AJPERES (last accessed 1 October 2018).

[25] Shemberg A, Stabilization Clauses and Human Rights. International Finance Corporation. World Bank Group, Report, 27 May 2009, https://www.ifc.org/wps/wcm/connect/9feb5b00488555eab8c4fa6a6515bb18/Stabilization%2BPaper.pdf?MOD=AJPERES (last accessed 1 October 2018).

[26] Shemberg A, Stabilization Clauses and Human Rights. International Finance Corporation. World Bank Group, Report, 27 May 2009, https://www.ifc.org/wps/wcm/connect/9feb5b00488555eab8c4fa6a6515bb18/Stabilization%2BPaper.pdf?MOD=AJPERES (last accessed 1 October 2018).

[27] Shemberg A, Stabilization Clauses and Human Rights. International Finance Corporation. World Bank Group, Report, 27 May 2009, https://www.ifc.org/wps/wcm/connect/9feb5b00488555eab8c4fa6a6515bb18/Stabilization%2BPaper.pdf?MOD=AJPERES (last accessed 1 October 2018).

ahead to enforce such laws without paying compensation, then the stabilisation clause may be relied on to bring international arbitral proceedings against the state.[28]

In the light of these findings, the study recommended that host states should exclude new social and environmental laws from the ambit of the stabilization clauses.[29] This would enable host states to apply dynamic social and environmental standards to investors.[30] This recommendation is particularly relevant to governments of mineral resource-rich African countries. This is the case because when compared with other regions of the world, the extractive industry of sub-Saharan Africa offers the most extensive form of stabilization clauses, protecting investors against changes in all types of laws.[31] Yet at the same time, it is the region with some of the world's weakest and poorly enforced regulatory frameworks leading to significant human rights abuses and environmental damage.[32] In other words, extractive companies enjoy the most far reaching protections from new human rights laws in the same region where there exists an acute need for the progressive enactment and implementation of human rights laws. The next section offers some possible reasons for this state of affairs.

3   Corruption, Transparency and Scope of Stabilisation Clauses

The lack of transparency and presence of corrupt practices (both real and perceived) in the extractive industry of many developing countries and their impact on sustainable development have already been well documented.[33] It is, however, useful to

---

[28] Shemberg A, Stabilization Clauses and Human Rights. International Finance Corporation. World Bank Group, Report, 27 May 2009, https://www.ifc.org/wps/wcm/connect/9feb5b00488555eab8c4fa6a6515bb18/Stabilization%2BPaper.pdf?MOD=AJPERES (last accessed 1 October 2018).

[29] Shemberg A, Stabilization Clauses and Human Rights. International Finance Corporation. World Bank Group, Report, 27 May 2009, https://www.ifc.org/wps/wcm/connect/9feb5b00488555eab8c4fa6a6515bb18/Stabilization%2BPaper.pdf?MOD=AJPERES (last accessed 13 August 2018). This is the recommendation several commentators including, Sheppard and Crockett (2011), pp. 329–350; Cotula (2008).

[30] Shemberg A, Stabilization Clauses and Human Rights. International Finance Corporation. World Bank Group, Report, 27 May 2009, https://www.ifc.org/wps/wcm/connect/9feb5b00488555eab8c4fa6a6515bb18/Stabilization%2BPaper.pdf?MOD=AJPERES (last accessed 1 October 2018); Sheppard and Crockett (2011) pp. 329–350; Cotula (2008).

[31] Shemberg A, Stabilization Clauses and Human Rights. International Finance Corporation. World Bank Group, Report, 27 May 2009, https://www.ifc.org/wps/wcm/connect/9feb5b00488555eab8c4fa6a6515bb18/Stabilization%2BPaper.pdf?MOD=AJPERES (last accessed 1 October 2018).

[32] Amnesty International, Nigeria: Petroleum, Pollution and Poverty in the Niger Delta. 2009, https://www.amnesty.org/download/Documents/44000/afr440172009en.pdf (last accessed 1 October 2018).

[33] See, for example, Rosenblum and Maples (2009), Kolstad and Søreide (2009), Marshall IE (2001) A Survey of Corruption Issues in the Mining and Mineral Sector. Report of Mining, Minerals and Sustainable Development Project, No. 15, http://pubs.iied.org/pdfs/G00949.pdf? (last accessed 1 October 2018).

summarise these issues in other to place them within the context of the present discussion.

From the perspective of developing countries' governments, the rationale for implementing policies to attract FDI is to enable them to access the huge financial resources required to fund measures to promote sustainable development.[34] For this reason, since the 1990s, developing countries have been encouraged and supported to create regulatory frameworks that attract FDI, especially to their extractive industries.[35] It was in this context that stabilisation clauses were portrayed as an essential tool for attracting investment.[36]

Thus in theory, developing countries accept stabilisation clauses in order to attract FDI to facilitate their sustainable development. This theory however diverges dramatically from reality as "many countries home to great resource wealth are also home to some of the world's poorest communities."[37] This is particularly the case in sub-Sahara Africa. Commentators agree that corruption is the main reason for this state of affairs.[38] The opaque nature of the contractual process in many developing countries, at least in the recent past, creates enough room for corruption. It enables government officials to act in their own personal interest rather than in the interest of the country and its citizens.[39] The particularly generous terms in these secret contracts when they are eventually made public are difficult to understand without assuming that some degree of corruption was involved in the contract negotiation.

A review of the stabilisation clauses in these contracts suggests that there is a link between the scope of stabilisation clauses granted by a country and the level of transparency in the country. The broadest and most rigid forms of the clauses are mostly found in contracts or legislation entered into or enacted by regimes known to or widely perceived to be corrupt and/or dictatorial. These contracts or legislation usually contain full stabilisation clauses drafted to protect investors from all types of laws, including human rights laws enacted by the country. Such contracts are also usually drafted to protect the investors for the entire duration of the contract or at least a significantly long period.

---

[34] See, for example, UN General Assembly, Agenda 21: A Programme for Action for Sustainable Development, UN Doc A/CONF 151/26, 13 June 1992, Annex I paras. 1.4, 2.23, 33.10 and 33.13.

[35] UN General Assembly, Agenda 21: A Programme for Action for Sustainable Development, UN Doc A/CONF 151/26, 13 June 1992, Annex I paras. 1.4, 2.23, 33.10 and 33.13.

[36] Shemberg A (2009) Stabilization Clauses and Human Rights. International Finance Corporation, World Bank Group, Report, http://www.ifc.org/ifcext/sustainability.nsf/content/publications_lessonslearned (last accessed 1 October 2018), p. 4.

[37] Transparency International, Promoting Revenue Transparency: 2011 Report on Oil and Gas Companies. 1 March 2001, http://www.transparency.org/news/feature/promoting_revenue_transparency_2011_report_on_oil_and_gas_companies (last accessed 1 October 2018).

[38] See, for example, Transparency International UK, Why Corruption Matters, http://www.transparency.org.uk/corruption/why-corruption-matters/#.WyoTKUxuK70 (last accessed 20 June 2018); Kolstad and Søreide (2009).

[39] See, for example, Marshall IE, A Survey of Corruption Issues in the Mining and Mineral Sector. Report of Mining, Minerals and Sustainable Development Project, No. 15. November 2001, http://pubs.iied.org/pdfs/G00949.pdf? (last accessed 1 October 2018); Kolstad and Søreide (2009).

For example, the agreements governing the Chad–Cameroon Oil Pipeline Project contain a combination of stringent freezing and economic equilibrium clauses protecting the investors for the entire duration of the project.[40] The governments agreed that they "shall not modify such legal, tax, customs, and exchange control regime in such a way as to adversely affect the rights and obligations" of the investors.[41] In addition, "no legislative, regulatory or administrative measure", which is contrary to the provisions of the agreement, shall apply to the investors "without their prior written consent."[42]

These clauses have already received extensive criticism in the literature on account of their broad scope and the effect they might have on the ability of Chad and Cameroon to protect human rights.[43] Chad signed its parts of the agreements between 1988 and 2004, first former president Hissène Habré who ruled Chad from 1982 until he was deposed in 1990 acted on behalf of Chad, and later president Idriss Déby, who has ruled Chad since 1992.[44] The regimes of both presidents at the time the clauses were agreed upon were well known for widespread corruption and dictatorship.

Hissène Habré fled to Senegal in 1990 after committing widespread misappropriations and human rights abuses, including political killings and systematic torture.[45] He was indicted in 2000 by Senegal and in 2005 by Belgium and was recently found guilty for crimes against humanity.[46] Idriss Déby, who has ruled Chad since

---

[40] These agreements include the 1988 Convention Agreement, the 2004 Convention Agreement that renewed it, the Convention of Establishment between the Republic of Cameroon and the Cameroon Oil Transportation Company (COTCO-Cameroon) 1998 and the Convention d'Etablissement between the Republic of Chad and the Tchad Oil Transportation Company (TOTCO-Chad), 10 July 1998.

[41] See generally Article 24.2 COTCO-Cameroon; Article 21 TOTCO-Chad; Article 34 of the 2004 Convention Agreement.

[42] Article 24.2 COTCO–Cameroon.

[43] See, for example, Hildyard N and Muttitt G, Turbo-Charging Investor Sovereignty: Investment Agreements and Corporate Colonialism. The Corner House. 11 February 2006, http://www.the-cornerhouse.org.uk/sites/thecornerhouse.org.uk/files/HGAPSA.pdf (last accessed 1 October 2018); Amnesty International, Contracting out of Human Rights: The Chad-Cameroon Pipeline Project. September 2005, https://www.amnesty.org.uk/files/pol340122005en.pdf (last accessed 1 October 2018).

[44] Gary I and Reisch N, Chad's Oil: Miracle or Mirage? Following the Money in Africa's Newest Petro-State. Catholic Relief Services and Bank Information Center, February 2005 Report, http://allafrica.com/download/resource/main/main/idatcs/00010386:1eb9d53b9c221def0b20cd18 35f99251.pdf (last accessed 1 October 2018), p. 16.

[45] For details, see United States Institute of Peace, Chad: Report of the Commission of Inquiry into the Crimes and Misappropriations Committed by Ex-President Habré, his Accomplices and/or Accessories. 7 May 1992, https://www.usip.org/sites/default/files/file/resources/collections/commissions/Chad-Report.pdf (last accessed 1 October 2018).

[46] For details, see the following, Human Rights Watch, Senegal New Court to try Chad Ex-Dictator in Senegal. 22 August 2012, https://www.hrw.org/news/2012/08/22/senegal-new-court-try-chad-ex-dictator-senegal (last accessed 1 October 2018); Human Rights Watch, The Case of Hissène Habré before the Extraordinary African Chambers in Senegal: Questions and Answers. 11 September 2012, https://www.hrw.org/sites/default/files/related_material/Q&A%20on%

1992 is also well known for perpetrating widespread human rights abuses and "extensive misuse of public funds".[47] In 2004 when the pipeline agreement was signed, the country appeared in Transparency International's Corruption Perception Index (hereafter 'CPI') for the first time and was ranked as third most corrupt country in the world.[48] The reputation of the regime in Cameroon was no different. The stabilization clauses in the 1998 COTCO- Cameroon-Agreement were granted under the regime of Paul Biya who has ruled Cameroon since 1982 to date. In 1998 when the Convention was signed, Cameroon was listed as the most corrupt country in the world by Transparency International, a position it retained the following year.[49]

Another example can be cited from the stabilization clauses related to the Nigeria Liquefied Natural Gas (hereafter 'NLNG') project.[50] Under these clauses, the government commits itself not to amend the fiscal regime governing the project without the prior written agreement of the investors.[51] The investors are further exempted from "new laws, regulations, taxes, duties, imposts, or charges of whatever nature which are not applicable generally to companies incorporated in Nigeria."[52] The clauses are to remain effective "so long as the Company or any successor thereto, is in existence and carrying on" its business.[53]

20Habre%20Case%20Before%20Extraordinary%20African%20Chambers%20in%20 Senegal%20EN.pdf (last accessed 1 October 2018); Maclean R, Chad's Hissène Habré found guilty of crimes against humanity. The Guardian UK. 30 May 2016 https://www.theguardian.com/ world/2016/may/30/chad-hissene-habre-guilty-crimes-against-humanity-senegal (last accessed 1 October 2018).

[47] Gary I and Reisch N, Chad's Oil: Miracle or Mirage? Following the Money in Africa's Newest Petro-State. Catholic Relief Services and Bank Information Center. February 2005 Report, http:// allafrica.com/download/resource/main/main/idatcs/00010386:1eb9d53b9c221def0b20cd18 35f99251.pdf (last accessed 20 June 2018); Bureau of Democracy, Human Rights, and Labour 2003, Country Report on Human Rights Practices for Chad 2003. United States Department of State. 25 February 2004, https://www.state.gov/j/drl/rls/hrrpt/2003/27719.htm (last accessed 1 October 2018).

[48] Transparency International, Corruption Perception Index 2004. https://www.transparency.org/ research/cpi/cpi_2004/0l (last accessed 1 October 2018).

[49] Transparency International, Corruption Perception Index 1998, https://www.transparency.org/ research/cpi/cpi_1998/0 (last accessed 1 October 2018); Transparency International, Corruption Perception Index 1999, https://www.transparency.org/research/cpi/cpi_1999/0 (last accessed 1 October 2018).

[50] See Nigerian LNG (Fiscal Incentives Guarantees and Assurances) (Amendment) Act 1993 (NLNG Act), http://www.eisourcebook.org/cms/Nigeria%20Liquified%20Natural%20Gas%20 Act.pdf (last accessed 18 April 2018). The Act was originally enacted as a military decree in 1993 but following the advent of democratic government, it is now deemed to be an Act.

[51] Section 9 (2), Nigerian LNG (Fiscal Incentives Guarantees and Assurances) (Amendment) Act 1993 (NLNG Act).

[52] Section 9 (3), Nigerian LNG (Fiscal Incentives Guarantees and Assurances) (Amendment) Act 1993 (NLNG Act).

[53] Section 9, Preamble, Nigerian LNG (Fiscal Incentives Guarantees and Assurances) (Amendment) Act 1993 (NLNG Act).

The scope of these stabilization clauses was rightly described as "rare" and "extensive" at the time they were granted.[54] The clauses were granted through a military decree signed by General Sani Abacha, who ran a remarkably corrupt and dictatorial government until his death in 1998. His government was characterized by extra-judicial killings, arbitrary imprisonment and draconian legislation.[55] At the same time, he was also well known for his remarkable corruption and was listed in a 2003 report by Transparency International as the world's fourth most corrupt leader in recent history.[56] Almost US\$3 billion of his looted funds have so far been traced and are still to be recovered and returned to the country.[57]

Before concluding this section, it is useful to state that the stringent stabilisation clauses in the BTC pipeline agreement which served as a catalyst for the debate over stabilisation clauses and human rights, also resulted from an opaque contractual process.[58] The stabilisation clauses, as well as other terms of the contracts, only became public when, following advice from the International Finance Corporation, the Consortium investors decided to publish the key project documents online in 2003.[59] It was following the publication that several terms of the agreements, and, in particular, the 'radical' nature of the stabilisation clauses received intense criticism by Amnesty International.[60]

Four months later, the consortium, in order to wade off mounting criticism, signed and published a Human Rights Undertaking, unilaterally excluding laws dealing with human rights, health, safety and environment from the scope of the

---

[54] Omorogbe (1996) p. 188.

[55] See generally: Human Right Watch Nigeria, The Price of Oil: Corporate Responsibility and Human Rights Violations in Nigeria's Oil Producing Communities. January 1999, http://www.legaloil.com/Documents/Library/HRW1999.pdf (last accessed 1 October 2018).

[56] Transparency International, Global Corruption Report 2003. 23 February 2003, https://www.transparency.org/whatwedo/publication/global_corruption_report_2003_access_to_information (last accessed 1 October 2018).

[57] For details, see, Transparency International, Impact of International Asset Recovery and Anti-money Laundering Efforts on Poverty Reduction and Political Accountability. 17 January 2010, https://www.transparency.org/files/content/corruptionqas/230_Impact_of_asset_recovery_and_money_laundering_on_poverty_reduction.pdf (last accessed 1 October 2018), p. 2; International Centre for Asset Recover, Selected Case(s): Sani Abacha, https://forum.assetrecovery.org/asset_recovery/cases (last accessed 1 October 2018); Windsor M, Nigeria, Switzerland Agree On Returning \$321M In Stolen Abacha Funds. International Business Times. 3 September 2016, http://www.ibtimes.com/nigeria-switzerland-agree-returning-321m-stolen-abacha-funds-2333157 (last accessed 1 October 2018).

[58] See Sect. 3 above.

[59] International Finance Corporation, The Baku-Tbilisi-Ceyhan (BTC) Pipeline Project. World Bank Group, Lessons of experience. September 2006, No. 2, https://www.ifc.org/wps/wcm/connect/d01d2180488556f0bb0cfb6a6515bb18/BTC_LOE_Final.pdf?MOD=AJPERES&CACHEID=d01d2180488556f0bb0cfb6a6515bb18 (last accessed 1 October 2018).

[60] Amnesty International UK (2003) Human Rights on the Line: The Baku-Tbilisi-Ceyhan Pipeline Project. https://www.amnesty.org.uk/press-releases/baku-tbilisi-ceyhan-pipeline-project-puts-human-rights-line (last accessed 1 October 2018).

clauses.[61] While this action is commendable, it goes to suggest that the scope of the stabilisation clauses went beyond what was legitimately required by the consortium. The incident further suggests that some stabilisation clauses granted in the extractive sectors of developing countries may not have been granted had the contracting process met minimal standards of transparency.

4   Transparency Initiatives and Stabilization Clauses: Some Case Studies

Concerns over the devastating effects of corruption and lack of transparency in the management of the extractive industries in sub-Sahara African countries led to the formation of several global initiatives to promote transparency and accountability in the extractive industries in developing countries. One such initiative is the Extractive Industry Transparency Initiative (EITI).[62]

The EITI is a coalition of governments, companies, investors, civil society groups and international organisations launched at the World Summit on Sustainable Development in 2002.[63] It is aimed at promoting transparency and accountability in the management of payments and receipts from the extractive industry. In its most current form, countries wishing to join the EITI must adhere to seven fundamental requirements before they can be recognised first as EITI Candidates and later as EITI Compliant countries.[64]

First, governments must set up an effective multi-stakeholder oversight mechanism, including a functioning multi-stakeholder group that involves the government, companies, and the full, independent, active and effective participation of civil society. In particular, civil society must be able to operate freely and express opinions about the EITI without restraint, coercion or reprisal.[65] Second, governments are required to disclose information related to the legal, regulatory and contractual frameworks that apply to their extractive sectors.[66] In particular, all contracts

---

[61] Baku-Tbilisi-Ceyhan Pipeline Company, BTC Human Rights Undertaking. 22 September 2003, https://subsites.bp.com/caspian/Human%20Rights%20Undertaking.pdf (last accessed 1 October 2018), Article 1.

[62] See also the chapter by Heidi Feldt in this volume.

[63] The EITI has 51 implementing countries, with 31 of them being "EITI Compliant" under the EITI Rules applicable until 2016. See http://eiti.org/eiti (last accessed 15 July 2016).

[64] EITI International Secretariat, The EITI Standard 2016. 15 February 2016, https://eiti.org/sites/default/files/migrated_files/english_eiti_standard_0.pdf (last accessed 1 October 2018), pp. 12–32. Note that the 2016 EITI Standard which replaced the 2011 EITI Rules changed the way countries are classified under the EITI.

[65] EITI International Secretariat, The EITI Standard 2016. 15 February 2016, https://eiti.org/sites/default/files/migrated_files/english_eiti_standard_0.pdf (last accessed 1 October 2018), pp. 13–17.

[66] EITI International Secretariat, The EITI Standard 2016. 15 February 2016, https://eiti.org/sites/default/files/migrated_files/english_eiti_standard_0.pdf (last accessed 1 October 2018 pp. 17–22.

and licenses containing the terms of the exploitation activities in the extractive industry are required to be disclosed.[67]

Third, the EITI Standard requires disclosure of information related to exploration activities, production data and export data enabling stakeholders to understand the potential of the sector.[68] Fourth, it requires a comprehensive reconciliation of company payments and government revenues from the extractive industries.[69] The fifth requirement is disclosure of information related to how the revenue received by the government is distributed, allocated, managed and expended.[70] The sixth requirement is disclosure of information related to social expenditures and the impact of the extractive sector on the economy, helping stakeholders to assess whether the extractive sector is leading to desirable social and economic impacts and outcomes.[71] The final requirement is related to outcomes and impact. It seeks to ensure that stakeholders are engaged, ensuring that EITI Reports contribute to wider public debate.[72]

Implementing the EITI therefore enhances access to information about the extractive industry of a country and empowers citizens to become active participants in the contractual process. Citizens are thus enabled to hold their governments to account throughout the process. The public scrutiny of the process should help reduce the opportunity for leakages in public expenditure. It is also expected to lead to contracts that better balance the profit making objectives of companies with the development objectives of host states. Based on the foregoing, if the claim that the broadest forms of stabilisation clauses are usually the outcome of an opaque contractual process is true, then the implementation of the EITI by a country, whose contractual process was hitherto secret, should lead to a reduction in the scope of stabilisation clauses. The next section examines some case studies to see if this hypothesis is valid.

4.1   Liberia

Liberia's rich mineral resources, including iron ore, diamonds and gold, constituted more than 65% of the country's exports prior to the civil war that took place between 1999 and 2003.[73] The war ended in 2003 with the formation of the National

---

[67] EITI International Secretariat, The EITI Standard 2016. 15 February 2016, https://eiti.org/sites/default/files/migrated_files/english_eiti_standard_0.pdf (last accessed 1 October 2018), pp. 17–22.

[68] EITI International Secretariat, The EITI Standard 2016. 15 February 2016, https://eiti.org/sites/default/files/migrated_files/english_eiti_standard_0.pdf (last accessed 1 October 2018), p. 22.

[69] EITI International Secretariat, The EITI Standard 2016. 15 February 2016, https://eiti.org/sites/default/files/migrated_files/english_eiti_standard_0.pdf (last accessed 1 October 2018), pp. 22–26.

[70] EITI International Secretariat, The EITI Standard 2016. 15 February 2016, https://eiti.org/sites/default/files/migrated_files/english_eiti_standard_0.pdf (last accessed 1 October 2018), pp. 26–28.

[71] EITI International Secretariat, The EITI Standard 2016. 15 February 2016, https://eiti.org/sites/default/files/migrated_files/english_eiti_standard_0.pdf (last accessed 1 October 2018), pp. 28–29.

[72] EITI International Secretariat, The EITI Standard 2016. 15 February 2016, https://eiti.org/sites/default/files/migrated_files/english_eiti_standard_0.pdf (last accessed 1 October 2018), pp. 29–31.

[73] Soto-Viruet Y, The Mineral Industry of Liberia. United States Geological Survey, 2010 Minerals

Transitional Government of Liberia (NTGL). The NTGL's tenure was characterized by reports of large scale corruption within the NTGL and the NTGL was severally described as a 'notoriously' and "exceedingly" corrupt government.[74]

In August 2005, few months to the end of its tenure, the NTGL signed a controversial Mineral Development Agreement (MDA) with Mittal Steel.[75] The negotiations leading to the signing of the MDA were conducted in secret despite widespread demands by stakeholders, including an unsuccessful court action by human rights groups, to stop the deal on grounds of lack of public scrutiny.[76] The terms of the signed MDA were kept secret until they were leaked by some local citizens. Their examination revealed that the MDA contained broad stabilization clauses, as well as other provisions that tilted the balance of the agreement heavily in favor of the company.[77] One of the stabilization clauses exempted the company from complying with "any modifications that could be made in the future to the Law as in effect" on the day the contract was signed.[78] The duration of the stabilization clause was potentially 50 years (an initial term of 25 years with the option of renewal for another 25 years).[79]

The stabilization clauses in the agreement were condemned by human rights groups.[80] They argued that the broad scope of the clauses allowed Mittal Steel to be

---

Yearbook, Liberia, August 2012, http://minerals.usgs.gov/minerals/pubs/country/2010/myb3-2010-li.pdf (last accessed 1 October 2018), p. 24.1.

[74] See, for example, UN Security Council, Sixth Progress Report of the Secretary-General on the United Nations Mission in Liberia, S/2005/177, 17 March 2005; Alley P, Ashworth N, Goinhas S, Mittal Steel did the right thing – will Firestone?. Global Witness, Press Release, 30 April 2007, https://www.globalwitness.org/en/archive/mittal-steel-did-right-thing%2D%2Dwill-firestone/ (last accessed 1 October 2018); Cook N, Liberia's Post-War Development: Key Issues and U.S. Assistance. Congressional Research Service, Report for Congress No. RL33185, 19 May 2010, https://fas.org/sgp/crs/row/RL33185.pdf (last accessed 1 October 2018), pp. 35–38.

[75] Mineral Development Agreement between the Government of Liberia and Mittal Steel Holdings AG and Mittal Steel (Liberia) Holdings Limited. 17 August 2005, http://liberia.arcelormittal.com/who-we-are/mineral-development-agreement.aspx (last accessed 1 October 2018).

[76] Global Witness, Heavy Mittal: A State within a State: The inequitable Mineral Development Agreement between the Government of Liberia and Mittal Steel Holdings NV. Report, October 2006, https://www.globalwitness.org/sites/default/files/pdfs/mittal_steel_en_oct_2006_low_res.pdf (last accessed 1 October 2018); Sayon M, Supreme Court Places "Stay Order", Firestone, Mittal Steel Agreements. The Inquirer, Monrovia, 7 November 2005, http://allafrica.com/stories/200511071075.html (last accessed 1 October 2018).

[77] Rosenblum and Maples, p. 52 and p. 99 endnote No. 123.

[78] Mineral Development Agreement between the Government of Liberia and Mittal Steel Holdings AG and Mittal Steel (Liberia) Holdings Limited. 17 August 2005, http://liberia.arcelormittal.com/who-we-are/mineral-development-agreement.aspx (last accessed 1 October 2018), Article XIX, Specific undertakings of the Government, p. 9.

[79] Mineral Development Agreement between the Government of Liberia and Mittal Steel Holdings AG and Mittal Steel (Liberia) Holdings Limited. 17 August 2005, http://liberia.arcelormittal.com/who-we-are/mineral-development-agreement.aspx (last accessed 27 June 2018), Article III, Terms of the Agreement, p. 2.

[80] See, for example, Global Witness, Heavy Mittal: A State within a State: The inequitable Mineral Development Agreement between the Government of Liberia and Mittal Steel Holdings

exempted from new social and environmental standards introduced subsequent to the conclusion of the contract.[81] The stabilization clauses would therefore have made it difficult for Liberia to meet its human rights obligations and improve its environmental, health or safety standards which had deteriorated significantly as a result of the civil war.[82]

In January 2006, Ellen Sirleaf Johnson was sworn in as Liberia's president after winning the presidential election that took place the year before. One of the key promises she made during the election campaign was to improve transparency and accountability in the management of the country's extractive industry.[83] In line with this promise, Liberia expressed its commitment to join the EITI that same year and the Liberia EITI was launched in 2007.[84] The country made impressive progress in implementing the EITI and by 2009 achieved Compliant status.[85] As part of measures to implement the EITI, the country enacted the Liberia EITI Act 2009 to formally establish the LEITI as an independent state entity. In line with a requirement of the Act, extractive industry contracts, concessions and agreements are now publicly available on the LEITI website.[86] These transparency measures have seen Liberia move from position 137 out of 159 countries in the 2005 Transparency International CPI[87] to position 83 out of 168 countries in the 2015 CPI.[88]

The improved transparency in the management of Liberia's extractive industry resulting from its implementation of the EITI has had a positive impact on the terms, and in particular, the stabilization clauses in Liberia's extractive industry contracts. In the first place, the Mittal Steel MDA was renegotiated in 2006 in line with the government's promise to review it.[89] The renegotiated agreement, signed in

---

NV. Report, October 2006, https://www.globalwitness.org/sites/default/files/pdfs/mittal_steel_en_oct_2006_low_res.pdf (last accessed 1 October 2018).

[81] Global Witness, Heavy Mittal: A State within a State: The inequitable Mineral Development Agreement between the Government of Liberia and Mittal Steel Holdings NV. Report, October 2006, https://www.globalwitness.org/sites/default/files/pdfs/mittal_steel_en_oct_2006_low_res.pdf (last accessed 1 October 2018).

[82] Global Witness, Heavy Mittal: A State within a State: The inequitable Mineral Development Agreement between the Government of Liberia and Mittal Steel Holdings NV. Report, October 2006, https://www.globalwitness.org/sites/default/files/pdfs/mittal_steel_en_oct_2006_low_res.pdf (last accessed 1 October 2018).

[83] Cook N, Liberia's Post-War Development: Key Issues and U.S. Assistance. Congressional Research Service, Report for Congress No. RL33185, 19 May 2010, http://www.fas.org/sgp/crs/row/RL33185.pdf (last accessed 1 October 2018), p. 11.

[84] See generally Liberia EITI, http://www.leiti.org.lr/ (last accessed 1 October 2018).

[85] Liberia EITI, http://www.leiti.org.lr/ (last accessed 1 October 2018).

[86] See Liberia Extractive Industries Transparency Initiative, https://eiti.org/document/20142015-liberia-eiti-report (last accessed 1 October 2018).

[87] Transparency International, Corruption Perception Index 2005, https://www.transparency.org/research/cpi/cpi_2005/0 (last accessed 20 June 2018).

[88] Transparency International, Corruption Perception Index 2015, https://www.transparency.org/cpi2015 (last accessed 1 October 2018).

[89] Reuters Staff, Liberia says has signed revised Mittal mining deal. Reuters. 21 January 2007, https://uk.reuters.com/article/liberia-mittal/liberia-says-has-signed-revised-mittal-mining-deal-idUKL2847972320061228 (last accessed 1 October 2018).

December 2006, substantially narrowed the scope of the stabilization clauses along-side other changes.[90] The new stabilization clauses only exempted the investor from changes in specific taxes and duties.[91] As a consequence, the Mittal Steel would no longer be exempted from complying with any new laws and regulations, including human rights laws enacted by Liberia, as was previously the case.

Beyond the Mittal Steel MDA, a review of stabilization clauses in recent extractive contracts in Liberia reveals that their scope is now limited and social, environmental and health and safety laws are explicitly excluded from its ambit. For example, the stabilization clause in a 2011 MDA only stabilizes specified taxes and duties.[92] The company is therefore obliged to comply with all other Liberian laws "in effect from time to time, including with respect to labor, environmental, health and safety, customs and tax matters."[93] Similarly, the stabilization clause in a 2013 Production Sharing Contract (PSC) which entitles the company to receive compensation for the cost of complying with changes in the laws of Liberia[94] goes on to provide that the company shall not be compensated "in respect of changes in Law which pertain to health, safety, security, labor and environment, and that are consistent with international standards and best practices and that are applied on a non-discriminatory basis."[95]

Unlike the formulation of stabilization clauses before Liberia joined EITI, the above formulations of stabilization clause, which now appears to be standard, do

---

[90] For example, previously granted tax holidays and exemption from withholding taxes were removed. See Government of Liberia, Summary of the Main Changes Brought About by the Review of the Mittal Mineral Development Agreement. 2005, 2006, http://www.emansion.gov.lr/doc/MittalAgreementFinalMitrix.pdf (last accessed 1 October 2018).

[91] Government of Liberia, Summary of the Main Changes Brought About by the Review of the Mittal Mineral Development Agreement. 2005, 2006, http://www.emansion.gov.lr/doc/MittalAgreementFinalMitrix.pdf (last accessed 1 October 2018).

[92] Mineral Development Agreement among the Government of the Republic of Liberia, Western Cluster Limited, Sesa Goa Limited, Bloom Fountain Limited and Elenilto Minerals & Mining LLC. 3 August 2011, http://www.leiti.org.lr/uploads/2/1/5/6/21569928/2067410-an-act-to-ratify-the-concession-agreement-between-the-republic-of-liberia-and-western-cluster-limited-sesa-gao-limited-bloom-fountain-limited-and-e.pdf, (last accessed 1 October 2018). Article 14(2) (b).

[93] Mineral Development Agreement among the Government of the Republic of Liberia, Western Cluster Limited, Sesa Goa Limited, Bloom Fountain Limited and Elenilto Minerals & Mining LLC. 3 August 2011, http://www.leiti.org.lr/uploads/2/1/5/6/21569928/2067410-an-act-to-ratify-the-concession-agreement-between-the-republic-of-liberia-and-western-cluster-limited-sesa-gao-limited-bloom-fountain-limited-and-e.pdf (last accessed 1 October 2018). Article 30(1).

[94] Restated and Amended Production Sharing Contract between Liberia by and through National Oil Company of Liberia and Exxon Mobil Exploration and Production Liberia Limited and Canadian Overseas Petroleum (Bermuda) Limited, with respect to offshore block 13. 8 March 2013, http://downloads.openoil.net/contracts/lr/lr_Block-LB-13_dd20111116_Asset-Purchase-Agree_Exxonmobil_Canadian-Overseas.pdf (last accessed 1 October 2018). Article 36 (1) (c).

[95] Restated and Amended Production Sharing Contract between Liberia by and through National Oil Company of Liberia and Exxon Mobil Exploration and Production Liberia Limited and Canadian Overseas Petroleum (Bermuda) Limited, with respect to offshore block 13, 8 March 2013, http://downloads.openoil.net/contracts/lr/lr_Block-LB-13_dd20111116_Asset-Purchase-Agree_Exxonmobil_Canadian-Overseas.pdf (last accessed 1 October 2018). Article 36 (1) (c).

not protect extractive companies against bona fide changes of social and environment laws. Thus, whatever impact stabilization clauses might have had on human rights is significantly limited, ensuring that investors cannot rely on these clauses to frustrate efforts by the host country to improve social and environmental standards.

4.2   Zambia

Zambia nationalized its mining industry in 1969 in view of the strategic role, especially of copper mining in the country's economy.[96] The country, however, came under pressure from the World Bank in the early 1990s to "quickly" privatize its mines as part of reforms to deal with the effects of the steep fall in commodity prices at the time.[97] After initial resistance, Zambia eventually privatized its mines after privatization had been made a pre-condition Zambia had to fulfil to continue to receive loans and other forms of support from the World Bank.[98]

However, the fact that the government came under enormous pressure from the World Bank to privatize the mines is only one side of the story. The other is that the privatization process was undertaken within a context of the rampant corruption that characterised Frederick Chiluba's presidency.[99] There was a culture of official secrecy throughout the privatisation period and neither consultation with stakeholders nor any form of public debate took place.[100] The eventual MDAs had an air of corruption hanging over them, made worse by the fact that their terms were kept secret for almost a decade.[101]

---

[96] On the strategic role of mining in Zambia prior to the privatisation, see, Ndulo (1986), pp. 5–6.

[97] For details, see Campbell (2010), pp. 197–217.

[98] See generally, Fraser A and Lungu J, For Whom the Windfalls? Winners and Losers in the Privatisation of Zambia's Copper Mines. Report, 2007, http://www.woek-web.de/web/cms/upload/pdf/kasa/publikationen/fraser_2006_for_whom_the_windfalls.pdf (last accessed 1 October 2018); Posthumus (2000); Scotland Aid Agency, Action for Southern Africa and Christian Aid, Undermining Development? Copper Mining in Zambia. October 2007, https://actsa.org/?s=under mining+development+Zambia+2007 (last accessed 1 October 2018), p. 6.

[99] Van Donge (2009); Fraser A and Lungu J, For Whom the Windfalls? Winners and Losers in the Privatisation of Zambia's Copper Mines. Report, 2007, http://www.woek-web.de/web/cms/upload/pdf/kasa/publikationen/fraser_2006_for_whom_the_windfalls.pdf (last accessed 1 October 2018), pp. 9–10.

[100] Van Donge (2009); Fraser A and Lungu J, For Whom the Windfalls? Winners and Losers in the Privatisation of Zambia's Copper Mines. Report, 2007, http://www.woek-web.de/web/cms/upload/pdf/kasa/publikationen/fraser_2006_for_whom_the_windfalls.pdf (last accessed 1 October 2018), pp. 9–10.

[101] Van Donge (2009); Fraser A and Lungu J, For Whom the Windfalls? Winners and Losers in the Privatisation of Zambia's Copper Mines. Report, 2007, http://www.woek-web.de/web/cms/upload/pdf/kasa/publikationen/fraser_2006_for_whom_the_windfalls.pdf (last accessed 1 October 2018), pp. 9–10.

The MDAs were negotiated in line with the Mines and Minerals Act 1995 enacted as part of the privatization process. The 1995 Act, apart from providing for generous incentives and exemptions for foreign investors, introduced stabilization clauses into Zambia's mining industry. Section 9(2) (d) of the Act gave the relevant Minister wide discretion to "make such stability commitments... as the Minister may consider necessary." In line with this provision, stabilization clauses were included in all the MDAs entered into as part of the privatization process.[102] The clauses exempted the mining companies from any laws that parliament might pass during the life of the project. For example, in one of such agreement, the government agreed not to apply any changes to legislation or regulations governing the operation of mines or related activities "which, individually or cumulatively, would have a Material Adverse Economic Effect" on the company.[103]

The potential impact of the stabilization clauses was exacerbated by the fact that the MDAs also contained generous exemptions with regard to the mining companies' environmental and social obligations. For example, under the Konkola MDA, mining companies were to apply a mandatory Environmental Management and Social Plan (EMSP).[104] The stabilization clauses prohibit the government from taking any action to enforce any applicable environmental laws "with the intent of securing a higher standard of compliance" or "imposing more onerous requirements than those specified in the EMSP."[105] In addition, the government cannot apply any change in legislation or regulations governing the terms and conditions of employment within Zambia to the company.[106] The stabilization clauses therefore give the EMSP precedence over Zambia's laws. This means for example, that if a new emission target is set which is higher than that contained in the EMSP, the company can legally exceed the target. It also means that if a new minimum wage law is enacted, the companies will be exempt from complying with it.

---

[102] Copies of these MDAs were subsequently leaked by several NGOs in Zambia, http://minewatchzambia.blogspot.co.uk/ (last accessed 1 October 2018).

[103] The Government of the Republic of Zambia and Konkola Copper Mines Plc, Amended and Restated Development Agreement (2004), http://www.mmdaproject.org/presentations/MMDA%20Zambia%202004%20Amended%20and%20Restated-1.pdf (last accessed 1 October 2018), Article 13.1.2.

[104] The Government of the Republic of Zambia and Konkola Copper Mines Plc, Amended and Restated Development Agreement (2004), http://www.mmdaproject.org/presentations/MMDA%20Zambia%202004%20Amended%20and%20Restated-1.pdf (last accessed 1 October 2018), Article 12.

[105] The Government of the Republic of Zambia and Konkola Copper Mines Plc, Amended and Restated Development Agreement (2004), http://www.mmdaproject.org/presentations/MMDA%20Zambia%202004%20Amended%20and%20Restated-1.pdf (last accessed 1 October 2018), Article 12.1.1.

[106] The Government of the Republic of Zambia and Konkola Copper Mines Plc, Amended and Restated Development Agreement (2004), http://www.mmdaproject.org/presentations/MMDA%20Zambia%202004%20Amended%20and%20Restated-1.pdf (last accessed 1 October 2018), Article 13.1.4.

In 2007, following widespread public discontent about the lack of transparency in the mining sector and its inability to benefit the country and its citizens,[107] the government requested assistance from the World Bank to undertake a scoping study to help it decide whether to implement the EITI or not.[108] The country eventually joined the EITI in 2009 as a candidate country and achieved Compliant status in 2012.[109] Within that period, Zambia's ranking in Transparency International's CPI improved from position 115 out of 180 countries in 2008 to position 76 out of 168 countries.[110]

The adoption of transparency initiatives by Zambia has significantly changed the form of MDAs in the mining sector particularly as regards the scope of stabilisation clauses. The 2008 Mines and Minerals Development Act no longer grants the relevant minister the power to negotiate stabilisation clauses. Rather, it provides that all existing MDAs shall cease to be binding with the entry into force of the Act "notwithstanding any provision to the contrary contained in any law or in the development agreement."[111] The legal effect of this provision was that mining companies were no longer exempted from complying with new laws.[112]

Apart from the removal of the power to grant stabilisation clauses, the 2008 Act contains elaborate provisions to ensure that mining companies' activities do not undermine the protection of human rights and the environment.[113] For example, unlike the 1995 Act, the 2008 Act imposes a clear statutory obligation on mining companies to assume liability and compensate affected individuals for any damage or harm caused by their operations.[114] The scope of liability was extended to include

---

[107] World Bank, Zambia What would it Take for Zambia's Copper Mining Industry to achieve its Potential?. Finance and Private Sector Development Unit Africa Region. Report No. 62378-ZM, June 2011, http://documents.worldbank.org/curated/en/461971468170956129/pdf/623780ESW0 Gray0e0only0900BOX361532B.pdf (last accessed 1 October 2018), p. 16.

[108] Zambia EITI, Background and Adoption of EITI in Zambia, http://www.zambiaeiti.org/index. php/ct-menu-item-17 (last accessed 1 October 2018).

[109] Zambia EITI, Background and Adoption of EITI in Zambia, http://www.zambiaeiti.org/index. php/ct-menu-item-17 (last accessed 1 October 2018).

[110] Transparency International, Corruption Perception Index 2015, https://www.transparency.org/ cpi2015, (last accessed 1 October 2018).

[111] Section 160 (1), The Mines and Minerals Development Act, Zambia. 2008, https://www.zambialii.org/zm/legislation/act/2008/7/mamda2008295.pdf (last accessed 1 October 2018).

[112] Note, however, that following threats of arbitration by investors on the basis of stabilisation clauses, the government agreed to allow existing stabilisation clauses to remain valid for 10 years subject to the companies agreeing to comply with all the provisions in the 2008 Act. See Ministerial Statements on the Status of Mining Taxation, 25 November 2010, http://www.parliament.gov.zm/ sites/default/files/images/publication_docs/Ministerial%20Statement%20Dr.%20Musokotwane. pdf (last accessed 1 October 2018), p. 6.

[113] Similar provisions are contained in The Mines and Minerals Act, Zambia. 2015, http://www. parliament.gov.zm/sites/default/files/documents/acts/The%20Mines%20and%20Minerals%20 Act%2C%202015.pdf (last accessed 1 October 2018), which has just replaced the 2008 Act. See generally section 87.

[114] Section 123, The Mines and Minerals Act, Zambia. 2015, http://www.parliament.gov.zm/sites/ default/files/documents/acts/The%20Mines%20and%20Minerals%20Act%2C%202015.pdf (last accessed 1 October 2018).

damage caused directly or indirectly to economy or social cultural conditions of any person or community.[115] In addition, any person or private organisation now has a statutory right and capacity to bring a claim and seek redress against mining companies "in respect of the breach or threatened breach of any provision relating to damage to the environment, biological diversity, human and animal health or to socio-economic conditions."[116] Such claims can be brought in the interest of the claimant, other persons, the public, as well as in the interest of protecting the environment or biological diversity.[117]

4.3   Tanzania

Like Zambia, Tanzania also privatized its mines in the 1990s under pressure from the World Bank.[118] The privatization process led to the enactment of the Mining Act 1998 which contained little or no provisions on transparency. Consequently, the negotiations leading to the signing of MDAs with mining companies were shrouded in secrecy and the eventual terms of the MDAs were kept secret for almost a decade.[119]

---

[115] Section 87 (5), The Mines and Minerals Act, Zambia. 2015, http://www.parliament.gov.zm/sites/default/files/documents/acts/The%20Mines%20and%20Minerals%20Act%2C%202015.pdf (last accessed 1 October 2018).

[116] Section 123. 7, The Mines and Minerals Act, Zambia. 2015, http://www.parliament.gov.zm/sites/default/files/documents/acts/The%20Mines%20and%20Minerals%20Act%2C%202015.pdf (last accessed 1 October 2018).

[117] Section 123.7 (a–e), The Mines and Minerals Act, Zambia. 2015, http://www.parliament.gov.zm/sites/default/files/documents/acts/The%20Mines%20and%20Minerals%20Act%2C%202015.pdf (last accessed 1 October 2018).

[118] Development Credit Agreement (Mineral Sector Development Technical Assistance Project) between Tanzania and IDA. 23 September 1994, http://www-wds.worldbank.org/external/default/WDSContentServer/WDSP/INF/2004/12/15/DDBE125D7A51E61B85256F0200829B88/1_0/Rendered/PDF/DDBE125D7A51E61B85256F0200829B88.pdf (last accessed 13 July 2016), Art III, sch 2 s 1; Policy Forum, The Demystification of Mining Contracts in Tanzania, 2010, http://www.sdsg.org/wp-content/uploads/2010/02/Article-re-Mining-Contracts-in-Tanzania.pdf (last accessed 18 June 2016); Bubelwa Kaiza B, Tanzania's Mining Boom: Initiatives for Increased Transparency and Accountability in the Starting Holes. Heinrich Böll, 8 July 2008, http://www.za.boell.org/web/resource-governance-570.html (last accessed 1 October 2018).

[119] Development Credit Agreement (Mineral Sector Development Technical Assistance Project) between Tanzania and IDA. 23 September 1994, http://www-wds.worldbank.org/external/default/WDSContentServer/WDSP/INF/2004/12/15/DDBE125D7A51E61B85256F0200829B88/1_0/Rendered/PDF/DDBE125D7A51E61B85256F0200829B88.pdf (last accessed 1 October 2018), Art III, sch 2 s 1; Policy Forum, The Demystification of Mining Contracts in Tanzania, 2010, http://www.sdsg.org/wp-content/uploads/2010/02/Article-re-Mining-Contracts-in-Tanzania.pdf (last accessed 18 June 2016); Bubelwa Kaiza B, Tanzania's Mining Boom: Initiatives for Increased Transparency and Accountability in the Starting Holes. Heinrich Böll, 8 July 2008, http://www.za.boell.org/web/resource-governance-570.html (last accessed 1 October 2018).

This fueled widespread perceptions that the MDAs contained unnecessary tax incentives and stabilization clauses.[120]

These perceptions were confirmed when leaked copies of several MDAs showed that they all contained a combination of full freezing and economic equilibrium clauses.[121] The clauses guaranteed the same tax rate for the mining companies for the entire duration of the contract.[122] They also committed the government not to make any legislative changes that would alter the terms of the mining license and "any other matter fundamental to the economic position of the company."[123] In the event that the government made any legislative changes that put the mining companies "in a worse off situation", the companies would receive compensation.[124] The stabilization clauses did not distinguish between fiscal and non-fiscal laws. They therefore formed a prima facie basis on which companies could avoid compliance with new social and environmental laws or seek compensation from the government for the cost of compliance.

The sentiment against the stabilization clauses and the generous incentives in the MDAs, coupled with the inability of a majority of Tanzanians to benefit from the mining sector led to demands for increased transparency and accountability in the mining sector.[125] It was against this background that President Jakaya Kikwete was elected in 2005, largely on a campaign promise to improve transparency in the extractive industry as well as to review all the MDAs concluded under opaque con-

---

[120] Development Credit Agreement (Mineral Sector Development Technical Assistance Project) between Tanzania and IDA. 23 September 1994, http://www-wds.worldbank.org/external/default/WDSContentServer/WDSP/INF/2004/12/15/DDBE125D7A51E61B85256F0200829B88/1_0/Rendered/PDF/DDBE125D7A51E61B85256F0200829B88.pdf (last accessed 1 October 2018), Art III, sch 2 s 1; Policy Forum, The Demystification of Mining Contracts in Tanzania, 2010, http://www.sdsg.org/wp-content/uploads/2010/02/Article-re-Mining-Contracts-in-Tanzania.pdf (last accessed 18 June 2016); Bubelwa Kaiza B, Tanzania's Mining Boom: Initiatives for Increased Transparency and Accountability in the Starting Holes. Heinrich Böll, 8 July 2008, https://za.boell.org/2010/07/08/tanzanias-mining-boom-initiatives-increased-transparency-and-accountability-starting (last accessed 1 October 2018).

[121] Policy Forum, 'The Demystification of Mining Contracts in Tanzania' (2010) http://www.sdsg.org/wp-content/uploads/2010/02/Article-re-Mining-Contracts-in-Tanzania.pdf (last accessed 1 October 2018) Gold Mine Development Agreement Between Tanzania and Pangea Minerals Ltd (Tulawaka Mine) December 2003, Article 11. This and other MDAs were leaked and analysed in Policy Forum, The Demystification of Mining Contracts in Tanzania. 2010, http://www.sdsg.org/wp-content/uploads/2010/02/Article-re-Mining-Contracts-in-Tanzania.pdf (last accessed 1 October 2018).

[122] Preamble, Articles 3.2 and 5, Gold Mine Development Agreement Between Tanzania and Pangea Minerals Ltd (Tulawaka Mine) December 2003.

[123] Article 9.2, Gold Mine Development Agreement Between Tanzania and Pangea Minerals Ltd (Tulawaka Mine) December 2003.

[124] Article 9.2, Gold Mine Development Agreement Between Tanzania and Pangea Minerals Ltd (Tulawaka Mine) December 2003.

[125] Policy Forum, The Demystification of Mining Contracts in Tanzania. 2010, http://www.sdsg.org/wp-content/uploads/2010/02/Article-re-Mining-Contracts-in-Tanzania.pdf (last accessed 1 October 2018).

ditions.[126] In line with this promise, Tanzania joined the EITI in 2009 and obtained Compliant status in 2012.[127]

One of the initiatives taken to implement the EITI was the enactment of the 2010 Mining Act.[128] As with several other countries that introduced transparency measures, the stabilization clauses that can be granted in Tanzania's mining sector were significantly affected. The 2010 Act limited the scope of stabilization clauses that can be included in MDAs to "applicable rates of royalties, taxes, duties and levies."[129] This means that mining companies can no longer be exempted from changes to social and environmental laws. In addition, the terms of MDAs, including stabilization clauses, are now made subject to a periodic review every 5 year.[130]

Tanzania's implementation of the EITI also facilitated the enactment of several laws to effectively regulate the country's petroleum sector. These laws include the Oil and Gas Revenues Management Act 2015 (OGRMA 2015),[131] the Tanzania Extractive Industries (Transparency and Accountability) Act 2015 (TEI Act 2015)[132] and the Petroleum Act 2015.[133] The OGRMA 2015 established an Oil and Gas Fund which will be used to maintain fiscal and macroeconomic stability, enhance social and economic development, and safeguard resources for future generations. The TEI Act 2015, amongst other provisions, makes it mandatory for all extractive industry concessions, contracts, and licenses to be published online or through widely accessible media.[134]

The most far reaching act is, however, the Petroleum Act 2015 which replaced the Petroleum Exploration and Production Act 1980 (PEPA).[135] Under the 1980 Act,

---

[126] HakiElimu, Government Promises II. August 2007, http://hakielimu.org/files/publications/document114govt_promises_II_en%20.pdf (last accessed 1 October 2018).

[127] Kråkenes A, Tanzania Discloses Mining Revenues in First EITI Report. Extractive Industries Transparency Initiative, 11 February 2011, https://eiti.org/news/tanzania-discloses-mining-revenues-in-first-eiti-report# (last accessed 1 October 2018).

[128] Oil and Gas Revenues Management Act. 23 April 2010, http://www.tmaa.go.tz/uploads/The_Mining_Act_2010.pdf, (last accessed 1 October 2018).

[129] Article 10.4(a) Section 10.4 (a), Tanzania, The Mining Act. 2010, http://www.tmaa.go.tz/uploads/The_Mining_Act_2010.pdf (last accessed 1 October 2018).

[130] Article 12, Tanzania, The Mining Act, 2010, http://www.tmaa.go.tz/uploads/The_Mining_Act_2010.pdf (last accessed 1 October 2018).

[131] Oil and Gas Revenues Management Act. 2015, http://parliament.go.tz/polis/uploads/bills/acts/1452057603-ActNo-22-2015-Book-21-25.pdf (last accessed 1 October 2018).

[132] The Tanzania Extractive Industries (Transparency and Accountability) Act. 2015, http://parliament.go.tz/polis/uploads/bills/acts/1452053429-ActNo-23-2015-Book-21-25.pdf, (last accessed 1 October 2018).

[133] Act Supplement, Petroleum Act. 2015, https://www.tanzania.go.tz/egov_uploads/documents/THE_PETROLEUM_ACT_2015_No_sw.pdf (last accessed 1 October 2018).

[134] Section 16, The Tanzania Extractive Industries (Transparency and Accountability) Act. 2015, http://parliament.go.tz/polis/uploads/bills/acts/1452053429-ActNo-23-2015-Book-21-25.pdf, (last accessed 1 October 2018).

[135] The Petroleum (Exploration and Production) Act. 1980, https://www.tanzania.go.tz/egov_uploads/documents/The_Petroleum_(Exploration_and_Production)_Act,_27-1980_sw.pdf (last accessed 1 October 2018).

full economic equilibrium clauses were included in the country's Model PSA[136] and in actual PSAs entered with petroleum companies. For example, a stabilization clause in a 2001 PSA specifies that the company shall be compensated for any change arising from the government's "'action or inaction, parastatal action or inaction, lapse of consent, court action or change in law."[137] The potential effect of the stabilization clauses on human rights and the environment was exacerbated by the weak human rights and environmental obligations imposed on companies in the PSA.[138]

The 2015 Act has however significantly altered the stabilization practice in Tanzania's petroleum sector, while also increasing the ability of the government to hold petroleum companies to account in respect of their human rights and environmental obligations. First, there is no provision authorizing the negotiation of stabilization clauses. In particular, it is no longer possible to include stabilization clauses in PSAs to exempt investors from changes in laws dealing with matters of public health and safety and the protection of the environment. This is because section 208 (1) makes it mandatory for petroleum companies to comply with the 'prevailing international standards, specifications and codes' related to matters of public health and safety and the protection of the environment.

Several provisions in the 2013 Model PSA also reduce the possibility of stabilization clauses exempting petroleum companies from complying with new health, safety and environmental laws. For example, petroleum companies must now comply with all relevant health, safety and environment laws and "other legislation at any time in force" in Tanzania.[139] The government is also empowered to "from time to time" require companies to take "necessary and adequate steps" to conduct their activities in a manner that protects the environment including human communities and settlements.[140]

---

[136] See, for example, Model Production Sharing Agreement between the Government of the United Republic of Tanzania and Tanzania Petroleum Development Corporation and ABC Oil Company, November 2004, http://www.tpdc-tz.com/wp-content/uploads/2015/04/1-MPSA-2004-Ver-7-0-12-11-2004.pdf (last accessed 1 October 2018), Article 30.

[137] Production Sharing Agreement between Tanzania, Tanzania Petroleum Development Corporation and Panafrican Energy Tanzania Limited relating to Songo Songo Gas Field. 11 October 2001, http://downloads.openoil.net/contracts%2Ftz%2Ftz_Songo-Songo-Gas-field_dd20060711_PSA_Panafrican.pdf (last accessed 1 October 2018), Article 28.17.

[138] Production Sharing Agreement between Tanzania, Tanzania Petroleum Development Corporation and Panafrican Energy Tanzania Limited relating to Songo Songo Gas Field. 11 October 2001, http://downloads.openoil.net/contracts%2Ftz%2Ftz_Songo-Songo-Gas-field_dd20060711_PSA_Panafrican.pdf (last accessed 1 October 2018), Article 25.

[139] Production Sharing Agreement between Tanzania, Tanzania Petroleum Development Corporation and Panafrican Energy Tanzania Limited relating to Songo Songo Gas Field. 11 October 2001, http://downloads.openoil.net/contracts%2Ftz%2Ftz_Songo-Songo-Gas-field_dd20060711_PSA_Panafrican.pdf (last accessed 1 October 2018), Article 25.

[140] Production Sharing Agreement between Tanzania, Tanzania Petroleum Development Corporation and Panafrican Energy Tanzania Limited relating to Songo Songo Gas Field. 11 October 2001, http://downloads.openoil.net/contracts%2Ftz%2Ftz_Songo-Songo-Gas-field_dd20060711_PSA_Panafrican.pdf (last accessed 1 October 2018), Article 25 (o).

4.4   Sierra Leone

Like Liberia, Sierra Leone went through a devastating civil armed conflict between 1991 and 2002 that negatively impacted its mining sector.[141] The conflict did not, however, prevent Sierra Leone from also adopting mining reforms in the 1990s. The 1994 Mining Act, enacted as part of the reforms, was very similar to that adopted by other African countries in the wake of the World Bank reforms. It contained several incentives and exemptions for foreign investors but lacked sufficiently detailed regulatory provisions on environmental, health, safety and social issues.[142] It also contained little or no provisions to promote transparency in the sector. For over a decade after the Act was enacted, the country's mining sector was characterized by an 'extreme lack of transparency.'[143] Mining agreements were negotiated in secret without public scrutiny while their contents were also kept secret.[144] This led to a widespread perception amongst civil society that these agreements were against the interests of the citizens and contained "stabilization and confidentiality clauses" which prevented the government from holding mining companies to account for their actions.[145]

The fears of citizens were confirmed in 2002 when the 2001 Sierra Rutile Agreement was published. The agreement had been negotiated secretly and kept secret but became a public document when, in order to strengthen the protections accorded to the investors, it was enacted as an act of parliament.[146] A review of the agreement revealed that it contained stabilization clauses exempting the company from complying with the provisions of existing laws where such provisions were

---

[141] Sierra Leone Embassy, An Overview of Sierra Leone Mining Sector, Washington DC USA, http://embassyofsierraleone.net/node/79 (last accessed 1 October 2018).

[142] Alix Y, Mining in Sierra Leone: an Overview of the Current Legal Framework, Herbert Smith Freehills LLP. 20 May 2015, https://www.lexology.com/library/detail.aspx?g=0f68dda3-1d7a-4770-b96a-d6df219e3fd0 (last accessed 1 October 2018).

[143] Curtis M (2009) Sierra Leone at the Crossroads: Seizing the Chance to Benefit from Mining. National Advocacy Coalition on Extractives (NACE), http://curtisresearch.org/wp-content/uploads/sierra-leone-at-the-crossroads.2.pdf (last accessed 1 October 2018).

[144] The only exception was the Agreement Between the Government of Sierra Leone and Sierra Rutile Limited (2001) which was reproduced in the Sierra Rutile Agreement (Ratification) Act 2002 (ratified 21 March 2002), Supplement to the Sierra Leone Gazette, Vol CXXXIII, No. 15. 21 March 2002, http://www.nma.gov.sl/home/wp-content/uploads/2015/07/Mineral-Agreement_Sierra-Rutile.pdf (last accessed 1 October 2018).

[145] Fofana L, Sierra Leone: Activists Cry Foul over Mining Policy, Inter Press Service. 26 August 2008, http://www.ipsnews.net/2008/08/sierra-leone-activists-cry-foul-over-mining-policy/ (last accessed 1 October 2018).

[146] Agreement Between the Government of Sierra Leone and Sierra Rutile Limited (2001) which was reproduced in the Sierra Rutile Agreement (Ratification) Act 2002 (ratified 21 March 2002), Supplement to the Sierra Leone Gazette, Vol CXXXIII, No. 15. 21 March 2002, http://www.nma.gov.sl/home/wp-content/uploads/2015/07/Mineral-Agreement_Sierra-Rutile.pdf (last accessed 1 October 2018).

inconsistent with the agreement.[147] Furthermore, the company was to be compensated for the cost of performing "more onerous obligations" caused by any new legislation or "changes in administrative rule or practice".[148] The broad scope of the clause meant that the company was to be exempted from all new laws whether they were fiscal (such as tax laws) or non-fiscal laws (such as human rights and environmental law).

The revelations of the terms of the Sierra Rutile Agreement, coupled with the perception that they had been corruptly obtained, created widespread mistrust of the government.[149] It was in this context that President Ernest Koroma was elected in 2007 on a "strong anti-corruption ticket."[150] One of the five 'core principles' of his manifesto was to ensure 'integrity, transparency and accountability in the conduct of public affairs.'[151] It also contained a promise to "review all exploration and mining contracts that are in operation."[152] In 2008, in line with the campaign promises, the government embarked on a review of the existing mining contracts to ensure greater benefits for the country and improve accountability and transparency "according to the EITI compliance model."[153] That same year, the country became an EITI candidate country, eventually attaining Compliant status in 2014.[154] As part of measures to implement the EITI, a number of laws and regulations were enacted

---

[147] Agreement Between the Government of Sierra Leone and Sierra Rutile Limited (2001) which was reproduced in the Sierra Rutile Agreement (Ratification) Act 2002 (ratified 21 March 2002), Supplement to the Sierra Leone Gazette, Vol CXXXIII, No. 15. 21 March 2002, http://www.nma. gov.sl/home/wp-content/uploads/2015/07/Mineral-Agreement_Sierra-Rutile.pdf (last accessed 1 October 2018), Article 11(e) 1 and 2.

[148] Agreement Between the Government of Sierra Leone and Sierra Rutile Limited (2001) which was reproduced in the Sierra Rutile Agreement (Ratification) Act 2002 (ratified 21 March 2002), Supplement to the Sierra Leone Gazette, Vol CXXXIII, No. 15. 21 March 2002, http://www.nma. gov.sl/home/wp-content/uploads/2015/07/Mineral-Agreement_Sierra-Rutile.pdf (last accessed 1 October 2018), Article 11(e) 3.

[149] Curtis M, Sierra Leone at the Crossroads: Seizing the Chance to Benefit from Mining. National Advocacy Coalition on Extractives (NACE), March 2009, http://curtisresearch.org/wp-content/uploads/sierra-leone-at-the-crossroads.2.pdf (last accessed 1 October 2018), p. 1.

[150] Doyle M, Can Sierra Leone Flush Away Corruption. BBC News Freetown, 23 January 2009, http://news.bbc.co.uk/2/hi/africa/7834228.stm (last accessed 1 October 2018).

[151] All Peoples Congress, Manifesto for 2007 Elections. Sierra Herald, Vol. 9 No. 1, http://www. sierraherald.com/apc-manifesto.htm (last accessed 1 October 2018).

[152] All Peoples Congress, Manifesto for 2007 Elections. Sierra Herald, Vol. 9 No. 1, http://www. sierraherald.com/apc-manifesto.htm (last accessed 1 October 2018), Section 14.2.b, see also Section 13.3.c.

[153] Bah S, Government to Review Mining Contracts for EITI Compliance. Awoko. 21 July 2011, http://awoko.org/2011/07/21/govt-to-review-mining-contracts-for-eiti-compliance/ (last accessed 1 October 2018), Koroma EB, Presidential Address to Parliament. Fifth Session of the Third Parliament of the Second Republic of Sierra Leone, in the Chamber of Parliament Building, 25 September 2012, http://www.sierra-leone.org/Speeches/koroma-092512.html (last accessed 1 October 2018), para. 80.

[154] Sierra Leone Extractive Industries Transparency Initiative, https://eiti.org/sierra-leone (last accessed 10 July 2018).

to promote transparency, accountability and good governance in the mineral sector.

The Environment Protection Agency Act 2008 was enacted to impose more oner-ous environmental standards on mining companies.[155] The following year, the Mines and Minerals Act 2009 was enacted, introducing several measures to improve trans-parency in the mining sector,[156] including a structured licensing process.[157] Subsequently, the National Minerals Agency Act 2012 established a National Minerals Agency to oversee the day-to-day implementation of the 2009 Act.[158] In line with its mandate, mining agreements and concessions entered into and granted by the government are all now publicly available at the Agency's website.[159] Data relating to revenues are now also publicly available online at an online repository launched in January 2012.[160]

The stabilization clauses in Sierra Leone's contracts were also affected by the new laws and measures. Under the previous Act, the Secretary of State was able to accept stabilization clauses in privately negotiated mining agreements by virtue of the wide discretionary power granted to him.[161] However, this provision was removed in the 2009 Act thereby limiting the possibility of stabilization clauses being legally negotiated in Sierra Leone's mining sector. On the basis of this change, the stabilization clauses, alongside other terms in a controversial 2009 agreement with London Mining were reviewed.[162] First, while the duration of the original sta-bilization clause was potentially 40 years,[163] the fiscal terms of the amended agreement are subject to review in 2020.[164] Secondly, while the scope of the original clauses covered changes in all laws,[165] the scope in the amended agreement was

---

[155] Environment Protection Agency Act. 2008, http://www.sierra-leone.org/Laws/2008-11.pdf, (last accessed 1 October 2018).

[156] See especially sections 159 to 160 of the Act, http://www.sierra-leone.org/Laws/2009-12.pdf (last accessed 1 October 2018).

[157] See, for example, sections 60.1, 63.7 and 72.1 of the Mines and Minerals Act, Sierra Leone. 2009.

[158] National Minerals Agency, Act. 2012, http://www.sierra-leone.org/Laws/2012-03.pdf, (last accessed 1 October 2018).

[159] National Minerals Agency, Mining Agreements, http://www.nma.gov.sl/home/mining-agree-ments/ (last accessed 1 October 2018).

[160] National Minerals Agency, Government of Sierra Leone, GoSL Online Repository, https://sier-raleone.revenuedev.org/dashboard (last accessed 1 October 2018).

[161] Section 22, Mineral Development Act, Sierra Leone. 1994, Act 525.

[162] Mining Agreement between Sierra Leone and London Mining Company Limited, December 2009.

[163] Sections 3(b) and 6(c) Mining Lease Agreement between the Government of Sierra Leone and London Mining Company Limited. 27 February 2012, http://www.nma.gov.sl/home/wp-content/uploads/2015/07/MiningAgreement_LondonMining.pdf (last accessed 1 October 2018).

[164] Section 6(8) Mining Lease Agreement between the Government of Sierra Leone and London Mining Company Limited. 27 February 2012, http://www.nma.gov.sl/home/wp-content/uploads/2015/07/MiningAgreement_LondonMining.pdf (last accessed 1 October 2018).

[165] Sections 3(b) and 6(c) Mining Lease Agreement between the Government of Sierra Leone and London Mining Company Limited. 27 February 2012, http://www.nma.gov.sl/home/wp-content/uploads/2015/07/MiningAgreement_LondonMining.pdf (last accessed 1 October 2018).

limited to cover a limited range of taxes.[166] Thus, unlike under the stabilization clauses in the original agreement, the company cannot rely on the clauses in the amended agreement to not comply with new social and environmental laws. Rather, the amended agreement explicitly provides that the company "shall comply with all health and safety standards and laws generally applicable in Sierra Leone from time to time"[167] and all environmental protection laws and regulations "as they may be amended from time to time."[168]

The above changes made to the London MDA are now standard provisions in MDAs entered into by the government since 2010.[169] It is therefore no longer possible for mining companies in Sierra Leone to rely on investor protection mechanisms, whether stabilization clauses or otherwise, to avoid complying with new social and environmental standards. This is particularly significant as the bulk of the regulations to implement health, safety, environmental and other social standards relating to the mining sector were formulated years after most of the existing mining agreements were signed.[170]

5   Concluding Remarks

Stabilization clauses insulate foreign investors from the adverse effects of changes in the laws of host states either by exempting them from the applicability of the changes or by entitling them to compensation for the cost of compliance. By exempting investors from changes in the laws of host states or requiring that investors are compensated for the cost of compliance, stabilization clauses reduce the policy space within which host states can effectively regulate investors and their investments in the future. For this reason, concerns over the impact of stabilization clauses on host states' ability to regulate in the area of human rights rose in 2003 leading to a huge literature on the potential impacts of stabilization clauses on

---

[166] Section 5.14 Mining Lease Agreement between the Government of Sierra Leone and London Mining Company Limited. 27 February 2012, http://www.nma.gov.sl/home/wp-content/uploads/2015/07/MiningAgreement_LondonMining.pdf (last accessed 1 October 2018).

[167] Section 4.14 Mining Lease Agreement between the Government of Sierra Leone and London Mining Company Limited. 27 February 2012, http://www.nma.gov.sl/home/wp-content/uploads/2015/07/MiningAgreement_LondonMining.pdf (last accessed 1 October 2018).

[168] Section 4.11 Mining Lease Agreement between the Government of Sierra Leone and London Mining Company Limited. 27 February 2012, http://www.nma.gov.sl/home/wp-content/uploads/2015/07/MiningAgreement_LondonMining.pdf (last accessed 1 October 2018).

[169] See, for example, Mining Lease Agreement Between Sierra Leone and Koidu Holdings S. A., relating to the Mining and Commercial Exploration of the Koidu Kimberlitiers in a Project to be known as "The Koidu Kimberlite Project", 2010, Articles 12 and 13.

[170] For example, the Environment Protection (Mines and Minerals) Regulations, http://www.azmec.co.zm/downloads/acts/SI%2029%20Mines%20and%20Minerals%20Act%20Environmental%20Regulations.pdf, (last accessed 1 October 2018) and the Mines and Minerals Operational Regulations were both enacted in July 2013.

human rights. The common recommendation arising from this literature is that social and environmental laws should be excluded from the ambit of stabilization clauses.

The findings in this chapter, however, suggest that whether or not a country follows this recommendation depends, to a large extent, on the presence of measures to improve transparency in its extractive industry. The reason is that the broadest forms of stabilization clauses, exempting investors from all laws, including human rights laws, are more likely to be found in contracts or legislation entered into, or enacted by, regimes known (or widely perceived) to be corrupt and/or dictatorial. These contracts or legislation usually contain full freezing or full economic equilibrium clauses or a combination of both. In most cases, they have been drafted to protect investors for the entire duration of the contract or at least a significantly long period from legislative change. They have also mostly been negotiated under opaque conditions and their contents were kept secret.

As exemplified by the case studies, citizens' demands for improved transparency and accountability in the extractive industries of several African countries have resulted in several governments becoming elected largely on campaign promises to increase transparency and accountability in the management of the extractive industries. In keeping with these promises, these governments joined the EITI and introduced transparency measures to implement the EITI. A noticeable effect of these initiatives is the elimination, or reduction in the scope of, stabilization clauses.

Before their involvement with the EITI, the four countries examined included broad forms of stabilization clauses in extractive industry contracts negotiated under opaque circumstances by corrupt governments. These clauses allowed investors to be exempted from the applicability of a change in law, including laws enacted to promote and protect human rights. The stabilization clauses therefore had the potential to limit the countries' abilities to implement their human rights obligations under international law. However, following increased transparency and accountability as a result of their involvement with the EITI, these countries either no longer employ stabilization clauses or negotiate more limited forms of the clause. In particular, stabilization clauses in these countries now exclude human rights and other socially desirable laws from their ambit.

The evidence therefore suggests that as transparency initiatives crystallize in countries, the use of broad forms of stabilization clauses diminishes. In other words, while governments appear willing to grant stabilization clauses when negotiations are conducted in secret, they seem unable to defend or justify the inclusion of such clauses when they are held to account by their citizens. This therefore suggests that as more African countries join the EITI and begin to implement measures to improve transparency in their extractive industries the potential detrimental impact of stabilization clauses on human rights diminishes.

References

Bernardini P (1998) The renegotiation of the investment contract. ICSID Rev Foreign Invest Law J 13(2):411–425

Campbell B (2010) Revisiting the reform process of African mining regimes. Can J Dev Stud 30(1–2):197–217

Cotula L (2008) Reconciling regulatory stability and evolution of environmental standards in investment contracts: towards a rethink of stabilization clauses. J World Invest Law Bus 1(2):158–179

Hirsch M (2011) Between fair and equitable treatment and stabilization clause: stable legal environment and regulatory change in international investment law. J World Invest Trade 12(6):783–808

Kolstad I, Søreide T (2009) Corruption in natural resource management: implications for policy makers. Resour Policy 34(4):214–226

Letnar Cernic J (2010) Corporate human rights obligations under stabilization clauses. Ger Law J 11(2):210–229

Maniruzzaman AFM (2008) The pursuit of stability in international energy investment contracts: a critical appraisal of the emerging trends. J World Energy Law Bus 1(2):121–157

Nassar N (1995) Sanctity of contracts revisited: a study in the theory and practice of long-term international commercial transactions. ICSID Rev Foreign Invest Law J 6(1):362–364

Ndulo M (1986) Mining legislation and mineral development in Zambia. Cornell Int Law J 19(1):1–34

Omorogbe Y (1996) Law and investor protection in the Nigerian natural gas industry. J Energy Nat Res Law 14(2):179–192

Oshionebo E (2010) Stabilization clauses in natural resource extraction contracts: legal, economic and social implications for developing countries. Asper Rev Int Bus Trade Law 10:1–33

Posthumus B (2000) ZCCM: a tale of heartbreak and tears. Afr Bus, 34–36

Rosenblum P, Maples S (2009) Contracts confidential: ending secret deals in the extractive industries. Revenue Watch Institute, New York

Sheppard A, Crockett A (2011) Are stabilisation clauses a threat to sustainable development? In: Segger MC, Gehring MW, Newcombe A (eds) Sustainable development in world investment law. Kluwer Law International, Alphen aan den Rijn, pp 329–350

Sikka P (2011) Accounting for human rights: the challenge of globalization and foreign investment agreements. Crit Perspect Account 22:811–827

Tienhaara K (2007) Unilateral commitments to investment protection: does the promise of stability restrict environmental policy development? Yearb Int Environ Law 17(1):139–167

Van Donge JK (2009) The plundering of Zambian resources by Frederick Chiluba and his friends: a case study of the interaction between national politics and the international drive towards good governance. Afr Aff 108:69–90

Wälde T, N'Di G (1996) Stabilising international investment commitments: international law versus contract interpretation. Tex Int Law J 31(2):215–267

Sotonye Frank   is lecturer at the Rivers State University and Senior Associate at the law firm of Ntephe, Smith & Wills, both in Port Harcourt. He studied law at Rivers State University, attended the Nigeria Law School and was subsequently called to the Nigerian Bar. He has an LLM from the University of Aberdeen and a PhD from the University of Nottingham. His research areas include international investment law, natural resource law, sustainable development law and policy, environmental law and human rights law.

Improving Tax Strategy Transparency in the Extractive Industries Sector for the Advancement of Human Rights

Wasima Khan

Contents

1 Introduction 142
2 The Emerging Link Between Taxation and Human Rights: Domestic Resource
   Mobilisation 147
3 State Actors, Taxation, Natural Resources, and Human Rights 148
4 Business, Taxation, and Human Rights 154
5 The Extractive Industries Sector and Tax Strategy Transparency 158
6 Conclusion 162
References 163

The most powerful weapon against inequality is tax. (…) To the super rich, I say: trickle-down is dead. To the elites and the kleptocrats in poor countries, I say: there's a limit to how high you can build the gates around your communities. The time has come to pay. Make sure the payment is in taxes.—Lilianne Ploumen, former Minister for Foreign Trade and Development Cooperation, The Netherlands[1]

---

[1] Ploumen EMJ (2016) Speech by Lilianne Ploumen, Minister for Foreign Trade and Development Cooperation, at 'Leaving No One Behind', a conference on inequality hosted by the Overseas Development Institute, London, 8 February 2016, https://www.government.nl/documents/speeches/2016/02/08/speech-by-minister-ploumen-at-the-conference-on-inequality-hosted-by-the-overseas-development-institute (last accessed 12 November 2018).

W. Khan (✉)
Erasmus University Rotterdam, Erasmus School of Law, Rotterdam, The Netherlands

© Springer Nature Switzerland AG 2019
I. Feichtner et al. (eds.), *Human Rights in the Extractive Industries*,
Interdisciplinary Studies in Human Rights 3,
https://doi.org/10.1007/978-3-030-11382-7_7

1 Introduction

The extractive industries sector[2] is one of the world's most profit-generating business sectors.[3] In 2010, profits from the extractive industries of 58 resource-rich countries totalled more than USD 2.6 trillion according to the Resource Governance Index.[4] Yet, many of the world's resource-rich countries are developing countries. They depend on their natural resource wealth but systematically fail to translate it into economic stability and growth and an enjoyment of basic human rights—such as access to health, education, and sanitation—for their citizens. Research from the United Nations Development Programme (UNDP) reveals that resource-dependent countries have a higher poverty number and rank lower in the Human Development Index than less endowed countries.[5] Widely cited as the "resource curse"[6] or the "paradox of plenty",[7] it is increasingly recognized that this problem may partially be caused by ineffective tax collection.[8]

---

[2] It is difficult to define exactly the "extractive industries sector" because interpretations vary. An UNCTAD report defines the extractive industry broadly as "processes that involve different activities that lead to the extraction of raw materials from the earth (such as oil, metals, mineral and aggregates), processing and utilization by consumers", see Sigam C and Garcia L, Extractive industries: Optimizing value retention in host countries. UN Conference on Trade and Development, http://unctadxiii.org/en/SessionDocument/suc2012d1_en.pdf (last accessed 1 October 2018), p. 3.

[3] Sigam C and Garcia L, Extractive industries: Optimizing value retention in host countries. UN Conference on Trade and Development, http://unctadxiii.org/en/SessionDocument/suc2012d1_en.pdf (last accessed 23 May 2018), p. 1, arguing that six out of the ten largest companies in terms of revenues were from the energy and mining sectors in 2010 and enjoyed record profits over the past few years; Stevens et al. (2013), p. 5; Halland et al. (2015), p. 3, mentioning that the extractive industry is characterized by "exceptional profits".

[4] Revenue Watch Institute, The 2013 Resource Governance Index: A measure of transparency and accountability in the oil, gas, and mining sector, http://www.resourcegovernance.org/sites/default/files/rgi_2013_Eng.pdf (last accessed 1 October 2018), p. 3.

[5] UN Development Programme, Extractive industries for sustainable development. April 2014, http://www.undp.org/content/dam/undp/library/Poverty%20Reduction/Extractive%20Industries/Extractive-Industries-Brochure.pdf (last accessed 1 October 2018). See also, Ross M, Extractive sectors and the poor. Oxfam America, 2001, https://www.oxfamamerica.org/static/media/files/extractive-sectors-and-the-poor.pdf (last accessed 23 May 2018), p. 5, "States that depend on mineral exports are among the most troubled states in the world today. They suffer from exceptionally slow rates of economic growth; their governments tend to be weak and undemocratic; and they more frequently suffer from civil wars than resource poor states".

[6] Auty (1993); Sachs and Warner (2001); Halland et al. (2015), pp. 4–7.

[7] The Economist, The paradox of plenty. 20 December 2005, http://www.economist.com/node/5323394 (last accessed 1 October 2018).

[8] Land (2009); Stürmer (2010); Le Billon (2011), arguing that much of the public revenues from extractive sectors in resource-rich developing countries is lost, partially due to tax evasion; Sigam C and Garcia L, Extractive industries: Optimizing value retention in host countries. UN Conference on Trade and Development, http://unctadxiii.org/en/SessionDocument/suc2012d1_en.pdf (last accessed 1 October 2018), pp. 10–11, mentioning the need for clear tax rules to avoid the negative impacts of dependence of governments' revenues on the extractive industry; Halland et al. (2015), pp. 12, 74–78, mentioning the need for an effective resource tax system to realize the large public revenue potential of the extractive industry.

The most telling example is the region of Africa,[9] home to about 30% of the world's mineral reserves, 10% of the world's oil, and 8% of the world's natural gas according to the World Bank.[10] Tax systems in Africa's resource-rich countries mainly rely on taxes from extractive industries, with resource taxes in the oil-exporting countries Equatorial Guinea, Republic of Congo, Angola, Gabon, Nigeria, and Chad amounting to around 70% to 90% of tax revenues.[11] There are no official figures but the African Union's High Level Panel on Illicit Financial Flows and the United Nations Economic Commission for Africa (UNECA) estimate that the continent is deprived of an annual amount of over USD 50 billion to USD 60 billion because of the many controversial tax abuse instances that mostly occur in the extractive industries sector.[12] This is more than the total amount of official development assistance (ODA) and foreign direct investment (FDI) coming into Africa.[13]

---

[9] Open Society Institute of South Africa et al., Breaking the curse: How transparent taxation and fair taxes can turn Africa's mineral wealth into development. March 2009, http://documents.twn-africa.org/breaking-the-curse-march2009.pdf (last accessed 1 October 2018), a report by African and international civil society organisations arguing for transparent and balanced mining tax regimes in African states in order to fund social and economic development and break the "resource curse".

[10] World Bank, Extractive industries – Overview, http://www.worldbank.org/en/topic/extractivein-dustries/overview#1 (last accessed 1 October 2018).

[11] Leibfritz (2015), p. 182.

[12] African Union and UNECA Conference of Ministers of Finance, Planning and Economic Development, Illicit financial flows: Report of the High Level Panel on illicit financial flows from Africa, http://www.uneca.org/publications/illicit-financial-flows (last accessed 1 October 2018). It is difficult to come up with hard numbers because reliable data is lacking, given the secretive nature of tax avoidance. Despite this limitation there is a wide range of studies describing the negative impact of tax avoidance and tax incentives provided to foreign companies in African countries, see e.g., Ndikumana (2015), p. 94, mentioning that, in 2011, Zambia may have lost tax revenue that was nearly equal to its total GDP in 2008, as a result of profit shifting and transfer pricing mechanisms by companies involved in international copper trade; Curtis M, Extracting minerals, extracting wealth. War on Want, October 2015, https://waronwant.org/sites/default/files/WarOnWant_ZambiaTaxReport_web.pdf (last accessed 1 October 2018), arguing that Zambia is losing USD 3 billion a year from corporate tax dodging; Otusanya (2011), describing how multinational companies in the oil, gas, and manufacturing sectors have used various tax schemes, ranging from off-shore intermediary companies to claiming recharges, royalties or technical fees and under-reporting of profit, to avoid paying tax in Nigeria. For a criticism of the "inflated" estimates of corporate tax abuse calculated by NGOs, see Forstater M (2015) Can stopping "tax dodging" by multinational enterprises close the gap in development finance? Center for Global Development CGD Policy Paper 069. October 2015, http://www.cgdev.org/content/publications/can-stopping-tax-dodging-multinational-enterprises-close-gap-development-finance (last accessed 1 October 2018). In any case, one notable exception to the bleak picture in Africa seems to be Botswana; a resource-rich country—exporter of diamonds, copper, and nickel—which has largely avoided the "resource curse" and undergone a transformation, due to mineral-led economic growth, from one of the poorest countries in the world at the time of independence in 1966 to an upper-middle income country, currently enjoying relatively low levels of corruption and environmental damage with open and transparent taxation, strong public finances and minimal debts, see Jefferis (2009).

[13] Sharples N and Jones T and Martin C, Honest accounts? The true story of Africa's billion dollar losses. Poverty Health Action et al., July 2014, http://curtisresearch.org/wp-content/uploads/Honest-Accounts-report-v4-web.pdf (last accessed 1 October 2018); Baker R, Financing for devel-

Recently, the Panama Papers also highlighted several major incidents of corporate tax avoidance in Africa, revealing, for example, how offshore oil profits from Nigeria have vanished and how a large oil and gas company in Uganda attempted to avoid a new capital gains tax through corporate restructuring.[14]

Multinational companies often circumvent local tax laws. They do not pay taxes in the countries in which they operate because they report their profits in more tax-friendly countries to minimise their tax liabilities.[15] A perverse incentive exacerbates the problem: In order to gain revenues, some developed countries negotiate tax treaties that favour the multinational companies which are seated in their jurisdictions but are highly unfavourable for developing countries.[16] In a vicious circle, such conduct explains to a great extent why African revenues disappear from the continent and domestic development is hindered.[17] In his foreword to the 2013 Africa Progress Report, the late Kofi Annan, former UN Secretary-General and chairman of the Africa Progress Panel, acknowledged the severity of the situation, and implicitly recognized the devastating impact of tax avoidance on the realisation of basic human rights, when he stated that "it is unconscionable that some companies, often supported by dishonest officials, are using unethical tax avoidance, transfer pricing and anonymous company ownership to maximize their profits, while millions of Africans go without adequate nutrition, health and education."[18]

---

opment: Enabling developing countries to tackle illicit flows. Global Finance Integrity, 8 February 2016, http://www.gfintegrity.org/press-release/financing-for-development-enabling-developing-countries-to-tackle-illicit-flows/ (last accessed 1 October 2018), a panel discussion speech by Global Financial Integrity President Raymond Baker at the 4th OECD Forum on Tax and Crime in Amsterdam, the Netherlands.

[14] These, and other, research findings are available at African Network of Centers for Investigative Reporting, Panama Papers: How the elite hide their wealth, https://panamapapers.investigativecenters.org/ (last accessed 1 October 2018).

[15] Jenkins (2005), p. 535.

[16] Developed countries in Europe play a large role in this regard, see Eurodad, Hidden profits: The EU's role in supporting an unjust global tax system. November 2014, http://www.eurodad.org/files/pdf/1546298-hidden-profits-the-eu-s-role-in-supporting-an-unjust-global-tax-system-2014-.pdf (last accessed 1 October 2018). Bilateral double taxation treaties based on the OECD model significantly constrain developing countries' rights to earn tax revenues on foreign business operations in their territories, see International Monetary Fund, Spillovers in international corporate taxation. 9 May 2014, https://www.imf.org/external/np/pp/eng/2014/050914.pdf (last accessed 1 October 2018). In general, many discussions about tax administration systems in Africa focus on dysfunctional and corrupted institutions in the continent's developing countries. Much less attention has been paid to the fact that developed countries exploit and perpetuate these weaknesses for their own capitalist benefit. To come to grips with how corruption in developing countries and Western capitalism are intertwined, we need more research that unravels how these two occurrences are linked.

[17] Open Society Institute of South Africa et al., Breaking the curse: How transparent taxation and fair taxes can turn Africa's mineral wealth into development. March 2009, http://documents.twnafrica.org/breaking-the-curse-march2009.pdf (last accessed 1 October 2018).

[18] Africa Progress Panel, Africa progress report 2013 – Equity in extractives: Stewarding Africa's natural resources for all. May 2013, http://www.africaprogresspanel.org/publications/policy-papers/africa-progress-report-2013/ (last accessed 1 October 2018), p. 7.

Developing countries are particularly vulnerable to the adverse consequences of international tax abuse because of their social, political, and administrative difficulties in establishing a sound public finance system.[19] Often, they lack the power capacity, financial resources and technical expertise to enforce legal standards on an international level.[20] If developing countries are able to find ways to increase their domestic extractive industries revenues by boosting the capacity to collect the taxes owed to them, they could achieve their full economic potential and obtain the public budgets needed to fund the advancement of human rights.[21] In line with the UN Guiding Principles on Business and Human Rights framework, both state actors and companies have a role to play in considering the adverse impact of their activities, including tax avoidance, on human rights.[22]

Under international law, states are granted the right to set up their own tax policies and systems. This right exists next to a human rights responsibility to generate and spend tax revenues for the benefit of the country's development, as well as a human rights responsibility to cooperate on an international level to safeguard other countries' ability to fulfil their responsibility (Sects. 2 and 3). Unfortunately, these human rights responsibilities are difficult to enforce. Instead of merely examining ways to improve the performance of state actors,[23] this chapter shifts the focus to the

---

[19] Deutsche Gesellschaft für Internationale Zusammenarbeit (2010), p. 6.

[20] Solheim (2012), p. ix, mentioning the example of Nigeria that made an attempt in the early 2000s to recover the funds that illegally fled the country but was confronted with out-dated rules and poorly trained staff in the domestic environment as well as bank secrecy, opaque corporate and trust vehicles, and time consuming procedures precluding cooperation overseas; Murphy (2012), pp. 287–288, mentioning that "the extractive industries are almost entirely immune to legislative changes affecting the way in which their tax liabilities are computed for periods of up to 30 years after signing mineral development agreements"; Calder (2014); Elbadawi and Mohammed (2015), pp. 249–250; UN Conference on Trade and Development (2015).

[21] Open Society Institute of South Africa et al., Breaking the curse: How transparent taxation and fair taxes can turn Africa's mineral wealth into development. March 2009, http://documents.twn-africa.org/breaking-the-curse-march2009.pdf (last accessed 1 October 2018), p. 15, "[t]here is a consensus among UNCTAD, UNECA and the IMF that the paramount development benefit of mining in Africa is the potential to generate public revenue through a transparent tax and budget system."; De Paepe and Dickinson (2014).

[22] International Bar Association's Human Rights Institute Task Force on Illicit Financial Flows, Poverty and Human Rights, Tax abuses, poverty and human rights. October 2013, https://www.ibanet.org/Article/NewDetail.aspx?ArticleUid=4A0CF930-A0D1-4784-8D09-F588DCDDFEA4 (last accessed 1 October 2018); Van Os R and McGauran K and Römgens I, Private gain – Public loss: Mailbox companies, tax avoidance, and human rights. SOMO, July 2013, https://www.somo.nl/wp-content/uploads/2013/07/Private-Gain-Public-loss.pdf (last accessed 1 October 2018), p. 8, arguing that "Dutch fiscal policy that facilitates tax avoidance by large multinationals has a negative impact on human rights in countries where extractive industry operations take place"; UN Human Rights Council, Illicit financial flows, human rights, and the post-2015 development agenda, UN Doc. A/HRC/28/60, 10 February 2015, para. 33.

[23] See e.g., G20, G20 targeted approaches to addressing corruption in the extractives sector. November 2015, http://g20.org.tr/wp-content/uploads/2015/11/Targeted-Approaches-to-Corruption-in-the-Extractives-Sector.pdf (last accessed 1 October 2018), mentioning the role of tax authorities to ensure maximum compliance and to minimise corruption risk in the collection of taxes on the extractives sector; Ploumen L, Why developing countries need to toughen up on taxes.

crucial role of multinational companies in the extractive industries sector to tackle tax avoidance. Large multinational companies are ultimately the ones responsible for deciding to deliberately and systematically engage in tax avoidance and with the means available to retain legal, accountancy, and banking services to hide and perpetuate such activities (Sect. 4).[24] If multinational extractive industry sector companies refrained from tax avoidance, they could prevent developing countries from being deprived of revenues that can have significant positive human rights impacts.[25] This chapter suggests the need for a legal requirement for multinational (extractive) companies to establish and publish a tax strategy (Sect. 5). The conclusion finishes with a summary and thoughts on the way forward (Sect. 6).

The Guardian, 7 July 2015, an article by the former Dutch Minister for Foreign Trade and Development Cooperation who argues that the full potential of developing countries can be achieved by their governments through domestic resource mobilisation starting with higher rates of tax revenue collection; Ploumen identifies three main areas of action: (a) ensuring fair taxation; (b) strengthening tax inspectors; and (c) broadening the tax base; The Report of the High-Level Panel of Eminent Persons on the Post-2015 Development Agenda, A new global partnership: Eradicate poverty and transform economies through sustainable development. 30 May 2013, http://www.un.org/sg/management/pdf/HLP_P2015_Report.pdf (last accessed 1 October 2018), p. 5: "Developed countries have a great responsibility to keep the promises they have made to help the less fortunate. The billions of dollars of aid that they give each year are vital to many low-income countries. But it is not enough: they can also co-operate more effectively to stem aggressive tax avoidance and evasion, and illicit capital flows. Governments can work with business to create a more coherent, transparent and equitable system for collecting corporate tax in a globalised world."

[24] African Union and UNECA Conference of Ministers of Finance, Planning and Economic Development, Illicit financial flows: Report of the High Level Panel on illicit financial flows from Africa. http://www.uneca.org/publications/illicit-financial-flows (last accessed 1 October 2018), p. 3. See also UN Office of the High Commissioner of Human Rights, Natural resources sector: UN expert calls for binding human rights treaty for corporations. 18 June 2015, http://www.ohchr.org/EN/NewsEvents/Pages/DisplayNews.aspx?NewsID=16097&LangID=E (last accessed 1 October 2018), UN Special Rapporteur on the Rights to Freedom of Peaceful Assembly and of Association, Maina Kiai, called upon States to enact a legally binding treaty that obliges businesses to respect fundamental human rights, arguing before the UN Human Rights Council that "corporations play an outsized role in the decision-making processes about exploitation of natural resources. But they are not subject to legally binding human rights obligations (…) It is time to address this issue more robustly; corporations must not escape responsibility to safeguard human rights".

[25] Developing countries are not the only ones to be affected. In the aftermath of the financial crisis, civil society organisations have expressed their concerns about the negative impact of tax avoidance among extractive sector companies on developed economies such as the UK, see e.g., Platform, Making a killing: Oil companies, tax avoidance and subsidies. February 2013, http://platformlondon.org/wp-content/uploads/2013/02/MakingAKilling-LOWRES.pdf (last accessed 1 October 2018), arguing that UK-based oil companies like BP and Shell receive major government support and pay very small amounts of UK tax in comparison to their global mega-profits at a time of massive public spending cuts.

2   The Emerging Link Between Taxation and Human Rights: Domestic Resource Mobilisation

Human rights cannot be realised without public resources.[26] This is why, in the past several years, novel ideas about ways to reduce the gap between the rich and poor have led a growing number of public policy practitioners and civil society organisations, e.g. the Center for Economic and Social Rights (CESR), the Task Force on Illicit Financial Flows, Poverty and Human Rights, the International Bar Association's Human Rights Institute (IBAHRI), Oxfam, and the Tax Justice Network (TJN), as well as inter-governmental bodies such as the European Union (EU), the International Monetary Fund (IMF), the Organisation for Economic Co-Operation and Development (OECD), the United Nations (UN), and the World Bank to take a look at taxation, which offers a powerful instrument to expand public budgets and realise development goals.[27] With a strong call to action, some of these individuals and organisations are at the forefront of launching long-term campaigns and practical approaches which ensure that effective tax policies in both developed and developing countries can be utilised as a redistributive tool to reduce inequality between and within countries.

At the heart of the efforts lies the concept of domestic resource mobilisation (DRM) that has recently gained attention, due to the agenda for sustainable development created at the beginning of this century with the adoption of the UN Millennium Development Goals (MDGs) and the subsequent 2030 Agenda for Sustainable Development enshrined in the Sustainable Development Goals (SDGs).[28] The gist of this core concept is the following: Taxes provide countries with domestic

---

[26] Elson et al. (2013), p. 13. See also Holmes and Sunstein (1999), arguing that all rights are public goods, financed through tax revenues.

[27] Center for Economic and Social Rights, Human rights in tax policy, http://www.cesr.org/article.php?list=type&type=229 (last accessed 1 October 2018); International Bar Association's Human Rights Institute Task Force on Illicit Financial Flows, Poverty and Human Rights, Tax abuses, poverty and human rights. October 2013, https://www.ibanet.org/Article/NewDetail.aspx?ArticleUid=4A0CF930-A0D1-4784-8D09-F588DCDDFEA4 (last accessed 1 October 2018); Byanyima W (2015) My message to world leaders: To finance development you must tackle tax. Oxfam International. 15 May 2015, https://blogs.oxfam.org/en/blogs/15-05-05-my-message-world-leaders-finance-development-you-must-tackle-tax (last accessed 1 October 2018); Tax Justice Network, Human rights, http://www.taxjustice.net/topics/inequality-democracy/human-rights/ (last accessed 27 July 2017); European Commission, Communication from the Commission to the Council, the European Parliament and the European Economic and Social Committee, Tax and Development: Cooperating with developing countries on promoting good governance in tax matters, COM (2010) 163; International Monetary Fund et al., Supporting the development of more effective tax systems: A report to the G-20 Development Working Group by the IMF, OECD, UN and World Bank, November 2011, https://www.imf.org/external/np/g20/pdf/110311.pdf (last accessed 1 October 2018).

[28] Shay (2013); Runde et al. (2014); UN, Outcome document of the Third International Conference on Financing for Development: Addis Ababa Action Agenda, 15 July 2015, UN Doc. A/Conf.227/L.1, https://documents-dds-ny.un.org/doc/UNDOC/GEN/N15/219/91/PDF/N1521991.pdf?OpenElement (last accessed 1 October 2018), paras. 20–34.

resources to pay for their own economic development and the delivery of public goods and services to their citizens for the realisation of basic human rights.[29] Tax revenues can be used to invest in health care, schools, roads, police, water systems, energy grids, and much more. Everyone benefits from taxes through the role they play in helping to shape safe, healthy, and accessible public environments.

Theoretically, a successful mobilisation of domestic resources is mainly determined by two aspects: the ability (1) to *generate* resources from taxes effectively and fairly, and (2) to *spend* resources from taxes effectively and fairly. This chapter predominantly focuses on the first aspect.[30] It looks at the human rights responsibilities of state actors to generate public resources from taxation, both generally and more specifically with regard to the extractive industries sector, and the "business and human rights" responsibility of multinational companies to not hinder the generation of revenues that can lead to successful domestic resource mobilisation.

Before taking a closer look at the role of multinational extractive companies, let us start first with examining the human rights responsibility of state actors in relation to the generation of public resources. From an international law perspective, state actors have fiscal sovereignty, i.e. a right of self-determination to formulate their own tax policies according to national and economic context. Yet, a closer look at several international human rights standards, in the next section, reveals that there may be limitations to the fiscal sovereignty of state actors when their policies conflict with the effective generation of public resources for the realisation of human rights.

3   State Actors, Taxation, Natural Resources, and Human Rights

State actors have a responsibility to generate a maximum amount of available resources to realise human rights. According to Article 2(1) of the International Covenant on Economic, Social and Cultural Rights (ICESCR), state actors have a duty to devote the maximum of their available resources to securing the realisation of economic, social and cultural rights of their citizens.[31] A state is in violation of the ICESCR if it fails to allocate the maximum of its available resources to realising human rights.[32] Although it remains unclear how to quantify and measure the "max-

---

[29] See e.g., the Lima Declaration on Tax Justice and Human Rights, http://www.cesr.org/downloads/Lima_Declaration_Tax_Justice_Human_Rights.pdf (last accessed 1 October 2018), "Taxation (…) plays a fundamental role in redistributing resources in ways that can prevent and redress gender, economic and other inequalities and reduce the disparities in human rights enjoyment that flow from them.".

[30] For a discussion of the second aspect, the question how to spend public resources and make effective budget decisions for successful domestic resource mobilisation and the realisation of human rights, see e.g. Nolan et al. (2013).

[31] International Covenant on Economic, Social and Cultural Rights (ICESCR), Art. 2(1).

[32] Maastricht Guidelines on Violations of Economic, Social, and Cultural Rights, para. 15(e).

imum of available resources", it has been acknowledged and emphasized that tax revenue generation plays an essential role in this regard. In a report on taxation and human rights to the UN, former UN Special Rapporteur on extreme poverty and human rights Magdalena Sepúlveda Carmona stressed that state actors' actions or omissions that diminish the maximum of available resources, for example "by allowing large-scale tax evasion or tax structures that have a disproportionate impact on the poorest segments of the population", could constitute a violation of this human rights obligation.[33]

The human rights responsibility of state actors regarding the effective generation of public resources for successful domestic resource mobilisation does not stop at the national border. Given the cross-border scope of tax abuse and the interdependence of state actors to enforce multi-jurisdictional tax legislation, there is a critical need for international coordination. Article 2(1) of the ICESCR recognizes the need for "international assistance and cooperation" for the fulfilment of economic, social and cultural rights.[34] Additionally, the Maastricht Principles on Extraterritorial Obligations of States in the Area of Economic, Social and Cultural Rights clarify that state actors have an extra-territorial obligation to refrain from conduct that impairs the ability of other states to comply with their own human rights commitments.[35] The latter obligation implies that state actors are also in violation of the ICESCR when their international tax policies fail to protect the realisation of economic and social rights in other countries. Enforcement of this extra-territorial obligation, however, remains problematic. There are no clear means to sanction state actors for non-compliance.[36]

In addition to the obligation to respect and protect the ability of countries to mobilise domestic revenues for the universal fulfilment of human rights, there are international standards that stipulate international cooperation for the economic development of developing countries with respect for their sovereignty over

---

[33] UN Human Rights Council, Report of the Special Rapporteur on Extreme Poverty and Human Rights, Ms. Magdalena Sepúlveda Carmona, on taxation and human rights, UN Doc. A/HRC/26/28, 22 May 2014, para. 5.

[34] International Covenant on Economic, Social and Cultural Rights (ICESCR), Art. 2(1).

[35] Maastricht Principles on Extraterritorial Obligations of States in the Area of Economic, Social and Cultural Rights, para. 21. Designed as a practical tool for public policymakers, the UN Guiding Principles on Extreme Poverty and Human Rights affirm that "states should take into account their international human rights obligations when designing and implementing all policies, including international trade, taxation, fiscal, monetary, environmental and investment policies" and "states must take deliberate, specific and targeted steps, individually and jointly, to create an international enabling environment conducive to poverty reduction, including in matters relating to bilateral and multilateral trade, investment, taxation, finance, environmental protection and development cooperation. This includes cooperating to mobilize the maximum of available resources for the universal fulfilment of human rights.", see UN Human Rights Council, UN Guiding Principles on Extreme Poverty and Human Rights, A/HRC/21/39, 18 July 2012, paras. 61 and 96.

[36] Balakrishnan and Heintz (2014), p. 164. For an interesting hypothetical inter-state communications complaint under Article 10(1) of the Optional Protocol to the ICESCR by Zambia against Switzerland for its conduct related to tax evasion and the adverse consequences for Covenant rights in Zambia, see Lusiani (2014).

domestic natural wealth and resources. The UN Resolution 1803 on the "Permanent Sovereignty over Natural Resources" of 1962 states:

> The right of people and nations to permanent sovereignty over their natural wealth and resources must be exercised in the interest of their national development and of the well-being of the people of the State concerned (…) International co-operation for the economic development of developing countries, whether in the form of public or private capital investments (…) shall be based upon respect for their sovereignty over their natural wealth and resources.[37]

This provision protects the means of resource-rich developing countries to exercise sovereignty and control over their natural resources to enable their economic and political development. The principle was affirmed in the Charter of Economic Rights and Duties of States, adopted by the UN General Assembly in 1974 as part of the economic rights and duties of state actors in the "New International Economic Order" (NIEO). Article 2 of the Charter mentions that:

> Every State has and shall freely exercise full permanent sovereignty, including possession, use and disposal, over all its wealth, natural resources and economic activities (…) Each State has the right to regulate and supervise the activities of transnational corporations within its national jurisdiction and take measures to ensure that such activities comply with its laws, rules and regulations and conform with its economic and social policies. Transnational corporations shall not intervene in the internal affairs of a host State. Every State should, with full regard for its sovereign rights, cooperate with other States in the exercise of the right set forth in this subparagraph.[38]

In practice, generating the maximum amount of available resources for successful domestic resource mobilisation remains an experiment in balancing competing interests. A significant challenge in our current era of economic globalisation is the phenomenon of international tax competition: In order to attract and retain foreign investment, some countries adjust their tax policies to the needs of multinational companies and provide them with substantial tax incentives.[39] Research from ActionAid and the Centre for Research on Multinational Corporations (SOMO) has pointed out that the Nigerian government has lost USD 3.3 billion in tax revenues because of major tax breaks—i.e. tax reductions or exemptions—provided to European shareholders of Shell, Total and ENI.[40] Developed countries also play an

---

[37] UN General Assembly, Permanent Sovereignty over Natural Resources, Res. 1803 (XVII), 14 December 1962, Art. 1, paras. 1, 6.

[38] UN General Assembly, Permanent Sovereignty over Natural Resources, Res. 1803 (XVII), 14 December 1962, Art. 2, paras. 1-2(2)(b).

[39] Russia, for example, was over-eager to attract investment in 1994, when it signed a contract with a consortium led by Royal Dutch Shell to develop oil and gas reserves off its Pacific coast. The Russian government agreed to forgo its share of the revenues until the foreign investors had recouped their costs. What Russia did not foresee was that the project would encounter major delays and that it would take a long time for the government to receive any tax payments. See The Economist, Barking louder, biting less. 8 March 2007, http://www.economist.com/node/8815008 (last accessed 30 July 2017).

[40] Van Dorp M, How Shell, Total and ENI benefit from tax breaks in Nigeria's gas industry. SOMO, January 2016, https://www.somo.nl/wp-content/uploads/2016/02/How-Shell-Total-and-Eni-benefit-from-tax-breaks-in-Nigerias-gas-industry.pdf (last accessed 1 October 2018).

important role in the race to design the most attractive fiscal climate for companies. Many of the world's largest extractive corporate groups maintain their holding company in the Netherlands because of its favourable investment climate including major tax benefits.[41] According to a 2013 policy paper by Oxfam, developing countries are annually deprived of EUR 460 million in revenues due to tax avoidance strategies that are facilitated by the legal tax system of the Netherlands.[42]

But in exceptional cases, developing countries do *de facto* use their rights of fiscal sovereignty and permanent sovereignty over natural resources to fight back and amend tax rules in order to generate more revenues and gain control over their resources.[43] In 2011, for example, Mongolia made headlines in tax newsletters and international fiscal circles when it decided to unilaterally cancel its tax treaties with the Netherlands, Luxembourg, Kuwait, and the United Arab Emirates, because the government believed it was not receiving its fair share of profits from the mining sector.[44] While the bilateral tax treaties had helped Mongolia to attract significant foreign investment in the past and were meant to avoid double taxation, the country realised they had now instead become a vehicle for treaty shopping[45] and aggressive international tax planning by major investors in the mining sector. Where mining companies in Mongolia would normally have to pay a 20% withholding tax on dividends, the tax treaty between the Netherlands and Mongolia allowed Netherlands-based companies to channel income from dividends, royalties and interest earned in Mongolia through their Dutch company, thus paying no withholding tax. Other Dutch treaties with states that charge little, or no, tax subsequently allowed the Netherlands-based companies to transfer that income from the Netherlands to tax havens. The Dutch-Mongolian treaty resulted in unnecessary revenue loss from the extractive industries sector for the Mongolian government whilst not contributing much to inbound investment.

Somewhat taken aback by Mongolia's "resource nationalism"[46] and pressured by civil society organisations, the Dutch government finally acknowledged its role in

---

[41] Van Os R and McGauran K and Römgens I, Private gain – Public loss: Mailbox companies, tax avoidance, and human rights. SOMO, July 2013, https://www.somo.nl/wp-content/uploads/2013/07/Private-Gain-Public-loss.pdf (last accessed 1 October 2018), p. 17.

[42] Berkhout (2013). Almost four decades ago, economist Raymond Vernon already predicted that "the mischief that can be produced in the future by the jungle of different national tax jurisdictions may prove to be considerable", see Vernon (1977), p. 127.

[43] Land (2009), pp. 158–159; Stevens et al. (2013), p. 68.

[44] Deutsch A and Edwards T, Special report: In tax case, Mongolia is the mouse that roared. Reuters, 16 July 2013, http://www.reuters.com/article/us-dutch-mongolia-tax-idUSBRE96F0B620130716 (last accessed 1 October 2018).

[45] The term "treaty shopping" generally refers to the practice of an investor forming a legal business entity in a country that has a favorable tax treaty with the "source" country, i.e. the country where the investment is made and the income in question is earned, often motivated by the goal to minimise tax payments.

[46] Resource nationalism may be defined as "the expression, by states, of their determination to gain the maximum national advantage from the exploitation of national resources". See Joffé et al. (2009), p. 4.

the facilitation of tax avoidance and proactively started making efforts in 2015 to tackle it when it agreed on the inclusion of anti-abuse provisions in tax treaties with five African developing countries (Ethiopia, Ghana, Kenya, Malawi, and Zambia), and initiated negotiations with 18 more developing countries.[47] Unsurprisingly, civil society organizations, such as SOMO, embraced the governmental initiative after many years of social activism,[48] while the business community—driven by the goal of profit maximisation—fiercely opposed the developments.[49]

One of the ways for multinational extractive companies to oppose and (temporarily) remain unaffected by tax reforms, is by seeking legal protection through the negotiation of a separate investment contract including stabilisation clauses,[50] as the mining company Rio Tinto had done in Mongolia.[51] Stabilisation clauses come in different forms and are a contractual, risk-mitigating device guaranteeing the investor that changing laws and regulations will be neutralized from an economic perspective. In general, they stipulate that foreign investors should be compensated for the cost of complying with legal reforms so that the investors remain in the same economic situation they would have been in had the laws not been changed. The main goal is to provide protection and legal certainty to foreign investors for the duration of a project and to prevent financial losses of foreign investors due to legal reforms.

Worldwide, half of all stabilisation clauses appear in contracts relating to projects in extractive industries.[52] Investments in the extractive industries sector are traditionally considered to be in greater need of stability, because they are long-term, capital-intensive projects that cannot be relocated.[53] Stabilisation clauses are typically offered in developing countries, because investors view these countries as more politically unstable than developed ones,[54] but also out of opportunistic

---

[47] Government of the Netherlands, Government stepping up support to developing countries on tax issues. 22 June 2015, https://www.government.nl/latest/news/2015/06/20/government-stepping-up-support-to-developing-countries-on-tax-issues (last accessed 1 October 2018).

[48] See e.g., SOMO, Many years of research by SOMO pays off. 25 September 2013, https://www.somo.nl/many-years-of-research-by-somo-pays-off/ (last accessed 1 October 2018).

[49] Steinglass M and Smyth J, Dutch tax avoidance crackdown sparks debate. Financial Times, 12 September 2013.

[50] For a thorough and critical analysis of such clauses and their impact on human rights in African developed counties, see *Frank's* chapter in this volume.

[51] Deutsch A and Edwards T, Special report: In tax case, Mongolia is the mouse that roared. Reuters, 16 July 2013, http://www.reuters.com/article/us-dutch-mongolia-tax-idUSBRE96F0B620130716 (last accessed 1 October 2018).

[52] Clinch D and Watson J, Stabilisation clauses – issues and trends. Lexology, 30 June 2010, http://www.lexology.com/library/detail.aspx?g=c5976193-1acd-4082-b9e7-87c0414b5328   (last accessed 1 October 2018).

[53] Tienhaara (2007), pp. 141–142.

[54] In practice, this argument is not completely valid. Not developing countries' as Russia's or Venezuela's, but rather Britain's fiscal policy is unpredictable as it "is constantly tinkering with its tax rates" according to energy consultant Saad Rahim, see Barking louder, biting less, 8 March 2007, http://www.economist.com/node/8815008 (last accessed 1 October 2018). See also Mansour M and Nakhle C, Fiscal stabilization in oil and gas contracts: Evidence and implications. The

motives on the part of investors: developing countries have relatively weak bargaining power combined with a strong desire to attract investment; they are more likely to agree to conditions that would not be accepted by developed countries.[55]

The desire for fiscal stability among multinational extractive companies can mainly be traced back to the need for legal protection against an increase in tax rates. When regulatory reforms take place during the lifetime of a project, foreign investors can enforce legally binding stabilisation clauses by means of the agreed upon dispute resolution mechanisms. They can seek redress through claims against the host state either under the contract or under investment treaties, if available. In practice, tax reforms have indeed been the subject of a significant number of international state-investor arbitration cases.[56] In Latin America, for example, Ecuador and Venezuela were subjected to international arbitrations by multinational extractive companies after the governments of these countries had introduced nationalistic policies and regulatory changes, including an increase in tax rates for the oil industry after oil prices had begun to rise, to reassert government control over the increased value of oil and gas resources.[57]

The validity of stabilisation clauses is questionable in general, but especially so in the realm of taxation. Requiring host states to compensate foreign investors financially for compliance with new laws, defeats the main purpose of tax reforms. State actors often introduce tax reforms to raise more revenues. These additional revenues cannot be adequately collected if the government has to pay them back instantly in the form of financial compensation due to stabilisation clauses.

Overall, state actors are faced with a troubling, paradoxical dilemma: generating sufficient tax revenues on the one hand and attracting foreign investment through an attractive low-tax climate on the other hand. As such, state actors find themselves in a catch 22–situation: they attempt to generate more jobs and revenues by attracting foreign companies, but in order to attract them, they are often forced to provide tax cuts and thus sacrifice revenues. In the worst case, an uncompetitive tax environment can drive multinational companies away to more favourable tax jurisdictions, leading to less foreign investment on the whole. The capacity of state actors alone to deal with the major tax problems, which currently challenge domestic resource mobilisation in resource-rich developing countries and have an adverse impact on the fulfilment of human rights, is limited.

Besides the responsibilities of state actors, it must be considered whether foreign multinational companies have a human rights responsibility not to hinder tax collection. Tax law is the framework through which the government puts the policies, structures, and hierarchies behind taxation into practice for the benefit of society, including the realisation of human rights. But some extractive companies

---

Oxford Institute for Energy Studies: SP 37, January 2016, https://www.oxfordenergy.org/wpcms/wp-content/uploads/2016/02/Fiscal-Stabilization-in-Oil-and-Gas-Contracts-SP-37.pdf   (last accessed 1 October 2018), p. 9: "The UK has long been a textbook example of fiscal instability."

[55] Tienhaara (2007), pp. 146–147.

[56] Land (2009), p. 158.

[57] Blackaby and Richard (2015).

significantly undermine the functioning of the legal framework of taxation for the advancement of their personal interests by engaging in tax avoidance.[58] This leads to a severe tax gap, i.e. a gap between the taxes owed and collected. In developing countries, the tax gap has a severe negative impact on the realisation of citizens' human rights. Therefore, one may argue, it is important that multinational companies, too, get actively involved in efforts for more effective tax collection.

4   Business, Taxation, and Human Rights

Taxation is increasingly becoming an important strategic consideration and reputational concern in top-level business decision-making among large multinational companies. The question is whether companies can actually claim to be acting socially responsibly when they continue to avoid taxes.[59] Society, at large, believes they cannot. Over the past decade, there has been an increased public awareness of corporate tax avoidance in the aftermath of the financial crisis and multiple data leaks (Swiss Leaks, Luxembourg Leaks, Panama Papers). The public response consisted of blaming and shaming of companies that engage in tax avoidance. This has taken place in the form of public protests, political statements, and social media calls for customer boycotts.[60] Is the public discomfort with tax avoidance, and the social expectation that multinational companies not engage in it, aligned with the legal perspective? Do companies have a tax responsibility, which obliges them to refrain from tax avoidance?[61]

From a corporate law perspective, the answer to the question whether a corporate tax responsibility exists, depends on how one interprets the purpose of a company and the corresponding directors' duties. Do the directors of a company merely owe a duty to their shareholders with the goal to maximise profits for the benefit of this constituency by any means possible, or do they owe a duty to a wider range of stakeholders—including society as a whole—with the goal to create value without causing societal harm? Interpretations regarding this issue vary across—and sometimes

---

[58] Pak (2012), describing how over USD 110 billion have "disappeared" through large scale mispricing of crude oil in the US and EU between 2000 and 2010 leading to a reduction of tax payments and profits moving from source countries' governments to extractive industry companies.

[59] The Economist, Social saints, fiscal fiends. 2 January 2016, https://www.economist.com/news/business-and-finance/21684770-social-saints-fiscal-fiends-opinions-vary-whether-firms-can-be-socially-responsible (last accessed 1 October 2018). Empirical evidence among American firms shows that companies with extensive CSR programs often also make the most efforts to avoid paying taxes; companies rationalise this behavior by stating that the less they pay in taxes, the more they can maximise their profits, which contributes to the common good, see Davis et al. (2016).

[60] Barford V and Holt G (2013) Google, Amazon, Starbucks: The rise of "tax shaming". BBC News Magazine. 21 May 2013, http://www.bbc.com/news/magazine-20560359 (last accessed 1 October 2018)

[61] In a similar sense, see Avi-Yonah (2014).

even within—jurisdictions among courts, business economists, and legal scholars.[62]

In the US state of Delaware—home to many Fortune 500 companies and the most influential state in the US for jurisprudence in matters of corporate governance—courts have addressed the question whether any legal standards are breached when directors decide not to minimise corporate tax payments. The answer: Directors are permitted but not obliged to minimise taxes. Whether they decide to do so or not, falls under their discretionary powers in managing the business and affairs of their company and is not a decision of shareholders. The Delaware Chancery Court held in the case *Seinfeld v. Slager* (2012) that:

> This Court has concluded that "there is no general fiduciary duty to minimize taxes." There are a variety of reasons why a company may choose or not choose to take advantage of certain tax savings, and generally a company's tax policy "typif[ies]" an area of corporate decision-making best left to management's business judgment, so long as it is exercised in an appropriate fashion." I am not foreclosing the theoretical possibility that under certain circumstances overpayment of taxes might be the result of a breach of a fiduciary duty. I am simply noting that a decision to pursue or forgo tax savings is generally a business decision for the board of directors. Accordingly, despite the Plaintiff's contentions, Delaware law is clear that there is no separate duty to minimize taxes, and a failure to do so is not automatically a waste of corporate assets. (footnotes omitted, WK)[63]

In the UK, company directors are required to promote the success of the company for the benefit of its members—i.e. the shareholders—according to Section 172 of the Companies Act 2006. But in doing so, they must take at least the following six factors into consideration: (1) the long-term consequences of their decisions; (2) the interests of employees; (3) the relationships with suppliers and customers; (4) the impact of corporate activities on the community and the environment; (5) the company's reputation for high standards of business conduct; and (6) the need for fairness between different members of the company. This legal provision represents an "enlightened shareholder view", indicating that directors must not merely maximise profits for the company's shareholders but must also take the interests of a wider range of stakeholders into account.

Both in the US and the UK, company directors seem to be legally permitted but certainly not obliged to engage in tax avoidance. In general, ideological arguments for and against tax avoidance traditionally center on questions about legal permissiveness. The debate on the side of some corporate taxpayers is often concluded with the statement that tax avoidance is permissible because it technically falls within the boundaries of tax law. From the viewpoint of state actors, however, each instance of tax avoidance has a harmful impact on government revenues which makes it *eo ipso* impermissible.[64] Both perspectives, each in their own way, are

---

[62] See e.g. Kay J, Directors have a duty beyond just enriching shareholders. Financial Times, 4 June 2013; Khan W, No obligation to avoid paying tax. Financial Times, 17 June 2013, for a comparison of the US and the UK.

[63] Court of Chancery of the State of Delaware, Civil Action No. 6462-VCG, *Seinfeld v. Slager*, 29 June 2012.

[64] Gravelle (2009); Mo (2003), p. 3. On June 1, 1937, President Franklin D. Roosevelt gave a

absolutist. In less polarizing and more nuanced debates that allow for ambivalence and complexity, the legal permissiveness of tax avoidance is put into question by mentioning that the boundaries between legitimate tax planning and unlawful tax evasion are not clear and that aggressive tax avoidance finds itself in an area with numerous shades of grey.[65]

This chapter adds another layer of nuance to the debate by focusing on the legal permissiveness of tax avoidance in a different way; not by accepting it undeniably, rejecting it flat-out, or putting it into a shady gray area, but by putting it in perspective with other rights, more specifically: human rights. In other words, this chapter does not revisit the debate whether tax avoidance is permissible in itself but rather questions whether it is permissible when it may come into conflict with existing responsibilities regarding human rights owed by those who are involved in it. The permissiveness of tax avoidance is not absolute, but relative; it depends on something more than tax law alone. The argument that the permissiveness of tax avoidance may be limited when it conflicts with international human rights law is fairly new. Not much has as yet been said or written about a corporate tax responsibility in relation to human rights. Some call corporate tax avoidance "the elephant in the room" on the business and human rights agenda.[66]

At the international level, human rights policy makers have only recently successfully advocated for a general corporate responsibility to respect human rights.[67] The Guiding Principles on Business and Human Rights—endorsed by the UN Human Rights Council in April 2011—include the corporate responsibility to respect human rights, which means that "business enterprises should act with due diligence to avoid infringing on the rights of others and to address adverse impacts

---

speech to the US Congress on tax evasion in which he mentioned: "Methods of escape or intended escape from tax liability are many. Some are instances of avoidance which appear to have the color of legality; others are on the borderline of legality; others are plainly contrary even to the letter of the law. All are alike in that they are definitely contrary to the spirit of the law. All are alike in that they represent a determined effort on the part of those who use them to dodge the payment of taxes which Congress based on ability to pay. All are alike in that failure to pay results in shifting the tax load to the shoulders of others less able to pay, and in mulcting the Treasury of the Government's just due." See Roosevelt FD, Message to Congress on tax evasion prevention. 1 June 1937, The American Presidency Project, online by G. Peters and J.T. Woolley, http://www.presidency.ucsb. edu/ws/?pid=15413 (last accessed 1 October 2018).

[65] Sikka (2014), p. 135. With subjectivity abound and the complication involved in trying to find a clear-cut definition, some argue that tax avoidance, like hardcore pornography, is definable only ostensively, referring to US Supreme Court Justice Potter Stewart's famous line "I know it when I see it" in the obscenity case *Jacobellis v. Ohio*, 378 U.S. 184 (1964), see Hern A, Why tax avoidance is like porn, 16 November 2012, New Statesman, http://www.newstatesman.com/econom-ics/2012/11/why-tax-avoidance-porn (last accessed 1 October 2018); Maugham J, Is tax avoidance like hardcore pornography?. Financial Times Alphaville, 10 June 2016, https://ftalphaville.ft. com/2016/06/10/2165878/is-tax-avoidance-like-hardcore-pornography/ (last accessed 1 October 2018).

[66] Darcy (2017).

[67] See also Khan (2013).

with which they are involved".[68] The Guiding Principles do not explicitly mention a responsibility for companies to pay taxes to ensure that citizens' human rights are fulfilled.[69] But given the adverse impacts of corporate tax avoidance on human rights, such a responsibility can be implied. Companies that knowingly engage in tax avoidance are "purposefully depriving countries of the resources they need to fulfil their human rights obligations".[70] As such, this activity amounts to a violation of the corporate responsibility to respect human rights under the Guiding Principles. Furthermore, the 2011 OECD Guidelines on Multinational Enterprises have dedicated a section to taxation, commenting that "corporate citizenship in the area of taxation implies that enterprises should comply with both the letter and the spirit of the tax laws and regulations in all countries in which they operate".[71]

Both the Principles and Guidelines are widely recognized yet they remain "soft law" instruments based on voluntary cooperation by companies; they do not have the effect of legally binding duties. As a consequence, there is no enforceable corporate tax responsibility as yet. In general, multinational companies enjoy a variety of considerable rights under international investment law and international human rights law, but they are not bound by a corresponding set of obligations.[72] This explains why human rights instruments so far have also had little chance to make an impact in the field of taxation. Yet, despite this current lacuna in the law, the public has voiced a call for greater corporate accountability regarding tax avoidance in the wake of the recent data leaks. One accountability tool that may have a visible impact on business conduct is a requirement for increased transparency.[73]

---

[68] UN Human Rights Council, Report of the Special Representative of the Secretary-General on the issue of human rights and transnational corporations and other business enterprises, John Ruggie. Implementing the United Nations "Protect, Respect and Remedy" Framework, UN Doc. A/HRC/17/31, 21 March 2011, p. 4.

[69] Aaronson and Higham (2013).

[70] UN Human Rights Council, Report of the Special Rapporteur on Extreme Poverty and Human Rights, Ms. Magdalena Sepúlveda Carmona, on taxation and human rights, UN Doc. A/HRC/26/28, 22 May 2014, para. 7. See also Interim report of the Independent Expert on the effects of foreign debt and other related international financial obligations of States on the full enjoyment of all human rights, particularly economic, social and cultural rights, Illicit financial flows, human rights and the post-2015 development agenda, February 10, 2015, UN Doc., para 33, stressing that the tax planning strategies of multinational companies have potential negative impacts on human rights.

[71] Organisation for Economic Co-operation and Development (2011), p. 60.

[72] See Wouters and Chané (2015).

[73] See also, European Commission, Communication from the Commission to the European Parliament, the Council, the European Economic and Social Committee and the Committee of the Regions, A renewed EU strategy 2011-14 for Corporate Social Responsibility, COM (2011) 681, p. 7, mentioning transparency as one of three principles that constitute good tax governance, the other two principles being "exchange of information" and "fair tax competition between state actors".

5   The Extractive Industries Sector and Tax Strategy Transparency

The idea to hold multinational extractive companies accountable to a greater extent through increased transparency has been recognized in the global political arena. At the G8 meeting in Northern Ireland on 17–18 June 2013, leaders agreed upon a set of principles in the Lough Erne Declaration including concrete commitments to fair taxation and transparency about payments to governments in the extractive industries sector.[74] The increased expectation among the public, markets and the legislature to obtain information about the activities in the extractive industries sector has led to country-wide reforms, for example in the US. On December 11, 2015, the US Securities and Exchange Commission proposed new rules under the Dodd-Frank Wall Street Reform and Consumer Protection Act that would require extractive companies listed on US stock exchanges to disclose payments made to the US federal government or foreign governments for the commercial development of oil, natural gas or minerals on a country-by-country and a project-by-project basis.[75] International soft law instruments, such as the OECD Principles to enhance the transparency and governance of tax incentives for investment in developing countries, also encourage companies to take up the responsibility to contribute adequately to the public finances of host countries and to comply with both the letter and spirit of the tax legislation of the countries in which they operate.[76]

The negative public perception of multinational companies on tax issues poses serious financial, operational and reputational business risks in the long term. To gain an adequate picture of long-term tax risks, transparent reporting on tax issues by multinational companies is also increasingly becoming important for investors.[77]

---

[74] See Gov. UK, G8 Lough Erne Declaration. 18 June 2013, https://www.gov.uk/government/publications/g8-lough-erne-declaration/g8-lough-erne-declaration-html-version (last accessed 1 October 2018). See also Gov.UK, 2013 Lough Erne G8 Leaders' Communiqué. 18 June 2013, https://www.gov.uk/government/uploads/system/uploads/attachment_data/file/207771/Lough_Erne_2013_G8_Leaders_Communique.pdf (last accessed 1 October 2018), paras. 27–29, 34–42. This agreement was in line with an earlier statement in a report by the High-Level Panel of Eminent Persons on the Post-2015 Development Agenda that "we need a transparency revolution, so citizens can see exactly where their taxes, aid and revenues from extractive industries are spent", see The Report of the High-Level Panel of Eminent Persons on the Post-2015 Development Agenda, A new global partnership: Eradicate poverty and transform economies through sustainable development. 30 May 2013, http://www.un.org/sg/management/pdf/HLP_P2015_Report.pdf (last accessed 1 October 2018), p. 9.

[75] SEC, Press release: SEC proposes rules for resource extraction issuers under Dodd-Frank Act. 11 December 2015, http://www.sec.gov/news/pressrelease/2015-277.html (last accessed 1 October 2018). For further discussion of these disclosure requirements, see *Keenan's* chapter in this volume.

[76] Organisation of Economic Co-operation and Development, Principles to enhance the transparency and governance of tax incentives for investment in developing countries. http://www.oecd.org/ctp/tax-global/transparency-and-governance-principles.pdf (last accessed 1 October 2018), p. 4.

[77] Hazra S, Tax me if you can: Game over. 27 October 2014, http://www.longfinance.net/pro-

In 2014, the Dow Jones Sustainability Index (DJSI)—a benchmark for investors who integrate sustainability considerations into their portfolios—was the first to introduce "tax strategy" as a sustainable investment criterion. The index now assesses three tax transparency-related issues: (1) tax strategy: whether or not companies have clearly defined tax policies that guide their approach to taxation and make them publicly available; (2) tax reporting: how detailed companies report on taxes in the countries and regions in which they operate; and (3) taxation risks: whether or not companies evaluate potential business and financial risks related to taxes.[78] Tax strategy-related risks could include direct financial risks due to changes in tax laws that come with higher tax rates, and the uncertain outcome of tax disputes, but also more indirect financial risks, such as negative impacts on a company's brand, reputation or relationships with key stakeholders (e.g. employees, governments, regulatory bodies).[79] In 2015, the UN Principles for Responsible Investment (UN PRI)—a network of investors representing USD 45 trillion of assets—published an engagement guide on corporate tax responsibility, encouraging investors to start a dialogue on tax issues with the companies they are investing in.[80] These risks come with potentially negative financial consequences, providing companies with *negative* incentives for good behaviour.

But what if we change the discussion on reputation from a risk-based discussion based on *negative* incentives for good behaviour to an opportunity-based discussion based on *positive* incentives for good behaviour? To put it in the words of the famed German writer and statesman Johann Wolfgang von Goethe: "Correction does much, but encouragement does more." Instead of merely constraining potential unethical conduct, it is useful to explore ways to incentivise ethical conduct through "naming and faming". Naming and faming could tap into the importance of reputation and market forces as an opportunity to influence the behaviour of companies in a positive way and be a pragmatic initiative to publicly reward companies that make efforts to curb tax avoidance practices. This is a more progressive alternative to regulatory punishment and the arbitrary practice of blaming and shaming. It is useful to look at recent developments to understand how a public reward for private conduct might be implemented concretely.

A promising inspiration can be found in the UK, where companies now have the opportunity to be accredited as "good tax-payers". In February 2014, a benchmark

---

grammes/london-accord/la-reports.html?view=report&id=475 (last accessed 1 October 2018); Deloitte, Responsible tax – Tax transparency developments in 2014. 2015 http://www2.deloitte. com/content/dam/Deloitte/uk/Documents/tax/deloitte-uk-transparency-developments-in-2014.pdf (last accessed 1 October 2018).

[78] RobecoSAM, DJSI 2014 review results, September 2014, http://www.sustainability-indices. com/images/DJSI_Review_Presentation_09_2014_final.pdf (last accessed 1 October 2018), p. 5.

[79] RobecoSAM, RobecoSAM's corporate sustainability assessment companion. April 2017, http:// www.robecosam.com/images/RobecoSAM-Corporate-Sustainability-Assessment-Companion-en. pdf (last accessed 1 October 2018), p. 41.

[80] Karananou A and Guha A, Engagement guidance on corporate tax responsibility: Why and how to engage with your investee companies. UN Principles for Responsible Investment, 2015, https:// www.unpri.org/download?ac=4536 (last accessed 1 October 2018).

label was introduced by the Fair Tax Mark, a non-profit co-operative that is the world's first independent fair tax accreditation scheme bringing together ethical consumers and UK businesses that promote tax fairness.[81] Fair Tax Mark believes not all companies aim to avoid taxes. The organisation has the aim to "offer businesses that know they are good taxpayers (or want to work towards becoming one) the opportunity to proudly display this to their customers."[82] The criteria required to get the Fair Tax Mark include: basic transparency about company structure and ownership; ensuring full accounts are in the public domain; understanding what tax has been paid and why; looking for a tax policy which commits to good practice; and for multinationals companies: public country-by-country reporting.[83] These criteria do not mention human rights, but there is a certain, albeit indirect, link between the Fair Tax Mark and the advancement of human rights. The Fair Tax Mark promotes responsible corporate tax behaviour, and responsible corporate tax behaviour contributes to not depriving state actors of resources that they need to realise human rights.

The efforts of UK-based Fair Tax Mark are exemplary of how *positive* financial incentives for good tax conduct could be put into practice through naming and faming. Yet, there would be an even greater public and market impact if the government would be involved in providing such positive financial incentives. Building further upon the aforementioned tax transparency initiatives and efforts, this chapter suggests to introduce a mandatory transparency requirement regarding tax strategy for multinational companies. Such a requirement could be designed after new legislation in the UK where large companies are now required to publish their tax strategy on the internet, on an annual basis.[84] The UK legislation stipulates that the published tax strategy must at least cover in relevant, up-to-date detail the approach of the UK group to risk management and governance arrangements in relation to UK taxation; attitude of the group to tax planning (so far as affecting UK taxation); level of risk in relation to UK taxation that the group is prepared to accept; and its approach toward dealings with the UK tax authority, HM Revenue and Customs. The tax strategy may be published with or as part of the group's financial statements. Companies face a penalty of GBP 7500 for each financial year that they fail to publish a tax strategy or fail to ensure that the tax strategy remains accessible on the internet for the prescribed period.

---

[81] Fair Tax Mark, Because fair tax is at the heart of society. http://www.fairtaxmark.net/ (last accessed 1 October 2018).

[82] Fair Tax Mark, What's the fair tax mark?. http://www.fairtaxmark.net/what-is-it/ (last accessed 1 October 2018).

[83] Fair Tax Mark, The criteria. https://fairtaxmark.net/criteria/ (last accessed 2 October 2017).

[84] For examples of tax strategy statements from large companies, see e.g., Unilever, Tax. https://www.unilever.com/sustainable-living/what-matters-to-you/tax.html (last accessed 28 July 2017); AkzoNobel, Tax principles, https://www.akzonobel.com/corporate_governance/policies/tax_principles/ (last accessed 28 July 2017); Philips, Tax principles, http://www.philips.com/b-dam/corporate/about-philips/investor-relations/governance/Philips_Tax_Principles_June2014.pdf   (last accessed 28 July 2017).

Because of the low cost of non-compliance—a financial penalty of GBP 7500—the UK requirement for tax strategy transparency will not deter some of the large multinational companies who were and still are strictly determined to avoid it, but the measure may nonetheless serve as a reference for good practice for other countries in changing corporate attitudes and mind-sets toward taxation. A mandatory tax strategy transparency requirement is an imperfect yet clear improvement compared to the previous widespread practice to avoid public disclosure of anything related to corporate tax matters.

From a business perspective, increased tax strategy transparency could reduce uncertainty and help critical investors and consumers with (a) monitoring and verifying that multinational companies are taking up the responsibility to curb tax avoidance through a thoughtful tax strategy, and (b) holding multinational companies accountable for inaction or non-compliance with both the letter and spirit of tax legislation.[85] It gives them the power to engage in business with companies that (pro)actively curb tax avoidance practices and that deal with tax issues in a socially accepted manner. In other words, mandatory tax transparency is not merely another compliance burden; it serves as a suitable positive incentive for companies because transparency from their part enables them to increase their public credibility and goodwill. On a macro-level, it provokes a race to the top; a higher market standard provides all companies with clear economic incentives and market demands to curb tax avoidance through a bottom-up approach in an uplifting manner.

From a legal perspective, the implementation of mandatory tax transparency is a way for state actors to fulfil their duty under the Guiding Principles to protect human rights, by taking an appropriate step to prevent human rights abuse by companies. This step can also prevent further legislative intervention and calls for a tighter tax code. Unlike sticks that stigmatise offenders,[86] the main benefit of using mandatory tax transparency is that it works as a carrot, as it becomes a market standard for ethical progress against tax avoidance. Mandatory tax transparency is an opportunity for multinational extractive companies to change their strategy from the risk-averse pathways of avoidance or mere compliance to the proactive pathway of using the law as a value-creating vehicle.[87] Ideally, this metric of ethical performance would serve as a reminder for companies to make better and more fulfilling entrepreneurial choices; to use their financial resources for legitimate business activities that lead to actual value creation to increase revenues instead of engaging in "paper

---

[85] See also Smith E and Rosenblum P, Enforcing the rules: Government and citizen oversight of mining. Revenue Watch Institute, 2011, https://resourcegovernance.org/sites/default/files/RWI_Enforcing_Rules_full.pdf (last accessed 23 May 2018), p. 19, arguing that transparency is a condition for effective monitoring and creates incentives for all stakeholders—governments, companies, and communities—to play by the rules.

[86] See also Blank (2009), discussing why the "shaming" sanction may not work and is rather counter-productive.

[87] For an analysis of five different corporate legal strategies (1. avoidance; 2. compliance; 3. prevention; 4. value; 5. transformation) with insights from business practice, see Bird and Orozco (2014).

entrepreneurialism"[88] by putting their money into the counterproductive activities of creation, implementation and defense of tax avoidance practices to decrease their costs.

6 Conclusion

Business, taxation, and human rights is a relatively young, both intellectually stimulating and practically relevant, research and policy field that has emerged out of the ground-breaking recognition that the goals of combatting tax avoidance among multinational companies and respecting human rights are connected. This chapter aims to move the field forward by encouraging a public debate on the phenomenon of tax avoidance by highly profitable multinational extractive industries sector companies and its detrimental impact on the advancement of human rights in developing countries.

Generally, states have fiscal sovereignty and are able to formulate their own tax policies according to their national and economic context. But fiscal sovereignty that leads to tax avoidance is incompatible with international (human rights) law. Tax avoidance by multinational extractive companies in developing countries, facilitated by the tax regimes of developing and developed countries: (1) limits the ability of developing countries to implement their obligations under international human rights law, i.e. the duty to devote the maximum of their available resources to securing the realisation of economic, social and cultural rights of their citizens[89]; (2) conflicts with the extra-territorial obligation under international law to refrain from conduct that impairs the ability of other states to comply with their own human rights commitments[90]; and (3) limits the right and obligation of developing countries under international law to exercise sovereignty and control over their natural resources to enable their own economic and political development.[91]

State actors are limited in their capabilities to combat tax avoidance alone. In the struggle against tax avoidance, an important question is how to improve tax compliance

---

[88] This term has been coined by the American political economist Robert Reich to identify the preoccupation of companies to increase shareholder value in the short term through paperwork on matters such as tax loopholes rather than in the long term through technological innovations and the development of new and better products. See Reich (1983). Another example of paper entrepreneurialism is the recent increase in share buybacks by directors of major listed companies, such as Apple, which leads to profits without prosperity. By reducing the number of outstanding shares, their value rises. This rise predominantly serves directors' own interests as their compensation is often heavily based on stock. The increase in corporate profits is distributed to shareholders instead of making reinvestments in the corporation—e.g. development of new products, creating new jobs, giving employees higher incomes—that would benefit the economy. See Lazonick (2014).

[89] International Covenant on Economic, Social and Cultural Rights (ICESCR), Art. 2(1); Maastricht Guidelines on Violations of Economic, Social, and Cultural Rights, para. 15(e).

[90] Maastricht Principles on Extraterritorial Obligations of States in the area of Economic, Social and Cultural Rights, para. 21.

[91] UN General Assembly, Permanent Sovereignty over Natural Resources, Res. 1803 (XVII), 14 December 1962, Art. 1, paras. 1, 6; UN General Assembly, Charter of Economic Rights and Duties of States, Res. 3281 (XXIX), 12 December 1974, Art. 2, paras. 1-2(2)(b).

among multinational extractive industries sector companies. Traditionally, multinational companies have a reputation for remaining obscure about their tax strategy, i.e. the long-term objectives on tax matters, the strategic goals, and the short-term tactics to achieve them. Many arrange their tax affairs through secrecy jurisdictions and tax havens. They do not provide information for the public to help them understand and evaluate the rationale behind the company's decisions on tax matters. As public scrutiny of tax avoidance has intensified in recent years, tax strategy transparency is increasingly becoming a matter of strategic importance to investors worldwide.

This chapter suggests complementing existing voluntary initiatives with improved mandatory tax strategy transparency, such as the new requirement recently introduced in the UK. Companies should define what their intentions in the conduct of tax policy are and how they plan to implement these intentions in their strategies. In addition to showing that they are complying with the letter of the law, it is equally important that companies increase their transparency about complying with the spirit of the law. Regular and detailed information allows investors and consumers to make better informed decisions. This measure could work in the long term as a necessary monitoring tool, not by "blaming and shaming", but instead "naming and faming" companies that proactively shun tax avoidance. It creates a new opportunity for both state actors and extractive industries sector companies to defend themselves against negative perceptions and to re-imagine their human rights commitments. The implementation of mandatory tax transparency is a way for state actors to fulfil their duty under the Guiding Principles on Business and Human Rights to protect human rights, and for companies to respect human rights.

If anything, the vibrant, opportunity-laden field of business, taxation, and human rights reveals one important lesson: The failure to realise human rights and achieve social justice is not due to a lack of capital, but a lack of redistribution of available capital. Tax avoidance is a main cause of that lack of redistribution. But this problem can be remedied. Economic development and social justice are compatible, if multinational companies do not avoid, but rather accept and proactively work together with governments on redistributive measures in the societies where they are located, and make their efforts known to the public. Achieving this goal is a work in progress; one that can benefit both business and society, and stimulate the advancement of human rights, now and for future generations.

Acknowledgements I am grateful to the conference organisers for the opportunity to address the topic of business, taxation, and human rights in the extractive industries sectors at the young scholars' workshop, where I received valuable feedback. I thank Prof. Markus Krajewski for his constructive comments and suggestions in a written review of this chapter's initial draft.

References

Aaronson SA, Higham I (2013) "Re-righting business": John Ruggie and the struggle to develop international human rights standards for transnational firms. Hum Rights Q 35(2):333–364
Auty RM (1993) Sustaining development in mineral economies: the resource curse thesis. Routledge, London

Avi-Yonah RS (2014) Corporate taxation and corporate social responsibility. NYU J Law Bus 11(1):1–29

Balakrishnan R, Heintz J (2014) Extraterritorial obligations, financial globalisation and macroeconomic governance. In: Nolan A (ed) Economic and social rights after the global financial crisis. Cambridge University Press, Cambridge, pp 146–166

Berkhout E (2013) De Nederlandse route: Hoe arme landen inkomsten mislopen via belastinglek Nederland [The Dutch route: how poor countries are deprived of revenues due to tax leakage in the Netherlands]. Oxfam Novib, The Hague

Bird RC, Orozco D (2014) Finding the right corporate legal strategy. MIT Sloan Manage Rev 56(1):81–89

Blackaby N, Richard C (2015) Regulatory change in oil and gas arbitration: the Latin American experience. In: Gaitis JM (ed) The leading practitioners' guide to international oil & gas arbitration. Juris Publishing, New York, pp 79–114

Blank JD (2009) What's wrong with shaming corporate tax abuse. Tax Law Rev 62(4):539–590

Calder J (2014) Administering fiscal regimes for extractive industries: a handbook. IMF, Washington DC

Darcy S (2017) "The elephant in the room": corporate tax avoidance & business and human rights. Bus Hum Rights J 2(1):1–30

Davis AK, Guenther DA, Krull LK, Williams BM (2016) Do socially responsible firms pay more taxes? Account Rev 91(1):47–68

De Paepe G, Dickinson B (2014) Tax revenues as a motor for sustainable development. In: Organisation of Economic Co-operation and Development (ed) Development co-operation report 2014: mobilising resources for sustainable development. OECD Publishing, Paris, pp 91–97

Deutsche Gesellschaft für Internationale Zusammenarbeit (2010) Addressing tax evasion and tax avoidance in developing countries. Deutsche Gesellschaft für Internationale Zusammenarbeit, Eschborn

Elbadawi IA, Mohammed NA (2015) Natural resources in Africa: utilizing the precious boon. In: Monga C, Lin JY (eds) The Oxford handbook of Africa and economics, vol II: policies and practices. Oxford University Press, Oxford, pp 247–256

Elson D, Balakrishnan R, Heintz J (2013) Public finance, maximum available resources and human rights. In: Nolan A, O'Connell R, Harvey C (eds) Human rights and public finance: budgets and the promotion of economic and social rights. Hart Publishing, Oxford, pp 13–40

Gravelle JG (2009) Tax havens: international tax avoidance and evasion. Natl Tax J 62(4):727–753

Halland H, Lokanc M, Nair A, Kannan SP (2015) The extractive industries sector: essentials for economists, public finance professionals, and policy makers. World Bank, Washington DC

Holmes S, Sunstein CR (1999) The cost of rights: why liberty depends on taxes. W.W. Norton & Company, New York

Jefferis K (2009) The role of TNCs in the extractive industry of Botswana. Transnatl Corp 18(1):61–92

Jenkins ROJ (2005) Globalization, corporate social responsibility and poverty. Int Aff 81(3):525–540

Joffé G, Stevens P, George T, Lux J, Searle C (2009) Expropriation of oil and gas investments: historical, legal and economic perspectives in a new age of resource nationalism. J World Energy Law Bus 2(1):3–23

Khan W (2013) Corporate power and the protection of human rights in equilibrium. Secur Hum Rights 24(1):29–42

Land B (2009) Capturing a fair share of fiscal benefits in the extractive industry. Transnatl Corp 18(1):157–173

Lazonick W (2014) Profits without prosperity. Harv Bus Rev, September:42–55

Le Billon P (2011) Extractive sectors and illicit financial flows: what role for revenue governance initiatives? U4 (13):1–32

Leibfritz W (2015) Fiscal policy in Africa. In: Monga C, Lin JY (eds) The Oxford handbook of Africa and economics, vol II: policies and practices. Oxford University Press, Oxford, pp 171–185

Lusiani NJ (2014) "Only the little people pay taxes": tax evasion and Switzerland's extraterritorial obligations to Zambia (Committee on Economic, Social and Cultural Rights). In: Gibney M, Vandenhole W (eds) Litigating transnational human rights obligations: alternative judgments. Routledge, London, pp 116–134

Mo PLL (2003) Tax avoidance and anti-avoidance measures in major developing economies. Greenwood Publishing Group, Westport

Murphy R (2012) Accounting for the missing billions. In: Reuter P (ed) Draining development? Controlling flows of illicit funds from developing countries. World Bank, Washington, DC, pp 265–308

Ndikumana L (2015) International tax cooperation and implications of globalization. In: Alonso JA, Ocampo JA (eds) Global governance and rules for the post-2015 era: addressing emerging issues in the global environment, The UN Series on Development. Bloomsbury, New York, pp 73–106

Nolan A, O'Connell R, Harvey C (2013) Human rights and public finance: budgets and the promotion of economic and social rights. Hart Publishing, Oxford

OECD (2011) OECD guidelines for multinational enterprises – 2011 edition. OECD, Paris

Otusanya OJ (2011) The role of multinational companies in tax evasion and tax avoidance: the case of Nigeria. Crit Perspect Account 22(3):316–332

Pak SJ (2012) Lost billions: transfer pricing in the extractive industries. Publish What You Pay Norway, Oslo

Reich RB (1983) The next American frontier. Time Books, New York

Runde DF, Savoy CM, Perkins CM (2014) Taxes and development: the promise of domestic resource mobilization. CSIS, Washington DC

Sachs JD, Warner AM (2001) The curse of natural resources. Eur Econ Rev 45(4–6):827–838

Shay SE (2013) Foreword. In: Brauner Y, Stewart M (eds) Tax, law, and development. Edward Elgar Publishing, Cheltenham, pp viii–xiii

Sikka P (2014) Tax avoidance and evasion. In: Atkinson R (ed) Shades of deviance: a primer on crime, deviance, and social harm. Routledge, Abingdon, pp 135–138

Solheim E (2012) Foreword. In: Reuter P (ed) Draining development? Controlling flows of illicit funds from developing countries. World Bank, Washington DC, pp ix–ix

Stevens P, Kooroshy J, Lahn G, Lee B (2013) Conflict and coexistence in the extractive industries. Chatham House, London

Stürmer M (2010) Let the good times roll? Raising tax revenues from the extractive sector in sub-Saharan Africa during the commodity price boom, Discussion Paper 7/2010. German Development Institute, Bonn

Tienhaara K (2007) Unilateral commitments to investment protection: does the promise of stability restrict environmental policy development? Yearb Int Environ Law 17(1):139–167

UN Conference on Trade and Development (2015) World Investment Report 2015: reforming international investment governance. United Nations Publications, Geneva

Vernon R (1977) Storm over the multinationals: the real issues. Harvard University Press, Cambridge

Wouters J, Chané AL (2015) Multinational corporations in international law. In: Noortmann M, Reinisch A, Ryngaert C (eds) Non-state actors in international law. Hart Publishing, Oxford, pp 225–252

Wasima Khan is currently a law lecturer at The Hague University of Applied Sciences. She has law degrees from the Erasmus University Rotterdam and is finishing a PhD in the research area of business, taxation, and human rights. In 2018, she published a Dutch law dictionary, including definitions of more than 10,000 legal terms.

Part II
Participation

The Evolving Duty to Consult and Obtain Free Prior and Informed Consent of Indigenous Peoples for Extractive Projects in the United States and Canada

Cathal M. Doyle

Contents

1   Introduction 169
2   Basis for and Content of the Duty to Consult in Canada and the US 172
3   US Context 175
    3.1   Statutory Duty to Consult 175
    3.2   Regulation and Executive Orders Addressing the Duty to Consult 177
    3.3   US Jurisprudence and the Duty to Consult 181
    3.4   Observations on Duty to Consult Under US Indian Law 185
4   Canadian Context 190
    4.1   Statutory Duty to Consult and Guidance of the Federal Government in Canada 190
    4.2   Canadian Jurisprudence Regarding Consultation, Accommodation and Consent:
          The Common Law Duty to Consult 195
    4.3   Observations on Canadian Duty to Consult and Obtain Consent 203
5   General Observations 207
6   Conclusion 212
References 216

1   Introduction

Canada and the United States (US), along with New Zealand and Australia, were the only countries to vote against the adoption of the UN Declaration on the Rights of Indigenous Peoples (henceforth UNDRIP or the Declaration) in the General Assembly in 2007.[1] One of the stated reasons for their position was the Declaration's affirmation of the duty to consult and cooperate in good faith with the Indigenous peoples through their own representative institutions in order to obtain their free and

---

[1] UN General Assembly, 61st Session, UN Doc. A/61/PV.107, 13 September 2007.

C. M. Doyle (✉)
Middlesex University School of Law, London, UK
e-mail: c.m.doyle@mdx.ac.uk

© Springer Nature Switzerland AG 2019
I. Feichtner et al. (eds.), *Human Rights in the Extractive Industries*,
Interdisciplinary Studies in Human Rights 3,
https://doi.org/10.1007/978-3-030-11382-7_8

informed consent (FPIC) to measures impacting on their rights and well-being.[2] In particular, objections were expressed to Articles 19 and 32 requiring FPIC "before adopting and implementing legislative or administrative measures that may affect them" and "prior to the approval of any project affecting their lands or territories and other resources, particularly in connection with the development, utilization or exploitation of mineral, water or other resources".[3]

Canada and the US finally endorsed the Declaration in 2010, but in so doing restated their positions on FPIC.[4] Canada objected to the principle of FPIC "when used as a veto", but stated that it was confident that it could now interpret it "in a manner that is consistent with its Constitution and legal framework".[5] Under the Harper government (2006–2015) Canada would not, however, clarify what it meant

---

[2] UN General Assembly, 61st Session, UN Doc. A/61/PV.107, 13 September 2007, pp. 11–12, 14; See also Hagen R, Explanation of vote on the Declaration on the Rights of Indigenous Peoples, U.S. Advisor, on the Declaration on the Rights of Indigenous Peoples, to the UN General Assembly, USUN Press Release #204(07), 13 September 2007.

[3] According to a joint 2006 statement of the US, New Zealand and Australia "there can be no absolute right of free, prior informed consent that is applicable uniquely to Indigenous peoples and that would apply regardless of circumstance", Statement of Vaughn P, On free, prior informed consent, 22 May 2006, http://unny.mission.gov.au/unny/soc_220506.html (last accessed 1 October 2018). The US also stated that "The text also could be misread to confer upon a sub-national group a power of veto over the laws of a democratic legislature by requiring indigenous peoples, free, prior and informed consent before passage of any law that "may" affect them (e.g., Article 19). We strongly support the full participation of indigenous peoples in democratic decision-making processes, but cannot accept the notion of a sub-national group having a "veto" power over the legislative process", Hagen R, Explanation of vote on the Declaration on the Rights of Indigenous Peoples, U.S. Advisor, on the Declaration on the Rights of Indigenous Peoples, to the UN General Assembly, USUN Press Release #204(07), 13 September 2007.

Canada explained its 2007 vote against the Declaration as, in part, deriving from significant concerns regarding "free, prior and informed consent when used as a veto", UN General Assembly, 61st Session, UN Doc. A/61/PV.107, 13 September 2007, p. 12. For an overview of the Canadian government's position at the time see Joffe (2010). See also UN Declaration on the Rights of Indigenous Peoples, Articles 19 and 32(2).

[4] Remarks by the President at the White House Tribal Nations Conference, The White House Office of the Press Secretary, December 16, 2010 https://obamawhitehouse.archives.gov/the-press-office/2010/12/16/remarks-president-white-house-tribal-nations-conference (last accessed 1 October 2018).

Announcement of U.S. Support for the United Nations Declaration on the Rights of Indigenous Peoples Initiatives to Promote the Government-to-Government Relationship & Improve the Lives of Indigenous Peoples, https://2009-2017.state.gov/s/srgia/154553.htm (last accessed 1 October 2018); Canada's Statement of Support on the United Nations Declaration on the Rights of Indigenous Peoples, 12 November 2010, http://www.aadnc-aandc.gc.ca/eng/1309374239861 (last accessed 26 January 2018).

[5] Canada's Statement of Support on the United Nations Declaration on the Rights of Indigenous Peoples, 12 November 2010, http://www.aadnc-aandc.gc.ca/eng/1309374239861 (last accessed 26 January 2018); Canada subsequently expressed its unqualified support for the UNDRIP in 2016, see UN Permanent Forum on Indigenous Issues, 16th Session, Speech for the Honourable Carolyn Bennett, Minister of Indigenous and Northern Affairs, 25 April 2017, https://www.canada.ca/en/indigenous-northern-affairs/news/2017/05/speaking_notes_forthehonourablecarolynbennettministerofindigenou.html (last accessed 1 October 2018).

by "veto" and refused to discuss this with Indigenous peoples.[6] In 2017, under the Trudeau government, Canada adopted a more constructive approach and formally retracted its concerns in relation to FPIC.[7]

In its qualified statement of support for the Declaration in 2011, the US recognized the significance of its provisions on FPIC with the caveat that it understood them "to call for a process of meaningful consultation with tribal leaders, but not necessarily the agreement of those leaders, before the actions addressed in those consultations are taken."[8] It committed to continued consultation with tribes "in accordance with federal law" and "where possible, ... obtaining the agreement of those tribes consistent with our democratic system and laws".[9]

The duty to consult with Indigenous peoples in the context of extractive or other development activities impacting on their rights and well-being is clearly established in Canadian and US law and policy, albeit differently in each jurisdiction.[10] In both jurisdictions, however, ambiguity remains regarding the nature of this duty to consult, including the degree to which Indigenous peoples' interests must be accommodated and the circumstances under which their consent may be required in the context of extractive industry projects. In order to fully appreciate the meaning and potential of this recent "support" for FPIC as articulated in the Declaration, it is therefore necessary to examine the legal frameworks governing Indigenous peoples' consultation and consent rights in these jurisdictions.

This chapter will focus on the primary areas where guidance on the duty to consult emerges in the two jurisdictions. It first addresses the US legislative, regulatory and jurisprudential context and then examines Canadian statutory requirements, the Federal Government's evolving position and the extensive body of Canadian jurisprudence on the topic. It offers a brief critique of the current situation with regard to

---

[6] Federal government representatives were not permitted to discuss the issue and it was therefore unclear if Canada understood "veto" to be synonymous with "consent" and "FPIC" as affirmed under IHRL, or if it regarded "veto" as an absolute right to say "no", irrespective of the facts and law in any given case.

[7] Bennett C, Speech at the United Nations Permanent Forum on Indigenous Issues. 16th Session: Opening Ceremony, 26 April 2017, https://www.canada.ca/en/indigenous-northern-affairs/news/2017/04/united_nations_permanentforumonindigenousissues16thsessionopenin.html (last accessed 1 October 2018). However, in 2016 Prime Minister Trudeau was reported as stating that indigenous peoples do not have a veto over energy projects, see Canadian Press, Trudeau says First Nations "don't have a veto" over energy projects, National Post, 20 December 2016, http://business.financialpost.com/news/trudeau-saysfirst-nations-dont-have-a-veto-over-energy-projects/wcm/a3b7313b-1c02-4769-84d0-96bceeba9d6a (last accessed 26 January 2018).

[8] Announcement of U.S. Support for the United Nations Declaration on the Rights of Indigenous Peoples Initiatives to Promote the Government-to-Government Relationship & Improve the Lives of Indigenous Peoples, https://2009-2017.state.gov/s/srgia/154553.htm (last accessed 1 October 2018).

[9] Announcement of U.S. Support for the United Nations Declaration on the Rights of Indigenous Peoples Initiatives to Promote the Government-to-Government Relationship & Improve the Lives of Indigenous Peoples, https://2009-2017.state.gov/s/srgia/154553.htm (last accessed 1 October 2018).

[10] McNeil (2009), p. 282; Richardson (2009), p. 54; Imai (2009), p. 302.

the duty to consult in each jurisdiction and concludes by addressing their incongruities from an international human rights law (IHRL) perspective and the steps that should be taken to align these national historically based legal regimes and doctrines with contemporary IHRL standards pertaining to FPIC.

2 Basis for and Content of the Duty to Consult in Canada and the US

The basis for the duty to consult under Canadian and US legal systems is found in treaty rights, jurisprudence addressing trust based and fiduciary responsibilities arising from colonial era international law doctrines, statutory requirements and administrative or regulatory requirements. Both Canada and the US have treaty based consultation requirements arising from the large body of treaties that were entered into with Indigenous peoples, primarily in the eighteenth and nineteenth centuries.[11] In both jurisdictions these treaties are granted constitutional protection. Indigenous peoples' rights established under historic and modern treaties are "recognized and affirmed" in the 1982 Canadian Constitution Act along with "Aboriginal rights".[12] Under the "supremacy clause" of the US Constitution treaties are classified as the "supreme law of the land", implying that they have the same force as federal laws, but leaving ambiguity as to the extent to which they are accepted as constitutional in nature.[13]

Similarly, in both Canada and the US, a trust or fiduciary duty has also been affirmed by the Courts, albeit interpreted differently in each jurisdiction, and provides an important basis for the duty to consult.[14] In Canada the fiduciary duty is embodied in Section 35 of the Constitution and arises from the sui generis nature of Aboriginal title as a property right to land, and the Crown's historic powers and responsibilities in relation to First Nations. It requires the Crown to act honourably, in the best interests of the First Nations and with "utmost loyalty".[15] The primary guidance on the content of the duty to consult flows from Canadian Supreme Court rulings addressing this fiduciary duty and the "special relationship" between the Crown and Aboriginal peoples as embodied in the principle of the "honour of the

---

[11] Williams (1999) and Prucha (1994).

[12] The Canadian Constitution Act, 1982, Sections 25 and 35. In negotiating s. 35(3) of the Constitution Act, 1982. Indigenous peoples took care to entrench their treaty rights and not the treaties themselves, as many of these treaties include "surrender" and/or "extinguishment" clauses that are at odds with IHLR principles. The Supreme Court of Canada has occasionally referred to such treaties as constitutional instruments, but without any legal analysis on this point. Communication from Joffe P on file with author.

[13] The Constitution of the United States, Article VI. For a commentary on the constitutional status of Indian treaties in federal courts see Fredericks and Heibel (2018).

[14] Supreme Court of Canada, Case no. 17507, *Guerin v. The Queen*, 2 S.C.R. 335.

[15] McNeil (2008).

Crown".[16] The Court has taken a broad approach, not only looking at compliance with statutory consultation obligations, but also expounding on the content of the common law duty to consult and Aboriginal rights under the 1982 Constitution. Based on this jurisprudence guidelines have been developed for federal officials on how to fulfil the duty to consult and legislative reviews are on-going to assess its compatibility with the UNDRIP.[17]

In the US, the federal trust based relationship with Indian tribes emerges from nineteenth century jurisprudence,[18] when Chief Justice Marshal affirmed that the "relation [of Indian tribes] to the United States resembles that of a ward to his guardian".[19] Together with statutory provisions and executive orders, this trust relationship constitutes the foundation for the duty to consult. The primary guidance in relation to the duty emerges from a combination of these provisions, administrative orders and jurisprudence addressing their implementation. In general, US Courts have only focused on whether consultations have complied with statutory requirements, rather than delve into the nature of the duty to consult itself.

The US and Canadian contexts also differ in a number of regards. In Canada constitutional recognition was afforded to Aboriginal rights in 1982, thereby restricting the potential for the legislature to extinguish rights,[20] unlike in the US where the only reference to tribes in the Constitution is found in the commerce clause. This clause has been problematically interpreted by the US Courts as supporting Congress's plenary power over Indian tribes, effectively providing it with the power to unilaterally extinguish tribal rights. Constitutional recognition in Canada also controversially opened the door for the Supreme Court to shape the content of Aboriginal rights. As a result, the Canadian Supreme Court has taken a more active role in addressing the content of and basis for the duty to consult, accommodate and potentially obtain consent of First Nations, which flows from their historical relationship with the Crown and the associated fiduciary duty.

A second differentiator between the US and Canada is that modern day treaties addressing land claims and self-governance rights have been under negotiation in Canada since the landmark *Calder v British Columbia* (1973) ruling.[21] In the US,

---

[16] Supreme Court of Canada, Case no. 29419, *Haida Nation v. British Columbia (Minister of Forests)*, SCC 73, 2004, para. 27.

[17] See discussion on Federal Government Initiatives below.

[18] The doctrine evolved from US Supreme Court jurisprudence in *Johnson v. McIntosh*, 21 U.S. 8 Wheat, 543, 1823; Case no. 42, *Cherokee Nation v. Georgia*, 30 U.S. 5 Pet. 1, 1831; Case no. 42, *Worcester v. Georgia*, 31 U.S. 6 Pet. 515, 1832.

[19] US Supreme Court, Case no. 42, *Cherokee Nation v. Georgia*, 30 U.S. 16-17, 1831. In 1941 the Supreme Court further expanded on this trust relationship clarifying that the US Federal Government had "charged itself with moral obligations of the highest responsibility and trust. Its conduct, as disclosed in the acts of those who represent it in dealing with the Indians, should therefore be judged by the most exacting fiduciary standards.", US Supreme Court, Case no. 348, *Seminole Nation v. United States*, 316 U.S. 286, pp. 296–297.

[20] For a commentary on rights extinguishment in Canada see McNeil (2002).

[21] Supreme Court of Canada, *Calder v. British Columbia*, S.C.R. 313, 4 W.W.R. 1.

land claims were effectively closed in 1978 with the termination of the controversial Indian Claims Commission which provided monetary compensation for non-consensual taking of tribal lands.[22] The situation with regard to unresolved land claims continues to have implications for consultation and consent duties in both jurisdictions.[23] A third differentiator is that self-government rights are generally afforded greater recognition in the US than in Canada, unless a self-government agreement has been negotiated.[24] An explicit right to self-government was not included in the Canadian Constitution and the Courts have yet to engage fully with the issue.[25] In the US, Indian tribes are recognized as maintaining a government-to-government relationship with the Federal government since the Nineteenth Century Marshall Supreme Court rulings. Finally, the political context in Canada changed significantly in 2015. A Liberal government advocating indigenous rights replaced the former Conservative government that had been strongly opposed to FPIC, and launched a number of initiatives reviewing statutory processes governing consultation and their alignment with the UNDRIP. Meanwhile, in the US the executive became significantly more hostile to indigenous peoples' consultation and consent rights in 2017 when President Trump replaced President Obama, offering promises and taking steps to fast track energy and extractive industry projects significantly impacting on tribes throughout the country.[26]

Given this context, the focus of the chapter differs significantly for the two jurisdictions. Greater emphasis is placed on the implementation of particular statutes and executive orders in the US context, while in the Canadian context the predominant focus is on the Supreme Court's evolving interpretation of the common law duty to consult and how this relates to FPIC under IHRL. The initiatives of the Canadian government to review its statutes and policies are also addressed, given their potentially important implications for FPIC recognition and implementation. In so doing, the chapter does not seek to compare the two jurisdictions. Instead, it seeks to engage with the issues that are of contemporary importance and relevance in each in the context of extractive industry activities in or near indigenous peoples' territories, while also offering suggestions applicable to both jurisdictions for a reformed approach to judicial, executive and legislative engagement with Indigenous peoples' rights.

---

[22] Richardson (2009), pp. 66–67.

[23] See discussion on the Western Shoshone case in the US, and the implications of recognition of Aboriginal title in the Canadian context, below.

[24] McNeil (1998a); Imai (2009); see also McNeil (1998b).

[25] Borrows (2015); Walters (2009), p. 49.

[26] As evidenced by the DAPL case, the order to the Secretary of State to expedite the review process for the Keystone XL Pipeline following the 24 January 2017, executive order inviting TransCanada to resubmit its permit application and the Resolution Copper Mine in Arizona impacting on cultural significant sites of the Sioux which the Trump administration is attempt to fast track.

3 US Context

3.1 Statutory Duty to Consult

In 1938, shortly after the Supreme Court recognized Indian ownership of subsoil resources in treaty and reservation lands,[27] the Indian Mineral Leasing Act (IMLA) was enacted to provide tribes with greater control over leasing processes for mining and oil and gas and to increase their revenues.[28] The Act requires consent of the tribal council and approval of the Secretary of the Interior for ten year mining leases on reservations. In 1982, the Indian Mineral Development Act (IMDA) (Melcher Act) was enacted enabling tribes to act as mineral developers on the basis that "Tribal autonomy and self-determination certainly should include the right to nego-tiate terms of contracts like any owner of valuable resources".[29] However, it is only in recent years that tribes have developed the legal and institutional capacity neces-sary to assert these rights and to negotiate fair agreements or block unwanted min-ing developments on tribal lands, which total some 48 million acres across the US.[30] Indeed, challenges remain for tribes to fully implement FPIC within their reserva-tions in accordance with their own customary laws and practices and their right to self-determination, with creative approaches being developed by tribes to this end.[31]

The consent requirement under the IMLA does not, however, apply to the vast traditional off-reservation territories that are now classified as Federal or public lands. The dispossession of tribes of these lands was based on "cession" in the form of land-surrender treaties entered into under duress, conquest in the context of the "Indian wars", or what effectively amounted to the application of the principle of terra nullius in the context of nomadic tribes.[32] This was compounded by the confis-cation of lands and extinguishment of Indian title by Congress under the plenary powers doctrine. These lands taken without consent total over 628 million acres, almost a third of the US landmass, and contain most of the areas of historical, cul-tural, religious or spiritual significance for Indian tribes.[33] As discussed below, under the extant legislative, regulatory and judicial frameworks, a duty to hold meaningful consultations, without an explicit associated duty to accommodate or

---

[27] US Supreme Court, Case no. 668, *United States v. Shoshone Tribe*, 304 U.S. 111.

[28] This followed the Indian Reorganization Act in 1934, which attempted to halt the widespread legislatively sanctioned dispossession of Indian lands.

[29] Hook and Banks (1993), quoting Senate Select Committee on Indian Affairs, Report S. REP. No. 472, 97th Cong., 2nd Sess., 1982.

[30] Ali et al. (2014).

[31] Fredericks (2016/2017), pp. 15–26.

[32] Williams (1990) and Borrows (1997).

[33] Galanda GS, The federal Indian consultation right: A frontline defense against tribal sovereignty incursion. Special Feature Article of the American Bar Association Federal Indian Law Newsletter Fall 2010, 2011, www.fedbar.org/Federal-Indian-Law (last accessed 1 October 2018), p. 2; Kinnison (2011), p. 1305.

obtain consent, applies in relation to extractive industry projects in these lands that impact on the rights of Indian tribes.[34]

Initial steps towards recognition of tribal self-determination and the requirement for consultations were taken in the late 1960s in response to the civil rights demands and mobilization of Native Americans[35] and were reflected in President Johnson's and Nixon's Special Messages to Congress on Indian Affairs in 1968 and 1970.[36] This in turn led the Bureau of Indian Affairs (BIA) to issue consultation guidelines in 1972.[37] The guidelines were limited to BIA personnel issues, and focused on information provision and on "obtaining the views of tribal governing bodies".[38] In 1975, the *Indian Self-Determination and Education Assistance Act*, which enabled the transfer of control of services from the BIA to Indian tribes, became the first legislative act to require consultations between federally recognized tribal governments and the Secretaries of the Interior, Health, Education, and Welfare in relation to its implementation.[39]

From the late 1960s to the 1990s, the duty to consult with indigenous peoples was affirmed in a number of US legislative acts addressing a broad range of issues, including the governance of natural resources.[40] Primary among these, in the context of natural resource extraction activities impacting on the rights of Indian tribes, were the *Archaeological Resources Protection Act* (1979),[41] the *Energy Policy* Act (1992),[42] the *National Environmental Policy Act* ("NEPA") (1969),[43] the *National Historic Preservation Act* ("NHPA") (1966, amended in 1992 to include properties of religious or cultural significance to tribes)[44] and the *Native American Graves Protection and Repatriation Act* (1990).[45] The latter, in addition to requiring consultation, also requires the consent of the appropriate Indian tribe for planned excavation

---

[34] Meaningful consultation is required under statutes, in particular where agencies are required to consult under Administrative Procedure Act (APA), Pub. L. 79-404, 60 Stat. 237, 1946.

[35] Imai (2009), pp. 288–289.

[36] Nixon R, Message from the President of the United States Transmitting Recommendations for Indian Policy, HR Doc. No. 91-363, 91st congress, 2nd Sess., 1970; Johnson L B, Special Message to Congress on the Problems of the American Indian: The Forgotten American, 1 Pub. Papers 336, 6 March 1968.

[37] The policy is quoted in US Court of Appeals, *Oglala Sioux Tribe of Indians v. Andrus*, 8th Cir. 1979, 603 F.2d 707, pp. 717–721.

[38] US Court of Appeals, *Oglala Sioux Tribe of Indians v. Andrus*, 8th Cir. 1979, 603 F.2d 707, pp. 717–721.

[39] The Act was amended in 1994 and incorporated into The Tribal Self-Governance Act of 1994, Pub. L. No. 103-413, 108 Stat. 4250.

[40] Haskew (1999), p. 21; There are at least 10 statutes requiring consultation, see Tsosie (2003), p. 285.

[41] Archaeological Resources Protection Act of 1979, 16 U.S.C., §§ 470aa–470mm, 2006.

[42] Energy Policy Act, 42 USC §§ 13201 et seq. Pub. L. No. 102-486, 1992.

[43] National Environmental Policy Act of 1969, 42 U.S.C., §§ 4321–4370, 2006.

[44] National Historic Preservation Act of 1966, 16 U.S.C., §§ 470 to 470x-6, 2006.

[45] Native American Graves Protection and Repatriation Act, 25 U.S.C., §§ 3001 et seq., 2006.

on tribal land.[46] This substantive consent requirement is exceptional in US legislative acts. Other statutes such as NEPA and NHPA are described as embodying a lesser requirement to "stop, look, and listen" with "agencies to consider how particular projects might affect the public interest" while also giving rise to "lenient standard[s] for granting a preliminary injunction".[47] They do not, however, constrain the federal agencies from prioritizing other concerns over tribal interests and do not contain a consent requirement irrespective of the extent of the impacts on tribal rights and interests.[48]

3.2 Regulation and Executive Orders Addressing the Duty to Consult

These and other legislative acts therefore impose a procedural obligation to consult on the four primary agencies responsible for managing federal lands, namely the Bureau of Land Management (BLM), the Fish and Wildlife Service, the National Park Service, and the Forest Service. They are accompanied by regulatory rules and guidance pertaining to consultation requirements issued by the administrative agencies responsible for their implementation. For example, the NHPA explicitly delegates authority to the Advisory Council on Historic Preservation (ACHP), an independent agency of the US government, to promulgate regulations interpreting and implementing its section 106 addressing consultations. The Council's guidelines build on the NHPA definition of consultations as

> the process of seeking, discussing, and considering the views of other participants, and, where feasible, seeking agreement with them regarding matters arising in the section 106 process.[49]

They clarify that "tribal consultation should commence early in the planning process" and that the agency "shall ensure that consultation provides the Indian tribe a reasonable opportunity to identify its concerns about historic properties" and to "participate in the resolution of adverse effects".[50] Consultations are to be "respectful of tribal sovereignty" and to "recognize the government-to-government relationship that exists between the Federal Government and federally recognized Indian tribes".[51] They also state that an Indian tribe "may enter into an agreement

---

[46] Native American Graves Protection and Repatriation Act, 25 U.S.C., §§ 3001 et seq., 2006.

[47] US Court of Appeals, Nos. 92-15635, 92-16288, 9th Cir. 1994, *Apache Survival Coalition v. United States*, 21 F.3d 895, p. 906.

[48] Kinnison (2011), p. 1311; Haskew (1999), p. 24.

[49] National Historic Preservation Act, 36 CFR Section 800.16 (f).

[50] Advisory Council on Historic Preservation, Consultation with Indian Tribes in the Section 106 Review Process: A Handbook, 25 November 2008, p. 7.

[51] Advisory Council on Historic Preservation, Consultation with Indian Tribes in the Section 106 Review Process: A Handbook, 25 November 2008, p. 8.

with a federal agency regarding any aspect of tribal participation in the review process…provided that no modification is made to the roles of other parties without their consent".[52] In 2013, the Council reportedly committed to incorporating the principle of FPIC in its programmes, policies and initiatives.[53] In 2017, responding to issues raised by tribal representatives in relation to the lack of a consent requirement in section 106, the ACHP noted that requiring FPIC in NHPA would necessitate congressional action.[54]

Similarly, the implementing regulations for NEPA require that when tribal interests may be affected by a project, Indian tribes be invited at the outset of the process to participate in the scoping exercises.[55] Orders issued by the secretariats responsible for the *Endangered Species Act of 1973* require consultations "when actions taken under authority of the Act and associated implementing regulations affect, or may affect, Indian lands, tribal trust resources, or the exercise of American Indian tribal rights".[56] In such an event, in keeping with the government-to-government relationship, the government departments are required to

> consult with, and seek the participation of, the affected Indian tribes to the maximum extent practicable. This shall include providing affected tribes adequate opportunities to participate in data collection, consensus seeking, and associated processes.[57]

Implementation of these consultation requirements is not homogenous across statutes and agencies, and compliance with the consultation requirements of one statute, such as NEPA, will not necessarily imply compliance with the consultation requirements of another statute, such as NHPA. Differences extend to who is to be consulted, with NEPA requiring government-to-government consultation with federally recognized tribal leaders, while NHPA requires consultation with federally recognized tribal leaders, traditional cultural leaders and other pertinent knowledge holders.[58] Furthermore, under both these statutes multiple federal agencies may be mandated to consult with Indian tribes in the context of a single project, and may or may not decide to designate a single agency to coordinate consultations. A degree

---

[52] Advisory Council on Historic Preservation, Consultation with Indian Tribes in the Section 106 Review Process: A Handbook, 25 November 2008, p. 7.

[53] UN Human Rights Council, Report of the Special Rapporteur on the rights of indigenous people on her mission to the United States of America, UN Doc. A/HRC/36/46/Add.1, 36th session, 9 August 2017, para. 23.

[54] Advisory Council on Historic Preservation, Improving Tribal Consultation in Infrastructure Projects, 24 May 2017, http://www.achp.gov/docs/achp-infrastructure-report.pdf (last accessed 1 October 2018), p. 4.

[55] US federal Government, Code of Federal Regulation, Title 40, §1501.7(a)(1); see also Bureau Land Management National Environmental Policy Act, Handbook H-1790-1, § 6.3.2.

[56] US Fish and Wildlife Service, Working with Tribes|American Indian Tribal Rights, Federal-Tribal Trust Responsibilities, and the Endangered Species Act, https://www.fws.gov/endangered/what-we-do/tribal-secretarial-order.html (last accessed 1 October 2018).

[57] US Fish and Wildlife Service, Working with Tribes|American Indian Tribal Rights, Federal-Tribal Trust Responsibilities, and the Endangered Species Act, https://www.fws.gov/endangered/what-we-do/tribal-secretarial-order.html (last accessed 1 October 2018).

[58] Stern (2009), p. 11.

of inconsistency and ambiguity also appears to exist over when consultation processes have to be conducted. In the name of flexibility, NHPA's ACHP regulations require consultations before the issuance of a license or permit, before approval of federal funding, or prior to ground-disturbing activities.[59]

In addition to these legislative acts and their implementing rules addressing the duty to consult, successive US presidents have issued executive orders (EOs) and memoranda addressing the measures to be taken by government agencies in accordance with the duty. Most notable among these are EO 13007 (1996) on Indian Sacred Sites[60] and EO 13175 (2000) requiring "meaningful consultation" issued under the Clinton administration together with the 2009 *Presidential Memorandum on Tribal Consultation* issued under the Obama administration which sought to give effect to EO 13175.[61] The latter executive order is significant in so far as it extends the Federal Government's consultation duty across the entire spectrum of the federal trust responsibility and resulted in the promulgation of consultation policies across the agencies of the Department of the Interior.[62] The stated objective of EO 13175 is

> to establish regular and meaningful consultation and collaboration with tribal officials in the development of Federal policies that have tribal implications, to strengthen the United States government-to-government relationships with Indian tribes, and to reduce the imposition of unfunded mandates upon Indian tribes.[63]

These orders are consequently broader in scope and more ambitious in their wording than existing statutory provisions, which tend to be limited to services or activities impacting on religious or cultural sites.[64] This principled approach to encouraging "meaningful consultation" is also reflected in guidance provided by the Attorney General on working together with Federally Recognized Indian Tribes.[65] It includes commitments by the Department of Justice to honour and strive "to act in accordance with the general trust relationship between the United States and tribes" and to further the government-to-government relationship with each tribe. The Department also commits to respect and support tribes' authority to exercise their inherent sovereign powers, including powers over ... their territory", to respect

---

[59] Stern (2009), p. 8.

[60] 61 Fed. Reg. 26771, 24 May 1996.

[61] Executive Order 13175, Consultation and Coordination with Indian Tribal Governments, 6 November 2000; Presidential Memorandum on Tribal Consultation, 5 November 2009.

[62] Haskew (1999), p. 74.

[63] Executive Order 13175, Consultation and Coordination with Indian Tribal Governments, 6 November 2000.

[64] Routel and Holth (2013), p. 450.

[65] See Office of the Attorney General, Attorney General Guidelines Stating Principles for Working With Federally Recognized Indian Tribes, Notice, Federal Register, Vol. 79, No. 239, at 73905–73906, 12 December 2014, Department of Justice, http://www.gpo.gov/fdsys/pkg/FR-2014-12-12/pdf/2014-28903.pdf (last accessed 1 October 2018).

tribal self-determination and autonomy and to promote and pursue the objectives of the UNDRIP.[66]

The executive orders have, however, been criticized on a number of grounds. One concern is that their content was not subject to consultation, a reality at odds with their stated aim.[67] Another is the absence of clear and enforceable obligations on federal agencies, as they stipulate that they do not grant or vest any right to any party, and their failure to adequately define what is meant by consultation and when the duty is triggered.[68] A related critique of the consultation processes pursuant to these executive orders and administrative regulations is that they create confusion by establishing a "non-binding"/"non-enforceable"/"non-remedial" consultation requirement, in addition to the binding/enforceable/remedial duty that flows from statutory consultation provisions.[69] As a result, the use of the single term "consulta-tion" for two apparently distinct requirements can cause confusion and may be counterproductive to the development of good faith relationships that are necessary for meaningful and effective consultations, potentially even giving rise to "bureau-cratic abuse and breach of faith".[70] This confusion is compounded by the Courts which in some instances have deemed administrative based consultation require-ments, such as those in the BIA guidelines, to be enforceable, while in other instances have affirmed the opposite in relation to the same administrative consulta-tion requirement.[71] This ambiguity is further compounded by the ad-hoc manner in which federal agencies implement consultations under the latest executive order.[72]

While the executive orders mention the government-to-government trust rela-tionship their silence on its implications has also been criticized. The fact that gov-ernment agencies can claim to have fulfilled their obligations toward Indigenous peoples by compliance with purely procedural and unenforceable processes is regarded as introducing the potential for consultations to sanction and legitimize incremental and systematic breaches of Indigenous rights instead of fulfilling their trust and fiduciary responsibilities.[73]

---

[66] See Office of the Attorney General, Attorney General Guidelines Stating Principles for Working With Federally Recognized Indian Tribes, Notice, Federal Register, Vol. 79, No. 239, at 73905–73906, 12 December 2014, Department of Justice, http://www.gpo.gov/fdsys/pkg/FR-2014-12-12/pdf/2014-28903.pdf (last accessed 1 October 2018).

[67] Haskew (1999), p. 33.

[68] Haskew (1999), p. 33.

[69] Haskew (1999), p. 62; Routel and Holth (2013), p. 451.

[70] Haskew (1999), p. 41.

[71] US Court of Appeals, *Oglala Sioux Tribe of Indians v. Andrus*, No. CIV 95-3034, 8th Cir. 1979, 603 F.2d, p. 721, versus, US District Court for the District of South Dakota, *Lower Brule Sioux Tribe v. Deer*, 911 F. Supp. 395, 1995, p. 400.

[72] UN Human Rights Council, Report of the Special Rapporteur on the rights of indigenous people on her mission to the United States of America, UN Doc. A/HRC/36/46/Add.1, 36th session, 9 August 2017, para. 16.

[73] Wood (1995a), p. 749.

3.3　US Jurisprudence and the Duty to Consult

A similar critique can be levied at the US Courts which have done little to clarify the substantive obligations and protections that the fiduciary duty could give rise to (beyond those specified in statutes) in the context of consultations pertaining to activities impacting on tribal rights, such as large scale extractive and energy industry projects.[74] In the US context, the basis for the Federal Government's trust relationship with tribes emerges from three rulings of Chief Justice Marshall, known as the Marshall Trilogy, issued between 1823 and 1832.[75] In these rulings, Marshall offered his interpretation of international law (then referred to as the law of nations) and the so-called 'doctrine of discovery' and the common law trust relationship it implied.[76] As noted earlier, according to Marshall, the relationship of native peoples "to the United States resembles that of a ward to his guardian".[77] Consequently, the Federal Government had a duty to protect the Indian tribes from states and individuals seeking access to, or control over, their lands. The Court recognized the inherent sovereignty of the tribes which continued following colonialization, albeit in diminished form.[78] Subsequent Supreme Court rulings clarified that this trust relationship constitutes a fiduciary duty in relation to tribal lands and resources.[79]

The Supreme Court's perspective on the implications of this trust, or fiduciary, responsibility evolved over time.[80] In the Marshall decisions, this responsibility is the corollary of inherent sovereignty and territorial rights of native peoples that were limited by, but nevertheless continued to be recognized under, colonial doctrines. Subsequently, during the late nineteenth and early twentieth centuries, the trust responsibility was construed as a means to deny those rights and to consequently deem consultation and consent unnecessary when appropriating Indian Lands.[81] This understanding was given legislative effect in 1871 in the Indian Appropriation Act when Congress officially halted the practice of treaty-making with Indian Nations.[82] The 1886 ruling in *U.S. v. Kagama* represented a further weakening of tribal sovereignty, classifying tribes as being in a state of pupillage and as wards of the State and extending and entrenching Congressional power over them.[83] This was compounded in 1903 by the US Supreme Court in *Lone Wolf v*

---

[74] Tsosie (2003), p. 290; see also Wood (1995b), p. 132.

[75] US Supreme Court jurisprudence in *Johnson v. McIntosh*, 21 U.S. 8 Wheat, 543, 1823; Case no. 42, *Cherokee Nation v. Georgia*, 30 U.S. 5 Pet. 1, 1831; Case no. 42, *Worcester v. Georgia*, 31 U.S. 6 Pet. 515, 1832.

[76] Anaya (2004), pp. 23–26; Williams (1999), p. 132; Williams (1990).

[77] US Supreme Court, *Cherokee Nation v. Georgia* 30 U.S. 5 Pet. 1, 1831, p. 17.

[78] US Supreme Court, *U.S. v. Kagama*, 1886, p. 118 U.S. 375.

[79] US Supreme Court, Case no. 72-1052, *Morton v. Ruiz*, 1974, p. 415 U.S. 199; US Supreme Court, Case no. 830, *Seminole Nation v. U.S.*, 1942, p. 316 U.S. 286.

[80] Ezra (1989); Riley (2011), pp. 207–208; Fletcher (2012), pp. 83–84; Williams (2005), pp. 47–122.

[81] US Supreme Court, Case no. 275, *Lone Wolf v. Hitchcock*, 1903, p. 187 U.S. 553.

[82] Indian Appropriations Act 1871, (and as amended later) 25 U.S.C. Section 71.

[83] US Supreme Court, *U.S. v. Kagama*, 1886, p. 118 U.S. 375.

Hitchcock—a case taken by Native Americans against the US government—which put an end to the notion that Indian consent was necessary prior to selling "surplus" tribal lands.[84] The rationale of the Court was that plenary power of Congress—which flowed from the dependant nature of Indian tribes and their trust relationship with the Federal Government and the Constitution's Commerce Clause[85]—could not be limited by a treaty and that the selling of Indian trust lands was "a mere change in the form of investment".[86] Indeed, in the face of the Indian arguments that the US had never taken land from tribes without their consent, the Court went so far as to reason that requiring their consent could be detrimental to the tribes well-being, as this was something which Congress was best placed to determine.[87] The guardian-ward relationship consequently had become a basis for Congress to deem Indian consent to be irrelevant in relation to disposing of their lands and resources, in particular their timber and mineral resources.[88]

In the modern "era of self-determination", recognition of Indian tribes' right to self-determination is nevertheless closely linked with the affirmation under Marshall era jurisprudence that they retain "those aspects of sovereignty not withdrawn by treaty or statute" and exist as "distinct political [societies], separated from others, capable of managing [their] own affairs and governing [themselves]".[89] While deficient in terms of IHRL recognition of indigenous peoples' right to self-determination, it does acknowledge their potentially significant self-determination based powers over the regulation of criminal justice, tribal membership and property, provided Congress does not regulate to limit those powers.[90] It also establishes the basis for the duty to consult. Federal Courts have addressed this duty on a number of occasions since self-determination was recognized as a policy objective. They have affirmed that the duty under federal common law arises from the trust relationship between the Federal Government and Indian tribes and extends to both on and off

---

[84] US Supreme Court, Case no. 275, *Lone Wolf v. Hitchcock*, 1903, p. 187 U.S. 553.

[85] US Supreme Court, Case no. 275, *Lone Wolf v. Hitchcock*, 1903, p. 187 U.S. 553, 565, Article I, Section 8, Clause 3, the Commerce Clause addresses the role of Congress in regulating commerce with Indian tribes. The Court in *Lone Wolf* interpreted this clause as providing Congress with political power over tribes that is "not subject to be controlled by the judicial department of the government".

[86] US Supreme Court, Case no. 275, *Lone Wolf v. Hitchcock*, 1903, p. 187 U.S. 553, 568; see also Miller (2015), p. 49; Fletcher (2012), p. 74.

[87] US Supreme Court, Case no. 275, *Lone Wolf v. Hitchcock*, 1903, p. 187 U.S. 553, 564.

[88] Routel and Holth (2013), p. 429.

[89] US Supreme Court, *Cherokee Nation v. Georgia*, 1831, 30 U.S. 5 Pet. 1, p. 17; Tsosie (2012), pp. 936–948; Imai (2009), pp. 293–294.

[90] The precarious and limited nature of tribal sovereignty, and by extension the duty to consult, is evident in US Supreme Court, Case no. 76-1629, *US v. Wheeler*, 1987, p. 435 US 313, 323, which held that tribal sovereignty "exists only at the sufferance of Congress and is subject to complete defeasance" and that "Indian tribes still possess those aspects of sovereignty not withdrawn by treaty or statute". It has also been argued that the trust doctrine should condition plenary power, see Skibine (2003).

reservation lands.[91] They also have clarified that the failure to comply with statutory consultation obligations constitutes a violation of trust duties,[92] and that the existence of a treaty implies a duty to consult under federal common law, irrespective of whether the treaty explicitly affirms this duty.[93]

In cases related to sewer construction, timber, geothermal, mining and hydroelectric projects, the US Courts have found both for and against tribes who challenged the compliance of government agencies with NHPA section 106, NEPA and other statutory consultation requirements.[94] In some cases sufficient studies demonstrating the non-existence of cultural resources were deemed to have satisfied consultation requirements,[95] while in others information provision was deemed inadequate to meet the criteria for informed consultations.[96] Courts have also held that the production of a large volume of documentation does not necessarily prove meaningful consultation occurred.[97] In cases of procedural breaches, where the "substantive duty" to consult on a government-to-government basis was not met, injunctive relief was available if irreparable harm was demonstrated and the injunction was deemed to be in the public interest.[98] Such injunctions have been issued in order to protect tribal resources such as timber.[99] In addition to granting injunctive relief, Courts have, on at least one occasion, issued a Writ of Mandamus, ordering

---

[91] *Klamath Tribes*, WL 924509, 1996, p. 8.

[92] US Court of Appeals, Case nos. 98-35043, 98-35231, *Muckleshoot Indian Tribe v. U.S. Forest Services*, 1999, 177 F.3d 800; US Court of Appeals, Case no. 13-16961, *Pit River Tribe v. U. S. Forest* Service, 2006, 469 F.3d 768.

[93] US District Court of Eastern District of Washington, Case no. 10-3050, *Confederated Tribes and Bands of the Yakama Nation v. U.S. Department of Agriculture*, 2010, WL 3434091; see also Galanda GS, The federal Indian consultation right: A frontline defense against tribal sovereignty incursion. Special Feature Article of the American Bar Association Federal Indian Law Newsletter Fall 2010, 2011, www.fedbar.org/Federal-Indian-Law (last accessed 1 October 2018), p. 9.

[94] For example in US Court of Appeals, Case nos. 98-35043, 98-35231, *Muckleshoot Indian Tribe v. U.S. Forest Services*, 1999, 177 F.3d 800 and US Court of Appeals, Case no. 13-16961, *Pit River Tribe v. U. S. Forest* Service, 2006, 469 F.3d 768, the Courts found in favour of the tribes while no breach of NEPA consultation requirements was found in, US Court of Appeals, Case no. 07-16336, *Te-Moak Tribe of W. Shoshone v. U.S. Dep't of the Interior*, 608 F.3d 592, 9th Cir., 2010, pp. 608–610; US Court of Appeals, Case nos. 05-72739, 05-74060, *Snoqualmie Indian Tribe v. Fed. Energy Regulatory Comm'n.*, 545 F.3d 1207, 9th Cir., 2008, pp. 1215–1216 and US Court of Appeals, Case no. 0 2-2672, *Narragansett Indian Tribe v. Warwick Sewer Auth.*, 334 F.3d 161, 1st Cir., 2003.

[95] US Court of Appeals, Case no. 93-36130, *Native Americans for Enola v. US Forest Service*, 832 F. Supp. 297, 1995.

[96] US Court of Appeals, Case no. 93-2188, *Pueblo of Sandia v. United States*, 50 F.3d, 1995, p. 857.

[97] US District Court, S.D. California, Case no. 10cv2241-LAB (CAB), *Quechan Tribe of the Fort Yuma Reservation v. U.S. Dep't of the Interior*, 755 F. Supp. 2d 1104, 2010, pp. 1118–119, 1122.

[98] US Court of Appeals, *Oglala Sioux Tribe of Indians v. Andrus*, No. CIV 95-3034, 8th Cir. 1979, 603 F.2d; *Klamath Tribes*, WL 924509, 1996; and US District Court of Eastern District of Washington, Case no. 10-3050, *Confederated Tribes and Bands of the Yakama Nation v. U.S. Department of Agriculture*, 2010, WL 3434091.

[99] *Klamath Tribes*, WL 924509, 1996; see also US District Court, S.D. California, Case no. 10cv2241-LAB (CAB), *Quechan Tribe of the Fort Yuma Reservation v. U.S. Dep't of the Interior*, 755 F. Supp. 2d 1104, 2010, pp. 1118–1119, 1122.

federal agencies to consult.[100] Courts, moreover, have held that increased tribal control over their resources implied an increased responsibility on the tribes' part, and lessened the fiduciary responsibilities of the Federal Government in relation to information provision.[101]

Another feature of Court decisions is their finding that consultation outcomes do not necessarily have to be respected, in particular where a "substantial burden" is not placed on the tribes,[102] and that Native traditional religious considerations do not "always prevail to the exclusion of all else".[103] In one instance this was held to be the case even when an Environmental Impact Assessment had recognized the difficult-to-assess, but nevertheless irretrievable impact a project could have on tribal beliefs and practices.[104]

The question of the extent to which government agencies are obliged to comply with their own consultation policies and guidelines has also come before a number of Courts of Appeal, but their findings have been inconsistent. One Court held that the BIA's failure to comply with its consultation policy "violate[d] 'the distinctive obligation of trust incumbent upon the Government in its dealings with these dependent and sometimes exploited people'",[105] while another Court (at the same level, but covering different geographical districts) held that the same consultation guidelines "do not establish legal standards that can be enforced against the Bureau".[106]

---

[100] See order in relation to the BIA in US District Court for the District of South Dakota, Case no. CIV 95-3034, *Lower Brule Sioux Tribe v. Deer*, 1995, p. 911 F. Supp. 395; see also Galanda GS, The federal Indian consultation right: A frontline defense against tribal sovereignty incursion. Special Feature Article of the American Bar Association Federal Indian Law Newsletter Fall 2010, 2011, www.fedbar.org/Federal-Indian-Law (last accessed 1 October 2018), p. 6.

[101] US Supreme Court, Case no. 01-1375, *United States v. Navajo Nation*, 203, p. 537 U.S. 488, see also Pevar SL, The federal-tribal trust relationship, Its origin, nature, and scope, 2009, http://www.saige.org/conf/12CO/TrustResponsibilityOutline%20SAIGE2012.doc (last accessed 28 January 2018).

[102] US Court of Appeals, Case nos. 81-1905, 81-1912, 81-1956, 82-1705, 82-1706 and 82-1725, *Wilson v. Block*, 1983, 708 F.2d 735, pp. 745–747, 464 U.S. 956; quoting U.S. District Court for the District of Arizona, Case no. Civ. 88-971 PHX-RGS, *Havasupai v. United States*, 1990, p. 752 F. Supp. 1471.

[103] US Court of Appeals, Case nos. 06-15371, 06-15436, 06-15455, *Navajo Nation v. United States Forest Service*, 2007, 479 F.3d 1024, p. 1063. For a commentary on the weakness of protections under the Act see Tsosie (2003), p. 289.

[104] US Court of Appeals, Case nos. 06-15371, 06-15436, 06-15455, *Navajo Nation v. United States Forest Service*, 2007, 479 F.3d 1024, pp. 1039, 1043, 1059.

[105] US Court of Appeals, *Oglala Sioux Tribe of Indians v. Andrus*, 8th Cir. 1979, 603 F.2d 707, para. 63; the Court was quoting from US Supreme Court, Case no. 72-1052, *Morton v. Ruiz*, 1974, p. 415 U.S. 199, 236; which in turn was quoting US Supreme Court, Case no. 348, *Seminole Nation v. United States*, 1942, p. 316 U.S. 286, 296.

[106] US Court of Appeals, Case no. 86-2861, *Hoopa Valley Tribe v. Christie*, 1986, 812, 1099 F.2d; see also Haskew (1999), p. 72, fn. 259.

3.4   Observations on Duty to Consult Under US Indian Law

The relatively small number of cases and the limited extent to which they address the duty to consult, along with the at times inconsistent findings of the Courts, make it difficult to draw clear conclusions from the case law as to the protections afforded by statutory consultation requirements and the trust doctrine. Rulings addressing the procedural aspects of consultations indicate that failure to consult with appropriate authorities, consult prior to decision-making, conduct adequate investigations in relation to the possible impacts, or provide available information, are all grounds for deeming that the duty to consult has not been adequately fulfilled. However, the lack of clear and uniform guidance as to what constitutes "meaningful consultation" means the threshold for some of these criteria remains somewhat obscure. While indirectly implying that consultation outcomes may have to be respected in some contexts,[107] there is little or no guidance in relation to accommodation of tribal interests or contexts when consent may be required. In addition, the notion that increased tribal control over decision-making lessens State obligations to inform tribes about facts affecting their right to benefit from projects is problematic from the perspective of a self-determination based duty to consult in order to obtain FPIC.

Other issues arise in relation to judicial review. The only substantive grounds upon which tribes can mount a judicial challenge to final decisions reached by US federal agencies is on the basis that those decisions were arbitrary, capricious or an abuse of discretion, as established in the Administrative Procedure Act (APA).[108] This is a limited recourse for two reasons. Firstly, it only applies at the end of the consultation process when a final decision has been reached and secondly the threshold of arbitrariness, capriciousness or abuse of discretion is very high.[109] The Dakota Access Pipeline (DAPL) case, discussed below, is illustrative of these limitations.[110] This situation gives rise to the general view that judicial review is unavailable in many cases where it is needed. Judicial review is furthermore restricted because provisions in executive orders negate judicial review and inconsistent Court rulings exist on their implications.[111] Restrictions also arise from failure of these orders to adequately contextualize the duty to consult within the broader framework

---

[107] US Court of Appeals, Case nos. 81-1905, 81-1912, 81-1956, 82-1705, 82-1706 and 82-1725, *Wilson v. Block*, 1983, 708 F.2d 735, pp. 745–747, 464 U.S. 956; quoting U.S. District Court for the District of Arizona, Case no. Civ. 88-971 PHX-RGS, *Havasupai v. United States*, 1990, p. 752 F. Supp. 1471; and US Court of Appeals, Case nos. 06-15371, 06-15436, 06-15455, *Navajo Nation v. United States Forest Service*, 2007, 479 F.3d 1024, p. 1063.

[108] Administrative Procedure Act (APA), Pub.L. 79–404, 60 Stat. 237 (1946); 5 U.S.C. §§ 551 to 599. The APA provides the necessary waiver of sovereign immunity to take a suit which other statutes do not provide.

[109] US Supreme Court, Case no. 82-354, *Motor Vehicle Mfrs. Ass'n of U.S., Inc. v. State Farm Mut. Auto. Ins. Co.*, 1983, p. 463 U.S. 29, 43.

[110] For an overview of the DAPL case see Fredericks and Heibel (2018).

[111] The Eight Circuit Court's rulings are an exception in relation to the BIA consultation guidelines.

of the Federal Government trust relationship with tribes,[112] and the prevalent judicial interpretation in the lower courts that the waiver of sovereign immunity is necessary in order for the right to consultation to be subject to judicial review unless it is tied to the violation of a specific statute.[113]

The fact that Supreme Court decisions have historically frequently been unfavourable to tribal sovereignty and are uninformed by IHRL is also relevant when considering the judicial position on the duty to consult.[114] The colonial doctrine basis upon which the Court continues to interpret and restrict tribal sovereignty does not bode well for the prospect of an empowering self-determination based duty to consult to emerge from its jurisprudence.[115] Indeed, the absence of an explicit acknowledgement that government agencies should, under certain circumstances, adhere to the wishes and decisions of tribes in relation to off-reservation measures that could significantly impact on their rights and interests is evidence of this. It is reflective of a core issue with tribal consultations in the US, namely that they are predominately procedural in nature with little emphasis placed on respecting their outcomes. This is coupled with an apparent lack of sensitivity in the judicial system and federal agencies to the importance of protecting tribal rights and cultural resources.[116] Despite these limitations, it has been argued that the 1995 US Appeal Court opinion in *Pueblo of Sandia v. United States* "indicates the federal courts should provide strong judicial review of agency actions [including consultations] under NHPA Section 106".[117] It has also been suggested that through greater proactive insistence on consultation, indigenous peoples can ensure that trust obligations are fulfilled in contexts where they would otherwise be systematically breached.[118] Another suggestion is that federal agencies establish independent mediation mecha-

---

[112] Routel and Holth (2013), p. 435.

[113] In general, the US government enjoys sovereign immunity from lawsuits unless it consents to waive that immunity. The government has included a limited waiver of immunity under the Indian Tucker Act 28 U.S.C. § 1505 (2006) provided the "claim is one arising under the Constitution, laws or treaties of the United States, or Executive orders of the President, or is one which otherwise would be cognizable in the Court of Federal Claims if the claimant were not an Indian tribe, band, or group". As Routel and Holth point out, this "should have no impact on tribal claims for declaratory or injunctive relief for breaches of the trust responsibility" as the Supreme Court has held that "no waiver of sovereign immunity is required if a plaintiff claims that a federal official has violated federal law (including federal common law) provided that the plaintiff names the federal official, rather than the agency itself, as the defendant". However, lower level courts have failed to make this distinction, thereby failing to "recognize the federal government's enforceable common law duty to consult with Indian tribes before taking actions that may impact them", see Routel and Holth (2013), p. 449.

[114] Williams (2005), pp. 186–194; Richardson (2009), p. 79.

[115] Williams (2005), pp. 193–194; Richardson (2009), p. 79; Imai (2009), p. 314.

[116] Wood (1995b), p. 221; Tsosie (2003), p. 289.

[117] Stern (2009), p. 12.

[118] Galanda GS, The federal Indian consultation right: A frontline defense against tribal sovereignty incursion. Special Feature Article of the American Bar Association Federal Indian Law Newsletter Fall 2010, 2011, www.fedbar.org/Federal-Indian-Law (last accessed 1 October 2018), p. 7.

nisms where tribes withhold consent.[119] Others regard a change from current consultation processes to FPIC as posing few challenges in the US context.[120] However, many continue to hold that despite improvements in consultation processes in recent decades, tribes remain deeply dissatisfied as they lack an effective voice in decision-making in relation to lands and resources in close proximity to their reservations as well as off-reservation lands and resources which they have traditionally or otherwise used or with which they maintain important spiritual or cultural connections.[121] This absence of a say over if, or how, off-reservation extractive and energy projects that impact on their rights and way of life, proceed is compounded by the frequent failure to realize the standard of meaningful good faith informed consultation in such contexts. Coupled with the general absence of judicial review of consultation procedures and the need to first exhaust administrative remedies, this situation contributes to the denial of basic protections for land, cultural and self-governance rights.[122]

This view is echoed in the 2017 US country mission report of the UN Special Rapporteur on the rights of indigenous peoples (UNSRIP) which focused on the energy sector. The Rapporteur found "few examples of meaningful consultation in the context of energy projects in the United States" and highlighted the need for a shift to an approach based on consultations in order to obtain FPIC rather than consultations as an end unto themselves.[123] The Rapporteur expressed particular concern in relation to the Dakota Access Pipeline (DAPL), an emblematic case that highlights deficiencies in the US consultation law, policy and practice in the context of potential impacts of energy projects on tribes.[124] The pipeline crosses the Great Sioux Nation traditional territories and treaty lands, comes within a kilometre of one of their reservations and has generated concerns with regard to its impact on sacred areas and tribal water supply.[125] The environmental assessment prepared by the Army Corps of Engineers in accordance with NEPA failed to address all these concerns when assessing the pipeline route.[126] Large scale protests ensued, involving all bands of the Great Sioux Nation and other indigenous peoples from around

---

[119] Kinnison (2011), p. 1332.

[120] Miller (2015), p. 38.

[121] Fishel (2007b), p. 621; Haskew (1999), p. 74; Miller (2015), p. 67; Kinnison (2011), p. 1323; Bluemel (2005), p. 529; Imai (2009), p. 302.

[122] Haskew (1999), p. 62.

[123] UN Human Rights Council, Report of the Special Rapporteur on the rights of indigenous peoples on her mission to the United States of America, UN Doc. A/HRC/36/46/Add.1, 36th session, 9 August 2017, para. 27.

[124] UN Human Rights Council, Report of the Special Rapporteur on the rights of indigenous people on her mission to the United States of America, UN Doc. A/HRC/36/46/Add.1, 36th session, 9 August 2017, paras. 63–74.

[125] UN Human Rights Council, Report of the Special Rapporteur on the rights of indigenous people on her mission to the United States of America, UN Doc. A/HRC/36/46/Add.1, 36th session, 9 August 2017, para. 64.

[126] US District Court for the District of Columbia, Civil Action, Case no. 16-1534 (JEB), *Standing Rock Sioux Tribe, et al., v. U.S. Army Corps of Engineers, et al*, 2017, p. 66.

the world, as well as climate change activists.[127] Private security forces and local law enforcement adopted a militarized and at times violent approach in response, arresting tribal members and protesters, some of whom remain in custody.[128]

According to the concerned tribes, the protests, which were largely non-violent, led to more constructive consultations and the promise by the Army Corps to conduct an environmental review in relation to easements.[129] The review was, however, cancelled following a directive by President Donald Trump, on 24 January 2017, enabling the pipeline to become operational, and according to the tribes, leading to the destruction of sacred areas.[130] In July 2017, the Columbia District Court found that the Army Corps had failed to adequately address the "impacts of an oil spill on fishing rights, hunting rights, or environmental justice, or the degree to which the pipeline's effects are likely to be highly controversial."[131] At the same time, the Court found that statutory consultation processes under section 106 of NHPA had been adequately fulfilled, despite tribal claims that attempts to consult them were made after key decisions relating to the pipeline route had already been taken, and that their request to conduct their own archaeological survey went unheeded.[132] The case demonstrates the piecemeal and disjointed nature of US consultation laws, policies, procedures and practices, the failure to involve tribes in a timely and sufficient manner in assessment processes, as well as the extent to which the executive has simply disregarded indigenous perspectives and wishes. It also points to the need for timely holistic participatory impact assessments, addressing the environmental, economic, social, cultural and spiritual impacts of proposed projects, that are necessary to inform meaningful consultations and for a greater emphasis on obtaining the consent of the impacted tribes.[133]

---

[127] UN Human Rights Council, Report of the Special Rapporteur on the rights of indigenous people on her mission to the United States of America, UN Doc. A/HRC/36/46/Add.1, 36th session, 9 August 2017, para. 67.

[128] UN Human Rights Council, Report of the Special Rapporteur on the rights of indigenous people on her mission to the United States of America, UN Doc. A/HRC/36/46/Add.1, 36th session, 9 August 2017, para. 72.

[129] UN Human Rights Council, Report of the Special Rapporteur on the rights of indigenous people on her mission to the United States of America, UN Doc. A/HRC/36/46/Add.1, 36th session, 9 August 2017, para. 69.

[130] UN Human Rights Council, Report of the Special Rapporteur on the rights of indigenous people on her mission to the United States of America, UN Doc. A/HRC/36/46/Add.1, 36th session, 9 August 2017, para. 70; see also Colwell C., Why Sacred Sites Were Destroyed for the Dakota Access Pipeline. 26 November 2016, https://www.ecowatch.com/sacred-sites-standing-rock-2103468697.html (last accessed 1 October 2018).

[131] US District Court for the District of Columbia, Civil Action, Case no. 16-1534 (JEB), *Standing Rock Sioux Tribe, et al., v. U.S. Army Corps of Engineers, et al*, 2017, p. 66.

[132] US District Court for the District of Columbia, Civil Action, Case no. 16-1534 (JEB), *Standing Rock Sioux Tribe, et al., v. U.S. Army Corps of Engineers, et al*, 2017, pp. 81–90; see also UN Human Rights Council, Report of the Special Rapporteur on the rights of indigenous people on her mission to the United States of America, UN Doc. A/HRC/36/46/Add.1, 36th session, 9 August 2017, para. 65.

[133] UN Human Rights Council, Report of the Special Rapporteur on the rights of indigenous people

The DAPL experience prompted a broader discussion between federal agencies and tribes in relation to infrastructure and extractive projects. Among the issues raised by tribes were the delegation of consultation and review duties by federal agencies to project applicants or private consultancies, and the inconsistency of such delegation with the notion of government-to-government consultations, and the associated lack of accountability mechanisms to ensure federal agencies fulfilled their consultation duties.[134] Communication, funding and training issues, including the importance of recognizing that no response from a tribe does not imply tribal consent, the lack of adequate funding and resources to participate in all consultations, and the lack of understanding of trust obligation and treaty rights among agency staff were also raised.[135] A core concern of the tribes related to the need for statutory recognition of their decision-making authority over infrastructure and extractive industry projects in line with UNDRIP's provision on FPIC.[136] This included ensuring that consultations involved comprehensive reviews of proposed projects and were geared towards obtaining the consensus of the tribes; were held sufficiently in advance of decision-making thereby enabling alternative options to be considered and tribes to act as partners in the decision-making process; valuing traditional knowledge on a par with archaeology and anthropology expertise; and the need for federal agencies to make use of their existing authority (or in the case of the ACHP to be granted greater authority) to refuse authorization to projects that significantly impacted on tribes.[137]

Responding to these and other critiques in the context of NHPA, the ACHP made a series of recommendations, including that "[f]ederal agencies and Indian tribes should develop Section 106 consultation agreements or protocols that define how they will consult" and "examine existing tribal consultation policies and incorporate principles for reaching consensus with Indian tribes" in the interest of ensuring more "efficient project delivery and better accommodation of tribal cultural concerns".[138]

---

on her mission to the United States of America, UN Doc. A/HRC/36/46/Add.1, 36th session, 9 August 2017, para. 88(g).

[134] Advisory Council on Historic Preservation, Improving Tribal Consultation in Infrastructure Projects, 24 May 2017, http://www.achp.gov/docs/achp-infrastructure-report.pdf (last accessed 1 October 2018), p. 4.

[135] Advisory Council on Historic Preservation, Improving Tribal Consultation in Infrastructure Projects, 24 May 2017, http://www.achp.gov/docs/achp-infrastructure-report.pdf (last accessed 1 October 2018).

[136] Advisory Council on Historic Preservation, Improving Tribal Consultation in Infrastructure Projects, 24 May 2017, http://www.achp.gov/docs/achp-infrastructure-report.pdf (last accessed 1 October 2018), pp. 4, 7.

[137] Advisory Council on Historic Preservation, Improving Tribal Consultation in Infrastructure Projects, 24 May 2017, http://www.achp.gov/docs/achp-infrastructure-report.pdf (last accessed 1 October 2018), pp. 7–10.

[138] Advisory Council on Historic Preservation, Improving Tribal Consultation in Infrastructure Projects, 24 May 2017, http://www.achp.gov/docs/achp-infrastructure-report.pdf (last accessed 1 October 2018), pp. 9–10, 15.

4   Canadian Context

4.1   Statutory Duty to Consult and Guidance of the Federal Government in Canada

In 2008, the Canadian Federal Government issued interim guidance outlining the responsibilities of federal agencies to fulfil the duty to consult as articulated in the common law and under statutory and contractual obligations, including specific consultation requirements under modern treaties.[139] The guidelines were updated in 2011 and identify a number of characteristics of meaningful consultation including that it be "carried out in a timely, efficient and responsive manner" and be "transparent and predictable; accessible, reasonable, flexible and fair".[140] Consultations are to be "founded in the principles of good faith, respect and reciprocal responsibility" and "respectful of the uniqueness of First Nation, Métis and Inuit communities" and to include "accommodation (e.g. changing of timelines, project parameters), where appropriate".[141] The guide envisages a four phase process applicable to the issuance of authorizations or approvals for resource extraction projects.[142] Phase one is the pre-consultation analysis and planning stage.[143] Phase two is focused on implementing and documenting the consultation.[144] Phase three relates to accommodation

---

[139] Minister of the Department of Aboriginal Affairs and Northern Development Canada, Aboriginal Consultation and Accommodation Interim Guidelines for Federal Officials to Fulfill the Legal Duty to Consult, February 2008, http://caid.ca/CanConPol021508.pdf (last accessed 1 October 2018).

[140] Minister of the Department of Aboriginal Affairs and Northern Development Canada, Aboriginal Consultation and Accommodation - Updated Guidelines for Federal Officials to Fulfil the Duty to Consult, March 2011, http://www.aadnc-aandc.gc.ca/eng/1100100014664/1100100014675 (last accessed 1 October 2018).

[141] Minister of the Department of Aboriginal Affairs and Northern Development Canada, Aboriginal Consultation and Accommodation - Updated Guidelines for Federal Officials to Fulfil the Duty to Consult, March 2011, http://www.aadnc-aandc.gc.ca/eng/1100100014664/1100100014675 (last accessed 1 October 2018), p. 13.

[142] Minister of the Department of Aboriginal Affairs and Northern Development Canada, Aboriginal Consultation and Accommodation - Updated Guidelines for Federal Officials to Fulfil the Duty to Consult, March 2011, http://www.aadnc-aandc.gc.ca/eng/1100100014664/1100100014675 (last accessed 1 October 2018), pp. 36–58.

[143] This involves describing the planned conduct, identifying potential adverse impacts, identifying Aboriginal groups in the area and their potential or established Aboriginal or treaty rights, determining if there is a duty to consult and accommodate and the scope of that duty, designing the consultation process and maximising collaboration opportunities, such as with provincial governments, while avoiding consultation fatigue for Aboriginal groups and developing a documentation system.

[144] This involves managing issues and concerns that arise in the process, including in relation to the proposed project and adjusting the consultation and accommodation process as necessary.

measures,[145] and the final phase is the implementation of the final decision.[146] Critically, neither the federal nor provincial governments tend to require that these final decisions address impacts on First Nations' rights.[147] To maximize efficiency, Aboriginal consultation is integrated into "environmental assessment and regulatory approval processes" with major projects requiring a Crown consultation coordinator who integrates the activities throughout these processes.[148]

The 2008 "interim guidelines" noted that "an 'established' right or title may suggest a requirement for consent from the Aboriginal group(s)".[149] This reference to consent was removed from the 2011 updated guidelines, arguably reflective of the Harper government's aversion to the concept. Since taking office in 2015, the current Federal Government has taken a more progressive stance and committed to implementing the UNDRIP. In its own words, taking steps towards "reversing the colonial and paternalistic approaches" and "breathing life into Section 35 of Canada's Constitution", which to date "has not been lived up to".[150]

The negotiation of impact benefit agreements (IBAs) between project proponents and First Nations is common practice in the extractive sector in Canada and is sometimes misunderstood as a manifestation of FPIC. While these agreements can complement consultations and consent seeking processes they cannot replace them. There is no government involvement in the processes and they are not underpinned by a legislative requirement to consult in order to obtain consent. Instead they are based on the presumption that extractive projects will be approved. In practice they are also often finalized prior to impact assessment completion, leading to decisions that are not properly informed in relation to potential impacts.

Two of the key legislative acts regulating consultations with First Nations pertaining to extractive industries in Canada are the Canadian Environmental Assessment Act (CEAA), 2012 and the National Energy Board Act (NEBA), 1985.[151] The former is implemented by the Canadian Environmental Assessment

---

[145] This consists of gathering information supporting the need for accommodation, identifying and selecting measures to realize accommodation and communicating and documenting accommodation measures.

[146] This includes accommodation measures and related communication, monitoring, follow-up and evaluation activities.

[147] Government of Canada, Expert Panel Report, Building Common Ground: A New Vision for Impact Assessment in Canada, 2017, p. 28.

[148] According to the guidelines a lead government agency is to be identified and is made accountable for "any consultation processes that may be carried out for federal government activities".

[149] Minister of the Department of Aboriginal Affairs and Northern Development Canada, Aboriginal Consultation and Accommodation Interim Guidelines for Federal Officials to Fulfill the Legal Duty to Consult, February 2008, http://caid.ca/CanConPol021508.pdf (last accessed 1 October 2018), p. 53.

[150] UN Permanent Forum on Indigenous Issues, 16th Session, Speech for the Honourable Carolyn Bennett, Minister of Indigenous and Northern Affairs, 25 April 2017, https://www.canada.ca/en/indigenous-northern-affairs/news/2017/05/speaking_notes_forthehonourablecarolynbennettministerofindigenou.html (last accessed 1 October 2018).

[151] National Energy Board Act (R.S.C., 1985, c. N-7).

Agency which conducts environmental impact assessments, provides support to review panels and acts as the Crown's consultation coordinator with First Nations. In the case of Energy projects, the National Energy Board (NEB) plays a central role in discharging the Crown's duty to consult. The extent to which Aboriginal rights are protected within these regulatory processes has been the subject of considerable discussion in recent years, and in the case of the NEBA has recently been addressed by the Supreme Court following litigation by indigenous peoples. The general consensus among indigenous people and independent experts is that they are failing to deliver on the promise of Constitutional recognition of Aboriginal rights and reconciliation and are instead increasing the potential for conflict.[152]

In 2016, the Federal Government commissioned expert review panels addressing environmental impact assessments (EIAs) and related consultations under the CEAA and the NEB's consultation procedures under the NEBA. The review panels concluded their reports in 2017. While the CEAA review was considerably more progressive than the NEB review, both reports found that consultation processes needed to be overhauled and be based on the principle of securing FPIC on matters affecting indigenous peoples' rights.[153] They also stressed the need for "equal consideration of Indigenous knowledge and ways of knowing", and the goal of co-decision-making "to the greatest extent possible" in accordance with the nation-to-nation relationship, as well as greater and more appropriately structured resourcing and support for indigenous peoples and their capacity building needs, including for building the conditions necessary for FPIC.[154] The CEAA review promoted the notion of "collaborative consent" and acknowledged that "Indigenous Peoples have the right to say no", qualifying this recognition on the basis that "this right must be exercised reasonably" and be subject to review.[155] The current approach to addressing Aboriginal rights in EIAs was described as "unclear, inconsistent and insufficient",[156] and a new collaboratively developed model of impact assessments [IAs] was recommended. This requires that "[r]ecognition of and support for Indigenous laws and inherent jurisdiction … be built into IA governance and

---

[152] Papillon M and Rodon T, Indigenous Consent and Natural Resource Extraction Foundations for a Made-in-Canada Approach, IRPP Insight 16, July 2017, http://irpp.org/wp-content/uploads/2017/07/insight-no16.pdf (last accessed 28 January 2018).

[153] Government of Canada, Expert Panel Report, Building Common Ground: A New Vision for Impact Assessment in Canada, 2017; and Government of Canada, Forward, Together Enabling Canada's Clean, Safe, and Secure Energy Future Report of the Expert Panel on the Modernization of the National Energy Board, 2017. The NEB report used the weaker language of "seek consent", rather than "obtain consent", and its practical proposals to ensure greater indigenous involvement are significantly weaker than the CEAA report.

[154] Government of Canada, Forward, Together Enabling Canada's Clean, Safe, and Secure Energy Future Report of the Expert Panel on the Modernization of the National Energy Board, 2017, p. 46; Government of Canada, Expert Panel Report, Building Common Ground: A New Vision for Impact Assessment in Canada, 2017, p. 32.

[155] Government of Canada, Expert Panel Report, Building Common Ground: A New Vision for Impact Assessment in Canada, 2017, p. 29.

[156] Government of Canada, Expert Panel Report, Building Common Ground: A New Vision for Impact Assessment in Canada, 2017, p. 30.

processes".[157] This position was reinforced in an Environmental and Regulatory Reviews Discussion Paper issued by the Federal Government in July 2017, in which it committed to "early and regular engagement and partnership with Indigenous peoples based on recognition of indigenous rights and interests from the outset, seeking to achieve [FPIC] through processes based on mutual respect and dialogue".[158] While weaker than the language used in the UNDRIP, and more conservative than the CEAA review recommendations, it represents a significant improvement on previous governmental positions and may provide the platform for the development of more meaningful consultation and consent seeking processes.

Canadian provinces conduct EIAs at the provincial level and are also bound by section 35 of the Constitution and the duty to consult. This adds an additional layer of complexity, as federal and provincial assessments can be required for a single project and despite the CEAA promise of "one project one assessment" this has not materialized.[159] Cooperation between federal, provincial and indigenous governments is essential for this to be realized, and as acknowledged in the CEAA review requires an approach by all parties that is premised on respect for Indigenous knowledge and FPIC.[160] Commitments of provinces, such as Alberta's in 2015 and British Columbia's in 2017, to the implementation of the UNDRIP are therefore of particular importance.[161]

In parallel to these reviews of statutory consultation processes, the Federal Government is also adopting a number of other progressive steps and positions in relation to FPIC, with potentially significant implications for extractive industry activities. On 21 April 2016, in an effort to harmonize federal laws with the UNDRIP, a legislative proposal, known as Bill C-262 which would effectively incorporate the Declaration into Canadian law, was tabled as a private members bill in the House of Commons.[162] The bill commenced its second reading in December 2017 and

---

[157] Government of Canada, Expert Panel Report, Building Common Ground: A New Vision for Impact Assessment in Canada, 2017, p. 29.

[158] Government of Canada, Environmental and Regulatory Reviews Discussion Paper, 2017, p. 15.

[159] See for example Taseko Mines Prosperity mine project that is strongly opposed by the Tsilhqot'in Nation, and despite having been rejected by the federal government following its EIA was approved at the provincial level EIA. For detailed documentation of the Federal government EIA process see http://www.ceaa-acee.gc.ca/050/documents-eng.cfm?evaluation=63928&type=1 (last accessed 1 October 2018).

[160] Government of Canada, Expert Panel Report, Building Common Ground: A New Vision for Impact Assessment in Canada, 2017, p. 23.

[161] The parties to the BC government are committed "as a foundational piece of their relationship... to support the adoption of UNDRIP, the Truth and Reconciliation Commission calls-to-action and the Supreme Court of Canada's Aboriginal title decision in Tsilhqot'in", see 2017 Confidence and Supply Agreement between the BC Green Caucus and the BC New Democrat Caucus, http://bcnd-pcaucus.ca/wp-content/uploads/sites/5/2017/05/BC-Green-BC-NDP-Agreement_vf-May-29th-2017.pdf (last accessed 1 October).

[162] UN General Assembly, UN Declaration on the Rights of Indigenous Peoples Act, Res. A/61/L.67 and Add. 1, 13 September 2007; An Act to ensure that the laws of Canada are in harmony with the United Nations Declaration on the Rights of Indigenous Peoples, http://www.parl.ca/DocumentViewer/en/42-1/bill/C-262/first-reading (last accessed 1 October). Previous attempts to

according to the Parliamentary Secretary to the Minister of Indigenous Affairs is supported by the government.[163] In 2017, the Federal Government announced that it was seeking a "complete renewal of Canada's nation-to-nation relationship with Indigenous peoples" and established a Working Group of Ministers responsible for reviewing federal laws, policies, and operational practices in relation to indigenous peoples.[164] It is tasked to

> help ensure the Crown is meeting its constitutional obligations with respect to Aboriginal and treaty rights; adhering to international human rights standards, including the [UNDRIP]; and supporting the implementation of the [2015] Truth and Reconciliation Commission's [TRC] Calls to Action.[165]

Among the calls of the TRC was that the Government develop a national action plan to achieve the goals of the UNDRIP and that all levels of government and the corporate sector fully adopt and implement the Declaration "as the framework for reconciliation", including through commitments "to meaningful consultation, building respectful relationships, and obtaining the [FPIC] of Indigenous peoples before proceeding with economic development projects".[166] This echoes the yet to be implemented recommendations of the Canadian Royal Commission on Aboriginal Peoples, which in 1996 had highlighted the need for FPIC and building a new relationship with Indigenous peoples based on mutual consent.[167]

In 2017 the Federal Government also issued a set of 10 principles aimed at renewing its government-to-government relationship with First Nations. The

---

get the Bill through the second reading had failed under the Conservative government.

[163] Bill C-262, https://openparliament.ca/bills/42-1/C-262/ (last accessed 1 October 2018).

[164] Trudeau J, Prime Minister announces Working Group of Ministers on the Review of Laws and Policies Related to Indigenous Peoples. 22 February 2017, http://pm.gc.ca/eng/news/2017/02/22/prime-minister-announces-working-group-ministers-review-laws-and-policies-related   (last accessed 1 October 2018); see also Trudeau J, Statement by the Prime Minister of Canada on advancing reconciliation with Indigenous Peoples. 15 December 2016, http://pm.gc.ca/eng/news/2016/12/15/statement-prime-minister-canada-advancing-reconciliation-indigenous-peoples (last accessed 1 October 2018).

[165] Trudeau J, Prime Minister announces Working Group of Ministers on the Review of Laws and Policies Related to Indigenous Peoples. 22 February 2017, http://pm.gc.ca/eng/news/2017/02/22/prime-minister-announces-working-group-ministers-review-laws-and-policies-related   (last accessed 1 October 2018).

[166] The Truth and Reconciliation Commission was established as an outcome of the Indian Residential Schools Settlement Agreement, the largest class-action settlement in Canadian history, to facilitate reconciliation. It was funded to the tune of 72$M by the Canadian government between 2007 and 2015. Montreal/Kingston: McGill-Queen's University Press, Truth and Reconciliation Commission of Canada, Canada's Residential Schools: Reconciliation, Final Report of the Truth and Reconciliation Commission of Canada, Vol. 6, 2015, p. 132, para. 92i.

[167] Canada Communication Group, Royal Commission on Aboriginal Peoples, Looking Forward, Looking Back, Report of the Royal Commission on Aboriginal Peoples, Vol. 1, 1996, pp. 481–482, 489. The Royal Commission on Aboriginal Peoples (RCAP) was established in 1991 by Order in Council and was mandated to investigate and propose solutions to the challenges affecting the relationship between Aboriginal peoples, the Canadian government and broader Canadian society.

principles specifically reference self-determination and self-government and state that "meaningful engagement with Indigenous peoples aims to secure their [FPIC] when Canada proposes to take actions which impact them and their rights, including their lands, territories and resources".[168] This is described as an acknowledgement of the "nation-to-nation...relationships that builds on and goes beyond the legal duty to consult" and is based on "the right of Indigenous peoples to participate in decision-making in matters that affect their rights".[169] Significantly, the principles also recognize that "the importance of [FPIC], as identified in the UN Declaration, *extends beyond title lands*" (emphasis added). This is particularly significant in a context where, to date, consent has only been considered in relation to established property rights by the Canadian Supreme Court.

4.2 Canadian Jurisprudence Regarding Consultation, Accommodation and Consent: The Common Law Duty to Consult

Since the enactment of the 1982 Constitution, the Canadian Supreme Court has issued a number of rulings affirming and elaborating on the common law duty to consult, to accommodate, and in certain circumstances to obtain consent. This duty has been derived from obligations under sections 25 and 35 of the Constitution and the Crown's trust and fiduciary relationship with First Nations. In 1950, the Supreme Court held that the Indian Act embodied "the accepted view that these aborigines are ... wards of the state, whose care and welfare are a political trust of the highest obligation."[170] In *Guerin v The Queen (1984)*, the Court explained that this implied a legal obligation as

[t]hrough the confirmation in s. 18(1) of the Indian Act of the Crown's historic responsibility to protect the interests of the Indians in transactions with third parties, Parliament has conferred upon the Crown a discretion to decide for itself where the Indians' best interests lie.[171]

Accordingly, the Court held that the Crown became a fiduciary, owing a fiduciary duty to the Band (i.e. the basic unit of government of a First Nation in Canada) "arising from its control over the use to which reserve lands could be put".[172] In *R.*

---

[168] Government of Canada, Principles respecting the Government of Canada's relationship with Indigenous peoples, http://www.justice.gc.ca/eng/csj-sjc/principles-principes.html (last accessed 1 October 2018).

[169] Government of Canada, Principles respecting the Government of Canada's relationship with Indigenous peoples, http://www.justice.gc.ca/eng/csj-sjc/principles-principes.html (last accessed 1 October 2018).

[170] Supreme Court of Canada, *St. Ann's Island Shooting & Fishing Club Ltd. v. R.*, [1950] S.C.R. 211, 1950; 2 D.L.R. 225, 1952, p. 232.

[171] Supreme Court of Canada, Case no. 17507, *Guerin v. The Queen*, 2 S.C.R. 335.

[172] Supreme Court of Canada, Case no. 17507, *Guerin v. The Queen*, 2 S.C.R. 335.

v. Sparrow (1990), the first case to be addressed following Constitutional recognition of Aboriginal rights, the Court expanded on this, holding that the fiduciary duty arose from the "sui generis nature of Indian title, and the historic powers and responsibility assumed by the Crown".[173] A "trust-like" relationship therefore existed between the government and Aboriginal peoples.[174] As a consequence, the Crown faced a "heavy burden", including conducting consultations with Aboriginal peoples, when justifying infringements on their rights and interests, in this case their inherent Aboriginal fishing rights.[175] The Court established a narrow basis for legitimate limitations, stating that it found "the 'public interest' justification to be so vague as to provide no meaningful guidance and so broad as to be unworkable as a test for the justification of a limitation on constitutional rights", while the justification of conservation and resource management on the other hand was uncontroversial.[176] In *Sparrow*, the Court also affirmed that prior to the 1982 Constitution Act consent of First Nations was not necessary for extinguishment of Aboriginal rights, provided there had been a "clear and plain" intent of the Crown to do so.[177] This aspect of the ruling was reaffirmed in *Delgamuukw v. British Columbia* (1997).[178] As Borrows notes, at no point in either ruling was there any "critical examination" of the legality of one nation extinguishing the rights of another "without their democratic participation or consent".[179] In *Delgamuukw*, the Supreme Court held that in addition to the requirement for consultation, the fiduciary duty could also trigger a consent requirement in order to justify infringements of established Aboriginal title. The Court clarified that the "special fiduciary relationship between the Crown and the aboriginal peoples" gives rise to the requirement to involve Aboriginal peoples in decisions taken with respect to their lands and to a duty that will in most cases "be significantly deeper than mere [good faith] consultation".[180] It further added that in some cases this "may even require the full consent of an aboriginal nation, particularly when provinces enact hunting and fishing regulations in relation to aboriginal lands".[181] The nature and scope of consultations, and the potential requirement for

---

[173] Supreme Court of Canada, Case no. 20311, *R. v. Sparrow*, 1 S.C.R. 1075, 1990, p. 1108.

[174] Supreme Court of Canada, Case no. 20311, *R. v. Sparrow*, 1 S.C.R. 1075, 1990, p. 1108.

[175] The charge under the Fishing Act was for "fishing with a drift net longer than that permitted by the terms of his Band's Indian food fishing licence".

[176] Supreme Court of Canada, Case no. 20311, *R. v. Sparrow*, 1 S.C.R. 1075, 1990, p. 1113.

[177] Supreme Court of Canada, Case no. 20311, *R. v. Sparrow*, 1 S.C.R. 1075, 1990, p. 1099; see also Borrows (2002), pp. 108, 240; and Supreme Court of Canada, Case no. 23603, *R v. Badger* [1996] 1 S.C.R. 771 (S.C.C).

[178] Supreme Court of Canada, Case no. 23799, *Delgamuukw v. British Columbia*, 3 S.C.R. 1010, 1997.

[179] Borrows (2002), p. 109. This authority to extinguish Aboriginal title was vested in Parliament under Statute of Westminster, 1931, see McNeil (2002).

[180] Supreme Court of Canada, Case no. 23799, *Delgamuukw v. British Columbia*, 3 S.C.R. 1010, 1997, para. 168.

[181] Supreme Court of Canada, Case no. 23799, *Delgamuukw v. British Columbia*, 3 S.C.R. 1010, 1997, para. 168.

consent, was therefore held to be contingent on the Aboriginal right in question and the extent of the infringement.

In *Haida Nation v. British Columbia* (2004), the Supreme Court addressed the duty to consult in the context of logging on lands under claim of title.[182] It clarified that the honour of the Crown, which began "with the assertion of sovereignty", is the basis for the fiduciary duty, but in cases where rights are "insufficiently specific", such as "asserted but unproven Aboriginal rights and title", the Crown is not mandated to act as a fiduciary.[183] In these contexts, the duty to consult, which the Court had classified as an "enforceable, legal and equitable duty",[184] continues to apply in relation to potential infringements on as yet unproven Aboriginal rights and title claims. However, it is derived directly from the honour of the Crown. This reasoning was based on the fact that (a) it was possible to arrive at a general idea and strength of the claimed right,[185] (b) the *Sparrow* test for infringements applied to unresolved claims and to government behaviour prior to the determination of rights,[186] (c) limiting reconciliation to "the post-proof sphere" was not honourable and led to it being "devoid of...meaningful content" as it could "deprive the Aboriginal claimants of some or all of the benefit of the resource",[187] and lead to "Aboriginal peoples ...find[ing] their land and resources changed and denuded".[188] The Court held that the extent of the obligation to consult varied with the strength of the claim, as well as the "seriousness of the potentially adverse effect upon the right or title claimed".[189] While the legal duty to consult established in *Delgamuukw* applies "as much to unresolved claims as to intrusions on settled claims",[190] it is "distinct from the fiduciary duty that is owed in relation to particular cognizable Aboriginal interests".[191] This fiduciary duty is only triggered in cases where the Aboriginal interest is sufficiently specific. Consequently the consent requirement

---

[182] Supreme Court of Canada, Case no. 29419, *Haida Nation v. British Columbia (Minister of Forests)*, SCC 73, 2004.

[183] Supreme Court of Canada, Case no. 29419, *Haida Nation v. British Columbia (Minister of Forests)*, SCC 73, 2004.

[184] Supreme Court of Canada, *Haida Nation v. British Columbia (Ministry of Forests)*, 6 W.W.R. 243, 2002, para. 33, p. 262.

[185] Supreme Court of Canada, Case no. 29419, *Haida Nation v. British Columbia (Minister of Forests)*, SCC 73, 2004, paras. 34, 36.

[186] Supreme Court of Canada, Case no. 29419, *Haida Nation v. British Columbia (Minister of Forests)*, SCC 73, 2004, para. 34.

[187] Supreme Court of Canada, Case no. 29419, *Haida Nation v. British Columbia (Minister of Forests)*, SCC 73, 2004, para. 27.

[188] Supreme Court of Canada, Case no. 29419, *Haida Nation v. British Columbia (Minister of Forests)*, SCC 73, 2004, para. 33.

[189] Supreme Court of Canada, Case no. 29419, *Haida Nation v. British Columbia (Minister of Forests)*, SCC 73, 2004, para. 37, 39.

[190] Supreme Court of Canada, Case no. 29419, *Haida Nation v. British Columbia (Minister of Forests)*, SCC 73, 2004, para. 24.

[191] Supreme Court of Canada, Case no. 29419, *Haida Nation v. British Columbia (Minister of Forests)*, SCC 73, 2004, para. 54.

does not appear to arise where claims have not yet been proven.[192] In the context of "potential, but yet unproven, interests", the honour of the Crown necessitates a case by case assessment of the obligations inherent in the duty to consult.[193] Where appropriate, the reasonable accommodation of Aboriginal concerns is required.[194] Accommodation, rather than consent, is the standard to be met where there is a high "risk of non-compensable damage".[195] In such cases, accommodation includes "steps to avoid irreparable harm or to minimize the effects of infringement, pending final resolution of the underlying claim".[196] If disagreement arises, "balance and compromise" would be necessary between societal and Aboriginal interests,[197] and potentially negotiation,[198] but there was no duty to reach agreement and "no veto over what can be done with land pending final proof of the claim".[199]

In another significant ruling, *Taku River Tlingit First Nation v. British Columbia* (2004), the Court concluded that the Tlingit First Nation had been adequately consulted and accommodated in relation to the construction of a road through their traditional territory which was necessary for a mining project but was strongly opposed by the First Nation.[200] The Court recognized that the Taku River Tlingit pending land claim "was relatively strong, supported by a prima facie case, as attested to by its acceptance into the treaty negotiation process", but nevertheless deemed that their interests had been accommodated in the decision to authorize the mining road.[201] As evidence of this, it pointed to the funding they had been allocated for monitoring and their role in the committee responsible for steering the impact assessment process.[202] The decision of the First Nation not to participate in some of the consultations was not deemed to have impacted the Crown's fulfilment of its

---

[192] Supreme Court of Canada, Case no. 29419, *Haida Nation v. British Columbia (Minister of Forests)*, SCC 73, 2004, para. 18.

[193] Supreme Court of Canada, Case no. 29419, *Haida Nation v. British Columbia (Minister of Forests)*, SCC 73, 2004, para. 27.

[194] Supreme Court of Canada, Case no. 29419, *Haida Nation v. British Columbia (Minister of Forests)*, SCC 73, 2004, paras. 10, 27.

[195] Supreme Court of Canada, Case no. 29419, *Haida Nation v. British Columbia (Minister of Forests)*, SCC 73, 2004, para. 44.

[196] Supreme Court of Canada, Case no. 29419, *Haida Nation v. British Columbia (Minister of Forests)*, SCC 73, 2004, para. 47.

[197] Supreme Court of Canada, Case no. 29419, *Haida Nation v. British Columbia (Minister of Forests)*, SCC 73, 2004, para. 45.

[198] Supreme Court of Canada, Case no. 29419, *Haida Nation v. British Columbia (Minister of Forests)*, SCC 73, 2004, para. 47.

[199] Supreme Court of Canada, Case no. 29419, *Haida Nation v. British Columbia (Minister of Forests)*, SCC 73, 2004, paras. 42, 45, 48.

[200] Supreme Court of Canada, Case no. 29146, *Taku River Tlingit First Nation v. British Columbia (Project Assessment Director)*, 2004 SCC 74, [2004] 3 SCR 550, para. 32.

[201] Supreme Court of Canada, Case no. 29146, *Taku River Tlingit First Nation v. British Columbia (Project Assessment Director)*, 2004 SCC 74, [2004] 3 SCR 550, para. 32.

[202] Supreme Court of Canada, Case no. 29146, *Taku River Tlingit First Nation v. British Columbia (Project Assessment Director)*, 2004 SCC 74, [2004] 3 SCR 550, paras. 3, 6, 7, 12.

duty to consult.[203] Echoing *Haida*, the Court stated that "[w]here consultation is meaningful, there is no ultimate duty to reach agreement".[204] Instead, accommodation involved achieving a reasonable balance between the potential impact on "aboriginal concerns" and "competing societal concerns", with compromise being "inherent to the reconciliation process".[205]

In *Tsilhqot'in Nation v. British Columbia* (2014) the Supreme Court made its first declaration of Aboriginal title and in so doing effectively established a retroactive consent requirement in certain contexts.[206] The Court held that

> if the Crown begins a project without consent prior to Aboriginal title being established, it may be required to cancel the project upon establishment of the title if continuation of the project would be unjustifiably infringing.[207]

While it does not establish a requirement for prior consent in relation to territories under Aboriginal title claim, it nevertheless constitutes an important step towards the presumption that prior consent should be obtained where land claims are pending resolution, as failure to do so could constitute a future unjustified infringement of Aboriginal title leading to project termination.

The ruling affirms that "[t]he right to control the land conferred by Aboriginal title means that governments and others seeking to use the land must obtain the consent of the Aboriginal title holders".[208] However, this unambiguous statement is immediately qualified by the statement that "[i]f the Aboriginal group does not consent to the use, the government's only recourse is to establish that the proposed incursion on the land is justified under s. 35 of the Constitution Act, 1982".[209] The ruling proceeds to address the basis upon which infringements of Aboriginal rights are permissible, stating that

> [t]o justify overriding the Aboriginal title-holding group's wishes on the basis of the broader public good, the government must show: (1) that it discharged its procedural duty to consult and accommodate, (2) that its actions were backed by a compelling and substantial objective; and (3) that the governmental action is consistent with the Crown's fiduciary obligation to the group.[210]

---

[203] This duty of the First Nations to consult was also addressed in Court of Appeal for British Columbia, *R. v. Douglas et al.*, 2007 BCCA 265, 278 D.L.R. (4th) 653, para. 45.

[204] Supreme Court of Canada, Case no. 29146, *Taku River Tlingit First Nation v. British Columbia (Project Assessment Director)*, 2004 SCC 74, [2004] 3 SCR 550, para. 2.

[205] Supreme Court of Canada, Case no. 29146, *Taku River Tlingit First Nation v. British Columbia (Project Assessment Director)*, 2004 SCC 74, [2004] 3 SCR 550, para. 2.

[206] Supreme Court of Canada, Case no. 34986, *Tsilhqot'in Nation v. British Columbia*, 2014 SCC 44, 2 SCR 257.

[207] Supreme Court of Canada, Case no. 34986, *Tsilhqot'in Nation v. British Columbia*, 2014 SCC 44, 2 SCR 257, para. 92.

[208] Supreme Court of Canada, Case no. 34986, *Tsilhqot'in Nation v. British Columbia*, 2014 SCC 44, 2 SCR 257, para. 76.

[209] Supreme Court of Canada, Case no. 34986, *Tsilhqot'in Nation v. British Columbia*, 2014 SCC 44, 2 SCR 257, para. 76.

[210] Supreme Court of Canada, Case no. 34986, *Tsilhqot'in Nation v. British Columbia*, 2014 SCC 44, 2 SCR 257, para. 77.

Echoing *Delgamuukw*, the Court held that extractive and energy projects consti-tuted a legitimate objective that could potentially justify limitations on Aboriginal rights,[211] subject to a possible consent requirement that can flow from the fiduciary obligation. The Court shed some light on the test to determine the trigger for con-sent by clarifying that the "fiduciary duty infuses an obligation of proportionality into the justification process".[212] This proportionality of impact necessitates that "the benefits that may be expected to flow from that goal are not outweighed by adverse effects on the Aboriginal interest".[213] Consequently, the determination of whether consent is necessary hinges on the assessment of impacts on the rights and interests of Aboriginal peoples balanced against an assessment of the economic benefits that can be derived from a project for society as a whole. Other particularly important features of the ruling were its recognition that: "the land in question belonged to, was controlled by, or was under the exclusive stewardship of the claim-ant group", and by logical extension that they exercised Aboriginal self-government[214]; the "notion of occupation must also reflect the way of life of the Aboriginal people, including those who were nomadic or semi-nomadic"; and the recognition of their territorial-wide title, beyond distinct site specific parcels of land.[215] Indeed, in light of these features, while acknowledging its deficiencies in terms of perpetuating colonial doctrines in relation to Crown underlying title and assertion of sovereignty, Borrows regards the ruling as setting "a new world stan-dard" and as representing a "large, liberal, and generous territorial view of Aboriginal rights", which helps to set "the stage for a robust recognition of Indigenous gover-nance over Indigenous lands" and can help erase the application of terra nullius.[216]

Therefore while *Haida* and *Tsilhqot'in* do not establish consent as a requirement in relation to territories under Aboriginal title claim, neither do they preclude recog-nition of the important role which FPIC should play as an interim solution while pending claims are being resolved in cases involving potentially significant impacts.[217] A similar argument applies to the implementation of the fiduciary duty based prohibition of activities that could deprive "future generations of the control and benefit of the land" in contexts where land claims are pending resolution.[218]

---

[211] This approach was questioned in her dissenting opinion by McLachlin CJ in Supreme Court of Canada, Case no. 23803, *R. v. Van der Peet*, 1996 2 S.C.R. 507.

[212] Supreme Court of Canada, Case no. 34986, *Tsilhqot'in Nation v. British Columbia*, 2014 SCC 44, 2 SCR 257, para. 87.

[213] Supreme Court of Canada, Case no. 34986, *Tsilhqot'in Nation v. British Columbia*, 2014 SCC 44, 2 SCR 257, para. 87.

[214] Borrows (2015), pp. 704, 714.

[215] Supreme Court of Canada, Case no. 34986, *Tsilhqot'in Nation v. British Columbia*, 2014 SCC 44, 2 SCR 257, para. 38.

[216] Borrows (2015), pp. 704, 714.

[217] Joffe P, "Veto" and "Consent" – Significant Differences, 26 March 2016, http://quakerservice. ca/wp-content/uploads/2016/03/Veto-and-Consent-Significant-differences-Joffe.pdf (last accessed 28 January 2018), p. 8.

[218] Supreme Court of Canada, Case no. 23799, *Delgamuukw v. British Columbia*, 1997 3 S.C.R. 1010, para. 117; Supreme Court of Canada, Case no. 34986, *Tsilhqot'in Nation v. British Columbia*, 2014 SCC 44, 2 SCR 257, para. 15.

Two rulings issued by the Supreme Court in 2017, *Clyde River v Petroleum Geo-Services Inc.* and *Chippewas of the Thames First Nation v Enbridge Pipelines Inc.*, also merit mention as they point to how, post *Tsilhqot'in*, the Supreme Court addresses the duty of regulatory tribunals to consult in contexts where Aboriginal title is not established. In *Chippewas of the Thames*, the Court upheld the National Energy Board (NEB) consultation process and its authority to authorize Enbridge to reverse the flow and increase the capacity of crude oil in a four decade old pipeline in the Anishinaabe peoples' territories, despite their objections to the NEB decision and to the form of consultation.[219] The Court also dismissed as irrelevant the fact that the community were not consulted in 1976 about the construction of the pipeline. In its view, "the duty to consult is not triggered by historical impacts" and consultation "is not the vehicle to address historical grievances".[220] The Court made no reference to consent, but did restate its view that the "duty to consult does not provide Indigenous groups with a 'veto' over final Crown decisions".[221]

In *Clyde River,* the Court rejected the NEB's consultation process, holding that it was "significantly flawed" "in view of the Inuit's established treaty rights [under the Nunavut Land Claims Agreement (1993)] and the risk posed by the proposed [seismic] testing to those rights".[222] The Court held that the NEB had failed to meet the duty of consultation at the "deep" end of the consultation spectrum, as required under *Haida.*[223] In addition to the NEB's failure to hold oral hearings and to answer questions regarding impacts on treaty rights, the ruling pointed to the Crown's failure to (a) inform the Inuit that the NEB process was the means through which it was fulfilling its duty to consult, (b) provide the First Nation with participant funding, as had been provided to the Chippewas of the Thames and the Taku River Tlingit, thereby preventing them from submitting their own scientific evidence or verifying that of the proponent, and (c) enable their participation in the design of the consultation processes.[224] However, the ruling did not question the authority of the NEB to make a final decision in relation to seismic testing in Inuit lands, provided it complied with the necessary procedural steps.

Legal commentators and First Nation representatives point to the fact that the NEB is a lower level administrative agency that has essentially been empowered to decide on matters of existential importance to indigenous peoples through the

---

[219] Supreme Court of Canada, Case no. 36776, *Chippewas of the Thames First Nation v. Enbridge Pipelines Inc.*, 2017 SCC 41, para. 66.

[220] Supreme Court of Canada, Case no. 36776, *Chippewas of the Thames First Nation v. Enbridge Pipelines Inc.*, 2017 SCC 41, para. 41.

[221] Supreme Court of Canada, Case no. 36776, *Chippewas of the Thames First Nation v. Enbridge Pipelines Inc.*, 2017 SCC 41, para. 59.

[222] Supreme Court of Canada, Case no. 36692, *Clyde River (Hamlet) v. Petroleum Geo-Services Inc.*, 2017 SCC 40, para. 52.

[223] Supreme Court of Canada, Case no. 36692, *Clyde River (Hamlet) v. Petroleum Geo-Services Inc.*, 2017 SCC 40, para. 47.

[224] Supreme Court of Canada, Case no. 36692, *Clyde River (Hamlet) v. Petroleum Geo-Services Inc.*, 2017 SCC 40, paras. 31, 47, 52.

conduct of a check list style consultation processes.[225] As noted by, Myeengun Henry, a chief of the Chippewas of the Thames, these rulings imply that "a decision from the NEB can effectively extinguish an Aboriginal and/or treaty right", which is not something the First Nations agreed to when sharing responsibility for land and resource management in their treaty relationships with the Crown.[226] He and others argue that, given the impacts on their lands, way of life, rights and cultural survival, these decisions need to be addressed in genuine good faith government-to-government consent based dialogues.

Finally, the cases addressed above relate to extractive and energy project specific consultation requirements, as addressed in Article 32 of the UNDRIP, but do not extend to legislative and administrative measures addressed in its Article 19. In *Courtoreille v. Canada* (2016) the Federal Court of Appeal held that legislative measures do not trigger a duty to consult.[227] The controversial ruling overturned a 2014 decision of the Federal Court upholding the duty to consult in relation to Omnibus legislation (Bills C-38 and C-45) that modified the environmental assessment regime under the 2012 Canadian Environmental Assessment Act (CEAA).[228] In 2017, the Mikisew Cree, who took the original case, appealed the decision to the Supreme Court. The Supreme Court had previously stated, in *Rio Tinto Alcan Inc. v. Carrier Sekani Tribal Council* (2010), that duty to consult extends "to strategic, higher level decisions" but did not clarify if this included legislative measures.[229] It therefore has an opportunity to clarify this duty in the case taken by the Mikisew Cree.

---

[225] See for example Lindberg T and Cameron A, SCC rulings suppress Indigenous peoples rights to their land, The Globe and Mail. 28 July 2017, https://beta.theglobeandmail.com/opinion/scc-rulings-suppress-indigenous-peoples-rights-to-their-land/article35828687/?ref=http://www.theglobeandmail.com& (last accessed 1 October 2018); see also Kanji A, Supreme Court's colonial roots are showing. The Star, 9 August 2017, https://www.thestar.com/opinion/commentary/2017/08/09/supreme-courts-colonial-roots-are-showing-kanji.html (last accessed 1 October 2018).

[226] Henry M, First Nation questions relationship with Canada following court ruling. The Star, 11 August 2017, https://www.thestar.com/opinion/commentary/2017/08/11/first-nation-questions-relationship-with-canada-following.html (last accessed 1 October 2018).

[227] Federal Court of Appeal, *Courtoreille v. Canada*, 2016 FCA 311.

[228] Abouchar J, Birchall C, Donihee J, Petersen N et al., Is There a Duty to Consult on Legislation? SCC May Decide. Willms & Shier Environmental Lawyers LLP, 22 February 2017, http://www.willmsshier.com/docs/default-source/articles/article%2D%2D-is-there-a-duty-to-consult-on-legislation-scc-may-decide-docx.pdf?sfvrsn=2 (last accessed 1 October 2018).

[229] Supreme Court of Canada, Case no. 33132, *Rio Tinto Alcan Inc. v. Carrier Sekani Tribal Council*, 2010 SCC 43, 2 SCR 650, para. 44.

4.3 Observations on Canadian Duty to Consult and Obtain Consent

A number of themes emerge from the evolving Canadian jurisprudence with regard to the duty to consult and obtain consent in the context of extractive industry projects when contrasted with FPIC under IHRL. This first relates to the discord between the protections for claimed, but as yet unproven, rights to Aboriginal title and those for "established rights". The *Delgamuukw* ruling provided for an extremely broad range of potentially permissible infringements on Aboriginal rights, which it controversially held were consistent with the Canadian concept of reconciliation.[230] At the same time, the ruling went some way towards mitigating this Aboriginal rights limiting assertion by establishing that, where Aboriginal title has been established, full consent to these infringements may be necessary in order for the State to comply with its fiduciary duty. The *Haida* ruling exposed the weakness in this approach in cases where land claims exist but Aboriginal title has not yet been established. In such cases, accommodation, as opposed to consent, becomes the standard of protection that the Crown is obliged to guarantee, as the Court reasoned that protections under Section 35 of the Constitution do not yet apply. *Tsilhqot'in* provided additional clarity and moderated the impact of the *Haida* ruling somewhat, by noting that the requirement for consent could potentially be retroactive in nature following the establishment of title, and that the trigger for the fiduciary duty based consent requirement was the proportionality of the impact on Aboriginal title rights. It nevertheless maintained *Haida's* logic that unestablished title claims did not merit Section 35 protection.

From an IHRL perspective this aspect of the Court's reasoning is problematic. The notion that consent is only required when title is formalized is inconsistent with the recognition of Aboriginal title as an "independent right" that pre-exists the Crown assertion of sovereignty and the affirmation that the principle of terra nullius never applied in Canada. Basing the requirement to obtain consent on a fiduciary duty that only comes into force following formalization of title, as opposed to deriving it from inherent self-determination, territorial and cultural rights, renders indigenous peoples' rights subject to limitations that are inconsistent with IHRL. It essentially severs the link between the consultation and consent duties and the inherent pre-existing rights they protect.

The Canadian Court has also reasoned that "[t]he constitutional duty to consult Aboriginal peoples is rooted in the principle of the honour of the Crown, which concerns the special relationship between the Crown and Aboriginal peoples as peoples".[231] The link between the honour of the Crown, consultations and the

---

[230] This built on the Supreme Court of Canada, Case no. 23803, *R. v. Van der Peet*, 1996 2 S.C.R. 507; and Supreme Court of Canada, Case no. 23801, *R. v. Gladstone*, 1996 2 SCR 723 rulings which had significantly expanded on Supreme Court of Canada, Case no. 20311, *R. v. Sparrow*, 1 S.C.R. 1075, 1990, narrow set of permissible infringements. See dissent of McLachlin J, in Supreme Court of Canada, Case no. 23803, *R. v. Van der Peet*, 1996 2 S.C.R. 507.

[231] Supreme Court of Canada, Case no. 33132, *Rio Tinto Alcan Inc. v. Carrier Sekani Tribal Council*, 2010 SCC 43, 2 S.C.R. 650, paras. 59–60.

inherent right to self-determination vested in "all peoples" under international law is implicit in this statement.[232] At the same time, the Court's reasoning is that inherent pre-existing property and self-determination rights are not entitled to full protection until they are formalized through State processes.

In effect the State is rendering it difficult and time consuming for Indigenous peoples to establish title and penalizing them in the form of lesser rights protections for this situation. Restricting the requirement to obtain consent until Aboriginal title is formalized also increases pressure on Indigenous peoples to conclude agreements in relation to extractive projects and weakens their negotiating position in land claim processes. Indeed, entering into such agreements has become a means of ensuring timely recognition of Aboriginal title. Under IHRL, respect for Indigenous peoples' collective rights is not contingent on State issued land titles, as the very premise of international law's Indigenous rights framework is that they are inherent rights, and therefore the State is duty bound to respect them, irrespective of the existence or efficiency of its titling processes.[233] Indeed, it could be argued that the requirement for Indigenous peoples' FPIC takes on even greater import before lands are demarcated and titles issued, as this is precisely when their rights are most vulnerable to violation.[234] As a result, to a certain degree the Court's logic facilitates the perpetuation of the colonial parental approach that section 35 sought to replace, whereby protection of Indigenous peoples' inherent rights effectively remain—as a restrictive positivist interpretation of the 1763 Proclamation would have held—subject to "the good will of the Sovereign".[235]

The potential for Indigenous peoples to negotiate for their claimed rights is also negatively affected by the Court's position that infringements on claimed rights that have yet to be negotiated or recognized are a part of the reconciliation process. As Christie has pointed out, an approach based on Section 1 of the Constitution[236] justifying infringements on Section 35 rights based on the interests of society as a whole should "never have been contemplated" by the Courts.[237] Instead, at this stage

---

[232] Common Article 1 of the International Covenant on Civil and Political Rights (1966) and International Covenant on Economic, Social and Cultural Rights (1966). See also Castellino (2000).

[233] This recognition of inherent land, territory and resource rights that are derived from possession and not from State grants is reflected in ILO Convention 107, ILO Convention 169 and the UN Declaration on the Rights of Indigenous Peoples as well as the jurisprudence of UN and regional human rights bodies. The duty to resect, protect and fulfil these inherent rights gives rise to the need for land titling. It is consequently illogical to hold that safeguards, such as FPIC, for those rights should not be required until titling processes has been completed. As Alston has noted in another context "[p]hilosophically, a right is a right, even if a government has refused to acknowledge that fact", Alston (2004), p. 476.

[234] See for example Inter American Court of Human Rights, *Saramaka v. Suriname*, 2007, para. 192.

[235] Royal Proclamation of 1763, issued on 7 October 1763.

[236] The Constitution Act, 1982, Section 1 states "The Canadian Charter of Rights and Freedoms guarantees the rights and freedoms set out in it subject only to such reasonable limits prescribed by law as can be demonstrably justified in a free and democratic society."

[237] Christie (2002), p. 69.

"in the process of reconciliation" the Courts should have affirmed what Slattery refers to as "sure and unavoidable" rights that protect Aboriginal interests.[238] The practical effect of such an approach would have been to "bring the governments of Canada to the negotiating table", and provide Aboriginal peoples with the power to bargain for what they regard as "fair accommodation" to remedy centuries of harm and for a "fair constitutional contract".[239] This was partially recognized in *Delgamuukw* when the Court affirmed that "best approach in these types of cases is a process of negotiation and reconciliation that properly considers the complex and competing interests at stake".[240] It was again acknowledged by the Court in *Tsilhqot'in Nation v. British Columbia (2007)*, when, in addressing Christie's arguments, the Court concluded that "[r]egrettably, the adversarial system restricts the examination of Aboriginal interests that is needed to achieve a fair and just reconciliation".[241] Unfortunately, the Court did not seem to see the contradiction between this preferred negotiated approach to reconciliation, and its affirmation— also in the name of reconciliation and ensuring the interests of others in society—of the legitimacy of non-consensual infringements on yet to be negotiated Aboriginal rights. The effect of this Court imposed conception of reconciliation is the continued subordination of pre-exiting Aboriginal legal rights and jurisdiction to the assertion of Crown sovereignty over them, something which requiring FPIC for proposed extractive industry activities while land title claims are being negotiated could have helped mitigate.

The possibility of a retroactive consent requirement as established in *Tsilhqot'in* (2014), while welcome in terms of its potential to incentivise efforts to obtain FPIC, is also inadequate from an IHRL perspective. Stopping a project when title is established may be too late to prevent significant or irreversible harm to the enjoyment of Aboriginal rights. It also exposes Canada to potential awards in international arbitration (under standards such as legitimate expectations and indirect expropriation) or in domestic Courts.[242] The regulatory chill effect of such awards on human rights is widely recognized.[243] In Canada, mining companies have already negotiated

---

[238] Christie (2002), pp. 69–70; Slattery (1983), pp. 251–253.

[239] Christie (2002), pp. 69–70.

[240] Supreme Court of Canada, Case no. 23799, *Delgamuukw v. British Columbia*, 3 S.C.R. 1010, 1997, para. 207.

[241] Supreme Court of British Columbia, *Tsilhqot'in Nation v. British Columbia*, 2007 BCSC 1700, para. 1358.

[242] By approving investments activities, such as mining, forestry or oil and gas concessions, the State establishes "legitimate expectations" of investors for which it can be held liable under contractual or international investment law. Prior warnings of the Supreme Court, such as that in *Tsilhqot'in* (2014), should be considered by investors when conducting human rights due diligence and should condition their expectations and inform investment tribunal decisions. However, under similar circumstances in other jurisdictions investors have taken governments to arbitration demanding hundreds of millions of dollars in compensation; see for example ICSID, Case no. ARB/14/2, *Bear Creek Mining Corporation v. Republic of Peru*; See also Human Rights Council, 33rd session, UN Doc. A/HRC/33/42, 11 August 2016.

[243] Human Rights Council, 33rd session, UN Doc. A/HRC/33/42, 11 August 2016.

multi-million dollar settlements where projects had to be stopped as a result of indigenous opposition following State authorizations. An example is the case of the Kitchenuhmaykoosib Inninuwug (KI) First Nation, where Canada compensated two mining companies a total of 8.5 million Canadian dollars so that they would abandon their claims following the KI's direct action preventing their projects from proceeding.[244] By requiring FPIC irrespective of whether title claims have been resolved or not, the State would provide the appropriate level of rights protection and legal certainty for all parties—be they Indigenous, corporate or the State and reduce the risk of irreparable violations of Indigenous peoples' rights.

Another related limitation of the Canadian jurisprudence is that to date the consent requirement arising from the fiduciary duty has only been affirmed in the context of Aboriginal title, and not in relation to other Aboriginal rights and interests. The Court's reasoning in *Tsilhqot'in* (2014) may, however, signal an increased willingness to engage with self-governance and territorial rights.[245] Logically, this should lead to a broader conception of when FPIC is required, as the Courts could no longer easily assume away the "underlying title and overarching governance powers that First Nations possess".[246] The introduction of the proportionality approach in *Tsilhqot'in* (2014) is also an important development, the implications of which have yet to be addressed. From an IHRL perspective, proportionality has to be considered in human rights terms and not in purely economic terms. This is expressed in Article 46 of the UNDRIP, which states that permissible limitations on Indigenous peoples' rights are to be determined "in accordance with international human rights obligations, ...[and must be] non-discriminatory...and strictly necessary solely for the purpose of securing due recognition and respect for the rights and freedoms of others...".[247] This establishes a very high threshold for the proportionality test, as what is at stake is the right of Indigenous peoples to self-determination—a peremptory legal norm which may arguably, in certain contexts, constitute a non-derogable right of Indigenous peoples, given that it constitutes the basis for their physical and cultural survival and is the foundation for the enjoyment of all their collective rights and interests as well as many of their individual rights.

The Supreme Court's position on "infringements" of Indigenous peoples' constitutionally and internationally recognized human rights is also somewhat problematic. Consistent with IHRL, the *Canadian Charter* and *Canadian Bill of Rights* hold that human rights may only be subject to "limitations",[248] while infringements are to

---

[244] See Kitchenuhmaykoosib Inninuwug First Nation (KI) case addressed in Doyle C and Cariño J, Making Free Prior & Informed Consent a Reality Indigenous Peoples and the Extractive Sector. May 2013, http://www.ecojesuit.com/wp-content/uploads/2014/09/Making-FPIC-a-Reality-Report.pdf (last accessed 1 October 2018), pp. 32–36; see also Ariss and Cutfeet (2012).

[245] Borrows (2015), p. 714.

[246] Borrows (2015), p. 742.

[247] UN General Assembly, UN Declaration on the Rights of Indigenous Peoples Act, Res. A/61/L.67 and Add. 1, 13 September 2007, Article 46(2).

[248] Constitution Act, 1982 (80) Canadian Charter of Rights and Freedoms (s. 1).

be protected against and remedied.[249] The Supreme Court has invoked relevant principles of international law, including IHRL, when interpreting *Charter* rights, holding that "the Charter should be presumed to provide at least as great a level of protection as is found in the international human rights documents that Canada has ratified".[250] However, the Court has not yet applied international human rights standards to interpret Indigenous peoples' human rights in section 35 of the Constitution. Instead, commencing with *R. v. Sparrow*,[251] it established a rule that constitutionally protected Aboriginal rights may be "infringed" or "denied"—provided the Crown has satisfied justification tests set out by the Court. In so doing it appears to be discriminating against Indigenous peoples' rights by applying a lower standard of protection to them than to the human rights of others.

The evolving approach to FPIC under Canadian jurisprudence therefore indicates that at present the Courts recognize that a fiduciary duty based obligation to obtain consent arises where Aboriginal title has been established and the potential impact of the proposed activity on Aboriginal title rights is disproportionate to the benefits to society as a whole. In addition "incursions on Aboriginal title... [that] would substantially deprive future generations of the benefit of the land" are prohibited where title is established.[252] Failure to obtain consent in the context of unproven claims could also lead to project cancelation once title is established. As outlined above, this represents significant progress but still falls short of IHRL standards and reasoning and leaves ample scope and need for further progressive jurisprudence.

5 General Observations

The trust-relationships and related duties established at the time of European assertion of sovereignty over the Americas continue to form the foundation for the duty to consult with Indigenous peoples in both the US and Canada. Conceptual tensions arise between these foundations and Indigenous peoples' right to self-determination

---

[249] The Charter provides that "Anyone whose rights or freedoms, as guaranteed by this Charter, have been infringed or denied may apply to a court of competent jurisdiction to obtain such remedy as the court considers appropriate and just in the circumstances." Canadian Charter S. 24. Similarly, the Canadian Bill of Rights, S.C. 1960, c. 44. affirms that "Every law of Canada shall ... be so construed and applied as not to abrogate, abridge or infringe or to authorize the abrogation, abridgment or infringement of any of the rights or freedoms herein recognized and declared ...".

[250] Supreme Court of Canada, Case no. 35423, *Saskatchewan Federation of Labour v. Saskatchewan*, 2015 SCC 4, para. 64. In 2014, in Supreme Court of Canada, Case no. 34986, *Tsilhqot'in Nation v. British Columbia*, 2014 SCC 44, 2 SCR 257, the Court described Part I (Canadian Charter) and Part II (Section 35) of the Constitution Act, 1982 as "sister provisions, both operating to limit governmental powers, whether federal or provincial".

[251] Supreme Court of Canada, Case no. 20311, *R. v. Sparrow*, 1 S.C.R. 1075, 1990, p. 1109.

[252] Supreme Court of Canada, Case no. 34986, *Tsilhqot'in Nation v. British Columbia*, 2014 SCC 44, 2 SCR 257, para. 15.

upon which FPIC is premised under IHRL.[253] Attempts to bridge these tensions have contributed to the establishment and evolution of the duty to consult in both jurisdictions. However, the results continue to fall short of international law standards, due in part to continued reliance of judicial reasoning on now discredited colonial doctrines. As IHRL addresses the issue of Indigenous rights from a principled rather than jurisprudential historical basis, it escapes the constraints of those racially discriminatory legal precedents which continue to underpin interpretations of Indigenous peoples' rights in many, if not most, national jurisdictions. By drawing from foundational principles of equality, non-discrimination and the indivisibility of rights, IHRL constructs a logically coherent and universally applicable framework of Indigenous peoples' rights. It consequently obliges States to reconceptualise the source, content and implications of those rights. Rights to land, territories and resources cannot be considered in isolation from self-determination, self-governance and cultural rights, and by extension Indigenous peoples' worldviews, legal regimes, and their perspectives on rights and duties. Nor can they be divorced from the self-determination based duty to consult in good faith with Indigenous peoples through their representatives in order to obtain their FPIC to measures impacting on those rights. This duty is derived from their rights and necessary for their realization.

For decades both the US and Canada have been subject to extensive review by, and guidance from, IHRL bodies concerned with Indigenous peoples' rights in the context of extractive industry projects.[254] The Committee on the Elimination of Racial Discrimination (CERD) has a particularly long history of engagement on the topic and has repeatedly called on States, including Canada and the US, to respect the requirement for FPIC.[255] Following the adoption of the UNDRIP, it has urged the US and Canada to use the Declaration as an interpretative guide in relation to the rights of Indigenous peoples under national law, including in the Constitution, and highlighted the disproportionate impact of mining and energy projects on their rights and well-being.[256] There is a significant divergence between this approach and the position of the US and Canada that the UNDRIP can or should be interpreted in a manner consistent with their existing legal frameworks.

In the US, the emblematic Western Shoshone case illustrates the gulf between national law and IHRL standards.[257] In 1978, the US Government successfully sued two Western Shoshone sisters, Carrie and Mary Dann, for trespass on their tradi-

---

[253] Routel and Holth (2013); Richardson (2009), p. 55; Skibine (1995); Tsosie (2012).

[254] For an overview of UN jurisprudence in relation to the extractive industry since the adoption of the UNDRIP see Doyle and Whitmore (2014).

[255] Office of the High Commissioner for Human Rights, 1st session, General Recommendation No. 23: Indigenous Peoples, CERD General Recommendation XXIII, 18 August 1997.

[256] Committee on the Elimination of Racial Discrimination, International Convention on the Elimination of All Forms of Racial Discrimination, UN Doc. CERD/C/SR.2142, 18th session, 2 March 2012, para. 39; Committee on the Elimination of Racial Discrimination, International Convention on the Elimination of All Forms of Racial Discrimination, UN Doc CERD/C/USA/CO/6, 72nd session, 8 May 2008, para 29.

[257] For an overview of the case see Fishel (2007a, b) and Kinnison (2011).

tional lands, despite their recognition as Shoshone lands under the 1863 *Treaty of Ruby Valley*. This Governmental position was based on the non-consensual acquisition of those lands following an Indian Claims Commission ruling in 1962 which held that "gradual encroachment" had rendered them public lands by 1872. In 1979, payment for those lands, at 1872 prices, was placed in a trust fund for Shoshone who never accepted to sell or cede their lands.[258] This non-consensual land taking was sanctioned by the US Supreme Court in 1985 in *US v Dann*, when the case was dismissed on procedural grounds.[259] Faced with the prospect of large-scale mining impacting on sacred areas, the Shoshone sisters appealed to the Inter-American Commission on Human Rights (IACHR), which in 2002 held that the US had violated their rights to property, due process and equality before the law, including by failing to obtain their informed consent.[260] The IACHR called on the US to revise its laws and policies to ensure they complied with international standards in relation to Indigenous peoples' rights. The US rejected the Commission's jurisdiction and the Shoshone took their case to CERD.[261] In March 2006, CERD issued a final decision under its urgent action/early warning procedure calling on the US to "freeze," "desist" and "stop" any further mining activities on Western Shoshone Territory until the land dispute was resolved in good faith. In light of the US inaction, CERD has repeatedly called on it to consult in good faith with the Shoshone and to reach a mutually acceptable solution, pending which no non-consensual mining activates should be conducted.[262] The Shoshone subsequently filed suit in the US courts claiming a breach of consultation duties under NHPA, however, in 2010, the Ninth Circuit Court of Appeals rejected their claim.[263] Other human rights treaty bodies, such as the Human Rights Committee have also recommended that the US consult in order to secure Indigenous peoples' FPIC in the context of extractive industry activities impacting on their sacred areas.[264] In her 2017 US country mission report, the UNSRIP called on the US to incorporate the UNDRIP into domestic law through statutes and regulations and recommended that "[c]onsent, not consultation, should be the policy to allow for the government-to-government relationship necessary to fulfil the principles set forth in the Declaration".[265]

---

[258] Fishel (2007a), p. 50.

[259] US Supreme Court, Case no. 275, *Lone Wolf v. Hitchcock*, 187 U.S. 553, 1903, p. 568 see also US Supreme Court, Case no. 83-1476, *United States v. Dann*, 470 U.S. 39, 1985, pp. 44–45.

[260] Canton S A, Executive Secretary of the Inter-American Commission on Human Rights, Report No. 75/02, *Mary and Carrie Dann v. United States*, Case 11.140, Inter-Am. C.H.R., OEA/Ser.L./V/II.117, Doc. 1 rev. 1, 27 December 2002, paras. 131–32.

[261] Fishel (2007a), p. 69.

[262] Committee on the elimination of racial discrimination, International Convention on the Elimination of All Forms of Racial Discrimination, UN Doc. CERD/C/USA/CO/6/Add.1, 5 February 2009, para. 19; CERD Follow up letter to the United States, 28 September 2009.

[263] US Court of Appeals, Case no. 07-16336, *Te-Moak Tribe of W. Shoshone v. U.S. Dep't of the Interior*, 608 F.3d 592, 9th Cir., 2010, pp. 608–610.

[264] Human Rights Committee, International Covenant on Civil and Political Rights, UN Doc. CCPR/C/USA/CO/4, 23 April 2014.

[265] UN Human Rights Council, Report of the Special Rapporteur on the rights of indigenous people

A similar recommendation was made by the UNSRIP to Canada in 2014, clarifying that "as a general rule resource extraction should not occur on lands subject to aboriginal claims without adequate consultations with and the free, prior and informed consent of the indigenous peoples concerned".[266] Over the past three decades Canada has also been subject to numerous reviews by human rights treaty bodies regarding its compliance with its obligations towards Indigenous peoples, including under the ICCPR individual complaint mechanism in the *Ominayak (Lubicon Lake Band) v Canada* (1990) in the context of oil and gas leases.[267] In 2017, CERD provided Canada with particularly relevant guidance on FPIC, calling on it to ensure "[FPIC] for all matters concerning [Indigenous peoples'] land rights", to prohibit "environmentally destructive development" in their territories and to allow them "to conduct independent environmental impact studies".[268] Addressing one of the on-going emblematic cases, the Site C dam in North-eastern British Columbia, CERD called on Canada to

> immediately suspend all permits and approvals for [its] construction. Conduct a full review in collaboration with Indigenous Peoples of the violations of the right to [FPIC], treaty obligations and [IHRL] from the building of this dam and identify alternatives to irreversible destruction of Indigenous lands and subsistence which will be caused by this project.[269]

Consistent with the recommendations of recent regulatory reviews, CERD urged the State to incorporate "the [FPIC] principle in the Canadian regulatory system, and amend decision making processes around the review and approval of large-scale resource development projects".[270] CERD also addressed one of the primary failings of the current consultation based approach, urging the State to "[e]nd the substitution of costly legal challenges as post facto recourse in place of obtaining meaningful [FPIC] of Indigenous Peoples".[271] Doing so would shift the burden from

---

on her mission to the United States of America, UN Doc. A/HRC/36/46/Add.1, 36th session, 9 August 2017, para. 87.

[266] Human Rights Council, General Assembly, Report of the Special Rapporteur on the rights of indigenous peoples, James Anaya, UN Doc. A/HRC/27/52/Add.2, 27th session, 4 July 2014, para. 98.

[267] UN Human Rights Committee, Communication No. 167/1984, U.N. Doc. Supp. No. 40 (A/45/40) at 1 (1990), *Lubicon Lake Band v. Canada*, 26 March 1990.

[268] Committee on the Elimination of Racial Discrimination, Concluding observations on the twenty-first to twenty-third periodic reports of Canada, UN Doc CERD/C/CAN/CO/21-23, 25 August 2017, para. 20.

[269] Committee on the Elimination of Racial Discrimination, Concluding observations on the twenty-first to twenty-third periodic reports of Canada, UN Doc CERD/C/CAN/CO/21-23, 25 August 2017, UN Doc CERD/C/CAN/CO/21-23, para. 20.

[270] Committee on the Elimination of Racial Discrimination, Concluding observations on the twenty-first to twenty-third periodic reports of Canada, UN Doc CERD/C/CAN/CO/21-23, 25 August 2017, UN Doc CERD/C/CAN/CO/21-23, para. 20.

[271] Committee on the Elimination of Racial Discrimination, Concluding observations on the twenty-first to twenty-third periodic reports of Canada, UN Doc CERD/C/CAN/CO/21-23, 25 August 2017, UN Doc CERD/C/CAN/CO/21-23, para. 20.

the Indigenous party to the State in cases where consent is not forthcoming and help avoid situations where bureaucratized consultation processes, with no obligation in relation to the outcome, risk masking an incremental erosion of Indigenous peoples' rights. The recommendations are timely given the Supreme Court's pending consideration of the duty to consult on legislative measures in *Courtoreille v. Canada*; the Working Group of Ministers analysis of the compatibility of existing legislation with Indigenous peoples' rights; and potential adoption of Bill C-262. All of these developments have potentially profound implications for Indigenous peoples' rights in the context of extractive and energy projects in and beyond Canada.

Another issue common to Canada and the US has been their equation of FPIC to an absolute veto right, rather than framing it as essentially equivalent to existing notions of consent under domestic laws, but applied in a culturally appropriate manner in accordance with indigenous peoples' collective decision-making processes and rights. The Declaration and other human rights instruments recognize that human rights may need to be balanced, and do not confer an absolute and indiscriminate power to Indigenous peoples. Under international law, the right to self-determination implies choice in relation to development options. It gives rise to a duty to consult in order to obtain consent whenever that right, and/or any other associated social, economic, political, cultural or territorial right, faces potentially significant limitations from the perspective of the rights holders. In such contexts Indigenous peoples are not exercising a veto power through the granting or withholding of consent. Instead, by granting FPIC they may be authorizing certain activities which would otherwise be prohibited based on the State's duty to respect, protect and fulfil their rights and by withholding it they are merely demanding this duty be fulfilled.[272] A heavy burden of proof therefore falls to the State to exhaustively justify any non-consensual rights infringements in accordance with IHRL standards. A veto, on the other hand, implies a polarized position whereby most FPIC processes would result in unreasonable Indigenous opposition to and rejection of proposed projects. As noted in the CEAA review, this is at odds with actual experience.[273] Instead, reviews have consistently found that FPIC was needed to foster a context in which Indigenous peoples, the State and project proponents can work together on the basis of mutual respect. This implies that the option to withhold consent must remain on the table. A reductionist equation of FPIC to a veto power is unhelpful and alarmist and misses the fundamental role of FPIC in transforming historically unjust and discriminatory relationship between States and indigenous peoples.[274] It is reflective of the one-sided colonial lens through which the nation-to-

---

[272] However, as noted by the Court in *Tsilhqot'in* (2014) there may be some activities that cannot be justified on the basis of obtaining FPIC.

[273] As the CEAA review noted "we did not hear strident opposition to the development of projects", see Government of Canada, Expert Panel Report, Building Common Ground: A New Vision for Impact Assessment in Canada, 2017, p. 10.

[274] See report of the UN Special Rapporteur on the rights of indigenous peoples discussing the importance of avoiding the use of veto language when discussing FPIC, Human Rights Council, Promotion and Protection of all Human Rights, civil, political, economic, social and cultural Rights, including the right to Development, UN Doc A/HRC/12/34, 14 July 2009. For a discussion

nation relationship has been viewed by the State and corporations. Viewed from the perspective of Indigenous peoples, it could be argued that the pursuit of their right to self-determined development is perpetually subject to "veto" by State and corporate actors. This is because Indigenous peoples' development plans and priorities cannot be formulated and implemented if they are under constant threat of non-consensual externally imposed projects with significant impacts on their rights that may be inconsistent with their plans and priorities and their aspired way of life. Genuine reconciliation and development requires that Indigenous peoples' world-views, aspirations and priorities be accorded equal respect in the context of consent based nation-to-nation negotiations and relationships. Rather than reduce their self-determination based aspirations and plans to the notion of a veto on third party proposed extractive and energy projects, what a constructive State should do is facilitate meaningful choices and build relationships within which FPIC can be exercised and self-determined development pursued.

6 Conclusion

The relevance of and potential role for contemporary international law on Indigenous peoples' rights is particularly clear in the US and Canadian legal contexts. Numerous commentators have pointed to the fact that the entire edifice of US Federal Indian law is premised on Chief Justice Marshall's nineteenth century understanding of international law.[275] In Canada, the Supreme Court has invoked Marshall's rulings on a number of occasions[276] and has also contextualized Aboriginal rights, and the duties to which they give rise, within the framework of colonial era international law doctrines pertaining to the acquisition of sovereignty and assertion of title to territory.[277] Ironically, the Canadian and US Courts' perspectives on these historical international law principles tend to be blind to the role which Indigenous sovereignty, consent and perspectives on nation-to-nation relationships played, or should have played, under legal theory legitimizing these then nascent States' title to territory and claim to sovereignty.[278] Given this legal backdrop, in essence, what US and Canadian Courts have been doing—since they first addressed the existence and

---

on the notion of consent as a veto power see Doyle (2015), pp. 161–168, see also Joffe P, "Veto" and "Consent" – Significant Differences, 26 March 2016, http://quakerservice.ca/wp-content/uploads/2016/03/Veto-and-Consent-Significant-differences-Joffe.pdf (last accessed 28 January 2018).

[275] Galanda GS, The federal Indian consultation right: A frontline defense against tribal sovereignty incursion. Special Feature Article of the American Bar Association Federal Indian Law Newsletter Fall 2010, 2011, www.fedbar.org/Federal-Indian-Law (last accessed 1 October 2018); Wood (1995b), Tsosie (2003), Williams (2005), Anaya (2004) and Newton et al. (2012).

[276] Jenkins (2001).

[277] Supreme Court of Canada, Case no. 34986, *Tsilhqot'in Nation v. British Columbia*, 2014 SCC 44, 2 SCR 257, para. 69.

[278] Doyle (2015), pp. 1–70.

legal rights of native peoples within their borders—is attempting to interpret what their responsibilities and duties towards those peoples are under international law. Rather than remaining trapped in the reasoning of discredited discriminatory, and at times misconstrued, colonial era antecedents, modern day Courts and legislatures have the opportunity to turn to contemporary international law, including the UNDRIP, for authoritative interpretative guidance. As pointed out by Williams, this can easily be justified jurisprudentially in the US by invoking the Marshall precedents in which international law formed the basis for the Supreme Court pronouncements on the rights of native peoples.[279] The Canadian Supreme Court, has in the past pointed to the persuasive interpretative role of international human rights declarations and treaties, and consequently has the option to inform its reasoning and interpretation of section 35 rights in line with the UNDRIP's FPIC requirement.[280] The option also exists in both jurisdictions for the re-alignment of legislation with IHRL pertaining to Indigenous peoples, including in relation to the requirement to consult in order to obtain FPIC to legislative and administrative measures—a prospect that, despite recent judicial setbacks, remains more plausible in Canada than in the US given the current political context. As Indigenous peoples in Canada have repeatedly stressed to their government, by effectively implementing the Declaration through Canadian legislation, Canada could set an important precedent that would help Indigenous peoples throughout the world.

The absence of good faith consultations in order to obtain FPIC in contexts where fundamental rights and cultural survival are in jeopardy, and serious legacy issues of extractive industry projects which remain unresolved, inevitably restrict Indigenous peoples' choices to a limited range of survival based responses. Some may decide that "the only thing worth spending energy on is learning to cope with the imposition of unacceptable alternatives".[281] Others, as seen in the Western Shoshone and Dakota Access Pipeline cases in the US, and the Kitchenuhmaykoosib Inninuwug and other cases in Canada, may adopt positions of resistance and direct action in order to assert their rights. One of the proactive responses of a growing number of Indigenous peoples in Canada, the US and elsewhere[282] has been to develop their own consultation and FPIC policies, protocols and regulations, including in relation to impact assessments, that go beyond national law and are grounded on their customary laws and principles of IHRL.[283] They regard this as an exercise of their right to self-determination and insist, through the use of all available legal, political and physical means, on compliance with them from government and corporate actors. Increasingly, indigenous peoples are also coming together to proactively assert their positions with respect to certain development projects and

---

[279] Williams (2005), pp. 161–195.

[280] Supreme Court of Canada, *Reference re Public Service Employee Relations Act (Alberta),* 1 S.C.R. 313, 1987, para. 57.

[281] Haskew (1999), p. 28.

[282] These include the Chippewas of the Thames First Nation. See Doyle and Carino (2013), pp. 29–40.

[283] Doyle and Carino (2013), pp. 29–40; Fredericks (2016).

principles.[284] They have been active internationally in the promotion of sustainable development and pushing states to recognize the need to protect their rights as integral to the Sustainable Development Agenda.[285] Commitments made to reach the nations and peoples who are the furthest behind first, and to protect their human rights and the planet's natural resources, are of vital importance to Indigenous peoples in Canada and the US. Canada's recognition in the Commission on Sustainable Development of the importance of the UNDRIP "in the context of global, regional, national and subnational implementation of sustainable development strategies" is important in this regard.[286] The *American Declaration on the Rights of Indigenous Peoples*, which contains similar FPIC provisions to the UNDRIP, also addresses the right of Indigenous peoples to ensure that resources in their territories are conserved and protected in a sustainable way and affirms Indigenous peoples' right to a "healthy, safe and sustainable environment".[287] These initiatives and achievements highlight the importance of FPIC as an enabler for Indigenous peoples' realization of their chosen form of sustainable self-determined development.

Indigenous peoples' lobbying has also resulted in international financial institutions such as the influential International Finance Corporation (IFC), the World Bank's private sector arm, in 2012 incorporating FPIC into their policies (having previously adopted the lesser standard of free prior and informed consultation), and by extension into the policies of all major private financial institutions that are party to the Equator Principles (EPs) on environmental and social risk management which apply to Indigenous peoples in developing countries.[288] This in turn has prompted a number of mining companies and the International Council for Mining and Metals (ICMM), which comprises of 23 major mining companies, to commit to "work to obtain FPIC", and multi-stakeholder initiatives in the sector to require FPIC for certification purposes.[289] These are particularly important developments in light of

---

[284] For example the signing of an accord by over 150 nations and tribes opposing the Tar Sands Pipeline "Indigenous Peoples Don't Consent To Pipelines. It's Time We Listened". 8 August 2017, http://www.huffingtonpost.ca/mike-hudema/indigenous-peoples-dont-consent-to-pipelines-its-time-we-list_a_23071485/ (last accessed 1 October 2018).

[285] General Assembly, Transforming Our World: The 2030 Agenda for Sustainable Development, UN Doc. A/RES/70/1, 25 September 2015 (adopted without a vote).

[286] Rio+20 United Nations Commission on Sustainable Development, The future we want, Rio de Janeiro, Brazil, 20–22 June 2012, UN Doc. A/CONF.216/L.1, 19 June 2012, para. 49. Endorsed by UN General Assembly, The future we want, UN Doc. A/RES/66/288, 27 July 2012 (adopted without vote).

[287] General Assembly, Draft Resolution, American Declaration on the Rights of Indigenous Peoples, Res. AG/doc.5537, adopted without vote by Organization of American States, Santo Domingo, Dominican Republic, 46th sess., 15 June 2016, Article XIX.

[288] IFC Performance Standard 7 on Indigenous Peoples, 2012, https://www.ifc.org (last accessed 1 October 2018); Equator Principles on Environmental and Social Management, http://www.equator-principles.com/ (last accessed 1 October 2018).

[289] ICMM Indigenous Peoples and Mining Position Statement (2013). See also FPIC requirements of the Initiative for Responsible Mining Assurance (IRMA), http://www.responsiblemining.net/ (last accessed 1 October 2018); and the Aluminium Stewardship Initiative (ASI), https://aluminium-stewardship.org/ (last accessed 1 October 2018).

the tendency of governments to (inappropriately from an IHRL and common law perspective) delegate consultation duties to companies. They provide another platform for indigenous rights advocacy in light of the independent responsibility of corporations to respect human rights affirmed in the UN Guiding Principles on Business and Human Rights.[290] In this regard, an interesting outcome of the protests in relation to the DAPL in the US is that some of the EP Banks funding the project became concerned about potential reputational damage. They consequently called on all EP members to apply FPIC policies uniformly across projects impacting on Indigenous peoples in developed and developing countries.[291] This would be particularly relevant in the Canadian context as junior companies make up a large proportion of the mining sector and are highly dependent on access to investment finance.

While these private sector policies have yet to translate into practice, and accountability mechanisms remain inadequate,[292] the contemporary reality in Canada and the US is that where potentially affected Indigenous peoples are opposed to projects on reasonable grounds, governments can no longer claim to have a moral or clear legal authority to proceed with those projects.[293] Even where national law, grounded on discriminatory colonial doctrines, may provide the basis for the government to proceed with a project, it is becoming increasingly politically and potentially financially infeasible to do so due to Indigenous peoples' sustained opposition and the proactive steps they are taking to assert their rights, including their right to give or withhold their FPIC, as recognized under international law.[294] Translating this de-facto exercise of self-determination into legal duties to consult in order to obtain FPIC would represent an important step towards genuine reconciliation and respect for inherent territorial, cultural and self-determination rights. This would breathe new life into relationships between Indigenous peoples and the contemporary nation states that now exist in their traditional territories.

---

[290] Human Rights Council, UN Guiding Principles on Business and Human Rights, UN Doc A/HRC/17/31, 21 March 2011.

[291] Torrance M, Banks look to apply free prior and informed consent in North America Why global banks may start to apply the concept of :free prior and informed consent: to North America. Canadian Mining Journal, 13 September 2017, http://www.canadianminingjournal.com/features/banks-look-apply-free-prior-informed-consent-north-america/ (last accessed 1 October 2018); see also BankTrack, Ten Equator banks demand decisive action on Indigenous peoples following DAPL debacle Banks from the Netherlands, France, Spain and Italy press Equator Principles Association for change. 16 June 2017, https://www.banktrack.org/news/ten_equator_banks_demand_decisive_action_on_indigenous_peoples_following_dapl_debacle (last accessed 1 October 2018).

[292] Coumans (2010).

[293] Hoberg G and Taylor S, Between Consent and Accommodation, What is the Government Duty to Accommodate First Nations Concerns with Resource Development Projects?. 2011, http://greenpolicyprof.org (last accessed 1 October 2018).

[294] Hoberg G, What is the Role of First Nations in Decision-Making on Crown Government Resource Development Projects?. 20 January 2015, http://greenpolicyprof.org/wordpress/?p=996 (last accessed 1 October 2018).

Acknowledgements The author wishes to thank Stefan Disko, Carla Fredericks, James Jide, Paul Joffe, and the editors Markus Krajewski and Ricarda Rösch for their comments and input. Any errors or omissions that remain are the author's sole responsibility.

References

Ali SH, Jorgensen M, Kalt JP, Krakoff S, McInnis A, Medford AB, Youpee-Roll A (2014) A Harvard Project on American Indian Economic Development, On improving tribal-corporate relations in the mining sector: a white paper on strategies for both sides of the table. Cambridge

Alston P (2004) Core human rights and the transformation of the international labour rights regime. Eur J Int Law 15:457

Anaya SJ (2004) Indigenous peoples in international law. Oxford University Press, Oxford

Ariss R, Cutfeet J (2012) Keeping the land, Kitchenuhmaykoosib Inninuwug, reconciliation and Canadian law. Fernwood Publishing, Nova Scotia

Bluemel EB (2005) Accommodating native American cultural activities on federal public lands. Idaho Law Rev 41:475–537

Borrows J (1997) Wampum at Niagara: the royal proclamation, Canadian legal history, and self-government. In: Auch M (ed) Aboriginal and treaty rights in Canada: essays on law, equality, and respect for difference. University of British Columbia Press, Vancouver, pp 155–172

Borrows J (2002) Recovering Canada: the resurgence of Indigenous law. University of Toronto Press, Toronto

Borrows J (2015) The durability of terra nullius: Tsilhqot'in nation v. British Columbia. UBC Law Rev 48(3):701–742

Castellino J (2000) International law and self-determination: the interplay of the politics of territorial possession with formulations of post-colonial national identity. Martinus Nijhoff Publishers, Leiden

Christie G (2002) Judicial justification of recent developments in aboriginal law. Can J Law Soc 17(2):41–71

Coumans C (2010) Alternative accountability mechanisms and mining: the problems of effective impunity, human rights, and agency. Can J Dev Stud 30(1–2):27–48

Doyle C (2015) Indigenous peoples, title to territory, rights and resources: the transformative role of free prior and informed consent. Routledge, London

Doyle C, Whitmore A (2014) Indigenous peoples and the extractive industries: towards a rights respecting engagement. Tebtebba, Middlesex University and PIPLinks, Manila

Ezra JBK (1989) The trust doctrine: a source of protection for native American sacred sites. Cathol Univ Law Rev 38(3):705–736

Fishel JA (2007a) The Western Shoshone struggle: opening doors for indigenous rights. Intercult Hum Rights Law Rev 2:41–92

Fishel JA (2007b) United States called to task on indigenous rights: the Western Shoshone struggle and success at the international level. Am Indian Law Rev 31:619–650

Fletcher MLM (2012) Tribal consent. Stan J Civ Rights Civ Liberties 8:45–112

Fredericks CF (2016/2017) Operationalizing free prior and informed consent. Albany Law Rev 80(2):429–482

Fredericks CF, Heibel JD (2018) Standing rock, the sioux treaties, and the limits of the supremacy clause. Univ Colo Law Rev 89:477–532

Haskew DC (1999) Federal consultation with Indian tribes: the foundation of enlightened policy decisions, or another badge of shame? Am Indian Law Rev 24(1):21–74

Hook J, Banks B (1993) The Indian Mineral Development Act of 1982. Nat Resour Environ 7(4):11–13, 52–54

Imai S (2009) Indigenous self-determination and the state. In: Richardson BJ, Imai S, McNeil K (eds) Indigenous peoples and the law. Hart Publishing, Oxford, pp 285–314

Jenkins D (2001) John Marshall's Aboriginal rights theory and its treatment in Canadian jurisprudence. UBC Law Rev 35:1–43

Joffe P (2010) UN Declaration on the Rights of Indigenous Peoples: Canadian government positions incompatible with genuine reconciliation. NJCLPJ 26:121–229

Kinnison AJ (2011) Indigenous consent: rethinking U.S. consultation policies in light of the U.N. Declaration on the Rights of Indigenous Peoples. Arizona Law Rev 53:1301–1332

McNeil K (1998a) Aboriginal rights in Canada: from title to land to territorial sovereignty. Tulsa J Comp Int Law 5(2):253–298

McNeil K (1998b) Defining Aboriginal title in the 90's: has the Supreme Court finally got it right?. 12th Annual Roberts Lecture, 25 March 1998, York University, Toronto, Ontario

McNeil K (2002) Extinguishment of Aboriginal title in Canada: treaties, legislation, and judicial discretion. Ottawa Law Rev 33(2):301–346

McNeil K (2008) Fiduciary obligations and aboriginal peoples. In: Berryman JB, Gillen MR, Woodman F (eds) The law of trusts: a contextual approach, 2nd edn. Emond Montgomery, Toronto, pp 907–976

McNeil K (2009) Judicial treatment of indigenous land rights in the common law. In: Richardson BJ, Imai S, McNeil K (eds) Indigenous peoples and the law. Hart Publishing, Oxford, pp 257–284

Miller RJ (2015) Consultation or consent: the United States' duty to confer with American Indian governments. North Dakota Law Rev 91:37–98

Newton NJ, Cohen F, Anderson R (2012) Cohen's handbook of federal indian law. LexisNexis, San Francisco

Prucha FP (1994) American Indian Treaties: the history of a political anomaly. University of California Press, Berkeley

Richardson BJ (2009) The Dydic Character of US Indian Law. In: Richardson BJ, Imai S, McNeil K (eds) Indigenous peoples and the law. Hart Publishing, Oxford, pp 51–80

Riley AR (2011) The apex of congress' plenary power over Indian affairs: the story of lone wolf v. Hitchcock. In: Goldberg C, Washburn KK, Frickey PP (eds) Indian law stories. Foundation Press, New York, pp 189–228

Routel C, Holth J (2013) Toward genuine tribal consultation in the 21st century. Univ Mich J Law Reform 46(2):417–475

Skibine AT (1995) Reconciling federal and state power inside Indian reservations with the right of tribal self-government and the process of self-determination. Utah Law Rev 4:1105–1156

Skibine AT (2003) Integrating trust doctrine into the constitution. Tulsa Law Rev 39(2):247–270

Slattery B (1983) The constitutional guarantee of aboriginal and treaty rights. Queen's Law J 8(1):232–273

Stern WE (2009) Developing energy projects on federal lands: tribal rights, roles, consultation, and other interests (a developer's perspective). Paper no. 15 A Rocky Mtn. Min. L. Fdn.

Tsosie R (2003) The conflict between the "public trust" and the "Indian trust" doctrines: federal public land policy and native nations. Tulsa Law Rev 39(2):271–311

Tsosie R (2012) Reconceptualizing tribal rights: can self-determination be actualized within the U.S. constitutional structure? Lewis Clark Law Rev 12(4):923–950

Walters MD (2009) The emergence of indigenous rights law in Canada. In: Richardson BJ, Imai S, McNeil K (eds) Indigenous peoples and the law. Hart Publishing, Oxford, pp 21–50

Williams RA Jr (1990) The American Indian in western legal thought: the discourses of conquest. Oxford University Press, Oxford

Williams RA Jr (1999) Linking arms together: American Indian treaty visions of law and peace 1600–1800. Routledge, New York

Williams RA Jr (2005) Like a loaded weapon: the Rehnquist Court, Indian rights, and the legal history of racism in America. University of Minnesota Press, Minneapolis

Wood MC (1995a) Fulfilling the executive's trust responsibility toward the native nations on environmental issues: a partial critique of the Clinton administration's promises and performance. Environ Law 25(3):733–800

Wood MC (1995b) Protecting the attributes of native sovereignty: a new trust paradigm for federal actions affecting tribal lands and resources. Utah Law Rev 1:109–238

Cathal M. Doyle is a Leverhulme Early Career Fellow at the School of Law, Middlesex University London (UK). He is a founding member of the European Network on Indigenous Peoples, a member of the boards of the Forest Peoples Programme (FPP) and the International Work Group for Indigenous Affairs (IWGIA), and a member of the International Law Association's Committee on the Rights of Indigenous Peoples. He specialises in the rights of Indigenous peoples under international and national law, and the interface with business and human rights and sustainable development, with a particular focus on the right to consultation and free prior and informed consent.

Asserting the Principle of Free, Prior and Informed Consent (FPIC) in Sub-Saharan Africa in the Extractive Industry Sector

Pacifique Manirakiza

Contents

1 Introduction 219
2 FPIC Normative Framework in Sub-Saharan Africa 222
3 Conceptualizing FPIC as a Right to Resist Power Imbalances and Raise Community
   Agency in the Extractive Industry Sector 226
4 Content and Scope of FPIC in Sub-Saharan Africa 230
   4.1 FPIC Content 231
      4.1.1 Unpacking the Concept 231
      4.1.2 FPIC and the Right to Veto Extractive Projects 233
   4.2 FPIC Scope: From Indigenous to Non-Indigenous Applicability 236
   4.3 FPIC Implementation Challenges in the Extractive Industry in Africa 238
      4.3.1 Shaky Legal Foundations of FPIC 239
      4.3.2 Lack of Technical Expertise and Agency 240
      4.3.3 Political Constraints 241
      4.3.4 Socio-Cultural Challenges 242
5 Conclusion 243
References 244

1 Introduction

Africa is a resource-rich continent.[1] For the last three decades, it has been subject to exploration and exploitation of natural resources,[2] mainly by multinationals backed by foreign governments.[3] Despite the fact that natural resources exploitation and

---

[1] According to Besada and Martin, Africa contains roughly 30% of the world's mineral reserves, much of it unexplored, see Besada and Martin (2015), p. 263.

[2] An author called the phenomenon a "new scramble for Africa", see Melber and Southall (2009), p. xxii.

[3] Major extractive corporations operating in Africa are registered in Canada (Barrick Gold, Nevsun

---

P. Manirakiza (✉)
University of Ottawa, Faculty of Law, Ottawa, ON, Canada
e-mail: pacifique.manirakiza@uottawa.ca

© Springer Nature Switzerland AG 2019
I. Feichtner et al. (eds.), *Human Rights in the Extractive Industries*,
Interdisciplinary Studies in Human Rights 3,
https://doi.org/10.1007/978-3-030-11382-7_9

development are ongoing, Africa is not fully benefitting from the extractive industry sector. Most of the extractive industry-generated revenues go back to home states where multinationals are registered and/or headquartered.[4] One can applaud the building of infrastructure such as roads, railways, hospitals, recreational and educational facilities along with the payment of royalties and taxes. However, even the small amount of revenues that accrue from the extractive sector has been mismanaged due to corruption practices that some states are marred with. Political elites and allied business people tend to benefit to the detriment of local communities living around extraction sites. In fact, local communities take the hit of the extractive industry. Most of the time, extraction results in armed conflicts, displacement and relocation of the population, pollution, soil and water sources contamination, impoverishment of the inhabitants, human rights violations, social tensions, land degradation and other environmental disasters.[5]

Despite the extractive industry's grave consequences borne by local communities, the latter's interests have been severely neglected in the industry. For a long time, the extractive industry sector has been a business partnership between states (governments) and extractive companies. Although states are duty-bound to ensure the well-being of their citizens, the extractive philosophy aiming at achieving economic growth at all costs constitutes an obstacle to the protection of local communities' rights. In fact, the modern extraction of African natural resources began under colonial regimes, where "...the state apparatus was (...) shaped as an extractive entity for the prosperity of the colonial empire rather than the local economy".[6] During that time, an organized pillage took place; natural resources were channelled to the colonial states.[7]

The Postcolonial State, which basically inherited the same structures from its colonial predecessor, is no better off in terms of protection of communities. After more than half a century of independence, affected communities rightly are still complaining about serious human rights violations associated with the extractive industry. There are ongoing local communities' mobilisation and resistance all over the world in order to ensure that their rights and interests are at the center of the industry. The latter cannot be sustainable without local communities' support, which requires a proper and direct engagement with them in order to secure their approval of projects affecting or likely to affect them. Therefore, local communities likely to be affected by the extractive projects ought to be consulted and give their

---

Resources, etc.), the United States of America (Anglo-American), the Netherlands (Shell Petroleum), Australia (Rio Tinto), China (China National Petroleum Corporation, CNPC), France (Areva), Malaysia (Petronas), etc.

[4] Carmody (2011), p. 4.

[5] For a detailed account of extractive industry-related violations of human and peoples' rights, see Manirakiza (2016), pp. 118–126; The African Commission on Human and Peoples' Rights, Report of the African Commission's Working Group of Experts on Indigenous Populations/Communities, DOC/OS(XXXIV)/345, 28th ordinary session, 14 May 2003, pp. 16–18.

[6] Buthelezi (2005), p. 14.

[7] Hönke (2009), p. 277.

consent to them prior to their implementation. Alongside their governments, they should have a special seat at the negotiating table and articulate their concerns and expectations as regards extractive industry projects.

One particular tool that has been developed and one which communities can resort to in their efforts to get their voices heard is the principle of free, prior and informed consent (FPIC). Although there is no internationally agreed definition as yet, FPIC is generally understood as the right of communities to give or withhold their consent to any project affecting their lands, livelihoods and environment.[8] In the indigenous context, FAO defines FPIC as "a collective right of indigenous peoples to make decisions through their own freely chosen representatives and customary or other institutions and to give or withhold their consent prior to the approval by government, industry or other outside party of any project that may affect the lands, territories and resources that they customarily own, occupy or otherwise use."[9] The decision must be freely expressed in the absence of coercion or manipulation. Consent should be "obtained prior to implementation of activities and be founded upon an understanding of the full range of issues implicated by the activity or decision in question".[10]

According to this broad definition, FPIC is a procedural right that is to enable the full enjoyment of substantive human rights. It envisages a platform for states, corporations and local communities to meet and shape the way extractive projects are designed and implemented. Using the governance theory of natural resources,[11] this chapter explores, from a human rights-based approach, the application of the FPIC principle in the context of the extractive industry in Africa. It first focuses on FPIC's legal bases (Sect. 2) before delving into the analysis of its conceptual framework (Sect. 3), its scope and content (Sect. 4) and the challenges of its implementation (Sect. 4.3).

---

[8] Colchester M et al., Free, Prior and Informed Consent: Guide for RSPO members. Roundtable on Sustainable Palm Oil, Human Rights Working Group, 21 January 2016, https://rspo.org/news-and-events/announcements/free-prior-and-informed-consent-guide-for-rspo-members-2015-endorsed (last accessed 1 October 2018), p. 8. See also Forest Peoples Programme, http://www.forestpeoples.org/en/guiding-principles/342 (last accessed 1 October 2018).

[9] Food and Agriculture Organisation of the UN, Respecting free, prior and informed consent, Practical guidance for governments, companies, NGOs, indigenous peoples and local communities in relation to land acquisition, Governance of Tenure technical Guide No. 3, 2014, http://www.fao.org/3/a-i3496e.pdf (last accessed 1 October 2018), p. 4.

[10] Colchester M and MacKay F, In search of Middle Ground: Indigenous Peoples, Collective Representation and the Right to Free, Prior and Informed Consent. Forest Peoples Programme, Paper presented to the 10th Conference of the International Association for the Study of Common Property Oaxaca, August 2004, http://www.forestpeoples.org/sites/fpp/files/publication/2010/08/fpicipsaug04eng.pdf (last accessed 1 October 2018), p. 9.

[11] Without delving into the theory, suffice it to mention that it seeks to ensure that a platform where states, corporations and local communities meet and shape extractive projects is designed and implemented. On the governance theory, see Ambe-Uva (2017), p. 84.

2 FPIC Normative Framework in Sub-Saharan Africa

The legal framework relevant to FPIC in the extractive industry sector in Africa is not clearly defined. African binding human rights instruments as well as relevant international instruments rarely provide explicitly for FPIC. When they do, they only refer to indigenous peoples, leaving outside FPIC's scope other communities which may potentially be affected by extractive and other investment projects. For instance, in international law, the FPIC is provided for in the International Labor Organization Convention No 169, especially for situations when indigenous or tribal peoples are facing evictions from their ancestral lands.[12] The United Nations Declaration on the Rights of Indigenous Peoples (UNDRIP) also provides for the right to FPIC in favor of indigenous peoples. In its Article 32(2) UNDRIP stipulates that "States shall consult and cooperate in good faith with the indigenous peoples concerned through their own representative institutions in order to obtain their free and informed consent prior to the approval of any project affecting their lands or territories and other resources, particularly in connection with the development, utilization or exploitation of mineral, water or other resources."

African states displayed a great deal of resistance to both instruments which provide for indigenous peoples' rights and they are still reluctant to become parties to or sign them, thereby problematizing and undermining their applicability in Africa. For instance, it is worth to mention that, almost 30 years after the adoption of ILO Convention No 169, only one African state, the Central African Republic, is party to it! Contrary to Latin American states which have legally recognized the rights of indigenous peoples to the greatest extent,[13] African indigenous rights are less protected. Similarly, one should recall that African states nearly opposed the adoption of the UNDRIP because of their concerns regarding "the political, economic, social and constitutional implications of the Declaration on the African Continent".[14] An advisory opinion from the African Commission on Human and Peoples (African Commission or the Commission) averted the derailment of the process. It recommended African states to "promote an African common position that will inform the United Nations Declaration on the rights of indigenous peoples

---

[12] "Where the relocation of these peoples is considered necessary as an exceptional measure, such relocation shall take place only with their free and informed consent. Where their consent cannot be obtained, such relocation shall take place only with their free and informed consent. Where their consent cannot be obtained, such relocation shall take place only following appropriate procedures established by national laws and regulations, including public inquiries where appropriate, which provide the opportunity for effective representation of the peoples concerned.", Convention concerning Indigenous and Tribal Peoples in Independent Countries, adopted in Geneva, 76th ILC session, 27 June 1989, Article 16 (2).

[13] Schilling-Vacaflor (2017), p. 1058.

[14] Assembly of the African Union, Decision on the United Nations Declaration on the Rights of Indigenous Peoples, Assembly/AU/Dec.141 (VIII), 8th Ordinary Session, 29–30 January 2007, para. 3.

with this African perspective so as to consolidate the overall consensus achieved by the international community on the issue."[15]

The African reluctance to espouse indigeneity in the African context stems from the deep belief addressed by the African Commission that every "African can legitimately consider him/herself as indigene to the continent".[16] However, this belief is not consonant with the reality on the ground: the very existence of a special category of indigenous peoples in Africa.[17] These are essentially African peoples that have suffered from discrimination, been subjected to marginalization and domination by the mainstream majority and dominant groups, due to their different lifestyles, cultures, or modes of production. According to the Working Group on the Indigenous Populations/Communities,[18]

They suffer from discrimination as they are being regarded as less developed and less advanced than other more dominant sectors of society. They often live in inaccessible regions, often geographically isolated and suffer from various forms of marginalisation, both politically and socially. They are subject to domination and exploitation within national political and economic structures that are commonly designed to reflect the interests and activities of the national majority. This discrimination, domination and marginalisation violates their human rights as peoples/communities, threatens the continuation of their cultures and ways of life and prevents them from being able to genuinely participate in deciding on their own future and forms of development.

Moreover, these groups are recognizable by their "special attachment to and use of their traditional land whereby their ancestral land and territory has a fundamental importance for their collective physical and cultural survival as peoples".[19]

In the interest of justice and equality, the African Commission recognizes the need for "affirmative action", which is not a way of granting these groups special rights but, simply of taking into consideration the legacy and the negative impact of the historical discrimination and subjugation they suffered.[20] That is why international human rights mechanisms implicitly recognize the right of African indigenous peoples to free, prior and informed consent in some situations. For instance, after finding that neither indigenous peoples nor their rights are recognized as such, the *Human Rights Committee*, recommended that Togo "take the necessary steps to guarantee the recognition of minorities and indigenous peoples" and "ensure that indigenous peoples are able to exercise their right to free, prior and informed

---

[15] African Commission on Human and Peoples' Rights, Advisory Opinion of the African Commission on Human and Peoples' Rights on the United Nations Declaration on the Rights of Indigenous Peoples, 41st session, 2007, para. 44.

[16] African Commission on Human and Peoples' Rights, Advisory Opinion of the African Commission on Human and Peoples' Rights on the United Nations Declaration on the Rights of Indigenous Peoples, 41st session, 2007, para. 13.

[17] The Working Group on Indigenous Communities/Populations provides examples of about 40 groups in Africa who identify themselves as indigenous peoples, see African Commission on Human and Peoples' Rights (ACHPR) (2006), pp. 15–16.

[18] African Commission on Human and Peoples' Rights Report (2006), p. 60.

[19] African Commission on Human and Peoples' Rights Report (2006), p. 63.

[20] African Commission on Human and Peoples' Rights Report (2006), p. 59.

consent."[21] Similarly, in Tanzania, several vulnerable communities, including pastoral and hunter-gatherer communities, have been forcibly evicted from their traditional lands for the purposes of large scale farming, the creation of game reserves and the expansion of national parks, mining, the construction of military barracks, tourism and commercial game hunting. The *Committee on Social, Economic and Cultural Rights* was concerned and deplored that these practices have resulted in a critical reduction in the communities' access to land and natural resources, particularly threatening their livelihoods and their right to food. It recommended that the establishment of game reserves, the granting of licences for hunting, or other projects on ancestral lands is preceded by free, prior and informed consent of the peoples affected.[22] Regarding the evictions of Botswana Basarwa/San people from their ancestral lands in the Central Kalahari Game Reserve, the Committee on the Elimination of Racial Discrimination recommended that "no decisions directly relating to the rights and interests of members of indigenous peoples be taken without their informed consent."[23]

On the regional level, the African Charter does not specifically provide for FPIC. However, a number of provisions have been interpreted as recognizing FPIC. For instance, in the famous *SERAC* case concerning the Ogoni people whose rights have been violated by extractive industry related activities in the Niger Delta region in Nigeria, the African Commission held that a joint reading of Articles 16 and 24 of the Charter implied a legal duty of State Parties to provide information to affected communities as well as "meaningful opportunities for individuals to be heard and to participate in the development decisions affecting their communities."[24] Similarly, in the *Endorois* case, the same Commission held that with respect to "any development or investment projects that would have a major impact within the Endorois territory, the state has a duty not only to consult with the community, but also to obtain their free, prior, and informed consent, according to their customs and traditions."[25] Moreover, the AU Convention on the Conservation of Nature and Natural Resources enjoins State Parties to "take the measures necessary to enable active participation by the local communities in the process of planning and man-

---

[21] Human Rights Committee, Consideration of reports submitted by State parties under article 40 of the Covenant concluding observations of the Human Rights Committee, Togo, CCPR/C/TGO/CO/4, 11 March 2011, para. 21.

[22] Committee on Economic, Social and Cultural Rights, Concluding observations on the initial to third report of the United Republic of Tanzania, adopted by the Committee, E/C.12/TZA/CO/1-3, 49th session, 12–30 November 2012, para. 22.

[23] Committee on the Elimination of Racial Discrimination, 60th session, 4–22 March 2002, 61st session, 5–23 August 2002, General Assembly Official Records 57th session, Supplement No. 18 (A/57/18), 30 November 2012, para. 304.

[24] African Commission on Human and Peoples' Rights, Case 155/96, *Social and Economic Rights Action Center (SERAC) and Center for Economic and Social Rights (CESR) v. Nigeria*, 2001, para. 53.

[25] African Commission on Human and Peoples' Rights, Case 276/03, *Centre for Minority Rights Development (Kenya) and Minority Rights Group (on behalf of the Endorois Welfare Council) v. Kenya*, 25 November 2009, para. 291.

agement of natural resources upon which such communities depend with a view to creating local incentives for the conservation and sustainable use of such resources."[26]

The African Commission's Resolution on a Human Rights-Based Approach to Natural Resources Governance, a soft law instrument, calls upon states to take all necessary measures to ensure participation, including the free, prior and informed consent of communities, in decision making related to natural resources governance.[27] The Pan-African Parliament followed suit by calling upon Member States to ensure effective consultations "with local communities and various people affected by investment projects and ensure that any investment is approved through free, prior, and informed consent of affected communities".[28] On the sub-regional level, the ECOWAS has spearheaded the move towards the protection of human rights in the extractive industry sector. According to one of its directives regulating the mining sector, "Member States and holders of mining rights shall ensure that the rights of the local communities are respected at all times."[29] Extractive companies are bound to "particularly respect the rights of local people and similar communities to own, occupy, develop, control, protect, and use their lands, other natural resources, and cultural and intellectual property."[30] Most importantly, they "shall obtain free, prior, and informed consent of local communities before exploration begins and prior to each subsequent phase of mining and post-mining operations."[31]

It becomes clear from the foregoing that FPIC as a legal principle is not clearly and firmly embedded in African human rights instruments. However, through soft law and caselaw, international and African regional human rights mechanisms have been innovative by interpreting relevant international and regional human rights rules in order to find and/or reinforce the legal foundations of the FPIC principle. A reading of the FPIC legal regime leads to the conclusion that the principle should be conceptualized as a right to resist power imbalances in the extractive industry sector.

---

[26] African Convention on the Conservation of Nature and Natural Resources, 2003, Article XVII (3).

[27] African Commission on Human and Peoples' Rights, Resolution on a Human Rights-Based Approach to Natural Resources Governance, Resolution 224, 2012.

[28] Pan-African Parliament, Recommendations and Resolutions, Ref: PAP(2)/RECOMS/(VI), 6th ordinary session, 16–20 January 2012.

[29] Economic Community of West African States, Directive C/DIR. 3/05/09 on the Harmonization of Guiding Principles and Policies in the Mining Sector, 2009, Article 15(2).

[30] Economic Community of West African States, Directive C/DIR. 3/05/09 on the Harmonization of Guiding Principles and Policies in the Mining Sector, 2009, Article 16 (2).

[31] Economic Community of West African States, Directive C/DIR. 3/05/09 on the Harmonization of Guiding Principles and Policies in the Mining Sector, 2009, Article 16 (3).

3 Conceptualizing FPIC as a Right to Resist Power Imbalances and Raise Community Agency in the Extractive Industry Sector

Following the neoliberal economic model inspired or imposed by the Bretton Woods institutions, African extractivism advocates for open markets with multinational corporations being key players, the intended but rarely achieved end result being economic growth for states. With the neoliberal policies, even states have been marginalized and disempowered in favor of transnational extractive companies. From the colonial era until recently, relevant laws favoured foreign direct investment. Tax advantages and other investment incentives are provided for in many African mining codes in order to attract and maintain foreign investment. Moreover, corporations are not under any contractual obligation to process natural resources locally so that local communities could benefit, for instance, in terms of employment or low cost of manufactured products. Corporations reap maximum profits to the detriment of local communities and, to some extent, the host state. However, the adoption of the African Mining Vision in 2010 at the African Union level operated as a paradigm shift in that it "prioritizes local development rather than attracting private mining companies as was the case with previous reforms undertaken by the WB and IMF,"[32] allowing states to regain control of their resources.

Nowadays, the main actors in the industry are governments and private extractive corporations. Still today, the latter are in a powerful position. They continue to be favoured by the neoliberal economic ideology and policies. Moreover, extractive transnational corporations enjoy, most of the time, active support and blessing from African governments[33] purportedly eager to promote economic growth and development. The support comes also from political elites and local leaders[34] who seek to maintain or reinforce their political power and influence. That dominant status coupled with advanced and up to date technical and legal expertise in this area result in corporations being powerful actors at the negotiation table. Although local communities are negatively impacted by the extraction of natural resources, they have not always been able to voice their concerns and articulate their interests in the sector. In fact, governments are supposed to represent them and ensure that they get maximum profits out of resource extraction. However, with undemocratic and corrupted

---

[32] Diallo (2016), pp. 2–3.

[33] Szablowski (2010), pp. 112–113.

[34] Lind, Research Briefing, Governing black gold: lessons from Oil finds in Turkana, Kenya. Institute for Development Studies, October 2017, https://opendocs.ids.ac.uk/opendocs/bitstream/handle/123456789/13279/Brief_IDSsaferworld_Turkana_Web.pdf;jsessionid=E2B19CE3F247E0A12E98AB68B32E167A?sequence=1 (last accessed 1 October 2018 p. 8: In Turkana County (Kenya) where oil has been discovered, "traditional elders and seers have been compromised by their involvement in and blessing of deals with investors that are thought to have few wider community benefits." A similar situation prevails in Sierra Leone where, comparing to local communities, "the relationship between chiefs and mining companies seems cordial on both sides"; see Werner (2017), p. 323.

governments, it has become clear that local communities' interests are not at the center of the extractive industry sector. Because of the prevailing presence of governments and multinationals, local communities still lack agency in the industry, despite some moves to open-up space for them. There are persisting asymmetries in power relations between local communities, governments and extractive industry corporations. Therefore, there is a need for a human rights based extraction; that is why, today, local communities are mobilising for their voices to be heard and eventually get a say in the extractive industry. It is in this context that the right to FPIC is now advocated for. FPIC is a tool that enables affected communities to ensure respect and protection of their substantive charter rights affected by the exploration and exploitation of natural resources. It "grants the real stakeholders the authority to define their own goals and destiny, and to have a meaningful say on development."[35]

In Africa, on a conceptual level, FPIC is to be located in the human rights theory of resistance. The theory of resistance dates back to the Enlightenment,[36] but it has now permeated the human rights domain. According to Finlay, human rights "exemplify the type of principles the violation of which may trigger a justification for resistance."[37] In fact, Heyns contends that "human rights are not about asking favours and they are not merely moral or rhetorical concepts; they are guides to action and triggers of resistance against what is perceived as the illegitimate use of power, in particular state power."[38] He further claims that "[h]uman rights is the flipside of the coin of legitimate resistance"[39]

In law, the right to resist was first provided for in the Declaration of the Rights of Man and Citizen.[40] Contemporary international human rights treaties do not specifically recognize a right to resist human rights violations.[41] The African human rights system, however, provides for the right to resist. This prerogative can be inferred from article 20 of the African Charter on Human and Peoples' Rights (African Charter), which states that "all peoples (...) shall have the unquestionable and

---

[35] Abebe (2009), p. 7.

[36] Locke (1689), para. 202: "[w]herever law ends, tyranny begins, if the breach of the law brings harm to someone else; and anyone in authority who exceeds the power given him by the law, using the force at his disposal to do to the subject things that aren't allowed by the law, thereby stops being an officer of the law; and because he acts without authority he may rightly be opposed, as may any other man who by force invades the right of someone else."; see also Rousseau (1920), p. 234.

[37] Finlay (2015), p. 26.

[38] Heyns (2001), p. 171.

[39] Heyns (2001), p. 171.

[40] Declaration of the Rights of Man and Citizen, approved by the National Assembly of France, 26 August 1789, Article 2: "The aim of all political association is the preservation of the natural and imprescriptible rights of man. These rights are liberty, property, security, and resistance to oppression."

[41] However, the Universal Declaration on Human Rights, in its preamble, alludes to this right: "whereas it is essential, if man is not to be compelled to have recourse, as a last resort, to rebellion against tyranny and oppression, that human rights should be protected by the rule of law.".

inalienable right to self-determination".[42] The right to self-determination implies, inter alia, that peoples "shall freely determine their political status and shall pursue their economic and social development according to the policy they have freely chosen."[43] According to Murphy, the right to resist acts at the same time as a mode of implementation and enforcement of the body of human rights and as an effective remedy against violations, a deterrent to violator regimes within the human security framework.[44] Previously, Honoré had contended that the right to resist is a secondary and not a primary right.[45] According to him, "its point is to provide a remedy in the event of the violation on a large scale of primary rights (…) The sustained denial of those rights may arguably amount to such oppression or exploitation as justifies rebellion."[46] In a nutshell, on a conceptual level, the right to resist is a legal remedy invoked and exercised when primary human rights have been violated.

As far as FPIC is concerned, its *raison d'être* is in fact to resist, balance and overcome power imbalances in the extractive industry sector. FPIC is an important component of the right to self-determination,[47] which is part of the foundation of the human rights theory of resistance. According to Wicomb and Smith, the right to self-determination potentially provides an appropriate platform for the protection of local communities' substantive and procedural rights and promotes their participation in decision-making in order for them to benefit from the development of their land.[48] In the area of natural resources, the right to self-determination implies peoples' sovereignty over their resources and wealth to which Article 21 of the African Charter speaks in unequivocal terms.[49] That situation triggers a legal duty of state parties to protect their peoples from exploitation by external economic powers, including extractive industry corporations.[50] Furthermore, states have to ensure that groups and communities, directly or through their representatives, are involved in decisions relating to the disposal of their wealth and the extraction of natural resources.[51] Popular sovereignty challenges the state's monopolization of control over natural resources on its territory.[52] Self-determination claims also explain

---

[42] African Charter, Article 20(1).

[43] African Charter, Article 20(1).

[44] Murphy (2011), p. 494.

[45] Honore (1988), p. 38.

[46] Honore (1988), p. 38.

[47] "The right of free, prior and informed consent needs to be understood in the context of indigenous peoples' right to self-determination because it is an integral element of that right.".

[48] Wicomb and Smith (2011), p. 422.

[49] African Charter, Article 21(1): "All peoples shall freely dispose of their wealth and natural resources. This right shall be exercised in the exclusive interest of the people. In no case shall a people be deprived of it".

[50] African Charter, Article 21(5); African Commission on Human and Peoples' Rights, Communication 328/06, *Front for the Liberation of the State of Cabinda v. Republic of Angola*, 2013, para. 129.

[51] African Commission on Human and Peoples' Rights, Communication 328/06, *Front for the Liberation of the State of Cabinda v. Republic of Angola*, 2013, para. 129.

[52] McNeish (2017), p. 1129.

growing demand and pressure from communities on the traditional key players in the extractive industry sector—governments and corporations—to open up space for them in order to allow them to substantively participate in the decision-making on projects affecting or likely to affect them.

A controversy around the scope of the right to self-determination soon arose in the first years of implementation of the African Charter. The debate centred on whether the right to self-determination is attributed only to the entire population of a particular state or whether it also extends to sub-groups within the state, such as the communities affected by extraction that are the focus of this chapter. Although the colonial context of the provision is easily and clearly discernible, African human rights mechanisms have interpreted the provision to apply both to the entire population and to its sub-groups. The African Commission had determined already that peoples who are entitled to self-determination include sub-groups within the population of a member state.[53] Quite recently, the African Court on Human and Peoples' Rights (African Court) followed suit and held that sub-groups of the population do enjoy Charter rights, especially the right to self-determination[54]; with some conditions attached, however. In the *Ogiek* case, the African Court held that groups or communities identifiable as peoples can enjoy the right to self-determination "provided such groups or communities do not call into question the sovereignty and territorial integrity of the state without the latter's consent".[55] The *Ogiek* judgment upholds the African Commission's prior position in the *Katanga* case, where it held that "Katanga is obliged to exercise a variant of self-determination that is compatible with the sovereignty and *territorial integrity of Zaire*".[56] Thus, sub-groups can also claim self-determination within the territorial confines of the state,[57] but the right does not give rise to a right to secession or rebellion. Self-determination therefore implies that peoples retain a certain sovereignty on natural resources as explained above. This peoples' sovereignty runs counter to and challenges the state's claim to monopolized control over natural resources on its territory.[58]

---

[53] African Commission on Human and Peoples' Rights, Case 276/03, *Centre for Minority Rights Development (Kenya) and Minority Rights Group (on behalf of the Endorois Welfare Council) v. Kenya*, 2009, para. 255; African Commission on Human and Peoples' Rights, Communication 328/06, *Front for the Liberation of the State of Cabinda v. Republic of Angola*, 2013, para. 131.

[54] African Court on Human and Peoples' Rights, Application 006/2012, *African Commission on Human and Peoples' Rights v. The Republic of Kenya*, 2017, para. 199.

[55] African Court on Human and Peoples' Rights, Application 006/2012, *African Commission on Human and Peoples' Rights v. The Republic of Kenya*, 2017, para. 199.

[56] African Commission on Human and Peoples' Rights (1995), Case 75/92, *Congrès du peuple katangais v. République du Zaire*, 1995, para. 6. See also African Commission on Human and Peoples' Rights, Advisory Opinion of the African Commission on Human and Peoples' Rights on the United Nations Declaration on the Rights of Indigenous Peoples, 41st session, 2007, paras. 6, 18.

[57] African Court on Human and Peoples' Rights, Application 006/2012, *African Commission on Human and Peoples' Rights v. The Republic of Kenya*, 2017, para. 199.

[58] McNeish (2017), p. 1129.

It can be concluded that, being embedded in the right to self-determination,[59] FPIC can be invoked and exercised when primary and substantive human and peoples' rights are affected or potentially affected by natural resource extraction and development. Charter rights which entail autonomy of decision-making include the right and ability to participate in the governance of one's state (African Charter, Article 13), the right to property (African Charter, Article 14), the right to freely dispose of wealth and natural resources (African Charter, Article 21), the right to economic, social and cultural development (African Charter, Article 22), the right to a healthy environment (African Charter, Article 24).[60] FPIC therefore acts both as a mode of implementation and enforcement of these rights and as an effective remedy against extraction-relative human rights violations. As an empowerment tool for local communities in Africa, FPIC immensely contributes to raise community agency in the extractive industry sector. Furthermore, as a right to resistance, it enables communities to resist against the colonial legal regime that has underpinned the extractive industry sector in Africa for decades. Recognizing FPIC, thus understood, would necessarily contribute to transform and decolonize the legal regime applicable to the extractive industry sector in Africa by ensuring a paradigm shift from the economic growth-based perspective to a human rights-based extraction.

4 Content and Scope of FPIC in Sub-Saharan Africa

Now that the legal and conceptual foundations of the FPIC principle have been dealt with, it is important to explore its content and scope in the African context.

---

[59] UN Human Rights Council, Final report of the study on indigenous peoples and the right to participate in decision-making, Report of the Expert Mechanism on the Rights of Indigenous Peoples, UN Doc. A/HRC/18/42, 17 August 2011, para. 20. As far as indigenous peoples' rights are concerned, "the right to self-determination (…) should be understood as encompassing a series of rights relative to the full participation in national affairs, the right to local self-government, the right to recognition so as to be consulted in the drafting of laws and programs concerning them, to a recognition of their structures and traditional ways of living as well as the freedom to preserve and promote their culture", see African Commission on Human and Peoples' Rights, Advisory Opinion of the African Commission on Human and Peoples' Rights on the United Nations Declaration on the Rights of Indigenous Peoples, 41st session, 2007, para. 27.

[60] As far as indigenous rights are concerned, according to the United Nations, numerous substantive rights may be implicated in natural resource development and extraction. They include the rights to property, culture, religion, and non-discrimination in relation to lands, territories and natural resources, including sacred places and objects; rights to health and physical well-being in relation to a clean and healthy environment; and rights to set and pursue their own priorities for development, including development of natural resources, as part of their fundamental right to self-determination. See Anaya, Report of the Special Rapporteur on the rights of indigenous peoples, A/HRC/21/47, 6 July 2012, para. 50.

4.1 FPIC Content

4.1.1 Unpacking the Concept

In accordance with the FPIC precepts, community consent must, first and foremost, be free. In the extractive industry sector, affected communities are entitled to be consulted and participate freely, without coercion, intimidation, manipulation,[61] gender or age-based discrimination in negotiations with extractive companies. Free participation in negotiations allows communities to articulate their concerns and interests vis-à-vis a proposed extractive industry project and ultimately to voluntarily consent to it. Second, community consent to extractive projects must be prior to their implementation. As a matter of principle, rights holders should consent to extractive industry projects "in advance of any authorization or commencement of activities, at the early stages of a development or investment plan."[62] In fact, communities need time to understand the added value of a project as well as its social, economic and environmental impacts. Therefore, consent may not be sought *ex post facto*. In the *Endorois* case, the Commission held that affected communities should be given an opportunity to shape the project before its implementation.[63] Thus, Kenya was found responsible for the violation of the right to development because the state carried out consultations with the *Endorois* indigenous community only after the decision had already been taken.[64] In the African context, as I wrote elsewhere, the African Commission "has set high the standard for consultations: communities must be informed of an impending development project not as a *fait accompli*."[65]

Third, community consent must be informed. Extractive companies must provide relevant information a long time before the proposed project actually kicks off and, in any case, "at the beginning or initiation of an activity, process or phase of implementation."[66] Therefore, communities are entitled to receive objective,

---

[61] Food and Agriculture Organization of the United Nations, Free Prior and Informed Consent, An indigenous peoples' right and a good practice for local communities. Manual for Practitioners, 2016, http://www.fao.org/3/a-i6190e.pdf (last accessed 1 October 2018), p. 15.

[62] Food and Agriculture Organization of the United Nations, Free Prior and Informed Consent, An indigenous peoples' right and a good practice for local communities. Manual for Practitioners, 2016, http://www.fao.org/3/a-i6190e.pdf (last accessed 1 October 2018), p. 15.

[63] African Commission on Human and Peoples' Rights, Case 276/03, *Centre for Minority Rights Development (Kenya) and Minority Rights Group (on behalf of the Endorois Welfare Council) v. Kenya*, 25 November 2009, para. 281.

[64] African Commission on Human and Peoples' Rights, Case 276/03, *Centre for Minority Rights Development (Kenya) and Minority Rights Group (on behalf of the Endorois Welfare Council) v. Kenya*, 25 November 2009, para. 281.

[65] Manirakiza (2015), pp. 3–9.

[66] African Commission on Human and Peoples' Rights, Case 276/03, *Centre for Minority Rights Development (Kenya) and Minority Rights Group (on behalf of the Endorois Welfare Council) v. Kenya*, 25 November 2009, para. 281.

complete and accessible information[67] on any possible risk or consequence of a proposed project or activity that may impact them. They should also be able to access independent information and experts on legal and technical issues.[68] Information must be provided on a continuous basis throughout the entire FPIC process, in the language of the interested communities and in a culturally sensitive manner.[69] In the famous *Kamanakao* case concerning the removal and relocation of indigenous peoples from the Central Kalahari Game Reserve, although consultations had been carried out, the High Court of Botswana found that "there was no free and informed consent because the government failed to take into account the specific socio-economic circumstances of the applicants. This included the fact that the applicants were generally a very poor, marginalized community with very little education and who spoke and understood Setswana to varying degrees. They were also of a culture that was markedly different from the Tswana culture. Thus, the form of meetings used for Tswana groups might not necessarily be so for non-Tswana groups."[70]

Finally, the information provided to each stakeholder has to indicate the reasons, the nature, the limitations, the scope, the scale, and the schedule of the respective project as well as the possibility to retreat from any proposed project or activity with negative social, economic or environmental impacts.[71] Unreliable, inaccurate and insufficiently detailed information perpetuates the imbalance of power between interested partners. Local communities with inadequate and imperfect knowledge can be persuaded to settle for less than they are due. Furthermore, communities that lack reliable information will find it difficult to mobilize their resources in their own best interests.[72]

---

[67] Food and Agriculture Organization of the United Nations, Free Prior and Informed Consent, An indigenous peoples' right and a good practice for local communities. Manual for Practitioners, 2016, http://www.fao.org/3/a-i6190e.pdf (last accessed 4 December 2017), pp. 15–16.

[68] Hill C, Guide to Free Prior and Informed Consent. June 2010, http://resources.oxfam.org.au/pages/view. php?ref=528 (last accessed 1 October 2018).

[69] Food and Agriculture Organization of the United Nations, Free Prior and Informed Consent, An indigenous peoples' right and a good practice for local communities, Manual for Practitioners, 2016, http://www.fao.org/3/a-i6190e.pdf (last accessed 1 October 2018), p. 16.

[70] Mentioned in: International Labour Organization and the African Commission on Human and Peoples' Rights on the constitutional and legislative protection of the rights of indigenous peoples in 24 African countries, Overview Report of the Research Project, ILO/ACHPR, 2009, http://www.ilo.org/wcmsp5/groups/public/%2D%2D-ed_norm/%2D%2D-normes/documents/publication/wcms_115929.pdf (last accessed 1 October 2018), p. 99.

[71] Pham et al. (2015), pp. 2409–2410.

[72] Szablowski (2010), p. 125.

4.1.2   FPIC and the Right to Veto Extractive Projects

As a resistance right, FPIC is a good tool for local communities to assert and claim their African Charter-based rights. Given that particular importance of the right to FPIC, one thorny issue concerns the question whether or not FPIC does imply the right to veto extractive projects. Some authors agree with the claim that an authentic FPIC process needs to offer the possibility of a veto.[73] Having the right to a veto on the table is both a valid option within a deliberative process and a rebalancing of the power differentials in the room.[74] For Goodland, consultation and participation ring hollow if potentially affected peoples cannot say "no".[75] Roesch nails it by affirming that "denying communities this right runs the danger of FPIC being used to legitimise projects implemented against the wishes of the local population. This would degrade it to a tool that possibly helps to avoid social unrest but fails to substantially mitigate the power imbalances between vulnerable communities and powerful corporations."[76]

This position in favour of the right to veto is sound from a rights perspective. It further enhances local communities' standing and power at the negotiations table. Conceptually, it even aligns well with the resistance theory alluded to above in that local communities can claim the right to resist non-consensual extractive industry activity. However, in the African context, the right to veto extractive activities, as an integral component of the right to self-determination is legally not well founded. In my view, the right to FPIC should be exercised within the confines of other compelling and relevant factors and interests. The first factor has to do with the African entrenched conception of rights which postulates that no right is absolute. The enjoyment and exercise of each Charter right should be balanced with others' rights and interests. This philosophy justifies the existence of claw-back and derogation clauses within the African Charter that limit the full enjoyment of rights. The exercise of some FPIC-related rights is limited by claw-back clauses attached to them. For example, the right to participate in government and the right to property are to be exercised respectively "in accordance with the provisions of the law"[77] and "in accordance with the provisions of appropriate laws".[78]

The second compelling factor to take into account is the notion of "national or public interest" underlying extractive industry policies in Africa and elsewhere. In the name of national solidarity, the exploration and development of natural resources shall not only benefit the affected communities. Resources are exploited in the

---

[73] Buxton A and Wilson E, FPIC and the extractive industries, A guide to applying the spirit of free, prior and informed consent in industrial projects. 2013, http://pubs.iied.org/pdfs/16530IIED.pdf (last accessed 1 October 2018); Roesch (2016), pp. 505–531; Goodland (2004), p. 68.

[74] Buxton A and Wilson E, FPIC and the extractive industries, A guide to applying the spirit of free, prior and informed consent in industrial projects. 2013, http://pubs.iied.org/pdfs/16530IIED.pdf (last accessed 1 October 2018), p. 23.

[75] Goodland (2004), p. 68.

[76] Roesch (2016), p. 523.

[77] African Charter, Article 13.

[78] African Charter, Article 14.

interest of the entire population and extraction should promote the development of the entire country. However, resource development should not take place at the expense of local populations. There is a need to protect them from the negative impacts of extractive activities. It has already been mentioned that frequently states fail to take the necessary protective measures, out of complicity with transnational corporations, lack of political will, powerlessness or incapacity to do so in the face of powerful transnational corporations usually backed-up by foreign governments and international financial institutions. The general fear that undemocratic governments will prioritize the protection of their interests at the expense of local communities explains why civil society organizations and citizens tend to strongly advocate for the right to a veto.

Finally, in most African legal regimes governing the extractive industry, states claim sovereignty and property rights over natural resources, especial subsoil resources.[79] Communities and other dwellers can, at best, claim surface rights if they own the land beneath which natural resources sit. Therefore, communities cannot claim a right to veto extraction agreements, provided that their governments compensate them for the loss of their land rights and for any other potentially negative impact on their livelihoods. Furthermore, Article 14 of the African Charter grants states leeway to expropriate citizens in the general interest of the nation. The right to property guaranteed in this provision includes land rights[80]; an eviction from land property "without prior consultation and without respecting the conditions of expulsion in the interest of public need" would amount to a violation of Article 14.[81] If the right to property as enshrined in the African Charter is not absolute, it would then be hard to think of a right to veto development activities/projects initiated or agreed to by a legitimate government.

In a nutshell, the recognition of the right to a veto that derives from FPIC may not be consistent with the legal regime of the African Charter. The right to a veto entails the risk of paralyzing extraction and development projects of the government. This scenario might lead to the lack of anticipated financial resources necessary for states to deliver on their promises and to comply with their Charter obligations to promote, fulfill and protect basic rights of its population, including local communities affected by the extractive industry. However, although FPIC should not entail the right to a veto, in my view, it should not be reduced simply to a public relations exercise or to mere consultations. According to Wilson, "for a deliberative process to work most effectively, all parties need to come to the table willing to open their minds to the views of others and seek mutually acceptable

---

[79] Zambia Lands (Amendment) Act, 1996, Article 3; Code minier du Burundi, 2012, Article 7 and 9; South Africa Mineral and Petroleum Resources Development Act No 28 of 2002, section 3(1).

[80] African Court on Human and Peoples' Rights, Application 006/2012, *African Commission on Human and Peoples' Rights v. The Republic of Kenya*, 2017, para. 131.

[81] African Court on Human and Peoples' Rights, Application 006/2012, *African Commission on Human and Peoples' Rights v. The Republic of Kenya*, 2017, para. 131.

solutions or agreement."[82] During the constructive dialogue and negotiations, some proposals can be vetoed, if an agreement cannot be reached. For instance, the Burkina Faso mining code explicitly requires community consent to mining activities that are to be carried out on or beneath a cemetery or holy place.[83] This does not mean, however, that the entire project is jeopardized. There is a need to craft a fair balance between national interests, corporate interests and those of affected communities. The latter should have a great stake and big share given the impact of extractive activities on their livelihoods compared to that on the rest of the population. In order to strike that balance, FPIC should enable local communities to give or withhold consent to extraction and development projects unless it can be shown that consent has been withheld unreasonably. At this particular juncture, one needs to distinguish between withholding consent and exercising a veto right. Communities can decide to withhold their consent after having been given clear and relevant information, along with the floor to voice concerns and articulate their own interests. To my understanding, withholding consent aims at reaffirming communities' right to fully and meaningfully participate in the decision-making processes related to extraction projects. Affected communities are entitled to disagree with other partners (governments and corporations) either on the very necessity of extraction projects or on how they should be implemented. However, the simple fact that local communities have withheld their consent does not necessarily end the project. While it is advisable that a responsible government would address their concerns in the best manner possible, other imperatives and interests are at play and, as I explained above, they can provide sufficient justification for a government's decision to pursue extraction projects. If a veto right were recognized, a local community's veto would imply the termination of the vetoed project. Given the importance of natural resources for a country and its entire population and economy, the right to veto cannot easily fit within the current African human rights perspective, which posits, as explained above, that no right is absolute.

Finally, negotiations should not be a forum for mainstream development thinking[84] and participation should not be equated to a mere "technical exercise that leaves the core assumptions of development untouched."[85] FPIC should ensure a proper engagement with the communities, their being valorized and included in extractive and development decision-making processes.

---

[82] Buxton and Wilson, FPIC and the extractive industries, A guide to applying the spirit of free, prior and informed consent in industrial projects. 2013, http://pubs.iied.org/pdfs/16530IIED.pdf (last accessed 1 October 2018), p. 38.

[83] Loi n° 036-2015/CNT portant Code Minier du Burkina Faso, JO N °44 du 29 October 2015, adopted 26 June 2015, Article 120.

[84] Leifsen et al. (2017), pp. 1045–1046.

[85] Leifsen et al. (2017), pp. 1045–1046.

4.2 FPIC Scope: From Indigenous to Non-Indigenous Applicability

Originally, as was alluded to earlier, FPIC was conceived as a right for indigenous and tribal peoples, in consideration of their material and spiritual attachment to ancestral lands, their history of domination and subjugation, and their constant desire to ensure continuity of their pre-colonial lifestyles. So far, there is no international or regional norm explicitly recognizing applicability of FPIC to other communities equally affected by the extractive industry. While this may be bearable in some other contexts, this situation can hardly be justified in the African context. First of all, natural resources are, most of the time, discovered and extracted in remote and often inaccessible areas. The inhabitants of those areas, regardless of their status as indigenous or not, are usually very poor, marginalized and vulnerable.[86] Non-indigenous communities, as well as the indigenous, depend on their lands and natural environment to ensure their food security, to get medicine and secure their well-being, to sustain their lifestyles, to perform their religious and other cultural ceremonies. There, thus, exists a special relationship between local communities and their lands and environment regardless of their non-indigenous status.

The second justification for extending FPIC to non-indigineous communities, related to the first one, is that extractive projects not only affect indigenous peoples but also other communities living close to extraction areas. Extraction-related activities on or beneath their lands may expose them, just like indigenous peoples, to adverse impacts such as human rights violations, disruption of their livelihoods and environment, food insecurity and diseases.[87] This situation requires a special protection which upholds their right to participate in decision-making processes that can potentially and negatively affect their lands and resources. While there is a clear differentiation between indigenous and non-indigenous communities in other contexts, this distinction is blurred in the African context. In the Americas, Australia and New Zealand for instance, indigenous peoples are natives of the land with different characteristics from the mainstream society mainly composed of settlers from Europe and elsewhere. The latter dominated the former; they discriminated against them and imposed their culture, legal systems, religion, lifestyles upon them to the point that one can easily claim that colonization is still ongoing in these areas. However, in the African context, as the African Commission put it, "the term

---

[86] For example, the Turkana County where oil is being exploited is "an area of sweeping rangelands in the reaches of Kenya's northwest. One of the poorest counties in the country, most inhabitants pursue livestock-keeping and a mix of opportunistic farming, charcoal burning and petty trade, see Lind, Research Briefing, Governing black gold: lessons from Oil finds in Turkana, Kenya. Institute for Development Studies, October 2017, https://opendocs.ids.ac.uk/opendocs/bitstream/handle/123456789/13279/Brief_IDSsaferworld_Turkana_Web.pdf;jsessionid=E2B19CE3F247E0A12E98AB68B32E167A?sequence=1 (last accessed 1 October 2018), p. 2. Similarly, the Basarwa people (Botswana) in the Kalahari desert stay in poor living conditions.
[87] Manirakiza (2016), pp. 118–126.

indigenous populations does not mean "first inhabitants" in reference to aboriginality as opposed to non-African communities or those having come from elsewhere."[88] Taking this peculiarity into account, the Commission was of the opinion that every African can claim to be indigenous to the continent.[89] Therefore, in most African countries, indigenous peoples are taken to form a component of local communities. In South Africa for instance, there is no distinction made for the purposes of application of the *Communal Land Rights* Act of 2004. Regarding the dispossession of lands prior to apartheid, the Constitutional Court indistinctly uses the term "indigenous" to allude to both indigenous and non-indigenous when it notes that:

> colonial settlement and expansion initiated a process whereby indigenous people were dispossessed of the land they occupied to a greater or lesser extent. The nomadic Khoi and San people in the Cape Colony were dispersed. After eight frontier wars all Xhosa people were finally colonised by the British by the end of the 19th century. So were the Zulu people in the colony of Natal. The Sotho people lost much of their land in the wars in the Orange Free State and eventually sought and found protection under the British in what is now Lesotho.[90]

As a consequence, the Court held that "communal law and indigenous law are so closely intertwined that it is almost impossible to deal with one without dealing with the other".[91]

Thus, on a conceptual level, there is no justification for excluding extraction-affected non-indigenous local communities from enjoying and exercising a right to FPIC.[92] Most of the time, in extractive industry contexts, indigenous and non-indigenous local communities are equally situated and therefore must be accorded equal treatment. Therefore, the consultation and consent standard should equally apply to non-indigenous communities affected or likely to be affected by the extractive industry sector. The African human rights law and the case law confirm this view. Although the African Charter does not specifically provide for FPIC as highlighted above, a number of its provisions have been interpreted as recognizing FPIC, both for indigenous and non-indigenous peoples affected by the extractive industry. For instance, the non-indigenous peoples of Cabinda alleged Angola's economic exploitation of Cabindan resources since the people of Cabinda were not allowed to

---

[88] African Commission on Human and Peoples' Rights, Advisory Opinion of the African Commission on Human and Peoples' Rights on the United Nations Declaration on the Rights of Indigenous Peoples, 41st session, 2007, para. 13.

[89] African Commission on Human and Peoples' Rights, Advisory Opinion of the African Commission on Human and Peoples' Rights on the United Nations Declaration on the Rights of Indigenous Peoples, 41st session, 2007, para. 13. However, this should not be interpreted as a negation by the African Commission of the existence of indigenous communities in Africa. Like other human rights mechanisms, the Commission does recognize that status and in fact, through its working group on indigenous communities/populations, it does work for the promotion and protection of indigenous communities identified as such.

[90] South African Constitutional Court, Case CCT 100/09, *Tongoane v Minister for Agriculture and Land Affairs*, (2010) 6 SA 214 (CC), fn. 12.

[91] South African Constitutional Court, Case CCT 100/09, *Tongoane v Minister for Agriculture and Land Affairs*, (2010) 6 SA 214 (CC), para. 88.

[92] Manirakiza (2013), pp. 6–9.

have any say in the grant of extraction licences and concessions, despite the negative impacts they endured.[93] The Commission reaffirmed its earlier jurisprudence that, in accordance with Article 21, the Charter is applicable in post-colonial Africa in favour of groups within States. It triggers an obligation on the part of the State Parties to protect their citizens from exploitation by external economic powers and to ensure that groups and communities, directly or through their representatives, are involved in decisions relating to the disposal of their wealth.[94] Similarly, in the above-mentioned SERAC case, the African Commission held that the non-indigenous Ogoni people should be consulted and participate in decision-making regarding their resources and development priorities.[95] Furthermore, as mentioned above, soft law and sub-regional law confirm the trend of non-discrimination between indigenous and non-indigenous peoples as concerns FPIC.

In a nutshell, FPIC in the African context applies both to indigenous and non-indigenous communities. This resonates very well with the spirit of the African Charter, which provides for and protects rights of groups, no matter their status or size. According to Ashuken, this principle can only be relevant in Africa if it is "applied beyond the context of indigenous and tribal people to include local communities and all other people who may be adversely affected by large-scale land acquisition activities, including land grabbing."[96] Accordingly, in the extractive sector, as the African Commission has held at numerous occasions, the affected communities, no matter their status, have the right to be consulted and to give their free, prior and informed consent to decisions concerning exploitation and extraction of their resources or any other development plan.

4.3   FPIC Implementation Challenges in the Extractive Industry in Africa

In Africa, the implementation of the FPIC principle in the extractive sector is problematic, mainly because rights holders (local communities) are disempowered and lack resources and expertise, basically for legal and political reasons. Socio-cultural circumstances also limit substantive participation and disempower some community members.

---

[93]African Commission on Human and Peoples' Rights, Communication 328/06, *Front for the Liberation of the State of Cabinda v. Republic of Angola*, 2013, para. 6.

[94]African Commission on Human and Peoples' Rights, Communication 328/06, *Front for the Liberation of the State of Cabinda v. Republic of Angola*, 2013, para. 129.

[95]African Commission on Human and Peoples' Rights, Case 155/96, *Social and Economic Rights Action Center (SERAC) and Center for Economic and Social Rights (CESR) v. Nigeria*, 2001, para. 53.

[96]Ashukem (2016), p. 6.

4.3.1   Shaky Legal Foundations of FPIC

The implementation of the FPIC principle in sub-Saharan Africa encounters legal challenges. The first of these challenges is that FPIC is not provided for domestic legislations of most countries. Although it can be inferred from the African Charter to which almost all African states are parties, State parties have failed to domesticate the FPIC principle. The silence of domestic laws as regards FPIC deprives right holders of the necessary legal basis to articulate their claims as to how natural resources should be managed and development carried out.[97] Even for indigenous peoples, it is worth noting as I mentioned above, that only one state so far is party to the relevant legal instruments. Therefore, right holders have to rely on regional instruments and mechanisms to vindicate their rights. Practice in this regard shows that this is a viable avenue, although there are still some legal hurdles to overcome. The first one has to do with the Charter claw-back and derogation clauses alluded to above, which impose limitations to the enjoyment of FPIC-related rights. The second relates to the relative inaccessibility of relevant regional mechanisms. For instance, any rights complaint before regional human rights mechanisms must satisfy the general admissibility conditions.[98] Moreover, the provisions of article 34(6) of the protocol establishing the African Court limit accessibility to the Court for citizens and NGOs absent a special declaration made by State parties to that effect. The limited capacity of adjudication bodies, along with non-implementation of their decisions is also cause for concern.

Finally, another legal constraint derives from the issue of ownership of natural resources. This thorny question is very important because ownership determines who has the final word in resource governance. In post-independence sub-Saharan Africa, most domestic legal orders uphold state ownership of subsoil natural resources. States, thus, claim that they are the sole legitimate actors in decision-making regarding non-renewable resource extraction. This seems to be a prolongation of colonial rule where the colonial state unilaterally decreed sole ownership over natural resources to the detriment of colonized or dominated peoples. During pre-colonial times, the owner of the land was also the owner of the sub-soil. Landowners could grant access to clay, cassiterite ore, etc. sitting beneath their lands. Under colonial rule, however, there have been some pushbacks from colonized or dominated peoples who have contested state ownership and reclaimed sovereignty over their resources.

In this area of "contested resource sovereignties",[99] one may contend that the rationale behind the emergence of the principle of peoples' permanent sovereignty over natural resources was to prevent well-intentioned but weak or myopic leadership from endangering the survival of the country through wide concessionary

---

[97] A handful of States including Burkina Faso have enacted legislation providing for FPIC, see Loi n° 036-2015/CNT portant Code Minier du Burkina Faso, JO N °44 du 29 Octobre 2015, adopted 26 June 2015.

[98] African Charter, Article 56.

[99] Schilling-Vacaflor (2017), p. 1061.

arrangements.[100] The principle imposes legal restraint or constraint on governments to avoid jeopardizing the rights and interests of affected communities. That is why some laws try to constrain state action by requiring governments to hold the ownership of and manage natural resources in the peoples' trust.[101] Nowadays, communities are also mobilizing for greater control over natural resources production and development. This is understandable because resources, with the exception of state owned land, are usually being extracted on or beneath their lands and extraction affects other commodities such as water or forests. Losing control over land and resource governance implies a loss of control over their own survival. For the communities, their land or surface rights extend to the sub-soil. The UN Special Rapporteur on the Rights of Indigenous Peoples is of the view that in the case of state owned sub-soil resources on indigenous peoples' lands, indigenous peoples still have the right to free, prior and informed consent for the exploration and exploitation of those resources and have a right to benefit-sharing arrangements.[102] Therefore, permits for extraction and even prospection of natural resources on indigenous land should not be granted if the activity prevents indigenous peoples from continuing to use and/or benefit from these areas or where the free, prior and informed consent of indigenous peoples concerned has not been obtained.[103] The same should also hold true for other local communities.

Given the argument made in this chapter in favor of local communities' rights, I would make the claim that the latter should also have a say in resources extraction beneath their lands, even if they actually lack legal ownership of sub-soil resources. In any case, extraction and development of resources will undoubtedly infringe their land rights and impact on their lives and lifestyles. Ascertaining FPIC in their favor will then depend on who holds land rights[104] and, as highlighted above, there is a growing demand for the recognition of substantive participation of local communities, be they indigenous or not, in extractive decision-making processes that may affect them.

4.3.2 Lack of Technical Expertise and Agency

FPIC assumes that affected communities have the power to make appropriate choices, weighing the costs and opportunities of a particular extractive project, and influence the way a particular project is designed.[105] However, that is not necessarily the case. Most of the time, natural resources are extracted in remote areas where

---

[100] Duruigbo (2014), p. 114.

[101] Zambia *Lands (Amendment) Act*, 1996, Article 3; South Africa *Mineral and Petroleum Resources Development Act No 28 of 2002*, section 3(1); Economic Community of West African States (2009), *Directive C/DIR. 3/05/09*, Article 3(3).

[102] United Nations Development Group Guidelines on Indigenous Peoples (February 2009).

[103] United Nations Development Group Guidelines on Indigenous Peoples (February 2009).

[104] Rutherford (2017), p. 257.

[105] Milne and Adams (2012), pp. 133–158.

local communities live in extreme poverty, with few resources and infrastructure and no access to resources to meet their basic needs in terms of health, education, food security, water, etc.[106] These extreme living conditions place them in a vulnerable situation. When facing extractive companies, very few communities are empowered to clearly and effectively articulate their concerns. Local communities' representatives face representatives of powerful corporations, who are well equipped with the technical and legal skills relevant in the extractive industry sector. Those skills are simply lacking in most local communities, which impedes their proper and substantive participation in complex and asymmetric negotiations with companies and governments over natural resource projects. Most of the time, as Wilson argues, local and national governments, as well as civil society organizations, act as intermediaries between companies and communities during the discussions.[107] However, government representation is ineffective and inadequate for political reasons as highlighted below. Some authors find the civil society intervention deplorable since it undermines the ability of the company to engage directly with the community and to undertake public consultation and disclosure in a meaningful way.[108] So there is a need for local communities to be empowered and assisted so that they can articulate their concerns and interests, and henceforth participate in direct negotiations with the extractive industries in a meaningful way. Civil society organizations should play a critical role in raising their agency and helping them to organize for better results. It is only under such conditions that local communities can substantively enjoy and exercise their right to FPIC.

4.3.3   Political Constraints

Political constraints can seriously hamper the substantive enjoyment of the right to FPIC in sub-Saharan African countries. In fact, most of the political rhetoric that every proposed extractive industry policy is solely in the national or collective interests does not necessarily conform to reality. The needs and interests of local communities are not the same as those of governments. For instance, the Nigerian government condones Shell's extractive activities despite their devastating impact on Ogonis' lives.[109] In Malawi, the main rivers were contaminated by uranium radiation due to the Kayelekera uranium mine.[110] In Botswana, the Basarwa were

---

[106] See above p. 21.

[107] Buxton and Wilson, FPIC and the extractive industries, A guide to applying the spirit of free, prior and informed consent in industrial projects. 2013, http://pubs.iied.org/pdfs/16530IIED.pdf (last accessed 1 October 2018), p. 44.

[108] Buxton and Wilson, FPIC and the extractive industries, A guide to applying the spirit of free, prior and informed consent in industrial projects. 2013, http://pubs.iied.org/pdfs/16530IIED.pdf (last accessed 1 October 2018), p. 44.

[109] African Commission on Human and Peoples' Rights, Case 155/96, *Social and Economic Rights Action Center (SERAC) and Center for Economic and Social Rights (CESR) v. Nigeria*, 2001, para. 54.

[110] Chareyon (2015), pp. 30–32.

evicted from their homeland so that the government could create a game reserve.[111] Moreover, most governments are engulfed in corruption practices; they are less committed to human rights and they tend to focus on their own interests which are synonymous with remaining in power. Thus, a corrupt, self-interested and power-hungry political elite will resist and oppose losing control over natural resources, which are the sources of its ill-acquired wealth. For example, according to Werner, "natural resources in Sierra Leone have been exploited by the elite at the expense of local development, and have thus contributed to civil war and general unrest."[112] He recounts that "under the government of Siaka Stevens from 1967 to 1996, mining rights were used by the government as a strategic tool to ensure the loyalty of sup-porters and to arm illicit diamond mining groups comprised mostly of unemployed youths who served as 'presidential forces' intimidating political opponents when necessary."[113] In Nigeria, Druigbo claims that "as oil and gas revenues play a key role in maintaining their hold on power, these politicians would view giving it up as suicidal."[114]

In a nutshell, political reasons can impede substantive participation of local com-munities in the democratic governance of the extractive industry sector. The inter-ests of local communities run the risk of being side-lined for the benefit of the "greater good" solely determined by governments at all levels. That's why Druigbo argues that "the immediate needs of the individuals in African petroleum-producing countries need to be taken into account beyond infrastructure provision, anti-corruption campaigns, or general nation-building efforts."[115]

4.3.4 Socio-Cultural Challenges

The promotion of democratic governance in the extractive industry is further ham-pered by the lack of a commonly accepted definition of "local communities". I concur with the definition suggested by Ashuken who presents a local community as "a group of people living in a given geographical area by reason of their ancestral lineage, and sharing common cultural and traditional characteristics, and having a strong relationship to their land, which serves as an important sacred ground for spiritual and traditional rituals and cleansing and on which they practise diverse economic activities such as hunting, food and cash crops farming, and pastoral farming, among other activities."[116] Local communities affected by the extractive industry are not homogenous and do not abide by the same traditions and rules. Like any rural communities in Africa, they have a range of social differentiation along

---

[111] Pham et al. (2015), pp. 2409–2410.

[112] Werner (2017), p. 315.

[113] Werner (2017), p. 315.

[114] Duruigbo (2014), p. 116.

[115] Duruigbo (2014), p. 116.

[116] Ashukem (2016), p. 5.

many social axes such as gender, class, ethnicity and kinship.[117] In this regard, ensuring that both groups and interest groups are represented on an equal footing is a daunting task. Yet, even if it may prove difficult, representatives should speak for the entire community.

Moreover, discrimination practices may jeopardize the ability of an important part of members of local communities to fully participate in the negotiations and ensure that their rights are upheld. For instance, women are among the most vulnerable and frequently victims of extraction projects.[118] And yet, most of them do not enjoy land rights and men may challenge their claim to participation in negotiations. Apart from women, other vulnerable groups such as the elderly, the disabled and children usually also face discrimination. Therefore, extractive industry corporations or community representatives should ensure *proprio motu* that the concerns of vulnerable and marginalized groups are also taken into consideration.

5 Conclusion

The exploration and extraction of natural resources affect substantive rights enshrined in the African Charter, which entail autonomy of decision-making in their exercise,[119] such as the right to property, the right to culture, the right to a healthy environment, the right to development, the right to self-determination, the rights to health and physical well-being and the right to freely dispose of wealth and natural resources. In order to mitigate the negative impact of the extractive industry on local communities, the right to FPIC ensures that the former are full participants at the negotiating table, along with governments and corporations. FPIC seeks to address the structural and power imbalances in the governance of natural resources. It enables affected communities to effectively articulate their concerns and interests in a domain where they have been historically excluded from the decision-making process. Originally conceived for indigenous and tribal peoples, this chapter argues, in the African context, that the right to FPIC should also benefit non-indigenous communities affected or likely to be affected by the extractive industry. Therefore, indigenous as well as non-indigenous peoples should have a big share and be both stakeholders and shareholders in the industry. Nevertheless, the chapter posits, in

---

[117] Rutherford (2017), p. 251.

[118] Galindo NJ, Environmental Security For Women In The Context of Extractive Industries. Bogotà, 2015, http://rednacionaldemujeres.org/phocadownloadpap/environmental_security.pdf (last accessed 1 October 2018); Kachika T, Gender & Legal Consultant. LawPlus, P.O. Box 2989, Lilongwe, Malawi, December 2014, https://mininginmalawi.files.wordpress.com/2013/05/2015-12-3-un-women-malawi-final-law-and-policy-analysis-dec-3-20141.pdf (last accessed 1 October 2018); Adamson (2017), pp. 24–31; Oxfam International, Position Paper on Gender Justice and the Extractive Industries. March 2017, https://www.oxfamamerica.org/static/media/files/EI_and_GJ_position_paper_v.15_FINAL_03202017_green_Kenny.pdf (last accessed 1 October 2018).

[119] Anaya, Report of the Special Rapporteur on the rights of indigenous peoples, A/ HRC/21/47, 6 July 2012, paras. 51.

accordance with African human rights, that the right to FPIC does not entail the right to a veto. It has to be exercised in relation to other compelling interests, in a way that the rights and interests of affected communities are balanced against the legitimate interests of the rest of the population to benefit from the resources of their motherland. Given the ongoing "African Springs"[120] with the African citizenry demanding better governance as concerns political, economic and social life, one thing we can be sure of is that communities affected by resource extraction are no longer passive and fully obedient to the government. FPIC is the necessary tool for effective and substantive participation as well as an empowering tool that can contribute to emancipatory transformation.[121]

References

Abebe AK (2009) The power of indigenous people to veto development activities: the right to free, prior and informed consent (FPIC) with specific reference to Ethiopia. University of Pretoria, Pretoria

Adamson R (2017) Vulnerabilities of women in extractive industries. Indian J Women Soc Change 2(1):24–31

Ambe-Uva T (2017) Whither the state? Mining codes and mineral resource governance in Africa. Can J Afr Stud/Revue canadienne des études africaines 51:81–101

Ashukem JCN (2016) Included or excluded: an analysis of the application of the free, prior and informed consent principle in land grabbing cases in Cameroon. Potchefstroom Electron Law J 19(1):1–29

Besada H, Martin P (2015) Mining codes in Africa: emergence of a "fourth" generation? Camb Rev Int Aff 28(2):263–282

Buthelezi S (2005) Regional integration in Africa: prospects and challenges for the 21st century. Ikwezi Afrika Publishers, East London

Carmody P (2011) The new scramble for Africa. Polity Press, Cambridge

Chareyon B (2015) Impact of the Kayelekera Uranium Mine, Malawi. EJOLT Report No. 21:30–32

Diallo P (2016) The Africa mining vision: a Panacea to the challenges of the African mining sector or another mirage? Leadersh Dev Soc 1(1):1–7

Duruigbo E (2014) Realizing the people's right to natural resources. Whitehead J Dipl Int Relat 12(1):111–123

Finlay CJ (2015) Terrorism and the right to resist: a theory of just revolutionary war. Cambridge University Press, Cambridge

Goodland R (2004) Free, prior and informed consent and the WB Group. Sustain Dev Law Policy 4:2

Heyns C (2001) A "struggle approach" to human rights. In: Soeteman A (ed) Pluralism in law. Springer, New York, pp 171–190

Hönke J (2009) Extractive orders: transnational mining companies in the nineteenth and twenty-first centuries in the Central African Copperbelt. In: Melber H, Southall R (eds) A new scramble for Africa? Imperialism, investment and development. University of KwaZulu-Natal Press, Durban, pp 274–298

Honore T (1988) The right to rebel. Oxf J Leg Stud 8(1):34–54

---

[120] Obse (2014), p. 817.

[121] Leifsen et al. (2017), p. 1045.

Leifsen E, Gustafsson MT, Guzmán-Gallegos MA, Schilling-Vacaflor A (2017) New mechanisms of participation in extractive governance: between technologies of governance and resistance work. Third World Q 38(5):1043–1057

Locke J (1689) Second treatise of government. Awnsham Churchill

Manirakiza P (2013) Loyola University Chicago International Law Symposium, Keynote address towards an African human rights perspective on the extractive industry. Loyola Univ Chicago Int Law Rev 11(1):6–9

Manirakiza P (2015) The extractive industry sector and human rights law in Africa. Min Law Rev 2016(2):3–15

Manirakiza P (2016) La protection des droits humains à l'ère de l'industrie extractive en Afrique. Criminologie 49(2):118–126

McNeish JA (2017) A vote to derail extraction: popular consultation and resource sovereignty in Tolima, Colombia. Third World Q 38(5):1128–1145

Melber H, Southall R (2009) A new scramble for Africa?. In: Melber H, Southall R (eds) A new scramble for Africa? Imperialism, investment and development. University of KwaZulu-Natal Press, Durban

Milne S, Adams B (2012) Market masquerades: uncovering the politics of community-level payments for environmental services in Cambodia. Dev Change 43(1):133–158

Murphy S (2011) Unique in international human rights law: Article 20(2) and the right to resist in the African Charter on Human and Peoples' Rights. Afr Human Rights Law 11(2):465–494

Obse K (2014) The Arab Spring and the question of legality of democratic revolution in theory and practice: a perspective based on the African Union normative framework. Leiden J Int Law 27(4):817–838

Pham TT, Jean-Christophe Castella JC, Lestrelin G, Mertz O, Ngoc Le D, Moeliono M, Nguyen TQ, Vu HT, Nguyen TD (2015) Adapting Free, Prior, and Informed Consent (FPIC) to local contexts in REDD+: lessons from three experiments in Vietnam. Forests 6:2409–2410

Roesch R (2016) The story of a legal transplant: the right to free, prior and informed consent in sub-Saharan Africa. Afr Human Rights Law J 16(2):505–531

Rousseau JJ (1920) The social contract & discourses. J.M. Dent & Sons Ltd/E.P. Duton & Co, London and Toronto/New York

Rutherford B (2017) Governance and land deals in Africa: opportunities and challenges in advancing community rights. J Sustain Dev Law Policy 8(1):235–258

Schilling-Vacaflor A (2017) Who controls the territory and the resources? Free, prior and informed consent (FPIC) as a contested human rights practice in Bolivia. Third World Q 38(5):1043–1057

Szablowski D (2010) Operationalizing free, prior, and informed consent in the extractive industry sector? Examining the challenges of a negotiated model of justice. Can J Dev Stud/Revue canadienne d'études du développement 30(1–2):111–130

Werner K (2017) The role of the state and the transnational in lifting the resource curse. J Sustain Dev Law Policy 8(1):309–330

Wicomb W, Smith H (2011) Customary communities as people and their customary tenure as culture: what we can do with the Endorois decision. Afr Human Rights Law J 11(2):422–446

Pacifique Manirakiza is associate professor at the Faculty of Common Law at the University of Ottawa. Previously, he was a member of the AU-led Commission of Inquiry on South Sudan, part of a defence team before the International Criminal Tribunal for Rwanda and a member of the African Commission on Human and Peoples' Rights. In this capacity he spent a lot of time advocating for the rights of communities affected by the extractive industries. He holds a law degree from Burundi and an LL.M, as well as a PhD from the University of Ottawa.

The Corporate Responsibility to Respect Consultation Rights in the Americas: How the Inter-American System Can Better Promote Free, Prior, and Informed Consent

C. Ignacio de Casas

Contents

1 Introduction 247
2 FPIC Standards in the Americas 249
   2.1 A Derivation from the Right to Property 250
   2.2 The Use of Exogenous Instruments: ILO Convention 169 and UNDRIP 252
   2.3 The Duty to Consult as a Principle of International Law 256
   2.4 FPIC as a Duty of the State in the Inter-American System 260
3 The Corporate Responsibility to Respect FPIC in the Inter-American System 262
   3.1 The State Due Diligence Standard: A Source of Indirect Responsibility of
      Corporations 262
   3.2 The Possibility of a Direct Responsibility of Corporations Under Inter-American
      Law 266
   3.3 The Delegation to Businesses of the State Duty to Consult 267
4 How the Organs of the Inter-American System Can Help to Promote a Direct
   Corporate Responsibility to Respect FPIC 273
   4.1 Constructing a Direct Corporate Responsibility in the IAHRS 273
   4.2 Tackling the Procedural Obstacles 276
5 Conclusion 277
References 278

1 Introduction

Two of the most rapidly developing issues in international law in recent years are the responsibilities of corporations to respect human rights, and the right of indigenous peoples to give or withhold free, prior, and informed consent for the use of their lands and resources (FPIC). In addition, both issues have points of

C. I. de Casas (✉)
Universidad Austral, Buenos Aires, Argentina
e-mail: idecasas@austral.edu.ar

© Springer Nature Switzerland AG 2019
I. Feichtner et al. (eds.), *Human Rights in the Extractive Industries*,
Interdisciplinary Studies in Human Rights 3,
https://doi.org/10.1007/978-3-030-11382-7_10

intersection, namely in the extractive industry sector, where corporations impact indigenous peoples' rights whenever they carry out their activities on the latter's ancestral lands.

Key moments in the "business and human rights" debate were the UN Human Rights Council's endorsement of the Protect, Respect and Remedy Framework in 2008, and the United Nations Guiding Principles on Business and Human Rights (UNGPs) in 2011. According to the UNGPs, corporations have a "responsibility to respect" human rights, which means that "they should avoid infringing on the human rights of others and should address adverse human rights impacts with which they are involved".[1] UNGP 12 provides:

> The responsibility of business enterprises to respect human rights refers to internationally recognized human rights –understood, at a minimum, as those expressed in the International Bill of Human Rights and the principles concerning fundamental rights set out in the International Labour Organization's Declaration on Fundamental Principles and Rights at Work.

Although the UNGPs do not explicitly discuss FPIC, the commentary to UNGP 12 adds that business enterprises may need to consider additional standards, including the UN instruments that have elaborated on the rights of indigenous peoples.[2] The UN Special Rapporteur on the Rights of Indigenous Peoples has affirmed that "the rights that corporations should respect include the rights of indigenous peoples as set forth in the UN Declaration on the Rights of Indigenous Peoples [UNDRIP, which includes FPIC in several provisions] and in other sources".[3] In summary, these sources confirm that general international law recognizes a corporate responsibility to respect FPIC.

In the Americas, however, despite being one of the regions where the development of FPIC has reached the highest standards,[4] this progressiveness contrasts with the comparatively slow development in the region of the responsibilities of corporations to respect human rights—and specifically indigenous rights.

---

[1] UN Human Rights Council, Guiding Principles on Business and Human Rights: Implementing the United Nations "Protect, Respect and Remedy" Framework, Un Doc. HR/PUB/11/04, 2011, UNGP 11.

[2] UN Human Rights Council, Guiding Principles on Business and Human Rights: Implementing the United Nations "Protect, Respect and Remedy" Framework, Un Doc. HR/PUB/11/04, 2011, Commentary to UNGP 12. See also Lehr, AK, Indigenous peoples' rights and the role of free, prior and informed consent: Good practice note endorsed by the UN Global Compact Human Rights and Labour Working Group. UN Global Compact, 20 February 2014, https://www.unglobalcompact. org/docs/issues_doc/human_rights/Human_Rights_Working_Group/FPIC_Indigenous_Peoples_ GPN.pdf (last accessed 1 October 2018), p. 6.

[3] UN Human Rights Council, Report of the Special Rapporteur on the rights of indigenous peoples, James Anaya, UN Doc. A/HRC/21/47, 6 July 2012, para. 59. See also Lehr, AK, Indigenous peoples' rights and the role of free, prior and informed consent: Good practice note endorsed by the UN Global Compact Human Rights and Labour Working Group. UN Global Compact, 20 February 2014, https://www.unglobalcompact.org/docs/issues_doc/human_rights/Human_Rights_Working_ Group/FPIC_Indigenous_Peoples_GPN.pdf (last accessed 1 October 2018), p. 6.

[4] Hanna and Vanclay (2013), pp. 151–152; see also Heyns and Killander (2013), p. 689.

This chapter focuses on the law—treaty-based and case law—of the Inter-American Human Rights system (IAHRS or "the Inter-American System"), which will be called "Inter-American law". It begins by explaining the development of FPIC in the IAHRS, and provisionally concludes that the regional system of protection restricts itself to the state obligation to protect and respect FPIC, rather than being also open to corporate responsibility (Sect. 2).

If the responsibility lies with the state, but sometimes arises from the unlawful activity of corporations, a corporation may still be found in some way responsible for violations of indigenous rights. The chapter finds that there are in fact implicit corporate responsibilities to be found in the case law. These arise from the due diligence standard, an Inter-American doctrine that holds that states are responsible for the actions of private parties, if those parties are under their jurisdiction and the state has not acted with "due diligence" to prevent those actions or to ensure the respect for human rights. That is the province of Sect. 3.1, which examines the role of corporations in the IAHRS jurisprudence, in order to determine whether they are required to comply with any human rights standards regarding indigenous peoples, pursuant to Inter-American law. Those responsibilities are termed "indirect" in this chapter.

The aim of the subsequent pages is to explore whether there are (or could be) certain "direct" responsibilities regarding indigenous peoples that corporations must abide by in the Inter-American law (Sect. 3.2). For that purpose the chapter addresses in particular the issue of the delegation of the duty to consult by the state to private corporations. The thesis is that if this kind of delegation is permitted in the IAHRS, it could give rise to a direct responsibility of corporations.

In Sect. 4.1, the chapter proposes one way in which direct corporate responsibilities could be framed based on the existing Inter-American human rights standards. Finally, in Sect. 4.2, some guidance is suggested on how the organs of the IAHRS could develop these responsibilities.

The conclusion argues that with direct and explicit corporate responsibilities the focus shifts from an exclusive duty-bearer (the state) to shared duty-bearers (the state and corporations), thus resulting in better protection for rights-holders.

2   FPIC Standards in the Americas

Across the different international legal regimes, two rights in particular are closely related to the protection of FPIC. They are the right to self-determination and the right to collectively own ancestral lands.[5] In other human rights systems FPIC has been derived from the former, in conjunction with a variety of other rights, notably the right to cultural development,[6] or has been expressly recognized in their legal

---

[5] Barelli (2012), p. 2.

[6] For example, the Human Rights Committee has also grounded this right in Article 27 of the International Covenant on Civil and Political Rights (the right to cultural development of minori-

instruments.[7] In the IAHRS, however, the basis of this collective right is generally held to be the right to collectively own ancestral lands (or right to communal property), as this section argues.

A review of the case law and reports of the Inter-American Commission on Human Rights (IACHR or "the Commission") and the Inter-American Court of Human Rights (IACtHR or "the Court") will reveal how FPIC was constructed in the Americas.[8]

2.1   A Derivation from the Right to Property

To begin with, neither FPIC nor consultation rights of any sort are expressly recognized in the text of the American Convention on Human Rights (ACHR) or the American Declaration of the Rights and Duties of Man (the "American Declaration"), the principal regional human rights instruments.[9] Instead, the organs of the IAHRS have created them, or derived them, from other legal provisions.[10]

---

ties), See UN Human Rights Committee, Communication No. 1457/2006, *Ángela Poma Poma v. Perú*, UN Doc. CCPR/C/95/D/1457/2006, 27 March 2009, para. 7. The Committee on Economic, Social and Cultural rights included FPIC in its general comment on the right to take part in cultural life enshrined in Article 15(a) of the ICECR, See UN Committee on Economic Social and Cultural Rights, General Comment No. 21, UN Doc. E/C.12/GC/21, 21 December 2009, paras. 37, 55. At the regional level, the African Commission has found lack of FPIC to constitute a violation of Article 22 of the African Charter, on the right to development, See African Commission on Human and Peoples' Rights, 276/2003, *Centre for Minority Rights Development (Kenya) v. Kenya*, 4 February 2010, paras. 281–298.

[7] e.g. ILO Convention No. 169, Article 6; UN Declaration on the Rights of Indigenous Peoples, Articles 19 and 32.

[8] The structure used in this section to describe the Inter-American standards follows the chronological development of the case law. This warning seems necessary for the readers may find that the Inter-American case law is not always coherent or clear. Sometimes it is not easy to distinguish between consultation and consent (or, for example, what role Environmental Impact Assessments play). For the purposes of this chapter, its author understands that it is not relevant to be able to make the distinction between consultation and consent, especially when it has been argued that "the Court [has] not comprehensively examine[d] the issue of consent or the consequences of the failure to obtain it." Brunner and Quintana (2012).

[9] An analogy between the American Declaration and Convention could be made with the Universal Declaration and the International Covenants (on Civil and Political Rights, and on Economic, Social, and Cultural Rights). This is to say, the Declaration is not legally binding *per se*, but as customary law, while the Convention is a treaty, and therefore, binding for those American states that have ratified it. See also footnote 15.

[10] Gómez et al. (2016), pp. 81 and 95–96.

The first cases on indigenous peoples' rights that these organs had to deal with addressed the issue of their right to "communal property" (yet another right that was not enshrined in those instruments).[11]

In *Awas Tingni Community v. Nicaragua* the Court found that the state had violated Article 21 ACHR, which notably protects the right to *individual* property. In order to reach this conclusion, the Court had to give the term "property" a different meaning, based on the idea that human rights treaties are living instruments that must be interpreted in an evolutionary fashion.[12] The Court held that:

> [A]rticle 21 of the Convention protects the right to property in a sense which includes, among others, the rights of members of the indigenous communities within the framework of communal property.[13]

The following year, the Commission issued a report in a case concerning members of the Western Shoshone indigenous people.[14] It is worth noting that the United States has not ratified the American Convention, so the IACHR only applied the American Declaration.[15]

In that case, the Commission mentioned consultation rights for the first time, as deriving from property rights.[16] The IACHR stated:

> [T]he American Declaration specially oblige[s] a member State to ensure that any determination of the extent to which indigenous claimants maintain interests in the lands to which they have traditionally held title and have occupied and used is based upon a process of fully informed and mutual consent on the part of the indigenous community as a whole.[17]

In another case before the IACHR, the Mayas of Toledo complained that Belize had systematically failed to consult them on the granting of logging and oil concessions to private companies, which threatened their rights to property, health and environment.[18]

---

[11] Inter-American Commission on Human Rights, Indigenous Peoples, Afro-Descendent Communities, and Natural Resources: Human Rights Protection in the Context of Extraction, Exploitation, and Development Activities, OEA/Ser.L/V/II. Doc. 47/15, 31 December 2015, para. 225.

[12] Inter-American Court of Human Rights, Series C No. 79, *Mayagna (Sumo) Awas Tingni Community v. Nicaragua (Merits, Reparations and Costs)*, Judgment 31 August 2001, para. 146.

[13] Inter-American Court of Human Rights, Series C No. 79, *Mayagna (Sumo) Awas Tingni Community v. Nicaragua (Merits, Reparations and Costs)*, 31 August 2001, para. 148.

[14] Inter-American Commission on Human Rights, Case 11.140, Report N° 75/02, *Mary and Carrie Dann (United States)*, 27 December 2002.

[15] Which is not a treaty, i.e., needs no ratification, and applies to all members of the Organization of American States simply by virtue of their membership status.

[16] Inter-American Commission on Human Rights, Case 11.140, Report N° 75/02, *Mary and Carrie Dann (United States)*, 27 December 2002, paras. 130-31.

[17] Inter-American Commission on Human Rights, Case 11.140, Report N° 75/02, *Mary and Carrie Dann (United States)*, 27 December 2002, para 140.

[18] Inter-American Juridical Committee, Corporate Social Responsibility in the Area of Human Rights and the Environment in the Americas, Second Report, OEA/Ser.Q, CJI/doc.449/14 rev.1, 11 March 2014, p. 17.

In its report, the Commission mentioned once again the need for "consideration and informed consultations" with the indigenous people, based on the right to use and enjoy property.[19] It also noted that third parties such as business enterprises could become perpetrators of violations of these rights, when acting with the tolerance or acquiescence of the state.[20]

2.2 The Use of Exogenous Instruments: ILO Convention 169 and UNDRIP

The first mention of the Indigenous and Tribal Peoples Convention of 1989 (ILO Convention 169) in relation to consultation in the IAHRS is found in *Yakye Axa Indigenous Community v. Paraguay*, concerning lands that the Yakye Axa considered their traditional habitat.[21]

In that case, when finding a violation of the right to property in Article 21 ACHR, the Court took into account the special meaning of communal property of ancestral lands for indigenous people, including the preservation of their cultural identity and its transmission to future generations.[22]

Accordingly:

[T]he Court deem[ed] it useful and appropriate to resort to other international treaties, aside from the American Convention, such as ILO Convention No. 169, to interpret its provisions in accordance with the evolution of the inter-American system, taking into account related developments in International Human Rights Law.

(…) ILO Convention No. 169 contains numerous provisions pertaining to the right of indigenous communities to communal property, which is addressed in this case, and said provisions can shed light on the content and scope of Article 21 of the American Convention.[23]

ILO Convention 169 is a treaty that is foreign to the Inter-American System, and as such the Court has no jurisdiction to apply it as law.[24] The mechanism that enabled the Court to use ILO Convention 169 in its reasoning is one expressly contained in the American Convention, namely Article 29 (b): "No provision of this Convention shall be interpreted as: (…) restricting the enjoyment or exercise of any right or

---

[19] Inter-American Commission on Human Rights, Case 12.053, Report N° 40/04, *Maya indigenous communities of the Toledo district (Belize), Merits*, 12 October 2004, para. 140.

[20] Inter-American Commission on Human Rights, Case 12.053, Report N° 40/04, *Maya indigenous communities of the Toledo district (Belize), Merits*, 12 October 2004, para. 140.

[21] Inter-American Court of Human Rights, Series C No. 125, *Yakye Axa Indigenous Community v. Paraguay (Merits, Reparations and Costs)*, 17 June 2005, para. 50.

[22] Inter-American Court of Human Rights, Series C No. 125, *Yakye Axa Indigenous Community v. Paraguay (Merits, Reparations and Costs)*, 17 June 2005, para. 124.

[23] Inter-American Court of Human Rights, Series C No. 125, *Yakye Axa Indigenous Community v. Paraguay (Merits, Reparations and Costs)*, 17 June 2005, paras. 127 and 130.

[24] On the use of foreign or exogenous instruments by the Court see Lixinski (2010), p. 597; Neuman (2008), p. 110.

freedom recognized by virtue of the laws of any State Party or by virtue of another convention to which one of the said States is a party". In the case, the Court noted that the state had ratified and included Convention 169 in its domestic legislation.[25]

Following this case, ILO Convention 169 became part of the reasoning of the Court in every indigenous peoples case, including its judgments on consultation rights, regardless of whether the state involved had ratified the ILO Convention.[26] The same happened with the UNDRIP, since its approval, in several cases.[27]

Interestingly, in *Saramaka People v. Suriname* the Court encountered difficulties when applying its previous interpretation of Article 21, as Suriname had not ratified ILO Convention 169. Noting that Suriname is a party to both International Covenants on Civil and Political Rights, and Economic, Social and Cultural Rights,[28] the Court found a solution to this problem, concluding that:

> [I]n the present case, the right to property protected under Article 21 of the American Convention, interpreted in light of the rights recognized under common Article 1 [of ICCPR and ICESCR, right to self-determination] and Article 27 of the ICCPR [cultural and religious rights of minorities], which may not be restricted when interpreting the American Convention, grants to the members of the Saramaka community the right to enjoy property in accordance with their communal tradition.[29]

This did not prevent the Court from referring to ILO Convention 169 in the judgment, to provide examples of the content of international instruments regarding different aspects of the right to property in a broad sense.[30]

With respect to consultations, the structure of the Court's reasoning is as follows. Indigenous and tribal peoples have property rights over their land and resources. Nevertheless, the protection of the right to property under Article 21 of the Convention is not absolute and may be subject to certain limitations and restrictions. Two requirements must be fulfilled in order for those restrictions to be valid. First,

---

[25] Inter-American Court of Human Rights, Series C No. 125, *Yakye Axa Indigenous Community v. Paraguay (Merits, Reparations and Costs)*, 17 June 2005, para. 130.

[26] See Inter-American Court of Human Rights, Series C No.146, *Sawhoyamaxa Indigenous Community v. Paraguay(Merits, Reparations and Costs)*, 29 March 2006, para. 117 (an example of a case against a state that ratified ILO 169); Inter-American Court of Human Rights, Series C No. 172, *Saramaka People v. Suriname (Preliminary Objections, Merits, Reparations, and Costs)*, 28 November 2007, para. 93 (a case concerning a state which was not a party to the Convention). See also Brunner and Quintana (2012).

[27] Inter-American Court of Human Rights, Series C No. 172, *Saramaka People v. Suriname (Preliminary Objections, Merits, Reparations, and Costs)*, 28 November 2007, para. 131; Inter-American Court of Human Rights, Series C No. 245, *Kichwa Indigenous People of Sarayaku v. Ecuador (Merits and reparations)*, 27 June 2012, fns. 218, 237, 242, etc.

[28] Inter-American Court of Human Rights, Series C No. 172, *Saramaka People v. Suriname (Preliminary Objections, Merits, Reparations, and Costs)*, 28 November 2007, paras. 92–94.

[29] Inter-American Court of Human Rights, Series C No. 172, *Saramaka People v. Suriname (Preliminary Objections, Merits, Reparations, and Costs)*, 28 November 2007, para 95.

[30] Inter-American Court of Human Rights, Series C No. 172, *Saramaka People v. Suriname (Preliminary Objections, Merits, Reparations, and Costs)*, 28 November 2007, paras. 137, 130, and fn. 128.

the general requirements for limiting anybody's property rights, namely that the limitation be (a) previously established by law; (b) necessary; (c) proportional; and (d) with the aim of achieving a legitimate objective in a democratic society.[31] Secondly, there is an additional requirement for the restriction of communal property: it should not deny the survival of the community as an indigenous or tribal people.[32]

In order to comply with the second requirement, the Court established that the state must abide by three safeguards:

> First, the State must ensure the effective participation of the members of the Saramaka people, in conformity with their customs and traditions, regarding any development, investment, exploration or extraction plan (...) within Saramaka territory. Second, the State must guarantee that the Saramakas will receive a reasonable benefit from any such plan within their territory. Thirdly, the State must ensure that no concession will be issued within Saramaka territory unless and until independent and technically capable entities, with the State's supervision, perform a prior environmental and social impact assessment. These safeguards are intended to preserve, protect and guarantee the special relationship that the members of the Saramaka community have with their territory, which in turn ensures their survival as a tribal people.[33]

The first of the safeguards is further explained by the Court under the heading "Right to consultation, and where applicable, a duty to obtain consent", as follows:

> [I]n ensuring the effective participation of members of the Saramaka people in development or investment plans within their territory, the State has a duty to actively consult with said community according to their customs and traditions (...). This duty requires the State to both accept and disseminate information, and entails constant communication between the parties. These consultations must be in good faith, through culturally appropriate procedures and with the objective of reaching an agreement. Furthermore, the Saramakas must be consulted, in accordance with their own traditions, at the early stages of a development or investment plan, not only when the need arises to obtain approval from the community, if such is the case. Early notice provides time for internal discussion within communities and for proper feedback to the State. The State must also ensure that members of the Saramaka people are aware of possible risks, including environmental and health risks, in order that the proposed development or investment plan is accepted knowingly and volun-

---

[31] Inter-American Court of Human Rights, Series C No. 172, *Saramaka People v. Suriname (Preliminary Objections, Merits, Reparations, and Costs)*, 28 November 2007, para. 127.

[32] Inter-American Court of Human Rights, Series C No. 172, *Saramaka People v. Suriname (Preliminary Objections, Merits, Reparations, and Costs)*, 28 November 2007, para. 128. *Survival as a people* means more than merely physical survival, and includes ensuring "that they may continue living their traditional way of life, and that their distinct cultural identity, social structure, economic system, customs, beliefs and traditions are respected, guaranteed and protected", cfr. ibid., para 121.

[33] Inter-American Court of Human Rights, Series C No. 172, *Saramaka People v. Suriname (Preliminary Objections, Merits, Reparations, and Costs)*, 28 November 2007, para. 129. These safeguards are drawn from the jurisprudence of UN treaty bodies, ILO Convention 169, and UNDRIP. Inter-American Court of Human Rights, Series C No. 172, *Saramaka People v. Suriname (Preliminary Objections, Merits, Reparations, and Costs)*, 28 November 2007, paras. 129–131, fn. 126, and paras. 128–130.

tarily. Finally, consultation should take account of the Saramaka people's traditional methods of decision-making.[34]

Next, the Court held that an additional protection should be established for communities when the development or investment plans are "large-scale" projects that would have a major impact within the territory. In such cases, mere consultation is not enough, but in addition their consent must be obtained.[35]

For the Court, in sum, consultation/consent rights are defined as one of the safeguards—that of effective participation of indigenous and tribal peoples—which are necessary to ensure that, in the determination of the acceptable restrictions on their right to communal property, their survival as a community is guaranteed.

At the end of 2009, the Commission published a thematic report entitled "Indigenous and Tribal People's Rights over their Ancestral Lands and Natural Resources". The Commission analysed the scope of indigenous and tribal peoples' rights over their territories, lands, and natural resources, based on the legal instruments of the IAHRS as interpreted by the Court and the Commission, and other standards "imported" from international human rights law.[36] Although the Commission did not purport to enact standards, by incorporating language from other sources—including the UN treaty bodies and reports of UN Special Rapporteurs—new standards were, in fact, established.

Chapter IX of the report describes FPIC at three levels. First, it explains "the general obligation" as a duty of the state to *consult* with indigenous peoples and guarantee their participation in decisions regarding any measure that affects their territory, taking into consideration the special relationship between indigenous peoples and their land and natural resources.[37]

Next, it explains the right to participation, with respect to decisions over indigenous people's natural resources, as a right to:

> [B]e involved in the processes of design, implementation, and evaluation of development projects carried out on their lands and ancestral territories (…). Natural resource exploitation in indigenous territories without the affected indigenous people's consultation and consent violates their right to property and their right to participate in government.

---

[34] Inter-American Court of Human Rights, Series C No. 172, *Saramaka People v. Suriname (Preliminary Objections, Merits, Reparations, and Costs)*, 28 November 2007, para. 133.

[35] Inter-American Court of Human Rights, Series C No. 172, *Saramaka People v. Suriname (Preliminary Objections, Merits, Reparations, and Costs)*, 28 November 2007, para. 134.

[36] Inter-American Commission on Human Rights, Indigenous and Tribal People's Rights over their Ancestral Lands and Natural Resources. Norms and Jurisprudence of the Inter-American Human Rights System, OEA/Ser.L/V/II. Doc. 56/09, 30 December 2009, para. 4.

[37] Inter-American Commission on Human Rights, Indigenous and Tribal People's Rights over their Ancestral Lands and Natural Resources. Norms and Jurisprudence of the Inter-American Human Rights System, OEA/Ser.L/V/II. Doc. 56/09, 30 December 2009, para. 273.

> Consequently there is a State duty to consult and, in specific cases, obtain indigenous peoples' consent in respect to plans or projects for investment, development or exploitation of natural resources in ancestral territories.[38]

The Commission lists the requirements of the right to consultation: it must be provided by an appropriate regulatory framework, prior, culturally adequate, informed, undertaken in good faith, aimed at reaching an agreement, and with the will to adapt the projects according to the outcomes of the consultation or to give reasoned decisions when this is not possible.[39]

Finally, the Report underscores the distinction between consultation and consent as established by the Court in *Saramaka,* and clarifies that the general obligation relates to the former, while the duty to obtain consent is limited. It repeats the "large-scale" threshold,[40] and provides a list of situations in which consent would be required.[41]

2.3   The Duty to Consult as a Principle of International Law

The IACtHR's *Kichwa Indigenous People of Sarayaku v. Ecuador*[42] judgement is arguably the most comprehensive and progressive to date regarding FPIC standards. It is a case in which the state expressly acknowledged its international responsibility, for failing—among other things—to consult with the community. Nevertheless, in the hearing before the IACtHR, the state "questioned its obligation to do so and argued that certain actions taken by the company satisfied the requirement to consult the indigenous communities of the area granted in concession".[43]

---

[38] Inter-American Commission on Human Rights, Indigenous and Tribal People's Rights over their Ancestral Lands and Natural Resources. Norms and Jurisprudence of the Inter-American Human Rights System, OEA/Ser.L/V/II. Doc. 56/09, 30 December 2009, paras. 289–290.

[39] Inter-American Commission on Human Rights, Indigenous and Tribal People's Rights over their Ancestral Lands and Natural Resources. Norms and Jurisprudence of the Inter-American Human Rights System, OEA/Ser.L/V/II. Doc. 56/09, 30 December 2009, paras. 298–328.

[40] Inter-American Commission on Human Rights, Indigenous and Tribal People's Rights over their Ancestral Lands and Natural Resources. Norms and Jurisprudence of the Inter-American Human Rights System, OEA/Ser.L/V/II. Doc. 56/09, 30 December 2009, paras 329–333.

[41] Inter-American Commission on Human Rights, Indigenous and Tribal People's Rights over their Ancestral Lands and Natural Resources. Norms and Jurisprudence of the Inter-American Human Rights System, OEA/Ser.L/V/II. Doc. 56/09, 30 December 2009, para 334. Those situations are: (1) Projects that imply a displacement of indigenous peoples from their traditional lands, i.e., their permanent relocation; (2) Cases where the plans or concessions would deprive indigenous peoples of the capacity to use and enjoy their lands and other natural resources necessary for their subsistence; (3) Storage or disposal of hazardous materials in indigenous lands or territories. The first and third of these cases arise from non-Inter-American sources.

[42] Inter-American Court of Human Rights, Series C No. 245, *Kichwa Indigenous People of Sarayaku v. Ecuador (Merits and reparations),* 27 June 2012.

[43] Inter-American Court of Human Rights, Series C No. 245, *Kichwa Indigenous People of Sarayaku v. Ecuador (Merits and reparations),* 27 June 2012, para. 124.

When analysing the obligation to guarantee the right to consultation, the Court began by recalling its own jurisprudence on the obligations that arise from the right to property in Article 21 as interpreted in previous cases. It cited the *Saramaka* precedent, including the three safeguards and in particular the duty to "conduct an appropriate and participatory process that guarantees the right to consultation, particularly with regard to development or large-scale investment plans".[44] The Court noted that Article 21 had been interpreted in the light of domestic law concerning the rights of indigenous peoples and of instruments like ILO Convention 169. It also mentioned—with many examples—that several states in the Americas have incorporated those standards in their national laws and in their domestic case law, taking into account the provisions of the ILO Convention, whether or not they had ratified it.[45] The Court concluded:

> [T]he obligation to consult, in addition to being a treaty-based provision, is also a general principle of international law.[46]

This is a very strong statement, and perhaps subject to dispute on various grounds. But leaving aside the issues pertaining to the status of the obligation to consult in international law, the Court was asserting that "nowadays the obligation of States to carry out special and differentiated consultation processes when certain interests of indigenous peoples and communities are about to be affected is an obligation that has been clearly recognized".[47] This was not a moot question, because Ecuador had not ratified ILO Convention 169 and did not introduce its standards into Ecuador's Constitution until 1998. The first acts that should have been consulted on (e.g. the call for proposals, contract signatures) were performed prior to that date. In any event, the Court ruled that since some exploration and other activities took place after that date, consultation rights had been violated.[48]

The ruling contains a very detailed list of standards on the nature and scope of the consultation duty, with several references to ILO Convention 169 and the UNDRIP: consultations must be prior, in good faith, adequate and accessible, provide information, and include an Environmental Impact Assessment (EIA).[49]

---

[44] Inter-American Court of Human Rights, Series C No. 245, *Kichwa Indigenous People of Sarayaku v. Ecuador* (*Merits and reparations*), 27 June 2012, para. 157.

[45] Inter-American Court of Human Rights, Series C No. 245, *Kichwa Indigenous People of Sarayaku v. Ecuador* (*Merits and reparations*), 27 June 2012, paras. 159–164.

[46] Inter-American Court of Human Rights, Series C No. 245, *Kichwa Indigenous People of Sarayaku v. Ecuador* (*Merits and reparations*), 27 June 2012, para. 164.

[47] Inter-American Court of Human Rights, Series C No. 245, *Kichwa Indigenous People of Sarayaku v. Ecuador* (*Merits and reparations*), 27 June 2012, para. 165.

[48] Inter-American Court of Human Rights, Series C No. 245, *Kichwa Indigenous People of Sarayaku v. Ecuador* (*Merits and reparations*), 27 June 2012, paras. 168–176.

[49] Inter-American Court of Human Rights, Series C No. 245, *Kichwa Indigenous People of Sarayaku v. Ecuador* (*Merits and reparations*), 27 June 2012, paras. 180-210. Note that an EIA was a different "safeguard" in the *Saramaka* scheme, but now appears here as a requirement of a sound consultation.

The decision makes it clear that both failure to consult and "engaging in consultations without observing their essential characteristics" constitute violations. One can only assume that this latter point refers to the concessionaire company's actions, since it was the only party that had engaged in any kind of consultation. Failure to observe those essential requirements implicated the state's international responsibility.[50]

Later on, in 2015, the IACtHR decided, on the same day, two cases against Honduras regarding Garífuna communities.[51] Both judgments applied the doctrine of consultation as a general principle of international law.[52]

In one of them, the Court considered the timing of the consultation, and recalled the requirement that this should be carried out at the earliest possible time during a project. One of the issues was that the state had granted a mining concession without consulting the community of Punta Piedra. Even though the exploration, let alone exploitation, phase had not started, the Court considered that the prior consultation standards were not met. Honduras had recognized the right to consultation by the time of the case (and would have probably consulted the communities) but domestic law on the timing of the consultation provided that it should be carried out immediately preceding the authorization for exploitation, and not earlier.[53] The Court concluded that regardless of how the issue is regulated in domestic law, the duty to consult, as a principle of international law, requires states to comply with specific standards as established in the key cases of *Saramaka* and *Sarayaku*, including the requirement that consultation should take place at the earliest stage and in any event prior to exploration.[54]

The final step in the evolution of the Court's case law is a case in which "neither the granting of mining concessions and licenses nor the establishment and permanence to date of (…) nature reserves were subject to any consultation procedure aimed at obtaining the [FPIC] of the *Kaliña and Lokono peoples*".[55] One of the key

---

[50] Inter-American Court of Human Rights, Series C No. 245, *Kichwa Indigenous People of Sarayaku v. Ecuador (Merits and reparations)*, 27 June 2012, para. 177.

[51] Inter-American Court of Human Rights, Serie C No. 304, *Comunidad Garífuna de Punta Piedra y sus miembros v. Honduras (Excepciones Preliminares, Fondo, Reparaciones y Costas)*, 8 October 2015; Inter-American Court of Human Rights, Serie C No. 305, *Comunidad Garífuna Triunfo de la Cruz y sus miembros v. Honduras (Fondo, Reparaciones y Costas)*, 8 October 2015. Both judgments only available in Spanish.

[52] Inter-American Court of Human Rights, Serie C No. 304, *Comunidad Garífuna de Punta Piedra y sus miembros v. Honduras (Excepciones Preliminares, Fondo, Reparaciones y Costas)*, 8 October 2015, para. 222; Inter-American Court of Human Rights, Serie C No. 305, *Comunidad Garífuna Triunfo de la Cruz y sus miembros v. Honduras (Fondo, Reparaciones y Costas)*, 8 October 2015, para. 158.

[53] Inter-American Court of Human Rights, Serie C No. 304, *Comunidad Garífuna de Punta Piedra y sus miembros v. Honduras (Excepciones Preliminares, Fondo, Reparaciones y Costas)*, 8 October 2015, paras. 216–221.

[54] Inter-American Court of Human Rights, Serie C No. 304, *Comunidad Garífuna de Punta Piedra y sus miembros v. Honduras (Excepciones Preliminares, Fondo, Reparaciones y Costas)*, 8 October 2015, para. 222.

[55] Inter-American Court of Human Rights, Series C No. 309, *Kaliña and Lokono Peoples v. Suriname (Merits, Reparations and Costs)*, 25 November 2015, para. 1.

elements of the judgment is the discussion of the timing of the obligation to consult. The mining concession was granted in 1958, when Suriname was not a party to any treaty that obliged it to consult. However, the preparatory works for the extractive activity began in the 1990s, and extraction itself in 1997, both following the establishment of the jurisdiction of the IACtHR.[56] According to the Court, the guarantee of effective participation should have been put into practice before the mining extraction operations, but effective participation was not carried out in this case.[57] Furthermore, the IACtHR held that the state should have ensured the effective participation of the Kaliña and Lokono peoples in relation to any development or investment plan, as well as any new exploration or exploitation operations that may be initiated in the future in these peoples' traditional territories.[58]

This is an interesting development with respect to the timing of consultation. It underscores the "prior" standard, but also emphasizes the idea that the obligation, once established, looks to the future. That is, even if consultations do not take place at the beginning of operations (because at that time consultation was not required) subsequent activity should not be considered exempt from the duty to consult, once this obligation is assumed by the state.

Judges Sierra Porto and Ferrer Mac-Gregor further clarify this point in a concurring opinion:

> [T]he obligation to consult comes into force prior to different moments. In this regard, a mining project is composed of different stages including exploration, feasibility, construction and exploitation, as well as that of project closure. Thus, the execution of each stage is an independent act, and although the stages are interrelated and are the result of the original act of the concession itself, owing to their characteristics, they should each be subject to prior consultation. (…)

> Evidently, since consultation is a constant process of dialogue, it should not be restricted merely to the initial stages of a project; rather, the obligation arises whenever there is a possible impact on the traditional indigenous or tribal life concerned.[59]

The issue remains as to whether failure to consult at an early stage of a project can be corrected by a subsequent consultation in the later stages of the same project. This issue could arise, for example, in a case in which the obligation to consult at an early stage was not very clear and in any case no consultation took place. If subsequently, in the same project, the same affected communities are engaged in consultation by the state, can these second consultations validate what was done initially without due authorization? These issues will be discussed in Sect. 4.

---

[56] Inter-American Court of Human Rights, Series C No. 309, *Kaliña and Lokono Peoples v. Suriname (Merits, Reparations and Costs)*, 25 November 2015, para. 200.

[57] Inter-American Court of Human Rights, Series C No. 309, *Kaliña and Lokono Peoples v. Suriname (Merits, Reparations and Costs)*, 25 November 2015, para. 207.

[58] Inter-American Court of Human Rights, Series C No. 309, *Kaliña and Lokono Peoples v. Suriname (Merits, Reparations and Costs)*, 25 November 2015, para. 211.

[59] Inter-American Court of Human Rights, Series C No. 309, *Kaliña and Lokono Peoples v. Suriname (Merits, Reparations and Costs)*, 25 November 2015, concurring opinion of Judges Sierra Porto and Ferrer Mac-Gregor, paras. 14–15.

Before concluding this section, it is worth mentioning two recent developments of the IAHRS with regards to indigenous peoples' rights. First, the most recent thematic report of the IACHR on extractive industries was published in 2016.[60] The report has a subsection on the "right to previous, free, and informed consultation and consent" that basically collects all the previously mentioned FPIC standards.[61] It also includes interesting new developments on the issue of consultation *vis-à-vis* consent, explaining the criteria to determine when a project is to be considered large-scale and, as such, requires the consent of the community.[62] This is important, as the IACtHR neither in *Saramaka* nor in *Sarayaku* had defined clearly when consent is mandatory.[63] Second, the General Assembly of the OAS adopted the American Declaration on the Rights of Indigenous Peoples (ADRIP) on 15 June 2016.[64] This declaration, which has a legal value analogous to that of the UNDRIP, was adopted by consensus—except for some of its provisions, notably some of those referring to FPIC. Several provisions therein include consultation rights and FPIC elements. One worth mentioning is Article XXIX on the Right to development, which says:

> States shall consult and cooperate in good faith with the indigenous peoples concerned through their own representative institutions in order to obtain their free and informed consent prior to the approval of any project affecting their lands or territories and other resources, particularly in connection with the development, utilization or exploitation of mineral, water or other resources.[65]

2.4 FPIC as a Duty of the State in the Inter-American System

One clear conclusion to be drawn from the material cited above is that, for the organs of the IAHRS, the state is the duty-bearer of the obligations regarding the consultation rights of indigenous and tribal peoples.

---

[60] Inter-American Commission on Human Rights, Indigenous Peoples, Afro-Descendent Communities, and Natural Resources: Human Rights Protection in the Context of Extraction, Exploitation, and Development Activities, OEA/Ser.L/V/II. Doc. 47/1, 31 December 2015. This report is also called by the IACHR "Indigenous Peoples, Communities of African Descent, Extractive Industries".

[61] Inter-American Commission on Human Rights, Indigenous Peoples, Afro-Descendent Communities, and Natural Resources: Human Rights Protection in the Context of Extraction, Exploitation, and Development Activities, OEA/Ser.L/V/II. Doc. 47/1, 31 December 2015, chapter 3.A.2.a.

[62] Inter-American Commission on Human Rights, Indigenous Peoples, Afro-Descendent Communities, and Natural Resources: Human Rights Protection in the Context of Extraction, Exploitation, and Development Activities, OEA/Ser.L/V/II. Doc. 47/1, 31 December 2015, paras. 183–193.

[63] Brunner and Quintana (2012).

[64] Organization of American States, American Declaration on the Rights of Indigenous Peoples, AG/RES. 2888 (XLVI-O/16), 15 June 2016.

[65] Organization of American States, American Declaration on the Rights of Indigenous Peoples, AG/RES. 2888 (XLVI-O/16), 15 June 2016, Article XXIX, section 4.

All of the cases discussed conclude with the Commission or the Court holding the state responsible for the violation of FPIC, even when in many of the cases studied third parties, specifically private enterprises, were involved, sometimes very actively and directly, in causing harm. The last thematic report of the IACHR confirms this trend, as it examines thoroughly state obligations and omits to mention any corporate responsibility.[66]

This is unsurprising, given the nature of the system under study: in the IAHRS, "the Court makes clear that the state is the principal guarantor of the human rights and that, as a consequence, if a violation of said rights occurs, the state must resolve the issue".[67]

As Faúndez Ledesma says, in arguably one of the books most widely used by the IAHRS officials, "the conduct of the State" is that which "may be characterized as a violation of human rights". For him, "[t]he function of the law of human rights is to regulate the exercise of public power vis-à-vis the individual".[68] And he concludes,

> The Court has held that the Convention places on the State the fundamental duties to respect and ensure human rights in such a way that 'any impairment of those rights which can be attributed under the rules of international law to the action or omission of any public authority constitutes an act imputable to the State, which assumes responsibility in the terms provided by the Convention'.[69]

This classic position is confirmed in *Advisory Opinion OC-14/94*, in which the Court held:

> As far as concerns the human rights protected by the Convention, the jurisdiction of the organs established thereunder refer exclusively to the international responsibility of states and not to that of individuals.[70]

Even in *Kaliña and Lokono*, in which the Court mentions the UNGPs for the first time, after noting that private agents carried out the activity that resulted in human rights violations,[71] this was not enough to breach the apparently rigid rule. The

---

[66] Inter-American Commission on Human Rights, Indigenous Peoples, Afro-Descendent Communities, and Natural Resources: Human Rights Protection in the Context of Extraction, Exploitation, and Development Activities, OEA/Ser.L/V/II. Doc. 47/1, 31 December 2015.

[67] Inter-American Court of Human Rights, Series C No. 157, *Acevedo Jaramillo et al. v. Peru (Interpretation of the Judgment of Preliminary Objections, Merits, Reparations and Costs)*, 24 November 2006, para. 66. Nevertheless, this seems to be a general feature of most human rights international procedures, as posited by Galvis (2011), pp. 12–13: "International human rights systems, which are set up to establish the responsibility of states, also have not proven to be an ideal venue for airing claims concerning the liability of private corporations".

[68] Faúndez Ledesma (2008), p. 6.

[69] Faúndez Ledesma (2008), p. 7. The internal reference is to Inter-American Court of Human Rights, Series C No. 4, *Velásquez Rodríguez v. Honduras (Merits)*, 29 July 1988, para. 164.

[70] Inter-American Court of Human Rights, Series A No. 14, Advisory Opinion OC-14/94, International Responsibility for the Promulgation and Enforcement of Laws in Violation of the Convention (Arts. 1 and 2 of the American Convention on Human Rights), 9 December 1994, para. 56. See also paras. 52–53.

[71] Inter-American Court of Human Rights, Series C No. 309, *Kaliña and Lokono Peoples v. Suriname (Merits, Reparations and Costs)*, 25 November 2015, para. 223.

reason, according to Carrillo-Santarelli, is that the Court is limited in its contentious jurisdiction to examining only state responsibility, due to procedural and substantive limitations.[72]

The IACHR's report on the extractive industries also mentions the UNGPs, but again it is only to support the idea of the state duty to protect—and to remedy—and no reference is made to the second pillar of Ruggie's framework (corporate responsibilities).[73]

3   The Corporate Responsibility to Respect FPIC in the Inter-American System

Having described in the introduction, albeit briefly, how general international law establishes a corporate responsibility to respect FPIC, this section will analyse the place of corporations in the jurisprudence of the Commission and the Court, and the nature and scope of the responsibilities imposed on them by the law applied and created by those organs.

3.1   The State Due Diligence Standard: A Source of Indirect Responsibility of Corporations

As previously stated, many of the cases studied in Sect. 2 involve the participation of business enterprises. Many cases were linked to the extractive industries, for example the logging concession-holders in the *Awas Tingni*,[74] *Maya communities of*

---

[72] Carrillo-Santarelli N, La Corte Interamericana de Derechos Humanos hace referencia a principios de responsabilidad corporativa, continuando con desarrollos en la región americana al respecto. Aquiescencia, 10 February 2016, https://aquiescencia.net/2016/02/10/la-corte-interamericana-de-derechos-humanos-hace-referencia-a-principios-de-responsabilidad-corporativa-continuando-con-desarrollos-en-la-region-americana-al-respecto/ (last accessed 1 October 2018).

[73] Inter-American Commission on Human Rights, Indigenous Peoples, Afro-Descendent Communities, and Natural Resources: Human Rights Protection in the Context of Extraction, Exploitation, and Development Activities, OEA/Ser.L/V/II. Doc. 47/1, 31 December 2015, paras. 52, 74, 99, and 131.

[74] The company Sol del Caribe, S.A. (SOLCARSA) was granted a concession for logging on the communal lands, without consultation, see Inter-American Court of Human Rights, Series C No. 79, *Mayagna (Sumo) Awas Tingni Community v. Nicaragua (Merits, Reparations and Costs)*, Judgment 31 August 2001, para. 6.

Toledo[75] and *Saramaka*[76] cases, or mining and hydrocarbon companies in *Maya communities of Toledo* and *Saramaka*, and in *Sarayaku*,[77] *Garífuna Punta Piedra*[78] and *Kaliña and Lokono.*[79] The other Garífuna case involved the tourism industry, specifically hotels.[80]

All of these cases resulted in liability being imposed on the state. The Commission or Court's reasoning is that since consultation is a duty of the state, the failure to consult prior to any activity, notwithstanding who carries out that activity, results in the international responsibility of the state.

Some authors have suggested that this responsibility may arise, in the case of violations committed by corporations, from the state's duty to protect and, especially, to *ensure* human rights in general. Thus, for Galvis,

> [T]he inter-American system has developed some jurisprudence that can be useful in inducing states to answer for the actions of corporations when the latter have been shown to violate conventional human rights.
>
> [... A] state may be held liable under inter-American law for the actions of private companies operating within its territory based on the jurisprudence relating to due diligence, the liability of private actors, state obligations, and the rights of indigenous peoples.[81]

---

[75] The government granted various logging concessions, including two sizeable concessions to two Malaysian timber companies, Toledo Atlantic International, Ltd. and Atlantic Industries, Ltd., see Inter-American Commission on Human Rights, Case 12.053, Report N° 40/04, *Maya indigenous communities of the Toledo district (Belize), Merits*, 12 October 2004, para 28.

[76] On the granting of "[l]and concessions for forestry and mining awarded by the State to third parties on territory possessed by the Saramaka people, without their full and effective consultation", see Inter-American Court of Human Rights, Series C No. 172, *Saramaka People v. Suriname (Preliminary Objections, Merits, Reparations, and Costs)*, 28 November 2007, paras. 124 and 157.

[77] The Ecuadorian State Oil Company (PETROECUADOR) signed a contract for oil exploration and exploitation with a consortium formed by the Compañía General de Combustibles S.A. (CGC) and Petrolera Argentina San Jorge S.A., see Inter-American Court of Human Rights, Series C No. 245, *Kichwa Indigenous People of Sarayaku v. Ecuador (Merits and reparations)*, 27 June 2012, para. 64.

[78] The mining company CANIXA S.A. obtained a concession for non-metal mining exploration, see Inter-American Court of Human Rights, Serie C No. 304, *Comunidad Garífuna de Punta Piedra y sus miembros v. Honduras (Excepciones Preliminares, Fondo, Reparaciones y Costas)*, 8 October 2015, para. 125.

[79] The mining company Suralco, a subsidiary of the Aluminum Company of America (ALCOA), had a concession to extract bauxite. Suralco began extraction operations alone, and some years later a joint-venture known as BHP Billiton-Suralco took over that mining exploitation, see Inter-American Court of Human Rights, Series C No. 309, *Kaliña and Lokono Peoples v. Suriname (Merits, Reparations and Costs)*, 25 November 2015, para 88.

[80] The Municipality sold lands from the area of the community to the company Inversiones y Desarrollos El Triunfo S.A. de C.V. (IDETRISA), for the construction of two tourism projects, "Club Marbella" and "Playa Escondida". Both were constructed and developed within the traditional territory, without consultation: Inter-American Court of Human Rights, Serie C No. 305, *Comunidad Garífuna Triunfo de la Cruz y sus miembros v. Honduras (Fondo, Reparaciones y Costas)*, 8 October 2015, paras. 74 and 165-7.

[81] Galvis (2011), p. 13.

The jurisprudence she refers to does not specifically relate to corporations, but may, in her view, be applied by analogy.[82] Sandri Fuentes makes a similar argument, explaining that according to the Court state obligations to respect and ensure human rights, as well as the duty to adopt measures under domestic law for their development, exist not only in relation to the behaviour displayed by its agents, whether or not authorized by the state. Those obligations also exist in relation to human rights violations by private parties where the state has not taken the necessary measures to prevent them from violating rights or has tolerated their violations of rights, thus establishing the *standard of due diligence*.[83]

The state due diligence standard can be expressed as follows:

[S]tates can be held liable for allowing corporations to engage in behaviors that violate international human rights law and for failing to ensure that such behaviors are appropriately punished in their territory.[84]

This is in fact the application of the most classic case law of the IAHRS,[85] and was confirmed with respect to corporations in the recent Commission's report on extractive industries:

When it is the State itself that implements a project, it has direct obligations to respect and guarantee the human rights involved. In contexts where third parties execute the projects at issue, *the State also has specific obligations to meet*. In this second scenario, (…) the international responsibility of the State for the acts of individuals has been addressed by the IACHR and the Inter-American Court, recognizing that *States have a duty to ensure the effectiveness of the human rights protected by the Inter-American instruments in the relations between individuals, as well as a duty to prevent with due diligence the violations of those rights*, and to investigate, punish and remedy their consequences.[86]

Even though corporations are included as possible perpetrators of human rights violations, the quote emphasises the state aspect of the responsibility.

The Court's most recent case also mentions the activities of corporations in FPIC-related matters, but the same caveats apply:

The Court notes that the mining activities that resulted in the adverse impact on the environment and, consequently, on the rights of the indigenous peoples, were carried out by private agents (…).

---

[82] Galvis (2011), p. 13.

[83] Sandri Fuentes (2014), pp. 222–223.

[84] Galvis (2011), p. 14.

[85] Inter-American Court of Human Rights, Series C No. 4, *Velásquez Rodríguez v. Honduras (Merits)*, 29 July 1988, para. 172: "An illegal act which violates human rights and which is initially not directly imputable to a State (for example, because it is the act of a private person [...]) can lead to international responsibility of the State, not because of the act itself, but because of the lack of due diligence to prevent the violation or to respond to it as required by the Convention".

[86] Inter-American Commission on Human Rights, Indigenous Peoples, Afro-Descendent Communities, and Natural Resources: Human Rights Protection in the Context of Extraction, Exploitation, and Development Activities, OEA/Ser.L/V/II. Doc. 47/1, 31 December 2015, para. 56. Emphasis added.

In this regard, the Court takes note of the "Guiding Principles on Business and Human Rights," endorsed by the Human Rights Council of the United Nations, which establish that businesses must respect and protect human rights, as well as prevent, mitigate, and accept responsibility for the adverse human rights impacts directly linked to their activities. Hence, as reiterated by these principles, "States must protect against human rights abuse within their territory and/or jurisdiction by third parties, including business enterprises. This requires taking appropriate steps to prevent, investigate, punish and redress such abuse through effective policies, legislation, regulations and adjudication."

Thus, the Special Representative of the Secretary-General of the United Nations on the issue of human rights and transnational corporations and other business enterprises has indicated that businesses must respect the human rights of members of specific groups or populations, including indigenous and tribal peoples, and pay special attention when such rights are violated.

Based on the above, *the Court finds that, because the State did not ensure that an independent social and environmental impact assessment was made prior to the start-up of bauxite mining, and did not supervise the assessment that was made subsequently, it failed to comply with this safeguard*; in particular, considering that the activities would be carried out in a protected nature reserve and within the traditional territories of several peoples.[87]

As previously mentioned, this was the first time that the Court referred to the UNGPs, and to what businesses ought to do, according to international law. However, it is clear from these passages that the emphasis is still on the state, as the party which must comply with the safeguards established in the IAHRS for the protection of indigenous peoples.

If the direct responsibility lies with the state, but arises from the unlawful activity of corporations, could it be said that some form of responsibility of corporations is implied in this due diligence standard, at least an indirect responsibility?

If pursuant to the due diligence standard states are obliged to investigate and prosecute corporations to the extent that their actions infringe human rights, a form of "indirect responsibility" of corporations may be ascertained pursuant to obligations contained in the American Convention. The consequence of such an indirect responsibility is that since the breaches of that treaty would eventually need to be investigated and punished by the state, corporations are ultimately held accountable.[88]

The UNGPs establish that the corporate responsibility to respect exists independently of the state duty to protect and does not diminish that duty.[89] It might be argued, therefore, that the responsibility described here is in fact more a direct responsibility. The position of this chapter, however, is that the responsibility of

---

[87] Inter-American Court of Human Rights, Series C No. 309, *Kaliña and Lokono Peoples v. Suriname (Merits, Reparations and Costs)*, 25 November 2015, paras. 223–226 (quotations omitted). Emphasis added.

[88] See Cantú Rivera (2013), p. 82.

[89] UN Human Rights Council, Guiding Principles on Business and Human Rights: Implementing the United Nations "Protect, Respect and Remedy" Framework, Un Doc. HR/PUB/11/04, 2011.

corporations described here is better explained as *indirect*. As John H. Knox expounds:

> A legal obligation that international law directly places on an individual differs from one that it imposes indirectly, through a duty on governments. In the first case, the international community as a whole exercises prescriptive jurisdiction over individuals in a way that makes them directly subject to international law apart from the mediating intervention of domestic law. In the second, domestic jurisdiction over individuals is left intact.[90]

Certainly in the *Kaliña and Lokono* precedent the Court opens the doors to direct responsibility by implying that corporations may violate (not just abuse) human rights.[91] Nevertheless, its language still maintains a "traditional, indirect approach to the horizontal application of human rights" based on the "traditional state-centric analysis" described above, which focuses solely on state duties, and "provides only an inexplicit condemnation of the conduct of non-state actors".[92]

Before concluding this subsection, it should be emphasized that the *standard of due diligence* used by the Inter-American organs is not to be confused with Ruggie's "human rights due diligence" *process* in UNGP 15.b and operational principles 17 onwards, sometimes referred to as "corporate due diligence." The standard described in this chapter is "state due diligence".[93]

3.2 The Possibility of a Direct Responsibility of Corporations Under Inter-American Law

Carrillo-Santarelli, among many others, considers that "it is important to also offer direct international protection from corporate abuse":

> Considering that corporations can abuse or participate in the violation of any human right, as John Ruggie has said, attention must be paid to the insufficiency of relying only on State

---

[90] Knox (2008), p. 29.

[91] Carrillo-Santarelli N, The intersection of business and human rights at the Inter-American Court of Human Rights (Part I). Oxford Human Rights Hub, 10 March 2016, http://ohrh.law.ox.ac.uk/part-i-the-intersection-of-business-and-human-rights-at-the-inter-american-court-of-human-rights/ (last accessed 1 October 2018) interpretation of Inter-American Court of Human Rights, Series C No. 309, *Kaliña and Lokono Peoples v. Suriname (Merits, Reparations and Costs)*, 25 November 2015, paras. 223–226.

[92] Carrillo-Santarelli N, The intersection of business and human rights at the Inter-American Court of Human Rights (Part I). Oxford Human Rights Hub, 10 March 2016, http://ohrh.law.ox.ac.uk/part-i-the-intersection-of-business-and-human-rights-at-the-inter-american-court-of-human-rights/ (last accessed 1 October 2018).

[93] For a comparison between these two concepts see Cantú Rivera (2013), p. 81; see also Gos (2017), pp. 864, 886. She explains—using different names—both state due diligence, as a form of attributing international responsibility to the state at the IAHRS, and corporate due diligence, arguing that the latter should be made legally binding at the domestic level, thus recognizing that it is not a legal duty creating obligations for corporations at the international level (neither direct nor indirect).

obligations. Why? Because those are obligations of means and due diligence, which implies that corporate abuses neither automatically nor always engage State responsibility. In such events, victims still have rights to protection and reparations, which must be fulfilled (…).

Additional arguments point to the importance of corporate human rights obligations: while they can have an impact on attitudes and pave the way for changes, voluntary initiatives themselves offer no certain prospects of protection (…). If neither voluntary standards nor State obligations ensure the protection of victims, something is missing. That void can be filled by regulating international corporate obligations, preventing gaps in domestic legal systems that can be taken advantage of by actors that, because of their nature and operations, can move across borders.[94]

The aim of the following pages is to explore whether there are (or could be) certain direct responsibilities regarding indigenous peoples that corporations must abide by in Inter-American law.

For the purpose of exploring direct business responsibilities this article will address in particular the issue of the delegation of the duty to consult by the state to private corporations. This means the assignment of a state responsibility to another actor, the potential transfer in whole or part of a legal responsibility from one party to another, and the consequent obtainment or acquisition of a duty or responsibility by that party. The next subsection explores whether such delegation is permitted in the IAHRS. It also describes how and under what conditions delegation could or should take place.

The thesis is that if this kind of delegation is permitted in the IAHRS, it could give rise to a direct responsibility of corporations recognized by Inter-American law, regardless of whether they have direct responsibilities under other sources of international law (such as the UNGPs). As will be explained, the newly born responsibility arising from delegation may not be of the same nature as the state's responsibility, since the latter cannot be avoided, and will not disappear. But the fact that states retain a duty would not mean that private parties cannot have any international responsibility under Inter-American law.

3.3   The Delegation to Businesses of the State Duty to Consult

To begin with, neither the Commission nor the Court have traditionally favoured direct responsibilities for corporations in these cases, appearing essentially to prohibit the delegation of consultation to private entities. The Commission expressly rejected this possibility in its 2009 thematic report, based not on Inter-American standards but on language from the UN Rapporteur on Indigenous Peoples:

---

[94] Carrillo-Santarelli N, Corporate human rights obligations: Controversial but necessary. Business & Human Rights Resource Centre, 25 August 2015, https://www.business-humanrights.org/en/regulating-companies'-human-rights-obligations-is-controversial-but-necessary-says-academic (last accessed 1 October 2018).

Carrying out consultation procedures is a responsibility of the State, and not of other parties, such as the company seeking the concession or investment contract. In many of the countries that form part of the Inter-American system, the State responsibility to conduct prior consultation has been transferred to private companies, generating a *de facto* privatization of the State's responsibility. The resulting negotiation processes with local communities then often fail to take into consideration a human rights framework, because corporate actors are, as a matter of definition, profit-seeking entities that are therefore not impartial. Consultation with indigenous peoples is a duty of States, which must be complied with by the competent public authorities.[95]

This doctrine was adopted by the Court more than 3 years later,[96] although with nuances, as will be shown.

The Commission's reference was to the then UN Special Rapporteur on Indigenous Peoples James Anaya's 2009 Report, in which he stated:

In accordance with well-grounded principles of international law, the duty of the State to protect the human rights of indigenous peoples, including its duty to consult with the indigenous peoples concerned before carrying out activities that affect them, is not one that can be avoided through delegation to a private company or other entity.[97]

Those "well-grounded principles" only prohibit the avoidance of the state responsibility by delegation, i.e., the total transfer of the duty (or "*de facto* privatization", in IACHR terms[98]) without the state retaining any responsibility. In other words, international law does not permit states to "wash their hands" of the duty. Long-established principles of international law require that the state ensure the protection of human rights including against infringement by private parties, and no form of delegation could ever imply that the state's duty disappears. In fact, in the same report Anaya clarifies that such delegations do not absolve the state of ultimate responsibility.[99] While not ruling out the possibility of delegation, he warns that the

---

[95] Inter-American Commission on Human Rights, Indigenous and Tribal People's Rights over their Ancestral Lands and Natural Resources. Norms and Jurisprudence of the Inter-American Human Rights System, OEA/Ser.L/V/II. Doc. 56/09, 30 December 2009, para. 291.

[96] Inter-American Court of Human Rights, Series C No. 245, *Kichwa Indigenous People of Sarayaku v. Ecuador* (*Merits and reparations*), 27 June 2012, para. 187: "It should be emphasized that the obligation to consult is the responsibility of the state; therefore the planning and executing of the consultation process is not an obligation that can be avoided by delegating it to a private company or to third parties, much less delegating it to the very company that is interested in exploiting the resources in the territory of the community that must be consulted".

[97] UN Human Rights Council, Report of the Special Rapporteur on the situation of human rights and fundamental freedoms of indigenous people, James Anaya, UN Doc. A/HRC/12/34, 6 July 2012, para 54.

[98] Inter-American Commission on Human Rights, Indigenous and Tribal People's Rights over their Ancestral Lands and Natural Resources. Norms and Jurisprudence of the Inter-American Human Rights System, OEA/Ser.L/V/II. Doc. 56/09, 30 December 2009, para. 291.

[99] UN Human Rights Council, Report of the Special Rapporteur, James Anaya, UN Doc. A/HRC/12/34, 6 July 2012, para 55. Draft Article 5 on Responsibility of States for Internationally Wrongful Acts [Conduct of persons or entities exercising elements of governmental authority] points to the same conclusion. It states that "The conduct of a person or entity which is not an organ of the State under article 4 but which is empowered by the law of that State to exercise elements of the governmental authority shall be considered an act of the State under international law,

handing on of a state's human rights obligations to a private company "may not be desirable, and can even be problematic".[100]

Although Anaya expressed similar concerns in his 2011 annual Report,[101] in an addendum he made reference to a country in which he observed that consultations had been delegated *de facto* to the enterprises responsible for the execution of certain projects, and the matter of concern was not the delegation itself but the fact that it was done "without due supervision of the State".[102]

The latter stance accords with the positions sustained by the Committee of Experts on the Application of Conventions and Recommendations of the ILO (CEACR). When interpreting ILO Convention 169 in a case concerning Ecuador, the CEACR accepted that the oil companies in charge of exploration and exploitation activities could carry out consultations.[103] The Committee found that the consultation was incomplete because only some groups of the Shuar people were consulted and due to representation problems, but not because the consultation was carried out by the contractors.[104]

The position of the IACHR and the UN Special Rapporteur may be understandable given the date at which those reports were issued. Anaya's 2009 report, quoted by the IACHR, still considered that "in strict legal terms" international law did not impose direct responsibility on companies to respect human rights, and that it was merely "ill-advised for companies to ignore relevant international norms for

---

provided the person or entity is acting in that capacity in the particular instance." (Draft articles on Responsibility of States for Internationally Wrongful Acts, with commentaries. Text adopted by the International Law Commission at its fifty-third session, in 2001, and submitted to the General Assembly as a part of the Commission's report covering the work of that session (A/56/10). The report, which also contains commentaries on the draft articles, appears in the Yearbook of the International Law Commission, 2001, vol. II, Part Two, as corrected.). However, it also has to be said that arguably FPIC is a duty under international law that, if imposed by international law also on a private party, the state would not be actually delegating it, and thus the breach of that duty by the entity would not be attributable to the state. As the *Commentary* to Draft Article 5 says, "entity" is "a narrow category".

[100] UN Human Rights Council, Report of the Special Rapporteur, James Anaya, UN Doc. A/HRC/12/34, 6 July 2012, para 55.

[101] UN Human Rights Council, Report of the Special Rapporteur on the rights of indigenous peoples, James Anaya: Extractive industries operating within or near indigenous territories, UN Doc. A/HRC/18/35,11 July 2011, para 63.

[102] UNHRC, Report of the Special Rapporteur on the rights of indigenous peoples, James Anaya: Extractive industries operating within or near indigenous territories. Addendum: Observations on the situation of the rights of the indigenous people of Guatemala with relation to the extraction projects, and other types of projects, in their traditional territories, UN Doc. A/HRC/18/35/Add.3, 7 June 2011, para 36.

[103] ILO Committee of Experts of the Application of Conventions and Recommendations, Observation, adopted 2002, published 91st ILC session, 2003 http://www.ilo.org/dyn/normlex/en/f?p=NORMLEXPUB:13100:0::NO::P13100_COMMENT_ID:2214938 (last accessed 1 October 2018).

[104] Gómez et al. (2016), p. 99.

practical reasons".[105] The adoption, subsequently, of the UNGPs could have altered the understanding of this issue in the IAHRS.

As previously noted, in *Sarayaku* the Court repeated the general prohibition against the transfer of responsibility with respect to the duty to consult,[106] but left the door open for a possible delegation. In fact, this was discussed explicitly for the first time because the state had alleged that some actions of "socialization and contact" conducted by the oil company were to be considered as forms of consultation.[107] Therefore, the Court considered that in the hypothetical case in which "such a consultation process could be delegated to private third parties" the state would have to indicate the measures it had taken to observe, supervise, monitor or participate in the process and thereby safeguard the rights of the people concerned.[108]

The Court went on to analyse whether the company's actions complied with the relevant consultation standards applicable to the state.[109] The Court concluded that "the search for an 'understanding' with the Sarayaku People, undertaken by the [company] itself, could not be considered a consultation carried out in good faith, inasmuch as it did not involve a genuine dialogue as part of a participatory process aimed at reaching an agreement".[110]

One can only speculate as to what the Court would have found if the corporation had in fact complied with the relevant standards. Certain parts of the ruling are encouraging for those who believe that the tribunal should develop the concept of direct corporate responsibility. Employing its traditional state-centred approach, the Court affirmed that:

> [T]he State not only partially and inappropriately delegated its obligation to consult to a private company, thereby failing to comply with the above-mentioned principle of good faith and its obligation to guarantee the Sarayaku People's right to participation, but it also

---

[105] UN Human Rights Council, Report of the Special Rapporteur, James Anaya, UN Doc. A/HRC/12/34, 6 July 2012, para. 56.

[106] Inter-American Court of Human Rights, Series C No. 245, *Kichwa Indigenous People of Sarayaku v. Ecuador* (*Merits and reparations*), 27 June 2012, para. 187.

[107] Inter-American Court of Human Rights, Series C No. 245, *Kichwa Indigenous People of Sarayaku v. Ecuador* (*Merits and reparations*), 27 June 2012, para. 188.

[108] Inter-American Court of Human Rights, Series C No. 245, *Kichwa Indigenous People of Sarayaku v. Ecuador* (*Merits and reparations*), 27 June 2012, para. 189.

[109] The Court found that they "failed to respect the established structures of authority and representation within and outside the communities", and "merely offered money and different economic benefits (…) in order to obtain their consent (…) without the state undertaking or monitoring a systematic and flexible process of participation and dialogue with them". It was also alleged "that the CGC had used fraudulent procedures to obtain signatures of support from members of the Sarayaku Community", and that although "numerous meetings took place between different local and state authorities, public and private companies, (…) there was a disconnect between these efforts and a clear determination to seek consensus, which encouraged situations of tension and dispute". The CGC actions in this respect were also not taken in due time, prior to exploration. See Inter-American Court of Human Rights, Series C No. 245, *Kichwa Indigenous People of Sarayaku v. Ecuador* (*Merits and reparations*), 27 June 2012, paras. 194, 198, 203, 211.

[110] Inter-American Court of Human Rights, Series C No. 245, *Kichwa Indigenous People of Sarayaku v. Ecuador* (*Merits and reparations*), 27 June 2012, para. 200.

discouraged a climate of respect among the indigenous communities of the area by promoting the execution of an oil exploration contract.[111]

Thus, there remains, nonetheless, a hint that an "appropriate delegation" might be possible.

The Court has not been called upon again to analyse corporate activity against the consultation standards usually applied to states. However, parts of *Kaliña and Lokono* could be interpreted as indirectly confirming the possibility of the delegation of consultation. In this case the EIA was carried out by a private entity subcontracted by the mining company.[112] It should be noted that the Court had never imposed an express ban on the "privatization" of EIAs, and therefore the analogy may not be instructive.[113] Yet, since the Court reaffirmed the interrelation of EIAs with the duty to ensure the effective participation of indigenous peoples, and emphasized the state's obligation to supervise these assessments, this leads to the possible interpretation that delegation of the consultation duty is possible on the condition that it is properly monitored by state agencies.[114]

Before concluding this section, it is important to note that in James Anaya's final Report as UN Special Rapporteur his position on delegation appeared to have shifted:

> The Special Rapporteur has observed that in many instances companies negotiate directly with indigenous peoples about proposed extractive activities that may affect them, with States in effect delegating to companies the execution of the State's duty to consult with indigenous peoples prior to authorizing the extractive activities. By virtue of their right to self-determination, indigenous peoples are free to enter into negotiations directly with companies if they so wish. Indeed, direct negotiations between companies and indigenous peoples may be the most efficient and desirable way of arriving at agreed-upon arrangements for extraction of natural resources within indigenous territories that are fully respectful of indigenous peoples' rights, and they may provide indigenous peoples opportunities to pursue their own development priorities.[115]

This new perspective may encourage the Court to continue on the path which it has tentatively taken.[116]

---

[111] Inter-American Court of Human Rights, Series C No. 245, *Kichwa Indigenous People of Sarayaku v. Ecuador (Merits and reparations)*, 27 June 2012, para. 199.

[112] Inter-American Court of Human Rights, Series C No. 309, *Kaliña and Lokono Peoples v. Suriname (Merits, Reparations and Costs)*, 25 November 2015, paras para. 215.

[113] The IACHR, however, did prohibit the privatization of EIAs in its 2009 thematic report: Inter-American Commission on Human Rights, Indigenous and Tribal People's Rights over their Ancestral Lands and Natural Resources. Norms and Jurisprudence of the Inter-American Human Rights System, OEA/Ser.L/V/II. Doc. 56/09, 30 December 2009, para. 252.

[114] Inter-American Court of Human Rights, Series C No. 309, *Kaliña and Lokono Peoples v. Suriname (Merits, Reparations and Costs)*, 25 November 2015, paras. 216, 221.

[115] UN Human Rights Council, Report of the Special Rapporteur on the rights of indigenous peoples, James Anaya: Extractive industries and indigenous peoples, UN Doc. A/HRC/24/41, 1 July 2013, para. 61.

[116] It is unclear why the IACHR still quotes in this regard Anaya's 2009 Report when his position has changed. See Inter-American Commission on Human Rights, Situation of Human Rights in Guatemala, OEA/Ser.L/V/II. Doc. 43/15, 31 December 2015, fn. 817; and Inter-American

This approach could be certainly rooted in what the Court had already clarified in its second ruling in the *Saramaka* case, when it held that:

> By declaring that the consultation must take place "in conformity with their customs and tradition", the Court recognized that it is the Saramaka people, not the State, who must decide which person or group of persons will represent the Saramaka people in each consultation process ordered by the Tribunal.[117]

Accordingly, it is also the indigenous people and not the IACHR or the IACtHR, who must decide whether the state, or a private party, is a suitable counterparty in the consultation process.

In conclusion this author argues that a limited delegation of the state duty to consult to private actors, with the persistence of that state duty under appropriate care/diligence, seems the most realistic and appealing scheme.[118] The core essence of the duty should remain with the state (its continuing and non-delegable duty to protect), and proper implementation both of the state and the corporate obligations should be complementary.

Therefore, in a context in which private corporations may carry out consultations directly with indigenous peoples, they must abide by all the international standards applicable to the rights of those people regarding FPIC. Thus, international law would be imposing direct responsibilities on them.[119] In the IAHRS, however, there are still some barriers or obstacles to this idea.

Commission on Human Rights, Indigenous Peoples, Afro-Descendent Communities, and Natural Resources: Human Rights Protection in the Context of Extraction, Exploitation, and Development Activities, OEA/Ser.L/V/II. Doc. 47/1, 31 December 2015, fn. 266.

[117] Inter-American Court of Human Rights, Series C No. 185, *Case of the Saramaka People v. Suriname (Interpretation of the Judgment on Preliminary Objections, Merits, Reparations, and Costs)*, 12 August 2008, para. 18.

[118] See a similar position in Lehr and Smith (2010), p. 12.

[119] Another area in which corporations are involved directly with indigenous rights, but that cannot be covered in this chapter, is the sharing of the benefits of exploitation and other development projects. Benefit-sharing—like FPIC—has a major role in the relationships between communities and corporations. Both corporations and states obtain benefits (revenue and others) from the extractive industry. Both should share their benefits with the communities, each one independently from the other. As benefit-sharing is one of the issues where relations between companies and communities may have no intermediation whatsoever from the state, it is a good example of a situation in which a direct responsibility of enterprises could be established, beyond and independently of the duty of states to share (and to ensure that private parties share). Unfortunately, the IACHR still considers this as a mere corporate social responsibility rather than a legally binding one, see Inter-American Commission on Human Rights, Indigenous Peoples, Afro-Descendent Communities, and Natural Resources: Human Rights Protection in the Context of Extraction, Exploitation, and Development Activities, OEA/Ser.L/V/II. Doc. 47/1, 31 December 2015, para. 223.

4   How the Organs of the Inter-American System Can Help to Promote a Direct Corporate Responsibility to Respect FPIC

As noted above, in the case of *Kaliña and Lokono* the Court encountered both *substantive* and *procedural* obstacles to finding corporations liable for breaches of the duty to consult.[120] This section will explore these obstacles.

4.1   Constructing a Direct Corporate Responsibility in the IAHRS

For a corporate responsibility to be really direct (as opposed to a responsibility deriving from the due diligence standard) this author understands that two requirements must be met: (1) it must be based on independent legal sources; (2) the breach of this responsibility must have legal consequences for the corporation, independently of the responsibility of the state.

The first requirement concerns the source of the obligation: it should be independent, i.e., distinct from the one imposing the obligation on the state. The "substantive obstacle" refers to the fact that the rights contained in the ACHR, including Article 21 (right to property), have traditionally been interpreted as giving rise to state obligations only.[121] This does not mean, however, that the ACHR cannot be a source of corporate responsibility.

Properly understood, many of the ACHR provisions could be interpreted so as to imply duties for corporations. For example, Article 29.a provides that no provision of the Convention shall be interpreted as permitting any state Party, *group, or person* to suppress the enjoyment or exercise of the rights. Article 6.3.a prohibits the placing of prisoners at the disposal of any *private party, company, or juridical person.* Similarly, Article 32.1 (*"Every person has responsibilities to his family, his community, and mankind."*) could be interpreted as obliging not only natural persons, but also juridical ones.[122] Finally, but importantly, another treaty which is part

---

[120] Carrillo-Santarelli N, La Corte Interamericana de Derechos Humanos hace referencia a principios de responsabilidad corporativa, continuando con desarrollos en la región americana al respecto. Aquiescencia, 10 February 2016, https://aquiescencia.net/2016/02/10/la-corte-interamericana-de-derechos-humanos-hace-referencia-a-principios-de-responsabilidad-corporativa-continuando-con-desarrollos-en-la-region-americana-al-respecto/ (last accessed 1 October 2018).

[121] Based on Article 1.1 "The States Parties to this Convention undertake to respect the rights and freedoms recognized herein and to ensure…".

[122] On the possibility of interpreting the term "person" of Article 1.2 American Convention on Human Rights as including juridical persons, see de Casas and Toller (2015), chapters VI and VII. To the contrary, the Inter-American Court of Human Rights has excluded that interpretation, at least in terms of the possibility of juridical persons being rights-bearers: Inter-American Court of Human Rights, Opinion OC-22/16, Entitlement of legal entities to hold rights under the Inter-

of Inter-American law, namely the Charter of the OAS, provides in Article 36 that "Transnational enterprises (...) shall be subject to (...) the international treaties and agreements to which [host] countries are parties". According to Shelton, Article 36 means that state parties "have accepted international responsibility of transnational companies and that transnational companies are to obey the treaties to which the states are parties".[123]

The answer may also lie in the evolution of the FPIC standards described in Sect. 2, and the recourse to other instruments, such as UNDRIP, the UNGPs, and ILO Convention 169. The latter, so ably employed by the Court in *Saramaka* against a state that was not a party to it, could also be extended to corporations.[124] Furthermore, the recognition of FPIC as a general principle of international law endows it with a legal force beyond treaty-based obligations.[125]

Assuming that corporations may be bearers of the duty/responsibility to consult, the standards applicable to them would be almost identical to those applicable to states, taking into account the differences that result from the state being the ultimate bearer of the duty to ensure rights. In Anaya's words:

> In accordance with the responsibility of business enterprises to respect human rights, direct negotiations between companies and indigenous peoples must meet essentially the same international standards governing State consultations with indigenous peoples, including – but not limited to– those having to do with timing, information gathering and sharing about impacts and potential benefits, and indigenous participation. Further, while companies must themselves exercise due diligence to ensure such compliance, the State remains ultimately responsible for any inadequacy in the consultation or negotiation procedures and therefore should employ measures to oversee and evaluate the procedures and their outcomes, and especially to mitigate against power imbalances between the companies and the indigenous peoples with which they negotiate.[126]

The second requirement (that the breaching of this responsibility must have legal consequences for the corporation, independently of the responsibility of the state) refers to the differentiation between the responsibilities of businesses and states. This is to say, that a corporation may be found responsible but not the state. Or vice

---

American Human Rights System (Interpretation and scope of Article 1(2), in relation to Articles 1(2), 8, 11(2), 13, 16, 21, 24, 25, 29, 30, 44, 46 and 62(3) of the American Convention on Human Rights, as well as of Article 8(1)(A) and (B) of the Protocol of San Salvador), Series A No. 22, 26 February 2016.

[123] Cited in Gonza (2017), p. 360.

[124] e.g. Article 6.1. (b), establishing the right to "freely participate (...) at all levels of decision-making in elective institutions and administrative and *other bodies* responsible for policies and programmes which concern them" (emphasis added), could be read to establish responsibilities of organs other than states. Also, Article XXIX.5 of the ADRIP includes "the right to compensation for any damage caused to them by the implementation of state, international financial institutions or *private business plans, programs, or projects*." (Emphasis added).

[125] See Sect. 2.3 of this chapter.

[126] UN Human Rights Council, Report of the Special Rapporteur on the rights of indigenous peoples, James Anaya: Extractive industries and indigenous peoples, UN Doc. A/HRC/24/41, 1 July 2013, para. 62.

versa, that a state may be responsible but a corporation is found to have complied with FPIC standards.

The dilemma can be posed in the following ways: If a state has not regulated FPIC in its domestic legal order, and therefore, there are no mechanisms for consultation, and the state does not carry out consultations, may the company do so? Would this consultation held by the corporation be valid for the purpose of compliance with the international standards, thus avoiding a finding that the rights of the community have been violated?[127] These are not moot questions. They are relevant to many of the situations which commonly arise and are likely to continue arising, as illustrated by the decided cases. For example, what would the Court have ruled if in the *Punta Piedra* case the Corporación Minera CANIXA had directly consulted the community, despite the local mining law not requiring consultation until the exploitation phase?[128] Or what would be the answer to the question posed earlier in this chapter, with respect to the possibility of correcting the omission through subsequent consultations in later stages of an unconsulted project?[129] In other words, can a corporation right a state's wrong, correcting its failure to consult or to establish in its law a framework for consultation?

A case like *Pascua-Lama,*[130] which—at the time of writing—is awaiting a decision on the merits from the IACHR, would have had interesting solutions if corporate responsibilities to consult were recognized, and these could correct the omissions of the state. *Pascua-Lama* was a case in which the company had attempted to obtain consent even where the state had already granted it the concession (in breach of its own duty, as this concession was granted without the state previously consulting the community for the relevant legal framework was absent).[131]

In sum, if the organs of the IAHRS wish to promote respect for FPIC by corporations, they should further explore, clarify, and confirm a direct corporate responsibility approach that accords with the approach of the UNGPs and other international soft and hard law instruments, and thus reflects the clear legal trend globally.[132]

---

[127] Gómez et al. (2016), p. 99.

[128] See text to footnote 53.

[129] See Sect. 2.3 *in fine*.

[130] Inter-American Commission on Human Rights, Report No. 141/09, Petition 415-07, *Diaguita Agricultural Communities of the Huasco-Altinos and the Members Thereof (Chile) Admissibility*, 30 December 2009.

[131] See The Globe and Mail, Barrick reaches deal with indigenous groups over Pascua Lama mine, 28 May 2014 (updated 12 May 2018), https://www.theglobeandmail.com/report-on-business/industry-news/energy-and-resources/barrick-reaches-deal-with-indigenous-groups-over-pascua-lama-mine/article18899708/ (last accessed 19 February 2019); and CBC News, Barrick reaches deal with Pascua-Lama opponents, 29 May 2014, https://www.cbc.ca/news/business/barrick-reaches-deal-with-pascua-lama-opponents-1.2658240 (last accessed 19 February 2019). At the present moment the project is suspended due to economic and domestic legal reasons.

[132] A trend that is reflected not only in the proliferation of soft law, but especially in the movement towards a binding treaty on business and human rights. To follow up this trend, visit the Business and Human Rights Resource Centre special site on the Binding Treaty, https://www.business-humanrights.org/en/binding-treaty (last accessed 19 February 2019).

They should do so by affirming its legal basis, and also by giving an independent treatment to the consequences of the activity of business enterprises, i.e. making them liable when they breach their responsibilities and also recognizing when they have complied with their duties.

4.2 Tackling the Procedural Obstacles

This task of establishing corporate responsibility must be undertaken in a system which was created to address mainly the consequences of state conduct. However, introducing more flexibility into the rigid scheme of state-only responsibility is possible through the current rules and organization of the IAHRS.

Galvis expressed the opinion that the Inter-American system has various mechanisms that could be activated in order to regulate the sphere of corporate activity with respect to human rights.[133] With respect to the Commission's powers, it should be noted that its mandate extends beyond providing international adjudication. As Boulin Victoria stresses:

> There is a key verb in all the legal structure of the Commission—present since its first decade of existence—which is "to promote." Since the very beginning the Commission has been in charge of promoting human rights in the region. The word "promote" reflects an open mission, not constrained by formal limits. In a way, from the first moment the Commission was able to go beyond its mandate because it was in charge of promoting human rights, and this could well mean to do whatever it takes to improve human rights situation in the region. In such a way, sooner rather than later the Commission expanded its scope of influence, performing functions that can be easily classified as political rather than adjudicative.[134]

This chapter would suggest that through exercising its political functions throughout the region the Commission might increase its effectiveness in promoting corporate respect for FPIC rights.[135]

Accordingly, the Commission could make use of press releases, public hearings, thematic reports, on-site observations, and many more possibilities pursuant to Articles 18 and 19 of the Statute of the IACHR. It could even have recourse to the mechanism of precautionary measures,[136] which are not strictly regulated, to set standards and establish a practice that includes corporations as parties sharing responsibility for respecting FPIC.[137] In fact, according to Gonza:

> The Commission has been granting these kinds of measures ordering the suspension of licensing process and projects' activities for a long time (…), but the Inter-American Court

---

[133] Galvis (2011), p. 14.

[134] Boulin Victoria (2015–2016), p. 49 (quotations omitted).

[135] Boulin Victoria (2015–2016), pp. 23 and 47.

[136] Article 25 of the Rules of Procedure of the Inter-American Commission on Human Rights.

[137] Some options mentioned here are suggested specifically for cases involving indigenous peoples rights in Ariza Santamaría (2013), pp. 80–81.

has rejected the idea of directly protecting land rights by ordering suspension of conces-sions or projects when the case is not yet under its consideration, because the Court consid-ers that it would be deciding the merits of the matter.[138]

Moreover, a creative use of the friendly settlement procedure, allowing corpora-tions to play an active role in the negotiations and to be a party to the resulting agreements, could certainly be helpful.[139]

The IACtHR is also in a good position to participate in advancing this cause, for example by exercising its advisory jurisdiction in a progressive manner with respect to corporate responsibilities.[140] As of yet, "the Court has emphasized state obliga-tions –but not what international human rights law requires specifically of corpora-tions in such circumstances. (…) But the experience at the Inter-American System shows that corporations, although not parties to the process and not directly account-able before the Court, are scrutinized internationally and feel the impact of the System's decisions".[141]

In its adjudicative role, the Court could give more leeway to states to delegate to corporations—within established limits—their duty to consult, with the consequent recognition of legal effects of the consultations conducted by corporations, as dis-cussed in Sect. 3.3, although this is more of a substantive rather than a procedural issue.

Finally, in its remedial approach, the Court could be more creative as well as more concrete. The *Kaliña and Lokono* case is a good start, for "it represents the first time that the Court designed a specific reparation to restore the indigenous ter-ritories, placing the obligation not only on the state but also 'in conjunction with the company'. The Court required Suriname to establish 'the necessary mechanisms to monitor and supervise the execution of the rehabilitation by the company'".[142]

5 Conclusion

Both the Commission and the Court have established a rich and progressive body of standards in relation to consultation and particularly FPIC. However, in doing so, they have focused on the responsibilities of states rather than those of businesses, rarely mentioning the latter as duty-bearers. This chapter has argued that there is a

---

[138] Gonza (2017), p. 361.

[139] Article sights 44–51 of the American Convention on Human Rights. See also Inter-American Commission on Human Rights, Impact of the Friendly Settlement Procedure, OEA/Ser.L/V/II. Doc. 45/13, 18 December 2013.

[140] Article 64 American Convention on Human Rights and 2.2 of the Statute of the Inter-American Court of Human Rights.

[141] Gonza (2017), pp. 362–363.

[142] Gonza (2017), p. 364. The internal references are to Inter-American Court of Human Rights, Series C No. 309, *Kaliña and Lokono Peoples v. Suriname (Merits, Reparations and Costs)*, 25 November 2015, para. 290.

legal basis for holding that those standards are also applicable to corporations in the IAHRS, and that it is practical and desirable for this idea to be further developed.

This regional system contains the seeds which could now be cultivated in order to adequately take into account the human rights challenges posed by the Americas' present realities: greater corporate power and the need to ensure it is channelled constructively, both in the interests of states and corporations, and especially in the interests of rights-holders.

The organs of the IAHRS have already established a strong doctrine with the due diligence standard, which ensures that states will be held responsible if corporations breach indigenous peoples' rights. This imposes, as has been argued in this chapter, an indirect responsibility on those corporations. But it is not enough.

Both the IACHR and the IACtHR should act pragmatically and creatively in order to promote and develop the corporate responsibility to respect FPIC. They can (and should) construct a direct corporate responsibility by affirming its legal basis, and by giving an independent treatment to the consequences of the activity of business enterprises, both rewarding positive corporate conduct and punishing negative conduct. They can also remove some procedural obstacles still existing in the system, for this corporate responsibility to be fully effective.

The proposals made in this chapter will not create a corporate responsibility entirely independent from state responsibility. For such corporate responsibility to be established, a reform of the Inter-American legal system might be necessary. Yet, it is crucial to underscore that, "[s]ince corporations have the factual capacity to violate human rights, an individual- and victim-centered international law (as it ought to be) must permit and require the full protection of all victims".[143] Ultimately, it is a matter of putting the focus not on the duty-bearer but on the rights-bearer.

Acknowledgements This chapter is based on the author's dissertation submitted for the Master of Studies degree in International Human Rights Law at the University of Oxford. He wants to thank his supervisor, Chip Pitts, and also Holly Buick, proof-reader of the first drafts. Both the positions held and the errors contained in this chapter should not be attributed to them.

References

Ariza Santamaría R (2013) Pueblos indígenas de Colombia ante el Sistema Interamericano de Derechos Humanos. Editorial Universidad del Rosario, Bogotá
Barelli M (2012) Free, prior and informed consent in the aftermath of the UN declaration on the rights of indigenous peoples: developments and challenges ahead. Int J Hum Rights 16(1):1–24
Boulin Victoria IA (2015–2016) Back to politics: lessons from the crisis of the Inter-American Commission on Human Rights. Buffalo Hum Rights Law Rev 22:21–66

---

[143] Carrillo-Santarelli N, Corporate human rights obligations: Controversial but necessary. Business & Human Rights Resource Centre, 25 August 2015, https://www.business-humanrights.org/en/regulating-companies'-human-rights-obligations-is-controversial-but-necessary-says-academic (last accessed 1 October 2018).

Brunner L, Quintana K (2012) The duty to consult in the Inter-American system: legal standards after Sarayaku. ASIL Insights 16(35)

Cantú Rivera H (2013) Regional approaches in the business and human rights field. L'Observateur des Nations Unies 35:53–84

de Casas CI, Toller FM (2015) Los derechos humanos de las personas jurídicas: Titularidad de derechos y legitimación en el Sistema Interamericano. Porrúa, Mexico

Faúndez Ledesma H (2008) The inter-American system for the protection of human rights: institutional and procedural aspects. IIDH, San José de Costa Rica

Galvis MC (2011) The obligation of states to prevent international law violations by private actors. Aportes DPLF 15:12–14

Gómez LE, Boulin Victoria IA, de Casas CI (2016) Las industrias extractivas frente al Sistema Interamericano de Derechos Humanos: Estándares jurisprudenciales en materia de derechos de los pueblos indígenas. Revista Argentina de Derecho de la Energía. Hidrocarburos y Minería 8:71–106

Gonza A (2017) Integrating business and human rights in the Inter-American human rights system. Bus Hum Rights J 1(2):357–365

Gos T (2017) La "responsabilidad de respetar" los derechos humanos y el establecimiento del deber de debida diligencia como una obligación legal para las industrias extractivas: desafíos y oportunidades en las Américas. Am Univ Int Law Rev 32(4):859–893

Hanna P, Vanclay F (2013) Human rights, Indigenous peoples and the concept of Free, Prior and Informed Consent. Impact Assess Proj Appraisal 31(2):146–157

Heyns C, Killander M (2013) Universality and the growth of regional systems. In: Shelton D (ed) The Oxford handbook of international human rights law. Oxford University Press, Oxford, pp 670–697

Knox JH (2008) Horizontal human rights law. Am J Int Law 102(1):1–47

Lehr AK, Smith GA (2010) Implementing a corporate free, prior, and informed consent policy: benefits and challenges. Foley Hoag eBook, Boston

Lixinski L (2010) Treaty interpretation by the inter-American court of human rights: expansionism at the service of the unity of international law. Eur J Int Law 21(3):585–604

Neuman GL (2008) Import, export, and regional consent in the inter-American court of human rights. Eur J Int Law 19(1):101–123

Sandri Fuentes A (2014) Negocios y derechos humanos: La responsabilidad de los Estados cuando intervienen empresas multinacionales en la violación de derechos humanos. In: Rey SA (ed) Los Derechos Humanos en el Derecho Internacional. Infojus, Buenos Aires, pp 213–228

C. Ignacio de Casas   is an adjunct professor at Austral University in Argentina. He is co-founder of the Centro Latinoamericano de Derechos Humanos (CLADH) and has been working for a law firm focussing on strategic litigation. He has law degrees from the University of Mendoza and University of Oxford and is a PhD candidate at Austral University.

Free, Prior, and Informed Consent in the Philippines: A Fourth World Critique

Armi Beatriz E. Bayot

Contents

1 Introduction... 282
2 A Fourth World Perspective of International Law... 283
3 State Sovereignty Doctrine and the Privileged Status of the State in International Law... 285
   3.1 Permanent Sovereignty Over Natural Resources..................................... 287
   3.2 Regalian Doctrine... 288
   3.3 Free, Prior, and Informed Consent as an International Legal Norm.................. 290
4 FPIC in the Philippines.. 293
   4.1 FPIC on the Ground: Text Versus Application....................................... 295
   4.2 FPIC Versus State Ownership of and Sovereignty Over Natural Resources......... 299
   4.3 Problematizing Indigenous Peoples' Rights in a State-Centric World: A Fourth
      World Critique of FPIC... 302
5 Indigenous Sovereignty: Participation in International Law-Making as an Exercise
   of Self-Determination.. 304
6 Conclusion.. 307
References.. 308

An earlier version of this chapter, focusing on Brazil, was submitted as a final paper in the research module *"Hard" Cases and Regulatory Challenges in Transnational Law and Global Governance* for the Transnational Law LL.M. Pathway at King's College London. This earlier paper helped earn for the author the Georg Schwarzenberger Prize in International Law from the Institute of Advanced Legal Studies, University of London in 2016. The author is indebted to Prof. Peer Zumbansen of King's College London for supervising her research.

A. B. E. Bayot (✉)
Faculty of Law, University of Oxford, Oxford, UK
e-mail: armi.bayot@law.ox.ac.uk

© Springer Nature Switzerland AG 2019
I. Feichtner et al. (eds.), *Human Rights in the Extractive Industries*,
Interdisciplinary Studies in Human Rights 3,
https://doi.org/10.1007/978-3-030-11382-7_11

1 Introduction

> It was her yielding that gave us life. We and the land are one! But who would listen? Will
> they listen? Those invisible ones, who, from unfeeling distance, claim the land is theirs
> because pieces of paper say so?—Macli'ing Dulag[1]

The norm of Free, Prior, and Informed Consent (FPIC) has gained widespread
recognition around the world. In fact, FPIC has been a statutory right in the
Philippines since the enactment of Republic Act (R.A.) No. 8371 or the Indigenous
Peoples' Rights Act (IPRA) in 1997. FPIC remains a regime of unfulfilled promise,
however, due to the power imbalance inherent in the relationship between states and
indigenous peoples. The unequal power relations mean that the very definition and
implementation of FPIC is left in the hands of a powerful party who has its own
interests in the natural resources found in indigenous territories. The determination
of whether the "C" in FPIC pertains to actual consent to resource use activities or to
a mere right to consultation has been left largely to states because it is states that
have the legal personality to create law both domestically and internationally; notably, they are also deemed to possess sovereign prerogatives over natural resources.

The supremacy of the state in international and domestic affairs, coupled with
the fragmented nature of international legal regimes, means that while states may
have ostensibly accepted the idea of indigenous peoples' rights, they can likewise
invoke other international norms, such as the norm of state sovereignty over natural
resources, to qualify these rights. Unless the content of other international legal
regimes also changes to accommodate indigenous peoples' concerns, existing protective norms such as FPIC will fall short in ensuring the physical, cultural, and
spiritual survival of indigenous peoples in today's world. And unless indigenous
peoples also gain access to the processes that create these other legal regimes in
competition with their rights, these parallel legal regimes will likely continue to
primarily reflect state aspirations.

This chapter will trace the development of state sovereignty doctrine in international law to show how its underlying rationale of domination and exclusion has
given shape to the power imbalances that characterize relations between states and
indigenous peoples and how this very rationale continues to animate the debate on
FPIC. Using a "Fourth World perspective," the chapter also analyses how the FPIC
norm as adopted and implemented in the Philippines has been framed within the
legal regime of state sovereignty over natural resources. Finally, it argues that there
is a legal basis to allow for the substantial participation of indigenous peoples in
international law-making and that allowing for such participation would provide
valuable parallel mechanisms to correct the distinct disadvantage that characterizes
the status of indigenous peoples not only in the domestic sphere, but in the international legal system as well. The chapter begins in Sect. 2 by laying down its

---

[1] Philippines: Philippines Remembers Indigenous Hero Macli'ing Dulag.' Indigenous Peoples
Human Rights Defenders http://iphrdefenders.net/philippines-philippines-remembers-indige-
nous-hero-macliing-dulag/ (last accessed 1 October 2018).

theoretical framework—a Fourth World perspective of international law. Section 3 explores the privileged status of states in international law, as illustrated by the concepts of permanent sovereignty over international law, the Regalian Doctrine, and FPIC itself as an international legal norm. Section 4 explores how FPIC, as conceptualized and operationalized in the Philippines, seems to merely perpetuate the unequal power relations between states and indigenous peoples in international law and ends with a Fourth World critique of FPIC. Section 5 explores indigenous sovereignty as a basis for participation in international law-making and the potential for such participation as an alternative means of rights-representation for indigenous peoples.

2   A Fourth World Perspective of International Law

In Third World Approaches to International Law (TWAIL), which are girded with the awareness of the colonial roots of international law, the justness of international law norms must be judged through the eyes of the peoples of the Third World. By peoples, TWAIL scholars refer to both the (post-colonial) states that represent peoples in the international fora and the various people groups who may not be sufficiently represented/heard because they fall short of the sovereignty requirement to be taken seriously in the international community, such as women, peasants, and other minorities. Thus, TWAIL not only looks into the effects that international law has upon the power relations between states, but also looks into the distribution of power between states and peoples.[2] TWAIL scholars note that the post-colonial state's adoption of the European concept of a "unitary state" disregards the diversity of its peoples along ethnic, gender, and class lines—leading to further marginalization of already minoritized groups.[3]

Taking off from the TWAIL tradition of assessing the justness of international law norms through the eyes of the peoples of the Third World, this chapter will critique the justness of the international norm of FPIC using the specific perspective of minoritized indigenous peoples or the Fourth World—a Fourth World approach to/perspective of international law. The Fourth World perspective reveals how state sovereignty doctrine—among the most enduring foundational legal concepts in international law that has permeated the whole world through colonialism—has created a power imbalance between states and indigenous peoples. It also reveals how state sovereignty doctrine has resulted in the relative powerlessness of indigenous peoples on the international stage, where they remain to be internationally unrecognized nations despite predating the modern state.

The term Fourth World was developed in the 1970s as a counterpoint to the post-World War II geopolitical blocs of sovereign states, namely the First World (referring to the European-American bloc that later included Japan), the Second World

---

[2] Anghie and Chimni (2003), p. 78.
[3] Mutua and Anghie (2000), p. 39.

(the communist-socialist bloc including the Soviet Union, China, North Korea, North Vietnam, and Eastern Europe), and the Third World (former colonies and newly independent states originally thought of as non-aligned states). It was only later that the term Third World began to take on a neo-colonial colour, in view of these new states' dependence on the First and Second Worlds. Because the older nations/indigenous communities from which these sovereign states were created were not themselves internationally recognized sovereign states, indigenous peoples began to assert a separate identity under the term Fourth World. Among the first proponents of the term Fourth World was Shuswap Chief George Manuel, who, with his co-author Michael Posluns, defined it in the book *The Fourth World: An Indian Reality* as "indigenous peoples descended from a country's aboriginal population and who today are completely or partly deprived of the right to their own territories and its riches."[4] Numbering around 370 million in about 70 different states, they have limited power and influence in a world where sovereign states are supreme.[5] Fourth World analyses and writings, according to Nietschmann, seek to correct the distortion that mainstream sovereign-state centred historical accounts have made regarding indigenous peoples' identities, geographies, and histories, with the end in view of resisting their continued oppression and exploitation.[6]

A Fourth World perspective of international law is essential in uncovering the unique status that indigenous peoples have in history, as well as their unique dilemmas within their states and within the wider international community. Unlike other marginalized people groups, indigenous peoples have a claim to a historical "tribal sovereignty"—a historical claim over their territories and the natural resources found therein, as well as a claim to the right to govern themselves using indigenous political structures and customary laws.[7] Significantly, these claims predate both the claims of newly-independent states and the claims of their former European colonial masters over indigenous peoples' territories and resources. From historical sovereigns, indigenous peoples have been relegated to the status of minority groups within modern states, and they are often seen as just another classification of vulnerable groups such as women, the urban poor, and farmers. Putting aside the obvious overlaps that these classifications ignore, it must be stressed that indigenous peoples' concerns go beyond the assertion of basic rights within the framework of the state to the assertion of the right to survival as peoples distinct from the state.

Through a Fourth World perspective, this chapter will critique FPIC by considering its place within international and domestic legal systems. In particular, FPIC should be understood vis-a-vis the primacy of the state sovereignty doctrine, the doctrine of permanent sovereignty over natural resources, and, in the Philippine context, the Regalian doctrine.

---

[4] Griggs R, The meaning of "nation" and "state" in the fourth world. Center for World Indigenous Studies (CWIS), CWIS Occasional Paper #18, 1992, http://cwis.org/GML/background/FourthWorld/ (last accessed 1 October 2018).

[5] Wiessner (2008), p. 1151.

[6] Nietschmann (1994), p. 230.

[7] Wiessner (2008), pp. 1145, 1166–1170.

3   State Sovereignty Doctrine and the Privileged Status of the State in International Law

State sovereignty is the cornerstone of law, both national and international. Wiessner notes that sovereignty denotes power both within and outside a state's territory. Within its territorial jurisdiction, a state has the power to issue rules binding upon the individuals and groups under its authority—in this way it creates domestic law. Internationally, a sovereign state is said to have the power to limit its power to the territorial limits of its jurisdiction in accordance with explicit agreements with other states or through consistent practice—in this way creating international law.[8] Sovereignty as power is a truism which draws life from the Westphalian notions of sovereign equality of states and state supremacy within territorial borders.[9]

While this concept of state sovereignty may seem, on its face, to promote equitable relations among states in the international community, Anghie asserts that the concept of state sovereignty, in fact, was born out of the exclusionary mindset of European states in the imperial age. In the age of empire, only European states were deemed sovereign; non-European states were "base," "backward," and "uncivilized"—lacking in sovereignty, and therefore lacking the standing to credibly resist conquest and colonization.

Anghie argues that international law, therefore, could be "seen as an attempt to establish a universal system of order among entities characterized as belonging to different cultural systems. This problem gives rise to what might be termed the 'dynamic of difference': international law posits a gap, a difference between European and non-European cultures and peoples, the former being characterized, broadly as civilized and the latter as uncivilized (and all this implies in terms of the related qualities of each of these labels). This gap having been established, what follows is the formulation of doctrines that are designed to efface this gap: to bring the uncivilized/aberrant/violent/backward/oppressed into the realm of civilization, the universal order governed by (European) international law. This distinction between the civilized and the uncivilized, the animating distinction of imperialism, is crucial to the formation of sovereignty doctrine, which can be understood as providing certain cultures with all the powers of sovereignty while excluding others."[10] This mindset, according to Anghie, is the foundation of the "civilizing mission" behind the colonial project. This distinction between the civilized and the uncivilized was the rationale for years of political subordination and economic exploitation of non-European peoples committed by Europeans through colonialism. Indeed, it was through colonial expansion that international law and sovereignty, as conceived in Europe, became universal.[11]

---

[8] Wiessner (2008), p. 1146.

[9] Anghie (2006), p. 740.

[10] Anghie (2006), p. 742.

[11] Anghie (2006), pp. 741–742.

And so, the "savage" non-European world was incorporated into the system of (European) international law as colonies of sovereign states that needed tutelage in "sophisticated" political thought and organization.

The incorporation of the non-European world continued in the process of decolonization, where former colonies were granted the status of being sovereign and equal members of the international community.[12] However, as aptly observed by Wiessner, "the choice as to the political future of colonized peoples was not given to the individual peoples conquered, but to the inhabitants of territories colonized by European conquerors, within the boundaries of the lines of demarcation drawn by colonizers." The post-colonial formation of states thus upheld the concept of *uti possidetis*.[13] The lines drawn made no distinction as regards unique ethnolinguistic groups and their customary lands—honouring only the colonizers' boundaries on the map. This rather arbitrary map-making disregarded indigenous peoples' unique political and social structures—indigenous peoples who had been exercising indigenous sovereignty according to their own customs over their own communities within their historical lands from time immemorial.[14] Thus, post-colonial states became subjects of international law, while indigenous peoples did not. While post-colonial states shed the image of the "savage," indigenous peoples within them continued to be regarded as uncivilized groups of people in need of the tutelage and guardianship of the post-colonial state.[15] In both the colonial and post-colonial eras, states (moulded after the European model of sovereign statehood) hold the monopoly on political power and international standing. While it was the European state that exclusively held power in colonial times, all states—including post-colonial states—now wield this power as full-fledged members of the international community. In both periods, the historical sovereignty that indigenous peoples exercise according to their own customs in their own territories is unrecognized, and consequently not honoured, for not resembling the contours of Eurocentric sovereignty.[16]

The colonial (and inequitable) origins of international law are evident in the privileged status of states vis-à-vis indigenous peoples in international law—in particular, in the context of certain international legal norms that affect indigenous peoples' rights, prerogatives, and, indeed, their very prospects for survival as distinct people groups.

---

[12] Anghie (2006), p. 740.

[13] "One should leave the place as one received it." See Wiessner (2008), p. 1150.

[14] Wiessner (2008), pp. 1150–1151.

[15] Miranda (2008), p. 425.

[16] Miranda (2008), p. 425; Wiessner (2008), pp. 1149–1150.

3.1 Permanent Sovereignty Over Natural Resources

Because colonization resulted in gross inequalities as regards power and the distribution of resources, the doctrine of permanent sovereignty over natural resources arose as a means of ensuring that peoples emerging from colonial rule would benefit from the exploitation of natural resources in their areas. It was also meant as a means of preventing foreign states or transnational businesses from infringing upon the sovereignty of newly independent states.[17] This doctrine is found in General Assembly Resolution 626 (VII) dated December 21, 1952 on the Right to Exploit Freely Natural Wealth and Resources. A key debate surrounding the interpretation of this instrument was identifying the juridical/legal entity that had the right to exercise sovereignty over natural resources. Because this doctrine developed during the decolonization process, the exercise of sovereignty was understood to be the right of newly-independent states, which they can assert vis-à-vis other states in the international community and internally within their territorial jurisdiction.[18] This understanding of sovereignty in the context of the decolonization process is crucial, considering that the resolution actually reads:

1. The right of peoples and nations to permanent sovereignty over their natural wealth and resources must be exercised in the interest of their national development and of the well-being of the people of the State concerned.

Despite the use of the term "peoples and nations" in the resolution itself, various iterations of the doctrine in succeeding instruments referred to "underdeveloped countries," "developing countries," and "states." Thus, the right has henceforth been interpreted as a right and prerogative of sovereign states, and is described in international law as "permanent," "absolute," and "inalienable." Since the underlying purpose of the doctrine at the time of decolonization was to strengthen the position of newly independent states versus former colonizers and other states, the term "peoples" was understood as referring to post-colonial states, and not constituent peoples. Post-colonial states, exercising permanent authority over natural resources, thus had exclusive authority to make decisions regarding natural resource use, with the end in view of strengthening their political and economic positions. Post-colonial states employed this doctrine to pursue various national development projects with aim of promoting the "national interest" or the "public welfare," i.e. the good of the whole post-colonial state—conflating the identities of various people groups with that of the state and establishing a new (forced) shared identity as one "people."[19]

It will be recalled that the presumed lack of sovereignty of non-European peoples over their lands was an underlying justification for European conquest and colonization. Sovereignty was not deemed inherent in the various non-European

---

[17] Miranda (2012), pp. 789–790.

[18] Miranda (2012), pp. 796–797.

[19] Miranda (2012), pp. 797–798.

polities that imperialists encountered in the course of the colonial project.[20] Sovereignty was later "granted" to former colonies under the auspices of the United Nations system, in most cases adhering to the boundaries drawn by the colonizers. Overlooked in this project were various indigenous people groups who had been exercising self-governance over their traditional lands according to customary laws that were independent of the European-imposed governance systems. Without regard to the distinctiveness of these indigenous peoples, they were included in brand-new post-colonial states who now had the right to exercise state sovereignty and, in particular, permanent sovereignty over natural resources within their territorial jurisdiction—including the lands over which indigenous peoples had been exercising their historical/indigenous sovereignty since time immemorial.[21] The argument could be made that indigenous peoples have been illegitimately deprived of sovereign control of their ancestral lands twice already—first during the colonial period and second during the decolonization era. Post-colonial states can exercise permanent sovereignty over natural resources because they exhibit the features of a Westphalian sovereign state. In the doctrine of permanent sovereignty over natural resources, the time immemorial possession and historical sovereignty of indigenous peoples over their traditional lands is subordinated to the sovereign state's authority, as well as its notions of what constitutes the "national good." This pursuit by post-colonial states of a unifying "public welfare" use of indigenous peoples' lands furthermore perpetuates the false model of a European-style unitary nation state where in fact what exists is a forced coexistence of nations and peoples.

3.2 Regalian Doctrine

The doctrine of permanent sovereignty over natural resources should also be read together with the colonial legal heritage that former colonizers left behind in their former colonies. One such legacy is the Regalian Doctrine, a legal framework that prevails in Spain and its former colonies—the Philippines, Mexico, and South America.[22] In the Philippines, the Regalian Doctrine provides that all lands and natural resources are owned by the state. Private title to agricultural land is obtained only through government grant; all other natural resources may not be subject to private ownership. It is the State that owns all natural resources, even when found on privately owned land.[23] It also has full control and supervision of the exploration, development, and utilization of such natural resources.[24]

---

[20] Anghie (2006), pp. 74–742.

[21] Wiessner (2008), pp. 1149–1151.

[22] Bocobo (1936), p. 151.

[23] Bocobo (1936), p. 151.

[24] Republic of the Philippines Supreme Court, G.R. No. 167707, *The Secretary of Environment and Natural Resources v. Yap*, 8 October 2008.

Lynch notes that the Regalian Doctrine was imposed upon the Philippine colony through Spanish occupation, and through it, the Spanish colonizers denied the indigenous peoples' sovereign and property rights over their territories:

> According to the doctrine, at some unspecified moment during the sixteenth century, the sovereign and property rights *(imperium and dominion)* of the Philippine peoples' forebears were unilaterally usurped by, and simultaneously vested in, the Crowns of Castille and Aragon. Although there appears to be no official determination, the only plausible date is Easter Sunday, March 31, 1521. On that day Ferdinand Magellan and his crew planted a large wooden cross on the Island of Limasawa. At that same five-hundred-year-old unspecified moment, every native in the politically undefined and still largely unexplored (not to mention unconquered) archipelago became a squatter, bereft of any legal rights to land or any other natural resources. The only way to reacquire sovereignty was to get it back from the colonial usurpers. The only way to remove the squatter label was by procuring a documented property right from the Spanish regime, or its state-successors.[25]

Despite the colonial and confiscatory roots of the Regalian Doctrine, it remains the foundation for Philippine land and natural resource laws. It is enshrined in Article XII, Section 2 of the Philippine Constitution:

> SECTION 2. All lands of the public domain, waters, minerals, coal, petroleum, and other mineral oils, all forces of potential energy, fisheries, forests or timber, wildlife, flora and fauna, and other natural resources are owned by the State. With the exception of agricultural lands, all other natural resources shall not be alienated. The exploration, development, and utilization of natural resources shall be under the full control and supervision of the State. The State may directly undertake such activities, or it may enter into co-production, joint venture, or production-sharing agreements with Filipino citizens, or corporations or associations at least sixty per centum of whose capital is owned by such citizens. Such agreements may be for a period not exceeding twenty-five years, renewable for not more than twenty-five years, and under such terms and conditions as may be provided by law. In cases of water rights for irrigation, water supply, fisheries, or industrial uses other than the development of water power, beneficial use may be the measure and limit of the grant.

Because "all lands of the public domain belong to the State," the state is the source of any asserted right to ownership of land. All lands not appearing to be clearly under private ownership are presumed to belong to the State, and public lands remain part of the inalienable land of the public domain unless the State has clearly reclassified or alienated them to private persons.[26] The Regalian Doctrine, in essence, invalidates all claims to land that have existed prior to the establishment of the colonial government in the Philippine islands or that claim to be independent of any government grant.

---

[25] Lynch (2011), pp. 6–7.

[26] Republic of the Philippines Supreme Court, G.R. No. 179987, *Malabanan v. Republic*, 3 September 2013.

3.3 Free, Prior, and Informed Consent as an International Legal Norm

The doctrine of permanent sovereignty over natural resources and the Regalian Doctrine both underscore the state's primacy, particularly as regards ownership and control over land and other natural resources. The emergence of the norm of FPIC can be thought of as a means to counter the state-centric nature of norms such as these.

A number of international instruments reflect a growing consensus that indigenous peoples are entitled to certain fundamental rights considering their special relationship with their traditional lands.[27] The notions of collective land ownership in the context of traditional territories, indigenous peoples' right to the physical enjoyment, control, and development of such lands, and their right to preserve them in the context of their spiritual significance, among others, stem directly from indigenous peoples' own customary laws.[28] These concepts can now be found in such instruments as the International Labor Organization (ILO) Convention No. 169 and the United Nations Declaration on the Rights of Indigenous Peoples (UNDRIP).[29] The growing consensus on indigenous peoples' rights has given rise to the norm of FPIC, which lays down guidelines for the participation of indigenous peoples in decision-making in relation to development activities in their territories, including the exploitation, development, and utilization of natural resources in their lands.[30] In theory, before states are to allow/embark upon such development activities, a procedure for consultation/FPIC must be completed.

However, even if it were to be conceded that FPIC has gained widespread recognition among states, it must be stressed that it is commonly asserted by states that FPIC generally only requires consultations with indigenous peoples and not consent. As Barelli notes, it secures a procedure for consultation and participation, but it does not grant an assurance with regard to outcome: as a general rule, FPIC does not actually grant indigenous peoples the power to grant or withhold consent to development activities in their territories.[31] This is apparent in the World Bank Operational Policy 4.10, which provides that before the World Bank agrees to financing a project that may affect indigenous peoples, the borrower must first engage in consultation, to wit: "a process of free, prior, and informed consultation with affected communities that (will lead to) broad support for the project."[32] The World Bank's use of the term "consultation" with the objective of gaining support militates against the argument that indigenous peoples can veto development projects. The World Bank policy is similar to what is provided in ILO Convention No.

---

[27] Barelli (2012), p. 2.

[28] Barelli (2012), p. 2; Wiessner (2008) pp. 1154–1155.

[29] Miranda (2008), pp. 429–432.

[30] Barelli (2012), p. 3.

[31] Barelli (2012), p. 2.

[32] Barelli (2012), pp. 3–5.

169, to wit: "the consultations carried out in application of this Convention shall be undertaken, in good faith and in a form appropriate to the circumstances, with the objective of achieving agreement or consent to the proposed measures."[33]

Even the UNDRIP does not guarantee consent in FPIC. Article 32 of the UNDRIP provides:

> 2. States shall consult and cooperate in good faith with the indigenous peoples concerned through their own representative institutions in order to obtain their free and informed consent prior to the approval of any project affecting their lands or territories and other resources, particularly in connection with the development, utilization or exploitation of mineral, water or other resources.

While at first blush, the provision seems to oblige states to obtain the consent of indigenous peoples before commencing upon any activity in their traditional lands, this interpretation is precluded by the drafting history of this provision. The earlier draft provided that indigenous peoples had "the right to require that States obtain their free and informed consent prior to the approval of any project affecting their lands, territories and other resources." States were concerned about the import of this provision and proposed alternative versions. Article 32 as finally drafted exhibits the compromise arrived at to accommodate the concern of various states.[34] The redraft of Article 32 from the original version indicates that there is no intention to grant indigenous peoples an absolute veto right against state projects in their lands in all instances.[35]

The Inter-American system has produced jurisprudence on the application of FPIC and provides a little more detail on the interpretation and application of this right.[36] Because of rampant encroachments upon their customary lands for purposes of the exploration, development, and utilization of natural resources, and because the indigenous peoples in Latin America could not consistently expect their state governments to honour their customary land laws, indigenous peoples in Latin America have engaged in various legal actions before the Inter-American Commission on Human Rights (IACHR) and the Inter-American Court of Human Rights (IACtHR). As a result of these legal actions, the Inter-American System has explicitly acknowledged indigenous peoples' special link with their lands and has underscored that FPIC is deemed a necessary component of indigenous peoples' meaningful exercise of their right to property.[37]

In *Saramaka People v. Suriname*,[38] the IACtHR was asked to rule on whether Suriname's awarding of logging and mining concessions to third parties over customary lands of the Saramaka people violated their right to property under Article 21 of the American Convention on Human Rights. The IACtHR ruling strikes a

---

[33] Barelli (2012), pp. 5–6.

[34] Barelli (2012), pp. 10–11.

[35] Heiniimki (2011), p. 225.

[36] See the chapter by de Casas in this volume.

[37] Miranda (2008) pp. 433–434.

[38] Inter-American Court of Human Rights, Series C No. 172, *Saramaka People v. Suriname*, Judgment (Preliminary Objections, Merits, Reparations, and Costs), 28 November 2007.

balance between state interest and indigenous peoples' right to property. The IACtHR clarified that Article 21 cannot be read as an absolute bar to state or state-authorized exploitation of resources in indigenous peoples' territory. It then applied a "sliding scale approach to participatory rights," clarifying that "the level of (indigenous peoples') effective participation (in decision making) is essentially a function of the nature and content of the rights and activities in question."[39] As a general rule, and consistent with Article 32 of the UNDRIP, Article 21 requires states to conduct consultations in good faith with the objective of reaching an agreement with indigenous peoples regarding extractive activity within indigenous territory, to the extent that indigenous peoples must be afforded "effective participation" in the "development or investment plans within their territory." As regards large-scale development activities, which would have a major impact within Saramaka territory, the IACtHR ruled that states have a duty not only to consult, but also to obtain their free, prior, and informed consent. The rationale for imposing the much more rigorous requirement of consent for large-scale activities is that these activities have the potential of creating such profound social, environmental, and economic changes that would negatively affect indigenous peoples' safety and survival.[40]

The sliding scale propounded in the *Saramaka* case should underscore the fact that even in the Inter-American System, good faith consultations are the norm and the consent requirement only applies in exceptional and extreme circumstances. The right to FPIC under Inter-American jurisprudence does not grant indigenous peoples the right to veto any and all extractive projects in their lands. The right to FPIC is carefully calibrated to accommodate state interests in the development of natural resources within their territorial jurisdiction on the one hand and the survival of indigenous peoples on the other. The debate on consultation and consent in the Inter-American system illustrates how the state is deemed to have authority in determining the propriety of development activities in the lands of indigenous peoples, especially if it is seen that such activities would redound to the common good.

FPIC exists within a world order where states are not only privileged over indigenous peoples as regards the ownership and control of land and natural resources, but they are also privileged with the exclusive power to create law both within their borders and internationally through binding treaties with other states. Indigenous peoples do not have this norm-creating power, and they are, therefore, hostage to the "beneficence" of states in the creation of international treaties that affect their rights. To date, for instance, the only treaty that establishes FPIC as a right on the part of indigenous peoples and as an international state obligation on a global level is the ILO Convention No. 169, and it has only been ratified by 22 states. Moreover, indigenous peoples are likewise hostage to state interpretation and implementation of

---

[39] Inter-American Court of Human Rights, Series C No. 172, *Saramaka People v. Suriname,* Judgment (Preliminary Objections, Merits, Reparations, and Costs), 28 November 2007, Barelli (2012), pp. 13–14.

[40] Inter-American Court of Human Rights, Series C No. 172, *Saramaka People v. Suriname,* Judgment (Preliminary Objections, Merits, Reparations, and Costs), 28 November 2007, Barelli (2012), pp. 14–15.

norms, formal or otherwise, that purport to protect indigenous peoples' rights—including the norm of FPIC. Such interpretation and implementation seem fundamentally skewed in favour of state prerogatives.

4   FPIC in the Philippines

The tension between state interests and prerogatives, on the one hand, and indigenous peoples' rights, on the other, persists even in the Philippines—a country where FPIC has long been adopted as part of the legal regime concerning land and land rights. The Philippines is not a party to ILO Convention No. 169, and, thus, the establishment of FPIC as a statutory right in the Philippines is not a matter of international obligation, but is rather a legislative "grant." The IPRA, which contains the FPIC guarantee, was enacted in 1997–20 years before the UNDRIP was adopted by the UN General Assembly.[41] The Philippines' vote for the UNDRIP is an affirmation of existing legislative policy as well as a further acknowledgment of indigenous peoples' rights.

The IPRA is a landmark law that mandates that the State shall recognize and promote the rights of indigenous cultural communities/indigenous peoples (ICCs/IPs) within the framework of national unity and development.[42] ICCs/IPs, as defined by the IPRA, refer to those who have continuously lived as organized communities on communally bounded and defined territories, under claims of ownership since time immemorial, sharing common bonds of language, customs, and other distinctive cultural traits and those who have resisted colonization and have therefore become historically differentiated from the majority of Filipinos. The term also includes their descendants, even if they have been displaced or have resettled away from their territories.[43]

The IPRA is noteworthy because, in an apparent break with the Regalian Doctrine, it honors *native title,* or "pre-conquest rights to lands and domains which, as far back as memory reaches, have been held under a claim of private ownership by ICCs/IPs, have never been public lands and are thus indisputably presumed to have been held that way since before the Spanish Conquest."[44] It guarantees the right of indigenous peoples to their ancestral domain, which it defines as all areas generally belonging to ICCs/IPs comprising lands, inland waters, coastal areas, and natural resources, held under a claim of ownership, occupied or possessed by ICCs/IPs, by themselves or through their ancestors, communally or individually since time immemorial.[45]

---

[41] It is believed, however, that the IPRA was influenced by early drafts of the UNDRIP, *see* Wiessner (2008), p. 1162.

[42] IPRA Section 2 (a).

[43] IPRA Section 3 (h).

[44] IPRA Section 3 (l).

[45] IPRA Section 3 (a).

The IPRA defines FPIC as the consensus of all members of the ICCs/IPs to be determined in accordance with their respective customary laws and practices, free from any external manipulation, interference and coercion, and obtained after fully disclosing the intent and scope of the activity, in a language and process understandable to them.[46] Ultimately, however, it is the National Commission on Indigenous Peoples (NCIP), the government agency mandated to implement the IPRA, through its Ancestral Domain Office, that makes a determination as to whether FPIC needs to be obtained or not, to wit:

Section 59. *Certification Precondition.* - all department and other governmental agencies shall henceforth be strictly enjoined from issuing, renewing, or granting any concession, license or lease, or entering into any production-sharing agreement, without prior certification from the NCIP that the area affected does not overlap with any ancestral domain. Such certificate shall only be issued after a field-based investigation is conducted by the Ancestral Domain Office of the area concerned: Provided, That no certificate shall be issued by the NCIP without the free and prior informed and written consent of the ICCs/IPs concerned: Provided, further, That no department, government agency or government-owned or -controlled corporation may issue new concession, license, lease, or production sharing agreement while there is pending application CADT:[47] Provided, finally, that the ICCs/IPs shall have the right to stop or suspend, in accordance with this Act, any project that has not satisfied the requirement of this consultation process.

As implemented by the NCIP, two FPIC scenarios are possible. Scenario One is where a proposed project will not overlap with or otherwise affect an ancestral domain, meriting the issuance by the NCIP of a Certificate of Non-Overlap. Scenario Two is where a proposed project will overlap with or otherwise affect an ancestral domain. In Scenario Two, the NCIP will conduct a lengthy FPIC procedure with the express purpose of obtaining the free, prior, and informed consent of the indigenous communities that will be affected by the proposed project. Once the FPIC of the relevant indigenous communities has been obtained, the NCIP will then issue a Certification Precondition to the project proponent.[48]

If the consultations reveal that the indigenous community/communities affected do not consent to the project, a Resolution of Non-Consent will be issued. The project proponent, however, has the right to seek a reconsideration of this resolution with the community/communities concerned. In seeking a reconsideration, the project proponent must make proposals to address the community/communities' reasons for not consenting to the project. In the event that the Resolution of Non-Consent is not reconsidered, another FPIC process for any similar proposal can be undertaken, but only after 6 months from the issuance of the said resolution.[49]

[46] IPRA Section 3 (g).

[47] Certificate of Ancestral Domain Title.

[48] NCIP Administrative Order No. 3. Series of 2012. The Revised Guidelines on Free and Prior Informed Consent (FPIC) and Related Processes of 2012. 13 April 2012, http://ncipro67.com.ph/wp-content/uploads/2015/09/NCIP-AO-3-Series-of-2012-FPIC.pdf (last accessed 1 October 2018), Sections 5(d), 5(e), and 15.

[49] NCIP Administrative Order No. 3. Series of 2012. The Revised Guidelines on Free and Prior Informed Consent (FPIC) and Related Processes of 2012. 13 April 2012, http://ncipro67.com.ph/

If the consultations result in the indigenous community/communities consenting to the project, the terms and conditions of such consent will be embodied in a Memorandum of Agreement (MOA) between the communities, the project proponent, the NCIP and other relevant stakeholders. Unless otherwise agreed upon in the MOA, the indigenous communities have the right to separate FPIC procedures for each major phase of a project, including exploration, development, contracting of operator and the like.[50]

During the consultations, the project proponent explains the cost, as well as the benefits, of the project to the indigenous communities and their ancestral domains. Any perceived disadvantages to the community must be addressed by the proponent with measures to avoid or mitigate such disadvantages.[51]

While the IPRA in Section 59 seems to imply that no government agency may issue, renew, or grant any concession, license, or lease, or enter into any production-sharing agreement with a project proponent for the exploration, development, and utilization of natural resources within an ancestral domain before the issuance of the Certification Precondition, this does not mean that the government does not award or approve of such contracts or otherwise embark on such projects itself prior to the completion of the FPIC process.

4.1 FPIC on the Ground: Text Versus Application

The Chico River, the longest river system in the Cordillera mountains in Northern Luzon, is the site of one of the most contentious, and most violent, disputes on resource use in the Philippines in the twentieth century. A World-Bank funded dam project that began in the 1970s was eventually shelved in the mid-1980s after attempts by government forces to implement the project resulted in an escalation of hostilities that culminated in the death of more than 100 persons. Macli'ing Dulag,[52] a Kalinga leader who led the opposition to the construction of the dam system, was shot dead in 1980 during a military raid in his town.[53]

---

wp-content/uploads/2015/09/NCIP-AO-3-Series-of-2012-FPIC.pdf (last accessed 1 October 2018), Sections 22 and 27.

[50] NCIP Administrative Order No. 3. Series of 2012. The Revised Guidelines on Free and Prior Informed Consent (FPIC) and Related Processes of 2012. 13 April 2012, http://ncipro67.com.ph/wp-content/uploads/2015/09/NCIP-AO-3-Series-of-2012-FPIC.pdf (last accessed 1 October 2018), Section 20.

[51] NCIP Administrative Order No. 3. Series of 2012. The Revised Guidelines on Free and Prior Informed Consent (FPIC) and Related Processes of 2012. 13 April 2012, http://ncipro67.com.ph/wp-content/uploads/2015/09/NCIP-AO-3-Series-of-2012-FPIC.pdf (1 last accessed 1 October 2018), Section 22.

[52] Whose quote appears earlier in the chapter.

[53] Indigenous Peoples Human Rights Defenders, Philippines: Philippines Remembers Indigenous Hero Macli'ing Dulag. 29 April 2013, http://iphrdefenders.net/philippines-philippines-remembers-indigenous-hero-macliing-dulag/ (last accessed 1 October 2018).

The local residents were not consulted by the Philippine government on the implementation of the project.[54] Bontocs and Kalingas, indigenous cultural communities who occupy the areas that would be affected by the project, both resisted the survey teams with such ferocity that the National Power Corporation eventually conducted its survey of the area by air.[55] The Philippine government, then under Martial Law under the former president Ferdinand E. Marcos, eventually militarized the area with the creation of the Civilian Home Defense Forces in Kalinga and the eventual deployment of the entire 60th Battalion of the Philippine Constabulary.[56]

The area covered by the Chico River Basin Development Project would have been the total catchment area of the Chico River—a total of 1400 km². This area coincides with a watershed including the municipalities of Sabangan, Sagada, Bontoc, Sadanga, and parts of Bauko and Barlig in Mountain Province and the municipalities of Tinglayan, Lubuangan, Pasil, and parts of Tabuk in Kalinga. It is estimated that had the project proceeded as planned, it would have displaced some 250,000 members of Bontoc and Kalinga indigenous communities as it would have flooded some 100,000 ha of their ancestral lands. These ancestral lands have been occupied by the Bontoc and the Kalinga since time immemorial and are used as residential areas, farm lands, and sacred burial sites.[57] Such a destruction would have struck a major blow to the locals' prospects for survival. Moreover, it would have severely impacted their cultural and spiritual heritage. The people in the Chico Valley have strong spiritual ties to the land and see the area as the accumulation of the toil of generations, guided by the spirit gods of the forests and the fields. The Bontoc and Kalinga see themselves as the guardians of this material and spiritual inheritance, and they believe that if they allowed the widespread destruction of their traditional lands, they would earn the unending ire of their ancestors and gods.[58]

On the part of the Philippine government, the Chico River dam project was a necessary step towards energy independence in the wake of the oil crisis in 1973. The OPEC's oil embargo resulted in a global price hike, and in the face of what was perceived as a looming energy crisis, the Chico River dam project would have provided a viable and reliable energy source for the island of Luzon. Local and international support for the Bontoc and Kalinga peoples' plight at the hands of government agents bent on implementing the project grew steadily over the years. By the

---

[54] Cariño (1980), p. 7.

[55] Malayang B S (1991) Rights and exclusion in tenure: implications to tenure policies in the Philippines. Paper read before the Second Annual Meeting of the International Association for the Study of Common Property at the University of Manitoba, Winnipeg, Canada, 26 September to 2 October 1991, p. 4.

[56] Cariño (1980), p. 8.

[57] Indigenous Peoples Human Rights Defenders, Philippines: Philippines Remembers Indigenous Hero Macli'ing Dulag. 29 April 2013, http://iphrdefenders.net/philippines-philippines-remembers-indigenous-hero-macliing-dulag/ (last accessed 1 October 2018).

[58] Cariño (1980), pp. 4–5.

mid-1980s, the backlash against the project had become so great that the World Bank had to pull out funding for the project.[59]

It is, therefore, perplexing that a new Chico River project has been approved by the Philippine government. The Department of Energy (DOE) awarded a contract for the Chico River Hydroelectric Power Project to private contractor San Lorenzo Ruiz Builders & Developers Group, Inc.[60] The proposed 240-MW plant in Tabuk, Kalinga will be connected to the Luzon power grid and is estimated to cost $680 million.[61] While the contract was awarded as early as 2015, the legally-mandated procedure for obtaining the indigenous communities' FPIC is yet to be concluded. The NCIP says that consultations with the communities have indicated local support for the project, but the communities—at the time of writing—are still in the middle of negotiations with the contractor to finalize a Memorandum of Agreement.[62] Despite there being a formal FPIC procedure in place, there appears to be growing opposition to the dam project. A petition submitted to the NCIP, signed by 200 locals, claims that those communities who were consulted and who have voted in favour of the project will not be directly affected by the project.[63] The petition further claims that the project will adversely affect the Kalingas' ancestral inheritance, livelihood, and ancestral burial grounds—leading to a fresh outbreak of violence.[64] Among the stakeholders opposing the project are members of the Naneng, Dallak, and Minanga sub-tribes in Kalinga and residents of Sitio Banat, Bagumbayan in Tabuk; it is feared that this *sitio* will be flooded once the project starts.[65] Thus, in an eerie parallel to the violent dispute that arose in the same area more than 40 years

---

[59] Malayang (1991) Rights and exclusion in tenure: implications to tenure policies in the Philippines. Paper read before the Second Annual Meeting of the International Association for the Study of Common Property at the University of Manitoba, Winnipeg, Canada, 26 September to 2 October 1991, pp. 3, 8.

[60] Department of Energy, Awarded Hydroelectric power Projects as of September 302,015, https://www.doe.gov.ph/sites/default/files/pdf/renewable_energy/awarded_hydropower_2015_09-30.pdf (last accessed 1 October 2018).

[61] Gonzales I, San Lorenzo Ruiz to pursue $2.5 B hydropower projects. 21 May 2014, http://www.philstar.com/business/2014/05/21/1325374/san-lorenzo-ruiz-pursue-2.5-b-hydropower-projects (last accessed 1 October 2018).

[62] Catajan M, Indigenous People commission approves Kalinga dam project. 4 May 2017, http://www.sunstar.com.ph/baguio/local-news/2017/05/04/indigenous-people-commission-approves-kalinga-dam-project-540019 (last accessed 1 October 2018).

[63] Catajan M, Chico river dam project awaits clearance. 4 July 2017, http://www.sunstar.com.ph/baguio/local-news/2017/07/05/chico-river-dam-project-awaits-clearance-551127 (last accessed 1 October 2018).

[64] Catajan M, Tribes oppose dam project in Chico River. 2 May 2017, http://www.sunstar.com.ph/baguio/local-news/2017/05/04/tribes-oppose-dam-project-chico-river-539748 (last accessed 1 October 2018).

[65] Catajan M, Tabuk City citizens hold anti-dam rally Sunday. 21 May 2017, http://www.sunstar.com.ph/baguio/local-news/2017/05/21/tabuk-city-citizens-hold-anti-dam-rally-543087 (last accessed 1 October 2018).

ago, the Philippine government is again facing mounting opposition from local communities regarding a hydroelectric project it has already approved.

The current Chico River hydroelectric project was awarded to the project proponent in 2015. As early as 2014, news reports regarding the project proponent's efforts to secure further investment for the project had begun to circulate.[66] It can be assumed that San Lorenzo Ruiz Builders & Developers Group, Inc. had already made substantial investments into the project by the time the FPIC procedure was conducted sometime in 2017, as documents on the DOE website dated 2015 to 2016 show that it has been steadily complying with project requirements during this period.[67] The FPIC procedure is yet to be concluded—no Certification Precondition has been issued to date.

The FPIC experience in the Chico River project 2.0 is not an anomaly. Similarly, the Jalaur River Multipurpose Project, Stage II in the province of Iloilo in Western Visayas was already in the works before the FPIC procedure was completed. The project, which includes the construction of a dam system, seeks to provide irrigation water to 12,000 ha of land and supplemental water to 22,340 ha of land already being serviced by the existing irrigation system. It will also generate 11.5 MW of hydroelectric power for the local communities. The Jalaur project was among the Aquino Administration's flagship economic projects and was already included in its list of priority Private-Public Partnership (PPP) Projects by the end of 2010.[68] However, the Certification Precondition for the Feasibility Study Stage was only issued to the National Irrigation Administration in 2012,[69] while the Certification Precondition for the Implementation Stage was only issued in 2015.[70] Assessments of the project from 2013 indicate that it will potentially inundate 900 ha of land and will affect the ancestral domain of the Bukidon-Halawodnon indigenous community.[71] The project is estimated to cost PhP 11.1 Billion, with PhP 8.9 Billion coming through a loan from the Korean Export-Import Bank.[72]

MacroAsia Corporation, on the other hand, was granted by the Department of Environment and Natural Resources a Mineral Production Sharing Agreement (MPSA) in 2005. Said MPSA covers an area of 1,113.983 ha straddling 5 barangays

---

[66] See Renewable Technology, San Lorenzo Ruiz to invest $2.5bn in hydropower projects, seeks partners. 20 May 2014, http://www.renewable-technology.com/news/newssan-lorenzo-ruiz-to-invest-25bn-in-hydropower-projects-seeks-partners-210514-4272982 (last accessed 1 October 2018).

[67] See Department of Energy, Awarded Hydroelectricpower Projects as of September 302015, https://www.doe.gov.ph/sites/default/files/pdf/renewable_energy/awarded_hydropower_2015_09-30.pdf (last accessed 1 October 2018).

[68] See Republic of the Philippines, Public-Private Partnerships Projects. 2010, http://ppp.gov.ph/wp-content/uploads/2011/02/brochure.pdf (last accessed 1 October 2018).

[69] NCIP Central Office, Official FPIC Documentation.

[70] Certification Precondition issued by the NCIP to NIA dated 11 August 2015.

[71] NCIP Central Office, Official FPIC Documentation.

[72] See Conserva LHU, Construction of Iloilos Jalaur Dam to start end-March. Business World Online, 15 March 2016, http://www.bworldonline.com/content.php?section=Economy&title=construction-of-iloilos-jalaur-dam-to-start-end-march&id=124517 (last accessed 1 October 2018).

in Brooke's Point, Palawan province and affecting the ancestral domain of the Palaw'an indigenous community.[73] According to MacroAsia, the MPSA is a conversion of old mining leases in the name of Infanta Mineral and Industrial Corporation dating back to the late 1970s.[74] The Certification Precondition for the Exploration Phase, however, was only issued in 2006.[75] In 2009, MacroAsia announced it was investing PhP 50 Million[76] to continue its exploration of the area.[77] Considering that there were controversies as to the conduct of the FPIC procedure for the Mining Operation Stage, the NCIP *En Banc* ruled that another FPIC procedure ought to be conducted for this stage.[78]

The cases of the Chico River, Jalaur, and MacroAsia projects are examples of projects where the decisions to undertake the exploration, development, and utilization of natural resources had already been made by the government long before the commencement of the FPIC process. Considering the government imprimatur on these projects and the considerable investments already put in by the project proponents *prior* to the FPIC procedure, it seems in these cases that the FPIC process provides a venue for the negotiation of the terms and conditions upon which the project is implemented, but it does not sufficiently empower indigenous communities to decide whether such projects should actually be done or not, as these decisions have long been made at the highest levels.

4.2   FPIC Versus State Ownership of and Sovereignty Over Natural Resources

Should the IPRA be interpreted to allow for a veto right on the part of ICCs/IPs on the basis of native title to ancestral domain (which, by definition, seems to include natural resources found therein)—a claim of ownership that predates the Regalian Doctrine? Unfortunately, the IPRA's history before the Philippine Supreme Court does not conclusively provide an affirmative answer to this question. The IPRA's legality in light of the Regalian Doctrine was questioned in the 2000 case of *Cruz v. Secretary of Environment and Natural Resources*.[79] The petitioners argued (among other grounds) that several provisions of the IPRA and its implementing rules, in

---

[73] NCIP En Banc Resolution No. 001-2012.

[74] See MarcroAsia Mining Corporation, Our Businesses, http://www.macroasiacorp.com/business-mmc.html (last accessed 1 October 2018).

[75] NCIP En Banc Resolution No. 001-2012.

[76] USD 968,000.00.

[77] See Rubio RAM, MacroAsia allots P50 million for exploration in Palawan. GMA News Online, 26 July 2009, http://www.gmanetwork.com/news/money/companies/168293/macroasia-allots-p50-million-for-exploration-in-palawan/story/ (last accessed 1 October 2018).

[78] NCIP En Banc Resolution No. 001-2012.

[79] Republic of the Philippines Supreme Court, G.R. No. 135385, *Cruz vs.DNR Secretary*, 6 December 2000.

granting comprehensive rights over ancestral lands and domains to indigenous peoples, amount to an unlawful deprivation of the state's ownership over the lands of the public domain, as well as the minerals and other natural resources therein, in violation of Article XII, Section 2 of the Constitution. After two rounds of deliberations, the Supreme Court *En Banc* votes ended up in a tie, with seven justices voting for the dismissal of the petition and seven voting for the granting of the same. Thus, the petition was dismissed pursuant to Rule 12, Section 2(a) of the Internal Rules of the Supreme Court. The split vote meant that there is no majority opinion laying down reasons for upholding the IPRA's constitutionality, as it was deemed constitutional on the basis of a technicality.

Moreover, even among the Justices who voted in favour of dismissing the petition, there was no support for the interpretation that the IPRA granted ownership rights over natural resources to indigenous peoples.

In his separate opinion,[80] Justice Puno clarified that the rights granted by the IPRA to indigenous peoples over natural resources in their ancestral domains merely give them, as owners and occupants of the land on which the resources are found, priority rights on said resources. Having priority rights over the natural resources does not necessarily mean ownership rights. The grant of priority rights implies that there is a superior entity that owns these resources and this entity has the power to grant preferential rights over the resources to whosoever it chooses. He argues that the IPRA does not mandate the State to automatically give priority to the indigenous peoples, and that there is nothing in the law which gives the indigenous peoples the exclusive right to undertake the large-scale development of the natural resources within their domain. They must undertake those endeavours under State supervision and control, which means the State does not lose control and ownership over the resources even in their exploitation. The IPRA simply gives due respect to the indigenous people who, as actual occupants of the land, have traditionally utilized these resources for their subsistence and survival.[81]

Justice Kapunan also argued that the mere fact that the IPRA defines ancestral domains as including the natural resources found therein does not *ipso facto* convert the character of such natural resources to private property of the indigenous people. It merely defines the coverage of ancestral domains, and describes the extent, limit, and composition of ancestral domains by setting forth the standards and guidelines in determining whether a particular area is to be considered as part of and within ancestral domains. It does not confer or recognize any right of ownership over the natural resources to the indigenous peoples. Its purpose is merely to define what ancestral domains are.[82]

---

[80] The separate opinions of Justices Puno, Vitug, Kapunan, Mendoza, and Panganiban, while differing from each other in terms of theoretical approaches, focus, and proposed conclusions, were all attached and made integral parts of the main Decision by the Supreme Court.

[81] Republic of the Philippines Supreme Court, G.R. No. 135385, *Cruz vs.DNR Secretary*, 6 December 2000, *Separate Opinion,* Justice Reynato Puno.

[82] Republic of the Philippines Supreme Court, G.R. No. 135385, *Cruz vs.DNR Secretary*, 6 December 2000, *Separate Opinion,* Justice Santiago Kapunan.

On the other hand, Justice Panganiban, who voted in favour of granting the petition and for declaring the IPRA unconstitutional, decried the IPRA for allegedly violating and contravening the Constitution of the Philippines insofar as "it recognizes or, worse, grants rights of ownership over 'lands of the public domain, waters, (…) and other natural resources' which, under Section 2, Article XII of the Constitution, 'are owned by the State' and 'shall not be alienated.'" He said that he rejects "the contention that 'ancestral lands and ancestral domains are not public lands and have never been owned by the State.'"[83]

These Justices' separate opinions show that the Regalian Doctrine is so fundamental to Philippine land law that any discussion regarding the IPRA's constitutionality must be framed within its parameters. Moreover, that the government is known to embark upon and to enter into contracts with third parties for the exploration, development, and utilization of natural resources within ancestral domains before they begin a consultation process with affected indigenous communities, as indicated in the examples above, seems to indicate the primacy of the Regalian Doctrine even in the minds of government decision-makers. For all intents and purposes, and despite the text of the IPRA as regards natural resources, as well as the necessity of a Certification Precondition prior to the award of any licenses or contracts for resource use, the Philippine government still acts in accordance with the Regalian Doctrine. That is, its acts are governed by the presumption of its ownership of all natural resources wherever found, as well as its authority to exercise full control and supervision over the exploration, development, and utilization of natural resources.

Even if indigenous peoples in the Philippines were to invoke international norms concerning their rights, including the UNDRIP, the resulting debate would not be that different. The text of the UNDRIP, for instance, seems to limit FPIC to good faith consultations. As illustrated by the drafting debates on FPIC in the UNDRIP, states retain their sovereign prerogatives over natural resources despite having made certain concessions as regards the participation of indigenous peoples in decision-making in resource use. In fact, in explaining the vote in support of the adoption of the UNDRIP, the Philippines took great pains to assert that its expression of support was "based on the understanding that land ownership and natural resources was vested in the State."

The idea of the state exercising ownership and control over natural resources is not only supported by the centuries-old Regalian Doctrine, but also by the doctrine of permanent sovereignty over natural resources, as discussed above. Under this doctrine, it is the post-colonial states who are granted permanent authority over natural resources and, consequently, the exclusive authority to make decisions regarding resource use. The Philippine government's exercise of authority over natural resources pursuant to this doctrine needs only to be in the name of the common good/public welfare of the "Filipino people" as a whole, and such common good/public welfare could conceivably qualify the protection of rights of ICCs/IPs. The

---

[83] Republic of the Philippines Supreme Court, G.R. No. 135385, *Cruz vs.DNR Secretary*, 6 December 2000, *Separate Opinion,* Justice Artemio V. Panganiban.

Constitution, in Article XII entitled "National Economy and Patrmimony" lays down the Regalian Doctrine in Section 2 and provides the following in Section 5:

> **Section 5.** The State, <u>subject to the provisions of this Constitution and national develop-</u><u>ment policies and programs</u>, shall protect the rights of indigenous cultural communities to their ancestral lands to ensure their economic, social, and cultural well-being.
>
> The Congress may provide for the applicability of customary laws governing property rights or relations in determining the ownership and extent of ancestral domain.[84]

4.3   Problematizing Indigenous Peoples' Rights in a State-Centric World: A Fourth World Critique of FPIC

Both the Regalian Doctrine and the doctrine of permanent sovereignty over natural resources deny the pre-existence and legitimacy of indigenous peoples' historic sovereignty over their traditional lands. With these two doctrines propping up Philippine state sovereignty over natural resources, FPIC is interpreted as a protective norm within the context of a unitary, post-colonial sovereign state. The Philippine state's acknowledgement and implementation of the FPIC norm does not put indigenous peoples on the same footing with the state as regards control over natural resources. It does not restore the "historical sovereignty"—the full ownership and control over territories—that indigenous peoples lost arbitrarily during colonization. The state has the prerogative to utilize resources within indigenous peoples' lands (with "adequate" consultation). A regime that is faithful to the historical sovereignty of indigenous peoples over their traditional lands would impose the opposite rule: indigenous peoples would have control over the use of their lands, and only in highly exceptional circumstances could they be compelled by the state to allow exploitative use of their resources.

As illustrated in the cases above, decisions to embark on resource use projects can be made well in advance of any FPIC proceeding. In light of the Regalian Doctrine and the doctrine of permanent sovereignty over natural resources, these decisions are sovereign acts. If at all, the FPIC mechanism only determines the conditions under which resource use would be acceptable to indigenous peoples, and the FPIC process is a negotiation of just such conditions. This is not quite the same as giving weight to indigenous peoples' position as to whether such a project ought to be embarked upon in the first place. Findings as to irregularities in the FPIC proceeding do not affect the state's prerogative to exploit the resources in question. The FPIC safeguards in Philippine law regarding the protection of indigenous peoples' rights in state and state-authorized activities in indigenous peoples' lands are statutory guarantees that coexist with a fundamental substantive norm (state sovereignty over natural resources) the strength of which trumps any protective intention that these guarantees may have. It is true that a growing number of

---

[84] Philippine Constitution, Article XII, Section 5.

international instruments now include references to indigenous concepts of ownership. This is a result of what Miranda refers to as the successful "uploading" by indigenous peoples of their indigenous conceptions of collective rights and land ownership to said instruments through their creative engagement with various transnational and international bodies. While indigenous peoples do not have the power to enter into international agreements, they have asserted themselves through advocacy work, as well as through international litigation.[85] Despite their success in "uploading" indigenous rights to international legal documents, indigenous peoples, however, have not affected or qualified the interpretation and application of regimes such as the Regalian Doctrine and the doctrine of permanent sovereignty over natural resources—a perfect example of the fragmented nature of international lawmaking. Miranda says that the various international regulatory regimes are "separate, often, impermeable boxes."[86] She further notes that:

> This broader contradiction within distinct realms of international law may continue to pose limits to indigenous peoples' on-the-ground progress.
>
> For example, in the context of extractive industry projects on indigenous lands, indigenous peoples' human rights over their ancestral lands and resources often collide with preexisting international law norms and other norms that continuously evolve under international trade and investment law. Indigenous peoples' rights over ancestral lands and resources exist outside of, and arguably in subordination to, other norms of international law such as state sovereignty over natural resources and states' rights to development.[87]

The fragmentation of international law-making, plus the foundational value ascribed to the doctrine of state sovereignty in international law in general, means that the victories of indigenous peoples in the UNDRIP and even in the Inter-American System have to contend with long-standing competing norms such as sovereignty over natural resources. The FPIC norm offers a mechanism of protection, within which indigenous peoples can only act from a position of weakness—seeking the implementation of a norm from the powerful party with competing (and "legally superior") interests. In fact, it can be argued that the very instruments that entreat states to "protect" indigenous peoples' rights and "consider their welfare" in national development policies perpetuate the very notion that indigenous peoples are under the control and tutelage of states. Such a framing of indigenous peoples' rights denies their historical sovereignty over their lands and communities; it is not empowering, it is, in fact, infantilizing—much in the way that the imperialists of old framed the colonial project as a civilizing mission. The injustice of merely laying down standards of behaviour for state action vis-à-vis indigenous peoples becomes clear when we realize that states would not possess the power to perform such sovereign actions in their jurisdictions if indigenous peoples had not been arbitrarily deprived of authority over their own lands in the first place.

---

[85] Miranda (2008), pp. 433–434.

[86] Miranda (2010), p. 260.

[87] Miranda (2010), p. 261.

FPIC, therefore, continues to exist in a system where sovereignty over natural resources is still interpreted in favour of states. It is also a system that places indigenous peoples under the charge of (post-colonial) states. This contradiction, underpinned by the unequal power relations between states and indigenous peoples poses severe limits on indigenous peoples' power to use, possess, enjoy, and control their lands and natural resources.

5   Indigenous Sovereignty: Participation in International Law-Making as an Exercise of Self-Determination

The assertion of an FPIC mechanism without effecting change in the norms of other competing regimes of international law has led to a somewhat hollow victory for indigenous peoples. As long as the content of contradictory international law regimes remains unchanged, and while the unequal power relations between states and indigenous peoples remain, any progress in indigenous peoples' rights seems illusory.

More spaces need to be opened to allow indigenous peoples to participate in international law-making.[88] Specifically, indigenous peoples must be allowed to participate in the political processes of international law-making (in particular, the negotiation and conclusion of treaties) in order for their interests and aspirations to be taken into account in the various overlapping (and often contentious) regulatory regimes spanning global activities today—activities which include natural resource extraction, energy production and regulation, environmental advocacy, and transnational trade, among others. Contemporary developments in international law point to the possibility of a new norm of indigenous sovereignty that could be the basis for participation in international law-making.

Lenzerini proposes that developments in international law upholding indigenous peoples' rights to self-determination and to the protection of their physical and cultural heritage indicate states' growing acquiescence to the existence of indigenous peoples' sovereignty rights under international law—a modern conception of indigenous sovereignty that co-exists with the sovereignty of the state. Indigenous sovereignty rights are not subject to statutory grant, but exist independently of such domestic legal acts—in parallel to, but not quite equal, to those of sovereign states. Thus, the exercise by indigenous peoples of this indigenous sovereignty could be regulated by states, but not precluded or prohibited by them. Lenzerini elaborates further that this indigenous sovereignty includes the right to live in traditional lands, the right to indigenous identity and culture, the right to self-government, and the right to effective participation at all levels of decision-making, in decisions which may affect them.[89]

---

[88] See United Nations Forum on Indigenous Issues http://undesadspd.org/IndigenousPeoples/AboutUsMembers.aspx (last accessed 1 October 2018).

[89] Lenzerini (2006–2007), pp. 187–188, underscoring supplied.

Lenzerini argues that the emergence of indigenous sovereignty, parallel to state sovereignty, provides indigenous peoples with some significant sovereign prerogatives that previously belonged to the State.[90] One such sovereign prerogative that indigenous peoples can arguably exercise in the context of indigenous sovereignty is participation in international law-making as an exercise of self-determination.

The classic definition of the right to self-determination is the right of sovereign states to exercise sovereignty within their territorial limits and to assert equal sovereign status in the international community.[91] With the emergence of the UNDRIP, however, self-determination can now be claimed by indigenous peoples as a right, as provided in Article 3 thereof.

> Article 3. Indigenous peoples have the right to self-determination. By virtue of that right they freely determine their political status and freely pursue their economic, social and cultural development.

The inclusion of self-determination was, at first, met with resistance by the international community on the ground that such claims pose the threat of secession by indigenous peoples from post-colonial states.[92] However, self-determination under the UNDRIP clearly pertains to self-determination within the context of a sovereign state, or internal self-determination:[93]

> Article 4. Indigenous peoples, in exercising their right to self-determination, have the right to autonomy or self-government in matters relating to their internal and local affairs, as well as ways and means for financing their autonomous functions.

Charters argues that the right of indigenous peoples to participate in international law-making is a meaningful exercise of their right to self-determination.[94] Indeed, indigenous peoples would be hard-pressed to "freely determine their political status and freely pursue their economic, social and cultural development" as provided in Article 3 of the UNDRIP without a modicum of participation in processes pertaining to their political and economic futures. Moreover, the UNDRIP specifically provides in Articles 18 and 19:

> Article 18. Indigenous peoples have the right to participate in decision-making in matters which would affect their rights, through representatives chosen by themselves in accordance with their own procedures, as well as to maintain and develop their own indigenous decision-making institutions.

> Article 19. States shall consult and cooperate in good faith with the indigenous peoples concerned through their own representative institutions in order to obtain their free, prior, and informed consent before adopting and implementing legislative or administrative measures that may affect them.

---

[90] Lenzerini (2006–2007), p. 189, underscoring supplied.

[91] Lenzerini (2006–2007), p. 174.

[92] Heiniimki (2011), p. 200.

[93] Charters (2010), p. 226.

[94] Charters (2010), pp. 228–230.

Charters proposes two conditions for such participation: (1) where the issue at stake is of substantial interest to indigenous peoples, and (2) indigenous peoples have not consented to being represented by their states. Thus, Charters clarifies that the right of indigenous peoples to participate in international law-making needs not be in the nature of participation as states, because her approach still proffers classic state espousal as a valid and viable option for interest representation. This distinction is important, considering the endurance of the state sovereignty principle in international law (as well as the resistance of states to measures that they deem threatening to their exclusive exercise of sovereignty). Charters pragmatically situates the right of indigenous peoples to participate in international law-making within the context of "contemporary political realities," i.e. the fundamental nature of the state sovereignty doctrine in international law and international relations. Hence indigenous peoples can participate directly in such law-making only when they have not consented to state representation. While Article 18 is usually read in the context of intrastate relations, she extends the application of the article to the international arena—with states (who have international standing) as indigenous peoples' representatives. It must be noted that the norm of FPIC is once again in play in the process of state representation, i.e., indigenous peoples could, of course, consent to states representing them internationally. But the option to consent or not must be given to indigenous peoples. This approach should not present such a challenge to state sovereignty as to be met with same resistance that self-determination was first met with during the drafting of the UNDRIP.[95]

Crucially, Charters notes that there appears to be an openness to interpreting self-determination as including the right to participate in international law-making. The World Bank Group, for instance, has been supportive of indigenous peoples' participation in climate change talks. Australia, Canada, New Zealand, and the United States have all previously opposed the UNDRIP at its vote in the UN General Assembly, but they have all expressed their support for such participation of indigenous peoples, saying that this would be crucial for the ultimate success of the UNDRIP. Denmark, Norway, Sweden, Chile, Bolivia, Fiji, Ukraine, Peru, Colombia, and the Russian Federation have similarly supported this kind of participation. The establishment of the Permanent Forum on Indigenous Issues, an advisory body to the Economic and Social Council of the United Nations, while not squarely addressing the issue of direct law-making participation by indigenous peoples, nevertheless points to the acknowledgment that indigenous peoples' voices—unfiltered by state representation—are essential in formulating international policy.[96]

According to Charters, extending Article 18 and 19 of the UNDRIP to international participation is more faithful to indigenous peoples' claims to historic sovereignty. She argues that "(t)here is a sense of historical wrong from the denial of recognition of indigenous peoples' sovereignty, coupled with the argument that this wrong must be both recognized and remedied, permeating indigenous peoples' discourse on self-determination law." While indigenous peoples do not seek self-

---

[95] Charters (2010), pp. 222, 228–230, 237–240.
[96] Charters (2010), pp. 218–221, 225–228.

determination in the sense that states exercise it, "their claim to self-determination is in part premised on their 'lost sovereignty' and the missed opportunity to have their statehood recognized, which is still felt today." It is also a means through which indigenous peoples seek redress for their exclusion in the decolonization project. It is their "arbitrary exclusion" from decolonization that has barred indigenous peoples from participating in most international law-making arenas. Acknowledging indigenous sovereignty and seeing this as a basis for allowing indigenous peoples to participate in international law-making would mitigate some of the harm that has befallen them because of this exclusion.[97]

6 Conclusion

Because long-existing international and domestic relations of power influence how the principle is defined and operationalized, FPIC seems to merely perpetuate unequal power structures that have beleaguered indigenous peoples since colonial times. The growing acceptance of FPIC, while successfully advancing the indigenous peoples' cause to a certain degree, has not succeeded in correcting the disadvantaged position that indigenous peoples have been forced into because of their lack of bargaining power in the context of a nation-state. This state of affairs is even more appalling if we recall that they are forgotten polities (or "unjustifiably excluded sovereigns"[98]) who have claims to historical sovereignty and who have been marginalized for far too long. Participation in international law-making, rooted in indigenous sovereignty, can help correct the imbalance that FPIC cannot remedy.

Participation in law-making, as an aspect of indigenous sovereignty, does not challenge the state-centric nature of the international legal regime. Just like FPIC, it plays by the rules—honouring state sovereignty doctrine as the foundational precept of international law. What difference could this proposed approach to participation make in terms of resisting the long-entrenched supremacy of the state? For one, it has the potential for restructuring the relationship between the state and indigenous peoples. As is apparent in the Philippine context, indigenous peoples are seen as groups that ought to be protected, a minoritized portion of the government's constituency. If indigenous peoples are welcomed into the heretofore state domain of international law-making, there is a potential for this relationship to be transformed into one of partnership, rather than of protection. Moreover, participation in international law-making (along with all the other sovereign prerogatives that indigenous sovereignty includes), will take indigenous peoples from being merely "forgotten polities" to something closer to the historical sovereigns they had been before the dawn of empire.

An awareness of the unequal power relations inherent in international law is crucial if advocates are to make realistic evaluations of the kinds of results they can

---

[97] Charters (2010), pp. 228–230, 240.

[98] Charters (2010), p. 240.

expect from international advocacy, international litigation, and FPIC procedures. While these mechanisms ought not to be completely abandoned, their limitations within a state-centric world should be clear in our minds. The fragmented nature of international legal regimes means that any affirmative rules that one legal regime may produce can be countered by competing and contradictory norms in other regimes. In the Philippines, the tension between indigenous peoples' rights and the state's sovereignty over natural resources has made the effective advancement of indigenous peoples' rights, particularly through FPIC, tricky at best. Moreover, the unequal power relations between the state and indigenous peoples make it possible for states to deem the state sovereignty norm superior to norms regarding indigenous peoples' rights. Therefore, it is imperative to open up other international legal regimes for indigenous peoples' participation in international law-making. The traditionally states-only arena of treaty-making need not be forever closed to indigenous peoples, considering contemporary developments in self-determination law that arguably support the idea of law-making participation on the part of indigenous peoples.

Of course, there is always the possibility that indigenous peoples' participation in international law-making may be similarly limited by continuing to exist in a state-centric world. But unlike advocacy work or international litigation, it has the best potential for addressing the unequal nature of the relations between states and indigenous peoples. By opening international law-making to indigenous peoples, the international community would be collectively moving towards the direction of correcting centuries of marginalization, minoritization, and exclusion of indigenous peoples. By not opening international law-making to indigenous peoples, the international community would be cursing itself to "re-enact the tragedy of colonialism."[99]

References

Anghie A (2006) The evolution of international law: colonial and postcolonial realities. Third World Q 27(5):739–753

Anghie A, Chimni B (2003) Third world approaches to international law and individual responsibility in internal conflicts. Chin J Int Law 2:77–103

Barelli M (2012) Free, prior and informed consent in the aftermath of the UN declaration on the rights of indigenous peoples: developments and challenges ahead. Int J Human Rights 16(1):1–24

Bocobo J (1936) The Regalian Doctrine. Philipp Law J XVI(4–5):151–153

Cariño J (1980) The Chico River basin development project: a case study in national development policy (an update). Agham-Tao 3(1):1–25

Charters C (2010) A self-determination approach to justifying indigenous peoples' participation in international law and policy making. Int J Minority Groups Rights 17:215–240

Heiniimki L (2011) Towards an equal partnership between indigenous peoples and states: learning from arctic experiences? Yearb Polar Law 3(1):193–246

---

[99] Charters (2010), p. 230, *citing* Michael Reisman in Macklem (2008), p. 208.

Lenzerini F (2006–2007) Sovereignty revisited: international law and parallel sovereignty of indigenous peoples. Tex Int Law J 42:155–189

Lynch O (2011) Colonial legacies of a fragile republic: Philippine land law and state formation. University of the Philippines College of Law, Diliman, Quezon City

Macklem P (2008) Indigenous recognition in international law: theoretical observations. Mich J Int Law 30(177):208

Miranda L (2008) Uploading the local: assessing the contemporary relationship between indigenous peoples' land tenure systems and international human rights law regarding the allocation of traditional lands and resources in Latin America. Or Rev Int Law 10:419–452

Miranda L (2010) Indigenous peoples as international lawmakers. Univ Pa J Int Law 32(1):203–263

Miranda L (2012) The role of international law in intrastate natural resource allocation: sovereignty, human rights, and peoples-based development. Vanderbilt J Transnatl Law 45:785–840

Mutua M, Anghie A (2000) What is Twail? Proceedings of the annual meeting. Am Soc Int Law 94:31–40

Nietschmann B (1994) The fourth world: nations versus states. In: Demko G, Wood W (eds) Reordering the world: geopolitical perspectives on the twenty-first century. Westview Press, pp 225–326

Wiessner S (2008) Indigenous sovereignty: a reassessment in light of the UN declaration on the rights of indigenous peoples. Vanderbilt J Transnatl Law 41:1141–1176

Armi Beatriz E. Bayot is currently a Doctor of Philosophy (DPhil) in Law student at the University of Oxford. She has worked as a lawyer for the Commission on Human Rights of the Philippines and for the Office of the Solicitor General. She was also a Senior Lecturer at the University of the Philippines College of Law. She holds a Juris Doctor degree from the University of the Philippines and a Master of Laws (LL.M.) in Transnational Law degree from King's College London.

Norm Contestation and (Non-)Compliance: The Right to Prior Consultation and FPIC in the Extractive Industries

Almut Schilling-Vacaflor

Contents

1 Introduction 311
2 Norm Contestation and Non-compliance 315
3 The (Contested) Right to Prior Consultation and FPIC According to International
  Standards 317
4 Norm Contestation in the Domestic Sphere: Bolivia, Colombia and Peru 320
  4.1 Prior Consultation and FPIC in Colombia 322
  4.2 Prior Consultation and FPIC in Peru 323
  4.3 Prior Consultation and FPIC in Bolivia 324
  4.4 Issues of Contestation: Who? How? When? and with What Results? 326
      4.4.1 Which Entity Leads Prior Consultation and FPIC Processes? 326
      4.4.2 Who Is to Be Consulted? 327
      4.4.3 Which Measures Require Consultation? 329
      4.4.4 When and How Shall the Consultation Take Place? 330
      4.4.5 What Is the Result of Consultation/FPIC Processes? 331
5 Discussion and Conclusions 333
References 335

1 Introduction

The power of international human rights does not primarily depend on their legal recognition, but rather on compliance with these rights on the ground. In general, compliance with human rights, defined as sustained behaviour and practices that conform to international human rights norms,[1] has been a difficult and challenging task. The United Nations Special Rapporteur on the Rights of Indigenous Peoples, Victoria Tauli-Corpuz, recently addressed the implementation gap of indigenous

---

[1] Risse and Ropp (2013), p. 10.

A. Schilling-Vacaflor (✉)
Osnabrück University, Institute for Social Sciences, Osnabrück, Germany
e-mail: aschillingva@uni-osnabrueck.de

© Springer Nature Switzerland AG 2019
I. Feichtner et al. (eds.), *Human Rights in the Extractive Industries*,
Interdisciplinary Studies in Human Rights 3,
https://doi.org/10.1007/978-3-030-11382-7_12

rights, especially in the ambit of resource extraction. In her statement to the Third Committee of the UN General Assembly on 12 July 2017, Ms. Tauli-Corpuz reminded states that they should harmonise their national legal frameworks with applicable international human rights standards regarding the rights of indigenous peoples, particularly the United Nations Declaration on the Rights of Indigenous Peoples (UNDRIP).[2] In addition, she highlighted the importance that legislation be effectively enforced and complied with.

More generally, Risse and Ropp[3] argue that the bottleneck of the power of human rights was the transition from the legal recognition of rights by states to rule-consistent behaviour. They also highlight the crucial role of norm contestation for explaining noncompliance and state that "[n]ormative conflict or contestation is not only the most interesting but also the least understood factor in research on international human rights impact".[4] This study emphasizes that the legal adoption of rights is not a straightforward issue, because when translating international human rights standards into domestic legislation, states usually interpret and regulate—and thereby change—the respective rights. This regulatory process is very powerful and important as it shapes the specific meaning of rights as interpreted domestically and, hence, is often extremely contested.

This chapter discusses the link between the strongly contested indigenous right to prior consultation and free, prior and informed consent (FPIC) and the frequent noncompliance with this right. The gap between rights in law and rights in practice has been particularly wide when rights—such as indigenous, participatory and environmental rights—are to be upheld against strategic economic interests, for instance, to carry out mining or hydrocarbon activities. In these cases, economic policy objectives very often have trumped human rights and environmental concerns. Studying such implementation gaps of human rights in Latin America is of particular interest, because in the past three decades many countries in the region on the one hand have legally recognized very comprehensive rights and on the other hand have experienced a new "commodity boom", which has threatened to undermine the established rights and has often provoked fierce conflicts with affected communities and civil society organizations. The expansion of the extractive frontiers in this region has been accelerating at an unprecedented rate since the 1990s.[5] Indigenous peoples, who use to maintain close relationships with ancestral lands and territories, have suffered disproportionally from the violation of all types of rights related to large-scale resource extraction. For instance, among the 200 assassinated defenders

---

[2] See UN Office of the High Commissioner of Human Rights, Statement of Ms. Victoria Tauli-Corpuz, United Nations Special Rapporteur on the Rights of Indigenous Peoples at the Tenth session of the Expert Mechanism on the Rights of Indigenous Peoples, Tenth Anniversary of the United Nations Declaration on the Rights of Indigenous Peoples. 12 July 2017, http://www.ohchr.org/EN/NewsEvents/Pages/DisplayNews.aspx?NewsID=21889&LangID=E (last accessed 1 October 2018).

[3] Risse and Ropp (2013).

[4] Risse and Ropp (2013), p. 36.

[5] Bebbington and Bury (2013a) and Burchardt and Dietz (2014).

of land and the environment in 2016 that were recorded by Global Witness, 40% self-identified as members of indigenous peoples.[6] This report argues that the main root cause of the reported attacks was the imposition of projects on communities without their FPIC. Obviously, when arguing in favour of FPIC, Global Witness refers to its own interpretation of FPIC, which implies considerable decision-making power of local populations.

Indigenous peoples' right to prior consultation and to FPIC, as well as their right to be compensated for adverse impacts from extraction projects and to receive a share of the benefits whenever possible, have been conceived of as safeguards for protecting the rights that might be at stake for local populations. Importantly, the right to prior consultation and to FPIC can be characterized as an umbrella right, because on the one hand it shall guarantee effective participation and on the other hand it shall contribute to protect all types of rights (to territory, water, self-government etc.) that might be affected by measures such as large-scale extraction projects.[7] Since the 1990s, the right to prior consultation and FPIC has been recognized in the form of hard law and soft law by United Nations institutions, by regional institutions such as the Inter-American human rights system[8] and by multilateral organizations like the World Bank and the Inter-American Development Bank.[9] The right to prior consultation and to FPIC lies at the heart of the International Labour Organization's Convention 169 (ILO C169) on the rights of indigenous peoples and tribal populations and of the UNDRIP. Among the 22 countries that have ratified ILO C169 to date are 15 Latin American and Caribbean countries. The ILO C169 and the UNDRIP establish that consultation and consent processes should be carried out in good faith prior to any planned measure affecting indigenous peoples, should involve representative persons and institutions of affected communities, and should be based on an intercultural dialogue. They also stipulate that the participants should be given complete and non-biased information about the measures at stake. These processes should conclude with a binding agreement and/or achieve the consent (or withholding of consent) of the participants.

Despite legal obligations and the emerging consensus that communities should be consulted with the objective of gaining their consent to planned resource activities, compliance with FPIC has been very rare. Hence, Szablowski's observation that "[i]n global policy circles relating to extractives, it seems that FPIC is everywhere discussed, but it is not much of an exaggeration to say that it is practised virtually nowhere"[10] holds largely true to date. We can distinguish three types of violations of the right to prior consultation and FPIC: (1) the absence of the right in practice, irrespective of its adoption in domestic legislation, (2) the implementation

---

[6] Global Witness, Defenders of the Earth. Global killings of land and environmental defenders in 2016.   2017,   https://www.globalwitness.org/en/campaigns/environmental-activists/defenders-earth/ (last accessed 1 October 2018).

[7] Doyle (2014).

[8] See the chapter by de Casas in this volume.

[9] Rodríguez et al. (2010).

[10] Szablowski (2010), p. 127.

of flawed processes of prior consultation and consent, measured against international human rights instruments and (3) the adoption of domestic legislation that regulates the right to prior consultation and FPIC in a way that violates international law. In theory, Szablowski[11] strictly distinguishes between the right to prior consultation, which does not involve the granting of decision-making authority to participants, and the right to FPIC that involves sharing or transferring authority. As a consequence, he argues, FPIC can be used by affected communities as leverage to shape decision-making, including to avoid projects that present them with greater risks than benefits. However, he shows that it can be difficult in practice to clearly distinguish between consultation and consent regimes, because the interpretation of consultation and consent rights often is contested, and formal requirements tend to be ambiguous or a hybrid.[12]

In most states worldwide, specific consultation and consent processes with indigenous peoples have been entirely absent and solely processes of public consultation, such as public hearings or informative events for the general citizenry, usually based on the domestic environmental legislation, have been organized. In Latin America, to date, only Bolivia, Colombia and Peru systematically have implemented prior consultation processes. Legal and political disputes about these rights in law and practice have been particularly strong in these Andean states. Previous research discussed the manifold shortcomings of these processes.[13] The discussion of frequent shortcomings of the implementation of the right to consultation and consent has been crucial to assess how this right is translated into concrete domestic and local contexts and to scrutinize to what extent it has been effective to protect indigenous rights.

This chapter draws on previous research on the right to prior consultation and consent and aims to discuss the root causes of the identified problems, by focusing on the role of norm contestation. To do so, it discusses both, contestations over the legal regulation of the right to consultation and consent, and contestations over concrete consultation processes as implemented in Bolivia, Colombia and Peru. After a brief theoretical section on norm contestation and norm compliance, I will outline the right to prior consultation and FPIC according to international standards. Subsequently, I will illustrate and discuss norm contestation of and noncompliance over the consultation and consent right in the domestic sphere, drawing on empirical examples from Bolivia, Colombia and Peru. I find that divergent claims of authority, territorial control and decision-making coexist within the analysed domestic contexts, all of which lie at the root of the existing norm contestations. In addition, such divergent claims or competing resource sovereignties are embedded within power

---

[11] Szablowski (2010).

[12] Szablowski (2010).

[13] See, for instance, Flemmer (2015); Flemmer and Schilling-Vacaflor (2016); Bebbington (2012); Pellegrini and Arismendi (2012); Rodríguez GA, De La Consulta Previa Al Consentimiento Libre, Previo E Informado a Pueblos Indígenas En Colombia (From the Prior Consultation to the Free, Prior and Informed Consent of Indigenous Peoples). 15 April 2015, https://papers.ssrn.com/sol3/papers.cfm?abstract_id=2592988 (last accessed 1 October 2018); Weitzner (2017).

asymmetries that clearly work in favour of strategic economic interests to extract natural resources and disadvantage strong indigenous and participatory rights. In the conclusions, I argue that the contestations over the right to prior consultation and FPIC are so profound that under current conditions the emergence of a shared understanding of this norm is very improbable. This chapter's findings aim to contribute to broader debates about the link between norm contestation and noncompliance with a focus on international human rights norms.

2 Norm Contestation and Non-compliance

To become effective, international human rights have to be translated and "vernacularized" into domestic and local contexts.[14] This translation process usually is twofold and includes (1) the translation of international rights into domestic legislation and (2) the implementation of domestic law in national and sub-national contexts. Norm contestation can occur at both stages; the contestations over the regulation and legal interpretation of a right often focus on a national scale, while the contestations about the implementation of a right tend to emerge on a local scale. In addition, we can distinguish between two different forms of norm contestation: either, actors' conceptions of what the applicable norm should look like may diverge, or, actors may disagree about whether a given practice complies with an agreed upon standard of appropriate behaviour.[15]

Norm contestation unfolds in an interplay between international and state norms with diverse local norms and conceptions of justice.[16] Hence, in this chapter law and legal norms are not equated merely with international and domestic (state) law, but are understood to also include plural legal norms that exist at the local level.[17] The underlying assumption is that the scope and meaning of different forms of participation and community engagement in extractive governance is being negotiated in situations of "interlegality", which is "the conception of different legal spaces superimposed, interpenetrated, and mixed in our minds as much as in our actions".[18]

Previous research about human rights translation into domestic contexts has highlighted that state law encompasses regulatory and repressive elements as well as emancipatory potentials.[19] Law is constantly negotiated and reshaped in a dynamic dialectic between hegemonic projections and counter-hegemonic actions.[20] Law may be used as "a form of violence with the legitimacy of formally constituted

---

[14] See Goodale and Merry (2007), Merry (2006) and Wilson (1999).

[15] Wiener (2009), Wiener (2014) and Dietz and Engels (2017).

[16] Von Benda-Beckmann et al. (2009) and Clarke and Goodale (2010).

[17] Merry (1988) and Von Benda-Beckmann (2001, 2002).

[18] De Sousa Santos (1987), pp. 297–298.

[19] Sieder (2011).

[20] De Sousa Santos (1987, 2002, 2003) and De Sousa Santos and Rodríguez-Garavito (2005).

authority",[21] providing states with a mode of social control and of enforcing power relations, particularly those linked to property rights.[22] For instance, the fact that the meanings of international norms are usually left vague intentionally, has allowed states to interpret rights in a restrictive way, thus watering down the respective rights' original aspirational character. However, legal norms limiting human rights often are contested by civil society actors applying different forms of resistance, such as collective actions (for instance, mobilisations, public statements, lawsuits) or more subtle forms of "everyday resistance".[23] With reference to Tully, Wiener[24] has underscored the importance of the struggling agents' objection to norms, as being part of the democratically legitimate role of citizens to realize their right to question the norms that govern them.

This chapter, moreover, shares Wiener's understanding that norm contestation does not only focus on the sanctioning of legal norms, but that the meaning of norms is embedded in social practices.[25] In the words of Taylor "the practice not only fulfils the rule, but also gives it concrete shape in particular situations. Practice is [...] a continual 'interpretation' and reinterpretation of what the rule really means".[26] I find the definition of the "practice of human rights" as formulated by Goodale[27] to be particularly useful: "The practice of human rights describes all of the many ways in which social actors across the range talk about, advocate for, criticize, study, legally enact, vernacularize, and so on the idea of human rights in its different forms. [...] In defining the practice of human rights in this way we draw attention to both the diversity of ways and places in which the idea of human rights – again, in its legal, conceptual, and discursive forms – emerges in practice, and the fact that the practice of human rights is always embedded in pre-existing relations of meaning and production".[28] Hence, for studying practices of rights, "ethnographies of human rights"[29] and the study of discursive interventions, for instance emerging from official documents, policy documents, political debates and media contributions[30] are particularly useful. Such methods can be applied for studying phenomena at different scales, whereby they can contribute to producing important findings for compliance research and to overcome the shortcomings of much previous research, which has suffered from what has been called "methodological nationalism".[31]

---

[21] Merry (1992), p. 369.

[22] Wilson (1999).

[23] Scott (2008).

[24] Wiener (2014).

[25] Wiener (2009).

[26] Taylor (1993), p. 57.

[27] Goodale (2007).

[28] Goodale and Merry (2007), p. 24.

[29] Wilson (1999).

[30] Wiener (2009).

[31] Zürn (2002).

Risse and Ropp also highlight the importance of discourses, such as naming and shaming, for explaining (non-)compliance.[32] However, naming and shaming can only be successful if either the target actors or an audience central to the change process actually believe in the social validity of the norm. Similarly, the persuasion approach, defined as "the process by which agent actions become social structure, ideas become norms, and the subjective becomes the intersubjective",[33] will only be effective when norms are perceived as socially and culturally valid. For instance, Jetschke[34] and Liese[35] showed that when governments managed to get widespread public approval for their justifications of human rights violations, by invoking reasons such as the necessity to protect state sovereignty or human security, it was almost impossible to force them to comply with their rights obligations.

Wiener clearly outlines the benefits of an approach that takes social practices into account and points to the link between norm contestation and (non-)compliance: "It follows that studying social practices in context opens analytical access to the interpretation of meaning which is constitutive for sustained compliance with norms as contestation sheds light on different meanings of a norm, thus enhancing the probability of establishing shared understanding of that norm".[36] Accordingly, the meaning of norms is contested, unless and until a mutually satisfactory interpretation is established. As a consequence, the contestation of norms and respective changes is understood as a crucial condition to enhance their legitimacy and, more broadly speaking, the legitimacy of global governance regimes.[37]

3   The (Contested) Right to Prior Consultation and FPIC According to International Standards

The comparison of the ILO C169 and the UNDRIP reveals the shifting focus in international standards from consultation to consent rights. While ILO C169 used the term "consult" seven times and the word "consent" only two times, the UNDRIP uses "consult" nine times and "consent" six times. Without any doubt, the consultation and consent approach has become a key principle for organizing the relations between states and indigenous peoples.

---

[32] Risse and Ropp (2013).

[33] Finnemore and Sikkink (1998), p. 914.

[34] Jetschke (2011).

[35] Liese (2009).

[36] Wiener (2009), p. 201.

[37] Wiener (2009).

The ILO C169 contains the following general rule on prior consultation: "In applying the provisions of this Convention, governments shall consult the peoples concerned, through appropriate procedures and in particular through their representative institutions, whenever consideration is being given to legislative or administrative measures which may affect them directly [...] The consultations carried out in application of this Convention shall be undertaken, in good faith and in a form appropriate to the circumstances, with the objective of achieving agreement or consent to the proposed measures".[38] It further includes the following more specific stipulation related to resource extraction: "The rights of the peoples concerned to the natural resources pertaining to their lands shall be specially safeguarded [...] In cases in which the State retains the ownership of mineral or sub-surface re-sources or rights to other resources pertaining to lands, governments shall establish or maintain procedures through which they shall consult these peoples, with a view to ascertaining whether and to what degree their interests would be prejudiced, before undertaking or permitting any programmes for the exploration or exploitation of such resources pertaining to their lands".[39]

The question of whether indigenous peoples have the right to prior consultation or to FPIC, has represented the bone of contention in international negotiations concerning the more recent international norm on indigenous rights, the UNDRIP. Largely due to divergent interpretations by the representatives of indigenous peoples and of states, it took over 20 years until the UNDRIP was finally adopted by the United Nations General Assembly on 13 December 2007. The Working Group on Indigenous Peoples' proposal for the UNDRIP originally included the stipulation that "indigenous peoples [...] have the right to require that states obtain their free and informed consent prior to the approval of any project affecting their lands, territories and other resources". This rather strong interpretation of the right to FPIC was eventually changed to "the states shall consult and cooperate in good faith with the indigenous peoples concerned [...] in order to obtain their free, prior and informed consent".[40] The latter formulation reflects the position adopted by most United Nations member states that states should not "obtain" but rather "seek" indigenous peoples' consent, leaving the crucial question of how to proceed when indigenous peoples withhold their consent open to further discussion.

Eventually, the UNDRIP came to include the following stipulations which are of special relevance for interpreting the right to FPIC: "Indigenous peoples have the right to self-determination. By virtue of that right they freely determine their political status and freely pursue their economic, social and cultural development"[41]; "Indigenous peoples shall not be forcibly removed from their lands or territories. No relocation shall take place without the free, prior and informed consent of the indigenous peoples concerned and after agreement on just and fair compensation

---

[38] Article 6, ILO C169.
[39] Article 15, ILO C169.
[40] Barelli (2012), p. 11.
[41] Article 3, UNDRIP.

and, where possible, with the option of return"[42]; "Indigenous peoples have the right to participate in decision-making in matters which would affect their rights, through representatives chosen by themselves in accordance with their own procedures, as well as to maintain and develop their own indigenous decision-making institutions"[43]; and "States shall consult and cooperate in good faith with the indigenous peoples concerned through their own representative institutions in order to obtain their free, prior and informed consent before adopting and implementing legislative or administrative measures that may affect them".[44] The most important provision concerning the right to FPIC about resource extraction is the following: "Indigenous peoples have the right to determine and develop priorities and strategies for the development or use of their lands or territories and other resources. States shall consult and cooperate in good faith with the indigenous peoples concerned through their own representative institutions in order to obtain their free and informed consent prior to the approval of any project affecting their lands or territories and other resources, particularly in connection with the development, utilization or exploitation of mineral, water or other resources".[45]

It has largely been due to the above-mentioned stipulations about the right to consultation and consent that four states (Australia, Canada, New Zealand and United States of America) opposed the adoption of the declaration. Since then, the four opposing states have changed their vote in favour of the declaration, however, with some reservations. For instance, the United States under President Obama declared its support of the UNDRIP, while at the same time providing specific weak interpretations of its meaning also concerning the right to consultation and consent, "which the United States understands to call for a process of meaningful consultation with tribal leaders, but not necessarily the agreement of those leaders, before the actions addressed in those consultations are taken".[46] In a similar vein, in its guiding principles, the World Bank has adopted an ambivalent and rather weak interpretation of this right by stipulating local populations' right to free, prior and informed *consultation*. This formulation has been replicated in the constitutions of Ecuador (2008) and Bolivia (2009), despite the harsh critique of many indigenous organisations, which demanded their right to free, prior and informed *consent*.

In response to highly controversial debates about the concrete interpretation of the right to prior consultation and consent according to international law, in his report on "The Extractive Industries and Indigenous Peoples", the former Special Rapporteur on the Rights of Indigenous Peoples James Anaya specified the meaning of these international norms.[47] Anaya clarifies: "The Declaration and various other

---

[42] Article 10, UNDRIP.

[43] Article 18, UNDRIP.

[44] Article 19, UNDRIP.

[45] Article 32, UNDRIP.

[46] US Department of State, Announcement of U.S. Support for the United Nations Declaration on the Rights of Indigenous Peoples. 12 January 2012, https://2009-2017.state.gov/s/srgia/154553. htm (last accessed 1 October 2018).

[47] UN Human Rights Council, Report of the Special Rapporteur on the rights of indigenous peoples, James Anaya Anaya. Extractive industries and indigenous peoples, UN Doc. A/HRC/24/41, 1 July 2013.

international sources of authority, along with practical considerations, lead to a general rule that extractive activities should not take place within the territories of indigenous peoples without their free, prior and informed consent. [...] In all instances of proposed extractive projects that might affect indigenous peoples, consultations with them should take place and consent should at least be sought, even if consent is not strictly required. [...] On the other hand, when indigenous peoples withhold their consent to extractive projects within their territories, no such presumption applies, and in order for a project to be implemented the State has the burden of demonstrating either that no rights are being limited or that, if they are, the limitation is valid".[48] According to Anaya, as a general rule, states should seek the FPIC of indigenous peoples affected by extraction projects. His interpretation, however, still leaves the door open for implementing resource activities against the will of local populations.

4 Norm Contestation in the Domestic Sphere: Bolivia, Colombia and Peru

The following section discusses processes of norm contestation in the domestic sphere, referring to both legal rules/lawsuits that address the right to prior consultation and FPIC and these norms' implementation. The respective disputes have been exacerbated in the context of the new commodity boom in Latin America since the 1990s. All countries of this region have increased the exported volumes of raw materials in the past few decades and many of them have massively expanded their extractive frontiers, very often affecting indigenous peoples and territories. In the Andean states—Bolivia, Colombia, Ecuador and Peru—primary goods currently represent more than 80%, or sometimes even more than 90%, of total export volumes.[49] The revenues from resource exploitation have been used partly for financing social policies and development programs, which has helped to reduce poverty rates: between 2003 and 2013, 72 million citizens from this region were able to escape poverty and in the same period, 94 million Latin Americans could rise from lower classes into the middle class.[50] The social uplifting of many Latin Americans could be financed without profound redistributive policies, which would have gone along with serious social conflicts fuelled by the region's still very powerful elites

---

[48] UN Human Rights Council, Report of the Special Rapporteur on the rights of indigenous peoples, James Anaya Anaya. Extractive industries and indigenous peoples, UN Doc. A/HRC/24/41, 1 July 2013.

[49] CEPAL, CEPALSTAT Database. Export of primary export as a share of total exports. http://interwp.cepal.org/sisgen/ConsultaIntegrada.asp?IdAplicacion=6&idTema=119&idIndicador=1910&idioma=I (last accessed 21 June 2016).

[50] UNDP, Regional Human Development Report for Latin America and the Caribbean Multidimensional progress: well-being beyond income. 2016, http://www.latinamerica.undp.org/content/rblac/en/home/library/human_development/informe-regional-sobre-desarrollo-humano-para-america-latina-y-e.html (last accessed 1 October 2018).

and oligarchs.[51] As a consequence of these developments, scholars of Latin America have discussed the existence of a broad "commodities consensus"[52] spanning conflicting political ideologies, the private and public sectors, social classes, rural and urban areas and different ethnicities. Bebbington and Bury state that subsoil resources in Latin America have been coupled with notions of sovereignty and nation, which means that the state and extraction are intimately bundled together.[53]

At the same time, indigenous movements and subnational entities have repeatedly challenged the state's claim to resource sovereignty, leading to different types of "contested resource sovereignties".[54] Indigenous organizations in Latin America largely centred their struggles on the recovering of ancestral territories, understood as a basis for the related rights to self-determination, autonomy, self-government and self-determined development. For example, in their life plan, Bolivia's Guaraní state that their main aim is to "search for the unity and autonomy of the Guaraní nation in the framework of our self-determination, self-management and self-government [...] We want to be autonomous, free and sovereign and we want to control, administer and utilise our natural resources".[55] Indigenous peoples movements in Latin America have been strengthened by the increased formal recognition of their rights in the past few decades, especially in the context of the "new Latin American Constitutionalism".[56] Here again, Andean states have been outstanding: Bolivia and Ecuador have legally recognized indigenous rights within their "plurinational states" to the greatest extent worldwide; Colombia has become globally known for the "rights revolution" driven by its strong and independent Constitutional Court[57]; and Peru has been the first country in the region to promulgate a specific framework law on the right to prior consultation in September 2011. To date, it is also the Andean countries that most systematically implement the right to prior consultation and FPIC. In addition, all three countries are members of the Organization of American States (OAS). Especially the jurisprudence of the Inter-American Court of Human Rights on indigenous rights has influenced the jurisprudence of domestic courts. In particular, the decision "Saramaka vs. Surinam" of the Inter-American Court of Human Rights, wherein the Court rules in favour of strong consent rights, has been an important reference for Latin American Constitutional Courts and for indigenous and human rights organizations. Moreover, the Inter-American Commission on Human Rights organized several hearings on alleged violations of the right to consultation and consent in the OAS member states.

---

[51] Burchardt and Dietz (2013), p. 189.

[52] Svampa (2015).

[53] Bebbington and Bury (2013b), p. 11.

[54] McNeish (2017).

[55] APG (2008).

[56] Nolte and Schilling-Vacaflor (2012).

[57] Pérez (2012).

4.1 Prior Consultation and FPIC in Colombia

Colombia is the Latin American country where most prior consultation processes have been concluded since 1994, a few years after the right to prior consultation was legally established in article 300 of Colombia's constitution in 1991. The role of the Colombian Constitutional Court (CCC) has been key for pressing the state to carry out consultation and consent processes. The CCC has defined the right to FPIC as a fundamental human right in 1997 and already has received 45 *tutela* actions (constitutional actions to guarantee fundamental rights) concerning alleged violations of this right.[58] In over 30 of these lawsuits, the CCC ruled in favour of the indigenous claimants and it has prescribed the suspension of several laws and specific extraction projects due to absent or flawed consultation and consent processes.

Between 2011 and 2014, only, the Colombian entity specialized on prior consultation within the Ministry of the Interior recorded the conclusion of a total of 4042 prior consultation processes; 201 of these processes concerned mining activities and 1300 processes concerned hydrocarbon activities.[59] Prior consultation processes that are part of environmental licensing procedures, for example for resource extraction projects, were led by Colombia's Ministry of the Environment. While there exists no specific law in Colombia regulating the right to consultation and consent, several sector-specific and general decrees and presidential directives aim to regulate and to limit this right.[60] These lower range norms have not been subject to prior consultation processes with organizations of indigenous peoples and Afro-descendants in Colombia.[61] These groups consider the unilaterally imposed norms as illegitimate. The decree 1320 from 1998 that regulates prior consultation in the ambit of natural resource exploitation was declared unconstitutional by the CCC in several rulings. The fact that there is no specific law on the right to FPIC in Colombia to date has been due to the widespread conviction among indigenous and Afro-descendent organizations in this country that the regulation of this fundamental right would only restrict and weaken it.[62]

While rejecting the adoption of state law regulating the consultation and consent right, several Colombian indigenous peoples formulated their own protocols to regulate how they are to be consulted.[63] Indigenous peoples' own norms usually diverge

---

[58] Domínguez (2015), p. 56.

[59] De Almenara and Linares (2017), p. 87.

[60] For an overview see Rodríguez (2015), pp. 102–103.

[61] According to international human rights standards, prior consultation and FPIC processes have to be carried out whenever legislative or administrate measures may affect indigenous peoples directly. Hence, indigenous peoples have to be consulted on laws and decrees affecting their rights, with the aim of reaching an agreement and/or their consent. In particular, the lack of prior consultation and consent processes concerning laws and decrees that regulate the right of consultation and consent has been criticized vehemently by indigenous organizations in many Latin American countries.

[62] Domínguez (2015), p. 46.

[63] See, for instance, Weitzner (2017).

clearly from and often openly contradict state law. An interesting example is the community protocol from the indigenous communities Resguardo Cañamomo Lomaprieto, wherein they specify in much detail how they are to be consulted.[64] Many of the provisions of the protocol were formulated in response to negative previous experiences with consultation processes and have the objective to prevent such shortcomings in the future. For instance, the protocol of the *Resguardo* stipulates that their assembly (and not individual authorities) has the decision power in consultation processes, that in addition to environmental and social impact assessment studies (ESIAs) specific human rights assessment studies have to be conducted, and that additional studies have to be carried out whenever the *Resguardo* misses important information for taking an informed decision about planned measures. There are also groups, such as the U'wa from Colombia's Sierra Nevada del Cocuy, who have adopted a more radical position towards consultation and consent processes. The U'wa have rejected the right to prior consultation and FPIC, arguing that it is a concept imposed by the "Law of white people".[65] The U'wa explained "We say no to prior consultation because we have our own laws and principles. Our ancestral legislators and divinities taught us that the territory is sacred and not negotiable [...] Prior consultation is a double-edged sword, every day we have to see how to defend our territory. We believe that the papers will not allow us to defend the territory, they rather lead to deception [...] We are not guided by the constitution or the ILO Convention 169; the U'wa are guided by Mother Earth".[66]

4.2 Prior Consultation and FPIC in Peru

Although Peru ratified ILO C169 in 1995, it has failed to implement the right to prior consultation until recently, when the framework law on the right to prior consultation (Law 29785) was adopted in September 2011, which is the first specific law regulating this right in Latin America. Before the adoption of this law only informative events with the general citizenry, which had a manipulative pro-extraction character, had been carried out.[67] The law that regulates the right to prior consultation (not to FPIC) was promulgated as a consequence of the yearlong mobilizations of Amazonian indigenous communities and their allies and the resulting violent conflicts in the province of Bagua in 2009, which had caused the death of at least 33 people. The reason for the mobilizations were the passing of nearly one hundred legislative decrees without prior consultation by former President Alan García, to adapt Peru's legislation to the Free Trade Agreement concluded with the United States. After the conflict had ended, a working group composed of indigenous and state actors was established with the task of drafting a law on the right to

---

[64] Herrera and García (2012).

[65] Howland et al. (2013), p. 26.

[66] Howland et al. (2013), p. 26.

[67] Schilling-Vacaflor et al. (2018).

prior consultation. During the drafting process and during the discussions in Peru's Congress, the original draft law elaborated by Peru's Ombudsperson was changed in order to weaken the indigenous peoples' right.[68] For instance, provisions specifying the right to FPIC and not just to prior consultation were completely eliminated. Nevertheless, President García vetoed the law. However, newly elected President Ollanta Humala promulgated it.

Thereafter, a contentious consultation process regarding a decree of implementation with the objective of regulating the consultation procedure in more detail was organized. This consultation involved the most important indigenous and peasant organizations of the country at the national scale and the resulting decree was adopted on 3 April 2012. While the indigenous organisations initially had hoped that the decree might correct the main deficiencies of the consultation law, powerful extractive corporations lobbied the state ministries to adopt a norm that would further restrict the indigenous rights contained in the law.[69] The analysis of the consultation process and its results reveal that more powerful state ministries (such as the Ministry of Energy and Mines and the Ministry of Finance) imposed their vision, overruling indigenous claims and interests. Despite the rejection of the implementation decree by the majority of the country's indigenous organizations, since its adoption, a total of 32 consultation processes have been concluded until April 2017, eleven of them concerning hydrocarbon projects and ten concerning mining activities.[70]

4.3 Prior Consultation and FPIC in Bolivia

Bolivia has undertaken comprehensive legal reforms in favour of indigenous rights since the inauguration of President Evo Morales in 2006, which culminated in the adoption of its new plurinational constitution in 2009. This constitution recognizes very comprehensive indigenous peoples' rights. In addition, in October 2007 Bolivia has been the first and to date the only country worldwide in adopting the UNDRIP as domestic law. Bolivia's president Morales also adopted progressive supreme decrees regulating the right to prior consultation and indigenous socio-environmental monitoring in Bolivia's hydrocarbon sector in 2007, which were co-formulated by indigenous organizations. Simultaneously, since 2005 the hydrocarbon sector in Bolivia has been re-nationalized and the government has used part of the additional revenues to finance social policies.

Unfortunately, since the passing of Bolivia's constitution, a retrogressive legal trend has taken place and a series of laws and decrees were put into force that severely restrict indigenous rights, some of them openly contradicting international

---

[68] Schilling-Vacaflor and Flemmer (2015).

[69] Flemmer and Schilling-Vacaflor (2016).

[70] De Almenara and Linares (2017), p. 87.

human rights norms.[71] These decrees were strongly opposed by indigenous organizations and the Bolivian Ombudsperson (*Defensoría del Pueblo*). In 2013, a government commission developed a draft law on the right to prior consultation after vehement public criticism concerning the lack of consultation over the construction of a road through the Indigenous Territory and National Park Isiboro Securé (TIPNIS). The indigenous organizations also drafted a law proposal and the original plan was to find a compromise in order to establish a shared norm that is acceptable to all parties. This plan failed, as the government ended up negotiating only with a few indigenous organizations close to the government and no consensus could be established between the state and more critical or more autonomous organizations, such as the Assembly of Guaraní Peoples (APG) that drafted a particularly well elaborated law proposal. The most important point of disagreement was the consultation participants' actual influence and decision-making power. The APG's proposal clearly stipulated that consultation had to obtain the participants' FPIC and that decisions taken in consultation processes were binding. The state's interpretation contradicted this proposal, arguing that the state should seek an agreement or consent *before the final decision was taken.* To leave no doubt, the government's proposal further added that "due to their strategic character and public interest, the execution and continuity of extractive activities will be guaranteed".[72] However, according to an expert working in the extractive industry, the plan to sanction a law on the right to prior consultation ultimately failed due to the strong opposition from the corporate sector.[73]

Despite the fact that norms about consultation and consent rights remain highly contested in Bolivia, approximately 70 consultation processes already have been concluded in the hydrocarbon sector, one consultation concerning the construction of a highway through the TIPNIS and since 2015 consultation processes have also been organized in the mining sector.[74] However, previous research into these practices revealed that they did not fulfil the criteria for prior consultation and FPIC established in international human rights instruments.

---

[71] The Bolivian government has released four supreme decrees (SD) that are directly related to extraction projects and indigenous rights, all of which have been vehemently opposed by indigenous organizations. SD 2195, from November 2014, established upper limits between 0.3 and 1.5% of the investment sums of hydrocarbon projects for compensation payments to the inhabitants of collective lands according to different project types. SD 2298 states that prior consultation processes should not surpass a maximum duration of 45 days; SD 2366 authorizes hydrocarbon activities in protected areas; and SD 2368 declares that gas ducts are of national interest. The three last decrees were adopted in May 2015. Schilling-Vacaflor (2017a).

[72] VII Comisión Nacional de la elaboración de la ley de consulta. Anteproyecto de Ley de Consulta Previa Libre e Informada [Proposal of the Law on Free, Prior and Informed Consultation]. La Paz, 2013.

[73] Interview with staff from the corporation Gas Trans Boliviano GTB, Santa Cruz, 18.11.2014.

[74] De Almenara and Linares, Buenas prácticas de las defensorías del pueblo de Bolivia, Colombia, Ecuador y Perú en procesos de consulta previa. 2017, https://www.business-humanrights.org/sites/default/files/documents/GIZ_BuenasPraGestion_16082017BAJA.pdf (last accessed 1 October 2018).

4.4   Issues of Contestation: Who? How? When? and with What Results?

While the experiences with consultation and consent rights and the respective contestations are shaped by the specific context conditions of each country and the
involved actors, a comparison reveals the existence of important cross-country similarities with regard to patterns of norm contestation. In the following, I will briefly
present some of the most contested issues, which are present in all of the three
countries.

4.4.1   Which Entity Leads Prior Consultation and FPIC Processes?

Undoubtedly, according to international human rights standards on indigenous peoples' rights, the state has the legal obligation to organize prior consultation and
FPIC processes. However, international norms do not specify which specific state
entity would be appropriate for leading consultations. In Bolivia and Peru, the state
entities leading consultation processes are subordinated to the ministries responsible for administering resource extraction (the Ministry of Hydrocarbons and Energy
and the Ministry of Mining in Bolivia, and the Ministry of Energy and Mining in
Peru). Indigenous organizations in both countries have criticized that due to this
institutional design the leading state entities would act as judge and party, taking
decisions that clearly favor economic interests and subordinate human rights and
environmental protection.

To create a more favorable institutional design, during the consultation about the
decree that regulates the Law on the Right to Prior Consultation in 2012/2013, the
Peruvian indigenous organizations demanded that the responsible entity for implementing consultations should be the specialized entity on indigenous issues (currently the Vice-Ministry of Intercultural Affairs) which, according to the indigenous
proposal, should be upgraded to a ministry, and not the Ministry of Energy and
Mining.[75]

In Bolivia, the Supreme Decree 29033 that regulates consultation processes in
the hydrocarbon sector establishes that the Ministry of Hydrocarbons and Energy
shall coordinate with the Ministry of the Environment and Water for carrying out
consultation processes. However, in practice it turned out that the staff from the
Environmental Ministry very often did not participate in consultation processes,
either due to a lack of personnel or resources or due to coordination problems with
the Hydrocarbon Ministry.[76] Experience shows that the Environmental Ministry,
when present in consultation processes, played an important role in upholding
indigenous rights, especially because it often supported the consultation participants' concerns about environmental impacts and their claims for more rigorous

---

[75] Schilling-Vacaflor and Flemmer (2015).
[76] Schilling-Vacaflor (2017b).

mitigation measures. Unfortunately, establishing close contact with the Environmental Ministry staff proved to be difficult for many affected communities and there has been a lot of political pressure directed towards ministry staff to grant environmental licenses to large-scale projects quickly and without obstacles.[77]

In Colombia, a specialized entity for prior consultation and FPIC processes was established within the Interior Ministry and the Environmental Ministry leads processes about extraction projects. While in general this solution seems to be much more appropriate compared to the Bolivian and Peruvian situations, indigenous and Afro-descendant organizations from Colombia have criticized the role that these state entities have played in consultation processes.[78] Indigenous and Afro-Colombian organizations have demanded that either the public ministry (*Ministerio Público*) or an entity from the judicial branch should be responsible for upholding the right to prior consultation and consent.

4.4.2   Who Is to Be Consulted?

International norms such as the UNDRIP do not adopt a clear definition of indigenous peoples in order to allow context-specific interpretations of the right-holders in diverse countries. The question of who are the holders of the right to prior consultation and FPIC is contested in the Andean countries. Largely due to the mobilization of communities and organizations of Afro-descendants, supported by human rights organizations and the CCC, Colombia has adopted an inclusive definition of the holders of indigenous and ethnic rights, granting rather strong collective rights to indigenous peoples, communities of Afro-descendants and the Rrom people.[79] Nevertheless, in several cases the consultation team from the Interior Ministry wrongly stated that in the places where extraction projects were planned none of such groups existed, denying them the right to prior consultation and FPIC.[80]

Bolivia has also opted for an inclusive definition of the holders of indigenous rights, granting these rights, according to its constitution and legislation, to first nations, indigenous peoples and peasant communities (*Naciones y Pueblos Indígenas Originarias Campesinas*). However, already during the Constituent Assembly and again during the debates about the law on the right to prior consultation, the indigenous lowland organizations and the traditional highland organizations (based on the *Ayllu*s) emphasized that they strongly disagreed with the granting

---

[77] Schilling-Vacaflor (2017b).

[78] Howland, Uprimny and Barsanti, Voces y Palabras Mayores de los pueblos étnicos de Colombia sobre el derecho a la consulta y al consentimiento previo, libre e informado. Oficina en Colombia del Alto Comisionado de Naciones Unidas para los Derechos Humanos. April 2013, http://www.acnur.org/fileadmin/scripts/doc.php?file=fileadmin/Documentos/Publicaciones/2013/9171 (last accessed 1 October 2018).

[79] The Rrom (or *gitano*) people, in English also referred to as Romani, have migrated to Colombia from Northern India over 1000 years ago. In the decree 2957 from 6 August 2010, the Colombian state recognizes the own ethnic identity of the Rrom people.

[80] Domínguez (2015).

of indigenous peoples rights, such as the right to prior consultation and FPIC, to peasant communities that hold individual land properties.[81] What is at stake here is that the inclusive definition of indigenous rights in several instances has disadvantaged specific indigenous groups. For example, a fund that was created to support indigenous peoples in Bolivia (*Fondo Indígena*) and financed with revenues from the hydrocarbon sector, which especially affects the Guaraní peoples from Bolivia's lowlands, has been accessible for all indigenous and peasant organizations of the country to the discontent of the groups bearing the main burdens from hydrocarbon activities. With regard to the consultation and consent right, it is important to clarify that in Bolivia these processes are linked to subsequent negotiations between the indigenous groups and the extraction corporations on compensation payments for negative, irreparable long-term impacts. The extension of the right to consultation and consent to peasant communities, thus, in practice implies the reception of lower compensation payments by the indigenous lowland peoples.

In contrast, in Peru the state has repeatedly aimed to limit indigenous rights exclusively to Amazonian groups and to exclude the peasant and coastal communities, which often share certain indigenous institutions (language, rituals, clothes etc.), but do not necessarily self-identify as indigenous. Measured against international norms, the new consultation legislation contains a more restrictive definition of indigenous peoples and Peru's former presidents García and Humala in several instances argued that they opposed the granting of indigenous rights and particularly of the right to prior consultation and consent to peasant communities.[82] This perspective was harshly criticized by the Peruvian Ombudsperson and by indigenous and peasant organizations. However, due to this dispute, consultation processes in the mining sector with peasant communities have had a very difficult beginning.

In addition to the above mentioned contestations, questions such as *Which organization is representative and at which scale (national, subnational, local)? How many persons are to be included in consultations? Shall decisions be taken by elected representatives or by more inclusive assemblies?* have been virulent and have contributed to often fierce contestations between state institutions and corporations on the one hand and indigenous actors on the other as well as within indigenous and Afro-descendant organizations and communities. Moreover, the inclusion of certain actors and organizations in consultation processes is often used strategically by state or corporate actors in all of the three countries, in order to give voice to pro-extraction forces and to exclude the more critical ones,[83] violating the principle that prior consultation and consent processes shall be characterized by good faith. Such informal practices are conducted in non-transparent ways and it has been very challenging or even impossible to hold state and corporate actors accountable

---

[81] Fontana and Grugel (2016).

[82] Flemmer and Schilling-Vacaflor (2016).

[83] Riaño DMM, Revisión crítica del derecho a la consulta previa de proyectos y sus procedimientos. Semillas, 55/56, http://www.semillas.org.co/es/revisi (last accessed 1 October 2018), pp. 54–26; Guzmán-Gallegos (2017); Schilling-Vacaflor and Eichler (2017).

for such practices. Through the misuse of prior consultation processes by manipulative or dividing actions, a right that should contribute to empowering indigenous peoples actually might be turned into a disempowering tool that weakens indigenous organizations and contributes to dispossessing communities of their territories and resources.

4.4.3   Which Measures Require Consultation?

According to international law on indigenous peoples' rights, all legislative and administrative measures that are likely to affect indigenous peoples have to be the subject of consultations. However, in practice it has been difficult to establish a shared rule that determines to which measures exactly this norm applies. For instance, one of the most contested issues concerning Peru's new consultation legislation is the question of whether extraction projects that are operative, but that were built after Peru ratified ILO Convention 169, have to undergo a consultation process according to the new legislation. The consultation legislation stipulates that only newly constructed projects require consultation. Yet, several indigenous organizations have challenged this restrictive interpretation. The Awajún and Wampis peoples recently won a lawsuit wherein they demanded the right to consultation and FPIC in relation to oil block 116. This block has been in place since 2006 and has a long contentious history. Peru's Supreme Court of Justice ruled on 28 March 2017 that, due to the violation of the indigenous right to consultation and consent, the contract to explore for and exploit hydrocarbons in block 116 be annulled and all related activities be suspended.

The necessity to consult with indigenous and Afro-descendant groups has also been related to the existence and severity of the planned projects' expected impacts. In the three Andean countries discussed here, groups of indigenous peoples and Afro-descendants have struggled for a broad definition of impacts, including both indirect impacts and impacts on ancestral territories that have not (yet) been titled in favor of the ethnic group involved. In Bolivia, only projects that are characterized as "category 1" projects by the Environmental Ministry—signifying that the expected impacts are considerable and either affect an indigenous group or a protected area— are the subject of a prior consultation process. However, in practice this unilateral definition by the state entity has often been challenged by indigenous communities and organizations, leading to mobilizations and even violent conflicts.

Similarly, one of the main points of contention regarding Colombia's decree 1320 that regulates prior consultation in the ambit of resource extraction has been that the decree establishes that consultation only has to take place when a resource project affects an indigenous reserve (*Resguardo*). In contrast, the organizations of Afro-descendants and indigenous peoples of the country have claimed that a broader concept of territory, which shall not be limited by legal recognition as collective lands and territories should be applied when determining whether consultation and consent processes shall take place.

4.4.4   When and How Shall the Consultation Take Place?

International norms point out that consultations shall conclude prior to the adoption
of planned measures. However, what does this mean exactly? In Colombia and
Bolivia prior consultation and consent processes have been organized before granting extraction projects the environmental license to operate. This means that at the
moment when consultations take place, the projects have already been designed and
the consultation participants have had little leeway to effectively shape decisions
affecting them. In Peru, prior consultation processes in the hydrocarbon sector have
been organized at a moment of time when actually nothing had to be decided, after
the size and shape of oil blocks had already been defined and before signing the
concession contract with the interested corporation.

Supported by international norms[84] and domestic norms,[85] indigenous organizations from Bolivia, Colombia and Peru have challenged the above-mentioned practices and have demanded that consultation and consent processes should not be
carried out solely at one moment of time, but rather they should occur at various
stages of an extractive project, from strategic planning to project closure.

Another point of contention has been the duration of consultation processes. In
the three Andean countries under analysis, the states have exercised considerable
time pressure to conclude consultation processes within limited timeframes. Peru's
consultation legislation limits the maximum duration of consultation processes to
120 days and in Bolivia the contested Supreme Decree 2298 from 2015 even pre-
scribes a time limit of 45 days for the conclusion of prior consultation processes in
the hydrocarbon sector. The indigenous organizations in these countries have
opposed the existence of such rigid timeframes and have demanded longer and
more flexible processes, which are adapted to their own norms and procedures and
rhythms of decision making.

Other issues of contestation concerning the consultation procedure include the
power asymmetries that often characterized these processes, which manifest themselves in the unilateral planning of consultation and consent processes; in the imposition of dominant knowledge such as the knowledge that usually is part of
corporate-financed environmental impact studies[86] and the neglect of local and
experiential knowledge; in the lack of egalitarian intercultural dialogues; and in the
use of manipulative strategies like the coupling of consultation processes with
unsatisfied basic needs, promising that in return for granting the social license to go
ahead with extraction projects, the communities would receive social investment
programs or compensation payments.[87] In addition, many organizations of indigenous peoples and Afro-descendants have criticized that supposedly binding

---

[84] UN Human Rights Council, Report of the Special Rapporteur on the rights of indigenous peoples, James Anaya. Extractive industries and indigenous peoples, UN Doc. A/HRC/24/41, 1 July
2013.

[85] For instance from the CCC, see Col. Sentencia T-129 de 2011.

[86] Referred to as "corporate science" by Kirsch (2014).

[87] See Leifsen et al. (2017).

consultation agreements have been disrespected in practice and that follow up mechanisms to supervise compliance with such agreements by corporations have often been missing.[88]

4.4.5   What Is the Result of Consultation/FPIC Processes?

According to international human rights norms, prior consultation and consent processes shall result either in the achievement of binding agreements or in the consent (or the withholding of consent) by the indigenous peoples involved. However, the question of how to interpret the state's obligation to seek indigenous peoples' and Afro-descendants' consent has been at the center of many political struggles and lawsuits. In general, indigenous and Afro-descendant communities and organizations have argued that they should have the right to oppose projects that would affect their (subnational) territories, demanding that states and corporations accept their decision as binding. For instance, indigenous peoples from the Colombian Sierra argued: "[t]here are situations or actions which, due to their dimension or impacts, must not be consulted. We cannot ask mother earth for giving us the permit to take away its vital organs".[89] In contrast, state governments have argued that they are entitled to take the final decision about extraction projects in their (national) territory. Hence, contradictory views about authority, territorial control and resource sovereignty at different but partly overlapping scales coexist, which are not easily reconcilable. Both actor groups have backed their viewpoints and convictions by referring to their own norms and often also by the selective use of international norms that are supportive of their claims or by expressing their own interpretation of international norms.

However, even across different state institutions within one country, interpretations of what the right to consultation and consent means exactly have often been contradictory. For instance, Colombia's presidential directive 001 from 2010, which has been opposed by indigenous peoples and Afro-descendant communities, states "the realization of prior consultation processes in the cases outlined in international agreements is obligatory, but the national ethnic groups exercising this fundamental right cannot veto the development of projects".[90] In contrast, supportive of strong consent rights, the CCC argues: "When large-scale investment projects with major impacts on Afro-descendent or indigenous territories are planned, it is the duty of the state not only to consult with these communities, but also to obtain their free, prior and informed consent, according to their customs and traditions. This is so

---

[88] Flemmer and Schilling-Vacaflor (2016).

[89] Howland T, Uprimny M and Barsanti P, Voces y Palabras Mayores de los pueblos étnicos de Colombia sobre el derecho a la consulta y al consentimiento previo, libre e informado. Oficina en Colombia del Alto Comisionado de Naciones Unidas para los Derechos Humanos. April 2013, http://www.acnur.org/fileadmin/scripts/doc.php?file=fileadmin/Documentos/Publicaciones/2013/9171 (last accessed 1 October), p. 22.

[90] Colombian presidential directive 001 (2010).

because due to the execution of exploration and exploitation activities in their habitat, these communities often suffer profound social and economic changes, such as
the loss of their traditional lands, the dispossession, migration, the reduction of
necessary resources for their physical and cultural subsistence, the destruction and
contamination of their traditional environment [...]".[91]

Similarly, an analysis of the court rulings from the constitutional courts and tribunals of Bolivia, Colombia and Peru reveal that these courts have formulated different and partly contradictory interpretations of the right to prior consultation and
FPIC with regard to the final decision making power of indigenous groups vs.
states.[92] For instance, diverging from the rather strong interpretation of the indigenous right to FPIC adopted by the CCC, the Peruvian constitutional tribunal stated
in one of its rulings: "The right to prior consultation [...] entails that the achieved
agreements must be respected, but what has been colloquially named the 'right to
veto' is excluded from the normative program of the right to consultation".[93]

While different actors' and institutions' positions within states range from weak
to strong interpretations of consultation and consent rights, a compromise has often
been to establish that the state takes the final decision about planned measures, but
that this decision has to be adequately justified, guaranteeing that the measure will
not violate indigenous rights. For instance, the CCC specified: "When it is not possible to achieve an agreement, the decision of the authority has to be devoid of
arbitrariness and authoritarianism; in consequence it has to be objective, reasonable
and proportional to the constitutional objective, that requests the state to protect the
social, cultural and economic identity of the indigenous community".[94] It has also
been argued that the indigenous decision-making power increases according to the
severity of the expected impacts.[95]

However, we can formulate reasonable doubts, fostered by previous negative
experiences, of whether the current Latin American states, characterized by power
asymmetries that clearly work in favour of extractive interests, will justify their
decisions in such a respectful way, doing justice to their human rights obligations.
One problem that has emerged with regard to the justification of the adoption of
measures against the ethnic communities' will is that states often refer to extraction
projects as being in the "national interest", representing a "public good" or being of

---

[91] CCC, Ruling T-769.

[92] See paper "La jurisprudencia de la CC de Colombia y el TC del Peru en casos con referencia al derecho a a la Consulta Previo de los PP II" presented by René Kuppe at the "Extracting Justice?" project meeting, Santa Cruz-Bolivia, 11.11.2015.

[93] Ruling of Peru's Constitutional Tribunal, 00025-2009-PI/TC.

[94] CCC, Ruling Col SU-039 from 1997.

[95] Doyle (2014), pp. 146–148; The CCC argued: "On the one side there is the prior consultation entailing the right to veto [...] on the other side there is the prior consultation consisting primarily in the provision of information. According to the court's perspective, the criteria that permits the reconciliation of these extremes depends on the grade to which the communities would be affected" (Col. Sentencia T-129 e 2011).

"national utility" in order to subordinate indigenous rights and interests as being of minor importance.[96]

5   Discussion and Conclusions

This chapter illustrates how different patterns of norm contestation over the right to prior consultation and FPIC contribute to the widespread noncompliance with this right, particularly in the extractive industries, which are of strategic economic importance for Latin American states. The analysis of the respective contestations over legal regulations and consultation processes in the Andean countries Bolivia, Colombia and Peru show that these disputes have deep roots, revealing the existence of competing resource sovereignties, i.e. divergent claims of territorial control and decision-making. In current Latin American contexts, it is difficult to imagine how to reconcile opposed views, which are tied to strong economic, political and cultural interests and values. The difficulty to establish shared ground rules concerning indigenous and participatory rights in the extractive industries also points to legitimacy problems in the ambit of resource governance.

As this study shows, when analysing norm contestation over consultation and consent rights in the extractive industries, legal pluralism—unfolding in the form of asymmetric inter-legal relations—has to be taken into account. Interestingly, my findings do not only point to divergent interpretations of rights according to international, state-sanctioned and local norms, but also to highly contested interpretations of the meanings of norms by different state institutions and within national fields of law. Due to unequal power relations that have largely worked in favour of economic interests and against indigenous rights, not only between states and indigenous peoples, but also between different state institutions involved, those interpretations restricting the right to consultation and consent have largely prevailed in shaping social practices on the ground. Against this background, the defenders of human rights and environmental concerns have been in a rather weak position.

The Andean governments have interpreted international human rights standards concerning the indigenous peoples' right to prior consultation and FPIC in a very restrictive manner and thereby they have counteracted a more empowering and influential understanding of this right. In all three countries analysed here, current domestic legislation regulating the right to prior consultation and FPIC comprises provisions that openly violate international human rights instruments. Relatedly, flawed consultation practices often have been interpreted in state discourses as

---

[96] Interestingly, with a critical stance towards such discriminatory interpretations, the CCC argued the following: "In the case of a conflict between the general interest and another interest that is constitutionally protected, [...] this is a conflict between two collective interests and not between one particular interest and the general interest. [...] The interest of the indigenous community possesses a major legitimacy when it is based on fundamental rights that are comprehensively protected by the Constitution." (COL T-428 de 1992).

being compliant with the right to prior consultation and consent, according to such restrictive or even rights-violating domestic legislation. As a consequence, it is pertinent to ask whether the Andean states have used this right in an instrumental way for legitimizing expansive extraction activities. Or, formulated in a more provocative way, *might the right to prior consultation and FPIC actually work like a wolf in sheep's clothing, being represented as a progressive right benefitting indigenous peoples, but actually contributing to dispossessing them of their territories and resources*? Whether we share such a critical stance or not, this study suggests that it is high time to ask how to protect indigenous peoples more effectively, not only from measures implemented without consultation and consent processes, but also from a misuse and misinterpretation of this right. The investigation of flawed regulations and consultation processes in domestic contexts can provide important feedback and information for global policy circles to rethink global norms and their specific meaning and to identify leverage points for transformation.

The limitation and violation of the right to prior consultation and FPIC has been justified in public discourses by referring to the need to advance resource extraction activities as a motor of states' economic development and for financing social policies. We can draw a parallel to the findings of other scholars regarding contexts where human rights violations have been justified by the need to protect citizens' security. In the cases studied here, human rights violations have been justified with the need to extract natural resources for financing the state's and its citizens' development and well-being. Taking the right to prior consultation and FPIC seriously and hence, to comply with it, would require that states challenge their conviction that resource extraction prevails over human rights and environmental concerns. Hence, states would need to be willing to discuss desirable futures without a predetermined conclusion in mind, opening up to the possibility of cancelling profitable projects and seeking alternative paths of development.

In addition, despite the inflationary spread of corporate social responsibility discourses—including the increased formal commitment by transnational corporations to the principle of FPIC—this study sheds light on the rights-limiting role that powerful extraction corporations have played in the Andean countries in contestations over strong vs. weak indigenous participatory rights in the extractive industries. Given that changes of corporate and state behaviour in the protection of human rights or the environment have mostly been driven by domestic mobilizations and/or transnational activism, the role of organized civil society and public discourses will be decisive for the future compliance or noncompliance with the right to prior consultation and FPIC. Hence, the future of the consultation and consent right in law and in practice and the question of whether it will be possible to create a shared understanding of this norm will largely depend on the degree to which the existing "commodities consensus" will be dismantled and substituted by other persuasive ideas and values.

References

APG (2008) Plan de Vida Guaraní [Guaraní life plan]. APG, Camiri

Barelli M (2012) Free, prior and informed consent in the aftermath of the UN Declaration on the Rights of Indigenous Peoples: developments and challenges ahead. Int J Hum Rights 16(1):1–24

Bebbington DH (2012) Consultation, compensation and conflict: natural gas extraction in Weenhayek territory, Bolivia. J Lat Am Geogr 11(2):49–71

Bebbington A, Bury J (2013a) Subterranean struggles: new dynamics of mining, oil, and gas in Latin America. University of Texas Press, Austin

Bebbington A, Bury J (2013b) Political ecologies of the subsoil. Subterranean struggles. In: Bebbington A, Bury J (eds) New dynamics of mining, oil, and gas in Latin America. University of Texas Press, Austin, pp 1–26

Burchardt HJ, Dietz K (2013) Extraktivismus in Lateinamerika – der Versuch einer Fundierung. In: Burchardt HJ, Dietz K, Öhlschläger R (eds) Umwelt und Entwicklung im 21. Jahrhundert. Nomos, Baden-Baden, pp 181–200

Burchardt HJ, Dietz K (2014) (Neo-) extractivism – a new challenge for development theory from Latin America. Third World Q 35(3):468–486

Clarke KM, Goodale M (2010) Mirrors of justice law and power in the post-cold war era. Cambridge University Press, Cambridge

De Sousa Santos B (1987) Law: a map of misreading. Toward a postmodern conception of law. J Law Soc 14(3):279–302

De Sousa Santos B (2002) Toward a new legal common sense: law, globalization, and emancipation. Cambridge University Press, Cambridge

De Sousa Santos B (2003) Poderá o direito ser emancipatório? Revista crítica de ciências sociais (65):3–76

De Sousa Santos B, Rodríguez-Garavito CA (eds) (2005) Law and globalization from below: towards a cosmopolitan legality. Cambridge University Press

Dietz K, Engels B (2017) Contested extractivism, society and the state: an introduction. In: Dietz K, Engels B (eds) Contested extractivism, society and the state. Palgrave Macmillan, London, pp 1–19

Domínguez DA (2015) El estado del arte ¿Es posible reglamentar la Consulta Previa? In: Rodríguez GA, Albán DA, Moncayo HL (eds) Las rutas de la consulta. Una discusión sobre la reglamentación de la consulta previa, libre e informada, pp 15–92

Doyle C (2014) Indigenous peoples, title to territory, rights and resources: the transformative role of free prior and informed consent. Routledge, London

Finnemore M, Sikkink K (1998) International norm dynamics and political change. Int Organ 52(4):887–917

Flemmer R (2015) Lecciones de los primeros procesos de la consulta previa en el sector de hidrocarburos en Perú. Iberoamericana 15(58):166–171

Flemmer R, Schilling-Vacaflor A (2016) Unfulfilled promises of the consultation approach: the limits to effective indigenous participation in Bolivia's and Peru's extractive industries. Third World Q 37(1):172–188

Fontana LB, Grugel J (2016) The politics of indigenous participation through "free prior informed consent": reflections from the Bolivian case. World Dev 77:249–261

Goodale M (2007) Locating right, envisioning law between the global and the local. In: Goodale M, Merry SE (eds) The practice of human rights: tracking law between the global and the local. Cambridge University Press, Cambridge, pp 1–38

Goodale M, Merry SE (eds) (2007) The practice of human rights: tracking law between the global and the local. Cambridge University Press, Cambridge

Guzmán-Gallegos MA (2017) Between oil contamination and consultation: constrained spaces of influence in Northern Peruvian Amazonia. Third World Q 38(5):1110–1127

Herrera F, García AF (eds) (2012) Estrategias y mecanismos de protección de pueblos indígenas frente a proyectos mineros y energéticos: La experiencia del Resguardo Indígena Cañamomo Lomaprieto. Resguardo Indígena Cañamomo Lomaprieto, Riosucio

Jetschke A (2011) Human rights and state security: Indonesia and the Philippines. University of Pennsylvania Press, Philadelphia

Kirsch S (2014) Mining capitalism: the relationship between corporations and their critics. University of California Press, Oakland

Leifsen E, Gustafsson M, Guzmán-Gallegos M, Schilling-Vacaflor A (2017) New mechanisms of participation in extractive governance: between technologies of governance and resistance work. Third World Q 38(5):1043–1057

Liese A (2009) Exceptional necessity – how liberal democracies contest the prohibition of torture and ill-treatment when countering terrorism. J Int Law Int Relat 5:17

McNeish JA (2017) A vote to derail extraction: popular consultation and resource sovereignty in Tolima, Colombia. Third World Q 38(5):1128–1145

Merry SE (1988) Legal pluralism. Law Soc Rev 22(5):869–896

Merry SE (1992) Anthropology, law, and transnational processes. Annu Rev Anthropol 21:357–377

Merry SE (2006) Human rights and gender violence: translating international law into local justice. University of Chicago Press, Chicago

Nolte D, Schilling-Vacaflor A (eds) (2012) New constitutionalism in Latin America: promises and practices. Routledge, London

Pellegrini L, Arismendi MOR (2012) Consultation, compensation and extraction in Bolivia after the "Left Turn": the case of oil exploration in the north of La Paz department. J Lat Am Geogr 11(2):103–112

Pérez JFJ (2012) Colombia's 1991 constitution: a rights revolution. In: Nolte D, Schilling-Vacaflor A (eds) New constitutionalism in Latin America: promises and practices. Routledge, London, pp 313–323

Risse T, Ropp SC (2013) Introduction and overview. In: Risse T, Ropp SC, Sikkink K (eds) The persistent power of human rights: from commitment to compliance. Cambridge University Press, Cambridge, pp 3–25

Rodríguez GA (2015) Hacia la progresividad del derecho a la consulta previa en Colombia. In: Rodríguez GA, Dominguez DA (eds) Las rutas de la consulta. Una discusión sobre la reglamentación de la Consulta Previa, libre e informada. ILSA and RRI, Bogotá, pp 95–124

Rodríguez CG, Morris M, Orduz Salina N, Buriticá P (2010) La consulta previa a pueblos indígenas. Los estándares del derecho internacional. Universidad de los Andes, Bogota

Schilling-Vacaflor A (2017a) Who controls the territory and the resources? Free, prior and informed consent (FPIC) as a contested human rights practice in Bolivia. Third World Q 38(5):1058–1074

Schilling-Vacaflor A (2017b) "If the company belongs to you, how can you be against it?" Limiting participation and taming dissent in neo-extractivist Bolivia. J Peasant Stud 44(3):658–676

Schilling-Vacaflor A, Eichler J (2017) The shady side of consultation: tactics of "Divide and Rule" in Bolivia's resource extraction. Dev Change 48(6):1439–1463

Schilling-Vacaflor A, Flemmer R (2015) Conflict transformation through prior consultation? Lessons from Peru. J Lat Am Stud 47(4):811–839

Schilling-Vacaflor A, Flemmer R, Hujber A (2018) Contesting the hydrocarbon frontiers: state depoliticizing practices and local responses in Peru. World Dev 108:74–85

Scott JC (2008) Weapons of the weak: everyday forms of peasant resistance. Yale University Press, New Haven

Sieder R (2011) "Emancipation" or "regulation"? Law, globalization and indigenous peoples' rights in post-war Guatemala. Econ Soc 40(2):239–265

Svampa M (2015) Commodities consensus: neoextractivism and enclosure of the commons in Latin America. South Atlantic Q 114(1):65–82

Szablowski D (2010) Operationalizing free, prior, and informed consent in the extractive indus-
try sector? Examining the challenges of a negotiated model of justice. Canadian Journal of
Development Studies/Revue canadienne d'études du développement 30(1–2):111–130
Taylor C (1993) To follow a rule. In: Calhoun CJ, LiPuma E, Postone M (eds) Bourdieu: critical
perspectives. Polity, Cambridge, pp 45–60
Von Benda-Beckmann FV (2001) Legal pluralism and social justice in economic and political
development. IdS Bull 32(1):46–56
Von Benda-Beckmann FV (2002) Who's afraid of legal pluralism? J Leg Pluralism Unofficial Law
34(47):37–82
Von Benda-Beckmann FV, Von Benda-Beckmann K, Eckert J (2009) Rules of law and laws of
ruling: law and governance between past and future. In: von Benda-Von Beckmann FV, von
Benda-Beckmann K, Eckert J (eds) Rules of law and laws of ruling. On the governance of law.
Law, justice and power. Ashgate, Aldershot, pp 1–30
Weitzner V (2017) "Nosotros Somos Estado": contested legalities in decision-making about
extractives affecting ancestral territories in Colombia. Third World Q 38(5):1198–1214
Wiener A (2009) Enacting meaning-in-use: qualitative research on norms and international rela-
tions. Rev Int Stud 35(1):175–193
Wiener A (2014) A theory of contestation. Springer, Berlin
Wilson R (1999) Human rights, culture and context. Anthropological perspectives. Pluto Press,
London
Zürn M (2002) From interdependence to globalization. In: Carlsnaes W, Risse T, Simmons BA
(eds) Handbook of international relations. Sage, London, pp 235–254

Almut Schilling-Vacaflor is postdoctoral researcher in the research project "Governance of
Environmental Sustainability in Telecoupled Systems (GOVERNECT)" at the University of
Osnabrück. Before that, she worked at the GIGA Institute of Latin American Studies and led two
research projects about the right to free, prior and informed consent (FPIC). She holds a degree in
sociology and a PhD in cultural and social anthropology from the University of Vienna. Her
research focusses on resource governance, law and society, participation, sustainability, socio-
environmental conflicts, human rights, indigenous peoples, the Andean countries and Brazil.

State-Investor Contracts and Human Rights: Taking a Critical Look at Transparency and Participation

Nora Götzmann

Contents

1 Introduction 339
2 State-Investor Contracts in the Extractive Industries 341
   2.1 The Role and Function of State-Investor Contracts 342
   2.2 State-Investor Contracts as a Governance Tool in the Mining Sector 343
   2.3 Contractual and Licensing Regimes 344
   2.4 Current Trends Concerning State-Investor Contracts 347
3 Key Human Rights Issues Associated with State-Investor Contracts 350
   3.1 Human Rights Coverage in State-Investor Contracts 350
   3.2 Asymmetry in Capacity and Information of Negotiating Parties 353
   3.3 Stabilisation Clauses and Regulatory Chill 355
   3.4 Transparency, Public Sector Oversight and Monitoring 359
   3.5 Access to Remedy and Dispute Settlement 364
4 Conclusions 370
References 373

1 Introduction

This chapter addresses the topic of state-investor contracts from a human rights perspective, focusing in particular on transparency and participation. A state-investor contract is an agreement between a host government and a foreign investor that governs the fiscal, regulatory and other governance aspects of a foreign direct

N. Götzmann (✉)
Human Rights and Business, The Danish Institute for Human Rights,
Copenhagen, Denmark

Centre for Social Responsibility in Mining, Sustainable Minerals Institute, The University of
Queensland, Brisbane, QLD, Australia
e-mail: nog@humanrights.dk

© Springer Nature Switzerland AG 2019   339
I. Feichtner et al. (eds.), *Human Rights in the Extractive Industries*,
Interdisciplinary Studies in Human Rights 3,
https://doi.org/10.1007/978-3-030-11382-7_13

investment (FDI) project.[1] Whilst there is a trend towards using the generally applicable domestic law of a country to govern FDI projects, state-investor contracts remain prominent in some global regions and industries, for example, the extractive industries[2] in Africa.

State-investor contracts as a governance tool in the extractive industries have considerable history. One of the main objectives from an investor's point of view is the stability and certainty that a state-investor contract seeks to provide, particularly in regulatory environments where applicable legislation (e.g. investment, environmental, labour and other relevant laws) is underdeveloped or subject to frequent changes, and other political and fiscal risks are prominent. Thus, on the one hand, it has been argued that state-investor contracts present a key tool for governments of the global south to attract and maintain FDI in the extractive industries. On the other hand, it has been suggested that such contracts are problematic from a human rights and good governance perspective,[3] for reasons such as lack of transparency and participation in the way they are negotiated, implemented and monitored. Critical perspectives on state-investor contracts contend, for example, that these can disincentivise host governments to regulate in the public interest; and make it harder for them to improve applicable domestic legislation, adequately monitor FDI projects, and secure fiscal terms that can be utilised to contribute to, for instance, the progressive realisation of economic, social and cultural rights. Rights-holders, such as workers and local community members who are impacted by an extractive industries FDI project, are not party to state-investor contract negotiations, limiting their participation and voice in how such contracts and the projects they govern are implemented. As both the negotiation and content of such agreements usually remain confidential, lack of transparency has been a further key point of critique.

By examining current trends and such critiques in more detail, in this chapter I seek to illustrate some of the main shortcomings of state-investor contracts from a human rights and good governance perspective, as well as to highlight initiatives and options put forward to improve transparency and stakeholder participation in the negotiation and implementation of such contracts. It will be suggested that the trend towards favouring the exclusive or prominent use of the generally applicable law to govern extractive industries FDI projects, rather than state-investor contracts, provides opportunities for greater transparency and participation in the way that agreements governing such projects are negotiated and implemented, and should therefore be encouraged; whilst acknowledging that reducing the use of state-investor contracts in isolation is unlikely to address prominent governance and

---

[1] Thomas Reuters Practical Law, Glossary: Host Government Agreement, https://uk.practicallaw. thomsonreuters.com/5-501-4985?transitionType=Default&contextData=(sc. Default)&firstPage=true&bhcp=1 (last accessed 1 October 2018).

[2] In this chapter defined as the exploration and exploitation of mineral, oil and natural gas reserves—with the primary focus being on mining in Africa.

[3] Defined here as the manner in which power and authority are exercised for sustainable development, including by promoting transparency, accountability, fairness and ownership—based on international human rights standards and principles.

human rights issues associated with FDI extractive industries projects. Furthermore, I will argue that significant opportunities exist to enhance transparency and participation in the use of state-investor contracts, which should be promptly realised irrespective of whether a jurisdiction favours a contractual or licensing regime for the governance of extractive industries FDI.

Following the introduction, the second part of the chapter will outline the nature and use of state-investor contracts in the context of extractive industries FDI, focusing predominantly on mining in Africa as state-investor contracts remain prominent in this region. The role and function of state-investor contracts in the international investment regime will be considered, as well as the respective merits of contractual and licensing regimes in the award of mineral exploration and exploitation rights in different jurisdictional contexts. Part three of the chapter will turn to examine five key human rights issues associated with state-investor contracts, namely: (1) human rights coverage in state-investor contracts; (2) asymmetry in capacity and information of negotiating parties; (3) stabilisation clauses and regulatory chill; (4) transparency, public sector oversight and monitoring; and (5) access to remedy and dispute settlement. The human rights issues and critiques that have been raised regarding these topics, focusing in particular on transparency and participation, will be discussed, and key frameworks and initiatives to address them—including the Principles for Responsible Contracts developed under the auspices of the United Nations Guiding Principles on Business and Human Rights, model mine development agreements (MMDAs), and the Extractive Industries Transparency Initiative (EITI)—will be considered. The chapter concludes by highlighting key opportunities for improving transparency and participation in state-investor contract negotiation and implementation, whilst noting the importance of considering these within the wider context of extractive industries FDI governance.

2　State-Investor Contracts in the Extractive Industries

This section of the chapter introduces state-investor contracts in the context of extractive industries. The different types of state-investor contracts will be briefly explained, including their role within the broader investment regime that also includes bilateral investment treaties (BITs) and free trade agreements (FTAs). The use and prevalence of state-investor contracts as a governance tool in the mining sector is contextualised, in particular drawing on examples from Africa. Lastly, the section will discuss how state-investor contracts relate to the generally applicable law that governs investments at the domestic level and the relationship between contractual regimes and licensing regimes. Observations regarding current trends in the use of state-investor contracts in the extractive industries conclude this section of the chapter.

2.1   The Role and Function of State-Investor Contracts

A state-investor contract is a legal agreement between a foreign investor and a host government governing the rights and obligations of the parties concerning the development, construction and operation of a project by the foreign investor.[4] These contracts are sometimes also referred to as "host government agreements". The material aspect is that the agreement is one between a host state[5] and a foreign investor, as opposed to two or more states (such as a BIT or FTA), or the investor and local communities (such as a community development agreement, land use agreement, impact benefit agreement, etc.).

In the mining context, state-investor contracts tend to have specific titles and there are several different types. The most common are "mining development" or "lease agreements", often called "concession agreements".[6] These tend to be comprehensive in scope, including content regarding: the granting of mining exploration and exploitation rights; financial arrangements; information exchange; applicable standards; state rights and obligations as well as investor rights and obligations; environmental and social provisions; and dispute resolution clauses. "Service agreements" were more common in the period following decolonisation but have been less prominent since the 1990s. Pursuant to these agreements, a government hires a company to perform its mining operations whilst retaining government control and ownership of the minerals being exploited.[7] "Investment promotion agreements" have become more common since the 1990s.[8] Specifically designed to promote investment by supplementing or supplanting national law, a notable feature of these agreements is the frequent inclusion of stabilisation clauses.[9] Such clauses either freeze the law at the time of signing of the investment agreement or compensate

---

[4] Thomas Reuters Practical Law, Glossary: Host Government Agreement, https://uk.practicallaw. thomsonreuters.com/5-501-4985?transitionType=Default&contextData=(sc. Default)&firstPage=true&bhcp=1 (last accessed 1 October 2018).

[5] A "host state" is usually defined as the state in which an FDI project is implemented, whereas a "home state" is the state in which the business enterprise is incorporated or has its primary location.

[6] Kienzler D et al., Natural Resources Contracts as a Tool for Managing the Mining Sector. Federal Ministy for Economic Cooperation and Development Germany, June 2015, https://www.bmz.de/ g7/includes/Downloadarchiv/Natural_Resource_Contracts.pdf (last accessed 1 October 2018), p. 7.

[7] Kienzler D et al., Natural Resources Contracts as a Tool for Managing the Mining Sector. Federal Ministy for Economic Cooperation and Development Germany, June 2015, https://www.bmz.de/ g7/includes/Downloadarchiv/Natural_Resource_Contracts.pdf (last accessed 1 October 2018), p. 7.

[8] Kienzler D et al., Natural Resources Contracts as a Tool for Managing the Mining Sector. Federal Ministy for Economic Cooperation and Development Germany, June 2015, https://www.bmz.de/ g7/includes/Downloadarchiv/Natural_Resource_Contracts.pdf (last accessed 1 October 2018), p. 18.

[9] See e.g., Shemberg A, Stabilisation Clauses and Human Rights. 27 May 2009, https://www.ifc. org/wps/wcm/connect/9feb5b00488555eab8c4fa6a6515bb18/Stabilization%2BPaper. pdf?MOD=AJPERES (last accessed 1 October 2018).

investors for the costs incurred due to compliance with updated laws and regulations (as discussed further below, such clauses have been extensively critiqued from a human rights perspective for arguably dis-incentivising states to regulate in the public interest[10]).

2.2 State-Investor Contracts as a Governance Tool in the Mining Sector

State-investor contracts have been a governance feature in the extractive industries to, first and foremost, promote FDI by providing certainty for investors through granting tenure rights and setting clear terms and conditions. In particular, such contracts have been used in contexts where domestic law might be weak, poorly implemented or subject to rapid and unpredictable changes.[11] Another context may be countries where the mining industry is new and associated laws and regulations not yet developed, i.e. contracts are used as an alternative to a well-developed legal and licensing regime.[12]

Essentially, this means that state-investor contracts are predominantly employed to govern extractive industries FDI projects in the global south.[13] Globally, there is a strong regional trend to use contracts and contract-based regimes for the mining sector in Africa, as well as some Asian countries with young mining sectors, for example Mongolia.[14] Contracts are used less in Latin America and the global north, including countries with mining-heavy economies such as Australia, Canada, or

---

[10] See also the contribution by Frank in this volume.

[11] Kienzler D et al., Natural Resources Contracts as a Tool for Managing the Mining Sector. Federal Ministy for Economic Cooperation and Development Germany, June 2015, https://www.bmz.de/g7/includes/Downloadarchiv/Natural_Resource_Contracts.pdf (last accessed 1 October 2018), p. 7; Smaller C, The IISD Guide to Negotiating Investment Contracts for Farmland and Water. IISD, November 2014, https://www.iisd.org/sites/default/files/publications/iisd-guide-negotiating-investment-contracts-farmland-water_1.pdf (last accessed 1 October 2018); UN Human Rights Council, Principles for Responsible Contracts. Integrating the Management of Human Rights Risks into State-Investor Contract Negotiations. Guidance for Negotiators, UN Doc. A/HRC/17/31/Add.3, 21 March 2011.

[12] Kienzler D et al., Natural Resources Contracts as a Tool for Managing the Mining Sector. Federal Ministy for Economic Cooperation and Development Germany, June 2015, https://www.bmz.de/g7/includes/Downloadarchiv/Natural_Resource_Contracts.pdf (last accessed 1 October 2018), p. 7.

[13] Halland et al. (2015), p. 71; Kienzler D et al., Natural Resources Contracts as a Tool for Managing the Mining Sector. Federal Ministy for Economic Cooperation and Development Germany, June 2015, https://www.bmz.de/g7/includes/Downloadarchiv/Natural_Resource_Contracts.pdf (last accessed 1 October 2018), p. 14.

[14] Kienzler D et al., Natural Resources Contracts as a Tool for Managing the Mining Sector. Federal Ministy for Economic Cooperation and Development Germany, June 2015, https://www.bmz.de/g7/includes/Downloadarchiv/Natural_Resource_Contracts.pdf (last accessed 1 October 2018), p. 7.

Chile, all of which favour the use of domestic law and licensing over the use of individually negotiated contracts.[15]

Signed early in the project lifecycle—often before an investor enters a country—state-investor contracts usually run for a long time. The duration of a mining project can easily be 50+ years; frequently, the initial contractual term will be for 25–30 years, with the possibility of extension for a further 10–25 years.[16] Whilst some agreements, in particular newer contracts, make provision for contract re-negotiation during this period—including to take account of legislative, regulatory and other changes and updates—many contracts run for a long time before they are re-negotiated (if at all).

2.3   Contractual and Licensing Regimes

In simple terms, the two primary regimes for granting and administering mineral rights are contractual and licensing regimes.[17]

In a contract-based regime, mineral exploration and exploitation rights and obligations are individually negotiated between the state and foreign investors for specific projects.[18] This means that in such a regime there may be a host of different contracts in place governing different mining projects according to varied terms and conditions. Negotiated contracts can have the benefit of being able to tailor the respective governing terms and conditions specifically to a particular project, including being able to take account of the location, commodity, community context, government and investor positions, and so forth.[19] In particular in the case of green-

---

[15] Kienzler D et al., Natural Resources Contracts as a Tool for Managing the Mining Sector. Federal Ministy for Economic Cooperation and Development Germany, June 2015, https://www.bmz.de/g7/includes/Downloadarchiv/Natural_Resource_Contracts.pdf (last accessed 1 October 2018), p. 7.

[16] Creative Commons, Mining Contracts: How to Read and Understand Them. International Senior Lawyers Project and Open Oil and Columbia Center on Sustainable Investment and Natural Resources Governance Institute, June 2014, https://s3.amazonaws.com/s3.documentcloud.org/documents/1279596/mining-contracts-how-to-read-and-understand-them.pdf (last accessed 1 October 2018), p. 102.

[17] Creative Commons, Mining Contracts: How to Read and Understand Them. International Senior Lawyers Project and Open Oil and Columbia Center on Sustainable Investment and Natural Resources Governance Institute, June 2014, https://s3.amazonaws.com/s3.documentcloud.org/documents/1279596/mining-contracts-how-to-read-and-understand-them.pdf (last accessed 1 October 2018), p. 12; Halland et al. (2015), p. 71.

[18] Creative Commons, Mining Contracts: How to Read and Understand Them. International Senior Lawyers Project and Open Oil and Columbia Center on Sustainable Investment and Natural Resources Governance Institute, June 2014, https://s3.amazonaws.com/s3.documentcloud.org/documents/1279596/mining-contracts-how-to-read-and-understand-them.pdf (last accessed 1 October 2018), p. 12; Halland et al. (2015), p. 71; Kienzler D et al., Natural Resources Contracts as a Tool for Managing the Mining Sector. Federal Ministy for Economic Cooperation and Development Germany, June 2015, https://www.bmz.de/g7/includes/Downloadarchiv/Natural_Resource_Contracts.pdf (last accessed 1 October 2018), p. 7.

[19] Kienzler D et al., Natural Resources Contracts as a Tool for Managing the Mining Sector. Federal Ministy for Economic Cooperation and Development Germany, June 2015, https://www.bmz.de/

field projects, new types of mining, or so-called "mega projects", it has been argued that contracts provide the flexibility to account for and respond to the specificity of the governance needs of a particular project.[20] On the other hand, contractual regimes are criticised as the multiplicity of different contracts pose additional challenges for the government as regulator—usually in contexts where government regulatory capacity is already weak—for example, by having to monitor different projects according to different standards specified in the various contracts.[21] Furthermore, the disparity in negotiation capacity between host governments and foreign investors has been raised as a key point of critique, noting that often foreign investors will have better access to geological data about deposits, fiscal modelling and prediction, as well as legal and negotiation expertise, as compared to often under-resourced host governments.[22] These and additional points are discussed further in section three of the chapter.

In a licensing regime, the process of granting mineral licences and all accompanying rights and obligations are defined and granted according to the generally applicable domestic law.[23] Such regimes are more prevalent in jurisdictions with well-developed legal systems and/or mining sectors.[24] It has been suggested that licensing regimes are favourable for several reasons, including: that there are fewer opportunities for corruption; that they reduce the information asymmetries often found in contract negotiations; that public oversight is increased and there is less burden on government administration; and that they provide investors with greater security of tenure.[25] Complexities and complications associated with having

---

g7/includes/Downloadarchiv/Natural_Resource_Contracts.pdf (last accessed 1 October 2018), p. 16.

[20] Dietsche E, Mineral Taxation Regimes. A review of issues and challenges in their design and application. Commonwealth Secretariat and International Council on Mining and Metals, Feburary 2009, https://www.icmm.com/website/publications/pdfs/social-and-economic-development/minerals-taxation-regimes (last accessed 1 October 2018), p. 32.

[21] Kienzler D et al., Natural Resources Contracts as a Tool for Managing the Mining Sector. Federal Ministy for Economic Cooperation and Development Germany, June 2015, https://www.bmz.de/g7/includes/Downloadarchiv/Natural_Resource_Contracts.pdf (last accessed 1 October 2018), p. 7.

[22] See e.g., Halland et al. (2015), p. 58.

[23] Halland et al. (2015), p. 71; Kienzler D et al., Natural Resources Contracts as a Tool for Managing the Mining Sector. Federal Ministy for Economic Cooperation and Development Germany, June 2015, https://www.bmz.de/g7/includes/Downloadarchiv/Natural_Resource_Contracts.pdf (last accessed 1 October 2018), p. 12.

[24] Kienzler D et al., Natural Resources Contracts as a Tool for Managing the Mining Sector. Federal Ministy for Economic Cooperation and Development Germany, June 2015, https://www.bmz.de/g7/includes/Downloadarchiv/Natural_Resource_Contracts.pdf (last accessed 1 October 2018), p. 7.

[25] See e.g., Dietsche E, Mineral Taxation Regimes. A review of issues and challenges in their design and application. Commonwealth Secretariat and International Council on Mining and Metals, Feburary 2009, https://www.icmm.com/website/publications/pdfs/social-and-economic-development/minerals-taxation-regimes (last accessed 1 October 2018), p. 9; Kienzler D et al., Natural Resources Contracts as a Tool for Managing the Mining Sector. Federal Ministy for Economic Cooperation and Development Germany, June 2015, https://www.bmz.de/g7/includes/

multiple contracts in play, disparity between progressive changes in legislation over time and fixed contractual terms, and corruption risks, arguably are avoided or lessened in licensing regimes, as the laws apply equally and the democratic process provides the necessary checks and balances.[26] However, licensing regimes may not provide the same level of flexibility as contractual regimes, for example, to respond to the specificity of particular projects. It should also be acknowledged that in the case of a licensing regime being implemented by an incompetent or corrupt government, the public policy arguments suggesting that greater transparency and democracy are to be found in a licensing regime may not carry the same weight.

Whilst contractual and licensing regimes thus can be compared and contrasted, in practice many regimes in fact contain a mixture of the two approaches, some relying more heavily on contracts, others more heavily on the generally applicable domestic law.[27] Whilst almost all jurisdictions have a mining law, only some provide for the possibility of negotiated contracts; countries in the global south tend to be on the contractual end of the spectrum.[28]

As such, the relationship between state-investor contracts and domestic law differs greatly depending on the particular jurisdiction. In short, three variants can be distinguished[29]: (1) pure licensing regime, i.e. all terms and conditions are governed by the generally applicable law; (2) the contract supplements the domestic law, i.e. the contract will refer to the domestic law and specific contractual provisions provide additional detail regarding terms and conditions that are not elaborated in the law—this model of supplementing the domestic law may be used in contexts where a country's mining laws are inadequate or underdeveloped; and (3) contractual terms supplant the domestic law—this is most commonly applied to fiscal provisions. Variants (2) and (3) may apply to a contract in its entirety, or a combination of the two approaches may also be used within a single contract; for example, one contractual provision may supplement the domestic law by elaborating specific local content provisions that are only specified in general terms in the domestic law, whereas another contractual clause in the same agreement may supplant an aspect of the domestic law, such as a tax exemption or incentive being granted by the terms of the agreement.

Downloadarchiv/Natural_Resource_Contracts.pdf (last accessed 1 October 2018), p. 12; Sachs et al. (2013), p. 367.

[26] Dietsche E, Mineral Taxation Regimes. A review of issues and challenges in their design and application. Commonwealth Secretariat and International Council on Mining and Metals, Feburary 2009, https://www.icmm.com/website/publications/pdfs/social-and-economic-development/minerals-taxation-regimes (last accessed 1 October 2018), p. 9.

[27] Halland et al. (2015), p. 71.

[28] Halland et al. (2015), p. 71; Kienzler D et al., Natural Resources Contracts as a Tool for Managing the Mining Sector. Federal Ministy for Economic Cooperation and Development Germany, June 2015, https://www.bmz.de/g7/includes/Downloadarchiv/Natural_Resource_Contracts.pdf (last accessed 1 October 2018), p. 16.

[29] Based on: Kienzler D et al., Natural Resources Contracts as a Tool for Managing the Mining Sector. Federal Ministy for Economic Cooperation and Development Germany, June 2015, https://www.bmz.de/g7/includes/Downloadarchiv/Natural_Resource_Contracts.pdf (last accessed 1 October 2018), p. 16.

The manner in which a state-investor contract comes into force will also vary depending on the type of jurisdiction and regime. In many countries, contracts are ratified by the legislature, essentially making them laws unto themselves.[30]

2.4 Current Trends Concerning State-Investor Contracts

Globally, there is a trend towards using licensing regimes that are based on the generally applicable domestic law, thereby reducing the exercise of discretion in the granting of mineral rights.[31] For example, Zambia's Mines and Minerals Development Act 2008 expressly prohibits the government from entering into any special agreements and annuls any existing development agreements.[32] Similarly, Liberia, Guinea and the Democratic Republic of the Congo (DRC) in recent years have all begun to move away from granting mineral rights pursuant to individually agreed contracts.[33]

The use of "model contracts" has also been on the rise. In 2011, the International Bar Association developed a MMDA, including a selection of good practice sample clauses as well as associated commentary.[34] Individual countries are increasingly developing their own model mining contracts.[35] Burkina Faso, the DRC, Guinea,

---

[30] Kienzler D et al., Natural Resources Contracts as a Tool for Managing the Mining Sector. Federal Ministy for Economic Cooperation and Development Germany, June 2015, https://www.bmz.de/g7/includes/Downloadarchiv/Natural_Resource_Contracts.pdf (last accessed 1 October 2018), p. 16.

[31] Barma NH et al., Rents to Riches? The Political Economy of Natural Resource-Led Development. World Bank, 2012, http://documents.worldbank.org/curated/en/545221468150583397/pdf/65957 0PUB0EPI10737B0Rents0to0Riches.pdf (last accessed 1 October 2018); Columbia Center on Sustainable Investment, Outcome, Governing Natural Resources. Lessons learned from good governance initiatives for extractive industry investments and large land-based agricultural investment, 11 November 2014, http://ccsi.columbia.edu/files/2014/11/Governing-Natural-Resources-Outcome-Note-Columbia-Center-on-Sustainable-Investment-1.pdf (last accessed 1 October 2018), p. 6; Kienzler D et al., Natural Resources Contracts as a Tool for Managing the Mining Sector. Federal Ministy for Economic Cooperation and Development Germany, June 2015, https://www.bmz.de/g7/includes/Downloadarchiv/Natural_Resource_Contracts.pdf (last accessed 1 October 2018), p. 16; Williams (2012), p. 422.

[32] Kienzler D et al., Natural Resources Contracts as a Tool for Managing the Mining Sector. Federal Ministy for Economic Cooperation and Development Germany, June 2015, https://www.bmz.de/g7/includes/Downloadarchiv/Natural_Resource_Contracts.pdf (last accessed 1 October 2018), p. 8.

[33] Kienzler D et al., Natural Resources Contracts as a Tool for Managing the Mining Sector. Federal Ministy for Economic Cooperation and Development Germany, June 2015, https://www.bmz.de/g7/includes/Downloadarchiv/Natural_Resource_Contracts.pdf (last accessed 1 October 2018), p. 8.

[34] International Bar Association, Model Mine Development Agreement, 4 April 2011, http://www.mmdaproject.org/presentations/MMDA1_0_110404Bookletv3.pdf (last accessed 1 October 2018).

[35] Columbia Center on Sustainable Investment, Outcome, Governing Natural Resources. Lessons learned from good governance initiatives for extractive industry investments and large land-based

Mongolia, Mozambique and Sierra Leone are examples of countries that currently are developing, or recently have developed such model agreements.[36] In some cases, a model contract may be stipulated for use by the government, or it may form the basis upon which an individualised contract is negotiated providing the parameters for the negotiation and the contract.[37] It has been suggested that model contracts may be a useful tool in moving towards a licensing regime, as they have the potential to put in place interim governance measures while the generally applicable law and licensing regime are developed and implemented.[38]

Lastly, there is a clear trend of more standards and initiatives promoting transparency of state-investor contracts. The EITI (an initiative promoting the open and accountable management of extractive industries resources[39]), for example, encourages its members to publish their mining contracts.[40] According to EITI Guidance Note 7 on contract transparency, implementing countries are encouraged to publicly disclose any contracts and licences that provide the terms attached to the exploitation of oil, gas and minerals.[41] It is also a requirement that the EITI country report documents a government's policy on disclosure of contracts and licences that govern the exploration and exploitation of oil, gas and minerals.[42] Consequently, several domestic EITI implementing acts are now requiring governments to publish state-investor contracts.[43] Similarly, the Open Government Partnership (a multilateral

agricultural investment, 11 November 2014, http://ccsi.columbia.edu/files/2014/11/Governing-Natural-Resources-Outcome-Note-Columbia-Center-on-Sustainable-Investment-1.pdf   (last accessed 1 October 2018), p. 6.

[36] Kienzler D et al., Natural Resources Contracts as a Tool for Managing the Mining Sector. Federal Ministy for Economic Cooperation and Development Germany, June 2015, https://www.bmz.de/g7/includes/Downloadarchiv/Natural_Resource_Contracts.pdf (last accessed 1 October 2018), p. 8.

[37] Kienzler D et al., Natural Resources Contracts as a Tool for Managing the Mining Sector. Federal Ministy for Economic Cooperation and Development Germany, June 2015, https://www.bmz.de/g7/includes/Downloadarchiv/Natural_Resource_Contracts.pdf (last accessed 1 October 2018), p. 8.

[38] See e.g., Kienzler D et al., Natural Resources Contracts as a Tool for Managing the Mining Sector. Federal Ministy for Economic Cooperation and Development Germany, June 2015, https://www.bmz.de/g7/includes/Downloadarchiv/Natural_Resource_Contracts.pdf (last accessed 1 October 2018), p. 12; Smaller C, The IISD Guide to Negotiating Investment Contracts for Farmland and Water. IISD, November 2014, https://www.iisd.org/sites/default/files/publications/iisd-guide-negotiating-investment-contracts-farmland-water_1.pdf (last accessed 1 October 2018).

[39] See also the chapter by Feldt in this volume.

[40] EITI, Contract Transparency in EITI Countries. A Review on How Countries Report on Government's Contract Transparency Policy, August 2015, https://eiti.org/sites/default/files/documents/eiti_brief_on_contract_transparency.pdf (last accessed 1 October 2018).

[41] EITI, Guidance notes and standard terms of reference, https://eiti.org/guidance (last accessed 1 October 2018).

[42] EITI, Guidance Note 7. Contract Transparency, September 2017, https://eiti.org/sites/default/files/documents/guidance-note-7-contract-transparency.pdf (last accessed 1 October 2018).

[43] EITI, Contract Transparency in EITI Countries. A Review on How Countries Report on Government's Contract Transparency Policy, August 2015, https://eiti.org/sites/default/files/documents/eiti_brief_on_contract_transparency.pdf (last accessed 1 October 2018), pp. 13–14.

initiative launched in 2011 that aims to secure concrete commitments from partici-pating governments to promote transparency, empower citizens and fight corrup-tion) includes a thematic area on natural resources that encourages the disclosure of extractive industries state-investor contracts.[44] Contract disclosure is also a priority area for extractive industries clients (i.e. investors) of the International Finance Corporation (IFC), which requires clients to commit to disclosing contracts, as well as revenue payments.[45] The International Monetary Fund's (IMF) Guide on Resource Revenue Transparency[46] and the Natural Resource Charter (a set of principles for governments and societies on how to best harness extractive resources for develop-ment[47]) consider publication of state-investor contracts to be good practice.

These trends should also be viewed in the context of new frameworks demanding business respect for human rights and attention to the role of business in sustainable development. For example, the United Nations Guiding Principles on Business and Human Rights, which were unanimously endorsed by the Human Rights Council in 2011, re-iterate the state duty to protect human rights from adverse human rights impacts of third parties, including businesses, as well as establishing the interna-tional norm of the "corporate responsibility to respect" human rights, meaning that businesses are expected to exercise due diligence to avoid and address any adverse impacts with which they are involved.[48] Relatedly, the 2030 Agenda for Sustainable Development and the Sustainable Development Goals refer to the need to ensure the responsible and sustainable governance of natural resources (Goal 12) and to pro-mote clean energy (Goal 7) in the interest of sustainable development.[49]

The implications of such trends in terms of facilitating greater transparency and participation for stakeholders, in particular rights-holders, in the governance of extractive industries FDI projects, is discussed further in the following section of the chapter.

---

[44] Open Government Partnership, Theme: Natural Resources, https://www.opengovpartnership.org/theme/natural-resources-0 (last accessed 1 October 2018). To become a member of the OGP, participating countries must endorse a high-level Open Government Declaration, deliver a country action plan developed in consultation with the public, and commit to independent reporting on their progress going forward.

[45] IFC, IFC's priorities in oil, gas and mining, http://www.ifc.org/wps/wcm/connect/industry_ext_content/ifc_external_corporate_site/ogm+home/priorities (last accessed 1 October 2018).

[46] IMF, Guidance on Resource Revenue Transparency, 2007, https://www.imf.org/external/np/pp/2007/eng/101907g.pdf, p. 6.

[47] NRGI, Natural Resource Charter. Second Edition, 2014, https://resourcegovernance.org/approach/natural-resource-charter (last accessed 1 October 2018).

[48] UN Human Rights Council, UN Guiding Principles on Business and Human Rights, UN Doc. A/HRC/17/31, 21 March 2011.

[49] See e.g., UN General Assembly, Transforming our world: the 2030 Agenda for Sustainable Development, UN Doc. A/RES/70/1, 21 October 2015; UN, Sustainable Development Knowledge Platform: Mining. 15 October 2015, https://sustainabledevelopment.un.org/topics/mining (last accessed 1 October 2018).

3 Key Human Rights Issues Associated with State-Investor Contracts

This section of the chapter takes a closer look at some of the key human rights issues that have been raised regarding the negotiation, content and implementation of state-investor contracts in the extractive industries. For the purposes of this discussion, this section is divided into the following five sub-sections:

1. human rights coverage in state-investor contracts;
2. asymmetry in capacity and information of negotiating parties;
3. stabilisation clauses and regulatory chill;
4. transparency, public sector oversight and monitoring; and
5. access to remedy and dispute settlement.

In particular, the shortcomings of state-investor contracts with regard to transparency and stakeholder participation will be noted, including reflections on how such shortcomings might be addressed. Specific governance frameworks and initiatives promoting greater transparency and participation in state-investor contract negotiations and implementation are referred to throughout.

3.1 Human Rights Coverage in State-Investor Contracts

Most state-investor contracts do not explicitly address human rights.[50] The length and level of detail provided by state-investor contracts governing mining projects vary considerably. Some contracts are very short and unspecific, whereas others provide a great level of detail regarding the rights and obligations of the state and the investor.

In recent years, discussion regarding the inclusion of human rights clauses in investment agreements, including state-investor contracts, has increased.[51] Some argue that the inclusion of such clauses is necessary and desirable to facilitate increased consideration of human rights in the implementation of investment agreements, including any potential dispute resolution or claims regarding non-compliance with such agreements. Discussion has included arguments both for the inclusion of "human rights clauses" as such (i.e. clauses that explicitly refer to international human rights standards and principles), and/or the inclusion of clauses that speak to human rights related topics, such as labour rights or environmental man-

---

[50] Kienzler D et al., Natural Resources Contracts as a Tool for Managing the Mining Sector. Federal Ministy for Economic Cooperation and Development Germany, June 2015, https://www.bmz.de/g7/includes/Downloadarchiv/Natural_Resource_Contracts.pdf (last accessed 1 October 2018); Mitchell L, Natural Resource Contracts: A Practical Guide. Environmental Law Alliance World, https://www.elaw.org/sites/default/files/images_content/general_page_images/publications/Natural_Resource_Contracts_Guide.pdf (last accessed 1 October 2018).

[51] See e.g., Cotula and Tienhaara (2013), p. 282; Gordon (2008).

agement (without explicitly referring to these topics in terms of international human rights standards and principles). Arguments for the inclusion of "human rights clauses" in state-investor contracts have been less prominent than for inclusion of such clauses in other types of investment agreements, such as BITs or FTAs. Instead, commentators have focused on the inclusion of clauses in state-investor contracts that[52]: (1) speak to specific human rights related topics, such as labour rights, community-level grievance mechanisms, security arrangements and so forth; (2) the avoidance of specific types of clauses that inhibit progressive legislative development of human rights relevant laws and regulations, e.g. stabilisation clauses, as discussed below; and (3) stipulating operating standards for projects that by implication will contribute to enhanced human rights enjoyment, e.g. contractually requiring the use of best practice standards for mine waste management, which as a follow-on effect would contribute to avoiding pollution which has an adverse impact on the rights to health and a clean environment.

Strengthening provisions relevant to human rights in state-investor contracts (e.g. on stakeholder participation, publication of the contract, dispute resolution, security arrangements) and/or the use of "human rights clauses" could make a significant contribution to enhancing transparency and participation in the implementation of projects governed by such contracts, and to set clear expectations that projects respect human rights.

The Principles for Responsible Contracts, developed under the auspices of the United Nations Guiding Principles on Business and Human Rights, for example, provide concrete and practical suggestions on the types of topics that might be included in state-investor contract negotiations and agreements.[53] The product of four years of research and inclusive multi-stakeholder dialogue, these ten principles represent a set of key areas where human rights should be considered at the state-investor contract negotiation stage. The Principles cover a range of subjects, including: negotiations planning; operating standards; stabilisation clauses; compliance and monitoring; transparency; security; grievance resolution; and community engagement. Each principle is supported by a brief explanation, a summary of key implications of the principle, and a checklist for state and company negotiators. Notably, the Principles focus on both the duties of the state, as well as the responsibilities of the investor, to include human rights considerations in state-investor contract negotiations. They are based on the premise that respect for human rights in the context of investment projects requires early identification and management of potential adverse human rights impacts, the establishment of clear roles and responsibilities for the management of such impacts, appropriate cost allocations for human rights management, and agreed procedures for managing human rights

---

[52] See e.g., UN Human Rights Council, Principles for Responsible Contracts. Integrating the Management of Human Rights Risks into State-Investor Contract Negotiations. Guidance for Negotiators, UN Doc. A/HRC/17/31/Add.3, 21 March 2011.

[53] UN Human Rights Council, Principles for Responsible Contracts. Integrating the Management of Human Rights Risks into State-Investor Contract Negotiations. Guidance for Negotiators, UN Doc. A/HRC/17/31/Add.3, 21 March 2011.

impacts throughout the project lifecycle. They also place an emphasis on the inclusion of topics in the state-investor contract that relate to both process and content, which is important from a human rights perspective as meaningful participation of rights-holders and other stakeholders in decision-making that affects them is both a key principle as well as a substantive right. For example, stakeholder engagement and grievance resolution have human rights process dimensions, potentially enabling the greater participation of rights-holders in decision-making related to the FDI project and the making of claims regarding non-compliance with due diligence and performance expectations. Similarly, the inclusion of content outlining the respective monitoring and inspection responsibilities of the state, investor, and independent third parties, can contribute to re-enforcing the respective roles and obligations of the state and investor with regard to human rights, i.e. the state duties to "respect, protect and fulfil" and the corporate "responsibility to respect".[54] This point is discussed below, in the context of public oversight and monitoring. The Principles take account of the fact that state-investor contracts are often agreed at an early stage in the project lifecycle, when not all specific needs of the project may be known yet, but point out that the contract can nevertheless make provisions for the subsequent development of the relevant plans and application of standards.[55] For example, whilst the precise structure and implementation of a project-level grievance mechanism may not be known at the signing of an early exploration agreement, the agreement could provide the commitment for the timely subsequent development and implementation of such a grievance mechanism. Importantly, the inclusion of such aspects into early agreements such as state-investor contracts can also facilitate the timely consideration and agreement regarding cost coverage for community engagement, grievance resolution, security provision and so forth, all of which have a direct relationship to the human rights enjoyment of workers and communities impacted by the project.[56] This can be critical for mining projects, where any subsequent disagreement regarding cost coverage and cost sharing between the state, investor and other relevant parties may result in lower resource allocation for human rights due diligence activities as compared to other operational priorities. Lastly, agreeing upon transparency of the contract content from the outset can be a way of contributing to enhanced transparency, both of state-investor contracts, as well as the subsequent due diligence processes that they may provide for (e.g. by including a commitment to publishing impact assessments for the project).

In summary, given that a state-investor contract constitutes a significant governance tool for a specific extractive industries FDI project—including attributing

---

[54] UN Human Rights Council, Principles for Responsible Contracts. Integrating the Management of Human Rights Risks into State-Investor Contract Negotiations. Guidance for Negotiators, UN Doc. A/HRC/17/31/Add.3, 21 March 2011, p. 20.

[55] UN Human Rights Council, Principles for Responsible Contracts. Integrating the Management of Human Rights Risks into State-Investor Contract Negotiations. Guidance for Negotiators, UN Doc. A/HRC/17/31/Add.3, 21 March 2011, p. 6.

[56] UN Human Rights Council, Principles for Responsible Contracts. Integrating the Management of Human Rights Risks into State-Investor Contract Negotiations. Guidance for Negotiators, UN Doc. A/HRC/17/31/Add.3, 21 March 2011, p. 22.

roles and responsibilities between different duty-bearers—the explicit inclusion of human rights relevant content can be a means of facilitating greater transparency, participation and protection for project-impacted rights-holders. Enhanced human rights due diligence and performance may be achieved through applying a human rights lens when shaping the various contractual clauses and/or the inclusion of a stand-alone human rights clause, recognising that these two approaches are of course not mutually exclusive. The Principles for Responsible Contracts and good practice model contracts can assist in guiding such integration.

3.2 Asymmetry in Capacity and Information of Negotiating Parties

One prominent human rights critique of state-investor contracts concerns the frequent asymmetries in the capacity and information of the negotiating parties. Such asymmetry is problematic because "there is a close connection between content and the process through which contracts are developed".[57]

Often, foreign direct investors in the mining industry have more industry experience, better access to geological data, fiscal know-how and predictions regarding the commodity market, and legal expertise in negotiation, than their state counterparts.[58] Moreover, host states are frequently hampered in state-investor negotiations by factors such as lack of human and financial resources, inconsistencies between government departments (creating multiple and potentially conflicting objectives for the negotiating team, as well as a potential lack of a clear mandate and negotiating position), and sometimes have more limited experience with the mining industry.[59]

To address such asymmetries, a number of initiatives have been put in place, primarily donor-driven and funded, to support host governments in contract negotiations, for example, through capacity building or facilitating access to independent technical support in negotiations.[60] Key current initiatives facilitating access to technical advisory services for host governments in negotiations include international

---

[57] Cotula and Tienhaara (2013), p. 286.

[58] Columbia Center on Sustainable Investment, Background Paper for Second Workshop on Contract Negotiation Support for Developing Host Countries. 18–19 July 2012, http://ccsi.columbia.edu/files/2014/01/Background_Paper_for_July_18-19_Negotiation_Assistance_Workshop.pdf (last accessed 1 October 2018), p. 27; Halland et al. (2015), p. 58.

[59] Columbia Center on Sustainable Investment, Background Paper for Second Workshop on Contract Negotiation Support for Developing Host Countries. 18–19 July 2012, http://ccsi.columbia.edu/files/2014/01/Background_Paper_for_July_18-19_Negotiation_Assistance_Workshop.pdf (last accessed 1 October 2018), p. 5; Halland et al. (2015), p. 58.

[60] See e.g., Halland et al. (2015), p. 58; Kienzler D et al., Natural Resources Contracts as a Tool for Managing the Mining Sector. Federal Ministy for Economic Cooperation and Development Germany, June 2015, https://www.bmz.de/g7/includes/Downloadarchiv/Natural_Resource_Contracts.pdf (last accessed 1 October 2018), p. 59.

workshops conducted by the World Bank[61] and BIOPAMA,[62] as well as specialist technical support services by various organisations including donors, multilateral financial institutions, non-governmental organisations, and legal service organisations and providers.[63]

As is evident from a compilation of host government support initiatives and services put together by the Columbia Center on Sustainable Investment, however, host government support tends to focus on fiscal and technical advisory services, rather than social, environmental and human rights aspects.[64] The fiscal arrangements around contracts of course have significant human rights implications—i.e. a well-structured contract resulting in good revenue and tax collection by the government from the project can lead to the spending of such funds on, for example, government essential services such as healthcare or education, having a direct impact on the human rights enjoyment of the country's citizens. Yet, the notable absence of the inclusion of environmental, social and human rights expertise and topics in host country negotiation support is reflected in the continued lack of consideration of such aspects in the negotiation of state-investor contracts. Arguably, this absence contributes directly to inhibiting the development of a more holistic approach to the role and implementation of FDI mining projects that adequately considers both the constraints and potential of the sector's contribution to sustainable development.

Whilst it is important to acknowledge and address the constraints faced by many host governments in state-investor contract negotiation—with the view to creating a more level playing field for such negotiations to take place—the role of the investor in the negotiation should also be addressed. Precisely for this purpose, the Principles for Responsible Contracts, introduced above, address the role of both negotiating parties, including guidance points that address the state specifically, the investor specifically, and points common to both negotiating parties.[65] In one subsequent guide, the points specific to the investor are further distilled into a checklist targeted

---

[61] World Bank, Building Negotiating Capacity in Africa to Make the Most from Mining Deals. 5 February 2015, http://www.worldbank.org/en/news/feature/2015/02/05/building-negotiating-capacity-in-africa-to-make-the-most-from-mining-deals (last accessed 1 October 2018).

[62] IUCN (2015), Building capacity for better negotiating skills: an inspiring solution for Africa. 8 April 2015, https://www.iucn.org/content/building-capacity-better-negotiation-skills-inspiring-solution-africa (last accessed 1 October 2018).

[63] See Columbia Center on Sustainable Investment, Background Paper for Second Workshop on Contract Negotiation Support for Developing Host Countries. 18–19 July 2012, http://ccsi.columbia.edu/files/2014/01/Background_Paper_for_July_18-19_Negotiation_Assistance_Workshop.pdf (last accessed 1 October 2018), for a useful overview of technical support services available.

[64] See Columbia Center on Sustainable Investment, Background Paper for Second Workshop on Contract Negotiation Support for Developing Host Countries. 18–19 July 2012, http://ccsi.columbia.edu/files/2014/01/Background_Paper_for_July_18-19_Negotiation_Assistance_Workshop.pdf (last accessed 1 October 2018).

[65] UN Human Rights Council, Principles for Responsible Contracts. Integrating the Management of Human Rights Risks into State-Investor Contract Negotiations. Guidance for Negotiators, UN Doc. A/HRC/17/31/Add.3, 21 March 2011.

specifically at company negotiators.[66] The Principles for Responsible Contracts and such subsequently developed tools may be interpreted to reflect that there is not only increased attention to the issue of human rights dimensions and implications of state-investor contracts but also that investors are becoming more open to considering human rights aspects in negotiations. The increased demand for human rights training for agreement negotiators in the extractive industries sectors may substantiate such assertions.[67] However, overall, literature as well as anecdotal evidence indicate that progress is slow, and that apart from some good practice exceptions, many investors and their negotiating teams continue to disregard human rights in negotiations and agreements. As such, state-investor contracts in mining arguably remain skewed towards concessions that favour investors over the public interest of rightsholders in host states. As one government official in a recent study put it: "People negotiate agreements because they want concessions in the law. The moment the government says 'Let's talk,' it is saying it is ready to go outside the law."[68]

In moving towards creating not only more equitable playing fields for state-investor contract negotiations, but also increasing the consideration of human rights by both negotiating parties, it will be essential to further promote the inclusion of human rights considerations in the mandate and capacity of both state and investor negotiating parties. The promotion of environmental, social and human rights expertise in technical support services, as well as training and capacity building of negotiators, may contribute to this end.

3.3   Stabilisation Clauses and Regulatory Chill

One particular type of contractual clause in state-investor contracts that has received significant attention and critique from a human rights and good governance perspective are the so-called "stabilisation clauses".[69]

The term "stabilisation clause" refers to the contractual clauses in state-investor contracts that address the issue of changes in law in the host state during the life of

---

[66] Götzmann N and Jensen M H, Human Rights and State Investor Contracts. Danish Institute for Human Rights. January 2014, https://www.humanrights.dk/sites/humanrights.dk/files/media/dokumenter/udgivelser/human_rights_and_stateinvestor_contracts_2014.pdf (last accessed 1 October 2018).

[67] Columbia Center on Sustainable Investment, Background Paper for Second Workshop on Contract Negotiation Support for Developing Host Countries. 18–19 July 2012, http://ccsi.columbia.edu/files/2014/01/Background_Paper_for_July_18-19_Negotiation_Assistance_Workshop.pdf (last accessed 1 October 2018), p. 8.

[68] Cited in Kienzler D et al., Natural Resources Contracts as a Tool for Managing the Mining Sector. Federal Ministy for Economic Cooperation and Development Germany, June 2015, https://www.bmz.de/g7/includes/Downloadarchiv/Natural_Resource_Contracts.pdf (last accessed 1 October 2018), p. 20.

[69] See also the chapter by Frank in this volume.

the project.[70] In short, there are three common types[71]: (1) freezing clauses—which are designed to make new laws inapplicable to the investment as they freeze the law of the host state at the time of the signing of the contract—such clauses may be "full freezing", i.e. applying to both fiscal and non-fiscal issues, or refer to a more limited set of legislative actions, by only applying, for example, to tax and customs issues; (2) economic equilibrium clauses—which provide that whilst new laws will apply to the investment, the investor will be compensated for the cost of complying with any updated laws and regulations; for example, if more stringent environmental legislation requires the company to spend additional resources to comply with the updated environmental standards, the investor will be able to seek monetary or other types of compensation (e.g. adjusted tariffs, extension of the concession, tax reductions) for the costs of such compliance; and (3) hybrid clauses—which combine some aspects of both of the other categories. As such, stabilisation clauses can either make foreign investments immune from *bona fide* laws (including social and environmental laws) that come into force after the effective date of the agreement, or require the host state to compensate the investor for compliance with those new laws.

A 2008 study regarding the prevalence of stabilisation clauses in FDI contracts found that full freezing clauses were prevalent in the extractive industries sectors, in particular mining, and that they remained prevalent in Africa.[72] Limited economic equilibrium clauses, on the other hand, were found to be more common in OECD countries.[73] On this point, it is worth noting that the OECD, amongst other actors, cautions against the use of full freezing clauses.[74]

Stabilisation clauses have been critiqued for contributing to a "regulatory chill" in host states; it is argued that host states may be dis-incentivised from improving laws and regulations where such improvements may result in the state having to compensate investors for compliance with updated laws (or investors not needing to comply with updated legislation at all).[75] Freezing clauses, and more specifically

---

[70] Shemberg A, Stabilisation Clauses and Human Rights. 27 May 2009, https://www.ifc.org/wps/wcm/connect/9feb5b00488555eab8c4fa6a6515bb18/Stabilization%2BPaper.pdf?MOD=AJPERES (last accessed 1 October 2018), p. 4.

[71] See e.g., Shemberg A, Stabilisation Clauses and Human Rights. 27 May 2009, https://www.ifc.org/wps/wcm/connect/9feb5b00488555eab8c4fa6a6515bb18/Stabilization%2BPaper.pdf?MOD=AJPERES (last accessed 1 October 2018), pp. 5–9.

[72] Shemberg A, Stabilisation Clauses and Human Rights. 27 May 2009, https://www.ifc.org/wps/wcm/connect/9feb5b00488555eab8c4fa6a6515bb18/Stabilization%2BPaper.pdf?MOD=AJPERES (last accessed 1 October 2018), p. 22.

[73] Shemberg A, Stabilisation Clauses and Human Rights. 27 May 2009, https://www.ifc.org/wps/wcm/connect/9feb5b00488555eab8c4fa6a6515bb18/Stabilization%2BPaper.pdf?MOD=AJPERES (last accessed 1 October 2018), pp. 24–25.

[74] Shemberg A, Stabilisation Clauses and Human Rights. 27 May 2009, https://www.ifc.org/wps/wcm/connect/9feb5b00488555eab8c4fa6a6515bb18/Stabilization%2BPaper.pdf?MOD=AJPERES (last accessed 1 October 2018), pp. 35–36.

[75] See e.g., Cotula (2014), p. 20; Shemberg A, Stabilisation Clauses and Human Rights. 27 May 2009, https://www.ifc.org/wps/wcm/connect/9feb5b00488555eab8c4fa6a6515bb18/Stabilization%2BPaper.pdf?MOD=AJPERES (last accessed 1 October 2018), p. 10; Tienhaara (2006), p. 75.

full freezing clauses, are the most problematic, as they not only provide investors with an opportunity to argue that they are not obligated to adhere to new laws, but may thereby also discourage the host state from application and enforcement and thus "work to reduce the effectiveness of new laws".[76] Whilst some scholars have questioned the binding nature of stabilisation clauses, arguing that states cannot limit their own sovereignty in this manner, in practice investment arbitral tribunals have consistently upheld these clauses.[77]

A state's ability to pass laws regulating the behaviour of private parties (including investors) is fundamental to human rights protection because legislation is a primary tool by which states implement their international human rights obligations—in particular the duty to protect human rights. For this reason, it has been argued that a stabilisation clause requirement to exempt investors from compliance with updated laws or to compensate them for such compliance is objectionable—as it denies the state its proper role as legislator, thus chilling or hindering progressive legislative and regulatory development, including the application of dynamic social and environmental standards over the life of a long-term mining project.[78] Furthermore, it has been argued that the negative effects of stabilisation clauses are exacerbated in host countries in the global south, where rapid legislative development and implementation is needed, rather than obstacles to the application of new laws.[79]

Scholars have also challenged the underlying rationale for stabilisation clauses, namely, that these are considered essential by investors to secure a stable investment environment and that usage of such clauses promotes FDI. Frank, for example, examines a number of empirical studies regarding the relationship between stabilisation clauses and FDI, concluding that "contrary to popular belief, stabilisation clauses do not play an 'essential' role in attracting FDI into developing countries"; but that rather, the use of such clauses is driven by political opportunism and that factors such as economics and resource location are far more compelling in investment decision-making.[80]

---

[76] Ingolfsson S H, Stabilisation Clauses in Investment Agreement: A Human Rights and Development Perspective. Graduate Thesis for the Lund University, 2012, http://lup.lub.lu.se/luur/download?func=downloadFile&recordOId=3359538&fileOId=3403760 (last accessed 1 October 2018), p. 54.

[77] Sornarajah (2004), p. 408; Tienhaara (2006), p. 84.

[78] See e.g., UN Economic and Social Council, Human Rights, Trade and Investment. Report of the High Commissioner for Human Rights, E/CN.4/Sub.2/2003/9, 2 July 2003, pp. 3–4, 20–21, 30–32.

[79] Shemberg A, Stabilisation Clauses and Human Rights. 27 May 2009, https://www.ifc.org/wps/wcm/connect/9feb5b00488555eab8c4fa6a6515bb18/Stabilization%2BPaper.pdf?MOD=AJPERES (last accessed 1 October 2018), p. 10.

[80] Frank (2015), p. 88. See also Cameron P D, Stabilisation in Investment Contracts and Changes of Rules in Host Countries: Tools for Oil & Gas Investors. Association of International Petroleum Negotiators, 5 July 2006, https://www.international-arbitration-attorney.com/wp-content/uploads/arbitrationlaw4-Stabilisation-Paper.pdf (last accessed 1 October 2018), p. 12; Mann H, Stabilisation in Investment Contracts: Rethinking the Context, Reformulating the Result. IISD, 7 October 2011, https://www.iisd.org/itn/2011/10/07/stabilization-in-investment-contracts-rethinking-the-context-reformulating-the-result/ (last accessed 1 October 2018).

In light of such considerations, several alternatives to the use of stabilisation clauses have been put forward. The first clear recommendation from a good practice perspective is to refrain from using freezing clauses, in particular full freezing clauses.[81] An alternative approach entails limiting the scope of stabilisation clauses through exempting socially desirable host state regulation from the remit of the stabilisation clause, including *bona fide* regulatory changes implemented in pursuit of meeting the state's human rights duties.[82] With regard to economic equilibrium clauses, a number of features fairly common in economic equilibrium clauses have been identified as being geared towards limiting the application of the stabilisation clause in some ways, ensuring fairness in its application, and preserving the long-term relationship necessary for long-term investments, such as mining projects.[83] For example, some economic equilibrium contracts contain stabilisation provisions that apply in both the investor's and the host state's favour. For changes in the law that create a windfall, lower costs, or higher revenues to the project, the host state shares in the benefit.[84] As such, the state may gain some benefits from economic equilibrium clauses that are not associated with full freezing clauses. Furthermore, some economic equilibrium clauses contain a threshold loss requirement below which no compensation or contract adjustment is due to the investor for changes in the law. Some economic equilibrium clauses explicitly require the investor to mitigate the cost implications of new legislation. Freezing clauses have been found to pose no such requirements.[85]

To summarise, it has been argued that the use of stabilisation clauses in state-investor contracts can have an adverse impact on human rights enjoyment and realisation as such clauses can have a chilling effect on host governments' *bona fide* efforts to make progressive regulatory and legislative changes to enhance human rights protection and meet their international human rights obligations. In particular,

---

[81] Shemberg A, Stabilisation Clauses and Human Rights. 27 May 2009, https://www.ifc.org/wps/wcm/connect/9feb5b00488555eab8c4fa6a6515bb18/Stabilization%2BPaper.pdf?MOD=AJPERES (last accessed 1 October 2018), p. 40.

[82] Cotula L, Regulatory Takings, Stabilisation Clauses and Sustainable Development. Global Forum on International Investment VII. 27–28 March 2008, http://www.oecd.org/investment/globalforum/40311122.pdf (last accessed 1 October 2018), p. 13; Shemberg A, Stabilisation Clauses and Human Rights. 27 May 2009, https://www.ifc.org/wps/wcm/connect/9feb5b00488555eab8c4fa6a6515bb18/Stabilization%2BPaper.pdf?MOD=AJPERES (last accessed 1 October 2018), p. 27.

[83] Shemberg A, Stabilisation Clauses and Human Rights. 27 May 2009, https://www.ifc.org/wps/wcm/connect/9feb5b00488555eab8c4fa6a6515bb18/Stabilization%2BPaper.pdf?MOD=AJPERES (last accessed 1 October 2018), p. 40.

[84] Shemberg A, Stabilisation Clauses and Human Rights. 27 May 2009, https://www.ifc.org/wps/wcm/connect/9feb5b00488555eab8c4fa6a6515bb18/Stabilization%2BPaper.pdf?MOD=AJPERES (last accessed 1 October 2018), p. 40.

[85] Shemberg A, Stabilisation Clauses and Human Rights. 27 May 2009, https://www.ifc.org/wps/wcm/connect/9feb5b00488555eab8c4fa6a6515bb18/Stabilization%2BPaper.pdf?MOD=AJPERES (last accessed 1 October 2018), p. 40.

full freezing clauses have been criticised, which has not kept them from remaining prominent in the extractive industries sectors in some world regions, in particular in Africa. Thus, it may be argued that such clauses should be avoided, and that instead, the investor's need for certainty and stability in the operating environment should be met through alternative means, such as through a stable, transparent and equitable licensing regime.

3.4   Transparency, Public Sector Oversight and Monitoring

Contractual regimes have been found to be more prone to corruption risks and lack of transparency in their allocation of mineral rights than licensing regimes for several reasons, most of which are associated with a higher level of discretion in the award of mineral exploration and exploitation rights in contractual regimes.[86] Lack of contract transparency has been noted as a key factor.[87]

In recognition of the problems associated with lack of transparency, several recent initiatives have focused on increasing transparency of state-investor contracts and associated documentation. A leading initiative is the EITI, introduced above. UNCTAD's 2015 Investment Policy Framework for Sustainable Development also provides a number of concrete suggestions for improving the transparency of international investment agreements.[88] Another initiative tailored to address some of these complexities is the Resource Contracts project—supported by the World Bank, the Natural Resource Governance Institute and the Columbia Center on Sustainable Investment—which includes a public website listing state-investor contracts (as well as other types of investment agreements), including analysis of contracts elaborating on the environmental, social and human rights content and potential implications.[89] The initiative also hosts a listing of support services available to stakeholders for negotiation support. The IFC and the IMF, likewise, have implemented requirements and made arguments in favour of revenue and contract disclosure.[90] The Principles for Responsible Contracts suggest that a "contract's

---

[86] See e.g., Halland et al. (2015), pp. 57, 71.

[87] See e.g., Kienzler D et al., Natural Resources Contracts as a Tool for Managing the Mining Sector. Federal Ministy for Economic Cooperation and Development Germany, June 2015, https://www.bmz.de/g7/includes/Downloadarchiv/Natural_Resource_Contracts.pdf (last accessed 1 October 2018), p. 12.

[88] UN Conference on Trade and Development, Investment Policy Framework for Sustainable Development, UN Doc. UNCTAD/DIAE/PCB/2015/5, 2015, p. 101. Whilst the Framework primarily addresses international investment treaties, rather than state-investor contracts, it includes a broad investment policy focus, the principles of which, by implication, can also be read as relevant to state-investor contracts.

[89] World Bank et al., Resource Contracts, http://www.resourcecontracts.org/ (last accessed 1 October 2018).

[90] Desai and Jarvis (2012), p. 118.

terms should be disclosed, and the scope and duration of exceptions to such disclosure should be based on compelling justifications."[91]

Countries are increasingly publishing their mineral agreements.[92] Afghanistan, the DRC, Guinea, Liberia, Mozambique and Sierra Leone, for example, all now publicly release their mining agreements.[93] This increase in transparency of state-investor contracts can be due to legislative requirements (e.g. in Liberia and Mozambique), voluntary commitments (e.g. in the DRC and Guinea), or as a result of the ratification of state-investor contracts by parliament (e.g. in Sierra Leone and Liberia).[94] One study found that recent contracts in Guinea, Liberia and Mongolia included clauses specifically making them public.[95] In other instances, companies have made agreements public through the filings and disclosures they are required to make to be listed on various stock exchanges, for example, including several mining agreements between SEMAFO and the Government of Burkina Faso.[96]

Despite considerable movement towards greater contract transparency, many state-investor contracts remain confidential.[97] This presents significant limitations in terms of rights-holders' and other interested stakeholders' ability to meaningfully participate in decision-making regarding the granting of mineral rights, implementation of specific projects and associated monitoring.[98] Furthermore, whilst there may be good reasons to keep the initial phases of a negotiation process confidential, "a failure to disclose the final agreement is far more difficult to justify".[99]

---

[91] UN Human Rights Council, Principles for Responsible Contracts. Integrating the Management of Human Rights Risks into State-Investor Contract Negotiations. Guidance for Negotiators, UN Doc. A/HRC/17/31/Add.3, 21 March 2011, p. 23.

[92] See also the chapter by Frank in this volume.

[93] Kienzler D et al., Natural Resources Contracts as a Tool for Managing the Mining Sector. Federal Ministy for Economic Cooperation and Development Germany, June 2015, https://www.bmz.de/g7/includes/Downloadarchiv/Natural_Resource_Contracts.pdf (last accessed 1 October 2018), p. 25.

[94] Kienzler D et al., Natural Resources Contracts as a Tool for Managing the Mining Sector. Federal Ministy for Economic Cooperation and Development Germany, June 2015, https://www.bmz.de/g7/includes/Downloadarchiv/Natural_Resource_Contracts.pdf (last accessed 1 October 2018), p. 26.

[95] Kienzler D et al., Natural Resources Contracts as a Tool for Managing the Mining Sector. Federal Ministy for Economic Cooperation and Development Germany, June 2015, https://www.bmz.de/g7/includes/Downloadarchiv/Natural_Resource_Contracts.pdf (last accessed 1 October 2018), p. 26.

[96] Kienzler D et al., Natural Resources Contracts as a Tool for Managing the Mining Sector. Federal Ministy for Economic Cooperation and Development Germany, June 2015, https://www.bmz.de/g7/includes/Downloadarchiv/Natural_Resource_Contracts.pdf (last accessed 1 October 2018), p. 26.

[97] Cotula and Tienhaara (2013), p. 286.

[98] Cotula and Tienhaara (2013), p. 284.

[99] Cotula and Tienhaara (2013), p. 287. See also Rosenblum P and Maples S, Contracts Confidential: Ending Secret Deals in the Extractive Industries. Revenue Watch. 2009, https://resourcegovernance.org/sites/default/files/RWI-Contracts-Confidential.pdf (last accessed 1 October 2018), pp. 17–18.

Discrepancies in the realities and benefits associated with contract disclosure between investors and states in terms of transparency have also been noted. For instance, a study by the IMF pointed out that contractual terms are likely to be known by industry (e.g. through expensive subscription services available to investors) and that for states there could actually be a strategic advantage in disclosure as knowledge of the general public may increase pressure on the government to negotiate a good deal.[100] Eliminating or restricting confidentiality clauses in contracts has therefore been suggested.[101]

Lack of transparency has been linked directly to increased corruption risks. For instance, it has been argued that in licensing regimes there are fewer opportunities for corruption because a generally applicable law sets out the same requirements, obligations and benefits for every investor.[102] Similarly, it has been suggested that the certainty and consistency provided by a stable licensing regime make these less arbitrary as responsibility for granting mineral rights is given to a particular government authority, thereby reducing government discretion in awarding or cancelling those rights.[103] A direct effect is an increased security of tenure for investors—one of the most important aspects of securing mineral rights for a foreign investment.[104] Without access to the contractual terms of state-investor contracts, citizens cannot effectively hold FDI mining projects to account.

In some contexts where contractual disclosure is now a requirement, in practice significant challenges remain in terms of rights-holders' and other interested stakeholders' ability to access such contracts and use them to participate in promoting and demanding accountability of states and investors to ensure that mining projects respect human rights. Corruption, lack of political will, or simple logistical issues can keep contracts hidden even in countries with transparency laws.[105] Furthermore, as put succinctly by Desai and Jarvis: "Disclosure does not in itself guarantee greater scrutiny or better governance of the sector."[106] On this point, it is important

---

[100] IMF, Guidance on Resource Revenue Transparency. 2007, https://www.imf.org/external/np/pp/2007/eng/101907g.pdf (last accessed 1 October 2018), p. 17. See also Cotula and Tienhaara (2013), p. 287; Halland et al. (2015), p. 73.

[101] See e.g., Cotula and Tienhaara (2013), p. 289; Rosenblum P and Maples S, Contracts Confidential: Ending Secret Deals in the Extractive Industries. Revenue Watch, 2009, https://resourcegovernance.org/sites/default/files/RWI-Contracts-Confidential.pdf (last accessed 1 October 2018).

[102] See e.g Halland et al. (2015), p. 71; Kienzler D et al., Natural Resources Contracts as a Tool for Managing the Mining Sector. Federal Ministy for Economic Cooperation and Development Germany, June 2015, https://www.bmz.de/g7/includes/Downloadarchiv/Natural_Resource_Contracts.pdf (last accessed 1 October 2018), p. 12.

[103] Halland et al. (2015), p. 68.

[104] Halland et al. (2015), p. 68.

[105] Kienzler D et al., Natural Resources Contracts as a Tool for Managing the Mining Sector. Federal Ministy for Economic Cooperation and Development Germany, June 2015, https://www.bmz.de/g7/includes/Downloadarchiv/Natural_Resource_Contracts.pdf (last accessed 1 October 2018), p. 26.

[106] Desai and Jarvis (2012), p. 120. See also Acosta A M, Annex 4. Natural Resource Governance. Review of Impact and Effectiveness of Transparency and Accountability Initiatives. Transparency

to acknowledge that whilst there is a clear move towards favouring transparency of state-investor contracts, there are also some underlying assumptions regarding the value of transparency which may fall short in practice. One of the primary assumptions underlying arguments in favour of greater transparency is that such transparency will reduce corruption and governments will be more accountable in terms of spending revenues generated from FDI projects in the public interest, such as for the pursuit of the progressive realisation of economic, social and cultural rights.[107] However, such causality cannot be presumed.[108] In many cases, when contracts are available, domestic education efforts are still needed to enable the public to understand these often complex agreements.[109] The time and effort required of civil society organisations, national human rights institutions and the public to hold a government accountable for the terms of each negotiated contract currently still remain much more significant than in a licensing regime with more uniform terms.[110] For example, in a study on Ghana, the country is said to have made great strides in terms of advancing the frontiers of transparency and accountability using the EITI framework, as a result of which at least there is some clarity and openness about how much revenue projects are making. However, it still faces several practical obstacles, including the separation of the Ghana EITI from corporate social responsibility efforts, challenges with the provision of data for EITI reports, conflicting stakeholder expectations and power relationships, general institutional disinterest in reforms, and the lack of correlation between recorded revenues and royalties and demonstrable positive developmental outcome(s) in local communities impacted by mining activities.[111] Despite such challenges, greater contractual transparency must

---

& Accountability Initiative, 2010, http://www.transparencyinitiative.org/wp-content/uploads/2017/03/impacts_annex4_final1.pdf (last accessed 1 October 2018), p. 4; Besada H and Martin P, Mining Codes in Africa: Emergence of a "Fourth" Generation?. The North-South Institute, May 2013, http://www.nsi-ins.ca/wp-content/uploads/2013/03/Mining-Codes-in-Africa-Report-Hany.pdf (last accessed 1 October 2018), p. 22; Cotula and Tienhaara (2013), p. 287.

[107] See e.g., Acosta A M, Annex 4. Natural Resource Governance. Review of Impact and Effectiveness of Transparency and Accountability Initiatives. Transparency & Accountability Initiative, 2010, http://www.transparencyinitiative.org/wp-content/uploads/2017/03/impacts_annex4_final1.pdf (last accessed 1 October 2018), p. 7; Desai and Jarvis (2012), pp. 109–110, speaking about transparency initiatives in natural resources management generally.

[108] Acosta A M, Annex 4. Natural Resource Governance. Review of Impact and Effectiveness of Transparency and Accountability Initiatives. Transparency & Accountability Initiative, 2010, http://www.transparency-initiative.org/wp-content/uploads/2017/03/impacts_annex4_final1.pdf (last accessed 1 October 2018), pp. 4–5; Hilson and Maconachie (2008), pp. 57, 91.

[109] Acosta A M, Annex 4. Natural Resource Governance. Review of Impact and Effectiveness of Transparency and Accountability Initiatives. Transparency & Accountability Initiative, 2010, http://www.transparency-initiative.org/wp-content/uploads/2017/03/impacts_annex4_final1.pdf (last accessed 1 October 2018), p. 11; Cotula and Tienhaara (2013), p. 284; Desai and Jarvis (2012), pp. 101, 110, 127.

[110] Kienzler D et al., Natural Resources Contracts as a Tool for Managing the Mining Sector. Federal Ministy for Economic Cooperation and Development Germany, June 2015, https://www.bmz.de/g7/includes/Downloadarchiv/Natural_Resource_Contracts.pdf (last accessed 1 October 2018), p. 27.

[111] Andrews (2016), p. 68.

be viewed as an essential component of improved extractive industries governance.

A further key point that has been noted is that of the heavy regulatory burden of having to monitor different contracts with different terms and conditions. In a licensing regime, there is arguably less burden on government administration, which in a contractual regime has to monitor a series of different individual agreements with varying terms and conditions.[112] This is particularly problematic in regulatory environments where governments are already over-stretched, under-resourced and/ or prone to corruption risks.[113] Furthermore, for any reference to international standards in contracts, including human rights standards, to be effective, proper funding of government oversight and monitoring is key.[114]

In sum, there are strong good governance policy and practical reasons for greater transparency of state-investor contracts, which are recognised by a number of international initiatives addressing FDI and extractive industries governance. Increasingly, these principles are also being integrated into relevant legislation, regulation and policy at the domestic level. However, in practice many challenges remain in terms of greater contract transparency being realised and translated into rights-holders' ability to utilise such information to demand greater accountability of governments and investors with regard to FDI projects.[115] Similarly, the nexus between contractual transparency, less corrupt extractive industries governance, and improved human rights conditions (e.g. through greater spending of extractive industries revenues on the realisation of human rights), is not a clear causal and linear relationship. Rather, for contractual transparency to play a meaningful role in this nexus, it must be considered within the wider agenda of extractive industries governance for sustainable development.[116] Here, again the arguments in favour of stricter licensing regimes remain persuasive, as these have the potential to reduce the regulatory burden on the state and corruption risks by virtue of there being more consistent and generally applicable terms for the granting of mineral rights. Finally, however, greater contractual transparency (or transparency generally regarding the award of mineral rights to investors) continues to be emphasised by scholars and practitioners as one of the absolutely necessary preconditions in working towards more transparency and participation in extractive industries governance for sustainable development.[117]

---

[112] Dietsche E, Mineral Taxation Regimes. A review of issues and challenges in their design and application. Commonwealth Secretariat and International Council on Mining and Metals, Feburary 2009, https://www.icmm.com/website/publications/pdfs/social-and-economic-development/minerals-taxation-regimes (last accessed 1 October 2018), p. 9.

[113] Cotula and Tienhaara (2013), p. 284.

[114] Cotula and Tienhaara (2013), p. 302; Halland et al. (2015), p. 74; Hilson and Maconachie (2008), p. 57.

[115] Cotula and Tienhaara (2013), p. 284; Desai and Jarvis (2012), pp. 101, 127.

[116] Desai and Jarvis (2012), pp. 101, 127; Hilson and Maconachie (2008), pp. 71, 84.

[117] See e.g., Desai and Jarvis (2012), p. 125: "Such information enables those affected to know whom to hold to account for what terms, and is the first step to building capacity more effectively to monitor the implementation of those terms, complementing existing government regulatory functions." See also Cotula and Tienhaara (2013), p. 287.

3.5 *Access to Remedy and Dispute Settlement*

Related to the topic of public sector oversight and monitoring, critiques have been levelled against state-investor contracts regarding access to remedy and dispute settlement, including: (1) that rights-holders' ability to raise concerns pursuant to the contractual agreement are limited; (2) that the interaction between state-investor contracts and other investment agreements (e.g. BITs) can act in a manner as to undermine domestic law; and (3) that there exists lack of transparency, limited stakeholder participation and a bias towards investors in commercial and investment arbitration. This section will address each of these three critiques in turn.

Third parties, such as rights-holders who are adversely impacted by an FDI project, because they are not parties to the state-investor contract, are not in a position to legally raise a claim pursuant to such a contract. One of the traditional arguments here has been that state-investor contracts are commercial contracts, subject to the general principles of contract law and that this lack of standing of third parties is therefore acceptable. However, critics have argued that because these contracts involve public resources and can impose significant externalities on communities and the country as a whole, these contracts should be regarded as public policy documents rather than commercial contracts.[118] As argued by Gathii and Odumosu-Ayanu: "We take it as a given that to assume the justness of extractive industries contracts between resource rich governments and investors outside of any external criteria for validity would be to reify an abstract notion of contractual freedom inconsistent with the duties states have to respect, protect, and fulfil rights under international human rights law."[119] Furthermore, scholars have noted that there is not necessarily a strict reason why rights-holders should be excluded from contracts, pointing to some examples of tripartite agreements, as well as an increase in state-investor contracts that refer to or require company-community agreements (including tripartite community development agreements involving communities, government actors and investors)—essentially increasing contractual avenues for rights-holders to hold investors to account.[120] Of course the practical challenges associated with such approaches should be acknowledged, for example, it needs to be clarified who represents the "community" and which interests are accounted for. However, the trend towards using contractual responsibilities to promote increased recognition and enforceability of the rights of project-impacted communities in the context of extractive industries FDI projects should be noted.

Regarding the second critique, state-investor contracts can pose a risk of undermining a country's domestic laws in different ways. Firstly, whilst state-investor contracts are generally subordinate to domestic law, in negotiating the contract the

---

[118] See e.g., Cotula and Tienhaara (2013), pp. 282, 287; Gathii and Odumosu-Ayanu (2015), pp. 70–71, 92.

[119] Gathii and Odumosu-Ayanu (2015), p. 72.

[120] See e.g., Cotula and Tienhaara (2013), p. 303; Gathii and Odumosu-Ayanu (2015), pp. 78, 85, 90.

parties can agree to the contract being subject to a law other than that of the host state, thereby essentially "internationalising" the contract.[121] In such a situation, not only are these contracts immune to changes in domestic laws, but significant concessions for the investor that bypass or contradict domestic laws can be made. In licensing regimes that rely on the generally applicable law, the rules applicable to FDI projects do not transcend domestic law in this way. Instead, licences to investors are awarded in accordance with domestic laws which are available to local communities and subject to a democratic process—meaning that rights-holders have both more avenues to raise objections to the award of mineral rights and any adverse impacts caused by a particular project, as well as greater participation opportunities in the design of mineral governance laws and regulations through a democratic process (at least in theory).

Another example of how state-investor contracts risk undermining domestic law is those cases where a state-investor contract interacts with an investment treaty (e.g. BIT or investment chapter in an FTA) in a manner that elevates the state-investor contract above domestic law, effectively allowing the investor to bypass or undermine domestic laws.[122] As flagged in the introduction, state-investor contracts must be distinguished from BITs (agreements between two countries for the reciprocal encouragement, promotion and protection of investments in each other's territories) and FTAs (several state parties entering into a legally binding commitment to liberalise access to each other's markets for goods and services and investments, some containing specific investment chapters). However, it is important to note the interplay between these agreements. In short, where there is a BIT or an investment chapter in an FTA, this will usually provide rights and remedies for the investor that are additional to those in domestic law or the state-investor contract. As such, an investor may challenge any laws or other government activity that are inconsistent with the treaty.[123] Investment case law is divided on the interpretation and so-called "umbrella clauses" in BITs that are being used by investors to challenge non-compliance with contractual provisions provided for in state-investor contracts; however, there have been cases in which investors have relied on such clauses to allege that a breach of a state-investor contract also constitutes a breach of host state

---

[121] See e.g., Johnson and Volkov (2013), pp. 370–371.

[122] Cordes K and Johnson L and Szoke-Burke S, Land Deal Dilemmas: Grievances, Human Rights and Investor Protection. Columbia Center on Sustainable Investment, March 2016, http://ccsi. columbia.edu/files/2016/03/CCSI_Land-deal-dilemmas.pdf (last accessed 1 October 2018), p. 17; Marshall F, Risks for Host States of the Entwining of Investment Treaty Contract Claims. IISD, August 2009, https://www.iisd.org/sites/default/files/publications/best_practices_bulletin_4.pdf (last accessed 1 October 2018), p. 1.

[123] Marshall F, Risks for Host States of the Entwining of Investment Treaty Contract Claims. IISD, August 2009, https://www.iisd.org/sites/default/files/publications/best_practices_bulletin_4.pdf (last accessed 1 October 2018), pp. 1, 15; Mann H and Smaller C, Foreign Land Purchase for Agriculture: What Impact on Sustainable Development?. United Nations. Sustainable Development Innovation Briefs Issue 8, January 2010, https://sustainabledevelopment.un.org/content/documents/no8.pdf (last accessed 1 October 2018), p. 4.

obligations under a BIT.[124] The use of an umbrella clause and/or equitable treatment obligation under an investment treaty may mean that the treaty "can potentially protect an entire investor-state contract (or provisions in that contract) that might otherwise be illegal or unenforceable under domestic law."[125] For example, a domestic court may deem a stabilisation clause invalid, whereas an investment arbitral tribunal may adopt a different view and enforce the clause under the umbrella or equitable treatment provision in the international investment treaty.[126] This interplay has the potential to not only undermine domestic law but can also result in "forum shopping" as investors can raise a claim in commercial arbitration for breach of the state-investor contract, as well as initiate international investment arbitration for breach of the treaty provision.[127]

Regarding the third critique, international arbitration has been criticised for lack of transparency, limited stakeholder participation, as well as a bias in favour of investors.[128] Whilst a distinction must be made between international commercial arbitration (for contract-based claims) and investment arbitration (for treaty-based claims) both are relevant given the interplay of contracts and treaties outlined above,

---

[124] See e.g., Cordes K and Johnson L and Szoke-Burke S, Land Deal Dilemmas: Grievances, Human Rights and Investor Protection. Columbia Center on Sustainable Investment, March 2016, http://ccsi.columbia.edu/files/2016/03/CCSI_Land-deal-dilemmas.pdf (last accessed 1 October 2018), p. 14; Marshall F, Risks for Host States of the Entwining of Investment Treaty Contract Claims. IISD, August 2009, https://www.iisd.org/sites/default/files/publications/best_practices_bulletin_4.pdf (last accessed 1 October 2018), pp. 11–15.

[125] Cordes K and Johnson L and Szoke-Burke S, Land Deal Dilemmas: Grievances, Human Rights and Investor Protection. Columbia Center on Sustainable Investment, March 2016, http://ccsi.columbia.edu/files/2016/03/CCSI_Land-deal-dilemmas.pdf (last accessed 1 October 2018), p. 2. See also Johnson L and Coleman J, International Investment Law and the Extractive Industries Sector. Columbia Center on Sustainable Investment, January 2016 http://ccsi.columbia.edu/files/2016/01/2016-01-12_Investment-Law-and-Extractives_Briefing-Note_1.pdf (last accessed 1 October 2018), p. 10.

[126] Cordes K and Johnson L and Szoke-Burke S, Land Deal Dilemmas: Grievances, Human Rights and Investor Protection. Columbia Center on Sustainable Investment, March 2016, http://ccsi.columbia.edu/files/2016/03/CCSI_Land-deal-dilemmas.pdf (last accessed 1 October 2018), p. 2, noting also that there are in fact examples where "even in the absence of a stabilisation clause, some investment arbitration tribunals have determined that promises of legal stability can be implied in certain circumstances."

[127] Marshall F, Risks for Host States of the Entwining of Investment Treaty Contract Claims. IISD, August 2009, https://www.iisd.org/sites/default/files/publications/best_practices_bulletin_4.pdf (last accessed 1 October 2018), pp. 1, 12; Mitchell L, Natural Resource Contracts: A Practical Guide. Environmental Law Alliance World, https://www.elaw.org/sites/default/files/images_content/general_page_images/publications/Natural_Resource_Contracts_Guide.pdf (last accessed 1 October 2018), p. 46.

[128] See e.g., Caron D, Light and Dark in International Arbitration: The Virtues, Risks and Limits of Transparency. The 9th Kaplan Lecture, 10 December 2015, http://neil-kaplan.com/wp-content/uploads/2016/10/2016_10_06-Caron-Light-and-Dark.pdf (last accessed 1 October 2018), p. 6; Marshall F, Risks for Host States of the Entwining of Investment Treaty Contract Claims. IISD, August 2009, https://www.iisd.org/sites/default/files/publications/best_practices_bulletin_4.pdf (last accessed 1 October 2018), p. 1; Tienhaara (2006).

and many of the critiques raised regarding international arbitration apply to both types.

The reach and function of international commercial arbitration should not be underestimated, with the majority of contracts that cross international borders falling under the remit of international commercial arbitration.[129] In this system disputes are adjudicated before private tribunals and the resulting awards are enforced in domestic courts—the resolution process itself being binding, non-judicial and private.[130] Important benefits of international commercial arbitration are considered to be the confidentiality the process provides as well as the flexibility as parties are able to select the procedural law that applies, the arbitrator(s) and the arbitral rules.[131] However, it is also precisely these factors that have been criticised from a human rights and good governance perspective, on the basis that they limit public participation and undermine due process and domestic legal accountability. Arbitral proceedings implicate public interest when they involve issues concerning the common interest, such as non-rival and non-excludable public goods like water or the environment, or the best interest of the state and its constituents.[132] Despite this public interest dimension, in both its processes and outcomes, international arbitration has been described as a system which "removes issues that directly affect citizens to a system that is inaccessible and structurally isolated from public input."[133]

Confidentiality, whilst serving as one of commercial arbitration's strongest selling points, has also been one of its most prominent sources of criticism. Confidentiality serves to expedite arbitrations, as well as to protect the privacy of information and reputation.[134] However, at the same time it severely limits public participation and involvement. As such, there is no guarantee or mechanism ensuring that the public will know about the claim brought, the positions taken by the parties, the process applied, the decisions issued by the tribunals and the tribunal's precise reasoning.[135] Non-disputant private parties have no access to the proceedings unless there is consent of the parties to open, or the tribunal in its discretion opens up, the proceedings to *amici curiae*, i.e. friends of the court.[136] There is also no general binding rule for the publication of awards and they generally remain confidential unless the parties to the dispute agree to disclose them.[137] As a result,

---

[129] See e.g., Myburgh (2016), p. 599, indicating that the estimate lies at 80% of international contracts containing recourse to international commercial arbitration.

[130] Myburgh (2016), pp. 597, 599.

[131] See e.g., Myburgh (2016), pp. 600–601.

[132] Choudhury (2008), p. 792.

[133] Choudhury (2008), p. 784.

[134] OECD, Transparency and Third Party Participation in Investor-State Dispute Settlement Procedures. OECD Working Papers on International Investment 2005/01, June 2005, https://www.oecd.org/daf/inv/investment-policy/WP-2005_1.pdf (last accessed 1 October 2018), p. 2.

[135] See e.g., Tienhaara (2006).

[136] Tienhaara (2006), p. 76.

[137] OECD, Transparency and Third Party Participation in Investor-State Dispute Settlement Procedures. OECD Working Papers on International Investment 2005/01, June 2005, https://www.oecd.org/daf/inv/investment-policy/WP-2005_1.pdf (last accessed 1 October 2018), p. 3.

international commercial arbitration between two parties may occur and run its course without the public even being aware of the dispute, let alone the outcomes. Although public participation in the form of *amicus* involvement or open public hearings has been permitted in limited cases, public participation in the arbitration process is more often the exception than the norm, and critics continue to point to the lack of transparency in the arbitration process.[138]

Investment arbitration, being private in nature, has also been criticised on the basis that it does not have the same accountability safeguards, impartiality and independence as domestic courts of law.[139] Given the potential interplay of state-investor contracts and international investment agreements (including access to international investment arbitration under these) as outlined above, critiques of international investment arbitration are also relevant to state-investor contracts. Regarding due process, it has been pointed out, for instance, that certain democratic restraints on administrative agencies do not apply to investment arbitral tribunals; that investment arbitration panels operate outside the formal adjudicatory process but effectively serve an adjudicatory and standard-setting function that affects the economic and social values of the general public.[140] Furthermore, in investment arbitration regimes there is no official system of precedent, resulting in a lack of consistency in arbitral decisions.[141] A domestic legal system, by contrast, is designed to follow established laws and precedent and "generally requires that an elected legislature both delegate the implementation of a specific statute to an administrative body and provide for independent judicial review of the administrative body's decisions to ensure that the administrative body is acting within the purview of its delegated statutory authority."[142] Furthermore, investment arbitration decisions are taken by international arbitrators appointed by the parties, rather than independent judges. The fact that arbitrators have a significant financial stake in arbitration has been criticised as a shortcoming, that arguably reduces their impartiality and independence.[143] Lastly, it has been noted that in terms of language used (usually English), resources and costs, international arbitration has a global north bias.[144] In practice, investment arbitral tribunals are often reluctant to consider the public policies supporting a state's regulations. As a result, the outcomes of investment disputes are

---

[138] See e.g., Choudhury (2008), pp. 786–787; Tienhaara (2006), p. 76.

[139] See e.g., Johnson L and Coleman J, International Investment Law and the Extractive Industries Sector. Columbia Center on Sustainable Investment, January 2016 http://ccsi.columbia.edu/files/2016/01/2016-01-12_Investment-Law-and-Extractives_Briefing-Note_1.pdf (last accessed 1 October 2018), pp. 6–7, for a useful overview of the differences between domestic court systems and international investment arbitration.

[140] Choudhury (2008), pp. 787–788.

[141] Tienhaara (2006), p. 77.

[142] Stewart cited in Choudhury (2008), p. 788.

[143] Garcia (2004), p. 352.

[144] See e.g., Tienhaara (2006), for a useful and comprehensive overview of these issues.

often weighted in favour of international investors and against host state interests.[145]

In light of such critiques of international investor state dispute settlement (ISDS), several reform processes are currently under way. For example, in 2017 the United Nations Commission on International Trade Law (UNCITRAL) entrusted its Working Group III with a broad mandate to identify concerns regarding ISDS, consider whether reform is necessary and develop relevant solutions to be recommended to the Commission.[146] This initiative builds on UNCITRAL's work on transparency standards for ISDS, the UNCITRAL Rules on Transparency in Treaty-based Investor-State Arbitration, adopted in 2013, which provide a procedural framework to make information on investment arbitration cases available to the public.[147] Another reform initiative is being led by the International Centre for the Settlement of Investment Disputes (ICSID), which in 2017 published a list of 16 potential areas for reform in the process of revision of its rules of procedure for arbitration.[148] Given the strong linkages between state-investor contracts and investment treaties, such reform processes could be utilised to also address concerns regarding state-investor contract dispute settlement and the interplay between commercial and investment arbitration.

In summary, the circumstance that rights-holders are not party to state-investor contracts limits their ability to influence how extractive industries FDI projects are implemented, including how any adverse impacts are avoided, mitigated and redressed. Relatedly, treating state-investor contracts as purely commercial and subject to general principles of contract law has been challenged by critics that argue that the interests that such contracts govern represent public interests and that therefore greater transparency and public involvement is warranted. Secondly, whilst there are varying interpretations of how state-investor contracts interact with international investment treaties, there is significant evidence that the interplay between such agreements can work in favour of investors by providing avenues whereby contractual claims can be elevated to fall under the protection of international investment agreements (e.g. BITs or investment chapters of FTAs). Thirdly, the international arbitration system used to resolve any potential disputes has been criticised for lack of transparency, limited stakeholder participation and a bias

---

[145] See e.g., Choudhury (2008), pp. 787–788; Dolzer (2005), pp. 953, 957.

[146] UN Information Service, Press release: UNCITRAL to consider possible reform of investor-state dispute settlement, 14 July 2017, http://www.unis.unvienna.org/unis/en/pressrels/2017/unisl250.html (last accessed 1 October 2018).

[147] The Rules apply to cases arising under relevant investment treaties concluded after 1 April 2014; the United Nations Convention on Transparency in Treaty-based Investor-State Arbitration (the "Mauritius Convention on Transparency") provides the mechanism for the application of these rules to cases concluded before 1 April 2014 and will enter into force in October 2017. See UN Commission on International Trade Law, United Nations Convention on Transparency in Treaty-based Investor-State Arbitration, 10 December 2014, http://www.uncitral.org/uncitral/uncitral_texts/arbitration/2014Transparency_Convention.html (last accessed 1 October 2018).

[148] ICSID, Amendment of ICSID's Rules and Regulations, https://icsid.worldbank.org/en/Pages/about/Amendment-of-ICSID-Rules-and-Regulations.aspx (last accessed 1 October 2018).

towards investors. Human rights perspectives regarding the potential for reform of the system range from arguments for outright abandonment to suggestions for procedural and substantive reforms that would increase transparency of international arbitration processes and outcomes, foster consistency in rule application and precedent, and promote impartiality and independence of decision-makers and decisions.[149] Given the continuing use of state-investor contracts in extractive industries FDI and the rapid proliferation of BITs and FTAs, arguably, such urgent calls for reform should be quickly realised if transparency and participation of rights-holders and other interested stakeholders in extractive industries FDI governance is to be improved.

4 Conclusions

This chapter has considered the topic of state-investor contracts from a human rights perspective, focusing in particular on transparency and participation. Whilst there is a trend towards using the generally applicable domestic law of a country to govern FDI, state-investor contracts remain prominent in some regions and industries, for example, the extractive industries in Africa. Therefore, the human rights critiques of these contracts must be noted, and opportunities for enhancing transparency and participation encouraged, if the adverse human rights impacts of extractive industries FDI projects are to be avoided and addressed. In this chapter, I have discussed five common areas of critique regarding state-investor contracts, and outlined potential measures, initiatives and standards put forward to address them.

Firstly, the majority of state-investor contracts continue to contain no or very marginal reference to human rights. Given the role that these contracts play in the governance of extractive industries FDI projects, this is problematic and the explicit inclusion of content relevant to human rights should be promoted as a means of facilitating greater transparency and participation for project-impacted rights-holders and other stakeholders. Contributing to enhanced human rights due diligence may be achieved through applying a human rights lens when shaping the various contractual clauses and/or the inclusion of a stand-alone human rights clause, recognising that these two approaches may be complementary rather than mutually exclusive. The application and use of good practice initiatives, such as the Principles for Responsible Contracts and model contracts, could go some way in addressing this important gap.

Secondly, the asymmetry in capacity and information between the negotiating parties has been identified as a key gap. In moving towards creating more equitable

---

[149] For a useful summary of potential reform measures see e.g., Choudhury (2008), pp. 807–830; Pahis S, Bilateral Investment Treaties and International Human Rights Law: Harmonization through Interpretation. International Commission of Jurists, 2011, https://www.icj.org/wp-content/uploads/2012/06/treaties-law-interpretation-thematic-report-2012.pdf (last accessed 1 October 2018), pp. 43–47; Sauvant (2016).

playing fields for state-investor contract negotiations, and increasing the consideration of human rights in such negotiations, it will be essential to further promote the inclusion of human rights in the mandate and capacity of both state and investor negotiating parties. This may also address the rights and interests of those project-impacted rights-holders most marginalised and at risk, recognising that the state negotiating party may not always be acting in the interest of these rights-holders. The promotion of environmental, social and human rights expertise in technical support services, as well as training and capacity building of negotiators, may contribute to this end.

Thirdly, it has been argued that the use of stabilisation clauses in state-investor contracts can have an adverse impact on human rights enjoyment and realisation as such clauses can have a chilling effect on host governments' *bona fide* efforts to make progressive regulatory and legislative changes to enhance human rights protection and meet their international human rights obligations. In particular, full freezing clauses have been criticised. Nonetheless they remain prominent in the extractive industries sectors in some world regions, in particular in Africa. These clauses should be avoided, and instead, the need of investors for certainty and stability in the operating environment should be met through alternative means, such as well-developed and functioning laws and regulations governing mineral rights at the domestic level.

Fourthly, there are strong good governance policy reasons for greater transparency of state-investor negotiation and contracts, which are recognised in a number of international initiatives addressing FDI and extractive industries governance. Increasingly, these principles are also being integrated into relevant legislation, regulation and policy at the domestic level. Nonetheless, in practice many state-investor contracts remain confidential and challenges remain in terms of increased contract transparency translating into rights-holders' ability to utilise such information to demand greater accountability of governments and investors with regard to FDI projects. Relatedly, the nexus between contractual transparency, less corruption in extractive industries governance, and improved human rights conditions (e.g. through greater spending of extractive industries revenues for the realisation of human rights), is not a clear causal and linear relationship. Rather, for contractual transparency to play a meaningful role in this nexus, it must be considered within the wider agenda of extractive industries governance for sustainable development. Here, again, the arguments in favour of stricter licensing regimes remain persuasive, as these have the potential to reduce the regulatory burden on the state and corruption risks by virtue of providing more consistent and generally applicable terms for the granting of mineral rights. However, greater contractual transparency (or transparency generally regarding the award of mineral rights to investors) must continue to be considered one of the absolutely necessary preconditions in working towards mineral governance for sustainable development.

Fifthly, the notion of treating state-investor contracts as purely commercial and subject to general principles of contract law has been challenged on the grounds that the interests that these contracts govern represent public interests and that therefore greater transparency and public involvement is warranted. The circumstance that rights-holders are not party to such contracts limits their ability to influence how extractive industries FDI projects are implemented and in theory there are no reasons why the contractual rights of rights-holders cannot be increased, for example, through better linkages between state-investor contracts and community development agreements, or through including strong rules on the rights and remedies of third-party beneficiaries in contracts. Whilst there are varying interpretations of how state-investor contracts interact with international investment treaties, there is significant evidence that the interplay between such agreements can work in favour of investors by providing avenues whereby contractual claims can be elevated to fall under the protection of international investment agreements. Given the persuasive critiques of the international arbitration system—including lack of transparency, undermining of domestic law and bias towards investors—and the rapid proliferation of BITs and FTAs, arguably, the urgent calls for reform of the international arbitration system should be quickly realised if transparency and participation of rights-holders and other interested stakeholders in extractive industries FDI governance is to be improved. For instance, current ISDS reform initiatives, such as those led by UNCITRAL and ICSID, could be leveraged to also address critiques regarding dispute settlement on the basis of state-investor contracts.

In conclusion, it should be re-iterated that the topic of state-investor contracts and human rights cannot and should not be considered in isolation from wider governance considerations regarding the human rights implications of extractive industries FDI. Factors such as corruption, transparency, participation, north-south dynamics, governance capacity and political will all continue to be critical topics in scholarly debates and applied practices regarding how the adverse impacts of extractive industries FDI projects can be avoided and addressed, and the role that these sectors can and should play in sustainable development. As indicated throughout this chapter, state-investor contracts are inextricably linked to these wider considerations and factors and any suggestions for reform regarding the content, negotiation and use of state-investor contracts should be considered within this wider context. Nevertheless, overall, it is arguable that the trend towards favouring the use of the generally applicable law to govern extractive industries FDI, rather than state-investor contracts, is positive in terms of improving opportunities for greater transparency and participation in the way that agreements governing mineral rights are executed and the respective projects are implemented, and should therefore be encouraged. In the meantime, opportunities to enhance transparency and participation in the use of state-investor contracts, such as those outlined in this chapter, should be realised irrespective of whether a jurisdiction favours a contractual or licensing regime for the governance of extractive industries FDI.

Acknowledgments I would sincerely like to thank Kaitlin Cordes, Mads Holst Jensen, Lise Johnson and Andrea Shemberg for their helpful comments on an earlier draft, as well as William Oon for his research assistance.

References

Andrews N (2016) A Swiss-Army knife? A critical assessment of the extractive industries transparency initiative in Ghana. Bus Soc Rev 121(1):59–83

Choudhury B (2008) Recapturing public power: is investment arbitration's engagement of the public interest contributing to the democratic deficit? Vanderbilt J Transnatl Law 41:775–831

Cotula L (2014) Do investment treaties unduly constrain regulatory space? Questions Int Law 9:19–31

Cotula L, Tienhaara K (2013) Reconfiguring investment contracts to promote sustainable development. In: Sauvant K (ed) Yearbook on international investment law and policy 2011–2012. Oxford University Press, Oxford, pp 281–310

Desai D, Jarvis M (2012) Governance and accountability in extractive industries: theory and practice at the World Bank. J Energy Nat Resour Law 30(2):101–128

Dolzer R (2005) The impact of international investment treaties on domestic administrative law. NYU J Int Law Polit 37:953–972

Frank S (2015) Stabilisation clauses and FDI: presumptions versus realities. J World Invest Trade 16(1):88–121

Garcia CG (2004) All the other dirty little secrets: investment treaties, Latin America, and the necessary evil of investor-state arbitration. Florida J Int Law 16:301–369

Gathii J, Odumosu-Ayanu I (2015) The turn to contractual responsibility in the global extractive industry. Bus Hum Rights J 1(1):69–94

Gordon K (2008) International investment agreements: a survey of environmental, labour and anti-corruption issues. In: Yannaca-Small C (ed) International investment law: understanding concepts and tracking innovations. OECD, Paris, pp 135–240

Halland H, Lokanc M, Nair A, Kannan SP (2015) The extractive industries sector: essentials for economists, public finance professionals, and policy makers. World Bank, Washington DC

Hilson G, Maconachie R (2008) "Good governance" and the extractive industries in Sub-Saharan Africa. Miner Process Extr Metall Rev 30(1):52–100

Johnson L, Volkov O (2013) Investor-state contracts, host-state "commitments" and the myth of stability in international law. Am Rev Int Arbitr 24(3):361–415

Myburgh A (2016) Does international commercial arbitration promote FDI? J Law Econ 59(3):597–627

Sachs L, Toledano P, Mandelbaum J, Otto J (2013) Impacts of fiscal reforms on country attractiveness: learning from the facts. In: Sauvant K (ed) Yearbook in international investment law and policy 2011–2012. Oxford University Press, Oxford, pp 345–387

Sauvant K (2016) The evolving international investment law and policy regime: ways forward. Invest Bridges Africa 5(5):1–12

Sornarajah M (2004) The international law on foreign investment, 2nd edn. Cambridge University Press, Cambridge

Tienhaara K (2006) What you don't know can hurt you: investor-state disputes and the protection of the environment in developing countries. Global Environ Polit 6(4):73–100

Williams P (2012) Global trends and tribulations in mining regulation. J Energy Nat Resour Law 30(4):391–422

Nora Götzmann is senior adviser at the Danish Institute for Human Rights, Denmark's national human rights institution. She is also adjunct researcher at the Centre for Social Responsibility in Mining at the University of Queensland, Australia. Nora's research and project work focuses on business and human rights, in particular on human rights and impact assessment, capacity building of national human rights institutions, extractive industries, access to remedy, gender, and investment and human rights.

Disruption and Institutional Development: Corporate Standards and Practices on Responsible Mining

Radu Mares

Contents

1 Introduction 375
2 Disruption and Institutional Development 378
    2.1 Disruption: Mere Presence and Irresponsible Operations 378
    2.2 Social Investments: Irrelevant or Even Problematic? 380
    2.3 Institutional Development: The Missing Link 382
3 Shifts in CSR Strategy 385
    3.1 Shifts in Social Investment 385
        3.1.1 Shift from Philanthropy to Community Investment 385
        3.1.2 Shift from Economic and Social Development to Institutional Development ... 386
    3.2 Shifts in Social Responsibility 389
        3.2.1 Shift from Punctual Interventions to More Encompassing Approaches 389
        3.2.2 Shift from Partnerships to Meaningful Partnerships 391
4 Operational Settings 396
    4.1 Water Management 397
    4.2 Security Provisions 398
    4.3 Contributions to Socio-Economic Development 403
    4.4 Revenue Transparency 408
5 Conclusions 411
References 412

1 Introduction

The far-reaching and diverse impacts of mining on local communities, the environment and national economies have been well documented.[1] Meanwhile mining companies have pointed to economic and social contributions and the opportunities

---

[1] World Bank, Extractive Industries Review. Striking a Better Balance. 17 September 2004, http://documents.worldbank.org/curated/en/961241468781797388/pdf/300010GLB.pdf (last accessed

---

R. Mares (✉)
Dr. Docent Raoul Wallenberg Institute of Human Rights and Humanitarian Law,
Lund, Sweden
e-mail: radu.mares@rwi.lu.se

© Springer Nature Switzerland AG 2019
I. Feichtner et al. (eds.), *Human Rights in the Extractive Industries*,
Interdisciplinary Studies in Human Rights 3,
https://doi.org/10.1007/978-3-030-11382-7_14

375

for advancing development their operations bring to host countries. At the same time, local communities in developing countries often associate mining with dispossession, repression, environmental degradation, conflict and social tensions, while benefits are felt mainly in capitals and the wider economy. The industry confronts a legitimacy problem. According to Ernst and Young the need for a social license to operate ranked third on the top ten list of industry-wide challenges.[2] Nowadays, obtaining this license is inconceivable without demonstrating respect for human rights.

The analysis in this chapter revolves around two notions: the disruption accompanying mining operations and local institutional development. Traditionally, the industry's social responsibility discourse has concentrated on compliance issues and contributions to economic and social development, but attention to deeper sources of risks and institutional capacities is increasingly surfacing in industry materials. For example, the International Council on Mining and Metals (ICMM) has a principle dedicated to contribution to "the social, economic and institutional development of host countries and communities."[3] The International Financial Corporation (IFC) writes that local capacity building "cannot be overemphasized;" furthermore it points out that the "local government is not always included in capacity-building considerations, yet it is frequently the critical 'missing link'."[4] Companies also show interest in more encompassing and integrated strategies to match the interlinkages and complexity in their social environment.[5]

The UN Guiding Principles on Business and Human Rights (UNGPs) stress that businesses should respect human rights and undertake human rights due diligence to address their activities' adverse impacts.[6] The responsibility not to infringe human rights is a minimum responsibility to be met by all businesses. This chapter

---

25 April 2018); UNCTAD, World Investment Report 2007: Transnational Corporations, Extractive Industries and Development. 2007, http://unctad.org/en/docs/wir2007_en.pdf (last accessed 1 October 2018).

[2] Ernst and Young, "Business Risks Facing Mining and Metals 2014–2015", referred to in ICMM, Understanding Company-Community Relations Toolkit. 2015, https://www.icmm.com/website/publications/pdfs/social-and-economic-development/9670.pdf (last accessed 1 October 2018).

[3] ICMM, Sustainable Development Framework: ICMM Principles. 2015, https://www.icmm.com/website/publications/pdfs/commitments/revised-2015_icmm-principles.pdf (last accessed 1 October 2018), Principle 9.

[4] IFC, Strategic Community Investment – A Good Practice Handbook for Companies Doing Business in Emerging Markets. 2010, https://www.ifc.org/wps/wcm/connect/f1c0538048865842b50ef76a6515bb18/12014complete-web.pdf?MOD=AJPERES&CACHEID=f1c0538048865842b50ef76a6515bb18 (last accessed 1 October 2018), pp. 74 and 51.

[5] The CEO of Anglo American writes that "all the issues we are faced with in our operating environment, such as inequality, distribution of wealth, corruption and lack of governance, are very clearly linked to the human rights of our stakeholders." Anglo American, Delivering Change, Building Resilience—Working In Partnership, Sustainability Report 2016, http://www.angloamerican.com/~/media/Files/A/Anglo-American-PLC-V2/documents/annual-reporting-2016/downloads/2016-sustainability-report.pdf (last accessed 1 October 2018), p. 14.

[6] UN Human Rights Council, UN Guiding Principles on Business and Human Rights, UN Doc. A/HRC/17/31, 21 March 2011.

accounts for the special context of mining and examines what "respecting" human rights means in the mining industry. Three questions are raised: Are social contributions[7] part of the corporate responsibility to respect under the UNGPs, and thus imperative, or are they optional, desirable, rather irrelevant or even problematic from a human rights perspective? Do industry strategies recognise institutional development as part of their social responsibility? Are there operational arrangements substantiating a shift in CSR strategy or does the shift remain largely confined to rhetoric and aspirations? The aim of the chapter is thus to clarify the relationship between social investments and respect for human rights. This should provide insight into what responsible human rights conduct in the mining sector entails in light of the UNGPs and latest corporate practices.

The analytical framework for this article revolves around institutional development—local capacities and good governance dynamics—which is essential from a human rights-based perspective.[8] The focus is on the capacities of two local stakeholders—local authorities and local communities—to cope with mining, and the positive or negative impact of mining companies on these capacities. Items such as participatory governance arrangements, capacity-building of local institutions, and corporate leverage to support good governance dynamics are highlighted. The analysis, thus, expands beyond the usual human rights accounts which tend to confine themselves to negative impacts and relegate positive social impacts to discussions on development.

In terms of sources, the chapter examines the latest reports from five of the largest mining companies[9] and the guidance from four organizations influential in the extractives sector[10] in order to discern their reasoning on the issue of institutional development. The companies were selected not as a representative sample but to serve as illustrations and ground the analysis in industry-generated materials. The four organizations guide and reflect thinking among industry stakeholders, and have touched directly on institutional development aspects.

The chapter has three delimitations. It covers primarily sources related to mining operations, rather than oil and gas as there are differences and similarities between

---

[7] The IFC refers to "strategic community investment" to mark a qualitative shift in CSR and have companies think creatively about the different ways to generate value for both business and neighboring communities IFC, Strategic Community Investment – A Good Practice Handbook for Companies Doing Business in Emerging Markets. June 2010, https://www.ifc.org/wps/wcm/connect/f1c0538048865842b50ef76a6515bb18/12014complete-web.pdf?MOD=AJPERES&CACHE ID=f1c0538048865842b50ef76a6515bb18 (last accessed 1 October 2018), pp. i–ii.

[8] UN HRBA Portal, The Human Rights Based Approach to Development Cooperation: Towards a Common Understanding Among UN Agencies. 2003, http://hrbaportal.org/the-human-rights-based-approach-to-development-cooperation-towards-a-common-understanding-among-un-agencies (last accessed 1 October 2018).

[9] BHP Billiton, Anglo American, Rio Tinto, Glencore, and Barrick Gold.

[10] The Extractive Industry Transparency Initiative (EITI) that pursues anti-corruption through disclosures on revenues generated and received; the Voluntary Principles on Security and Human Rights (VPI) that promote security arrangements that do not infringe human rights; the International Council on Mining and Metals (ICMM) as a leading industry association on sustainability issues, and the International Finance Corporation (IFC) belonging to the World Bank group.

the two industries.[11] Furthermore responsible mining encompasses mineral exploitation and trading of minerals along global supply chains, but this analysis covers only exploitation. Finally, the focus here is on large scale mining operated often by multinationals, not on small and artisanal mining.

The structure is as follows: Sect. 2 sets out the framework for human rights analysis to encompass disruption and social investments. Section 3 uses this more comprehensive analytical framework to identify shifts in industry strategy putting more emphasis on local institutional capacities and holistic solutions to facilitate good governance dynamics. Section 4 continues the analysis of the strategic shifts in four specific areas where they are particularly discernible: water management, security provision, contributions to development, and revenue transparency. Based on this examination it becomes possible to assess whether the responsibility to respect human rights takes a distinct shape in a context like mining characterised by (unavoidable) disruption.

2 Disruption and Institutional Development

The starting point is to recognize the dislocation, i.e. the far reaching impacts that a large mine's presence and its (irresponsible) operations have on host communities. The dislocation is mitigated or aggravated by the institutional capacities of local communities and local authorities to handle the harms and opportunities caused by mining. Therefore, CSR strategies in this industry must be measured by their contribution—positive or negative—to good governance dynamics. Issues of participation, capacity-building, and corporate leverage are particularly relevant. Corporate human rights policies should be measured by their depth, i.e. how they affect—beneficially or detrimentally—deeper factors leading to violations of human rights in mining areas.

2.1 Disruption: Mere Presence and Irresponsible Operations

Even when a mine with a large footprint operates rather responsibly and neither directly infringes rights nor harms the environment, the mere presence of the mine can be disruptive and produce sources of risks for communities and company alike.

---

[11] For differences between oil/gas and mining, see World Bank, Implementing the Extractive Industries Transparency Initiative – Applying Early Lessons from the Field. 2008, https://openknowledge.worldbank.org/bitstream/handle/10986/6399/439590PUB0Box310o nly109780821375013.pdf?sequence=1&isAllowed=y (last accessed 1 October 2018), p. 25 and OECD, Due Diligence Guidance for Meaningful Stakeholder Engagement in the Extractive Sector. 2017, https://read.oecd-ilibrary.org/governance/oecd-due-diligence-guidance-for-meaningful-stakeholder-engagement-in-the-extractive-sector_9789264252462-en#page4 (last accessed 1 October 2018), pp. 20–22.

The far reaching adverse impacts can take the form of side effects of population influxes, increased security risks due to military presence, displacement of previous occupations and livelihoods, new divisions within communities and aggravation of pre-existing tensions, transformation of traditional institutions with authority in the community, and so on.[12] Poorly managed, such sources of risk reinforce each other and nurture a downward spiral that deteriorates company-community relations and inhibits good governance dynamics. Social investments meant to break the vicious circle become difficult to implement as such social investments often require collaboration to achieve significant impact. As accidents and other harmful impacts occur they further compound distrust and the downward spiral.

These are reinforcing negative dynamics that diminish social capital and retard local institutional capacities on which resilient communities depend. Sand is thrown in the wheels of local and international, private and public actors that work to respect and ensure human rights of host communities. Therefore, the relation between respecting human rights and social investments needs to be placed in an operational context characterised by disruption. Respecting human rights—addressing the direct and indirect impacts of the operation—cannot be understood in separation from the responsibility and role of the business in managing that disruption.

Both mining presence as well as mining closure have far-reaching impacts for local communities. BHP Billiton, for example, recognises "the significant risks associated with ineffective closure and seek(s) to minimise these through our closure governance framework. BHP Billiton's closure framework integrates resource planning and development, health, safety and environment, stakeholder engagement, finance and assurance into business operational design."[13] The disruption caused by mine closure points to the corresponding need for local institutional development to reduce risks and grasp opportunities. The mining industry will close many large operations over the next decade. Rio Tinto writes that "[i]n many jurisdictions where we operate, regulatory frameworks for large mine closure remain undeveloped or untested. With our peers we are working on the challenges and engaging with governments on good closure policy and regulation."[14]

---

[12] IFC refers to "indirect or 'induced' impacts (such as population influx, food security, or an increased incidence of HIV/AIDS)". IFC, Strategic Community Investment – A Good Practice Handbook for Companies Doing Business in Emerging Markets. June 2010, https://www.ifc.org/wps/wcm/connect/f1c0538048865842b50ef76a6515bb18/12014complete-web.pdf?MOD=AJPE RES&CACHEID=f1c0538048865842b50ef76a6515bb18 (last accessed 1 October 2018), p. 9. See also ICRC, Addressing Security and Human Rights Challenges in Complex Environments. 2016, http://www.securityhumanrightshub.org/sites/default/files/publications/ASHRC_Toolkit_V3.pdf (last accessed 1 October 2018), Sect. 4.4.

[13] BHP Billiton, Taking the long view. Sustainable Report 2015, 2016, https://www.bhp.com/~/media/bhp/documents/society/reports/2016/160509_sustainabilityreport2015_chileanoperations.pdf (last accessed 1 October 2018), p. 15.

[14] Rio Tinto, Partnering for Progress 2016. 5 April 2017, http://www.riotinto.com/documents/170405_Partnering_for_progress_presentation_slides.pdf (last accessed 1 October 2018), p. 57.

Mining can be seen as a fragile environment due to the disruption caused by a mining presence, its (irresponsible) operations and its closure. As Ganson and Wennmann explain, in post-conflict and other fragile environments, large-scale investments in the extractive industries, commercial agriculture and infrastructure "often create stresses at the community level and also present conflict triggers for broader political, economic, social, and ecological systems" and argue that "collaborative action is required to tackle the stress factors and conflict dynamics in the context of large scale investment."[15] Their research reveals that there is "growing convergence around understandings that proactive, multi-layered, multi-sectoral, and locally-rooted initiatives represent the most promising practice for lasting conflict prevention and risk mitigation."[16]

2.2   Social Investments: Irrelevant or Even Problematic?

The UNGPs lay down a corporate responsibility to respect human rights that requires a company to act diligently when it causes, contributes or is linked to adverse impacts through its business relationships. Can the UNGPs account for social investments? Are they even relevant for a discussion on respect for human rights, understood to demand that human rights not be infringed? The answer is affirmative.

Mines operate in volatile contexts where sources of risks compound each other, particularly in developing countries displaying multiple governance gaps. To deal with such risks and weaknesses, the UNGPs call on companies to employ "human rights due diligence".[17] The latter is a proactive process meant to prevent and address harms. The more far-reaching the disruptive effects of mining, the more numerous are the actors that get involved and the harder it is to control the risks by individual actions of the company. Collaboration and comprehensive packages of measures are needed as a modality to discharge due diligence effectively. So the UNGPs can easily accommodate social investments through its human rights due diligence provisions. Furthermore, when social investments are geared toward local institutional development, they have direct significance for the other two pillars in the UNGPs regarding the capacities of public authorities (pillar 1) and rightholders (pillar 3). And the UNGPs recognize that the three pillars are mutually reinforcing: "Each pillar is an essential component in an inter-related and dynamic system of preventative and remedial measures".[18]

---

[15] Ganson and Wennmann (2012), p. 3.

[16] Ganson and Wennmann (2012), p. 3.

[17] UN Human Rights Council, UN Guiding Principles on Business and Human Rights, UN Doc. A/HRC/17/31, 21 March 2011, Principle 17.

[18] UN Human Rights Council, UN Guiding Principles on Business and Human Rights, UN Doc. A/HRC/17/31, 21 March 2011, Introduction, para. 6.

Once disruption and multiple sources of risk in a volatile context are factored into the corporate responsibility to respect human rights, the clear-cut distinction between respect for human rights and development contributions begins to break down. This is acknowledged in the 2015 UNGPs Reporting Framework: "The Reporting Framework focuses on [the baseline expectation of] respect for human rights [and] does not, therefore, address any social investment or philanthropic activities to support or promote human rights, *except where these form part of a deliberate strategy to address a risk to human rights related to the company's salient human rights issues.*"[19] Therefore, in higher risk mining settings, social investment measures are firmly situated within the corporate responsibility to respect human rights and constitute imperative rather than discretionary expenses. They should not be seen as irrelevant to a human rights analysis, as mere charity, but as commendable development contributions.

Presenting such social investments as a human rights issue might be problematic as they can distract attention and confuse audiences about what responsible mining entails. While desirable, social contributions are problematic if part of a strategy to buy the social license to operate not by reducing harms, but by continuing business as usual with add-on, check-writing programs. Therefore the UNGPs warn against such offsetting approaches: "Business enterprises may undertake other commitments or activities to support and promote human rights, which may contribute to the enjoyment of rights. But this does not offset a failure to respect human rights throughout their operations."[20] As the OHCHR writes, "there is no equivalent of a carbon off-set for harm caused to human rights: a failure to respect human rights in one area cannot be cancelled out by a benefit provided in another."[21]

The concern regarding offsetting appears also in the context of the Sustainable Development Goals (SDGs),[22] where the private sector is seen as a key vehicle for development, from the financing to the implementation stage. Ruggie warns that this global framework covering business conduct should not end up de-emphasizing respect for human rights: "business has a critical role to play in achieving the Sustainable Development Goals. This role must be founded on respect for human rights and *not on philanthropy or social investment*, much as they too are needed. Sustainable development depends not just on *generous* business, but first and foremost on responsible business."[23]

---

[19] Shift and Mazars LLP, UN Guiding Principles Reporting Framework. 2015, https://www.ungpreporting.org/wp-content/uploads/UNGPReportingFramework_2017.pdf (last accessed 1 October 2018), p. 5. (emphasis added).

[20] UN Human Rights Council, UN Guiding Principles on Business and Human Rights, UN Doc. A/HRC/17/31, 21 March 2011, Principle 11, Commentary.

[21] OHCHR, The Corporate Responsibility to Respect Human Rights. An Interpretive Guide, UN Doc. HR/PUB/12/02, June 2012, pp. 14–15.

[22] UN General Assembly, Transforming our world: the 2030 Agenda for Sustainable Development, A/RES/70/1, 21 October 2015.

[23] John Ruggie in H&M, Conscious Actions Sustainability Report 2015, https://sustainability.hm.com/content/dam/hm/about/documents/en/CSR/2015%20Sustainability%20report/HM_SustainabilityReport_2015_final_FullReport_en.pdf (last accessed 1 October 2018), p. 68. (emphasis added).

The argument in this chapter is that social investments are particularly relevant to a human rights analysis if they advance local institutional capacities and good governance dynamics. This indicator may be used to expose social contributions as a smokescreen when companies actually retard institutional development. For example, reports from Nigeria indicate that a multinational won oil licenses with an offer much inferior to that of competitors, possibly due to corruption.[24] Yet, bribery retards institutional development. Also it is common for companies to negotiate significant tax rebates just to beat the drum loudly afterwards for their voluntary social contributions worth a fraction of the tax rebate. Both these versions of offsetting are problematic as they diminish institutional capacities: the rule of law is weakened and public budgets are deprived of revenues for essential services.

2.3   Institutional Development: The Missing Link

A focus on institutional development and good governance dynamics in host communities is warranted as they help to cope with the disruption caused by mining. Some businesses set up operational grievance mechanisms that meet the criteria of the UNGPs[25] as part of their commitment to respect human rights which is a worthwhile contribution to institutional development. More companies are keen to highlight their contribution to development. They insist on *economic* development wherein companies contribute jobs, taxes, business opportunities, credit schemes, training for local entrepreneurs and employees, and *social* development wherein companies support social services such as education, health, and sanitation. Such economic and social contributions are also cross-referenced with the SDG framework.[26] They are further understood as "community investment" which implies that companies consider them strategic and measurable just like other business investments normally are assessed.[27]

Overall, however, in corporate reports contributions to institutional development tend to drown among expositions of economic and social contributions. They are not highlighted conceptually and tracked systematically. At times, relevant aspects

---

[24] Global Witness, Probe into Murky ExxonMobil Deal Shows Why Strong U.S. Transparency Rules are Needed for Oil Companies, 24 June 2016, https://www.globalwitness.org/en/press-releases/probe-murky-exxonmobil-deal-shows-why-strong-us-transparency-rules-are-needed-oil-companies/ (last accessed 1 October 2018).

[25] UN Human Rights Council, UN Guiding Principles on Business and Human Rights, UN Doc. A/HRC/17/31, 21 March 2011, Principle 31.

[26] For an example, BHP Billiton, Integrity Resilience Growth Sustainability Report 2016. 2016, https://www.bhp.com/-/media/bhp/documents/investors/annual-reports/2016/bhpbillitonsustainabilityreport2016.pdf (last accessed 1 October 2018).

[27] IFC, Strategic Community Investment – A Good Practice Handbook for Companies Doing Business in Emerging Markets. June 2010, https://www.ifc.org/wps/wcm/connect/f1c0538048865 842b50ef76a6515bb18/12014complete-web.pdf?MOD=AJPERES&CACHEID=f1c0538048865 842b50ef76a6515bb18 (last accessed 1 October 2018), pp. i–ii.

such as the unintended effects of CSR creating dependency and divisions among host communities have been highlighted.[28] As the next sections shows, a wealth of industry materials is now recognising these aspects. But a systematic assessment of corporate impacts on institutional development and capacity constraints faced by two local actors—local governments and local communities—is still underdeveloped.[29] The need is however pressing if the far reaching effects of mining are to be addressed effectively. To begin with, *local governments* often fall short in human resources, logistics, ability to attract financial resources, or ability to function in a stifling legal framework. When local authorities are weak, ineffective, or corrupt, vulnerability increases further if *local communities* also fall short in their capacities to organise under an effective, knowledgeable, representative leadership, to network externally to enhance their leverage, to use the legal system, to effectively engage in participatory development following decentralisation, and to hold local officials accountable.

A rare analysis of these aspects in a corporate report comes from Anglo American which indicates that "Good local institutional capacity depends on at least six building blocks:

- Participation of citizens in the public processes and decisions that affect their lives, including planning and budgeting.
- Partnerships among local governmental institutions, community-based organisations (CBOs) and the private sector for transparent, accountable and equitable service delivery and local development.
- Capacity of local institutions to respond to peoples' needs and facilitate local development and governance processes.
- Effective information channels for communication between state and non-state actors.
- Accountability between local representatives and their constituents (including citizens and CBOs), and between government bodies (both local and national).
- Appropriate administrative, fiscal, political and legal frameworks for local governments to function effectively."[30]

To date, institutional development is far from being recognised as an essential cross-cutting issue for evaluating CSR performance.[31] Some companies continue to

---

[28] Warner and Sullivan (2004); McPhail, Sustainable Development in the Mining and Minerals Sector. May 2008, http://nrc.resourcegovernance.org/sites/default/files/Rei-Essay-FINAL.pdf (last accessed 1 October 2018).

[29] Bebbington A et al., Mining and Development in Peru. 2007, http://www.perusupportgroup.org.uk/files/fckUserFiles/file/FINAL%20-%20Mining%20and%20Development%20in%20Peru.pdf (last accessed 1 October 2018); Bebbington (2011) (discussing institutional development in the mining industry).

[30] Anglo American, Social-Economic Assessment Toolbox. Version 3. 2012, http://www.foretica.org/wp-content/uploads/2015/12/SEAT-Toolbox-Angloamerican.pdf (last accessed 1 October 2018), p. 185.

[31] For example, "At Barrick, we believe strong relationships with communities are about getting the simple things right: managing our impacts (such as dust, noise and traffic), doing what we say we

concentrate on delivering and measuring contributions to economic and social development.[32] Companies often touch on institutional development narrowly by referring to their policies on corruption and revenue transparency. For example, BHP Billiton recently launched its Global Signature Programs encompassing two projects on anti-corruption led by Transparency International and on financial transparency led by World Bank; their aims are to "enhance citizens' ability to use data and improve the governance capacity of institutions."[33] Indeed, bribery and secrecy around revenues generated by mining are classic ways in which the extractive sector has historically retarded local institutional development. Anti-bribery laws in home states as well as the Extractive Industry Transparency Initiative[34] offer detailed standards and guidance on how to counter bribery and secrecy. These two areas are entry points for businesses beginning to focus on institutional development.

Sometimes the importance of institutional development is clearly stated but is yet to be elaborated meaningfully. For example, the leading industry organization, ICMM dedicates one of its foundational principles to institutional development of both local authorities and local communities: "Pursue continual improvement in social performance and contribute to the social, economic and institutional development of host countries and communities."[35] However, the notion of institutional development is hardly developed in the sub-paragraphs. These refer to social and economic development while institutional development is replaced by vague notions of partnership and collaboration.

In sum, focusing on institutional development is essential for managing the disruption accompanying mining. But are the CSR strategies of mining companies conceived and implemented in ways that enhance local capacities? The next section analyses a number of shifts appearing in the industry from simpler models of CSR towards more comprehensive assessments and holistic responses.

---

will, resolving grievances, and buying and hiring locally." Barrick Gold Corporation, Advancing Together. 2016 GRI Content Index, https://www.unglobalcompact.org/system/attachments/cop_2017/391931/original/Barrick_2016_GRI_Content_Index.pdf?1497042875, (last accessed 1 October 2018), p. 107.

[32] For example Glencore launched in 2015 its socio-economic contribution scorecard which does not refer to institutional capacity aspects and focuses on socio-economic contributions: "While the most significant [contributions] derive from employment and procurement, we also have a responsibility to *minimise dependency* on our operations, and *promote diversified and resilient local economies*." Glencore, Sustainability Report 2016, http://www.glencore.com/sustainability/reports-and-presentations (last accessed 1 October 2018), p. 43.

[33] BHP Billiton, Integrity Resilience Growth Sustainability Report 2016. 2016, https://www.bhp.com/-/media/bhp/documents/investors/annual-reports/2016/bhpbillitonsustainabilityreport2016.pdf (last accessed 1 October 2018), p. 19.

[34] See the chapter by Feldt on the EITI in this volume.

[35] ICMM, Sustainable Development Framework: ICMM Principles. 2015, https://www.icmm.com/website/publications/pdfs/commitments/revised-2015_icmm-principles.pdf (last accessed 1 October 2018), Principle 9.

3 Shifts in CSR Strategy

The previous section emphasized that social investments fall squarely within the corporate responsibility to respect human rights, and that contribution to institutional development should be a key indicator for assessing corporate performance. This section argues that the way in which the industry accounts for disruption and sources of risk is shifting. There are signs that institutional development is emerging as a cross-cutting dimension in corporate strategic documents. This section covers this shift at the strategic level while the next section shows how the shift has played out in four operational settings.

Industry documents point to two main shifts in CSR thinking. One shift regards social contributions: there is a move away from philanthropy to *community investment*, and from economic and social development towards the inclusion of *institutional development* aspects also. The other shift regards overall CSR strategies: there is a shift from punctual interventions towards more *encompassing strategies* and from partnerships to *"meaningful partnerships"* in ways that address both negative and positive impacts through more holistic assessments and solutions tackling deeper causes. Thus, there is a growing emphasis on effective local institutions and local governance dynamics able to build resilient communities able to cope with mining. What is being analysed here might be more profound than a mere partnership approach; indeed such collaborations and collective action have been around for a while and the partnership rhetoric has been used in CSR for the last two decades.

This section assesses strategic level documents from both individual companies and influential organizations within the industry. They reflect the latest conceptualisation of CSR and are based on lessons learned from past experiments. They explain why these shifts are necessary and what the nature of the CSR task is. As the analytical spotlight is on institutional development, a number of components will be tracked: *participatory (inclusive) governance* mechanisms, *capacity-building* of local stakeholders, corporate *leverage* to support good governance dynamics and remove a myriad of bottlenecks, and encompassing strategies accounting for the interaction of *negative and positive impacts*.

3.1 Shifts in Social Investment

3.1.1 Shift from Philanthropy to Community Investment

The shift away from philanthropy to community investment is compellingly explained in the IFC Handbook on Strategic Community Investment.[36] The IFC draws on the "lessons and practical experiences of IFC, its client companies, and

---

[36] IFC, Strategic Community Investment – A Good Practice Handbook for Companies Doing Business in Emerging Markets. June 2010, https://www.ifc.org/wps/wcm/connect/f1c0538048865

other organizations focused on the private sector in emerging markets"[37] to explain how good practice regarding community investment continues to evolve. Participatory approaches and institutional development are two issues increasingly mentioned as some companies move away from hand-outs and mere compliance with (imperfect) local laws. The IFC eloquently presents 12 reasons why "old-style" community investment has underperformed despite the considerable time, goodwill, and resources invested[38] and observes:

> Companies are moving away from philanthropic donations and ad hoc practices to more sophisticated and strategic ways of planning and delivering their community investment programs. There is greater emphasis on the business case—on viewing CI [community investment] through the lens of risk and opportunity, and on creating "shared value" by aligning business goals and competencies with the development priorities of local stakeholders. Other trends include a focus on building social capital and local ownership through multi-stakeholder processes; factoring sustainability and handover strategies into project design; and measuring and communicating results to optimize the business value derived from CI.[39]

3.1.2 Shift from Economic and Social Development to Institutional Development

The shift from economic and social development to institutional development appears clearly in BHP Billiton's Social Investment Framework. It covers three themes: governance, human capability and social inclusion, and environment.[40] The "governance" theme has two components: institutional strengthening, and transparency and corruption. However, while the latter two areas—revenue secrecy and bribery—are well conceptualized in detail, "institutional strengthening" appears as only an incipient issue.[41] Indeed, in its policy paper dedicated to communities BHP

842b50ef76a6515bb18/12014complete-web.pdf?MOD=AJPERES&CACHEID=f1c0538048865 842b50ef76a6515bb18 (last accessed 1 October 2018).

[37] IFC, Strategic Community Investment – A Good Practice Handbook for Companies Doing Business in Emerging Markets. June 2010, https://www.ifc.org/wps/wcm/connect/f1c0538048865 842b50ef76a6515bb18/12014complete-web.pdf?MOD=AJPERES&CACHEID=f1c0538048865 842b50ef76a6515bb18 (last accessed 1 October 2018), p. ii.

[38] IFC, Strategic Community Investment – A Good Practice Handbook for Companies Doing Business in Emerging Markets. June 2010, https://www.ifc.org/wps/wcm/connect/f1c0538048865 842b50ef76a6515bb18/12014complete-web.pdf?MOD=AJPERES&CACHEID=f1c0538048865 842b50ef76a6515bb18 (last accessed 1 October 2018), p. 1.

[39] IFC, Strategic Community Investment – A Good Practice Handbook for Companies Doing Business in Emerging Markets. June 2010, https://www.ifc.org/wps/wcm/connect/f1c0538048865 842b50ef76a6515bb18/12014complete-web.pdf?MOD=AJPERES&CACHEID=f1c0538048865 842b50ef76a6515bb18 (last accessed 1 October 2018), p. i.

[40] BHP Billiton, Community – Our Requirements. 7 April 2017 https://www.bhp.com/-/media/ documents/ourapproach/governance/160404_community.pdf?la=en, (last accessed 1 October 2018), pp. 2–3.

[41] For latest details and indicators, BHP Billiton, Integrity Resilience Growth Sustainability Report 2016. 2016, https://www.bhp.com/-/media/bhp/documents/investors/annual-reports/2016/bhpbillitonsustainabilityreport2016.pdf (last accessed 1 October 2018), p. 38.

Fig. 1 BHP Billiton's social investment framework (BHP Billioton, Taking the long view. Sustainability Report 2015. 2016, https://www.bhp.com/~/media/bhp/documents/society/reports/2016/160509_sustainabilityreport2015_chileanoperations.pdf (last accessed 1 October 2018))

Billiton does not elaborate on "institutional strengthening", which receives only cursory attention (Fig. 1).[42]

Anglo American offers a comprehensive framework that visualizes how inputs translate into outcomes as they are mediated by the market sector interacting with the social sector. Part of the social sector are elements of "government capacity building" and "social investment". The company appears to direct resources towards these two elements. Furthermore, the graphic indicates the interdependency between the company's economic and social contributions. While institutional development is not front and center in this graphic, it is indicated clearly as part of the social performance of the company (Fig. 2).

The IFC analyses how the presence and interventions of the company affect stakeholders and their relationships. The Handbook mentioned above draws attention to the imperative of understanding "the local ecosystem".[43] Such understanding is essential for implementing community investment (CI) smoothly as well as for grasping the far reaching impacts of CI on local stakeholders and local dynamics. In a graphic the IFC maps a multitude of elements ("variables") grouped in four clusters. Two clusters refer to local actors: one mentions institutions and their capacities while another cluster refers to communities and their (social) capital. This dovetails the emphasis in this chapter on local authorities and local communities as essential for coping with a mine's impacts. A third cluster captures "risk factors" and obstacles to CI that revolve around weaknesses in local institutional development, such as elite capture, corruption, and low capacity. Based on this graphic it follows that community investment should concentrate more on institutional development aspects and not remain fixated on economic and social benefits. Finally this emphasis on the local context and institutional weaknesses carries insights beyond CI for other strategic approaches that tackle the negative impacts of mining (Fig. 3).

---

[42] BHP Billiton, Community – Our Requirements. 7 April 2017 https://www.bhp.com/-/media/documents/ourapproach/governance/160404_community.pdf?la=en (last accessed 25 April 2018), pp. 2–3.

[43] IFC, Strategic Community Investment – A Good Practice Handbook for Companies Doing Business in Emerging Markets. June 2010, https://www.ifc.org/wps/wcm/connect/f1c0538048865 842b50ef76a6515bb18/12014complete-web.pdf?MOD=AJPERES&CACHEID=f1c0538048865 842b50ef76a6515bb18 (last accessed 1 October 2018), p. 25.

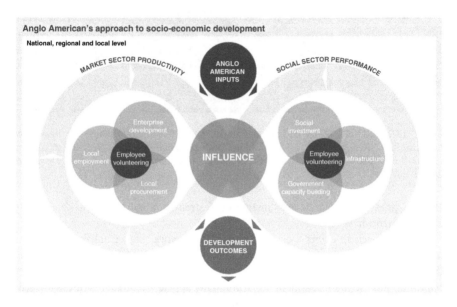

Fig. 2 Anglo American's approach to development (Anglo American, Delivering Change, Building Resilience—Working In Partnership, Sustainability Report 2016, http://www.angloamerican.com/~/media/Files/A/Anglo-American-PLC-V2/documents/annual-reporting-2016/downloads/2016-sustainability-report.pdf (last accessed 1 October 2018), p. 47)

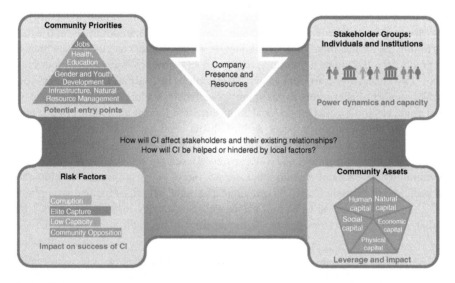

Fig. 3 IFC on community investment and variables of the local context (IFC, Strategic Community Investment—A Good Practice Handbook for Companies Doing Business in Emerging Markets. June 2010, https://www.ifc.org/wps/wcm/connect/f1c0538048865842b50ef76a6515bb18/12014complete-web.pdf?MOD=AJPERES&CACHEID=f1c0538048865842b50ef76a6515bb18 (last accessed 1 October 2018), p. 25)

3.2 Shifts in Social Responsibility

3.2.1 Shift from Punctual Interventions to More Encompassing Approaches

There is a shift in CSR thinking from punctual interventions towards more comprehensive framing and integrated solutions. As the complexity of the local context is appreciated more, understanding grows on how the negative impacts (infringements) from mining interact in the volatile local context. Even attempts to deliver positive impacts (benefits) can become sources of risk. These are sources of risk that interact, compound each other and shortcut efforts for responsible mining and satisfactory company-community relations. Therefore isolated assessment and compartmentalised efforts to comply or deliver socio-economic benefits tend to fall short. These efforts are not able to address either the interrelations among the sources of risks or the deeper causes of abuses, including those having to do with a weak local institutional set-up.

Anglo American puts forward an "integrated approach to managing all of our risks and impacts".[44] In its strategy paper Social Way, the company defines social performance as encompassing "stakeholder engagement, management of social risks and impacts, human rights and our approach to socio-economic development... [A]ll Anglo American managed sites [have] to ensure that systems are in place to: engage with affected and interested stakeholders; avoid, prevent, mitigate and, where appropriate, remediate adverse social impacts; and maximise development opportunities."[45]

The ICMM also offers a holistic framework and discusses institutional capacity. Its Toolkit on why community support may be lacking places corporate inputs and impacts into context. Thus it identifies three external, "contextual factors": sociopolitical and governance context, equity and social capital considerations, and reputational context (of the broader industry). These factors are deemed "critical to understanding community–company relationships since they help define the environment in which those relationships take place."[46]

Regarding the sociopolitical and governance context the Toolkit explains that "good governance for the mining sector includes, at a minimum, a clear and reputable legal framework combined with the institutional capacity to execute that

[44] Anglo American, Social Way. Version 2. 2014 http://www.angloamerican.com/~/media/Files/A/Anglo-American-PLC-V2/documents/approach-and-policies/social/aa-social-way-singles-v2.pdf (last accessed 1 October 2018), p. 6.

[45] Anglo American, Social Way. Version 2. 2014 http://www.angloamerican.com/~/media/Files/A/Anglo-American-PLC-V2/documents/approach-and-policies/social/aa-social-way-singles-v2.pdf (last accessed 1 October 2018), p. 6.

[46] ICMM, Understanding Company-Community Relations Toolkit. 2015, https://www.icmm.com/website/publications/pdfs/social-and-economic-development/9670.pdf (last accessed 1 October 2018), p. 17.

framework in an accountable and reliable manner."[47] This helps create a conducive environment. "Conversely, governance and political frameworks that lack credibility, effectiveness and accountability, with weak institutional capacity, tend to inhibit healthy community–company relationships."[48] Moreover, the Toolkit welcomes simultaneous emphasis on both negative human rights impacts ("implementation of impact management measures") and positive impacts ("social investment").[49] In sum, the ICMM's comprehensive approach prevents isolated assessments and emphasises local institutional capacity in order to enhance community support and move towards responsible mining.

The IFC recommends a "Holistic Approach to Community Relations" based on four components: "When it comes to managing company-community relationships, *community investment* [CI] is only one part of the equation [and] should not be thought of as the company's primary means for *risk management, stakeholder engagement*, or local *job creation*."[50] The IFC, thus, indicates that CI should not offset other ways to minimize harm (risk mitigation) or essential ways to produce positive impacts (in particular create jobs).[51] However, although holistic strategies to manage interacting sources of risk are important, they are not always necessary, the IFC maintains. The Handbook distinguishes here between "higher risk" contexts and other less challenging settings.[52] The higher risk contexts are those where there are "significant project impacts on local communities, where basic needs and expectations for benefits are high, or where the affected communities do not have the

---

[47] ICMM, Understanding Company-Community Relations Toolkit. 2015, https://www.icmm.com/website/publications/pdfs/social-and-economic-development/9670.pdf (last accessed 1 October 2018), p. 17.

[48] ICMM, Understanding Company-Community Relations Toolkit. 2015, https://www.icmm.com/website/publications/pdfs/social-and-economic-development/9670.pdf (last accessed 1 October 2018), p. 17.

[49] How these inputs translate into impacts depends on the context where governance and social capital must be highlighted. Figure H.2: Input–output–outcome–impact analysis. ICMM, Understanding Company-Community Relations Toolkit. 2015, https://www.icmm.com/website/publications/pdfs/social-and-economic-development/9670.pdf (last accessed 1 October 2018), p. 71.

[50] IFC, Strategic Community Investment – A Good Practice Handbook for Companies Doing Business in Emerging Markets. June 2010, https://www.ifc.org/wps/wcm/connect/f1c0538048865842b50ef76a6515bb18/12014complete-web.pdf?MOD=AJPERES&CACHEID=f1c0538048865842b50ef76a6515bb18 (last accessed 1 October 2018), p. 9. (emphasis added).

[51] IFC, Strategic Community Investment – A Good Practice Handbook for Companies Doing Business in Emerging Markets. June 2010, https://www.ifc.org/wps/wcm/connect/f1c0538048865842b50ef76a6515bb18/12014complete-web.pdf?MOD=AJPERES&CACHEID=f1c0538048865842b50ef76a6515bb18 (last accessed 1 October 2018), p. 9.

[52] The IFC indicates that "[n]ot every project needs to have a CI program. In fact, many projects can reduce their social risks by managing project impacts well and adjusting their business practices and procedures to increase local economic benefits." IFC, Strategic Community Investment – A Good Practice Handbook for Companies Doing Business in Emerging Markets. June 2010, https://www.ifc.org/wps/wcm/connect/f1c0538048865842b50ef76a6515bb18/12014complete-web.pdf?MOD=AJPERES&CACHEID=f1c0538048865842b50ef76a6515bb18 (last accessed 1 October 2018), p. 5.

ability (i.e. skills or resources) to take advantage of development opportunities being created by private investment".[53] Apparently, the mining operations that make it onto the human rights agenda invariably fall into the higher risk context which then requires indeed the kind of holistic approach the IFC puts forward.

BHP Billiton uses the comprehensive framework of the SDGs to explain its performance in terms of socio-economic benefits as well as the way the company seeks to work in a rights-respecting and inclusive manner:

> In addition to the role the resources we produce play in improving the quality of life of billions of people around the world, we contribute towards the achievement of the SDGs in three ways. Firstly, through our business activities, including the direct and indirect employment we create through our workforce and supply chains. Secondly, through the use by our host governments of the taxes and royalties we pay. And thirdly, through our voluntary social investment. Importantly, we also *contribute through how we work* – for example, through our respect for human rights, zero tolerance for bribery and corruption, minimising our environmental footprint, recognition of gender equality, diversity and inclusiveness and support for reconciliation with Indigenous peoples.[54]

In their study of large-scale investments in fragile environments, Ganson and Wennmann placed "locally-rooted capabilities and systems" at the centre of their framework for action:

> [S]trong and resilient local actors are required to identify and mobilize appropriate responses to stress factors, tensions, and risks from whatever source. Whether the goal is characterized as a "stable operating environment" or "peace", all actors share common questions in these contexts. The first is how best to strengthen dispute resolution and prevention capacities that better manage the overlapping, diverging and conflicting interests of communities, state authorities, and companies, as well as the multiple risks to which these interests are exposed. The second question is the role of various national and international actors in supporting such capacities and risk mitigation strategies.[55]

3.2.2   Shift from Partnerships to Meaningful Partnerships

There is also a shift from partnerships to "meaningful" partnerships,[56] that is, collaborations that highlight aspects of capacity-building and inclusion. The partnership approach stems from the realisation that by-passing local authorities,

---

[53] IFC, Strategic Community Investment – A Good Practice Handbook for Companies Doing Business in Emerging Markets. June 2010, https://www.ifc.org/wps/wcm/connect/f1c0538048865 842b50ef76a6515bb18/12014complete-web.pdf?MOD=AJPERES&CACHEID=f1c0538048865 842b50ef76a6515bb18 (last accessed 1 October 2018), p. 5.

[54] BHP Billiton, Integrity Resilience Growth Sustainability Report 2016. 2016, https://www.bhp.com/-/media/bhp/documents/investors/annual-reports/2016/bhpbillitonsustainabilityreport2016.pdf (last accessed 1 October 2018), p. 10.

[55] Ganson B and Wennmann A, Confronting Risk, Mobilizing Action. A Framework for Conflict Prevention in the Context of Large-scale Business Investments. December 2012, http://library.fes.de/pdf-files/iez/global/09577.pdf (last accessed 1 October 2018), p. 5.

[56] OECD, OECD Due Diligence Guidance for Meaningful Stakeholder Engagement in the Extractive Sector. 2017, https://read.oecd-ilibrary.org/governance/oecd-due-diligence-guidance-

communities and rightholders generates a litany of negative effects such as ineffective interventions, unsustainable results, dependency, community divisions and conflict, and mistrust. The benefits and risks of partnerships are well documented, and some benefits hint directly at good governance dynamics: leverage, capacity-building, and sustainability of benefits. The IFC identifies five strategic reasons to partner: risk sharing, ability to leverage resources, extended reach, scalability, and enhanced likelihood of successful outcomes (for example shared ownership and sustainability).[57] Anglo American discusses both benefits and risks of partnerships, with benefits including "diverse perspectives, skills and solutions; improved understanding of partner organisations; credibility amongst stakeholders; reduced dependency and enhanced sustainability (particularly relevant in the context of mine closure); capacity-building among partners; opportunities to leverage resources; and reputational benefits.[58]

Once the decision not to by-pass local actors has been taken, it is essential to move to meaningful partnership. Partnership does not automatically ensure participation. The latter requires tackling the multitude of bottlenecks that disable participation. Insufficient capacity to participate and exclusionary dynamics are such bottlenecks that speak directly to the idea of institutional development and participatory local governance. As the IFC writes, every program is an opportunity to build institutional capacity[59] and exercise leverage over public authorities.[60] For Anglo

---

for-meaningful-stakeholder-engagement-in-the-extractive-sector_9789264252462-en#page4 (last accessed 1 October 2018) emphasises "meaningful stakeholder engagement".

[57] IFC, Strategic Community Investment – A Good Practice Handbook for Companies Doing Business in Emerging Markets. June 2010, https://www.ifc.org/wps/wcm/connect/f1c0538048865 842b50ef76a6515bb18/12014complete-web.pdf?MOD=AJPERES&CACHEID=f1c0538048865 842b50ef76a6515bb18, (last accessed 1 October 2018), pp. 89–91.

[58] The potential risks of partnering include "reputation impact, potential for conflict, slower decision-making, corruption, reduced control and, potentially, additional bureaucracy." Anglo American, Social-Economic Assessment Toolbox. Version 3. 2012, http://www.foretica.org/wp-content/uploads/2015/12/SEAT-Toolbox-Angloamerican.pdf (last accessed 1 October 2018), p. 154.

[59] The Handbook offers tips regarding strategic community investment such as "Choose the option that builds local ownership and capacity." IFC, Strategic Community Investment – A Good Practice Handbook for Companies Doing Business in Emerging Markets. June 2010, https://www.ifc.org/wps/wcm/connect/f1c0538048865842b50ef76a6515bb18/12014complete-web.pdf?MOD=AJPE RES&CACHEID=f1c0538048865842b50ef76a6515bb18 (last accessed 1 October 2018, p. iv).

[60] Another tip is to "Move away from doing it yourself to making sure it gets done. Instead of substituting for government by providing health and education services, companies are increasingly using their access and leverage to ensure that local community needs are met. This can be done by lobbying the government to provide services, using contacts to attract external donor funds and forge partnerships, or building the capacity of communities to take these types of actions themselves… [When] communities trust that a company is willing to support them over a longer time-frame, they are more likely to prioritize skills training and capacity building." IFC, Strategic Community Investment – A Good Practice Handbook for Companies Doing Business in Emerging Markets. June 2010, https://www.ifc.org/wps/wcm/connect/f1c0538048865842b50ef76a6515bb1 8/12014complete-web.pdf?MOD=AJPERES&CACHEID=f1c0538048865842b50ef76a651 5bb18 (last accessed 1 October 2018), p. iv.

American, "Developing local institutional capacity is increasingly seen as a vital step in promoting good governance and sustainable development. Capacity development can encourage this by bringing local government closer to citizens, allowing constituents to participate more effectively, tailoring decisions to local needs, and enabling more effective provision of public services."[61] The IFC further observes:

> Capacity building is one of the least understood yet most important aspects of development work. Building human and social capital is integral to strategic community investment because it leverages and multiplies the impact of CI resources by strengthening local partner organizations, promoting self-reliance, and increasing the likelihood of project success. Effective capacity building benefits both the company and local stakeholders by generating inclusive processes that strengthen trust and build commitment and good relationships.[62]

Inviting cooperation with and among local stakeholders overturns governance dynamics where previously marginalized communities might not want the government involved, or where governments do not support or facilitate company-community agreement processes.[63] The IFC suggests that government representatives and traditional authorities might fear that community-led planning processes threaten the status quo.[64] Therefore grasping the local context is essential if interventions are to be effective. Elite capture,[65] local governance issues,[66] inclusion

---

[61] Anglo American, Social-Economic Assessment Toolbox. Version 3. 2012, http://www.foretica. org/wp-content/uploads/2015/12/SEAT-Toolbox-Angloamerican.pdf (last accessed 1 October 2018), p. 185.

[62] IFC, Strategic Community Investment – A Good Practice Handbook for Companies Doing Business in Emerging Markets. June 2010, https://www.ifc.org/wps/wcm/connect/f1c0538048865 842b50ef76a6515bb18/12014complete-web.pdf?MOD=AJPERES&CACHEID=f1c0538048865 842b50ef76a6515bb18 (last accessed 1 October 2018), p. 49.

[63] Rio Tinto, Why agreements matter. March 2016, http://www.riotinto.com/documents/Rio_ Tinto_Why_Agreements_Matter.pdf (last accessed 1 October 2018), pp. 89.

[64] IFC, Strategic Community Investment – A Good Practice Handbook for Companies Doing Business in Emerging Markets. June 2010, https://www.ifc.org/wps/wcm/connect/f1c0538048865 842b50ef76a6515bb18/12014complete-web.pdf?MOD=AJPERES&CACHEID=f1c0538048865 842b50ef76a6515bb18 (last accessed 1 October 2018), p. 29.

[65] "Some communities can be highly stratified, with power structures dominated by traditional "elites" who control most of the community decisions regarding resource use and management… It undermines representation, participation, and fairness in the distribution of benefits." IFC, Strategic Community Investment – A Good Practice Handbook for Companies Doing Business in Emerging Markets. June 2010, https://www.ifc.org/wps/wcm/connect/f1c0538048865842b50ef76 a6515bb18/12014complete-web.pdf?MOD=AJPERES&CACHEID=f1c0538048865842b50ef76 a6515bb18 (last accessed 1 October 2018), p. 28.

[66] The government can be hindered by corruption and vested interests, lack of resources and institutional capacity, power dynamics between elected and traditional authorities, historical distrust between government authorities and communities, and patronage politics. "Past lessons point to the importance of promoting CI without circumventing local government, and implementing initiatives to build local government capacity and promote accountability and inclusiveness." IFC, Strategic Community Investment – A Good Practice Handbook for Companies Doing Business in Emerging Markets. June 2010, https://www.ifc.org/wps/wcm/connect/f1c0538048865842b50ef76 a6515bb18/12014complete-web.pdf?MOD=AJPERES&CACHEID=f1c0538048865842b50ef76 a6515bb18 (last accessed 1 October 2018), p. 29.

and gender,[67] historical legacy,[68] conflict,[69] and availability of local partners[70] should be taken into account.

Inclusion is thus inherent in the idea of meaningful partnership. There is a strong focus on intra-community dynamics in some industry materials. For example, the ICMM requires in its Principles companies to "[e]nsure that appropriate systems are in place for ongoing interaction with affected parties, making sure that minorities and other marginalized groups have equitable and culturally appropriate means of engagement."[71] Indeed, the government, social groups in the community, or even the rightholders might be excluded. To prevent such exclusion, BHP Billiton calls on its staff regarding community investment projects to "never… implement a community development project that will intentionally, or likely replace, take over or destabilise

---

[67] "Some communities may not historically favor participation and inclusion; others do. … Experience shows that without specific measures to ensure their inclusion, the most vulnerable groups are typically excluded from, or underrepresented in, the development process." Companies are advised to use a range of techniques to address for example gender imbalances and promote women's participation: participatory techniques, awareness raising, support around the non-traditional roles women can perform, use of gender-sensitized facilitators, timing meetings to accommodate women's schedules, and organizing separate women's meetings. IFC, Strategic Community Investment – A Good Practice Handbook for Companies Doing Business in Emerging Markets. June 2010, https://www.ifc.org/wps/wcm/connect/f1c0538048865842b50ef76a6515bb18/12014c omplete-web.pdf?MOD=AJPERES&CACHEID=f1c0538048865842b50ef76a6515bb18 (last accessed 1 October 2018), p. 28.

[68] Past actions of governments and private companies have left a legacy of mistrust "in response to environmental damage, land disputes, unfair compensation, broken promises, corrupt practices, non-transparent behavior, and/or human rights abuses." IFC, Strategic Community Investment – A Good Practice Handbook for Companies Doing Business in Emerging Markets, June 2010, https:// www.ifc.org/wps/wcm/connect/f1c0538048865842b50ef76a6515bb18/12014complete-web.pdf? MOD=AJPERES&CACHEID=f1c0538048865842b50ef76a6515bb18 (last accessed 1 October 2018), p. 28.

[69] The risks lies in CI creating or exacerbating existing tensions around CI resources; "Done well, [CI] can play an important role in bringing groups together around shared interests, facilitating collaborative processes, and strengthening the capacities of local actors." IFC, Strategic Community Investment – A Good Practice Handbook for Companies Doing Business in Emerging Markets. June 2010, https://www.ifc.org/wps/wcm/connect/f1c0538048865842b50ef76a6515bb18/12014c omplete-web.pdf?MOD=AJPERES&CACHEID=f1c0538048865842b50ef76a6515bb18 (last accessed 1 October 2018), p. 29.

[70] "Experience has shown that even where there are local NGOs and CBOs [community-based organizations], these organizations can lack capacity, accountability, transparency, or representativeness. CBOs in particular are often informal in structure and tend to reflect the power structures and cultural values of their communities." Companies should "be prepared to invest time and patience in a long-term process of capacity building and mutual learning." IFC, Strategic Community Investment – A Good Practice Handbook for Companies Doing Business in Emerging Markets. June 2010, https://www.ifc.org/wps/wcm/connect/f1c0538048865842b50ef76a6515bb1 8/12014complete-web.pdf?MOD=AJPERES&CACHEID=f1c0538048865842b50ef76a651 5bb18 (last accessed 1 October 2018), p. 29.

[71] ICMM, Sustainable Development Framework: ICMM Principles. 2015, https://www.icmm.com/ website/publications/pdfs/commitments/revised-2015_icmm-principles.pdf (last accessed 1 October 2018), Principle 9.

the authority of any level of government."[72] The company should not intentionally sow divisions along political, religious or ethnic lines. Its "approach to community investment specifically excludes contributions to any religious organization for religious purposes, as they may be considered socially exclusive."[73]

This shift toward meaningful partnerships comes at a time when the rhetoric of partnership is prevalent throughout the industry. Anglo American has incorporated the partnership approach in its very vision as an organization—"To be partners in the future"—and states: "It is our belief that Anglo American, and mining as an industry, has both the potential and responsibility to act as a development partner, for the long term benefit of society."[74] Barrick includes in its Human Rights Compliance Program five core principles. One is about "partnership and collaboration" covering global and local partnerships, dealing with negative and positive impacts, given that "We continue to face human rights dilemmas that defy easy answers."[75] Rio Tinto also emphasizes partnerships: "Partnership is make or break for our industry and for Rio Tinto... This allows us to manage risk in the short term, in relation to our existing operations, and gives us the ability to secure new deposits in the medium and the long term."[76] For companies extorting the virtues of partnership, focusing on institutional development aspects is an opportunity to turn rhetoric into meaningful partnerships.

Meaningful partnerships are an illustration of good governance dynamics with spill over effects beyond the specific objective of each partnership. Furthermore, partnerships are not confined to social contributions where benefits are simply shared in a participatory fashion. Instead they are a collaborative mode of dealing with negative as well as positive impacts. Negative impacts caused by third parties often require companies to enter into partnerships such as the VPI and the EITI. Indeed to effectively exert leverage over third parties often requires collective action through multi-stakeholder schemes. But even negative impacts within a company's own control might require collaboration as in participatory water monitoring; it is necessary to generate trust in complex technical processes. Furthermore,

---

[72] BHP Billiton, Working with integrity. Code of Business Conduct. August 2014, https://www.bhp.com/-/media/bhp/documents/aboutus/ourcompany/code-of-business-conduct/160310_code-ofbusinessconduct_english.pdf?la=en (last accessed 1 October 2018), p. 30.

[73] BHP Billiton, Working with integrity. Code of Business Conduct. August 2014, https://www.bhp.com/-/media/bhp/documents/aboutus/ourcompany/code-of-business-conduct/160310_code-ofbusinessconduct_english.pdf?la=en, (last accessed 1 October 2018), p. 30.

[74] Anglo American, Delivering Change, Building Resilience—Working In Partnership, Sustainability Report 2016, http://www.angloamerican.com/~/media/Files/A/Anglo-American-PLC-V2/documents/annual-reporting-2016/downloads/2016-sustainability-report.pdf   (last accessed 1 October 2018), p. 11.

[75] Barrick Gold Corporation, Advancing Together. 2016 GRI Content Index, https://www.unglobal-compact.org/system/attachments/cop_2017/391931/original/Barrick_2016_GRI_Content_Index.pdf?1497042875, (last accessed 1 October 2018), p. 94.

[76] Rio Tinto, Partnering for Progress 2016. 5 April 2017, http://www.riotinto.com/documents/170405_Partnering_for_progress_presentation_slides.pdf (last accessed 1 October 2018), p. 5.

exercising leverage to support local institutional development is relevant both within partnerships—capacity to collaborate—and outside partnerships—capacity of local institutions to discharge their respective mandate and public role.

In sum, focusing on local institutional development repositions the company as a facilitator of good governance dynamics. A fundamental element is to seek out not to bypass local institutions as the company goes forward addressing negative and positive impacts. Their role and capacity should be reinforced. Working collaboratively and for ensuring sustainable improvements requires multiple repositioning from a company.[77] This section documented four shifts regarding social investment and general CSR strategy. These shifts are consistent with a stronger focus on institutional development. They help reflecting on what the corporate responsibility to respect entails in the context of mining. What appears at first glance as social contributions outside "respecting" human rights prove to be essential ingredients for actually achieving respect for human rights in a difficult operational context like mining.

These shifts are compellingly articulated at the strategic level and appear to be at the incipient stages of elaboration and operationalisation. The risk is that they remain confined to the declaratory and the aspirational. The next section analyses latest developments in four concrete settings where companies are beginning to operationalize these strategic approaches and move beyond rhetoric.

4   Operational Settings

This section concentrates on four settings: water, security, socio-economic development, and revenue transparency. The first two settings correspond directly to human rights, namely the right to water and basic civil rights, while the other two settings are about an enabling environment for human rights free from corruption and poverty. Some of these areas benefit from global partnerships (security and revenue transparency) while others evolve through local partnerships (water and socio-economic development). Some settings deal with direct negative impacts from mining (water and security) while the other settings cover the positive contributions mining can make to host societies (revenue transparency and socio-economic development. However, all these settings, partnerships and impacts can and should be assessed in terms of contributing to or reducing institutional development as a cross-cutting issue.

---

[77] The company's interventions should be strategic, aligned, multi-stakeholder driven, sustainable, and measurable. IFC, Strategic Community Investment – A Good Practice Handbook for Companies Doing Business in Emerging Markets. June 2010, https://www.ifc.org/wps/wcm/connect/f1c0538048865842b50ef76a6515bb18/12014complete-web.pdf?MOD=AJPERES&CACHE ID=f1c0538048865842b50ef76a6515bb18, (last accessed 1 October 2018), p. i.

4.1 Water Management

All five companies dealt with in this chapter are members of ICMM, which in 2015 developed a water management guide.[78] It covers a highly sensitive issue that can escalate and stop projects in their tracks. The key element of ICMM's approach is the "catchment-based approach" meant "both to limit material risks and maximize opportunity".[79] It is grounded in the need to "Understand the true value of water".[80] The Guide promotes a shift in water management from treating water as an operational issue[81] to taking "a holistic view of the social, cultural, environmental and economic value of water at a catchment scale."[82] Thus the ICMM puts forward

> A catchment-based approach to managing water resources [that] looks at activities and issues in the catchment as a whole, rather than considering different aspects separately. It requires a diverse range of processes to be considered, including the hydrology and land use, as well as broader political, economic, social and ecological dynamics that influence water availability and quality. A catchment-based approach encourages organizations to consider holistically how competing demands on water resources from a range of stakeholders (domestic water users, industry, regulators, politicians) can create pressures and lead to conflict if not appropriately managed. It also requires that people from different sectors be brought together to identify issues and agree priorities for action, and ultimately build local partnerships to put these actions in place.[83]

This comprehensive approach requires engagement with stakeholders. The guide refers to the opportunities, benefits and risks of partnerships, and recommends that

---

[78] ICMM, Practical guide for catchment-based water management for the mining and metal industry. 2015, https://www.icmm.com/website/publications/pdfs/water/practical-guide-catchment-based-water-management_en (last accessed 1 October 2018).

[79] ICMM, Practical guide for catchment-based water management for the mining and metal industry. 2015, https://www.icmm.com/website/publications/pdfs/water/practical-guide-catchment-based-water-management_en (last accessed 1 October 2018), p. 6.

[80] ICMM, Practical guide for catchment-based water management for the mining and metal industry. 2015, https://www.icmm.com/website/publications/pdfs/water/practical-guide-catchment-based-water-management_en (last accessed 1 October 2018), p. 16. ("Water is fundamental to life, human dignity and functional ecosystems. Water is also the lifeblood of many industries, from agriculture to manufacturing, energy generation and mining.")

[81] The ICMM explains that "Historically, the industry has approached water as an operational issue – one that is largely managed 'inside the fence' with a focus on water use efficiency and control over effluent discharges to demonstrate good practice and minimize risk... Successful risk management must be based on understanding the complete suite of water issues within the catchment and finding solutions that work for the business and other water users." ICMM, Practical guide for catchment-based water management for the mining and metal industry. 2015, https://www.icmm.com/website/publications/pdfs/water/practical-guide-catchment-based-water-management_en (last accessed 1 October 2018), p. 5.

[82] ICMM, Practical guide for catchment-based water management for the mining and metal industry. 2015, https://www.icmm.com/website/publications/pdfs/water/practical-guide-catchment-based-water-management_en (last accessed 1 October 2018), p. 6.

[83] ICMM, Practical guide for catchment-based water management for the mining and metal industry. 2015, https://www.icmm.com/website/publications/pdfs/water/practical-guide-catchment-based-water-management_en (last accessed 1 October 2018), p. 15.

"companies should understand their own internal capacity and consider the ambition and capacity of other partners (i.e. communities, NGO groups, government or other mining and metals operations) to meaningfully engage"[84] before proceeding with a specific catchment-based response. The ICMM approach builds on lessons learned: "Poor social management of water (for example, lack of inclusive community engagement, participatory monitoring programs, etc) can lead to the erosion of stakeholder relationships and ultimately the loss of the company's social licence to operate."[85]

The ICMM also refers explicitly to institutional development aspects. There is detailed advice on the need to get clarity on the regulatory framework and gauge institutional capacities:

> In addition to institutional arrangement and regulatory timeframes, the institutional strength and capacity of local authorities to deliver services and manage catchment challenges as they arise should also be assessed. Limited resources of local government institutions may have implications for the expectations communities have of mining operations and other industrial water users in the catchment along with implications for the reliability of water supply over time.[86]

With its catchment-based approach, the ICMM offers a compelling example of a shift to more encompassing and integrated approaches to addressing a negative impact of mining (on water). Industry approaches to security issues offer another example of how negative impacts need to be addressed broadly to deal with compounding sources of risk in volatile environments.

4.2 Security Provisions

The Voluntary Principles on Security and Human Rights Initiative (VPI) is a global multistakeholder partnership set up in 2000 to "guide *companies in maintaining the safety and security of their operations within an operating framework that encourages respect for human rights.*"[87] *The scheme covers three sets of issues: risk assessment, public security, and private security. Governments, businesses and NGOs*

---

[84] ICMM, Practical guide for catchment-based water management for the mining and metal industry. 2015, https://www.icmm.com/website/publications/pdfs/water/practical-guide-catchment-based-water-management_en (last accessed 1 October 2018), p. 51.

[85] ICMM, Practical guide for catchment-based water management for the mining and metal industry. 2015, https://www.icmm.com/website/publications/pdfs/water/practical-guide-catchment-based-water-management_en (last accessed 1 October 2018), p. 17.

[86] ICMM, Practical guide for catchment-based water management for the mining and metal industry. 2015, https://www.icmm.com/website/publications/pdfs/water/practical-guide-catchment-based-water-management_en (last accessed 1 October 2018), p. 23.

[87] Initiative of the Voluntary Principles on Security and Human Rights, Voluntary Principles on Security and Human Rights. 2000, http://www.voluntaryprinciples.org/wp-content/uploads/2013/03/voluntary_principles_english.pdf (last accessed 1 October 2018), Introduction.

participate.[88] *As a partnership, the VPI evolved from a rather opaque multistake holder initiative into a more transparent one.*[89] *Its transparency, however, is mainly internal transparency towards participating organizations; information is shared within the confidential setting of the VPI in order to secure* engagement and "full and open dialogue" among participants.[90] Reputable NGOs are engaged in the VPI and lend it credibility.

The VPI progressively has adopted measures to make it more likely that genuine learning and collaboration takes place. With its emphasis on measurement and learning, the VPI offers the opportunity to inquire whether institutional development aspects are given due emphasis at the strategic and operational levels. Nowadays the VPI reporting system emphasizes measurability, including the development and sharing of key performance indicators (KPI), and lessons learned. All companies follow the Reporting Guidelines[91] and companies that voluntarily have opted into the Verification Framework,[92] complete self-assessments according to KPIs.[93] To stimulate the lesson-sharing process, NGOs are also asked to report to the VPI and concentrate on evaluation techniques and key learnings.[94] Work on KPIs commenced in 2012 and has been supported by the UN Global Compact.[95]

---

[88] For the list of participants, see www.voluntaryprinciples.org (last accessed 1 October 2018).

[89] For a concise table comparing reporting requirements expected from the three groups of stakeholders see Global Compact Canada, Auditing Implementation of Voluntary Principles on Security and Human Rights. 2016, http://globalcompact.ca/wp-content/uploads/2016/08/Auditing-Implementations-of-VPs-on-Security-and-Human-Rights.pdf (last accessed 1 October 2018), pp. 66–67.

[90] Initiative of the Voluntary Principles on Security and Human Rights, Participation Criteria, 2007/2016, http://voluntaryprinciples.org/files/VPs_Participation_Criteria_Final_-_127000_v1_FHE-DC.PDF (last accessed 1 October 2018), pp. 1–2.

[91] Initiative of the Voluntary Principles on Security and Human Rights, Corporate Pillar Reporting Guidelines. 2017, http://www.voluntaryprinciples.org/wp-content/uploads/2016/08/VPI-Corporate-Pillar-Reporting-Guidelines-July-2016.pdf (last accessed 1 October 2018).

[92] Initiative of the Voluntary Principles on Security and Human Rights, Corporate Pillar Verification Framework. 2017, http://www.voluntaryprinciples.org/wp-content/uploads/2015/05/Corporate-Pillar-Verification_Framework-May-2015.pdf (last accessed 1 October 2018).

[93] The VPI constructed six categories of KPIs and explains that "a significant component of the accountability framework for any participating organization is the selection of a suite of organizationally appropriate performance indicators." Initiative of the Voluntary Principles on Security and Human Rights, Corporate Pillar Verification Framework. 2017, http://www.voluntaryprinciples.org/wp-content/uploads/2015/05/Corporate-Pillar-Verification_Framework-May-2015.pdf (last accessed 1 October 2018), p. 1.

[94] NGOs are asked to share their evaluation techniques and present in-depth case studies with specific methodologies employed. Initiative of the Voluntary Principles on Security and Human Rights, NGO Pillar Verification Framework. 2015, http://www.voluntaryprinciples.org/wp-content/uploads/2015/05/NGO-Pillar-Verification-Framework-May-2015.pdf (last accessed 1 October 2018).

[95] Global Compact Canada, Auditing Implementation of Voluntary Principles on Security and Human Rights. 2016, http://globalcompact.ca/wp-content/uploads/2016/08/Auditing-Implementations-of-VPs-on-Security-and-Human-Rights.pdf (last accessed 1 October 2018), p. 2.

Naturally, institutional development aspects feature high in the VPI. It is public forces that often provide security to mining facilities and the host government itself regards mining operations as a strategic asset. Among the challenges identified are lack of capacity of host governments to support VPI implementation; resistance to the VPI within the host country government at local or national levels; and the VPI being seen as "interference" in the affairs of the host country government.[96] Therefore the VPI extensively deals with both capacity constraints of security forces as well as leverage over host governments to deliver security responsibly. Attention to and action on these challenges is essential for tackling a root cause of human rights infringements, that is, an underlying cause stemming from deficiencies of public authorities.

Companies in the VPI are invited to use their leverage to strengthen the functioning of governmental institutions within their "roles and responsibilities".[97] For example companies should support the rule of law "to the extent feasible in each operating context" in different ways: by recording and reporting credible allegations of abuse, urging investigation, actively monitoring investigation status and pressing for proper resolution; and supporting efforts by states and civil society organizations to strengthen state institutions.[98] The International Committee of the Red Cross (ICRC) also discusses leverage issues in its Guide and recommends coordination with other stakeholders and strengthening their capacities and role.[99]

Local capacity constraints come in diverse forms. The ICRC indicates that "Public security forces may suffer from insufficient human resources, low salaries, inadequate training and poor equipment. This may increase the risk that they engage in criminal activity or human rights violations."[100] Weak capacity might take the form of a poor understanding of human rights and rules of engagement, arrests and

---

[96] Initiative of the Voluntary Principles on Security and Human Rights, Implementation Guidance Tools. 2011, http://www.voluntaryprinciples.org/files/Implementation_Guidance_Tools.pdf (last accessed 1 October 2018), p. 21.

[97] Initiative of the Voluntary Principles on Security and Human Rights, Guidance on Certain Roles and Responsibilities of Governments. 2014, http://www.voluntaryprinciples.org/wp-content/uploads/2014/10/VPs_-_Roles_and_Responsibilities_-_Government_Pillar.pdf (last accessed 1 October 2018).

[98] Initiative of the Voluntary Principles on Security and Human Rights, Guidance on Certain Roles and Responsibilities of Governments. 2014, http://www.voluntaryprinciples.org/wp-content/uploads/2014/10/VPs_-_Roles_and_Responsibilities_-_Government_Pillar.pdf (last accessed 1 October 2018), p. 1.

[99] ICRC, Addressing Security and Human Rights Challenges in Complex Environments. 2016, http://www.securityhumanrightshub.org/sites/default/files/publications/ASHRC_Toolkit_V3.pdf (last accessed 1 October 2018), p. 23.

[100] ICRC, Addressing Security and Human Rights Challenges in Complex Environments. 2016, http://www.securityhumanrightshub.org/sites/default/files/publications/ASHRC_Toolkit_V3.pdf (last accessed 1 October 2018), p. 45.

detentions, damaged health of people in custody, and torture or degrading treatment.[101] However, even apparently non-controversial actions a company might take, such as training to build local capacity, can be problematic in the security area.[102]

The ICRC indicates that another capacity weakness—the lack of appropriate equipment—may lead to excessive use of force by security forces.[103] The VPI explains that "In many countries, public security providers are underresourced and will make requests to the company for the transfer of equipment (lethal and nonlethal), fuel, or access to vehicles... Receiving requests from public security providers for equipment (e.g. fuel, use of vehicles, communications equipment, etc) can be very common."[104] That creates risks that transferred equipment will be sold illicitly or be used to commit human rights abuses. To address risks and gaps in the public security provider's ability to deliver on the VPI, the VPI offers advice.[105]

Sources of risk compound each other in the security context which then calls for more comprehensive assessments and solutions. Thus, the VPI draws attention to how "Security measures that are viewed as 'heavy-handed' may end up creating, rather than reducing security risks by endangering parallel efforts to develop community trust [e.g. through social investment and CSR activities]."[106] The ICRC also highlights the multiple sources of risks that require a comprehensive assessment:

> Community-related security risks are frequently the result of unaddressed concerns, negative impacts, or misunderstandings about non-security related issues such as employment, land, environment, compensation, resettlement, and negative legacies from previous company projects, to name a few. When concerns and grievances go unaddressed or unmitigated, these issues can escalate into tensions and may eventually result in situations of violence.[107]

---

[101] Initiative of the Voluntary Principles on Security and Human Rights, Implementation Guidance Tools. 2011, http://www.voluntaryprinciples.org/files/Implementation_Guidance_Tools.pdf (last accessed 1 October 2018), p. 42.

[102] Examples from Colombia and the DRC reveal governmental restrictions on what training companies are allowed to offer to public security forces on international standards. ICRC, Addressing Security and Human Rights Challenges in Complex Environments. 2016, http://www.securityhumanrightshub.org/sites/default/files/publications/ASHRC_Toolkit_V3.pdf (last accessed 1 October 2018), pp. 60–61.

[103] ICRC, Addressing Security and Human Rights Challenges in Complex Environments. 2016, http://www.securityhumanrightshub.org/sites/default/files/publications/ASHRC_Toolkit_V3.pdf (last accessed 1 October 2018), p. 70.

[104] Initiative of the Voluntary Principles on Security and Human Rights, Implementation Guidance Tools. 2011, http://www.voluntaryprinciples.org/files/Implementation_Guidance_Tools.pdf (last accessed 1 October 2018), p. 43.

[105] For example, installing tracking devices on equipment, company personnel to accompany the equipment, third-party monitoring, and supporting other stakeholders involved in security sector reform. Initiative of the Voluntary Principles on Security and Human Rights, Implementation Guidance Tools. 2011, http://www.voluntaryprinciples.org/files/Implementation_Guidance_Tools.pdf (last accessed 1 October 2018), p. 43 and p. 72.

[106] Initiative of the Voluntary Principles on Security and Human Rights, Implementation Guidance Tools. 2011, http://www.voluntaryprinciples.org/files/Implementation_Guidance_Tools.pdf (last accessed 1 October 2018), p. 20.

[107] ICRC, Addressing Security and Human Rights Challenges in Complex Environments. 2016, http://www.securityhumanrightshub.org/sites/default/files/publications/ASHRC_Toolkit_V3.pdf (last accessed 1 October 2018), p. 146.

As often in conflict analysis,[108] attention goes to root causes: "The company may be faced with community-related security issues caused by unidentified root causes, unaddressed impacts of the operation or unfulfilled commitments. In these situations, tensions with communities may persist despite efforts by the company to address them."[109] Therefore the ICRC recommends comprehensive baseline studies and risk assessments[110] that use participatory methodologies. This attention to the depth of CSR responses to security risks results in recommending an encompassing approach. Indeed such a comprehensive approach transpires from the ICRC Guide as it recommends "both a prevention and a conflict management approach" to corporate-community relations given that "understanding why companies, at times, face opposition from local communities, crime and violence, and how to change the situation, remains elusive."[111] This holistic approach is warranted as "corporate-community relations do not happen in a vacuum":

> Community concerns and grievances targeted at the company will often be the result of weak governance, poor public services, and lack of genuine engagement on the part of the host government. Companies, therefore, must assess how all aspects of their operations, beyond just security measures, interact with the existing context. Critical analysis must be applied to understand whether the company's actions are reinforcing inequalities, increasing competition for resources, and reducing the extent to which community members have a voice in decision-making, or whether, conversely, company actions are reinforcing good governance, respecting human rights, and safeguarding human security. In this respect, while companies cannot and should not replace the government, efforts can be made to support a stronger government role.[112]

Rio Tinto offers an example of a comprehensive strategy to security risks at its Peruvian mine and explains why that proved necessary. The company decided to move from its previous narrow approach to security to a broader one encompassing other human rights issues. Previously the company's "main approach was to focus on the interaction between company security personnel, local and national security

---

[108] Ganson B and Wennmann A, Confronting Risk, Mobilizing Action. A Framework for Conflict Prevention in the Context of Large-scale Business Investments. December 2012, http://library.fes.de/pdf-files/iez/global/09577.pdf (last accessed 1 October 2018).

[109] ICRC, Addressing Security and Human Rights Challenges in Complex Environments. 2016, http://www.securityhumanrightshub.org/sites/default/files/publications/ASHRC_Toolkit_V3.pdf (last accessed 1 October 2018), p. 148.

[110] "Consider all direct and indirect impacts of the company's operations on local communities, including: immigration, displacement, loss of land, loss of livelihood, loss of biodiversity, all forms of pollution, prices of goods, services and accommodation, rise in violence and crime, effects on community health, damage to religious, spiritual or cultural sites of significance, and increased socio-political tensions, strife or conflict." ICRC, Addressing Security and Human Rights Challenges in Complex Environments. 2016, http://www.securityhumanrightshub.org/sites/default/files/publications/ASHRC_Toolkit_V3.pdf (last accessed 1 October 2018), p. 150.

[111] ICRC, Addressing Security and Human Rights Challenges in Complex Environments. 2016, http://www.securityhumanrightshub.org/sites/default/files/publications/ASHRC_Toolkit_V3.pdf (last accessed 1 October 2018), p. 146.

[112] ICRC, Addressing Security and Human Rights Challenges in Complex Environments. 2016, http://www.securityhumanrightshub.org/sites/default/files/publications/ASHRC_Toolkit_V3.pdf (last accessed 1 October 2018), p. 147.

forces, and surrounding communities."[113] The company sought however a broader understanding of "how existing social conflicts and intra-community issues might exacerbate security and human rights issues, and how company behaviour could in turn aggravate these."[114] That led the company to conclude that "the primary source of peace and security for the La Granja project lay in the project's ability to work with local communities and organisations... to manage the social and economic changes brought by the project."[115] The recognition resulted in diversified and expanded forums (roundtables) covering security and other issues. Furthermore, the company reviewed "its local employment, social investment and community engagement activities to better understand and anticipate socioeconomic impacts and strengthen the integration of project activities into the local economic and social context."[116]

In sum, the security area offers a compelling example of a negative impact of mining that requires local institutional development. Contributions to local capacities and exercising corporate leverage are crucial. The fact that the security related documents cited in this section refer to social investment show the interlinkages between security, human rights and development. The VPI offers evidence of a global partnership that has been evolving and substantiates the observation that emerging shifts in CSR strategy appear to trickle down to the operational level.

4.3 Contributions to Socio-Economic Development

The economic and social contributions to the development of host communities are front and centre in CSR reports. They also appear as commitments to the SDGs—the integrative framework covering both contributions and compliance aspects—[117] which some companies use now as a framework for their CSR policies. Both positive and negative impacts should be discussed under a common umbrella of human rights. Indeed the way both positive and negative impacts are handled can enhance or reduce social and human capital (institutional development) within host

---

[113] Rio Tinto, Why Human Rights Matter. January 2013, http://www.riotinto.com/documents/ReportsPublications/Rio_Tinto_human_rights_guide_-_English_version.pdf (last accessed 1 October 2018), p. 39.

[114] Rio Tinto, Why Human Rights Matter. January 2013, http://www.riotinto.com/documents/ReportsPublications/Rio_Tinto_human_rights_guide_-_English_version.pdf (last accessed 1 October 2018), p. 39.

[115] Rio Tinto, Why Human Rights Matter. January 2013, http://www.riotinto.com/documents/ReportsPublications/Rio_Tinto_human_rights_guide_-_English_version.pdf, (last accessed 1 October 2018), p. 41.

[116] Rio Tinto, Why Human Rights Matter. January 2013, http://www.riotinto.com/documents/ReportsPublications/Rio_Tinto_human_rights_guide_-_English_version.pdf, (last accessed 1 October 2018), p. 41.

[117] UN General Assembly, Transforming our world: the 2030 Agenda for Sustainable Development A/RES/70/1, 21 October 2015, para 67.

communities and thus reverberate well beyond the specific impact being addressed. As the OECD explains, "if stakeholder engagement activities are not properly supported, developed or executed, their due diligence function may not be realised, and adverse impacts may not be avoided or addressed. Furthermore, poor stakeholder engagement can in and of itself give rise to actual or perceived adverse impacts and jeopardise potential benefits to stakeholders."[118]

Anglo American offers a compelling analysis of the context of mining and the ways to address sustainability challenges.[119] The company hints to the disruption brought about by mining when it sees "value in pursuing business strategies that are socially inclusive and environmentally responsible, with the aim of minimising relevant local root causes that drive social instability."[120] In terms of development contributions, it acknowledges the "expectation that the industry acts as a catalyst for socio-economic development."[121] The way forward to address risks and expectations lies in a comprehensive and integrated strategy that refers to institutional development:

> Our strategic focus is on improving the productivity of local markets and public institutions. The aim is to support sustainable job creation and effective public service delivery, to ensure that local economies are able to deliver opportunities even after mine closure. Our strategy recognises the importance of implementing programmes that build on existing successful initiatives and strengthen the capacity of local institutions, as opposed to isolated projects.[122]

Anglo American illustrates this strategy with its development strategy in South Africa. This is an example of a strategy extending beyond the usual coverage of surrounding communities. The company explains why a confined strategy would not

---

[118] OECD, Due Diligence Guidance for Meaningful Stakeholder Engagement in the Extractive Sector. 2017, https://read.oecd-ilibrary.org/governance/oecd-due-diligence-guidance-for-meaningful-stakeholder-engagement-in-the-extractive-sector_9789264252462-en#page4 (last accessed 1 October 2018), p. 18 (identifying also common challenges to meaningful stakeholder engagement, pp. 71–74).

[119] Anglo American, Delivering Change, Building Resilience—Working In Partnership, Sustainability Report 2016, http://www.angloamerican.com/~/media/Files/A/Anglo-American-PLC-V2/documents/annual-reporting-2016/downloads/2016-sustainability-report.pdf, (last accessed 1 October 2018), pp. 8–10.

[120] Anglo American, Delivering Change, Building Resilience—Working In Partnership, Sustainability Report 2016, http://www.angloamerican.com/~/media/Files/A/Anglo-American-PLC-V2/documents/annual-reporting-2016/downloads/2016-sustainability-report.pdf, (last accessed 1 October 2018), p. 9.

[121] Anglo American, Delivering Change, Building Resilience—Working In Partnership, Sustainability Report 2016, http://www.angloamerican.com/~/media/Files/A/Anglo-American-PLC-V2/documents/annual-reporting-2016/downloads/2016-sustainability-report.pdf, (last accessed 1 October 2018), p. 8.

[122] Anglo American, Delivering Change, Building Resilience—Working In Partnership, Sustainability Report 2016, http://www.angloamerican.com/~/media/Files/A/Anglo-American-PLC-V2/documents/annual-reporting-2016/downloads/2016-sustainability-report.pdf, (last accessed 1 October 2018), p. 47.

address effectively the sources of risk. The background is one of social instability and deprivation in the Limpopo province:

> Many of the protests have their roots in poor public service delivery and unemployment. Persistent drought in the region has exacerbated socio-economic challenges and social sensitivities, heightening negative sentiment around mining, and raising expectations for mining companies to deliver socio-economic benefits.... We have placed a particular strategic focus on mitigating social conflict and promoting socio-economic development across Limpopo province.[123]

Anglo American adopted "a regional approach to development opportunity identification": "we needed to move from being a single actor to a regional partner; from a participant in the development debate to a leader and facilitator. As a result, we embarked on work to catalyse collaboration and partnership on systemic, cross-sector, transformational sustainable development in Limpopo."[124] In operational terms, the company engaged in spatial analysis and planning in order "to develop a detailed understanding of the opportunities [across a range of sectors] based on the bio-physical and social conditions of the province" and employed "the collective impact model, which hinges on the idea that in order for organisations to create lasting solutions to social problems on a large scale, they need to co-ordinate their efforts and work together around a clearly defined goal."[125]

More broadly, but also on operational matters, Anglo American expects all its sites to have Socio-Economic Development (SED) plans[126] touching on three main elements: Long-term SED strategy,[127] Optimal package,[128] and Partnership. The

---

[123] Anglo American, Delivering Change, Building Resilience—Working In Partnership, Sustainability Report 2016, http://www.angloamerican.com/~/media/Files/A/Anglo-American-PLC-V2/documents/annual-reporting-2016/downloads/2016-sustainability-report.pdf,   (last accessed 1 October 2018), p. 40.

[124] Anglo American, Delivering Change, Building Resilience—Working In Partnership, Sustainability Report 2016, http://www.angloamerican.com/~/media/Files/A/Anglo-American-PLC-V2/documents/annual-reporting-2016/downloads/2016-sustainability-report.pdf   (last accessed 1 October 2018), p. 38.

[125] Anglo American, Delivering Change, Building Resilience—Working In Partnership, Sustainability Report 2016, http://www.angloamerican.com/~/media/Files/A/Anglo-American-PLC-V2/documents/annual-reporting-2016/downloads/2016-sustainability-report.pdf   (last accessed 1 October 2018), p. 38.

[126] Anglo American, Social Way. Version 2. 2014 http://www.angloamerican.com/~/media/Files/A/Anglo-American-PLC-V2/documents/approach-and-policies/social/aa-social-way-singles-v2.pdf (last accessed 1 October 2018), p. 14.

[127] The SED strategy is "developed with external stakeholders in *a participative and inclusive manner* to ensure SED articulates *a vision for long-term, multi-sector development* and provides *a platform for collaboration* with critical stakeholders such as local and regional government, other private sector actors and social investment partners." Anglo American, Social Way. Version 2, 2014 http://www.angloamerican.com/~/media/Files/A/Anglo-American-PLC-V2/documents/approach-and-policies/social/aa-social-way-singles-v2.pdf (last accessed 1 October 2018), p. 14. (emphasis added).

[128] The package contains components such as "local employment, local procurement, employee volunteering, infrastructure synergies, municipal capacity building, enterprise development and corporate social investment." Anglo American, Social Way. Version 2. 2014 http://www.angloamer-

company also reports on "supporting institutional capacity" of local institutions to enhance the delivery of public services. The company exemplifies partnerships in South Africa and Latin America involving development banks[129] and explains how its local infrastructure can be shared with local communities at marginal cost and with benefits for both company and communities.[130]

Rio Tinto is notable for its approach to community benefit agreements which constitutes a formalised approach to promote good governance dynamics.[131] The company documents its shift towards agreements in the context of the late 1980s; a significant trigger was litigation and law (the Native Title Act) in native Australia and severe unrest at its Papua New Guinea operations.[132] In operational terms, in 2014, the company made community benefit agreements mandatory for its operations globally and thus shapes the social performance standards where long-term projects are planned; this approach will benefit indigenous and traditional land-connected peoples.[133]

In its "Why Agreements Matter" guide,[134] the company draws on its experience with more than 150 community agreements extending over the last two decades. One insight is that "it takes time to negotiate mutual agreements and the process can be as important as the final agreement itself."[135] The company flags its Cooperation Agreement in Mongolia at its Oyu Tolgoi copper-gold operation.[136] Concluding

---

ican.com/~/media/Files/A/Anglo-American-PLC-V2/documents/approach-and-policies/social/aa-social-way-singles-v2.pdf (last accessed 1 October 2018), p. 14.

[129] Anglo American, Delivering Change, Building Resilience—Working In Partnership, Sustainability Report 2016, http://www.angloamerican.com/~/media/Files/A/Anglo-American-PLC-V2/documents/annual-reporting-2016/downloads/2016-sustainability-report.pdf (last accessed 1 October 2018), p. 50.

[130] Anglo American, Delivering Change, Building Resilience—Working In Partnership, Sustainability Report 2016, http://www.angloamerican.com/~/media/Files/A/Anglo-American-PLC-V2/documents/annual-reporting-2016/downloads/2016-sustainability-report.pdf (last accessed 1 October 2018), p. 179.

[131] By comparison, Anglo American is much less committed to Benefit Sharing Agreements for which it takes a case-by-case approach: "The development of these agreements is complex, can have unintended consequences and may set precedents (intentionally or otherwise) for other Anglo American operations." Anglo American, Social Way. Version 2. 2014 http://www.angloamerican.com/~/media/Files/A/Anglo-American-PLC-V2/documents/approach-and-policies/social/aa-social-way-singles-v2.pdf (last accessed 1 October 2018), p. 23.

[132] Rio Tinto, Why agreements matter. March 2016, http://www.riotinto.com/documents/Rio_Tinto_Why_Agreements_Matter.pdf (last accessed 1 October 2018), pp. 15–25.

[133] Rio Tinto, Partnering for Progress 2016. 5 April 2017, http://www.riotinto.com/documents/170405_Partnering_for_progress_presentation_slides.pdf (last accessed 1 October 2018, p. 19).

[134] Rio Tinto, Why agreements matter. March 2016, http://www.riotinto.com/documents/Rio_Tinto_Why_Agreements_Matter.pdf, (last accessed 1 October 2018).

[135] Rio Tinto, Partnering for Progress 2016. 5 April 2017, http://www.riotinto.com/documents/170405_Partnering_for_progress_presentation_slides.pdf, (last accessed 1 October 2018), p. 34.

[136] Rio Tinto, Cooperation Agreement. 2015, http://www.sdsg.org/wp-content/uploads/2011/06/OT_Cooperation_Agreement_EN.pdf (last accessed 1 October 2018). The agreement covers seven

such an agreement was obligatory under the 2009 Investment Agreement with the Mongolian state. The agreement was concluded in 2015 after a 4 year process. The company explains local government capacity constraints, representation of communities within Mongolian law and tradition, and highlights the novelty of this agreement as a governance framework with a "high degree of detail about rules, obligations and governance committees in a formal agreement" for the country.[137]

BHP Billiton describes its program in rural Colombia that "works to address the root causes of poverty and provide opportunities for families to break the poverty cycle."[138] The program is clear about economic and social development aspects: it provides increased access to basic services (education, healthcare, water, sanitation and housing) as well as economic opportunities (training in agricultural practices, support for entrepreneurship). But there is also an institutional development facet in this "integrated development approach [that] builds resilience in rural Colombia."[139] In terms of impacts on local institutional development, BHP Billiton documents an increase in the capacity of local public administrations[140] and in their links to the central government.[141] This is part of a general orientation "not to duplicate or displace existing agencies and services, but rather strengthen and support local capacity development."[142] On the capacities of local communities, the company reports that a priority was to establish Community Management Committees in 40 rural communities "to provide a forum for discussion, dialogue, analysis and identification of issues."[143] One outcome has been the Community Development Plans

---

topics: water management, environmental management, traditional animal husbandry and pasture management, natural history, culture and tourism, social services, local business development and procurement, and infrastructure and capital projects.

[137] Rio Tinto, Why agreements matter. March 2016, http://www.riotinto.com/documents/Rio_Tinto_Why_Agreements_Matter.pdf (last accessed 1 October 2018), p. 82.

[138] BHP Billiton, Taking the long view. Sustainable Report 2015. 2016, https://www.bhp.com/~/media/bhp/documents/society/reports/2016/160509_sustainabilityreport2015_chileanoperations.pdf (last accessed 1 October 2018), p. 57.

[139] BHP Billiton, Taking the long view. Sustainable Report 2015. 2016, https://www.bhp.com/~/media/bhp/documents/society/reports/2016/160509_sustainabilityreport2015_chileanoperations.pdf (last accessed 1 October 2018), p. 57.

[140] The evaluation showed that "local administrations have improved by an average of nine per cent in areas such as planning, resource management, monitoring, evaluation and accountability." BHP Billiton, Taking the long view. Sustainable Report 2015. 2016, https://www.bhp.com/~/media/bhp/documents/society/reports/2016/160509_sustainabilityreport2015_chileanoperations.pdf (last accessed 1 October 2018), p. 57.

[141] The links have improved as the company "offers technical assistance to municipalities in the formulation and submission of proposals for the national Royalty Fund and other government programs." BHP Billiton, Taking the long view. Sustainable Report 2015. 2016, https://www.bhp.com/~/media/bhp/documents/society/reports/2016/160509_sustainabilityreport2015_chileanoperations.pdf (last accessed 1 October 2018), p. 57.

[142] BHP Billiton, Taking the long view. Sustainable Report 2015. 2016, https://www.bhp.com/~/media/bhp/documents/society/reports/2016/160509_sustainabilityreport2015_chileanoperations.pdf (last accessed 1 October 2018), p. 56.

[143] BHP Billiton, Taking the long view. Sustainable Report 2015. 2016, https://www.bhp.com/~/media/bhp/documents/society/reports/2016/160509_sustainabilityreport2015_chileanoperations.pdf (last accessed 1 October 2018), p. 57.

through which the communities indicated "their long-term vision; their tangible and non-tangible assets; prioritization of needs; possible solutions; and key partners for development."[144]

This subsection highlighted participatory approaches that are commonly described nowadays by leading companies regarding their benefit-sharing and development programs. Institutional development aspects are still not a commonly used indicator for assessing such programs, or if such assessment takes place, it remains at a higher level of generality in brief case studies. There are signs that the shifts in CSR are happening and are trickling down from the strategic to the operation level. Contributions to development should be seen as a human rights-relevant matter and important for dealing with the disruption created by mining. From a human rights perspective institutional development should be emphasised: depending on the way they are implemented, social investments can facilitate rights-based participatory governance dynamics in host communities.

The next subsection shows another type of positive contribution mining companies can make, and that institutional development aspects are not confined to the local level. Institutional development plays out at the national level, too, when it comes to states managing the vast revenues the industry generates.

4.4 Revenue Transparency

The EITI is "a global standard to promote the open and accountable management of oil, gas and mineral resources"[145] launched in 2002 and covering now 52 resource-rich countries. At the heart of the EITI is a multistakeholder approach and the principle of transparency regarding revenues generated by the extractive sector. Fundamentally, EITI builds on the belief that "a public understanding of government revenues and expenditure over time could help public debate and inform choice of appropriate and realistic options for sustainable development."[146]

The initial focus has been on the reconciliation of revenues paid by companies and received by governments to detect misalignments.[147] However, the initiative has evolved well beyond this initial aim and in 2013 the EITI was subject to a major revision.[148] The focus has now expanded to other expenditures such as transfers

[144] BHP Billiton, Taking the long view. Sustainable Report 2015. 2016, https://www.bhp.com/~/media/bhp/documents/society/reports/2016/160509_sustainabilityreport2015_chileanoperations.pdf (last accessed 1 October 2018), p. 57.

[145] EITI, Who We Are, https://eiti.org/who-we-are#aim-of-the-eiti (last accessed 1 October 2018).

[146] EITI, The EITI Standard 2016. 24 May 2017, https://eiti.org/sites/default/files/documents/the_eiti_standard_2016_-_english.pdf (last accessed 1 October 2018).

[147] "Payments and revenues are reconciled by a credible, independent administrator applying international auditing standards." EITI, The EITI Standard 2016. 24 May 2017, https://eiti.org/sites/default/files/documents/the_eiti_standard_2016_-_english.pdf (last accessed 1 October 2018), Para. 4.9.

[148] EITI, History of the EITI, https://eiti.org/history (last accessed 1 October 2018).

from the central government to subnational entities (with revenue distribution frameworks), and social expenditures by companies. Such revisions were made due to the limited impact of EITI's previously narrow focus. As a 2011 assessment concluded: "little impact at the societal level can be discerned ... largely due to [EITI's] lack of links with larger public sector reform processes and institutions".[149] That shows how a limited approach had to evolve towards a more comprehensive assessment and action framework to tackle revenue opacity.

In 2015, EITI adopted the protocol "Participation of civil society".[150] To become an EITI candidate country, states have to fulfill five conditions among which are civil society engagement and the establishment of a multi-stakeholder group.[151] The EITI requires "effective multi-stakeholder oversight, including a functioning multi-stakeholder group that involves the government, companies, and the full, independent, active and effective participation of civil society."[152] The EITI Standard contains specific provisions regarding civil society engagement. To be part of the EITI the government must ensure "an enabling environment for civil society participation" and that the "fundamental rights of civil society" are respected.[153] To increase representation of voices heard in the multi-stakeholder group, the EITI emphasizes inclusiveness and representation also within the civil society sector: "Each stakeholder group must have the right to appoint its own representatives, bearing in mind the desirability of pluralistic and diverse representation."[154] At a time of shrinking space for civil society globally, the EITI affirms the important role of NGOs and remarkably so in a sensitive area such as the collection and management of massive revenues. This illustrates a genuine shift at the operational level from partnership to meaningful partnership.

Issues of capacity are addressed in the Guidance on how to establish and manage an effective multi-stakeholder group (MSG).[155] The EITI identifies five common challenges, among which is the "lack of capacity to engage in technical discussions and carry out activities foreseen in the workplan". The MSG has to carry out "an assessment of capacity constraints and include actions for addressing capacity

---

[149] Scanteam, Achievements and Strategic Options Evaluation of the Extractive Industries Transparency Initiative. May 2011, https://www.scanteam.no/images/scanteam/pdfs/reports2010/2010_1041.pdf, (last accessed 1 October 2018).

[150] EITI, The EITI Standard 2016. 24 May 2017, https://eiti.org/sites/default/files/documents/the_eiti_standard_2016_-_english.pdf (last accessed 1 October 2018), pp. 41–44.

[151] EITI, The EITI Standard 2016. 24 May 2017, https://eiti.org/sites/default/files/documents/the_eiti_standard_2016_-_english.pdf (last accessed 1 October 2018), Requirement 1.

[152] EITI, The EITI Standard 2016. 24 May 2017, https://eiti.org/sites/default/files/documents/the_eiti_standard_2016_-_english.pdf (last accessed 1 October 2018), Requirement 1.

[153] EITI, The EITI Standard 2016. 24 May 2017, https://eiti.org/sites/default/files/documents/the_eiti_standard_2016_-_english.pdf (last accessed 1 October 2018), Para 1.3 (b).

[154] EITI, The EITI Standard 2016. 24 May 2017, https://eiti.org/sites/default/files/documents/the_eiti_standard_2016_-_english.pdf (last accessed 1 October 2018), Para 1.4 (a).

[155] EITI, Guidance note 14. Establishment and governance of multi-stakeholder groups. May 2016, https://eiti.org/document/guidance-note-14-on-establishment-governance-of-multistakeholder-groups, (last accessed 1 October 2018).

gaps".[156] Furthermore, data generated must be accessible to users, thus the MSG is asked to undertake "capacity-building efforts, especially with civil society and through civil society organisations, to increase awareness of the process, improve understanding of the information and data from the reports, and encourage use of the information by citizens, the media, and others."[157] For the EITI the priority is that the "EITI Report is comprehensible, actively promoted, publicly accessible and contributes to public debate" as otherwise the disclosure of extractive industry data is of "little practical use".[158]

With these operational measures, the EITI seeks to secure a role—a place at the table—for civil society, and increase their capacity to use the information local EITIs produce. It is an operationalization of a participatory and genuinely inclusive approach to governance. The evolution beyond the focus on revenue collection towards how the revenue is spent further strengthens the contribution of EITI to national and now also local good governance dynamics. Indeed the EITI produces now more information about resource flows at the local level. One EITI requirement concerns the allocation of revenue from the central to the local levels of government.[159] Another requirement refers to social and economic spending by companies thus enabling stakeholders to assess "whether the extractive sector is leading to the desirable social and economic impacts and outcomes."[160] This captures social investment by companies, in addition to taxes paid, as both mandatory (by law or contract) and voluntary (discretionary) corporate spending is covered.[161]

The companies that are the subject of this chapter are supportive of revenue transparency and tend to be members of the EITI. Such support extends to the new wave of transparency laws adopted in developed countries.[162] For example, BHP Billiton indicates its support for "appropriate national and extra-territorial mandatory corporate reporting to complement the EITI, and provide a globally consistent regulatory framework for all extractive industry companies."[163] Thus, benefiting

---

[156] EITI, Guidance note 14. Establishment and governance of multi-stakeholder groups. May 2016, https://eiti.org/document/guidance-note-14-on-establishment-governance-of-multistakeholder-groups, (last accessed 1 October 2018), p. 3.

[157] EITI, The EITI Standard 2016. 24 May 2017, https://eiti.org/sites/default/files/documents/the_eiti_standard_2016_-_english.pdf (last accessed 1 October 2018), Para 7.2 (d).

[158] EITI, The EITI Standard 2016. 24 May 2017, https://eiti.org/sites/default/files/documents/the_eiti_standard_2016_-_english.pdf (last accessed 1 October 2018), Requirement 7.

[159] This is meant to enable stakeholders "understand how revenues are recorded in the national and where applicable, subnational budgets." EITI, The EITI Standard 2016. 24 May 2017, https://eiti.org/sites/default/files/documents/the_eiti_standard_2016_-_english.pdf (last accessed 1 October 2018).

[160] EITI, The EITI Standard 2016, 24 May 2017, https://eiti.org/sites/default/files/documents/the_eiti_standard_2016_-_english.pdf (last accessed 1 October 2018), Requirement 6.

[161] EITI, Guidance note 17. Social expenditures. June 2016, https://eiti.org/sites/default/files/documents/guidance_note_17_social_expenditure_en_2016.pdf, (last accessed 1 October 2018).

[162] Mares (2018) (analysing disclosure laws on sustainability, slavery, conflict minerals, and revenue transparency).

[163] BHP Billiton, Taking the long view. Sustainable Report 2015. 2016, https://www.bhp.com/~/media/bhp/documents/society/reports/2016/160509_sustainabilityreport2015_chileanoperations.pdf, (last accessed 1 October 2018), p. 14.

from good levels of corporate support, with its strategic orientation and unique operationalization mechanisms, the EITI has evolved to be the leading initiative on revenue transparency. It thus demonstrates the shifts in CSR around institutional development aspects.

5 Conclusions

The chapter set out to clarify the meaning of respect for human rights in a complex context such as mining and to examine the (ir)relevance of ubiquitous corporate contributions to development for a human rights analysis. The analytical focus has been on the issue of institutional development and local capacities. Of the three questions raised, the first was whether social contributions fall under the corporate responsibility to respect as defined in the UNGPs. This was answered in the affirmative and the analysis explained that the responsibility to respect takes a distinct shape in a context like mining characterised by disruption in host communities. This finding remains within the confines of the UNGPs and does not appear as an exception from the do-no-harm principle, but as a particular manifestation of the responsibility to respect in a complex and volatile context, particularly so in high risk developing countries beset by governance gaps. In such a context, sources of risks compound each other and generate a downward spiral for both the protection of human rights and a company's attempts to manage its impacts and break the vicious cycle. The key point is that an analytical focus on institutional development is helpful to break the cycle and should receive attention from both risk management and human rights-based perspectives.

The second question was whether there is evidence in industry strategies that CSR is shifting to recognise the importance of local institutional development. Significant evidence in this direction comes from both corporations and industry organizations. There is an explicit and growing emphasis on local capacities and institutional development aspects. The analysis documented four shifts regarding social contributions and general CSR that are consistent with a stronger focus on institutional development. While these shifts are welcome and eloquently articulated at the strategy level, there is also a possibility that these shifts might remain confined to the declaratory and the aspirational.

The third question asked was whether at the operational level there is also evidence substantiating these shifts in CSR strategy. A closer look at four policy settings covering both issues of compliance (negative impacts) and social contributions (positive impacts) documented advances in operationalisation. Local institutional development aspects feature prominently in these four settings. Individually or collectively, some companies are moving beyond rhetoric and are operationalizing new CSR strategies. Some global multistakeholder schemes have evolved remarkably from humbler beginnings.

In sum, a discussion on responsible mining has to evaluate the impacts on economic, social and institutional development of a mine's presence and its CSR interventions. Institutional development is emerging as a cross-cutting dimension that creates an opportunity for increased participation of rightholders, mines and external actors in constructing a rights-based and development-enhancing approach to mining. This participation of stakeholders aims at systemic changes in mining governance that are able to addresses deeper causes of abuse through encompassing strategies. Placing emphasis on local capacities and institutional development is indispensable for advancing towards a rights-based framework for mining to which companies have a responsibility to contribute.

References

Bebbington A (ed) (2011) Social conflict, economic development and extractive industry. Routledge, Abingdon

Mares R (2018) Corporate transparency regulations: a hollow victory? Netherlands Quarterly of Human Rights 36(3):189–213

Warner M, Sullivan R (eds) (2004) Putting partnerships to work - strategic alliances for development between Government, the private sector and civil society. Greenleaf, Sheffield

Radu Mares is a senior researcher and the team leader of "Economic Globalisation and Human Rights" at Raoul Wallenberg Institute of Human Rights. He holds a Doctor of Law and an Associate Professor degree from Lund University. He is specialised in the area of business and human rights, with a focus on multinational enterprises and global supply chains.

Part III
Resistance

Taking Sides in Scientific Research? The Struggle for the Right to Participate in Public Decision-Making Related to a Mining Project in Brazil

Aline Rose Barbosa Pereira

Contents

1 The Minas-Rio Iron Ore Mining Project and the Struggle of Local Communities 416
  1.1 Background 416
  1.2 Theoretical Contextualization 418
2 Overview of the Environmental Licensing Process: The Logics of Legal
Proceduralization in Legislation 420
  2.1 The Rights to Information and Participation in Environmental Law: The
       Potential for Democratic Proceduralization 422
  2.2 Two Tentative Interpretations of Participation: An Intrinsic Requisite of
       Democracy, a Functional Demand in Proceduralization 426
3 The Rights to Information and Participation in the Minas-Rio 428
  3.1 The Right to Information 430
       3.1.1 Controlling Knowledge Production 430
       3.1.2 Restricting Access to Information 432
  3.2 The Right to Participation 435
       3.2.1 Participation: To Which End? 435
       3.2.2 Coping with Physical Obstacles to Participate and Pushing Institutional
              Ones 437
  3.3 Frustrating Information and Participation: Demobilizing and Fostering
       Mobilization 442
4 The Emptying of Rights to Information and Participation in Brazil: A Brief Reflection
on the Challenges and Potential Benefits of Action Research 444
  4.1 Action Research 444
  4.2 Choosing the Case 446
  4.3 Redefining the Research Object Together with Participants 447
  4.4 Worldview, Positionality and Subjectivity 448
  4.5 Double Accountability and Pitfalls of Action Research 449
References 452

A. R. Barbosa Pereira (✉)
Center for Development Research (ZEF), University of Bonn, Bonn, Germany
e-mail: alinerbpereira@daad-alumni.de

© Springer Nature Switzerland AG 2019
I. Feichtner et al. (eds.), *Human Rights in the Extractive Industries*,
Interdisciplinary Studies in Human Rights 3,
https://doi.org/10.1007/978-3-030-11382-7_15

1   The Minas-Rio Iron Ore Mining Project and the Struggle of Local Communities

1.1   Background

When the Minas-Rio open pit iron ore mining project was announced in late 2006, many people in Conceição do Mato Dentro, despite being engaged in different projects to diversify the local economy, had never heard of it.[1] Conceição do Mato Dentro (CMD) is a small town in the countryside of the state of Minas Gerais, Brazil, with nearly 18,000 inhabitants in urban and rural areas. The village was established due to gold mining in colonial times. After the exhaustion of the mines in the nineteenth century,[2] subsistence agriculture had been the main economic activity. In the 25 years preceding the project announcement, the CMD municipal government, together with non-governmental organizations, had been advancing a series of policies to promote ecotourism as a development alternative based on one of a few agreements reached between different political groups in the city.[3] These common efforts, *inter alia*, led to the acknowledgement of Conceição do Mato Dentro as the state capital of ecotourism and of the Espinhaço mountain range as a biosphere reserve.

The change of focus from environmental protection and ecotourism development to mining, thus, came as a surprise for most of the inhabitants of the city. Political scientist Luzia Costa Becker, who has been studying strategies of political, economic and social development in, and the political culture of Conceição do Mato Dentro for over 15 years, describes the recent inclusion of mining as a development strategy in the region as the result of a coalition that began to develop in 2003 between local politicians, the government of the state and entrepreneurs.[4] The majority of the population only became aware of the ambitious mining project[5]

---

[1] Becker (2009), p. 340.

[2] Costa (1975).

[3] A detailed analysis of tourism as a development policy in Conceição do Mato Dentro, as well as of social mobilization around ecotourism in CMD, is the object of Becker (2009).

[4] Becker (2009), pp. 324, 339.

[5] The Minas-Rio Project encompasses an open-pit mine and processing plant in Conceição do Mato Dentro, Alvorada de Minas and Dom Joaquim (covering an area of around 3880 hectares of land), a mineral-duct of 525 km crossing 32 municipalities in the states of Minas Gerais and Rio de Janeiro, which connects the processing plant to the Açu Port (the port itself was built in connection with the project in order to export iron ore). With initial investments of 3 billion dollars and predicted production of 26.6 million tons of iron ore per year (Prates 2014, p. 11), the project had already cost 8.8 billion dollars by 2013 (according to Miller JW and Kiernan P, Miner, billions over budget, slogs ahead in rural Brazil. The Wall Street Journal, 9 June 2013, http://www.wsj.com/articles/SB10001424127887323582904578487090505277214 (last accessed 1 October 2018). Its water demand according to the EIS (3123 m^3 per hour), and its pressure on local water resources has been one of the main problems raised by affected families and environmentalists (see Becker 2009, p. 340; Becker and Pereira 2011).

when it was announced to the larger public (in Minas Gerais and in Brazil), through the media, in 2006.

The news initially led an educated urban middle class in Conceição do Mato Dentro to mobilize in order to understand the consequences mining could have for the little colonial village (both in terms of opportunities for the local economy, as well as regarding environmental degradation and social disruption). This small urban group initiated the Fórum Conceição do Mato Dentro (FórumCMD) in December 2006, an organized movement that included online mobilization (and online documentation of all their activities on a platform with the same name) and many local initiatives, such as smaller meetings and workshops, cultural activities and walks. The FórumCMD organized a one-week conference with experts on various aspects of mining projects (including environmental, social, legal, urban and developmental issues) that was open to the public.

The reactions of different groups in Conceição do Mato Dentro to the possibility of mining were by no means homogeneous. Many of those working in local commerce saw growth potential for their businesses, as more capital would circulate in the region. Others, who had been engaged in promoting ecotourism, saw a threat to their projects.[6] Urban dwellers welcomed the investment and job generation promises and feared the possibility of sudden population increase (through migrants attracted by the mining project) and disorderly urban growth putting yet more pressure on traffic, housing, and the fragile public services (including local public hospitals and schools). By organizing many educational events on mining, the FórumCMD triggered strong demands by urban and rural communities of Conceição do Mato Dentro to be properly informed about the consequences of the Minas-Rio and to participate in the environmental licensing of the mining project. Local groups (especially rural communities who would be potentially affected and some founders of the FórumCMD) have consistently and strongly questioned the mining project and opposed its advancement, making their voices heard in the arenas coordinated by the environmental authority of Minas Gerais or by CMD's municipal government (e.g., public hearings and public meetings organized by the municipal authorities; public hearings and meetings organized by the Minas Gerais state environmental authorities; meetings organized by the FórumCMD and by other resistance movements).

The environmental licensing is an administrative process (steered by the competent environmental authority) in which the "environmental viability" of a project is assessed, resulting in environmental permits to the company or in their denial. It is an essential requirement to pursue mining (and virtually all industrial activities, or activities with considerable potential to affect the natural environment) under

---

[6]Yet, in the first year of the environmental licensing process, some of those who were already involved in paving the way to ecotourism in the region, and who were initially members of the FórumCMD, created a competing group with a similar name (Fórum Conceição Sustentável) and started to organize events in order to persuade the local population that mining would be the best development strategy, as long as they were able to push for good environmental compensation (e.g. financing of reforestation and recuperation of water springs and riparian vegetation). There was considerable resistance, nonetheless, as we will see below.

Brazilian legislation. It is defined by principles of equitable access to natural resources; sustainable development; public participation, information and transparency; reparation; and the right to a healthy quality of life, to mention just a few. Depending on the activity, its environmental impact, its consequences for human life (and other forms of life), the permit can be denied, granted, or—as happens in most of the cases—granted with "conditionalities". These conditionalities include environmental and social compensation and mitigation measures discussed and agreed among the interested parties.

1.2 Theoretical Contextualization

I theoretically frame the case of Conceição do Mato Dentro as an instance of legal proceduralization.[7] Proceduralization not only blurs the lines between the public and the private, but also the distinctions between norm-making, norm-enforcement and norm-revision become harder to trace.[8] To some extent, legal proceduralization involves the replacement of rules of defined substantive content with procedures in which the affected parties negotiate and create the material content of the rules.[9] Procedural forms of regulation—besides being more adaptable to specific contexts and more responsive to the needs of a constantly changing globalized economy[10]—can be understood as a pragmatic solution[11] to cope with a reality of growing complexity and specialization of knowledge,[12] in which the state alone (the executive, elected parliaments, or even the judiciary) does not have the expertise, or the necessary cognitive (and economic) resources to produce appropriate legal solutions to all emerging challenges.[13] Moreover, procedural forms of regulation are often associated with more democratic processes and outcomes, as the affected parties are allowed to participate more directly in norm- and decision-making. A strategy especially welcomed after the broadly discussed legitimacy crisis of western representative democracies in the 1970s.[14]

Environmental licensing in Brazil emerged in the 1980s in the context of strong popular demand for more participation in decision-making processes and the campaigns for re-democratization that led to the 1988 Constitution (known as citizen

---

[7] On proceduralization, see Ladeur (2004), Teubner (2004), Sassen (2004), Black (2000, 2008), Simon (2010). The works of Mercado Pacheco (2012) and Estévez Araújo (2006) are central references to the discussion in the Spanish, as well as the work of Faria (2009, 2011) in the Brazilian context.

[8] Mercado Pacheco (2012), pp. 38–42.

[9] Estévez Araújo (2006), p. 99.

[10] Faria (2011), p. 51; Teubner (2004), p. 76.

[11] Faria (2009), p. 18.

[12] Ladeur (2004), pp. 7–10; Teubner (2004), p. 76.

[13] Ladeur (2004), p. 6.

[14] Mercado Pacheco (2012), p. 41.

constitution).[15] At the same time, and especially at the beginning of the 1990s, a series of reforms in the administrative structure of the state reduced its role as a guarantor of rights, shrinking some of its social responsibilities while transferring others to civil society,[16] which was invited to participate more directly in norm- and decision-making processes through a series of deliberative councils. This model is also reflected in the structure of the environmental authorities, which include both at the federal level and at the state level, a technical division (responsible for assessing the environmental impact studies and steering environmental licensing procedures) and a deliberative council formed by representatives of the government and of different sectors of civil society.

Environmental licensing contains a series of elements that contribute to its procedural rationality. It demands highly specialized knowledge in the assessment of the possible impacts and risks of a given project, and, still, every decision will involve a margin of uncertainty: there is always the possibility of unexpected or unknown outcomes, which explains the centrality of the environmental law principles of precaution and prevention.[17] The rights to information, participation and the ample involvement of civil society in environmental licencing are justified as necessary to enhance the democratic quality and scientific soundness of decisions.

Against this background, I focus in this chapter on the rights to information and participation of the actors involved in environmental licensing, offering a reflection on how these rights are understood by different groups and which consequences these divergent interpretations have. First, I consider how participation rights are established by Brazilian environmental law. Second, I briefly present two interpretations of the right to participation: as holding an intrinsic value for democracy and as holding a functional value in procedural decision-making.[18] This distinction is important to the subsequent discussion of grassroots resistance to enforce rights to information and participation in the environmental licensing process of the Minas-Rio project.

Based on the data I have collected,[19] I argue that affected communities, environmentalists and their allies (researchers from local universities and other movements) push for an interpretation of the rights to information and participation as holding intrinsic value for democracy. The environmental authorities of the state of Minas Gerais and the mining company, by contrast, tend to support a weaker conception of the rights to information and participation, adopting a more functional view of participation. While the former has the potential to democratize procedural regulation, the later favors *privatized proceduralization.* In privatized proceduralization, the power to determine the concrete content of the applicable law—formed by the environmental permits and their conditionalities—is not distributed between the participants. On the contrary, norm- and decision-making power is transferred to (or appropriated by)

[15] Dagnino (2004), p. 143.

[16] Dagnino (2004), p. 142.

[17] Milaré (2011), p. 1069.

[18] Mercado Pacheco (2012), p. 59.

[19] Further detailed in the final session, where I present a critical analysis of my research methods.

the most resourceful actors—who, in many cases, are not those who will be affected most by the project.

2   Overview of the Environmental Licensing Process: The Logics of Legal Proceduralization in Legislation

In Brazil the construction, installation, expansion and operation of any activity that makes use of environmental resources, modifies the environment, pollutes it or has the potential to do so (e.g. building new industrial parks, roads, railways or hydro-electric dams, establishing a farm area, mining, oil extraction) has to undergo an administrative process known as environmental licensing.[20] The competence for environmental licensing can lie with the federal level (the Union), with a state or with a municipality. The licensing of the open pit mine of the Minas-Rio project fell within the jurisdiction of the environmental authority of the state of Minas Gerais.[21]

The process consists of several stages, three of which result in different environmental permits: the preliminary license (*licença prévia*), the installation license (*licença de instalação*) and the operation license (*licença de operação*).[22] At the first stage, the environmental feasibility of the project is assessed. On the basis of an assessment that takes into account the location and the initial conception of the project, a *preliminary license* is issued, establishing basic requirements and conditionalities (e.g. environmental control, compensation and mitigation measures).[23] At the second stage, the company needs to elaborate and present more detailed and concrete plans, programs and projections of its activity, together with environmental control measures. If the legal requirements and conditionalities are met, the *installation license* is issued,[24] usually combined with more conditionalities. This second permit forms the basis for yet another assessment. At the third stage the project is

---

[20] Brazil, National Council for the Environment (CONAMA) Resolution 001/1986, Article 2, http://www.mma.gov.br/port/CONAMA/res/res86/res0186.html (last accessed 1 October 2018); CONAMA Resolution 237/1997, Article 2, http://www.mma.gov.br/port/CONAMA/res/res97/res23797.html (last accessed 1 October 2018).

[21] A fact that has been questioned by resistance movements: once the pipeline goes from the state of Minas Gerais to the state of Rio de Janeiro, where the logistics of the project also demanded the construction of a port, the Union could as well have jurisdiction with respect to the project as a whole.

[22] The open pit mine of the Minas-Rio Project was licensed in four stages—the installation license being divided into installation license 1 (LI-1) and installation license 2 (LI-2), which was interpreted by many researchers (Becker and Pereira 2011; Becker 2009, p. 340) and locals (MAM, 2017) as a strategy to fragment the process and, thus, make it harder to assess the total impacts of the project.

[23] CONAMA Resolution 237/1997, Article 8, I, http://www.mma.gov.br/port/CONAMA/res/res97/res23797.html (last accessed 1 October 2018).

[24] CONAMA Resolution 237/1997, Article 8, II, http://www.mma.gov.br/port/CONAMA/res/res97/res23797.html (last accessed 1 October 2018).

evaluated regarding the environmental law, as well as all the conditions and criteria established by the environmental authority (and interested parties) at the previous stages. If the project meets all requirements, the *operation license* is issued.[25] Only then the core activities of the project—in our case, iron ore extraction—can begin.

For projects of higher environmental impact or complexity (such as open pit iron ore mining), a specific study called Environmental Impact Study (*Estudo de impacto ambiental*, EIS[26]) is required. The environmental authority decides whether an EIS is required at a screening stage. It can also decide that an EIS is not necessary, that simpler environmental studies are enough: "The competent environment authority, verifying that the project or activity cannot potentially cause significant environmental degradation, will determine which are the pertinent environmental studies to the respective licensing process".[27] The *minimum content* of an Environmental Impact Study (EIS) is defined by law. First, an environmental diagnosis of the area directly affected by the project is undertaken. It has to encompass descriptions of the *physical environment,* the *biological environment* and *natural ecosystems* including areas of permanent preservation, and the *socioeconomic environment,* including land use and occupation, water resources use, socioeconomic aspects of the affected areas, highlighting archeological sites, historical and cultural monuments of the community, dependency relations within local society, the potential future use of environmental resources.[28]

Second, the EIS must include an analysis of the environmental impacts of the project and its alternatives. It has to identify probable relevant impacts, predicting their extent and interpreting their importance; indicate positive and negative impacts, direct and indirect impacts, short and long-term impacts, temporary and permanent impacts, to which degree the impacts are reversible, cumulative and synergetic; as well as how the disadvantages and benefits of the project will be socially distributed.[29] Third, the EIS must define mitigation measures, control equipment and systems

---

[25] CONAMA Resolution 237/1997, Article 8, III, http://www.mma.gov.br/port/CONAMA/res/res97/res23797.html (last accessed 1 October 2018).

[26] EIA in Portuguese does not correspond to the same acronym in English, which stands, as well known, for Environmental Impact Assessment. It refers just to a particular type of Environmental Impact Study. To avoid confusion, I will, in this chapter, refer to the study as EIS.

[27] National Council for the Environment (CONAMA) Resolution 237/1997, Article 3, sole paragraph, http://www.mma.gov.br/port/CONAMA/res/res97/res23797.html (last accessed 1 October 2018).

All translations of legal texts, interviews and literature originally in Portuguese or Spanish are my own, unless indicated otherwise.

[28] CONAMA Resolution 001/1986, Article 6, I, http://www.mma.gov.br/port/CONAMA/res/res86/res0186.html (last accessed 1 October 2018).

[29] CONAMA Resolution 001/1986, Article 6, II, http://www.mma.gov.br/port/CONAMA/res/res86/res0186.html (last accessed 1 October 2018).

to treat waste and emissions, evaluating how efficient they are[30]; and elaborate on monitoring and follow-up programs concerning positive and negative impacts.[31]

The environmental licensing process at its initial stages is characterized by dialogue between the applicant for a license and the environmental authority with the aim to determine whether an EIS will be necessary, or if simpler types of environmental studies (or other documents) can replace the EIS. Afterwards, the dialogue goes on to define what the EIS (or replacing studies) must encompass (scoping).[32] This "[…] screening stage is crucial in the process. Mistakes in framing the proposals can allow projects to be installed without the proper environmental controls, or unfairly impose costly and sluggish processes of environmental assessment and control on potentially non-impacting projects".[33]

In most cases only the company and the environmental authority take part in these stages of the licensing procedure. However, also the broader public can be invited to participate at this early stage of environmental licensing. Local people will probably know their surroundings better than the environmental authority based in another city.[34] Locals cannot only provide questions and opinions that contribute to richer and more encompassing environmental studies, they can also help the environmental authority to better understand the potential effects of a project and correctly decide if an EIS is necessary or not.[35]

2.1 The Rights to Information and Participation in Environmental Law: The Potential for Democratic Proceduralization

The Brazilian Constitution attributes to "[…] the Public Power and the whole community the duty to defend and preserve the environment".[36] The rights to information and participation are corollaries of these constitutional duties. The applicable

---

[30] CONAMA Resolution 001/1986, Article 6, III, http://www.mma.gov.br/port/CONAMA/res/res86/res0186.html (last accessed 1 October 2018).

[31] CONAMA Resolution 001/1986, Article 6, IV, http://www.mma.gov.br/port/CONAMA/res/res86/res0186.html (last accessed 1 October 2018).

[32] In Minas Gerais, this initial dialogue stage in practice lumps screening and scoping in rather informal consultations between the professionals who will elaborate the EIS and the Environmental Authority.

[33] Fonseca (2015), p. 32.

[34] The environmental authority for the open pit mine of CMD is located in Diamantina, Minas Gerais, approximately 150 km away from CMD. The road trip takes around 3 h. By the time of my field research (which coincided with the end of the operation license stage) I often needed 4 h, as the road only has two lanes (one in each direction) and it was undergoing construction in several places.

[35] Fonseca (2015), p. 32.

[36] Brazil. Constitution of 1988, Article 225, http://www.planalto.gov.br/ccivil_03/constituicao/constituicaocompilado.htm (last accessed 1 October 2018).

national and local legal frameworks for the environmental licensing process grant rights to environmental information[37] (on different sorts of impacts caused by the intended activities) and to participation[38] to all interested citizens.

The law on the National Environmental Policy (law 6938/1981), for example, establishes in article 4, V, that the national environmental policy will aim at "[...] the divulgation of environmental data and information, and at the formation of public awareness about the necessity of preserving the environmental quality and the ecological balance". The same law establishes as instruments of the National Environmental Policy an environmental information system (article 9, VII), and includes "[...] the guarantee of providing information that regards the environment, the Public Power being obliged to produce such information, in the case it is inexistent" (article 9, XI).

Besides the Environmental Impact Study, which usually results in an extensive report with the same name (the EIS of the Minas-Rio open pit, for example, has 1150 pages), the applicant must also present a *report of environmental impacts* (RIMA, for *relatório de impacto ambiental*).[39] The RIMA is an instrument to ensure the right to environmental information. Based on the EIS, the RIMA is a shorter and more accessible version of the report, a summary containing *inter alia* the conclusions of the EIS. Most importantly, *"[t]he RIMA must be presented objectively and in a comprehensible way. The information must be presented in accessible language, illustrated by maps, charts, boxes, graphs and other visual communication techniques, so as to allow understanding of the advantages and disadvantages of the project, as well as of all environmental consequences of its implementation"*.[40]

The right to participation in the environmental licensing process, too, is further determined in specific legislation. The National Council for the Environment (CONAMA), for example, establishes in its resolution 237/1997, article 3, that the environmental permit for activities that actually or potentially cause significant environmental degradation hinges upon the EIS-RIMA "[...] to which due publicity will be given, assured public hearings, when applicable, in accordance with regulations". Resolution 009/1987 of CONAMA determines, in its article 2, that "[w]

---

[37] See: Brazil. Law 6938, 31 August 1981, Article 9, XI, and Article 4, V, http://www.planalto.gov.br/ccivil_03/leis/L6938.htm (last accessed 24 August 2017); Law 10650, April 16 2003, especially Article 2, http://www.planalto.gov.br/ccivil_03/leis/2003/L10.650.htm (last accessed 1 October 2018); Constitution of the Federal Republic of Brazil from 1988, Article 5, XIV and XXXIII, Article 225 §1° IV and VI, http://www.planalto.gov.br/ccivil_03/constituicao/constituicaocompilado.htm (last accessed 1 October 2018).

[38] See: Constitution of the Federal Republic of Brazil from 1988, Article 225, §1°, IV; National Council for the Environment (CONAMA) Resolution 237/1997, Article 3, http://www.mma.gov.br/port/CONAMA/res/res97/res23797.html (last accessed 1 October 2018); CONAMA Resolution 009/1987, Article 2, http://www.mma.gov.br/port/CONAMA/res/res87/res0987.html (last accessed 1 October 2018); CONAMA Resolution 001/1986, Article 11 §2°, http://www.mma.gov.br/port/CONAMA/res/res86/res0186.html (last accessed 1 October 2018).

[39] These reports are usually referred to together as EIA-RIMA.

[40] CONAMA Resolution 001/1986, Article 9, Sole paragraph, http://www.mma.gov.br/port/CONAMA/res/res86/res0186.html (last accessed 1 October 2018), highlighted.

henever it is deemed necessary, or when it is requested by a civil entity, by the Government Agency for Law Enforcement and Prosecution,[41] or by fifty (50) or more citizens, the Environmental Authority shall conduct a public hearing". Finally, CONAMA resolution 001/1986, article 11, §2°, requires that the competent environmental authority "[...] determine a deadline for receiving comments [on the EIS-RIMA] from public agencies and other interested parties and, whenever it deems necessary, will conduct hearings to inform the public about the project and its impacts and to discuss the RIMA".

Public participation is prescribed, furthermore, as concerns the elaboration of rules and norms[42] by the National Council for the Environment (and by corresponding state councils), and as concerns the formulation and execution of environmental policies.[43] Participation of directly impacted communities is, however, unusual, either because there are no appropriate channels to connect communities directly to the environmental authorities, or because councils of the environmental authority, despite their representative role, tend not to have balanced representation of government, environmental and community organizations, and companies. Thus, the environmental licensing procedure gains in importance as one of the only channels where affected communities can directly voice their interests and defend their rights.[44]

In Minas Gerais and in most states in Brazil, as well as at the federal level, the environmental authority has several departments and divisions. In Minas Gerais, a state that is larger than metropolitan France, the environmental authority has regional subdivisions. Each of those territorial subdivisions encompasses a predominantly technical division that works together with an advisory and deliberative council. The former, called SUPRAM,[45] is responsible for the screening; for determining the scope of the environmental studies (the terms of reference); for evaluating impact studies and projects and producing technical opinions about them.

---

[41] I opted for this expression (instead of Public Prosecution Office, commonly found in translations from Brazilian Portuguese to English) to refer to the *Ministério Público* because this institution has no correspondence in English-speaking common law countries. This public authority is independent from the executive, from the judiciary and from the legislature and is also known as a fourth power in Brazil. It exists at the federal (Ministério Público Federal (MPF)) and the state level— (Ministério Público Estadual (MPE)). Its constitutional mandate designates it as "a permanent institution that is essential to the jurisdictional function of the state" (Brazilian Constitution, Article 127); apart from criminal prosecution, it is mandated to defend the legal order, democracy, and social interests and inalienable individual interests. In the environmental licensing, the member of the Government Agency of Law Enforcement and Public Prosecution acts as guardian of the law, defendant of the legal order and of community rights. Throughout this chapter, I refer to the Minas Gerais Government Agency for Law Enforcement and Prosecution (Ministério Público de Minas Gerais) as MPMG.

[42] The CONAMA resolutions determine, for example, parameters to emissions, standards to air and water resources quality, among others.

[43] Brazil. Law 6938, 31 August 1981, Article 8, VII, http://www.planalto.gov.br/ccivil_03/leis/L6938.htm (last accessed 1 October 2018).

[44] Milaré (2011), p. 230.

[45] SUPRAM stands for superintendência regional de meio ambiente.

SUPRAM also monitors the implementation of projects after the environmental permits have been issued. The advisory and deliberative council, called URC,[46] is formed by representatives of the government, civil society (usually NGOs dedicated to environmental protection) and industry representatives.[47] URC members (councilors) deliberate and vote on granting or denying the environmental permits based on the technical analysis provided by SUPRAM. The ordinary and extraordinary sessions of URC are public and provide some space for communities to directly voice their concerns, questions, criticisms and suggestions.

Public hearings and sessions of URC are, in practice, the main occasions at which affected communities and other interested parties can participate in environmental licensing: mainly by asking questions and expressing their concerns. At neither do citizens have a right to vote. Public hearings are, furthermore, an essential legal requirement. If the prescribed public hearings are not carried out, the environmental permit can be declared void by the executive or by the judiciary.[48] Public hearings are, however, not binding on the environmental authority, they are merely informative.

Brazilian legal scholarship on the rights to information and participation tends to acknowledge the importance of engaging society at all stages of the environmental licensing process, and not only through public hearings or URC deliberative sessions in which the council votes on the environmental permit. Yet, not only the legal literature recognizes that participation in practice remains insufficient[49]; also the Brazilian sociological and anthropological literature on socio-environmental conflicts holds the rights to information and participation to be systematically violated in environmental licensing processes.[50] Not everybody who proclaims the importance of the right to participation shares the same understanding of what this right means. How participation is interpreted depends ultimately on how we understand

---

[46] URC stands for Unidade Regional Colegiada. The Minas-Rio open pit mine falls within the jurisdiction of SUPRAM-Jequitinhonha and its respective council, URC-Jequitinhonha.

[47] According to the legislation applicable from 2007 to 2016 (period under analysis) to environmental licensing in Minas Gerais, the Decree 44.667/2007, Article 23: "Each URC, observing the equal representation criterion, is composed by the maximum of twenty members, representation is guaranteed of the following segments: I. state public power; II. federal public power; III. municipal public power, IV. representative entities of the productive sector; V. liberal professions related to environmental protection; VI. non-governmental organizations legally constituted for protection, conservation and improvement of the environment; VII. regional entities whose activities are related to the development of environmental protection policies; VIII. entities of acknowledged dedication to teaching, research, or technological or scientific development in the area of environment or improvement of life quality". The URC Jequitinhonha has twenty councilor positions, ten representing the government, ten representing civil society (encompassing both the "productive sector", as the mining industry; and environmental protection NGOs). Not all positions are filled all times. https://www.almg.gov.br/consulte/legislacao/completa/completa.html?tipo=Dec&num=44667&ano=2007 (last accessed 14 June 2018).

[48] CONAMA Resolution 009/1987, Article 2, § 2°, http://www.mma.gov.br/port/CONAMA/res/res87/res0987.html (last accessed 1 October 2018); Milaré (2011), p. 549.

[49] Milaré (2011), p. 230; Fonseca (2015), p. 32.

[50] Bermann (2014), p. 98.

democracy, a question open to debate. In the next session I address but two possible understandings of participation that have very different practical implications.

2.2 Two Tentative Interpretations of Participation: An Intrinsic Requisite of Democracy, a Functional Demand in Proceduralization

The value of participation to the advancement of democracy and to the promotion of all human rights is broadly acknowledged not only in the core conventions on human rights, but also in the Brazilian national legal order (in the constitution and in several national and state laws). The Office of the United Nations High Commissioner for Human Rights (UNOHCHR) stresses: "The right to directly and indirectly *participate in political and public life* is important in empowering individuals and groups, and is one of the core elements of human rights-based approaches aimed at eliminating marginalization and discrimination".[51] Participation can be understood as citizen participation in the construction of a public sphere, in its broadest sense,[52] and is closely connected to a core assumption of democracy itself: the idea that all citizens have equal political competence and reasoning capacity to participate in, debate and decide public matters.[53] Participation thus understood is self-determined and holds value per se in a democratic order. It empowers individuals and groups that, just by actively taking part in public debates and arenas, exercise and demand respect for their citizenship and their dignity.

However, participation can also be understood more narrowly, as taking part in specific administrative decision-making procedures within the government structures—in the case here analyzed, within the space provided by the environmental authorities. Participation, thus understood, holds different value: it becomes a tool to improve decision-making, especially in contexts of risk, uncertainty and complex challenges to which there exist no ready-made solutions.[54] As concerns environmental licensing, participation thus becomes a component of environmental

---

[51] OHCHR, Equal participation in political and public affairs. In: United Nations Office of the High Commissioner for Human Rights, http://www.ohchr.org/EN/Issues/Pages/EqualParticipation.aspx. (last accessed 1 October 2018).

[52] This is, for example, the idea behind Habermas' model of deliberative democracy. See, among others, Habermas (1996), Porte and Nanz (2004), p. 269 and Mercado Pacheco (2012) p. 47.

[53] Equality of citizens' capacity to reason and to participate in politics justifies majority rule in classical democracy and modern forms of representative democracy. Equality, however, is more than a formal premise: it also becomes a central objective of democratic regimes. This brings with it the need for an educational system that prompts autonomous thinking and critical capacity. This argument is elaborated by Castoriadis (1998), pp. 222–223. Although Castoriadis deconstructs the notion of purely procedural democracy, like Habermas he highlights the importance of citizen participation in the public sphere for a functioning democracy.

[54] Following Mercado Pacheco (2012), I derive this concept of participation from the experimentalist governance debates.

governance. According to the latter concept of participation, citizens and groups holding divergent—and sometimes incompatible—interests can enrich the debate and facilitate rational problem-solving characterized by cooperation and mutual learning.[55] I refer to this narrower concept of participation as *functional participation.*[56]

It is important to mark the difference between citizen participation as fundamental to democracy and functional participation, or the participation of interested parties (stakeholders[57]) in specific decision-making procedures. The latter, despite its potential to enhance democratic practices, differs from citizen participation in relevant aspects. First, functional participation relates less to the broader social context (to a public sphere or to discussions about how to live together, as a collective), and more to the respective stakeholders' particular interests in a certain decision or their respective expertise. Second, participation as an element in experimentalist governance demands that participants possess certain qualities and resources (e.g., being part of an NGO or other organization[58]; holding certain types of knowledge); citizen status alone is not sufficient. In the case of URCs, for example, those entitled to become councilors are either environmental NGOs and other representatives of certain interests (e.g. government, the mining industry or other industries, labor movements), or actors with a particular kind of expertise (e.g. "those exercising liberal professions related to environmental protection; entities of acknowledged dedication to teaching, research, or technological or scientific development in the area of environment or improvement of life quality"[59]). As highlighted by Mercado Pacheco, who has extensively researched new governance and new forms of regulation in the context of the European Union and Spain, this selective participation compromises the equality principle that underlies democratic decision-making.[60] Citizen participation is replaced by participation based on certain selection criteria. As the selection criteria are not always coherent (or even explicit) in practice, the aforementioned democratic potential is weakened.

Another criticism of the functional understanding of participation holds that the experimentalist model fails to acknowledge that material inequalities among participants are more often than not unsurpassable. Thus, the stakeholders holding more knowledge (and/or economic resources, political influence, etc.)—that is, the most powerful actors—can distort the outcomes. According to Mercado Pacheco,

---

[55] As explained, *inter alia*, by Mercado Pacheco (2012) and Estévez Araújo (2006), Wilkinson (2012).

[56] Mercado Pacheco (2012), p. 57.

[57] The stakeholder category encompasses companies, public powers, NGOs and other actors, besides natural persons.

[58] This is the case of representation through councilors in the URCs in the environmental licensing of Minas Gerais.

[59] Minas Gerais, Decree 44.667/2007, Article 23, V and VIII, https://www.almg.gov.br/consulte/legislacao/completa/completa.html?tipo=Dec&num=44667&ano=2007 (last accessed 14 June 2018).

[60] Mercado Pacheco (2012), p. 59.

reducing participation to its functional aspect results in privileging expert groups and specific interests groups (stakeholders) to the detriment of citizens' participation:

> The result of this selective process [of who participates] is the inequality of participants. Power asymmetries distort the results of the participative and consensual instruments of governance and democratic experimentalism. The participants of the horizontal coordination games, negotiation and cooperation in governance are not equal. The most powerful, most homogeneous, better organized groups, and those who enjoy a better strategic view of their own interests are the ones who accumulate greater opportunities for succeeding in the participatory and cooperative game that governance suggests to us.[61]

Furthermore, functional participation reduces political conflicts and opposition to questions of problem solving presented as an exercise of rational discussion in which the best arguments prevail. The rational problem-solving approach assumes that disagreements result merely from information asymmetries that can be addressed through sharing knowledge and through debate. It thus ignores that diverging and conflicting ideas of how to live together are a key feature of pluralist societies. As long as these differences exist, they will lead to conflicts that cannot be resolved exclusively with the help of scientific knowledge.

This approach also tends to insufficiently account for the many uncertainties involved in scientifically predicting the actual social and environmental impacts of administrative decisions, such as the licensing of large-scale mining projects; in mitigating these impacts; and in estimating the actual economic benefits of the respective project.[62] Given these uncertainties (many times unsurpassable despite the best scientific knowledge), debate on whether or not to grant a license will necessarily involve aspects beyond technical knowledge. Yet, the reduction of opposing political views to issues that can be resolved by applying expert knowledge has been very common in the environmental licensing process of the Minas-Rio project. In this process, the environmental authority in different ways, which I describe in the next section, has weakened, if not undermined, the rights to information and participation by favoring a functional interpretation of participation.

3   The Rights to Information and Participation in the Minas-Rio

The Minas-Rio case reveals the following deficits in the licensing process with respect to the rights to information and participation: (1) flaws in how information is produced in the EISs and in their evaluation by the environmental authority; (2) restrictions (intentional or not) of the right to information of locals from Conceição

---

[61] Mercado Pacheco (2012), p. 60, my translation.

[62] The environmental studies just make predictions, which may have been established following the most reliable methods and available information. They can never eliminate the risk of unexpected outcomes, be they negative or positive.

do Mato Dentro, (3) constraints on the right to participation. Control of knowledge production and barriers to access to information contributed to undermining the right to participation. There was strong mobilization against the infringements of the rights to information and participation. Against this background I argue that, despite its democratizing potential, in practice the environmental licensing process has been favoring functional participation and, therefore, privatized legal proceduralization.

I have collected the data from which I derive these findings through direct observation of public meetings during 2014 and 2015 in rural and urban areas of Conceição do Mato Dentro and in Diamantina,[63] and 28 in-depth semi-structured interviews with key informants. All interviews were conducted in Portuguese. I have initially interviewed persons who were part of the conflict since the beginning of the environmental licensing process,[64] and later on experts in EIS-RIMAs, lawyers specialized in mining and environmental law (some of which also helped to elaborate Minas Gerais' environmental legislation in the 1980s), and lawyers working for affected communities. Depending on the interviewee's background, the focus of the interview was on the history of the case (how the conflict unfolded), and specifically on the Minas-Rio environmental licensing process, or on general aspects of environmental licensing processes of mining activities in Minas Gerais (this was the case, for example, with experts on environmental licensing and EISs). I have also collected extensive documentation of this process at the environmental authority archives in order to compare the information gained from interviews with the case files of the Minas-Rio licensing process. My time at the SUPRAM archives in Diamantina became, furthermore, an important opportunity to observe the routines of people working at SUPRAM and their interactions with different actors involved in the conflict.

It goes without saying that my own subjectivity, worldview and positionality have influenced my data collection and analysis, not to mention changes in the research objectives that I made after several rounds of discussion with research participants in the field.

---

[63] The total of 18 public meetings encompassed sessions organized by affected families without the presence of the mining company; one meeting organized by the affected families with the mining company, mediated by the local prosecutor; meetings organized by municipal authorities with the mining company and with attendance of affected families; meetings organized by municipal authorities because of affected families' pressure (without the presence of the mining company); meetings organized by state environmental authorities with the mining company, environmental councillors and prosecutor (without affected families or anyone representing them); and URC public sessions to deliberate on the environmental permit (with considerable attendance of affected families and mining company representatives and workers).

[64] Members of affected families and resistance groups, municipal authorities, environmental authorities and technical staff (including legal experts) who participated in the case since its beginning and, therefore, know it thoroughly, environmentalists and members of the MPMG.

3.1   The Right to Information

3.1.1   Controlling Knowledge Production

Barriers to the right to information arise even before demands for information are voiced and are due to the way that technical environmental information, which is to inform the decision-making process, is produced. As described earlier in this chapter, a company presents an EIS, which is then evaluated by the technical branch of the environmental authority (SUPRAM). SUPRAM's technical staff (coming from different backgrounds, including agronomy, engineering and economics) is responsible for the assessment. However, not only is SUPRAM insufficiently staffed, it also lacks equipment and resources for sufficient field visits (for verification during the analysis). Increases in SUPRAM's budget are necessary to allow the environmental authority to employ more (and more experienced) environmental experts; to finance field visits (and equipment) in order to verify data in the EIS and supervise mining projects. The existing qualified staff works under several constrains, such as excessive workload and the scarcity of resources for field visits. What staff members have pointed out in interviews, however, was the excess of political intervention in their work on the Minas-Rio project.

These environmental experts indicated that when the drafts of their Opinions contained information that could have delayed the Minas-Rio project or made it more costly, or when they identified violations of environmental regulations, they were often required to eliminate such information from the final Opinions[65] (or from memoranda). Referring to my archival research at SUPRAM, one employee, an environmental expert, observed:

> Ahhh, there are so many documents that were taken out of there [the environmental licensing process file]! Yes, she [the superintendent of SUPRAM[66]] said so in a meeting. She said that she had removed these documents from the file and that whenever she found this kind of documents there she would remove them again. She exactly said so: "I took them out and I will always do so. Whenever I find them. You are not supposed to add any memorandum to this process file". And in the meetings [internal SUPRAM meetings], you should have seen the power that Anglo had. For example, when I requested more information, or concluded that the studies were insufficient, then the secretary [State Secretary for the Environment] came here to tell me that this was not the case [that more information was not needed], that I should just leave everything as it was.[67]

---

[65] Drafts of Opinions are solely for internal use at SUPRAM. The final Opinions (Parecer Único—PU) are the only documents that become part of the case file, and, thus, can become available to the public. Sometimes the case file also includes memoranda, short summaries of the discussions among the technical staff. As reported by the interviewee, though, there were superior orders not to file any memoranda.

[66] The highest officer at SUPRAM.

[67] Interview with SUPRAM environmental expert (technical staff). Minas Gerais, May 22nd, 2015. I do not mention the gender, specific position within the SUPRAM, background or age of any of these interviewees, in order to protect their anonymity. The staff to which I refer as technical or environmental experts encompasses environmental engineers, civil engineers, hydraulic engineers, mechanical engineers, geographers, agronomists, etc.

Apart from reporting that they were being pressured by their superiors, the SUPRAM environmental experts I interviewed or with whom I had informal talks[68] also said they had little independence in conducting and reporting their environmental analysis of the Minas-Rio due to the constant presence of the mining company's staff in internal meetings of SUPRAM's staff. According to the latter, mining company's staff unduly tried to influence the Opinions.

According to the SUPRAM technical staff members I interviewed, the order to omit information and suppress documents that could be detrimental to the project came, in most cases, from the superintendent, following orders from the State Secretary for the Environment[69] and from the governor of Minas Gerais. At some occasions, the State Sub-Secretary or the Secretary for the Environment even came to talk to them in person at SUPRAM. Thus, mechanisms to assure the independence of the environmental authority's technical staff would be essential to assure the quality of information produced in the environmental licensing and, thus, the right to information. An environmental expert who had been working for the environmental authority for more than 10 years said:

> When I reported things that went against what the company wanted, they [superiors of this environmental expert] changed the technical Opinion. This also happened in another mining project now [not only in the Minas-Rio]. I wrote the Opinion, and afterwards they took out everything that could somehow be contrary to the interests of the company. I obviously didn't sign this Opinion. There is no autonomy. In the environmental authority, whoever worked on the Minas-Rio project had no independence working in this process. The political pressure to just let the project pass was huge. They [superiors of this environmental expert] even told us [the technical staff]: "This project will pass. You better put in conditionalities, because it will pass". And that is what we had in the end. An environmental permit with more than two hundred conditionalities, can it be feasible? If there are more than two hundred measures that the project has to fulfil so that it can be installed, how can something like that be feasible?[70]

The superintendent reported that she had always been open to all information verified by SUPRAM's technical staff, independently of whose interest this information could affect, and also to alternative sources of information, such as studies presented by the Government Agency for Law Enforcement and Prosecution or by research groups supporting affected communities. Her only objection to these researchers was that they were too critical and often, in her view, too late with their submissions. Apart from declaring her openness to the various sources of information and to the participation of various actors, the SUPRAM superintendent also stated that the outcome of the environmental licensing process was predetermined from above, even before the process had started. In my opinion this contradicts the possibility of real openness to other sources of information and to participation:

> Ahh... I believe that the licensing process, as Dr. José Carlos de Carvalho [Former Secretary for the Environment and Sustainable Development of Minas Gerais and former Minister for

---

[68] Some were afraid of talking to me in recorded interviews.

[69] The highest positions in the Environmental Bureaucracy in the whole state, only subordinated to the Governor.

[70] Interview with SUPRAM environmental expert (technical staff). Minas Gerais, 22 May 2015.

the Environment of Brazil] used to say, even before the process is formalized, there is already a decision, right? What is the project, it is a strategic project for the state, so… in other words, this decision is already taken beforehand, even before any licensing procedure has formally started, right? Now, the problem that I see there is that… all right, the project interests the government. So what is necessary, if it [the project] interests the government, then the government should take this project with all its problems and try to find a solution to all these problems, and not leave everything to the licensing process. The mistake is in leaving a project that is strategically important for the government to be treated only within the environmental licensing. It is impossible, right?[71]

Further contradicting the openness of the licensing process, a member of the Minas Gerais Government Agency for Law Enforcement and Prosecution (MPMG)—which also presented independent studies that put into question SUPRAM's technical opinions—reported that he had heard from SUPRAM interns that, whenever external studies were submitted, the superintendent ordered the technical staff not to take these studies into account.[72] Becker also shows that external studies presented during the preliminary license stage (e.g. by the FórumCMD, by the MPMG technical support center and by some councilors) were ignored, together with all the risks and flaws of the EIS-RIMA that SUPRAM itself had described in its Opinion to the preliminary license.[73]

The wording of SUPRAM's Opinion preceding the preliminary license provides further evidence of political pressure.[74] The Opinion highlights that the project was bound to result in considerable environmental losses and no environmental gains. It further states that eventual social gains would depend on political decisions and could not, yet, be assessed. Therefore, the Opinion proceeds, there was no justification for granting environmental permits for the project.[75] Nonetheless, the conclusion of the Opinion highlights the project's importance within the economic development strategy of the government of Minas Gerais and recommends that the URC grants the preliminary license.

3.1.2 Restricting Access to Information

While the quality of the information produced within the environmental licensing procedure can be questioned on many grounds, access to information presents yet additional challenges. I already mentioned that CMD's population (including those who were working on local development) only learned about the Minas-Rio project

---

[71] Interview with SUMPRAM superintendent. Diamantina, Minas Gerais, 29 May 2015.

[72] Interview with MPMG member, Belo Horizonte, Minas Gerais, 6 March 2015.

[73] Becker (2009), p. 352.

[74] Minas Gerais, Parecer Único SISEMA n° 001/2008. P.A COPAM n°472/2007/001/2007, the author has it on file.

[75] Minas Gerais, Parecer Único SISEMA n° 001/2008. P.A COPAM n°472/2007/001/2007, the author has it on file.

through the newspapers. The project was presented as bound to happen before any discussion with locals from CMD (and from other affected cities) took place.[76]

Even after newspapers had started reporting that the environmental licensing process had begun, locals said they did not have access to information related to the project and to the EIS-RIMA.[77] According to the law, a copy of these documents should have been made available for public consultation at the city hall in Conceição do Mato Dentro.[78] Members of the FórumCMD reported, though, that whenever someone from the FórumCMD requested access to the EIS-RIMA, the reply was that the studies were somewhere else; or that someone had taken them out to make copies and had not yet returned them; or that the person who could allow taking the documents out of the city hall for copies was not there; etc. Therefore, locals critical of the project initially mobilized in order to demand access to information. They did gain access to the EIS-RIMA, not at the municipal level, but only at the Minas Gerais state level, through the state environmental authority.[79]

All along the licensing process, access to information has been an issue for resistance movements. The online platform of the Minas Gerais environmental authority is hard to access and, at critical moments of the licensing process (e.g. shortly before URC meetings), relevant documents (e.g. the SUPRAM Opinions) were not accessible.[80] At the beginning of my field research, I also tried to find documents of the case online, but the website was confusing and I did not manage to find many documents there. This made trips to the countryside city where the competent environmental authority is located (Diamantina, Minas Gerais) necessary. When I first went to SUPRAM and requested access to their archives, on 16 December 2014, in order to see the whole Minas-Rio environmental licensing process files, those working at SUPRAM seemed surprised both by my request and by the presence of a researcher there.

---

[76] Becker (2009), pp. 339–357.

[77] This complaint was made in many informal talks in CMD between September 2014 and June 2015 by founders of the FórumCMD and other actors involved in the opposition to the project.

[78] The person who worked at the city hall at the time and who had access to the EIS-RIMA said, in an interview (Conceição do Mato Dentro, 19 March 2015) that the document was available for public consultation at all times. But those who initially mobilized to understand the project and its potential consequences, and whom I have also interviewed (resistance supporter, Belo Horizonte, 28 July 2014; resistance initiator, Belo Horizonte, 27 May 2015; community leader, Conceição do Mato Dentro, 29 March 2015), contradicted this information. Many local residents also mentioned the fact in informal conversations during the first semester of 2015.

[79] Becker (2009), p. 346. According to Becker, who did her research while the preliminary license was being discussed in CMD (between 2006 and 2008), political groups that were in power at the municipal level (and had initially supported the FórumCMD) decided to support the mining company around July 2007. From this moment on, the municipal secretary for the environment and other municipal authorities restricted popular access to official documents and decisions about the Minas-Rio project in CMD. Those interested in this information, thus, pursued it at the Minas Gerais state level.

[80] The absence of the relevant documents online was criticized by the communities through the MPMG member at the URC, for example, on the URC meeting on 18.09.2014 (see minutes of the 85th URC-JEQ meeting, lines 95 to 110 (on file with the author)).

Administrative acts and procedures (such as the environmental licensing procedure) in Brazil, by law, are public and case files must be made accessible upon a
simple request.[81] The Brazilian federal law 10650, from 16 April 2003, specifically
regulates the duty of environmental authorities to provide society with all information regarding environmental licensing processes. Yet, the first time I attempted to
see the case file, access was denied to me; I was being told that the files were in the
capital, Belo Horizonte. I filed another written request and waited. Aware of my
rights and the environmental authority's obligation to provide access to information,
I talked to MPMG members in the capital, Belo Horizonte, and in Diamantina. They
advised me to talk directly to the legal department of the environmental authority,
which I did on the same day. The legal department granted me access to the (public)
documents, which had been in Diamantina all the time. Some months after that, an
interview with a former member of the technical staff of Minas Gerais environmental authority, who is now working in the private sector as an expert on EIS, suggested that this episode was not exceptional. When I asked about the right to
participation in the environmental licensing process, the interviewee mentioned
restrictions to the right to information:

> I believe that this participation… I believe that the government, especially the previous one
> [the party in power in Minas Gerais between 2003-2014], the government has restricted
> participation a little. In former times, when I worked for the environmental authority, if you
> were there analysing a document and some interested person came to see this document –
> because the process is public, right? Every process that is there is public. So if an interested
> person would come, you would receive a call "hey, so and so is here and wants to see a
> certain document". At the same time this document was sent there and the person had
> access. To take pictures, or make copies, analyse… and afterwards the document was sent
> back to us. As far as I know, after I left [between 2005 and 2006], this kind of access has
> been restricted. They always replied that the document was somewhere else, not in the place
> it was supposed to be, that is, in the environmental authority building.[…] So, until this
> person got access, it often took months. […] My impression is that this group in power
> [politicians]… it is trying to restrict this action by social groups. Especially by those groups
> that are interested in these big projects. […] At the time I worked there [at the environmen-
> tal authority] there was this perception that social participation was way too much. It was
> an obstacle. Because it does generate obstacles, right? Because other people read, ques-
> tion… there were also groups related to the university that analysed the documents. But I
> believe that this [participation] contributes more than it hampers. At least as I see it.
> Everybody has his or her interests, that are legitimate, and there… in this discussion this is
> excellent. Of course you [the environmental authority staff] will suffer more pressure. You
> are there, exposed, every day. The COPAM[82] meeting happens every month. And I felt as if

---

[81] As established in Article 37 of the constitution in what can be translated as "publicness principle"
or "openness principle" of administrative acts and in article 5, XXXIII, all Brazilians and resident
foreigners are entitled to receive information from public authorities relevant to their private interest, or the general or collective interest, except for information related to national security
matters.

[82] COPAM—Conselho Estadual de Política Ambiental (State Council for Environmental Policy)
has jurisdiction over the whole state of Minas Gerais (not only over a sub-region, as the URCs). At
the time the interviewee worked at the environmental authority of Minas Gerais, all decisions on
permits were taken at the COPAM public sessions. After decentralization reforms in Minas Gerais
(that started around 2005), decisions on permits started to be taken at the regional level, at the
URCs meetings.

> I was going to a slaughterhouse in every day of [COPAM] meeting. Because this is the day you [environmental authority staff] were totally exposed. You had to expose your work. So once a month you got naked and showed everything there, openly. But this was good. Professionally, it was good as well… even to learn how to cope with these issues, especially with these conflict issues".[83]

Finally, the Opinions are often made public only ten days before an URC ordinary meeting (5 days if it is an extraordinary meeting). Councilors, affected communities and environmentalists consider this time insufficient to understand these often complex and lengthy documents.[84] Both knowledge production control and barriers to access to information undermine the right to participation.

3.2   The Right to Participation

3.2.1   Participation: To Which End?

Another barrier that affects both the right to information and the right to participation is the mistrust that some of those working at SUPRAM express towards leaders of affected communities, research groups, environmentalists and, generally, towards actors that the higher officer at SUPRAM considered too critical of SUPRAM's work:

> Everybody knows that the processes are under analysis… GESTA [a well-known socio-environmental conflicts research group in Minas Gerais] never came after us. Then they come to the [URC] meeting… I am sure that the Professor Andrea Zhouri [coordinator of this research group] would have many contributions to make to SUPRAM. But she comes to URC and starts to criticize. This is not to add something. This is not to be a partner, right? These various actors, it is important… the more actors who can act, the better, because each one brings his view, but to contribute, not to criticize, right?[85]

While the environmental authority tends to regard the company as a partner, who cooperates with SUPRAM by providing all information necessary for the environmental analysis, it resents how other actors participate because of their critical assessment of the information provided by the company, the Opinions and, generally, the environmental licensing process. The complaint of the superintendent of SUPRAM relates, furthermore, to a fundamental weakness of the experimentalist governance logic (and the idea of a functional participation); to the underestimation of conflict situations in which diverging interests cannot be reconciled through

---

[83] Interview with environmental authority's former technical staff (environmental expert). Belo Horizonte, Minas Gerais, 18 May 2015. Again I do not indicate gender, age or exact position of the person in order to ensure anonymity.

[84] This is a common issue mentioned by URC councilors in interviews and publically, during URC meetings. See, for example, the minutes of the 90th URC-JEQ meeting, lines 213–214 (on file with the author).

[85] Interview with SUPRAM superintendent, Diamantina, 29 May 2015.

"rational debate" or scientific knowledge. The dispute is not only about "the facts", but also about how different groups interpret and valuate these "facts".

As we have seen, the procedural logic according to which the environmental licensing was conceived assumes that different actors are willing to share information and cooperate towards common ends and that the ends themselves can be debated and reviewed along the process. The objectives of environmental law include the rational use of environmental resources, the preservation of the environment and sustainable development. It is these objectives that the environmental licensing procedure is meant to further. While the concept of sustainable development, in particular, is open to interpretation,[86] it would be hard to argue for an understanding that excludes environmental protection or that does not demand a minimum of equity in the distribution of risks and benefits of economic projects. By law, environmental licensing aims at promoting sustainable development and encompasses, as a possibility, the denial of environmental permits for projects that do not comply with environmental legal frameworks. Yet, in practice, the aim of the procedure seems to be the legalization of projects that—even if not compliant with environmental law—the state considers economically and strategically relevant. This objective determines the selection of whose views are taken into account (and whose are disregarded) and which information is considered valid (and which information is distorted, or simply ignored).

The view that the superintendent of SUPRAM expressed in the interview I conducted conforms to the government of Minas Gerais' promotion of mining, which it considers of high importance to the state's economic development. Thus, information and participation that contributes to the furtherance and implementation of mining projects is welcome. By contrast, participation of actors such as affected communities, environmentalists, the mentioned university group and other researchers who analyze the conflict from different disciplinary backgrounds[87] (and, as a result, question the benefits that mining brings to the state) is being restricted. The state government and SUPRAM superintendent, therefore, do not consider the participation of these actors (and the information they bring to the process) as functional to the environmental licensing. It is a participation that "does not add" to the envisaged aim of promoting mining even if it comes with high socioeconomic and environmental costs.

---

[86] And the literature on strong and weak concepts of sustainable development, or on strong and weak senses of the sustainability principle is also countless, see, for example, Mercado Pacheco (2013), Zhouri (2014) Maping environmental inequalities in Brazil: mining, environmental conflicts and impasses of mediation. desiguALdades.net Working Paper Series 75; Sampaio (2011), p. 167; Zhouri et al. (2005).

[87] Becker (2009), Becker and Pereira (2011), Carvalhosa (2016), Ferreira (2016), Prates (2014), Tôrres (2014); among others.

3.2.2 Coping with Physical Obstacles to Participate and Pushing Institutional Ones

A series of well-known practical barriers also contribute to undermining the right to participation. These include the geographical distance from CMD (where affected families live) to Diamantina (where decisions concerning the Minas-Rio permits are taken at URC meetings), the time and cost of travel.[88]

Even if these material barriers and inequalities did not exist, there would be other obstacles to participation. Importantly, there exist too few (and too limited) opportunities for true popular participation. A former legal expert of the environmental authority—who was a key figure in the elaboration of the environmental legislation in Minas Gerais in the 1980s, and is now legal advisor of one of the biggest law firms of the state that focus on environmental and mining law—expresses this criticism:

> But above all, one thing that Brazil has not changed yet, has not improved, and I still believe that is very precarious, is the popular participation in these things. The public hearings aren't good, they aren't good. You know? Even the discussion of the RIMA. That's how I see it… a company will conduct a discussion in a public hearing. It just throws a bundle of information on an audience that has little means to absorb all that [information]. It is very complicated. Maybe we should change the process, you know? […] The instrument is weak; the public hearing is not enough.[89]

This view is shared by a legal expert of SUPRAM:

> And also this question of the public hearings, how they happen, this has to be reviewed, because it is not one day [that will assure participation]. And other mechanisms for society's participation when these big projects come, they must be reviewed. They have to be enlarged, the discussion spaces. Beyond the public hearing, the public hearing is just a legal formality: "I did it, check".[90]

While the dialogue between the mining company and SUPRAM is constant—even considered excessive by some SUPRAM technical staff—the environmental authority does not have the same capacity to deal with participation demands by affected communities and other actors critical of the project:

> In the case of bigger projects, I believe SUPRAM was not prepared for it [popular participation demands]. It was a shock, I believe that this confrontation was a huge shock, and until now the state is not yet prepared. Neither the state nor the entrepreneur was prepared to deal

---

[88] The road trip from CMD to Diamantina takes around three and a half hours by bus. For interested persons from local communities (including affected families) and other actors critical of the project, participation in URC meetings means that they miss one day of work and the corresponding income. Furthermore, they must fund their own expenses. The mining company, by contrast, has staff that attends these meetings and covers all their costs. Despite these constraints, community members and other interested actors (including activist researchers) have participated in the public deliberative sessions in order to discuss and vote on each permit—and they maintain doing so to date.

[89] Interview with legal advisor of a mining and environmental law firm. Belo Horizonte, 15 June 2015.

[90] Interviews with legal expert of SUPRAM. Diamantina, 22 May, 2015 and 1 June, 2015.

with the participation demand by the community. [...] We, the state, we haven't been there [in Conceição do Mato Dentro] before the project, the state hasn't been there. The state doesn't know who the people are. The state didn't have a picture of the situation before. All that is produced, all the information that is produced, is brought to us by the company, this is the system, you understand? [...] Indeed, I believe this should change, this relation between company, state, I believe this should be maybe reverted. I believe the state has to assume its role more... impartially. [...].[91]

Apart from the obstacles to community participation, the interviewee criticizes the state's lack of impartiality towards different groups and interests, and, again, mentions the insufficiency of information, especially concerning the socio-economic impacts of the Minas-Rio project. The socio-economic impacts of the project and the number of affected families were not known by the time the preliminary license was approved (in December 2008). On 10 June 2010, at the 43rd URC meeting, that is, one and a half years after the preliminary license had been granted, and 6 months after the installation license-1 (LI-1) had been issued, a conditionality was approved in order to oblige the mining company to finance a study (to be carried out by independent experts suggested by the affected communities) in order to determine the extent of areas (and, thus, of families) directly and indirectly impacted by the Minas-Rio project. This happened after many families had been resettled and entire villages were already vacated.[92]

The affected community members, too, noticed the lack of impartiality of the state. They were dissatisfied with the participation they were granted and which, in their view, was a mere formality and could not possibly influence the outcome of the process.[93] In an interview a family (mother [M] and son [S]) who live in the rural area that will be impacted by the open pit mine in its second stage (Sapo community), voiced their disappointment with the weak participation, or worse, with the appropriation (and distortion) of this weak participation in order to legitimate decisions:

S   I didn't use to believe that, but it is a planned theatre. All environmental licensing [processes] that happened were planned theatres. Everybody already arrived there with their own conviction: "It will be this way". "It will!" All is fine, the procedure rolls normally, but in the end the votes are a stacked deck. For you to see that there is nothing.

M   That's why I don't like to join these things.

---

[91] Interviews with a legal expert of SUPRAM. Diamantina, 22 May, 2015 and 1 June, 2015.

[92] The consultancy company Diversus carried out the field research of this first study between August and December 2010, with the report being published in August 2011. Diversus then had to write an addendum to the study (published in August 2012). And as the discussions and doubts about the socio-economic impacts of the project; flaws (and frauds) in land negotiation processes; and about how to define which families could be considered affected went on, Diversus produced two further studies, published in August and September 2014. These issues to the present days remain disputed. See Diversus (2011, 2012, 2014a, b), as well as the minutes of the 43ª URC-JEQ meeting, the author has it on file.

[93] De Oliveira Vieira (2015), p. 65.

S   I don't like to say that to people, because people... in my case, right? A resi
     dent from here, we can't lose hope, but unfortunately we have to recognize the
     truth. What is happening is stacked deck. All the meetings for licensing of
     anything, everything is well organized before. One arrives there, some are talk-
     ing bad, others are talking good [of the project], you think it is favourable [to
     the affected families]. But in the end, indeed, you see that the sum of the votes
     is always in favour [of the project], it is always bigger.[94]

Environmentalists, some URC councilors and activist researchers, as well, frequently complained that they were heard solely to fulfil legal requirements of participation and, thus, to legitimate the decision-making process, but that their
arguments and demands for change were rarely taken into account.[95]

The member of the MPMG in Conceição do Mato Dentro has mentioned more
than once that he considers the rights to information and participation as among the
most seriously violated rights within the Minas-Rio licensing process, and added:

Although participation is assured in the law, formally, it is... the communities don't have an
active voice. The environmental licensing procedures should be much stronger in the guarantee of these rights to information and participation. A recent example [related to the
licensing of the second stage of the Minas-Rio Project] is the public hearing meant to
explain to the communities what they are calling "optimization" of the mining cave. No one
knew about this public hearing. Who did know about it? There were no posters in the city,
the hearing was not advertised... there was a formal statement in the radio, but it really
didn't inform what was about to happen, right? A few persons knew what the hearing would
be about. At the end there was no hearing for now, but I am almost sure that, if there had
been a hearing at this moment, 90% of the audience would be workers of the company, who
are obliged to go in order to make big numbers, to make a strong choir. [...] We [the
MPMG] have been informed here that some people were invited [to take part in the hear-
ing], but they didn't know what would be discussed there. The language that is used, is it
accessible to this audience? Do they understand the information? And even if they are duly
informed, this doesn't fulfil the right... do they have an active voice to say "no", or "we
want it this or that way"? [...] But it [participation] is just for the record. Right? Thus "I've
fulfilled the legal requirement". Right? This right to participation, of... having an active
voice, power to influence the results, this is absent; it is completely absent in practice. It
shouldn't be, but it is.

An illustration of this participation "just for the record" are public hearings and
URC meetings. While local dwellers were granted turns of two or three minutes to
present their position, the company, when explaining the project, was often not subjected to the same time limits.[96] The company is, after all, regarded by the state as
the main information provider, the one that can give the answers demanded by community and councilors. It is, thus, no surprise that, after some time trying to influence the outcomes through taking part in the meetings and presenting their
complaints in the little time they had, resistance movements started to adopt

---

[94] Interview, Conceição do Mato Dentro, 24 March 2015.

[95] De Oliveira Vieira (2015), p. 69.

[96] Direct observation, September 2014.

contentious strategies to raise awareness for their situation, such as protests within URC meetings and blocking roads in Conceição do Mato Dentro.[97]

While citizen presence and participation at meetings seems to be just for the record, URC councilors are expected to provide their respective expertise. Councilors are expected to have relevant knowledge on environmental issues and to cast informed votes at the URC meetings based on the Opinions of the environmental authority.[98] Nonetheless, they often come unprepared or do not fully understand the technical information presented in the Opinions.[99] Sometimes, lack of preparedness may be due to the fact that these documents are only made available five or ten days before an URC meeting; in other cases because councilors are not fully aware of their role and responsibility, or because they also suffer pressure from their superiors. An environmental expert from SUPRAM expressed his frustration about this situation:

> I feel enraged, the councilors do not… participate, you know? This process of shared decision-making at the Council [URC], it just pulverizes the responsibility. Because they [the councilors] don't read. They sometimes don't even know what they are doing there… they are a mere political instrument, because most of them are just representing the state. So he goes there and votes for the state. The state votes in favour, and it stays this way. At the end, the organ [the environmental authority] works to legitimate the degradation.[100]

Yet, also when councilors put effort into understanding the studies and Opinions within the little time available, and attempt to responsibly participate, their participation is limited when their views do not conform to the outcome envisaged by the government. As reported by an environmental expert who worked at SUPRAM at the time of the preliminary license procedure:

---

[97] I could observe one such protest at the 85th URC Extraordinary meeting, on 18 September 2014. According to the agenda a vote was to be taken on the operation permit for the first stage of the Minas-Rio project. About 2 weeks before, a lot of fish had suddenly appeared floating on a creek in the surroundings of the tailings dam of the project. Local communities that depend on this creek for their own water consumption, for their crops, fruit gardens and animals, had long been saying that the creek had been polluted and its water was no longer healthy, not even for animals. Demanding clean-up of the creek and access to water, these communities brought iceboxes filled with dead fish and plastic bottles with water from the creek in order to show the authorities what they were talking about, thus generating turmoil at the meeting. In the end, the MPMG member requested more time to examine the case file and the voting was postponed to 29 September 2014. Local dwellers organized road blockades at several occasions, when I was in the field, on 29 April 2015, and later in 2015, 2016 (as reported by Prates 2017, p. 28) and more recently, in March 2018. See Rodrigues W, Como prometido, manifestantes bloqueiam acesso à Anglo em Conceição do Mato Dentro. De Fato Online 12 March 2018, https://www.defatoonline.com.br/como-prometido-manifestantes-bloqueiam-acesso-anglo-em-conceicao-do-mato-dentro/ (last accessed 1 October 2018).

[98] See the selection filters determining who can become a councilor in the aforementioned legislation, *supra* footnote 47.

[99] This was mentioned in interviews with EIS-RIMA elaboration experts on 6 May 2015; with SUPRAM staff (Diamantina, 22 May 2015; 29 May 2015), with URC councilors themselves (Diamantina, 8 May 2015), among others.

[100] Interview with SUPRAM environmental expert, Diamantina, 29 May 2015.

> The most horrendous thing was the URC meeting to vote on the Preliminary License, in 2008. December 2008. The company, they wanted to get the permit at any cost, all right? There was even duress on the councilors. Just like that, in our face. You might have heard that already. The DNPM [National Department of Mineral Production] voted, he said his vote was against issuing the permit, because of the iron content of the iron ore, he explained... he showed that there are more advanced technologies, that the sludge dam as they [the company] were proposing, the impacts... he went on explaining everything, telling that he was against issuing the permit. Suddenly his phone rang, and he said something like that... he never came back to URC meetings, by the way. He said something like that "personally, I am against it... but as I have been told now, I am here for the institution, and I am obliged to vote in favour of the permit".[101]

The superintendent of SUPRAM said the following on the topic of councilor participation (and on community participation at the URC meetings):

> We believe that it is much easier to discuss the problem with the involved parties. And there at the URC [public meetings] this is complicated, right? Because they lack information, when they have to discuss the problem there, information lacks. Sometimes there are councilors who make absolutely inappropriate suggestions. Instead of helping to solve, the suggestions will bring more problems. But the problem is lack of information... and then they have to decide, do you understand? So, today our experience, there, when there is a presentation, one of the first things I've done is that "Dear all, this is a presentation, there will be no deliberation, any pending issue, exactly because this is a complex process, any pending issues regarding certain conditionalities, what are we going to do? We will have another meeting to discuss the issue separately with the involved parties". And from there we formed a working group. I believe that now, based on this experience we had with Anglo, I believe that... the URC itself acquires this experience and agrees with this... this alternative, to discuss our practice. Because there you can discuss everything calmly and you already take the question more or less settled, agreed, to the URC, to the deliberation there. It is much easier. Why? At the time of the deliberation, there at URC, the atmosphere is heavy. Because people are... they are in this logic of being in favour or against, of not respecting the opinion of others, so... people's spirits there, the atmosphere is tumultuous for you to decide properly, right? So, I believe that this working group idea is an interesting alternative.

Indeed, the meetings—that used to happen once a month during 2015, and before that once every 2 to 3 months—are not enough to explain to the councilors, and the broader public, complex reports and analyses. Thus, when suggesting the establishment of working groups to debate controversial or pending issues, I believe the superintendent is really trying to find solutions that allow the councilors to discuss the issues in depth and thus to contribute to improved decision-making. It called my attention, however, that SUPRAM's superintendent seemed to exclude the broader public that attends URC meetings (such as affected communities and environmentalists) from what she considers "involved parties", even though many of these persons are the ones dealing with impacts of the project on a daily basis. I believe this interview demonstrates, thus, the superintendent's perception that participation of affected families and environmentalists is counter-productive to the decision-making process. Other authorities in Minas Gerais share this perception.

---

[101] Interview with SUPRAM environmental expert (technical staff). Minas Gerais, 22 May 2015.

The massive public presence at URC meetings aimed at pushing the institutional actors to take the local communities' demands, narratives and views into account and at building up pressure on councilors and SUPRAM's expert staff. Once the public debate of "pending issues" and "pending conditionalities" was permeated by opposition and protest, the solution that the chief authority at SUPRAM found was to allow "presentations" without deliberation. To move controversial discussions to more restricted sessions. And when councilors, too, presented questions or seemed insecure in issuing their votes (a frequent occurrence given the considerable public pressure that affected families and other participants exert in public URC meetings), to create working groups to discuss these specific issues removed from public pressure and public scrutiny.

As highlighted by a councilor at a URC meeting (where the superintendent shared her idea of smaller working groups):

> We have to ponder the issue of transparency towards others, as well as documentation in minutes. As interesting as it is, if things are not documented in minutes, as is the case here [in the URC meeting], and other councilors cannot come to these debates, and other persons will also not be aware of the debated information, then I believe that, although, on the one hand, these smaller separate meetings are interesting, on the other hand I believe the debates must be carried out here at the council [URC]. Because this is what gives transparency, a democratic quality, and makes more clarity about the licensing possible. I believe this is good for the technical staff, good for the councilors, and good for the company.[102]

Moving controversial discussions to closed spaces weakens transparency, infringes on rights to information and participation, and promotes selective and unequal participation.

3.3 Frustrating Information and Participation: Demobilizing and Fostering Mobilization

While the process reveals severe restrictions to the rights to information and participation, it is also important to highlight how the flaws in the licensing process, even if frustrating and demobilizing, have also contributed to mobilization and strengthening resistance. A kind of network grassroots resistance re-emerged and took different forms through the years.[103] The incipient resistance group mentioned supra, for example, founded the "Forum for Sustainable Development CMD"[104] (FórumCMD) on 8 December 2006 and created an online platform with the same name on 27 March 2007.[105] After a thorough assessment of the EIS-RIMA, the

---

[102] Minas Gerais. Minutes of the 90th URC Jequitinhonha ordinary meeting. Diamantina, 11 December 2014, lines 228–235.

[103] For more detail on different resistance configurations, see De Oliveira Vieira (2015).

[104] "Fórum de Desenvolvimento Sustentável CMD", in Portuguese.

[105] The digital archives of the forum are accessible upon approval by the forum administrators.

FórumCMD published a comprehensive document pointing to a series of inconsistencies and missing information in the EIS-RIMA.[106]

Demobilization of the FórumCMD[107] after the preliminary license (in late 2008) did not mean demobilization of all of its members. Many continued to pressure the government and the company for more transparency and participation, calling out rights violations in the course of the environmental licensing process and elsewhere, i.e. in meetings of the municipal environmental authority, meetings of the municipal legislative, meetings organized by the affected communities together with researchers from local universities and a series of public meetings organized by the MPMG.[108] Between 2011 and 2013, groups of activist researchers also started to present their own technical opinions supporting community demands in the environmental licensing process.[109] Actors whose participation had been restricted have persisted in disputing the information produced within the environmental licensing process and reaffirming their right to participate.

By affirming certain kinds of information, in particular information provided by the company, as relevant and valid (and discrediting other kinds of information) and by discriminating against certain affected communities and their demands, the state has transferred to the company much of the power to determine the rules governing the case (including conditionalities and environmental compensation measures). What this shows is that, by adopting a functional concept of participation, the state has contributed to privatized proceduralization.

The success of the resistance movements in pursuing specific demands (e.g., acknowledgement of all families impacted by the Minas-Rio; resettlement of the families living downstream of the tailings dam and in other areas of risk; holding the company accountable for water pollution in local creeks and for drying up of water

---

[106] Documento de manifestação da comunidade conceicionense com questionamentos e solicitação de esclarecimentos sobre o Eia/Rima (mina a céu aberto) do Empreendimento Mineração Minas-Rio da MMX na região de Conceição do Mato Dentro (on file with the author). To date this document forms a reference document for resistance groups, as many of the problems it articulates persist and are materializing now. Environmental analysts of SUPRAM confirmed many of the critiques in their technical Opinion to the preliminary license.

[107] The issuance of the preliminary license in December 2008 marked the beginning of the demobilization of the FórumCMD. A founding member of the FórumCMD reported, however, that even before, supporters of the mining project had attempted to demobilize resistance initiatives. For example, by announcing inexistent meetings of the FórumCMD, or informing the population that a meeting that would take place had been cancelled. Even the organization of the seminar mentioned above was, according to members of the FórumCMD, very difficult, once some of the invited experts received calls informing them that their lives would be at risk if they came to Conceição do Mato Dentro (Interview with one of the founders of the Fórum Desenvolvimento Sustentável CMD, Belo Horizonte, 27 May 2015).

[108] For more on the meetings organized by the MPMG between 2013 and 2014 and how resistance groups appropriated them as a space of mobilization, see De Oliveira Vieira (2015), Prates (2014) and Ferreira (2015).

[109] A technical opinion by the "Studies Group in Environmental Thematics" (Grupo de Estudos em Temáticas Ambientais, GESTA) was added to the case file on 18 September 2013. The opinion mentions that this activist research group had been studying and supporting the affected families of the Minas-Rio project in Conceição do Mato Dentro since 2011.

springs; company compliance with conditionalities) can be debated. Their mobilization around the environmental licensing process and beyond, nonetheless, is an affirmation of their right to participation and a loud complaint against its violation. It helped keeping track of how the documents and technical studies the community and their allies had produced have been ignored, and providing support to strategic litigation (and other resistance actions) in cooperation with other groups resisting mining in Brazil and internationally.[110] While the functional view of participation ends up diminishing the democratic potential of new forms of governance, resistance movements are defending, through their sustained and well-informed opposition, the intrinsic value of participation and, thereby, strengthening the young—and still fragile—Brazilian democracy.

4 The Emptying of Rights to Information and Participation in Brazil: A Brief Reflection on the Challenges and Potential Benefits of Action Research

4.1 Action Research

The narrative presented so far results from a troubled research process, which reflects well the difficulties of doing research in conflict scenarios. At the outset of my research, I had a loose idea that I wanted to investigate legal enforcement and rights violations in the mining sector. I also knew that I intended to contribute to knowledge production that could help, primarily, the most vulnerable groups in this kind of conflict. It was clear to me, therefore, that I should follow an action research approach.

Holding the view that politics permeates knowledge production, and that theory must be combined with practice, action researchers aim at understanding how social structures produce inequalities, marginalization and oppression in order to promote or stimulate change. "The aim of participatory action research is to change practices, social structures, and social media which maintain irrationality, injustice, and unsatisfying forms of existence".[111] Thus, action researchers are committed to the normative ideal that science (and, thus, universities and their research agendas) should strive to improve the life of marginalized groups and individuals, instead of being indifferent to existing structures of oppression. While writing my research proposal and doing fieldwork, I was especially influenced by the ideas of the Brazilian popular educator and philosopher Paulo Freire.

---

[110] A first initiative had requested a thematic hearing (about rights violations in the mining sector) at the Inter-American Commission on Human Rights (IACHR) in 2016. See Oliveira A, Comissão Interamericana denuncia Brasil à OEA por tragédia em Mariana. El País, 07 June 2016, https://brasil.elpais.com/brasil/2016/06/07/politica/1465319140_029773.html (last accessed 1 October 2018).

[111] McTaggart as cited in Reason and Bradbury (2001), p. 1.

Paulo Freire became well known for his theoretical and practical work in teaching literacy. He criticized prevailing models of formal education, based on tedious repetition of books' contents that had little to do with students' lives, and advanced a new methodology. His methodology embedded learning to read and to write in the life contexts of those who joined what he called cultural circles. In these circles, and the following is a simplified account, people learn to write and read while telling their own stories and discussing them with the other members of the circle, which stimulates reflection about the world in which they live, how they interpret it, and how they position themselves in it. Paulo Freire conceived of education as a practice of liberty and strove in his practice as educator to promote his ideal of an emancipatory, critical and humanist education. His work has become very influential across countries and disciplines, making him a key thinker for participatory action research from the 1970s onwards.[112] Furthermore, his conception of knowledge and education has been very influential in adult education, research and extension projects in Brazil, including in the projects in which I have worked.[113]

Freire sees education as a collective learning process where action and reflection (theorization), understood as inseparable (praxis), prompt the development of the critical consciousness of all involved actors (teachers and students). In this process, each one contributes with his or her unique experiences in less hierarchical relations. In a similar vein, researchers and researched subjects in action research should act, reflect and produce knowledge together. In this process, all participants would have the chance to develop a more critical, active and questioning attitude towards the structural inequalities of their respective life worlds.

One methodological consequence of Freire's ideas for action research concerns the question how the researcher should deal with the persons with whom she engages in her research process. In action research, these persons are not seen as *study objects*, but as subjects, collaborators and co-authors in a knowledge-production process that attempts to mitigate—if not deny—sharp distinctions between subject and object, reflection and action, encouraging all participants at all

---

[112] See, among others, Torres (1992), Reason and Bradbury (2001), p. 3; Baum et al. (2006), p. 854; Kindon et al. (2007), p. 10; Reason and Bradbury (2008), p. 1.

[113] Influenced by decades of social mobilization and by the critiques of Paulo Freire, *extensão*, which literally translates as *extension*, acquired a different meaning in Brazilian public universities. It refers to the insertion of universities (including their practices and research agendas) within communities, as well as opening the university (and the knowledge it builds through research and through teaching and learning) to these communities. Ideally, extension projects go much beyond science outreach. They bring the university closer to the communities and the communities closer to the university, in a process that enables both to generate new knowledge, relying on traditional knowledge as well as on scientific knowledge, and aiming to overcome the theory-practice divide. *Extension* embodies an ethical commitment of universes with the communities with whom they work and develop projects, acknowledging their cultural diversity, advocating social justice and pursuing emancipation. Indeed, according to the Brazilian Constitution of 1988, Article 207, the universities must observe the principle of inseparability between teaching, research and extension. For more on the concept of extension in Brazil, see De Paula (2013), p. 18.

stages to constantly think about their practice and act upon their world based on the knowledge they develop.[114]

Thus, it becomes important to create conditions in which research subjects are acknowledged as agents, capable to think and speak for themselves and tell their own story. It is important to be open to their perspectives and to allow for them to reflect and criticize our own position as researchers; what we researchers define as research problems; and our data collection strategies. Last but not least, we need to be open to discuss and potentially re-evaluate all steps of our research and their possible implications. Otherwise we could unwittingly contribute to reproduce or reinforce existent forms of discrimination and oppression. Qualitative research methods—such as semi-structured interviews, participant observation and group discussions—are suitable for action research, as they allow participants to express their views and opinions of the issue under analysis on their own terms, without forcing them to think and formulate within the categories previously selected by the researcher.

4.2 Choosing the Case

As I was generally interested in the right to participation (which voices are taken into account, how and why) during legal enforcement, three main criteria oriented the selection of the case I would study through an in-depth qualitative analysis. The first related to content: as my interest was in participation and mobilization, I was looking for a case that encompassed these elements. Mining with the strong contestation it provokes appeared as a suitable field. Moreover, the contested mining project should have already been the subject of at least one legal decision with respect to environmental licensing, as otherwise I would not have enough material for the document analysis. The second criterion was time: I looked for a case that had started from 2005 onwards, in order to be able to interview persons who had witnessed the case, besides having access to documents, in order to work with and compare these two sources of information. Preferably, also direct observation should be possible (joining public deliberative sessions, public hearings, self-organized community meetings and protest actions would allow me to develop my own perceptions of the case). The third criterion was my access to the data needed. As I already had access to networks in Minas Gerais (also the main so-called mining state in Brazil, together with Pará), doing the research in Minas Gerais would facilitate my access to data. In Pará, overcoming issues of mistrust would be harder and, furthermore, the risks would be considerably greater, as Pará stands out as the Brazilian state with the highest number of murders of human rights defendants.[115]

---

[114] See among others, Freire (2002) and Torres (1992).

[115] Brum, E, Massacre anunciado na Anapu de Dorothy Stang. El País, 30 July 2018, https://brasil. elpais.com/brasil/2018/07/30/opinion/1532957463_995238.html (last accessed on 9 August 2018).

4.3 Redefining the Research Object Together with Participants

During the first 3 months of my research I spent considerable time getting to know people who had been directly involved in this conflict and discussing my research with them. I mainly got in touch with environmentalists, community leaders and other researchers who had worked (or were still working) in Conceição do Mato Dentro. Thinking about participation and strategies to influence decision-making, I was quite intrigued about how such a small group[116] had managed to delay the Minas-Rio project so much, achieving acknowledgement by the authorities that further families were affected by the project and producing rich studies and materials about the case. However, my interest in participation and in the resistance groups' strategies to influence decision-making raised suspicion among some community leaders and environmentalists—given prior episodes of cooptation and betrayal. How could a study of their strategies be in any way helpful to them? Due to this suspicion community leaders never shared their plans related to protest actions or other oppositional strategies with me before taking action.

Nonetheless, seeing me as a potential collaborator, they more than once highlighted the importance of following more closely the environmental licensing process and understanding it better. Some were quite convinced that everything could be explained with corruption, but most of them believed that an analysis of the documents and legal argumentation within the environmental licensing process had the potential to add to the knowledge they needed in order to support their claims of rights violations. I hold this knowledge not only to be beneficial to my research participants, but more generally, to foster critical reflection and improve the practices of environmental licensing. Thus, in dialogue with research participants, I decided to adapt my research questions and to follow the environmental licensing process more closely in order to investigate if and how the rights of affected families and environmental protection had been sidelined along legal enforcement.

There exists no uniform body of practices and methods orienting action research, as it is mostly driven by specific real-life problems and methods always are context-dependent. Collaboration with research participants in less hierarchical relations is a central feature of the approach—ideally, all along the research process. The intensity of this collaboration varies from case to case and how much collaboration is required for research to be considered action research is a disputed question. Some argue that research can only be considered action research when it is devised in collaboration with the people it is meant to benefit.[117] Other authors consider themselves to be action researchers[118] even when employing traditional positivist research

---

[116] From CMD's nearly 20,000 inhabitants, the resistance was most of the time organized around less than ten persons, who were decisive in sharing information on the project, on actions of the local municipal authorities and about the environmental licensing and in sparking mobilization.

[117] Hale (2006), p. 98, for example, explicitly claims that the difference of activist research to other approaches must be seen in the methods all along the research process.

[118] Or activist researchers; it is not an objective of this chapter to differentiate these approaches.

methods, provided that their research findings have the potential to benefit marginalized groups.[119]

The participants who shared in the process of refining my own research questions were mainly environmentalists, affected families engaged in opposition to the project, community leaders, and local authorities from CMD. Yet, also in informal conversations and semi-structured interviews with other research subjects (who had less influence on my research design), I strived to keep an open attitude to my interlocutors and to their criticism towards my research, as they were the experts on the history of the conflict and how it had unfolded. I also had the chance to discuss with all of them the relevant data to be collected and how to collect it (e.g. which archives to visit; snow-ball sampling of interviewees).

4.4 Worldview, Positionality and Subjectivity

Throughout my research I reflected on questions of objectivity and how subjectivity (my own beliefs, predispositions, biases) defined my research approach, design and results. John Creswell, a well-known professor of educational psychology and author of several books on methods and research design, invites scholars in general to reflect on their own worldviews and on how these worldviews influence their research practices. He defines worldview as "[...] a basic set of beliefs that guide action", "a general philosophical orientation about the world and the nature of research that a researcher brings to a study".[120] This approach calls for more transparency and awareness of our own philosophical assumptions and how they influence—whether we admit it or not—our attitudes and choices regarding research design and methods.

Our positionality and worldview[121] inform the questions we choose to investigate, the methods we use to address them, what information we consider "data" and what we discard as irrelevant during the research process. Many further *pre-scientific* factors condition our work as researchers, including ontological and epistemological assumptions.

Instead of denying this basic condition that pervades research, we can embrace it, make it explicit and problematize it. In other words, we can try to incorporate reflexivity in each step of our research and be transparent about our positionality and how it shapes our theoretical and methodological choices. Such an attitude,

---

[119] Cancian (1993), p. 100.

[120] Creswell (2014), p. 6.

[121] Although the terms worldview and positionality are closely related, they are not synonymous. A person's positionality encompasses relevant aspects of her identity, such as age, gender, socioeconomic status, educational background, colour of the skin, ethnical identification, etc. All of those also play a role in how this person will be able to conduct her field research, especially when it involves t relating to other persons, as is the case when we do interviews (even close-ended surveys), and participant observation.

common In the action research tradition, is reflected in the frequent use of the first person and clear positioning in the choice of research questions.[122]

The decision of which topic to address in which way is not only a methodological, but also a political one. Following Paulo Freire's knowledge conception, if knowing the world implies positioning ourselves in it, knowledge construction itself has an inherent political dimension that makes neutrality impossible. Admitting that knowledge cannot be neutral does not mean, however, that anything counts as valid knowledge, nor giving up on objectivity. In Paulo Freire's philosophy, our subjectivity is a condition of our understanding of the world, and it does not preclude the existence of an objective reality.[123] Although our perceptions of the world are inevitably subjective, we are still talking about a collectively and historically constructed social reality that is objective. Our perceptions can confront each other as well as enrich each other in a dialogic knowledge construction process from which we all learn. Thus, our subjectivity enables the production of objective knowledge of reality through inter-subjectivity.

4.5 Double Accountability and Pitfalls of Action Research

For an action researcher, the need to produce scientifically sound knowledge that can be assessed by peers and strengthen her academic position does not preclude the commitment to collaborate with the proposed beneficiaries of the research. Collaboration does not mean abdicating rigor along the research process. To the contrary, it can increase the workload and it enlarges the public to whom we are accountable. In my experience, this double accountability—to peers and research participants—has enhanced my diligence and made me think about different standards of knowledge relevance. I believe this contributes positively to the research outcome and to my development as a researcher.

Taking the voice of research participants seriously—not only as passive objects, but also as subjects actively contributing to the research process—matters, thus, to validate the research findings not only in academia, but also outside of it.[124] As explained by Charles R. Hale—an anthropologist who has researched indigenous resistance in Latin America and written about activist research methods:

> Activist anthropologists attempt to be loyal both to the space of critical scholarly production and to the principles and practices of people who struggle outside the academic setting. These dual political commitments transform our research methods directly: from the formulation of the research topic to the dissemination of results they require collaboration,

---

[122] Despite an academic rhetoric prone to hide the researcher (the author) in an attempt to mark—also in the language—the impersonality and distance considered essential in the scientific realm (a rhetoric that is also characteristic of jurisprudence and legal practice, we could add), real persons are behind all scientific research and reflexivity is important whether we do action research or not.

[123] Freire (2002), p. 37.

[124] Gordon et al. (2003), p. 370.

dialogue, and standards of accountability that conventional methods can, and regularly do, leave out of question.[125]

The idea of double accountability is shared by a number of researchers that attempt to adopt an action research approach.[126] Accountability to research participants presupposes a different take on knowledge production, disrupting—or at least putting into question—the authority of so-called *experts* and valuing local knowledge. One strategy entails organizing small workshops with our research participants in order to discuss our research at each step of the process. This implies typically logistic challenges (how to bring a group together; where; how may the setting of the meeting influence the discussion; etc.) and it is time-consuming, both for the researcher and the participants. I intend to go back to CMD and organize a workshop to discuss my research and results with those who participated in elaborating the research questions and reflecting upon data collection methods. However, I believe it would have been much better to do it during a second field visit, after completing data analysis and before submitting my dissertation. By doing it afterwards, I am prioritizing academic accountability.

Attention to coherence (and incoherencies), rigour in analysing different sources of information, and the duty to provide evidence for our claims are not exclusive to science—as jurists and those who participated in my research are well aware. Quite often, however, scientific standards require endorsing theoretical frames and categories that are not necessarily shared by research participants. Of course research participants involved in a conflict theorize and reflect about their practice, sometimes more critically than researchers do. Yet, research participants, more focused on direct action, do not always see the immediate relevance of the researcher's analytical frames and categories. Researchers may not always be successful in translating theoretical categories in ways that people can appropriate (or see some sense in appropriating). I believe, at least for now, this to be the case with my theoretical framework concerning proceduralization. For me it was pertinent to understand the case while participants do not see it as directly useful for their struggles.

In a recent academic event dedicated to the role of law in conflicts involving extractive industries and land grabbing I had the chance to present my analytical framework. In the coffee break, an environmentalist approached me to share his disappointment with my presentation. In his view, I had dedicated too little time to the exposition of the factual situation on the ground in this specific case. Although I acknowledge his point and how important it is to make visible to broader audiences the problems that people on the ground are facing, a pure description of arbitrary decisions and of the human suffering they generate would not have met the demands of an academic event, nor of research—a point with which my interlocutor agreed.

The production of useful materials to support participants in their immediate struggles might require extra-work (e.g. assisting participants in the production of reports and legal opinions, or co-writing booklets, helping to organize workshops to

---

[125] Hale (2006), p. 104.
[126] Cancian (1993), p. 93; cfr. Russell (2015).

discuss the research results in a more practice-oriented manner, etc.), or some translation of the theorization of the case into more practical language. Due to my study, I have been invited by the human rights organization Coletivo Margarida Alves (that provides legal counselling and assistance to affected families and community leaders in CMD) to help with a document describing the Minas-Rio project. This was presented at the Inter-American Commission on Human Rights.[127] Yet, this kind of work is not usually taken into account in academic evaluations.

Anyone engaging in action research must have a clear idea both of the features that characterize and distinguish this kind of research from more conventional approaches, as well as about how difficult action research can be in practice, particularly in the more restricted timeframes of post-graduate programmes. Getting truly involved and building rapport within a community can take considerable time, especially in conflict contexts where trust, solidarity and collaboration have been weakened, in many cases by co-optation of local leaders and other key actors.

My experiences while in the field and afterwards made me realize the value of relational and horizontal research. It gave me access to information that I might not have accessed if I had not shown a more open attitude to the participants of my research and to their criticism. More importantly, open debate with research participants at the initial stages not only helped me to gain rapport and access to data, it also allowed me to reframe my research questions in ways that might have more practical relevance to them.

I believe it is not always easy to reconcile academic and societal objectives of a research project—maybe mostly because of predominant models of research evaluation. The issue has been recently touched upon in a comment published in Nature under the title "A better measurement of research from the global south".[128] That the discussion of what is taken as relevant in academia has now reached high impact journals might be seen as a sign of improvement, a movement towards inserting the university within its social context, as demanded by the principle of inseparability of teaching, research and extension. However, it is still too early to be optimistic given how universities are predominantly run today (globally, and also in Brazil) favouring research with a high "impact factor" (sometimes absolutely disconnected from social problems) to the detriment of teaching and extension.

Acknowledgements The research on which this chapter is based would not have been possible without intense and enriching dialogue with many persons in Conceição do Mato Dentro, Diamantina and Belo Horizonte, Minas Gerais, Brazil, who shared their time, their knowledge and

---

[127] The final document reporting many cases of rights violations in the mining sector in Brazil was written by a network of human rights organizations from different parts of the country. My contribution via Coletivo Margarida Alves was exclusively related to the Minas-Rio case. The full document was presented to the IACHR in June 2016 (on file with the author). The video record of the hearing is available at: https://www.youtube.com/watch?v=1RAfL10Jfmk#action=share (last accessed 1 October 2018). See Oliveira A, Comissão Interamericana denuncia Brasil à OEA por tragédia em Mariana. El País, 07 June 2016, https://brasil.elpais.com/brasil/2016/06/07/politica/1465319140_029773.html (last accessed 1 October 2018).

[128] Lebel and McLean (2018).

much of their daily lives with me from June 2014 to June 2015. I also thank ZEF and the DAAD for the resources and support provided to my doctoral studies and to my field research in Brazil. I thank my colleagues from the Doctoral Program of the University of Barcelona Law School and Doctor Antonio Giménez Merino for the invaluable discussions and learning opportunities that helped me to advance data analysis and writing my dissertation and for the support during the elaboration of this chapter.

References

Baum F, MacDougall C, Smith D (2006) Participatory action research. J Epidemiol Community Health 60:854–857

Becker LC (2009) Tradição e modernidade: O desafio da sustentabilidade do desenvolvimento na Estrada Real. Instituto Universitário de Pesquisas do Rio de Janeiro

Becker LC, Pereira DC (2011) O projeto Minas-Rio e o desafio do desenvolvimento territorial integrado e sustentado: a grande mina de Conceição do Mato Dentro. In: Fernandes Fernandes FRC, Rodrigues da Silva Enríquez MA, De Carvalho Jimenez Alamino R (eds) Recursos minerais e sustentabilidade territorial: grandes minas. CETEM/MCTI, Rio de Janeiro, pp 229–258

Bermann C (2014) A desconstrução do licenciamento ambiental e a invizibilização social nos projetos de usinas hidrelétricas. In: Zouri A, Valencio N (eds) Formas de matar, de morrer e de resistir: limites da resolução negociada de conflitos ambientais. Belo Horizonte, Editora UFMG, pp 95–109

Black J (2000) Proceduralizing regulation: Part I. Oxf J Legal Stud 20:597–614

Black J (2008) Constructing and contesting legitimacy and accountability in polycentric regulatory regimes. Regul Gov 2:137–164

Cancian FM (1993) Conflicts between activist research and academic success: participatory research and alternative strategies. Am Sociol 24:92–106

Carvalhosa NM (2016) Fora daqui não sei andar: movimentos de roça, transformações sociais e resistência da honra em comunidades rurais de Minas Gerais. Universidade Federal do Rio de Janeiro, Rio de Janeiro

Castoriadis C (1998) El acenso de la insignificancia. Ediciones Cátedra, Madrid

Costa JR (1975) Conceição do Mato Dentro: fonte da saudade. Livraria Itatiaia Editora, Belo Horizonte

Creswell JW (2014) Research design: qualitative, quantitative, and mixed methods approaches, 4th edn. SAGE Publications, Thousand Oaks

Dagnino E (2004) Construção democrática, neoliberalismo e participação: os dilemas da confluência perverse. Revista Política e Sociedade 3(5):139–164

De Oliveira Vieira LP (2015) O Projeto Minas-Rio e a mineração em Conceição do Mato Dentro/MG: Uma análise a partir dos discursos, dos conflitos e da resistência. Universidade Federal de Minas Gerais, Belo Horizonte

De Paula JA (2013) A extensão universitária: história, conceito e propostas. Interfaces – Revista de Extensão da UFMG 1:53–23

Diversus (2011) Diagnóstico socioeconômico da área diretamente afetada e da área de influência direta do empreendimento Anglo Ferrous Minas-Rio Mineração S.A. (Ex-MMX Minas-Rio Mineração S.A.) - Lavra a Céu Aberto com Tratamento a úmido de minério de ferro - Conceição do Mato Dentro, Alvorada de Minas e Dom Joaquim/MG - DNPM N°: 830.359/2004 -PA/N° 00472/2007/004/2009- Classe 06. Belo Horizonte

Diversus (2012) Adendo ao diagnóstico socioeconômico da área diretamente afetada (ADA) e área de influência direta (AID) da Mina da Anglo Ferrous Minas-Rio Mineração S/A – Conceição do Mato Dentro, Alvorada de Minas e Dom Joaquim. Belo Horizonte

Diversus (2014a) Estudo de definição sobre as comunidades/famílias a serem reassentadas: área diretamente afetada (ADA) e área de entorno da cava licenciada e estruturas correlatas – Municípios de Conceição do Mato Dentro, Alvorada de Minas e Dom Joaquim. Belo Horizonte

Diversus (2014b) Avaliação socioambiental dos processos de negociação fundiária e reestruturação produtiva das famílias atingidas – Empreendimento Anglo Ferrous Minas-Rio S.A. – Municípios de Conceição do Mato Dentro, Alvorada de Minas e Dom Joaquim. Belo Horizonte

Estévez Araújo JA (2006) El revés del derecho: transformaciones jurídicas en la globalización neoliberal. Universidad Externado de Colombia, Bogotá, Colombia

Faria JE (2009) Few certainties and many doubts: law after financial crisis. Revista Direito GV 5:003–024

Faria JE (2011) O Estado e o direito depois da crise. Saraiva, São Paulo

Ferreira IL (2016) Mineração e conservação ambiental em Conceição do Mato Dentro: desafios de uma (des)ordenação territorial. Universidade Federal de Minas Gerais, Belo Horizonte

Ferreira LSS (2015) "O QUE A GENTE QUER É JUSTIÇA": Conflito, mobilização e a luta por justiça dos atingidos pela mineração nas reuniões da Rede de Acompanhamento Socioambiental (REASA), em Conceição do Mato Dentro/MG. Universidade Federal de Minas Gerais, Belo Horizonte

Fonseca A (2015) A avaliação de impacto ambiental e o seu vínculo com o licenciamento ambiental. In: Ribeiro JCO (ed) Licenciamento Ambiental: herói, vilão ou vítima?. Arraes Editores, Belo Horizonte, pp 27–41

Freire P (2002) Pedagogia do oprimido. 32nd edn. Paz e Terra, Rio de Janeiro

Gordon ET, Gurdián GC, Hale CR (2003) Rights, resources, and the social memory of struggle: reflections on a study of indigenous and black community land rights on Nicaragua's Atlantic coast. Hum Org 62:369–381

Habermas J (1996) Between facts and norms: contributions to a discourse theory of law and democracy. MIT Press, Cambridge

Hale CR (2006) Activist research v. Cultural critique: Indigenous land rights and the contradictions of politically engaged anthropology. Cult Anthropol 21:96–120

Kindon S, Pain R, Kesby M (2007) Participatory action research: origins, approaches and methods. In: Kindon S, Pain R, Kesby M (eds) Participatory action research approaches and methods: connecting people, participation and place. Routledge, London, pp 9–18

Ladeur KH (2004) Globalization and public governance - a contradiction?. In: Ladeur KH (ed) Public governance in the age of globalization. Ashgate, Burlington, pp 1–22

Lebel J, McLean R (2018) A better measure of research from the global south. Nature 559:23–26

Mercado Pacheco P (2012) Experimentalismo democrático, nuevas formas de regulación y legitimación del derecho. Anales de la Cátedra Francisco Suárez 46:37–68

Mercado Pacheco P (2013) Derechos insostenibles. In: Estévez Araújo, JA El libro de los deberes: las debilidades e insuficiencias de la estrategia de los derechos. Trotta, Madrid, pp 139–166

Milaré E (2011) Direito do ambiente: a gestão ambiental em foco: doutrina, jurisprudência, glossário, 7a. ed. rev., atualizada e reformulada. Editora Revista dos Tribunais, São Paulo, SP, Brasil

Porte C, Nanz P (2004) The OMC – a deliberative-democratic mode of governance? The cases of employment and pensions. J Eur Public Policy 11(2):267–288

Prates CG (2014) Mineração em Conceição do Mato Dentro: uma análise da REASA como instância de "resolução" de conflito. Universidade Federal de Minas Gerais, Belo Horizonte

Prates CG (2017) Efeitos derrame da mineração, violências cotidianas e resistências em Conceição do Mato Dentro-MG. Universidade Federal de Minas Gerais, Montes Claros

Reason P, Bradbury H (2001) Handbook of action research: participative inquiry and practice. Sage Publications, London

Reason P, Bradbury H (2008) The Sage handbook of action research: participative inquiry and practice, 2nd edn. Sage Publications, London

Russell B (2015) Beyond activism/academia: militant research and the radical climate and climate justice movement(s): beyond activism/academia. Area 47:222–229

Sampaio RS (2011) Direito Ambiental: doutrina e casos práticos. Elsevier-FGV, Rio de Janeiro

Sassen S (2004) De-Nationalized State Agendas and privatized norm-making. In: Ladeur KH (ed) Public governance in the age of globalization. Ashgate, Burlington, pp 51–67

Simon WH (2010) New governance anxieties: a Deweyan response - symposium: new governance and the transformation of law - Wisconsin Law Review Symposium Afterword: Part II. Wis Law Rev 2010(2):727–736

Teubner G (2004) Global private regimes: neo-spontaneous law and dual constitution of autonomous sectors?. In: Ladeur KH (ed) Public governance in the age of globalization. Ashgate, Burlington, pp 71–87

Torres CA (1992) Participatory action research and popular education in Latin America. Int J Qual Stud Educ 5:51–62

Tôrres MA (2014) Histórias de água e minério: os efeitos do Projeto Minas-Rio em Água Quente, Conceição do Mato Dentro. Universidade Federal de Minas Gerais, Belo Horizonte

Wilkinson MA (2012) Dewey's 'Democracy without politics': on the failures of liberalism and the frustrations of experimentalism. LSE Legal Studies Working Paper n. 6/2012. Available at: https://doi.org/10.2139/ssrn.2150100. Last accessed 10 August 2017

Zhouri A (2014) Maping environmental inequalities in Brazil: mining, environmental conflicts and impasses of mediation. desiguALdades.net Working Paper Series 75

Zhouri A, Laschefski C, Pereira D (2005) Introdução: desenvolvimento, sustentabilidade e conflitos ambientais. In: Zhouri A, Laschefski C, Pereira D (org) A insustentável leveza da política ambiental. Autêntica, Belo Horizonte

Aline Rose Barbosa Pereira graduated in law from the Federal University of Minas Gerais (2009) and holds a LLM in Legal Philosophy (2012). She has worked as lawyer from 2009 to 2013, and as a researcher in the action research project "Cidade e Alteridade: convivência cultural e justiça urbana" from 2011 to 2013. Since 2014 she is external collaborator of the human rights defendants' network "Coletivo Margarida Alves", based in Belo Horizonte, Brazil. She is currently doing her doctoral research at the Center for Development Research (ZEF), University of Bonn, Germany, on legal practices in mining-related conflicts.

Building the Case for a Home-State Grievance Mechanism: Law Reform Strategies in the Canadian Resource Justice Movement

Charis Kamphuis

Contents

1 Introduction: Context, Issues and Debates 456
2 Establishing the Nature of the Problem with Empirical Research (1999–2017) 459
   2.1 Canadian Global Dominance in Resource Extraction and Canadian
        State Support 459
   2.2 Problematizing the Impacts of Canadian Resource Companies Abroad 462
   2.3 Problematizing the Canadian State's Support for Companies 468
3 Canada's Corporate Social Responsibility Policy Response (2009–2017) 471
   3.1 CSR Policy and CSR Counsellor: 2009–2014 472
   3.2 CSR Policy and CSR Counsellor: 2014–2017 474
   3.3 Canada's National Contact Point 477
4 Empirical, Normative and Political Critiques of Canada's CSR Policy 479
   4.1 Critiques of Canada's National Contact Point 480
   4.2 Critiques of Canada's 2014 CSR Policy and Counsellor 482
5 Building Strong Consensus with International Human Rights Bodies (2002–2017) 485
6 Creating and Advocating for Concrete Law Reform Proposals (2009–2016) 488
   6.1 Draft Legislation: The *Business & Human Rights Act* (2016) 489
   6.2 Administrative Body, Regulatory Objectives and Jurisdiction 490
   6.3 Standards 493
   6.4 Investigatory Powers and Recommendations 495
   6.5 Potential Sanctions 500
   6.6 Analysis of the Draft *Business & Human Rights Act* 501
7 The Canadian Ombudsperson for Responsible Enterprise (January 2018) 502
8 Conclusion and Future Research 504
References 508

C. Kamphuis (✉)
Thompson Rivers University, Kamloops, BC, Canada
e-mail: ckamphuis@tru.ca

© Springer Nature Switzerland AG 2019
I. Feichtner et al. (eds.), *Human Rights in the Extractive Industries*,
Interdisciplinary Studies in Human Rights 3,
https://doi.org/10.1007/978-3-030-11382-7_16

1   Introduction: Context, Issues and Debates

On May 26, 2017, a group of Canadian activists belonging to the Toronto-based Mining Injustice Solidarity Network occupied the office of Liberal Member of Parliament Michael Levitt, chairperson of the Subcommittee on International Human Rights, a committee of the Canadian federal Parliament.[1] Their stated goal was to protest "Canadian mining abuses abroad" as well as the federal government's inaction in response to draft legislation proposed in 2016 by the Canadian Network for Corporate Accountability (CNCA).[2] The proposal, called *The Global Leadership in Business and Human Rights Act: An act to create an independent human rights ombudsperson for the international extractive sector*,[3] contemplates an International Extractive Industry Ombudsperson with the power to investigate complaints against Canadian companies and make recommendations to the Canadian government, the company and/or the complainant, including with respect to remedies. The proposed legislation also contained some limited incentive and enforcement tools.

The civil disobedience referred to represents one position in a long history of debate in Canada on the issues raised by the protestors. This debate began to take shape in Canada in the late 1990s, and consistently revolved around two interrelated issues. The first point of controversy arose from competing views of the nature of the problem to be addressed. Advocates raised serious allegations about the conduct of Canadian resource extraction companies abroad and the human rights impacts of their operations. They alleged that Canadian companies are routinely causing or contributing to a long list of harms in developing countries with impunity.[4] In contrast, some industry supporters asserted that alleged or documented abuses signal the behavior of only "a few bad apples" who are the anomaly, and not indicative of a prevalent or systemic problem.[5] Others said that Canadian companies are

---

[1] Saunders S, Activists occupy Liberal MP Michael Levitt's office to protest Canadian mining abuses. Now Magazine, 31 May 2015, https://nowtoronto.com/news/mining-abuse_1/ (last accessed 1 October 2018).

[2] Formed in 2005, the Canadian Network for Corporate Accountability (CNCA) brings together 30 environmental, human rights, religious, labor and solidarity groups from across Canada. The CNCA's mission is to ensure that Canadian mining, oil and gas companies respect human rights and the environment when working abroad. To do this, it advocates for policy and law reform in Canada: Canadian Network for Corporate Accountability, What we do, http://cnca-rcrce.ca/about-us/what-we-do/ (last accessed 1 October 2018); Canadian Network for Corporate Accountability, How we work, http://cnca-rcrce.ca/about-us/how-we-work/ (last accessed 1 October 2018).

[3] Canadian Network on Corporate Accountability, The Global Leadership in Business and Human Rights Act: An Act to Create an Independent Human Rights Ombudsperson for the International Extractive Sector, Draft Model Legislation. 2 November 2016, http://cnca-rcrce.ca/wp-content/uploads/2016/03/The-Global-Leadership-in-Business-and-Human-Rights-Act-An-act-to-create-an-independent-human-rights-ombudsperson-for-the-international-extractive-sector-11022016.pdf (last accessed 1 October 2018).

[4] Section 2 will review the main sources and content of these allegations.

[5] Freeman S, The case for – and against – an ombudsperson to resolve mining disputes. Financial Post, 7 March 2017, http://business.financialpost.com/business/the-case-for-and-against-an-ombudsperson-to-resolve-mining-disputes (last accessed 1 October 2018). See for example the

improving, and learning from past mistakes.[6] Some individuals in industry and government also took the view that "anti-mining" groups invent or exaggerate their claims and manipulate local communities.[7]

The second point of debate in Canada has centered on the nature of the appropriate government response to the problem, however defined. Between 2005 and 2016, Canadians were presented with a litany of law and policy initiatives and proposals in response to this issue. This included a parliamentary committee report in 2005, a series of national roundtables in 2006 and a multi-stakeholder expert report in 2007. In response, the federal government unveiled two voluntary Corporate Social Responsibility (CSR) policies on point, first in 2009, followed by a modified version in 2014. Civil society's dissatisfaction with these government responses was reflected in four different legislation proposals from opposition Members of Parliament and/or civil society groups between 2008 and 2016. Finally, international institutions weighed in. Between 2002 and 2017, Canada's policy position and refusal to develop a legal framework was the subject of as many as twelve statements from international human rights bodies and three dedicated hearings before the Inter-American Commission on Human Rights.

While these discussions on the nature of the problem and the nature of the appropriate Canadian government response have been wide-ranging, Canadian civil society organizations have significantly focused their efforts on advocating for the creation of an effective state-based non-judicial grievance mechanism. This chapter's objective is to record the advocacy strategies that these organizations, in collaboration with affected communities around the world, used to pursue law and policy reform in Canada with a special focus on non-judicial grievance mechanisms. This chapter picks up the story of this debate where previous writing on these issues left off, while at the same time filling in some empirical gaps.[8]

This story, as told here, is structured in accordance with the advocacy strategies it depicts. Section 2 surveys how advocates attempted to document and report on the nature of the problem from the perspective of affected communities. Section 2 also shows how advocates moved beyond case studies to develop empirically informed general descriptions of the harms associated with Canadian resource extraction abroad. It also tracks how advocates endeavoured to document and problematize

---

terms of the debate on the following recent TV Ontario (TVO) interviews: Paikin S, Toronto: Mining Capital of the World. TVO, 31 May 2017, https://www.youtube.com/watch?v=6NDn1LqKA3A (last accessed 10 December 2017); Paikin S, Canadian Mining Accountability Abroad. TVO, 31 May 2017, https://www.youtube.com/watch?v=Oem4r7zLTEY (last accessed 1 October 2018).

[6] Las mineras canadienses gestionan mejor los conflictos que otras de propiedad extranjera. Revista ENERGIMINAS, 14 August 2017, http://www.energiminas.com/las-mineras-canadienses-gestionan-mejor-los-conflictos-que-otras-de-propiedad-extranjera/ (last accessed 1 October 2018).

[7] This assumption informed Canada's 2009 CSR Policy which allowed companies to complain to the CSR Counsellor about communities to NGOs: Kamphuis (2012). It was also present in industry rhetoric in key debates over law reform: Seck (2011), p. 73. Most recently, this position appeared in a report issued by the Canadian CSR Counsellor, see Sect. 3.2.

[8] Seck (2011, 2012), Simons (2015), Kamphuis (2012) and Coumans (2012).

related forms of Canadian government support for the sector. Section 3 examines how the Canadian government responded to these problematizations with the development of a voluntary CSR policy for the Canadian extractive industry abroad. This part summarizes the CSR policy status quo in Canada between 2009 and 2017 with a focus on the relevant portions of the 2014 CSR framework. This sets the context for Sect. 4, which profiles a second set of advocacy strategies, namely the development of informed critiques of Canada's CSR policy and associated non-judicial grievance mechanisms. These critiques were primarily rooted in experience, accumulated as advocates tested these mechanisms' efficacy by supporting affected communities to file complaints. To a lesser extent, but no less important, some critics invoked international standards for non-judicial grievance mechanisms as a metric for critiquing Canadian CSR policy.

In tandem with the strategies of research-based descriptions of the nature of the problem (Sect. 2) and experience-based critiques of the government's CSR policy response (Sect. 4), advocates further took up a third strategy. This involved presenting this body of research and experience to international human rights bodies at every possible opportunity. Section 5 catalogues the resulting statements of numerous international bodies and summarizes their main themes. Finally, Sect. 6 describes a fourth and final strategy, the development of concrete proposals for law reform to create a more effective home-state grievance mechanism. Advocates pressured the Canadian government to consider their proposals, either in the parliamentary process or through direct political pressure and lobby efforts. This section introduces the history of the law and policy proposals put forward in Canada between 2005 and 2014 before undertaking an in-depth review of the groundbreaking 2016 CNCA Ombudsperson proposal.

This study of law reform advocacy in Canada on the issue of home-state non-judicial grievance mechanisms will be of interest to activists and academics participating in wider global conversation on transnational corporate accountability for harms caused in developing countries. Attention to home-state law and policy responses in this context became a permanent feature of mainstream international legal debate following the UN Human Rights Council's endorsement of the *Guiding Principles on Business and Human Rights* in 2011.[9] While there is no clear consensus over the nature of home-state responsibility in international law or the most appropriate responses, there is common ground that global society is facing a serious problem of corporate impunity, due in part to the "governance gap".[10] This

---

[9] UN Office of the High Commissioner of Human Rights, Guiding Principles on Business and Human Rights: Implementing the United Nations "Protect, Respect and Remedy" Framework. UN Doc HR/PUB/11/04, 2011. The Guiding Principles were endorsed by the Human Rights Council in 2011: UN Human Rights Council, Human rights and transnational corporations and other business enterprises, UN Doc A/HRC/RES/17/4, 6 July 2011, para 1.

[10] G Gagnon, A Macklin and P Simons cited in Simons and Macklin (2014). Also see ETOS for human rights beyond borders, Maastricht principles on extraterritorial obligations of states in the area of economic, social and cultural rights. 2013, http://www.etoconsortium.org/en/main-navigation/library/maastricht-principles/ (last accessed 1 October 2018), p. 3; UN Human Rights Council, Elaboration of an international legally binding instrument on transnational corporations and other

refers to law's global and systemic failure to prevent, ensure accountability, and provide remedy for corporate human rights abuses in the developing countries that host their operations.[11] There is also common ground that home states like Canada must play an important role in addressing this issue by preventing human rights violations and ensuring access to effective remedies. It is also widely agreed that home-state non-judicial grievance mechanisms form an important part of these efforts.

The Canadian experience is highly pertinent to these international conversations for at least three reasons: first, due to the size of the Canadian resource extraction industry internationally; second, given the unparalleled intensity of the Canadian debate on home-state non-judicial grievance mechanisms over nearly two decades; and third, given advocates' unprecedented success in early 2018 when the Canadian government announced a ground-breaking decision to create the Canadian Ombudsperson for Responsible Enterprise, a new and more robust state-based non-judicial grievance mechanism.

This chapter is fundamentally an account of civil society strategies to address questions of global economic injustice by pursuing law and policy reform in a developed capital-exporting country. In conclusion, I will analyze these strategies, their achievements and limitations, and identify future areas of research. This chapter may also be of interest to those concerned generally with global economic injustice. It will be of particular value to those interested in tracking the ways in which states like Canada actively shape economic relationships in the global economy, as well as the ways in which social justice advocates might problematize these relations and imagine legal responses.

2   Establishing the Nature of the Problem with Empirical Research (1999–2017)

2.1   Canadian Global Dominance in Resource Extraction and Canadian State Support

For at least two decades, Canadian companies have been among the most significant players globally in resource extraction, especially in mining.[12] The majority of large and junior mining companies are incorporated in Canada and Canadian stock

---

business enterprises with respect to human rights, UN Doc A/HRC/26/L.22/Rev, 25 June 2014, para 1.

[11] Simons and Macklin (2014).

[12] For 2005 statistics, see Advisory Group Report, National Roundtables on Corporate Social Responsibility (CSR) and the Canadian Extractive Industry in Developing Countries. 1 May 2007, http://www.pdac.ca/docs/default-source/priorities/public-affairs/csr-national-roundtables-background.pdf?sfvrsn=720e9e50_12 (last accessed 1 October 2018), pp. 3–4. For 2008 statistics, see Global Affairs Canada, Building the Canadian Advantage: A Corporate Social Responsibility

exchanges list more mining companies than any other exchange in the world.[13] In 2013, over 50% of the world's publically listed exploration and mining companies were headquartered in Canada, numbering approximately 1500, with junior companies accounting for 90% of the total count.[14] That same year, the foreign presence of Canadian mining companies extended to 107 countries worldwide and Canadian companies accounted for nearly 31% of global expenditures on exploration.[15] In 2015, Canadian stock exchanges accounted for more than half of the equity capital raised globally for mining.[16] Generally, the largest regional destination for Canadian mining investments is Latin America, with Africa in second place.[17] In 2013, nearly half of the total value of Canada's overseas mineral assets was in Latin America[18] and 41% of the largest companies in Latin America were Canadian.[19]

Without a detailed historical study, it is difficult to determine exactly why the Canadian mining industry has gained such significant size and global dominance. What is clear though is that the Canadian state supports the industry in a variety of ways. Some authors have observed that the Canadian government has historically

(CSR) Strategy for the Canadian International Extractive Sector. March 2009, http://www.international.gc.ca/trade-agreements-accords-commerciaux/topics-domaines/other-autre/csr-strat-rse-2009.aspx?lang=eng (last accessed 1 October 2018). In 2008, 75% of the world's exploration and mining companies were headquartered in Canada with an interest in over 100 countries around the world.

[13] Kamphuis (2012), p. 1457. Also see UN Office of the High Commissioner of Human Rights, Statement at the end of visit to Canada by the United Nations Working Group on Business and Human Rights, 1 June 2017, http://www.ohchr.org/EN/NewsEvents/Pages/DisplayNews.aspx?NewsID=21680&LangID=E (last accessed 1 October 2018).

[14] Global Affairs Canada, Canada's Enhanced Corporate Social Responsibility Strategy to Strengthen Canada's Extractive Sector Abroad – Doing Business the Canadian Way: A Strategy to Advance Corporate Social Responsibility in Canada's Extractive Sector Abroad. 2014, http://www.international.gc.ca/trade-agreements-accords-commerciaux/assets/pdfs/Enhanced_CS_Strategy_ENG.pdf (last accessed 1 October 2018); Natural Resources Canada, Canadian Mining Assets: Information Bulletin. December 2014, https://www.nrcan.gc.ca/mining-materials/publications/17072 (last accessed 1 October 2018).

[15] Natural Resources Canada, Canadian Mining Assets: Information Bulletin. December 2014. https://www.nrcan.gc.ca/mining-materials/publications/17072 (last accessed 1 October 2018).

[16] Marshall B, Facts and Figures of the Canadian Mining Industry: F&F 2016. Mining Association of Canada, 2016 http://mining.ca/sites/default/files/documents/Facts-and-Figures-2016.pdf (last accessed 1 October 2018), p. 36.

[17] Global Affairs Canada, Building the Canadian Advantage: A Corporate Social Responsibility (CSR) Strategy for the Canadian International Extractive Sector. March 2009, http://www.international.gc.ca/trade-agreements-accords-commerciaux/topics-domaines/other-autre/csr-strat-rse-2009.aspx?lang=eng (last accessed 1 October 2018).

[18] Marshall B, Facts and Figures of the Canadian Mining Industry: F&F 2016. Mining Association of Canada, 2016 http://mining.ca/sites/default/files/documents/Facts-and-Figures-2016.pdf (last accessed 1 October 2018), p. 81.

[19] Canadian Network for Corporate Accountability & Justice & Corporate Accountability Project, Human Rights, Indigenous Rights and Canada's Extraterritorial Obligations. Inter-American Commission on Human Rights, Thematic Hearing for 153rd Period of Sessions. 28 October 2014, http://cnca-rcrce.ca/wp-content/uploads/2016/05/canada_mining_cidh_oct_28_2014_final.pdf (last accessed 1 October 2018), p. 6.

welcomed and promoted mining, both at home and abroad.[20] Others note that a favourable tax regime is one major explanation for the concentration of the global mining sector in Canada,[21] along with a securities industry designed to promote mining.[22] A cluster of mining-related equipment and service providers with wide-ranging expertise has grown up around the Canadian mining industry.[23] The Canadian government also provides direct financial support to the industry with favourable loans from Export Development Canada (EDC) and through the provision of development assistance to promote corporate social responsibility at specific mining projects.[24]

Beyond favourable loans, tax arrangements, and stock markets, the Canadian government also provides robust legal protection and political support for the sector. In these latter areas, state support for global mining significantly ramped up during the Conservative government's time in power, between 2006 and 2015. In this time period Canada dramatically expanded its Foreign Investment Promotion and Protection Agreements (FIPPAs)[25] and by 2016 Canada had signed 33 FIPPAs in Latin America and 12 in Africa. Political support for Canadian mining companies abroad was also formalized and strengthened. In 2007, the federal government announced the Global Commerce Strategy, followed in 2013 by the Global Markets

---

[20] See generally: Hughes et al. (2016) and Barton (1993).

[21] Deneault (2015); Natural Resources Canada, Canada's Positive Investment Climate for Mineral Capital: Information Bulletin. November 2014, https://www.nrcan.gc.ca/mining-materials/publications/8782 (last accessed 1 October 2018); Wach T, Jim Flaherty's corporate tax overhaul made Canada competitive. The Globe and Mail, 20 March 2014, https://beta.theglobeandmail.com/report-on-business/economy/economy-lab/jim-flahertys-corporate-tax-overhaul-made-canada-competitive/article17590384/?ref=http://www.theglobeandmail.com& (last accessed 1 October 2018).

[22] Canadian Network for Corporate Accountability & Justice & Corporate Accountability Project, Human Rights, Indigenous Rights and Canada's Extraterritorial Obligations. Inter-American Commission on Human Rights, Thematic Hearing for 153rd Period of Sessions. 28 October 2014, http://cnca-rcrce.ca/wp-content/uploads/2016/05/canada_mining_cidh_oct_28_2014_final.pdf (last accessed 1 October 2018), p. 6.

[23] Natural Resources Canada, Canadian Mining Assets: Information Bulletin. December 2014, https://www.nrcan.gc.ca/mining-materials/publications/17072 (last accessed 1 October 2018).

[24] Canadian Network for Corporate Accountability & Justice & Corporate Accountability Project, Human Rights, Indigenous Rights and Canada's Extraterritorial Obligations. Inter-American Commission on Human Rights, Thematic Hearing for 153rd Period of Sessions. 28 October 2014, http://cnca-rcrce.ca/wp-content/uploads/2016/05/canada_mining_cidh_oct_28_2014_final.pdf (last accessed 1 October 2018), p. 8; Keenan K and Hamilton K Export Credit Agencies and Human Rights: Failure to Protect. Halifax Initiative, Both Ends, CounterCurrent, Forum Suape and Rios Vivos. 2015, http://77.104.146.242/~aboveground/wp-content/uploads/2015/06/Failure-to-Protect.pdf (last accessed 1 October 2018); Brown (2012).

[25] Mertins-Kirkwood H and A Losing Proposition: The Failure of Canadian ISDS Policy at Home and Abroad. Canadian Centre for Policy Alternatives, August 2015, https://www.policyalternatives.ca/sites/default/files/uploads/publications/National%20Office/2015/08/Losing_Proposition.pdf (last accessed 1 October 2018); Marshall B, Facts and Figures of the Canadian Mining Industry: F&F 2016. Mining Association of Canada, 2016 http://mining.ca/sites/default/files/documents/Facts-and-Figures-2016.pdf (last accessed 1 October 2018), p. 81.

Action Plan. These policies involve "economic diplomacy", promising that "all Government of Canada diplomatic assets are harnessed to support the pursuit of commercial success by Canadian companies and investors."[26] This includes the Canadian Trade Commissioner Service, which offers companies "privileged access to foreign governments, key business leaders and decision-makers."[27] The policy claims that "other countries are doing the same, and Canada…must be more aggressive and effective than…the competition."[28] The policy of economic diplomacy remains in place to date.[29]

2.2 Problematizing the Impacts of Canadian Resource Companies Abroad

This section chronicles the various ways in which government, industry and civil society actors have studied the conduct of Canadian resource companies abroad empirically. Initially, the Canadian government worked with industry, civil society and academia to lead or enable three major studies of the issue. The first was an in-depth case study of Talisman Energy Inc., undertaken in 1999 by the Canadian Assessment Mission to Sudan, also known as the Harkat Mission. The Canadian government convened this independent fact-finding initiative in response to international pressure and allegations that Talisman was benefiting from grave human rights abuses in relation to its operations in Sudan. The Harkat Mission concluded that oil extraction and development was fuelling Sudan's civil war. It also found that the Sudanese government was using oil company infrastructure to bomb civilian populations in combination with violent ground operations, including forced displacement, rape, murder and kidnapping, in order to clear a swath of land around oil operations to ensure their security in the midst of the war.[30]

---

[26] Global Affairs Canada, Global Markets Action Plan: The Blueprint for Creating Jobs and Opportunities for Canadians through Trade. 2013, http://international.gc.ca/global-markets-marches-mondiaux/plan.aspx?lang=eng#1b (last accessed 1 October 2018).

[27] Canadian Trade Commissioner Service, What we can do for you. 2017, http://tradecommissioner.gc.ca/how-tcs-can-help-comment-sdc-peut-aider.aspx?lang=eng (last accessed 1 October 2018).

[28] Global Affairs Canada, Global Markets Action Plan: The Blueprint for Creating Jobs and Opportunities for Canadians through Trade. 2013, http://international.gc.ca/global-markets-marches-mondiaux/plan.aspx?lang=eng#1b (last accessed 1 October 2018).

[29] Interestingly, in 2016 the federal government announced a new policy elaborating on Canadian embassies' commitment to supporting human rights defenders in the countries where they are located. However, this new policy did not modify or change economic diplomacy: Canada, Voices at risk: Canada's guidelines on supporting human rights defenders. 2016, http://international.gc.ca/world-monde/issues_development-enjeux_developpement/human_rights-droits_homme/rights_defenders_guide_defenseurs_droits.aspx?lang=eng (last accessed 1 October 2018).

[30] Simons and Macklin (2014), pp. 1–3, 22–78.

After the Harkat Mission, the Parliamentary Sub-committee on Human Rights and International Development held several rounds of hearings on the activities of Canadian resource companies in developing countries. It heard evidence from an array of expert witnesses, industry representatives, Canadian civil society leaders, and leaders from affected communities. The sub-committee's 2005 final report was adopted by the Standing Committee on Foreign Affairs and International Trade (SCFAIT) and submitted to the Canadian Parliament. The report found that:

> mining activities in some developing countries have had adverse effects on local communities, especially where regulations governing the mining sector and its impact on the economic and social wellbeing of employees and local residents, as well as on the environment, are weak or non-existent, or where they are not enforced.[31]

In response to the SCFAIT report, in 2006 the Canadian government formed an Advisory Group of experts representing industry, NGOs and academia with a mandate to convene the Canadian National Roundtables on Corporate Social Responsibility and the Extractive Industry in Developing Countries. In their 2007 consensus report, the Advisory Group summarized the concerns at issue in terms of: environmental concerns, community relations, human rights, security and armed conflict, labour relations, indigenous peoples' rights, compatibility of resource development with national and local economic priorities, benefit sharing with local communities, ineffective legal systems and the potential for corruption.[32]

Following the Harkat, SCFAIT and Advisory Group reports, the Canadian government refrained from further research-based study of these issues for about 10 years. In this vacuum, many academics and civil society groups continued to study the problem empirically, albeit without support or endorsement from the Canadian government. Initially, advocates focused primarily on researching and publishing case studies that documented connections between specific Canadian mining companies and human rights violations in affected communities around the world.[33]

Advocates' grassroots research into specific company misconduct enabled a handful of affected communities to bring civil claims against Canadian companies to Canadian courts. However, between 1998 and 2011 a number of attempts to

---

[31] House of Commons Standing Committee on Foreign Affairs and International Trade, Mining in Developing Countries: Corporate Social Responsibility. 38th Parl, 1st Sess, 14th Rep. 2005, http://www.ourcommons.ca/DocumentViewer/en/38-1/FAAE/report-14 (last accessed 1 October 2018).

[32] Advisory Group Report, National Roundtables on Corporate Social Responsibility (CSR) and the Canadian Extractive Industry in Developing Countries. 1 May 2007, http://www.pdac.ca/docs/default-source/priorities/public-affairs/csr-national-roundtables-background.pdf?sfvrsn=720e9e50_12 (last accessed 1 October 2018), pp. 4–5.

[33] For some examples see: Imai, Mehranvar and Sander (2007); Rights and Democracy, Human Rights Impact Assessment of Foreign Investment Projects: Learning from Community Experiences in the Philippines, Tibet, the Democratic Republic of Congo, Argentina, and Peru. 2007, http://publications.gc.ca/collections/collection_2007/dd-rd/E84-21-2007E.pdf (last accessed 1 October 2018); Halifax Initiative, Canadian Mining Map. Blog, 21 February 2007 https://miningwatch.ca/blog/2007/2/21/halifax-initiative-publishes-canadian-mining-map (last accessed 1 October 2018); McGee (2009); Walter and Martinez-Alier (2010).

access Canadian courts failed to overcome procedural objections from the company defendant at a preliminary stage.[34] Nonetheless, advocates persisted and between 2013 and 2016 they succeeded in convincing Canadian courts to try claims against three different Canadian mining companies.[35] In 2013, an Ontario provincial court ruled that a group of plaintiffs have an arguable case against Hudbay Minerals Inc and sent the parties to trial. These suits claim damages from serious bodily harm, gang rape and death perpetrated by security forces at Hudbay's Fenix nickel mine in Guatemala.[36]

In 2016 a British Columbia (BC) provincial court sent another suit to trial, finding that BC is the most appropriate forum to hear claims against Nevsun Resources in relation to its Bisha mine in Eritrea.[37] In this case, the plaintiffs claim that they endured forced labour conditions at the mine, in violation of Canadian and international law. Finally, in 2017 the BC Court of Appeal found that that BC is the most appropriate jurisdiction to hear claims against Tahoe Resources in relation to its El Escobal mine in Guatemala.[38] The plaintiffs claim of serious bodily harm, caused when Tahoe security guards shot at them during a peaceful protest, will now be heard on the merits.[39]

The alleged facts in these cases certainly garnered public attention, as did their success in overcoming significant jurisdictional and procedural obstacles. However, it quickly became clear to advocates that case studies and litigation alone had limited power to influence broad policy or law reform responses. Individual studies could not reveal the severity or extent of the problem at the industry, regional or global level, and were too easily written off as examples of just "a few bad apples".

---

[34] Québec Superior Court, 2011 QCCS 1966, *Association canadienne contre l'impunité (ACCI) c Anvil Mining Ltd*, reversed Québec Court of Appeal, [2012] JQ no 368, leave to appeal to Supreme Court of Canada refused, 34733, 1 November 2012; US Court of Appeals for the Second Circuit, Case No. 07-0016-cv, *Presbyterian Church of Sudan v Talisman Energy*, 2 October 2009; Québec Supreme Court, 1998 QJ no 2554 (QL), *Recherches Internationales Québec v Cambior Inc*; Court of Appeal for Ontario, 2011 ONCA 191, 332 DLR (4th) 118, *Piedra v Copper Mesa Mining Corp*, affirming Superior Court of Justice Ontario, 2010, 2421.

[35] See: Above Ground, Transnational Lawsuits in Canada Against Extractive Companies: Developments in Civil Litigation, 1997–2016. October 2016, http://www.aboveground.ngo/wp-content/uploads/2016/02/Cases_Oct2016_LO.pdf (last accessed 1 October 2018); Bennett N, Wave of Foreign Lawsuits against Local Miners hits Canadian Courts: Human Rights Groups are Backing Several Claims against Firms Operating in Guatemala, Eritrea. Business in Vancouver, 19 April 2016, https://www.biv.com/article/2016/4/wave-foreign-lawsuits-against-local-miners-hits-ca/ (last accessed 1 October 2018).

[36] Superior Court of Justice Ontario, 2011 ONSC 1414, [2011] OJ No 3417 (QL) (Ont SCJ), *Choc v Hudbay Minerals Inc*.

[37] Court of Appeal for British Columbia, 2017 BCCA 401, *Araya v Nevsun Resources Ltd*, affirming 2016 BCSC 1856.

[38] Court of Appeal of British Columbia, 2017 BCCA 39, *Garcia v Tahoe Resources Inc*, reversing Supreme Court of British Columbia, 2015 BCSC 2045, *Garcia v Tahoe Resources Inc*.

[39] Tahoe on Trial, Security Footage Outside Escobal Mine. Video, 27 April 2013, https://tahoeon-trial.net/2015/11/19/security-footage-april-27-2013/ (last accessed 1 October 2018).

Following the high-water mark of the Advisory Group report, it also became clear to advocates that the Canadian government and industry were no longer interested in collaborating with civil society to undertake larger scale studies or to create a transparent system for proactively monitoring conflicts and allegations against Canadian mining companies. One infamous example of this is a 2009 report, secretly commissioned by the Prospectors and Developers Association of Canada (PDAC) and leaked to civil society groups in 2010.[40] The PDAC report studied the rates of Canadian involvement in severe ethical, environmental, human rights and occupational incidents in developing countries.[41] It did so by surveying reports and complaints involving the activities of all mining and exploration companies operating in developing countries over the previous 10 years. On this basis, it identified 171 incidents of human rights violations.[42] Of these, Canadian companies represented 33% of total violations, four times the number attributed to any other country.[43] Importantly, PDAC commissioned this study in the midst of an intense debate in the Canadian Parliament over proposed legislation that aimed to create a home-state non-judicial grievance mechanism. Nonetheless, PDAC did not disclose the study's findings but rather lobbied vigorously against the proposed legislation.[44]

In this context, civil society and academic research groups began to work toward their own general, research-based description of the problem from the perspective of affected communities. Their first attempt was a 2013 report to the Inter-American Human Rights Commission (IAHRC), submitted by the Latin American Working Group on Mining and Human Rights. The Working Group, comprised of six prominent organizations, collected information from grassroots organizations across eleven Latin American countries.[45] It found commonalities across 22 case studies tracked over a period of 3 years. On this basis, the Working Group's final report summarized the human rights issues associated with Canadian companies in terms of: damage to the environment, including to water, livelihood and health; and lack of participation and consent, including inadequate consultation, imposition of

---

[40] Simons (2015), p. 3.

[41] Canadian Centre for the Study of Resource Conflicts, Corporate Social Responsibility: Movements and Footprints of Canadian Mining and Exploration Firms in the Developing World. October 2009, http://caid.ca/CSRRep2009.pdf (last accessed 1 October 2018), p. 4.

[42] Canadian Centre for the Study of Resource Conflicts, Corporate Social Responsibility: Movements and Footprints of Canadian Mining and Exploration Firms in the Developing World. October 2009. http://caid.ca/CSRRep2009.pdf (last accessed 1 October 2018), pp. 6–7. The report described violations under the categories of: occupational, unlawful, unethical, human rights, environmental and community conflict.

[43] Canadian Centre for the Study of Resource Conflicts, Corporate Social Responsibility: Movements and Footprints of Canadian Mining and Exploration Firms in the Developing World, October 2009, http://caid.ca/CSRRep2009.pdf (last accessed 1 October 2018), p. 7.

[44] Seck (2011) and Coumans (2012).

[45] The six organizations included were from Chile, Colombia, Honduras, Mexico, Peru and the United States: see ETO Consortium, For human rights beyond borders: How to hold States accountable for extraterritorial violations, Handbook. September 2017, http://www.etoconsortium. org/nc/en/main-navigation/library/documents/detail/?tx_drblob_pi1%5BdownloadUid%5D=204 (last accessed 1 October 2018), p. 42.

projects in spite of opposition, and irregularities in property acquisition.[46] The report also informed that local communities are not benefiting equitably and economically from mining projects.[47]

In addition to capturing social, environmental and economic impacts, the Latin American Working Group report described problems with civil liberties. In this regard, it reported that some Canadian mining projects had led to large-scale social conflicts and the criminalization of protest and dissent. A 2015 MiningWatch report picked up on this theme. It undertook detailed case studies of four Latin American countries and found a connection between Canadian mining interests and the growing trend of criminalization of dissent and social protest involving land and environmental defenders.[48]

This focus on civil liberties intensified with a 2016 report published by the Justice & Corporate Accountability Project (JCAP). This report remains the most comprehensive study undertaken to date on these issues. It systematically documents reported incidents of violence and criminalization associated with Canadian mining companies operating in Latin America over a 15-year period, from 2000 until 2015.[49] Using a recognized, rigorous and replicable research methodology, JCAP found that 44 people were killed, over 400 people were injured and over 700 people were criminalized in conflicts related to Canadian mining companies in Latin America in the period under study.[50] On the basis of this data, the report concluded that there is close *proximity* between Canadian mining companies abroad

---

[46] Working Group on Mining and Human Rights in Latin America, The impact of Canadian Mining in Latin America and Canada's Responsibility: Executive Summary of the Report submitted to the Inter-American Commission on Human Rights. 2013, http://www.dplf.org/sites/default/files/report_canadian_mining_executive_summary.pdf (last accessed 1 October 2018), pp. 10–19.

[47] Working Group on Mining and Human Rights in Latin America, The impact of Canadian Mining in Latin America and Canada's Responsibility: Executive Summary of the Report submitted to the Inter-American Commission on Human Rights. 2013, http://www.dplf.org/sites/default/files/report_canadian_mining_executive_summary.pdf (last accessed 1 October 2018), pp. 10–19.

[48] Notably, the MiningWatch study adopted a broader definition of criminalization than the JCAP Report. It defines criminalization as "the systematic manipulation of concepts of law and order – whether administrative, civil, or criminal – and the use of the punitive powers of the state and its organs of justice – whether initiated by state or non-state actors or some combination of the two – to forbid, dissuade and/or prosecute legitimate dissent that are portrayed by state/non-state actors as contrary to fundamental social values." See Moore J, In the National Interest?: Criminalization of Land and Environment Defenders in the Americas. MiningWatch Canada, August 2015, https://miningwatch.ca/sites/default/files/inthenationalinterest_fullpaper_eng_1.pdf (v), p. 14. The study's fifth case study is of Indigenous communities in Canada.

[49] Imai S, Gardner L and Weinberger S, The "Canada Brand": Violence and Canadian Mining Companies in Latin America. Osgoode Legal Studies Research Paper No. 17/2017, 17 December 2016, https://ssrn.com/abstract=2886584 (last accessed 1 October 2018), p. 8.

[50] Imai S, Gardner L and Weinberger S, The "Canada Brand": Violence and Canadian Mining Companies in Latin America. Osgoode Legal Studies Research Paper No. 17/2017, 17 December 2016, https://ssrn.com/abstract=2886584 (last accessed 1 October 2018), p. 4. The JCAP study defined criminalization as legal complaints or warrants again activists, arrests, detentions and charges. The study did not capture criminalizing discourse from public authorities or companies.

and violence.[51] Notably, the JCAP research did not include death threats, property destruction, displacement, attempted assassination without injury, environmental contamination or psychological trauma in its definition of violence.[52] In addition to the concept of proximity, the JCAP report also explored the concept of *complicity* in order to understand the relationship between companies and violence.[53]

In a similar vein, international organizations also began to compile data on violence against human rights defenders across sectors and on a global scale. In 2017, the Business & Human Rights Resource Centre published statistics from its database tracking human rights defenders, working on corporate accountability issues, who were attacked, harassed or killed in 2015 and 2016.[54] In this 2-year period, the Centre identified over 400 cases worldwide, with the largest concentration of cases in the mining sector (30%). Moreover, one-quarter of all cases were connected to companies headquartered in China, the United States or Canada. The fact that this global study tracked the nationality, not only of human rights defenders but also of companies, meant that its findings further corroborated research focused exclusively on Canada, like the reports from JCAP, the Latin America Working Group and MiningWatch.

The shift in the civil society research agenda, to move beyond case studies to aggregate data in order to describe the problem more generally, had a major impact on the debate in Canada. The JCAP report in particular appears to have had far-reaching effects. It received significant media attention in the Canadian press and was mentioned in international press, including in the *New York Times*. Its authors presented their findings to lawmakers in Canada and numerous human rights bodies internationally. Importantly, the shift to aggregate data also involved a narrow focus on civil rights and on violence in particular. Undoubtedly the quantitative clarity of statistics on violence was an effective strategy for attracting the attention of the public and policy makers. It was also methodologically rigorous and much simpler

---

[51] The report found a link between a Canadian mining project and violent conflict where at least two independent reports provide information or analysis that credibly establishes that the project's presence is likely to have made a substantial contribution to violence or criminalization, Imai S, Gardner L and Weinberger S, The "Canada Brand": Violence and Canadian Mining Companies in Latin America. Osgoode Legal Studies Research Paper No. 17/2017, 17 December 2016, https://ssrn.com/abstract=2886584 (last accessed 1 October 2018), p. 11.

[52] Imai S, Gardner L and Weinberger S, The "Canada Brand": Violence and Canadian Mining Companies in Latin America. Osgoode Legal Studies Research Paper No. 17/2017, 17 December 2016, https://ssrn.com/abstract=2886584 (last accessed 1 October 2018), p. 5.

[53] Imai S, Gardner L and Weinberger S, The "Canada Brand": Violence and Canadian Mining Companies in Latin America. Osgoode Legal Studies Research Paper No. 17/2017, 17 December 2016, https://ssrn.com/abstract=2886584 (last accessed 1 October 2018), p. 28. The report uses the concept of complicity to refer to an act, or failure to act, that enables violence to occur, exacerbates the occurrence of abuse, or facilitates abuses.

[54] Business & Human Rights Resource Centre, Business & Human Rights Defenders: Key Database Findings. February 2017 https://business-humanrights.org/en/key-findings-from-the-database-of-attacks-on-human-rights-defenders-feb-2017 (last accessed 1 October 2018). Global Witness also tracks annual incidences of violence against environmental defenders.[54] See: Global Witness (2016).

than producing large scale aggregate data on the full range of social, economic and environmental impacts of projects.

While the production of quantitative aggregate data was an invaluable strategy, detailed individual case studies also made a very important contribution. Case studies helped inform the framing of aggregate studies and captured critical details about the scope of the human rights concerns at issue. A small number of case studies also became the basis for civil suits in Canada, which helped demonstrate the cogency of the alleged facts. In combination, these strategies raised the public profile of the issues and strengthened the credibility of advocates' fundamental message: that the impacts of Canadian resource companies' operations abroad raise concerns that require a legal response from Canadian authorities.

2.3   Problematizing the Canadian State's Support for Companies

Canadian civil society has developed another important research strategy that, although garnering less attention to date than the research described above, is no less important. This refers to a stream of research that has documented and problematized Canadian state policies and practices that support Canadian mining operations abroad. In this regard, advocates' research has focused primarily on three main modalities of support: loans from Export Development Canada (EDC); equity held by the Canadian Pension Plan (CPP) in the form of investor shares, and political support from the Canadian foreign service, known as "economic diplomacy" (see description in Sect. 2.1). Both the CPP and EDC are publically owned Crown corporations that operate at arm's length from the federal government.

Early forms of research in the area of financial and political support began with case studies. In 2007 an organization called the Halifax Initiative published a collection of 23 short case studies that tracked the quantum of EDC and CPP financial support for each Canadian resource company and briefly summarized the problems allegedly associated with each companies' overseas operations.[55] In an early case that raised concerns about political support, a Canadian documentary filmmaker sued the former Canadian Ambassador to Guatemala for defamation. The filmmaker had taken live video footage of the violent forced displacement of a community of Indigenous Guatemalans in 2007 by the Guatemalan military, police, private security companies, and employees of a Canadian mining company. After the video was posted online, the Ambassador publicly accused the filmmaker of having fabricated the footage. In 2010, an Ontario judge found that the Ambassador had slandered the filmmaker by making false statements about his film.[56]

---

[55] Halifax Initiative, Canadian Mining Map, MiningWatch Canada Blog. 2007, https://mining-watch.ca/blog/2007/2/21/halifax-initiative-publishes-canadian-mining-map (last accessed 1 October 2018).

[56] Voices-Voix, Steven Schnoor, July 2013, http://voices-voix.ca/en/facts/profile/steven-schnoor (last accessed 1 October 2018).

Following this early work, advocates began to develop of a more comprehensive and detailed description of the full range of Canadian public supports for companies abroad. For example, the 2013 Latin American Working Group report to the IAHRC, referred to above, included numerous examples of the Canadian state's political, legal and economic supports for companies. In addition to CPP, EDC and diplomatic support, it described the impact of Canada's free trade agreements, development aid and interference in other countries' domestic policies.[57] A second report to the IAHRC, this time submitted by the CNCA and JCAP in 2014, repeated concerns with these policies and argued that Canada lacks effective accountability mechanisms to oversee company conduct *as well as* the provision of state support.[58]

Building on these general descriptions of policy, advocates began to develop detailed empirical accounts of the government's modalities of support for Canadian companies in specific cases. The first line of research in this area focused on the Canadian state's political support for companies abroad. In 2013 and 2015, a coalition of Canadian organizations published two substantial reports based entirely on documents obtained through federal access to information requests. The reports profiled two different case studies in Mexico, where Canadian embassy staff and Trade Commissioners had acted to defend Canadian mining companies in spite of strong opposition from affected communities and in the face of serious and credible allegations of human rights violations or risks of violations.[59] In both cases, violence occurred against community members and in one case, a high-profile community leader was assassinated. Also in 2015, MiningWatch published a report that built on these two studies to identify a wide range of specific *policies* and actions of the Canadian state and its representatives in four Latin American counties.[60] The

[57] Working Group on Mining and Human Rights in Latin America, The impact of Canadian Mining in Latin America and Canada's Responsibility: Executive Summary of the Report submitted to the Inter-American Commission on Human Rights. 2013, http://www.dplf.org/sites/default/files/report_canadian_mining_executive_summary.pdf (last accessed 1 October 2018), pp. 25–29.

[58] Canadian Network for Corporate Accountability & Justice & Corporate Accountability Project, Human Rights, Indigenous Rights and Canada's Extraterritorial Obligations. Inter-American Commission on Human Rights, Thematic Hearing for 153rd Period of Sessions. 28 October 2014, http://cnca-rcrce.ca/wp-content/uploads/2016/05/canada_mining_cidh_oct_28_2014_final.pdf (last accessed 1 October 2018), pp. 6–10, 17–18.

[59] Moore J and Colgrove G, Corruption, Murder and Canadian Mining in Mexico: The Case of Blackfire Exploration and the Canadian Embassy. MiningWatch Canada, United Steelworkers and Common Frontiers. May 2013, https://miningwatch.ca/sites/default/files/blackfire_embassy_report-web.pdf (last accessed 1 October 2018). Moore J (2015) Unearthing Canadian Complicity: Excellon Resources, the Canadian Embassy, and the Violation of Land and Labour Rights in Durango, Mexico. MiningWatch Canada & United Steelworkers, https://miningwatch.ca/sites/default/files/excellon_report_2015-02-23.pdf (last accessed 1 October 2018).

[60] See: Moore J, In the National Interest?: Criminalization of Land and Environment Defenders in the Americas. MiningWatch Canada, February 2015, https://miningwatch.ca/sites/default/files/inthenationalinterest_fullpaper_eng_1.pdf (last accessed 1 October 2018), p. 14. Also see: MiningWatch Canada, Backgrounder: A Dozen Examples of Canadian Mining Diplomacy. MiningWatch Canada Blog, 8 October 2013, https://miningwatch.ca/blog/2013/10/8/backgrounder-dozen-examples-canadian-mining-diplomacy#sthash.poxyIirH.dpbs (last accessed 1 October 2018).

report argued that these actions and policies had exacerbated specific conflicts with Canadian companies, escalating the risk of harm for affected communities and human rights defenders. Much of the research presented in these reports appeared in a 2016 book published by two Canadian political scientists who tracked many different forms of Canadian political intervention and influence in a number of Latin American countries to the benefit of Canadian resource companies.[61]

In addition to studying the Canadian state's political support for companies, advocates continued to raise the issue of public financial support through the CPP and EDC. The primary strategy in this regard was to publish credible research on the human rights record of companies receiving such support. A 2016 report by a coalition of organizations profiled five complaints against Canadian resource companies brought to Canada's National Contact Point (to be discussed in Sects. 3 and 4). Among its many findings, the study tracked the quantum of EDC loans and CPP equity holdings in each company. It found that in three of five cases, companies facing serious allegations of human rights abuse and environmental harm continued to receive substantial financial support from these government agencies.[62]

These findings were further supported by an extremely detailed 2017 case study of serious human rights allegations against a Canadian company with operations in Brazil. The study found that despite credible, well known and ongoing allegations, EDC issued five loans to the company between 2012 and 2017 totally $850 million in financing, the CPP maintained an equity interest in the company worth 460 million, and the Canadian embassy continued to offer the company diplomatic support.[63] On the basis of these studies, advocates have called for reforms to ensure due diligence, transparency and accountability in the decision making of government agencies when it comes to the provision of political and financial support for companies abroad. Advocates have also called on the CPP to divest and EDC to deny loans to companies facing serious and credible allegations of human rights violations.[64]

The previous pages have referred to numerous studies published between 1999 and 2017 by the Canadian government, civil society and academics documenting a wide range of human rights and environmental concerns directed at Canadian mining companies' overseas operations. Government support for these efforts was relatively short-lived and consisted of funding three studies and the resulting reports,

---

[61] Gordon and Webber (2016).

[62] Above Ground, MiningWatch Canada and OECD Watch, "Canada is Back" but Still Far Behind – An Assessment of Canada's National Contact Point for the OECD Guidelines for Multinational Enterprises, https://miningwatch.ca/sites/default/files/canada-is-back-report-web_0.pdf (last accessed 1 October 2018), p. 20.

[63] Above Ground and JusticiaGlobal, Swept Aside: An Investigation into Human Rights Abuse at Kinross Gold-s Morro Do Ouro Mine. March 2017, http://aboveground.ngo/wp-content/uploads/2017/12/Swept-Aside-Kinross-Morro-do-Ouro-report.pdf (last accessed 1 October 2018).

[64] MiningWatch Canada, Almost a Quarter-Million People Worldwide Join Call for Nevsun Resources Investors to Divest over Abuses at Eritrea Mine, News Release. 3 May 2017, https://miningwatch.ca/news/2017/5/3/240000-people-worldwide-join-call-nevsun-resources-investors-divest-over-abuses (last accessed 1 October 2018).

published between 1999 and 2007 (the Harkat Report, 1999, the SCFAIT Report, 2005, and the Advisory Group Report, 2007). Following this period, advocates continued this research, combining detailed case studies with regional, global or industry level studies. Beginning in 2013, some advocates intensified their efforts to document the breadth of the Canadian state's economic, legal, political and policy support for the sector. These efforts consisted of general descriptions of state policy in these areas, as well as a handful of detailed case studies of conflicts between Canadian companies and local communities. In terms of the later, this research strategy also tracked the quantum of the Canadian state's financial support and/or specific practices of diplomatic support in the context of specific conflicts.

3   Canada's Corporate Social Responsibility Policy Response (2009–2017)

In response to the research described in Sect. 2, between 2009 and 2017 the Canadian government developed a Corporate Social Responsibility (CSR) policy framework consisting of three main elements: (1) a CSR policy document; (2) the office of the CSR Counsellor; and (3) the Canadian National Contact Point (NCP). The CSR policy and Counsellor's office were first introduced in 2009 and updated in 2014. The Canadian NCP, first established in 2000 pursuant to Canada's membership in the Organization of Economic Cooperation and Development (OECD), became a central component of Canada's 2014 CSR policy.[65] In this period, the NCP and the CSR Counsellor each oversaw a state-based non-judicial grievance mechanism available for mediating conflicts arising between Canadian companies and those affected by their operations abroad.

This section begins by establishing the main features and outcomes of the 2009 CSR policy before moving on to describe the 2014 updated policy and NCP mechanism in terms of their regulatory components: objectives, standards, procedures and potential incentives and disincentives. This summary of Canadian's CSR policy in the period in question is important, not only because it constituted the status quo policy response for nearly 9 years to the problematizations described in the previous section, but also because it formed the basis of a further suite of law reform advocacy strategies, analysed in Sects. 4 and 5 of this chapter.

---

[65] Global Affairs Canada, Canada's National Contact Point (NCP) for the Organisation for Economic Co-operation and Development (OECD) Guidelines for Multinational Enterprises (MNEs). 2016, http://www.international.gc.ca/trade-agreements-accords-commerciaux/ncp-pcn/index.aspx?lang=eng&menu_id=1&menu=R (last accessed 1 October 2018).

3.1   CSR Policy and CSR Counsellor: 2009–2014

In 2009 the Canadian government launched *Building the Canadian Advantage: A Corporate Social Responsibility (CSR) Strategy for the Canadian International Extractive Sector.*[66] Its objective was to "improve the competitive advantage of Canadian international extractive sector companies by enhancing their ability to manage social and environmental risks."[67] To this end, the policy encouraged companies to sign on to voluntary CSR Principles[68] and included the statement that the government "expects and encourages Canadian companies operating abroad to respect all applicable laws and internationally-agreed principles of responsible business conduct."[69] Any reference to human rights was notably absent from the policy's text.

The CSR strategy also involved the creation of an Office of the Extractive Sector CSR Counsellor with a mandate to review the CSR practices of Canadian extractive companies operating abroad and to advise them on the implementation of CSR guidelines.[70] This Office included a voluntary dispute resolution mechanism whereby an individual, group or community who "reasonably believes that it is being or may be adversely affected by the activities of a Canadian extractive sector company in its operations outside Canada" could ask the CSR Counsellor to initiate a review.[71] Surprisingly, the 2009 policy also allowed companies to file a complaint against individuals or civil society groups.[72] Notably, the Counsellor could only undertake reviews with the consent of all parties involved and reviews consisted of informal or formal mediation.

---

[66] Global Affairs Canada, CSR Counsellor, About Us. 2017, http://www.international.gc.ca/csr_counsellor-conseiller_rse/About-us-A-propos-du-bureau.aspx?lang=eng (last accessed 1 October 2018).

[67] Global Affairs Canada, Building the Canadian Advantage: A Corporate Social Responsibility (CSR) Strategy for the Canadian International Extractive Sector. March 2009, http://www.international.gc.ca/trade-agreements-accords-commerciaux/topics-domaines/other-autre/csr-strat-rse-2009.aspx?lang=eng (last accessed 1 October 2018).

[68] The International Finance Corporation's Performance Standards on Social & Environmental Sustainability, the Voluntary Principles on Security & Human Rights, the Global Reporting Initiative and the OECD Guidelines for Multinational Enterprises.

[69] Global Affairs Canada, Building the Canadian Advantage: A Corporate Social Responsibility (CSR) Strategy for the Canadian International Extractive Sector. March 2009, http://www.international.gc.ca/trade-agreements-accords-commerciaux/topics-domaines/other-autre/csr-strat-rse-2009.aspx?lang=eng (last accessed 1 October 2018).

[70] Global Affairs Canada, Office of the Extractive Sector Corporate Social Responsibility (CSR) Counsellor. 2017, http://www.international.gc.ca/csr_counsellor-conseiller_rse/index.aspx?lang=eng (last accessed 1 October 2018).

[71] Global Affairs Canada, Building the Canadian Advantage: A Corporate Social Responsibility (CSR) Strategy for the Canadian International Extractive Sector. March 2009, http://www.international.gc.ca/trade-agreements-accords-commerciaux/topics-domaines/other-autre/csr-strat-rse-2009.aspx?lang=eng (last accessed 1 October 2018).

[72] For more details on this strange provision see: Kamphuis (2012).

The first CSR Counsellor served from October 2009 to October 2013.[73] During this time advocates and affected communities brought six cases or "requests for review" to the Counsellor's office. These cases involved allegations of labour rights violations, serious environmental damage, and lack of consultation with affected communities. In three cases the process ended because the company refused to participate.[74] In a fourth case, the requesters asked to keep their identities confidential and ultimately neither the company nor the requesters responded to the Counsellor's mediation efforts.[75] In another case the affected community members declined to participate in the review process.[76] In a final case, after informal mediation the company agreed to raise awareness of its site level grievance process and adopt best practices for dispute resolution.[77] However, there is no indication that the CSR Counsellor oversaw the implementation of this agreement or followed up on the resolution of the community's original complaints. In sum, in only one of six cases did the parties participate in a mediation process leading to an agreement and there is no evidence in any case that the conflicts improved or that the issues were resolved. The first CSR Counsellor resigned at the end of 2013 before completing her term.[78]

[73] Global Affairs Canada, CSR Counsellor, About Us. 2017, http://www.international.gc.ca/csr_counsellor-conseiller_rse/About-us-A-propos-du-bureau.aspx?lang=eng (last accessed 1 October 2018).

[74] Global Affairs Canada, Closing Report – Request for review file #2011-01-MEX. October 2011, http://www.international.gc.ca/csr_counsellor-conseiller_rse/publications/2011-01-MEX_closing_rep-rap_final.aspx?lang=eng (last accessed 1 October 2018); Global Affairs Canada, Closing Report – Request for Review File Number 2012-03-ARG. October 2012, http://www.international.gc.ca/csr_counsellor-conseiller_rse/publications/2012-03-ARG_closing_report-rapport_final.aspx?lang=eng (last accessed 1 October 2018); Global Affairs Canada, Closing Report – Request for Review File Number 2013-05-ARG. September 2013, http://www.international.gc.ca/csr_counsellor-conseiller_rse/publications/2013-05-ARG_closing_report-rapport_final.aspx?lang=eng (last accessed 1 October 2018).

[75] Global Affairs Canada (2013) Closing Report – Request for Review File Number 2013-06-ARG. October 2013, http://www.international.gc.ca/csr_counsellor-conseiller_rse/publications/2013-06-ARG_closing_report-rapport_final.aspx?lang=eng (last accessed 1 October 2018).

[76] Global Affairs Canada (2017) Closing Report – Request for Review File Number 2013-04-MEX. May 2017, http://www.international.gc.ca/csr_counsellor-conseiller_rse/publications/2017-05-ARG_closing_report-rapport_final.aspx?lang=eng (last accessed 1 October 2018).

[77] Global Affairs Canada (2012) Closing Report – Request for Review File Number 2011-02-MAU, February 2012. http://www.international.gc.ca/csr_counsellor-conseiller_rse/publications/2011-02-MAU_closing_report-rapport_final.aspx?lang=eng (last accessed 1 October 2018).

[78] Global Affairs Canada, CSR Counsellor, About Us. 2017, http://www.international.gc.ca/csr_counsellor-conseiller_rse/About-us-A-propos-du-bureau.aspx?lang=eng (last accessed 1 October 2018).

3.2   CSR Policy and CSR Counsellor: 2014–2017

Advocates intensely criticized the 2009 CSR policy and its merger results, including at hearings before the IAHRC in 2013 and 2014. This criticism in combination with the refusal of some companies to participate in the 2009 dialogue mechanism likely informed the Canadian government's decision to launch a second CSR policy called *Doing Business the Canadian Way: A Strategy to Advance Corporate Social Responsibility in Canada's Extractive Sector Abroad*.[79] This new policy described Canadian companies as being on the "leading edge of CSR practice."[80] In terms of standards, it stated that Canada expects its companies operating abroad to "integrate CSR throughout their management structures so that they operate abroad in an economic, social and environmentally sustainable manner."[81] It also articulated the expectation that companies "respect human rights and all applicable laws, and… meet or exceed widely-recognized international standards for responsible business conduct."[82] Where local laws are not consistent with "Canadian values", the policy encouraged companies to rethink their investment.[83] Notably, while the policy promoted a number of international CSR policies as sources of guidance for companies, it did not define the standard of "Canadian values" and did not refer directly to international human rights law.[84]

---

[79] Global Affairs Canada, Canada's Enhanced Corporate Social Responsibility Strategy to Strengthen Canada's Extractive Sector Abroad – Doing Business the Canadian Way: A Strategy to Advance Corporate Social Responsibility in Canada's Extractive Sector Abroad. 2014, http://www.international.gc.ca/trade-agreements-accords-commerciaux/assets/pdfs/Enhanced_CS_Strategy_ENG.pdf (last accessed 1 October 2018).

[80] Global Affairs Canada, Canada's Enhanced Corporate Social Responsibility Strategy to Strengthen Canada's Extractive Sector Abroad – Doing Business the Canadian Way: A Strategy to Advance Corporate Social Responsibility in Canada's Extractive Sector Abroad. 2014, http://www.international.gc.ca/trade-agreements-accords-commerciaux/assets/pdfs/Enhanced_CS_Strategy_ENG.pdf (last accessed 1 October 2018), p. 6.

[81] Global Affairs Canada, Canada's Enhanced Corporate Social Responsibility Strategy to Strengthen Canada's Extractive Sector Abroad – Doing Business the Canadian Way: A Strategy to Advance Corporate Social Responsibility in Canada's Extractive Sector Abroad. 2014, http://www.international.gc.ca/trade-agreements-accords-commerciaux/assets/pdfs/Enhanced_CS_Strategy_ENG.pdf (last accessed 1 October 2018), p. 3.

[82] Global Affairs Canada, Canada's Enhanced Corporate Social Responsibility Strategy to Strengthen Canada's Extractive Sector Abroad – Doing Business the Canadian Way: A Strategy to Advance Corporate Social Responsibility in Canada's Extractive Sector Abroad. 2014, http://www.international.gc.ca/trade-agreements-accords-commerciaux/assets/pdfs/Enhanced_CS_Strategy_ENG.pdf (last accessed 1 October 2018), p. 3.

[83] Global Affairs Canada Canada's Enhanced Corporate Social Responsibility Strategy to Strengthen Canada's Extractive Sector Abroad – Doing Business the Canadian Way: A Strategy to Advance Corporate Social Responsibility in Canada's Extractive Sector Abroad. 2014, http://www.international.gc.ca/trade-agreements-accords-commerciaux/assets/pdfs/Enhanced_CS_Strategy_ENG.pdf (last accessed 1 October 2018), p. 3.

[84] Adding to the CSR standards incorporated into the 2009 policy Global Affairs Canada, Building the Canadian Advantage: A Corporate Social Responsibility (CSR) Strategy for the Canadian International Extractive Sector. March 2009, http://www.international.gc.ca/trade-agreements-

While the 2014 policy retained an economic rationale for responsible corporate conduct (also prominent in the 2009 policy), it added a moral dimension. It argued that CSR will lead to "win-win outcomes" by "creating value" for companies and generating benefits and development for communities.[85] In this policy, "doing business the Canadian way" involved being economically successful *and* reflecting "Canadian values". Like its 2009 predecessor, the 2014 policy referred to local concerns as "environmental and social risks" to the company.[86] It made the "business case" for CSR, advising companies that CSR is good for "traditional notions of profit" and that investors care about CSR "alignment". At the same time, the policy reminded companies that it is also "intrinsically valuable" to contribute to society.[87]

Within this framework, the CSR Counsellor's role was that of an expert educator and an informal complaint mediator. The Counsellor was to offer "advice and guidance for all stakeholders on implementing CSR performance guidelines" with special expertise in providing guidance on effective and meaningful dialogue with affected communities.[88] The Counsellor could also "review the CSR practices of Canadian extractive sector companies operating outside Canada."[89] A review could

---

accords-commerciaux/topics-domaines/other-autre/csr-strat-rse-2009.aspx?lang=eng   (last accessed 10 December 2017), the 2014 policy endorses the OECD Due Diligence Guidance for Responsible Supply Chains of Minerals from Conflict-Affected and High-Risk Areas and the United Nations Guiding Principles on Business and Human Rights: Global Affairs Canada, Canada's Enhanced Corporate Social Responsibility Strategy to Strengthen Canada's Extractive Sector Abroad – Doing Business the Canadian Way: A Strategy to Advance Corporate Social Responsibility in Canada's Extractive Sector Abroad. 2014 http://www.international.gc.ca/trade-agreements-accords-commerciaux/assets/pdfs/Enhanced_CS_Strategy_ENG.pdf (last accessed 1 October 2018), pp. 6–7.

[85] Global Affairs Canada, Canada's Enhanced Corporate Social Responsibility Strategy to Strengthen Canada's Extractive Sector Abroad – Doing Business the Canadian Way: A Strategy to Advance Corporate Social Responsibility in Canada's Extractive Sector Abroad. 2014, http://www.international.gc.ca/trade-agreements-accords-commerciaux/assets/pdfs/Enhanced_CS_Strategy_ENG.pdf (last accessed 1 October 2018), pp. 2–3.

[86] Global Affairs Canada, Canada's Enhanced Corporate Social Responsibility Strategy to Strengthen Canada's Extractive Sector Abroad – Doing Business the Canadian Way: A Strategy to Advance Corporate Social Responsibility in Canada's Extractive Sector Abroad. 2014, http://www.international.gc.ca/trade-agreements-accords-commerciaux/assets/pdfs/Enhanced_CS_Strategy_ENG.pdf (last accessed 1 October 2018), p. 3.

[87] Global Affairs Canada, Canada's Enhanced Corporate Social Responsibility Strategy to Strengthen Canada's Extractive Sector Abroad – Doing Business the Canadian Way: A Strategy to Advance Corporate Social Responsibility in Canada's Extractive Sector Abroad. 2014, http://www.international.gc.ca/trade-agreements-accords-commerciaux/assets/pdfs/Enhanced_CS_Strategy_ENG.pdf (last accessed 1 October 2018), p. 8.

[88] Global Affairs Canada, Canada's Enhanced Corporate Social Responsibility Strategy to Strengthen Canada's Extractive Sector Abroad – Doing Business the Canadian Way: A Strategy to Advance Corporate Social Responsibility in Canada's Extractive Sector Abroad. 2014, http://www.international.gc.ca/trade-agreements-accords-commerciaux/assets/pdfs/Enhanced_CS_Strategy_ENG.pdf (last accessed 1 October 2018), p. 4.

[89] Global Affairs Canada, Canada's Enhanced Corporate Social Responsibility Strategy to Strengthen Canada's Extractive Sector Abroad – Doing Business the Canadian Way: A Strategy to

be requested by an affected individual, community, or by the company. In response, the Counsellor attempted to bring the parties together for informal dialogue aimed at reaching a "mutually beneficial result". Where formal mediation was required, the Counsellor could refer the parties to Canada's NCP, although the policy did not define this threshold. Notably referral was also not necessary since parties can elect to bring a complaint directly to the NCP according to its procedures.

The 2014 CSR policy also offered more detail on Canada's official policies and mechanisms for politically supporting Canadian companies. It stated that Canada's Trade Commission Service (TCS) will assist extractive companies who are contributing to Canada's economic growth, have a demonstrated capacity for internationalization, and have strong potential to add value to Canada's economy.[90] It described TCS assistance as on the ground intelligence, practical advice, local contacts, problem solving and market assessment.[91] The CSR policy also made reference to Canada's longstanding economic diplomacy policy (see Sect. 2.1), which it defined as a suite of services for companies including letters of support, advocacy efforts and participation in trade missions.[92]

According to the 2014 policy, companies that aligned their operations with the policy would receive "enhanced Government of Canada economic diplomacy".[93] It offered no further details or descriptions of what this involves. However, the policy did envision a new CSR related role for Canadian embassies and the TCS with respect to Canadian companies. It suggested that these agencies might support companies' CSR practices by helping them conduct social risk analyses, form

---

Advance Corporate Social Responsibility in Canada's Extractive Sector Abroad. 2014, http://www.international.gc.ca/trade-agreements-accords-commerciaux/assets/pdfs/Enhanced_CS_Strategy_ENG.pdf (last accessed 1 October 2018), p. 4.

[90] Global Affairs Canada, Canada's Enhanced Corporate Social Responsibility Strategy to Strengthen Canada's Extractive Sector Abroad – Doing Business the Canadian Way: A Strategy to Advance Corporate Social Responsibility in Canada's Extractive Sector Abroad. 2014, http://www.international.gc.ca/trade-agreements-accords-commerciaux/assets/pdfs/Enhanced_CS_Strategy_ENG.pdf (last accessed 1 October 2018), p. 5.

[91] Global Affairs Canada, Canada's Enhanced Corporate Social Responsibility Strategy to Strengthen Canada's Extractive Sector Abroad – Doing Business the Canadian Way: A Strategy to Advance Corporate Social Responsibility in Canada's Extractive Sector Abroad. 2014, http://www.international.gc.ca/trade-agreements-accords-commerciaux/assets/pdfs/Enhanced_CS_Strategy_ENG.pdf (last accessed 1 October 2018), p. 9.

[92] Global Affairs Canada, Canada's Enhanced Corporate Social Responsibility Strategy to Strengthen Canada's Extractive Sector Abroad – Doing Business the Canadian Way: A Strategy to Advance Corporate Social Responsibility in Canada's Extractive Sector Abroad. 2014, http://www.international.gc.ca/trade-agreements-accords-commerciaux/assets/pdfs/Enhanced_CS_Strategy_ENG.pdf (last accessed 1 October 2018), p. 12.

[93] Global Affairs Canada, Canada's Enhanced Corporate Social Responsibility Strategy to Strengthen Canada's Extractive Sector Abroad – Doing Business the Canadian Way: A Strategy to Advance Corporate Social Responsibility in Canada's Extractive Sector Abroad. 2014, http://www.international.gc.ca/trade-agreements-accords-commerciaux/assets/pdfs/Enhanced_CS_Strategy_ENG.pdf (last accessed 1 October 2018), p. 5.

partnerships with civil society groups, facilitate dialogue with local communities, and identify opportunities for social support programs.[94]

Finally, the 2014 policy included some limited tools to encourage "alignment" with its CSR guidance and participation in dialogue. A company that refused to participate in the voluntary review and dialogue process, offered by either the NCP or the CSR Counsellor, would face the withdrawal of TCS and "other Government of Canada advocacy support abroad".[95] The situation would also be made public. If a company did not participate *and* did not "embody CSR best practice", it would further be denied economic diplomacy (as defined above) and Export Development Canada (EDC) would take its non-compliance into consideration in decisions about financing or other supports.[96] The policy offered no further detail with respect to how EDC would take these facts into consideration. Moreover, according to the terms of the policy, as long as a company participated in the dialogue process proposed, it would continue to receive government supports even if its practices were in fact contrary to the policy's standards.

3.3   Canada's National Contact Point

This section describes Canada's National Contact Point (NCP) complaint system given that it also qualifies as a home-state non-judicial grievance mechanism. As a country belonging to the Organization for Economic Cooperation and Development (OECD), Canada is required to maintain a NCP mechanism. NCPs are mandated to further the effectiveness of the OECD *Guidelines for Multinational Enterprises*, promote their implementation, and help resolve issues including through mediation. They are required to operate in an accessible, transparent, predictable and accountable manner and to effectively and impartially deal with any issues covered in the *Guidelines*.[97]

---

[94] Global Affairs Canada Canada's Enhanced Corporate Social Responsibility Strategy to Strengthen Canada's Extractive Sector Abroad – Doing Business the Canadian Way: A Strategy to Advance Corporate Social Responsibility in Canada's Extractive Sector Abroad. 2014, http://www.international.gc.ca/trade-agreements-accords-commerciaux/assets/pdfs/Enhanced_CS_Strategy_ENG.pdf (last accessed 1 October 2018), pp. 9–10.

[95] Global Affairs Canada, Canada's Enhanced Corporate Social Responsibility Strategy to Strengthen Canada's Extractive Sector Abroad – Doing Business the Canadian Way: A Strategy to Advance Corporate Social Responsibility in Canada's Extractive Sector Abroad. 2014, http://www.international.gc.ca/trade-agreements-accords-commerciaux/assets/pdfs/Enhanced_CS_Strategy_ENG.pdf (last accessed 1 October 2018), p. 12.

[96] Global Affairs Canada, Canada's Enhanced Corporate Social Responsibility Strategy to Strengthen Canada's Extractive Sector Abroad – Doing Business the Canadian Way: A Strategy to Advance Corporate Social Responsibility in Canada's Extractive Sector Abroad. 2014, http://www.international.gc.ca/trade-agreements-accords-commerciaux/assets/pdfs/Enhanced_CS_Strategy_ENG.pdf (last accessed 1 October 2018), pp. 12–13.

[97] Organisation for Economic Co-operation and Development (2011), pp. 68, 71–72.

The *Guidelines*, first introduced in 2000, were updated in 2011.[98] They are also listed among the standards endorsed in Canada's 2014 CSR Policy. The *Guidelines* provide "non-binding principles and standards for responsible business conduct in a global context consistent with applicable laws and internationally recognized standards."[99] They include standards that refer to the social, economic, environmental and human rights impacts of companies on the societies in which they operate. The human rights chapter, a 2011 addition, establishes that multinational enterprises should respect human rights, avoid causing or contributing to human rights impacts, address adverse consequences, carry out human rights due diligence and provide legitimate processes for remediation of adverse impacts.[100] The *Guidelines* are significant because they represent the only multilaterally endorsed comprehensive code of conduct that numerous governments around the world have committed to promote.[101]

The Canadian NCP's procedural guide sets out the various phases of review that may occur when a complaint is filed alleging that a Canadian company has violated the *Guidelines*.[102] If an initial assessment reveals that the issues merit further examination, the NCP will offer to facilitate dialogue between the parties, which may include non-adversarial conciliation or mediation.[103] If an agreement is not reached, the NCP will issue a public statement and if an agreement is reached, it will issue a report. According to the procedural guide, these documents will contain, at a minimum, information about the issues and the procedures initiated.[104] While participation in the NCP review is voluntary, Canada's Department of Foreign Affairs at the time stated "there are consequences if Canadian companies do not participate, or do not engage in good faith." This likely refers to the potential withdrawal of certain

---

[98] Organisation for Economic Co-operation and Development (2011), pp. 3–4.

[99] Organisation for Economic Co-operation and Development (2011), p. 3.

[100] Organisation for Economic Co-operation and Development (2011), pp. 31–34. In the Guidelines, due diligence means accessing actual and potential human rights impacts, integrating and acting upon findings, communicating how impacts are addressed, including risks to rights holders: Organisation for Economic Co-operation and Development (2011), p. 34.

[101] Global Affairs Canada, Canada's National Contact Point (NCP) for the Organisation for Economic Co-operation and Development (OECD) Guidelines for Multinational Enterprises (MNEs). 2016, http://www.international.gc.ca/trade-agreements-accords-commerciaux/ncp-pcn/index.aspx?lang=eng&menu_id=1&menu=R (last accessed 1 October 2018).

[102] Global Affairs Canada, Procedures Guide for Canada's National Contact Point for the Organisation of Economic Co-operation and Development (OECD) Guidelines for Multinational Enterprises. 2016, http://www.international.gc.ca/trade-agreements-accords-commerciaux/ncp-pcn/procedures_guide_de_procedure.aspx?lang=eng (last accessed 1 October 2018).

[103] Global Affairs Canada, Procedures Guide for Canada's National Contact Point for the Organisation of Economic Co-operation and Development (OECD) Guidelines for Multinational Enterprises. 2016, http://www.international.gc.ca/trade-agreements-accords-commerciaux/ncp-pcn/procedures_guide_de_procedure.aspx?lang=eng (last accessed 1 October 2018), section 3.

[104] Global Affairs Canada, Procedures Guide for Canada's National Contact Point for the Organisation of Economic Co-operation and Development (OECD) Guidelines for Multinational Enterprises. 2016 http://www.international.gc.ca/trade-agreements-accords-commerciaux/ncp-pcn/procedures_guide_de_procedure.aspx?lang=eng (last accessed 1 October 2018), section 3.

forms of government support, as specified in the 2014 CSR policy. In 2015, the Canadian NCP reported on the first and only known case to date where this sanction was contemplated. When the company China Gold refused to respond to the NCP's efforts to convene a dialogue, the NCP stated that its non-participation "will be taken into consideration in any applications...for enhanced advocacy support from the Trade Commissioner Service and/or Export Development Canada (EDC) financial services".[105] At the time China Gold was not receiving EDC loans and the Canadian government has not since disclosed any further information to indicate whether or not this sanction was ever in fact applied to China Gold.

4   Empirical, Normative and Political Critiques of Canada's CSR Policy

While Canada's voluntary CSR policy framework was in place, civil society groups in Canada and around the world consistently called upon the Canadian government to improve its policy, including by developing a legal framework that regulates the human rights and environmental impacts of Canadian companies operating abroad, and provides remedies for harms. In their most political form, these calls took the form of global and national letter writing campaigns. In 2016 more than 49 organizations sent individual letters to Prime Minister Trudeau and more than 200 organizations signed a joint letter communicating this message.[106] In 2017, more than 80 Canadian university professors sent a letter to Prime Minister Trudeau with the same call for action.[107] These letters all urged the implementation of an effective non-judicial grievance mechanism like the one proposed in the CNCA's *Business & Human Rights Act* (see Sect. 6). Canadian and international civil society rallied

---

[105] Global Affairs Canada, Final Statement on the Request for Review regarding the Operations of China Gold International Resources Corp Ltd, at the Copper Polymetallic Mine at the Gyama Valley, Tibet Autonomous Region. 2015, http://www.international.gc.ca/trade-agreements-accords-commerciaux/ncp-pcn/statement-gyama-valley.aspx?lang=eng (last accessed 1 October 2018).

[106] Canadian Network on Corporate Accountability, From Guatemala to Zambia, people affected by Canadian mining plea for a Human Rights Ombudsperson for Extractive Industries. 3 March 2017, http://cnca-rcrce.ca/recent-works/from-guatemala-to-zambia-people-affected-by-canadian-mining-plea-for-a-human-rights-ombudsperson-for-extractive-industries/ (last accessed 1 October 2018); Jimenez M, Honduran activist wants Trudeau to pressure Canadian mining companies on human rights abuses. The Star, 16 August 2016, https://www.thestar.com/news/world/2016/08/16/honduran-activist-wants-trudeau-to-pressure-canadian-mining-companies-on-human-rights-abuses.html (last accessed 1 October 2018); Canadian Network on Corporate Accountability, Nearly 200 organizations write to PM urging stronger accountability of Canadian mining overseas. 25 April 2016, http://cnca-rcrce.ca/recent-works/latin-american-organizations-hope-for-stronger-accountability-of-canadian-mining-overseas/ (last accessed 1 October 2018).

[107] Imai S et al., Open Letter to the Prime Minister Calling for Independent Investigation of Allegations against Mining Companies. 24 March 2017, https://www.osgoode.yorku.ca/wp-content/uploads/2017/03/Open-Letter-to-the-Prime-Minister-final.pdf (last accessed 1 October 2018).

around the normative claim that it is wrong for the Canadian government to continue to promote and benefit from mining abroad without putting effective mechanisms into place to ensure accountability.[108]

This section surveys the empirical and normative strategies that advocates employed to question the efficacy of the Canadian government's voluntary CSR policies, in place from 2009 to 2017. As stated in this chapter's introduction, in January 2018 the Canadian government announced its plans to replace the 2014 policy with a new home-state non-judicial grievance mechanism: the Canadian Ombudsperson for Responsible Enterprise (CORE). While few details are available at time of writing, according to the announcement, the new mechanism will respond to civil society proposals and will be the first of its kind in the world.[109] This unexpected development after a prolonged impasse makes the Canadian civil society strategies critiquing the voluntary CSR status quo all the more important.

4.1 Critiques of Canada's National Contact Point

After Canada's updated CSR policy was published in 2014, civil society advocates and academics undertook to analyse its effectiveness. Recall that the policy relied on and incorporated Canada's NCP, which it described as a "robust and proven" complaint mechanism.[110] To test this assertion, three reputable NGOs studied the NCP's performance in five complaints involving Canadian mining companies and allegations of serious harm.[111] All five complaints were filed with the NCP after Canada's 2014 CSR policy was put into place. Following a detailed study of each complaint, the 2016 NGO report identified numerous shortcomings in the Canadian NCP: lack of independence, lack of investigative procedures; ineffective recommendations and follow-up; lack of transparency; unjustified delays; inaccessibility

---

[108] Canadian Network for Corporate Accountability & Justice & Corporate Accountability Project, Human Rights, Indigenous Rights and Canada's Extraterritorial Obligations. Inter-American Commission on Human Rights, Thematic Hearing for 153rd Period of Sessions. 28 October 2014, http://cnca-rcrce.ca/wp-content/uploads/2016/05/canada_mining_cidh_oct_28_2014_final.pdf (last accessed 1 October 2018).

[109] Global Affairs Canada, The Government of Canada brings leadership to responsible business conduct abroad, News Release. 17 January 2018, https://www.canada.ca/en/global-affairs/news/2018/01/the_government_ofcanadabringsleadershiptoresponsiblebusinesscond.html (last accessed 1 October 2018).

[110] Global Affairs Canada, Canada's Enhanced Corporate Social Responsibility Strategy to Strengthen Canada's Extractive Sector Abroad – Doing Business the Canadian Way: A Strategy to Advance Corporate Social Responsibility in Canada's Extractive Sector Abroad. 2014, http://www.international.gc.ca/trade-agreements-accords-commerciaux/assets/pdfs/Enhanced_CS_Strategy_ENG.pdf (last accessed 1 October 2018), p. 12.

[111] Above Ground, MiningWatch Canada and OECD Watch, "Canada is Back" but Still Far Behind – An Assessment of Canada's National Contact Point for the OECD Guidelines for Multinational Enterprises. November 2016, https://miningwatch.ca/sites/default/files/canada-is-back-report-web_0.pdf (last accessed 1 October 2018).

of the mechanism due to high threshold for accepting complaints; and ineffective penalties.

The report noted that while each OECD country has discretion in how to structure its NCP, some countries have ensured that their NCP is completely independent of the government. In contrast, Canada's NCP is composed entirely of government representatives and is chaired by Global Affairs Canada, whose mandate includes expanding trade and investment and providing special support to Canada's natural resources sector abroad. The NGO report argued that this raises questions about the NCP's impartiality on the basis that Global Affairs may have a conflict of interest in hearing complaints against the very companies it is mandated to support.[112]

Another major area of concern in the NGO report was that the Canadian NCP will not investigate complaints or make any findings: it is only available to facilitate dialogue between disputing parties. When the NCP makes recommendations, these often fail to address the issues between the parties, lack justification and lack appropriate follow up mechanisms.[113] The report also found problems with transparency. While the Canadian NCP's procedural guidelines require it to publish either a public statement or a report following a complaint,[114] the NGO study found that in practice this does not always occur and any reporting that does occur is sparse.[115]

Further, the NGO report found that it is unclear how the penalties specified in Canada's 2014 CSR policy are being applied. Recall that the policy stated that a company's failure to participate in dialogue and align with the policy will result in the withdrawal of trade support and may be taken into account by Export Development Canada (EDC). In the NGO study, companies named in credible complaints nonetheless continued to receive significant government support and financing from EDC and the Canadian Pension Plan. Moreover, the report found that the threat of penalty and the penalty itself was ineffective. For example, it pointed out that China Gold had refused to participate in any dialogue regardless of the threat of withdrawal of trade support. Moreover, even after the NCP found the requisite conditions to withdraw federal Trade Commissioner Services (TCS) from China Gold,

---

[112] Above Ground, MiningWatch Canada and OECD Watch, "Canada is Back" but Still Far Behind – An Assessment of Canada's National Contact Point for the OECD Guidelines for Multinational Enterprises. November 2016, https://miningwatch.ca/sites/default/files/canada-is-back-report-web_0.pdf (last accessed 1 October 2018), p. 17. Also see Simons (2015), pp. 26–27.

[113] Above Ground, MiningWatch Canada and OECD Watch, "Canada is Back" but Still Far Behind – An Assessment of Canada's National Contact Point for the OECD Guidelines for Multinational Enterprises. November 2016, https://miningwatch.ca/sites/default/files/canada-is-back-report-web_0.pdf (last accessed 1 October 2018), pp. 18–19.

[114] Global Affairs Canada, Procedures Guide for Canada's National Contact Point for the Organisation of Economic Co-operation and Development (OECD) Guidelines for Multinational Enterprises. 2016, http://www.international.gc.ca/trade-agreements-accords-commerciaux/ncp-pcn/procedures_guide_de_procedure.aspx?lang=eng (last accessed 1 October 2018).

[115] Above Ground, MiningWatch Canada and OECD Watch, "Canada is Back" but Still Far Behind – An Assessment of Canada's National Contact Point for the OECD Guidelines for Multinational Enterprises. November 2016, https://miningwatch.ca/sites/default/files/canada-is-back-report-web_0.pdf (last accessed 1 October 2018), pp. 17, 19.

the company nonetheless subsequently participated in a trade mission organized by the provincial government of British Columbia.[116]

Finally, the NGO report noted that even if supports from EDC and the TCS are withdrawn, other government services are not impacted. There are also no consequences or penalties for a company that participates in dialogue but is not compliant with the OECD *Guidelines*. On the basis of all of its findings, the NGO report concluded that the Canadian NCP is failing to prevent harm, improve conditions and facilitate access to remedy.[117]

4.2   Critiques of Canada's 2014 CSR Policy and Counsellor

Shortly after the 2014 CSR policy was announced, Canadian law professor Penelope Simons evaluated the extent to which it met Canada's obligations to protect human rights and to ensure that victims have access to effective remedies as set out in the UN *Guiding Principles on Business & Human Rights*.[118] In her analysis, Simons acknowledged some advances in the 2014 policy, including the statement that Canadian companies are expected to respect human rights. However, Simons pointed out that the policy does not define any of the standards it refers to, namely CSR, Canadian values, or human rights, nor does it refer to how companies should meet these standards.[119] For example, it fails to clearly set out the expectation that companies should engage in comprehensive and ongoing human rights due diligence as recommended by the *Guiding Principles*.[120] Simons also argued that merely endorsing a list of intergovernmental or international multi-stakeholder initiatives is not helpful for the purposes of establishing clear standards.[121]

Perhaps most importantly, Simons firmly concluded that Canada's 2014 CSR policy and NCP procedures, as voluntary consensus-based dialogue and dispute resolution mechanisms, do not help fulfil Canada's obligation to take measures to

---

[116] Above Ground, MiningWatch Canada and OECD Watch, "Canada is Back" but Still Far Behind – An Assessment of Canada's National Contact Point for the OECD Guidelines for Multinational Enterprises. November 2016, https://miningwatch.ca/sites/default/files/canada-is-back-report-web_0.pdf (last accessed 1 October 2018), pp. 5, 20.

[117] Above Ground, MiningWatch Canada and OECD Watch, "Canada is Back" but Still Far Behind – An Assessment of Canada's National Contact Point for the OECD Guidelines for Multinational Enterprises. November 2016, https://miningwatch.ca/sites/default/files/canada-is-back-report-web_0.pdf (last accessed 1 October 2018), p. 21. These findings are consistent with the conclusion reached in a 2015 report by OECD Watch in a comprehensive study of the efficacy of NCPs around the world. It concluded that the overwhelming majority of complaints failed to bring an end to corporate misconduct or provide remedy for past or on-going abuses, leaving complainants in the same or worse position as they were in beforehand: Daniel et al. (2015), p. 9.

[118] Simons (2015).

[119] Simons (2015), p. 12.

[120] Simons (2015), p. 17.

[121] Simons (2015), p. 13.

ensure victims' access to remedy.[177] Simons also found that the CSR Counsellor's review mechanism does not meet at least some of the criteria set out in the *Guiding Principles* for an effective non-judicial grievance mechanism.[123] For example, it lacks features to ensure that outcomes are rights-compatible and the policy's potential sanction tool, namely conditioning or withdrawing some forms of government support, fails to ensure access to justice for victims.[124] Simons also pointed out that the policy failed to offer a basis or guideline for measuring non-alignment with the policy such that the withdrawal of support would be warranted.[125]

Notably, Simons' analysis, undertaken shortly after the publication of the 2014 CSR Policy, was entirely textual. Experience with the implementation of the policy and complaint mechanisms between 2015 and 2017 revealed further weaknesses in practice. In 2015 the federal government appointed Jeffrey Davidson to the CSR Counsellor position. Davidson had 35 years of experience working for a number of mining companies as well as the World Bank on community relations strategies.[126] Following Davidson's appointment, there is no record of a single request for review (or complaint) being brought to his office between 2015 and 2017.[127] Given the ongoing reports of harms linked to Canadian extractive companies abroad in this period (see Sect. 2), this absence suggests that civil society and affected communities lacked trust in the CSR Counsellor's review process from the very beginning. According to the Counsellor's 2015/2016 Annual Report, Davidson primarily dedicated his time to public presentations and informal meetings with a wide variety of mining companies, civil society organizations, academics, industry associations, and CSR consultants.[128] There is no indication that these meetings involved a mediated dialogue of any kind.

In August 2016, Counsellor Davidson made his first reported country trip to Honduras for a period of approximately 12 days. The purpose was to explain and promote CSR expectations, develop a better understanding of the local context, issues and challenges, and establish a foundation for effective advisory support and constructive intervention if required.[129] In his country trip report, published about a

---

[122] Simons (2015), p. 29. Also see Coumans (2012), p. 685.

[123] Simons (2015), p. 24.

[124] Simons (2015), pp. 26, 30.

[125] Simons (2015), p. 21.

[126] Global Affairs Canada, Jeffrey Davidson, Extractive Sector Corporate Social Responsibility (CSR) Counsellor. 2017, http://www.international.gc.ca/csr_counsellor-conseiller_rse/jeffrey-davidson.aspx?lang=eng (last accessed 1 October 2018).

[127] Global Affairs Canada, Registry of Request for Review. 2017, http://www.international.gc.ca/csr_counsellor-conseiller_rse/Registry-web-enregistrement.aspx?lang=eng (last accessed 1 October 2018).

[128] Global Affairs Canada, 2016 Annual Report to Parliament: May 2015–May 2016. November 2016, http://international.gc.ca/csr_counsellor-conseiller_rse/publications/2016_annual_report-rapport_annuel_2016.aspx?lang=eng (last accessed 1 October 2018).

[129] Global Affairs Canada, Honduras Country Trip Overview: Office of the Extractive Sector Corporate Social Responsibility (CSR) Counsellor. 27 June–7 August 2016, http://www.international.gc.ca/csr_counsellor-conseiller_rse/trip_overview_Honduras-apercu_voyage_Honduras.

year later, Davidson described his meetings with stakeholders and the concerns he heard with respect to the negative impacts of extractive activities in Honduras. However, the report also contained a series of controversial statements in a section called "The Canada NGO Connection," where the Counsellor stated that foreign and local NGOs have contributed to the strained and tense situation around extractive activities in Honduras. In this section, Davidson accused two Canadian NGOs in particular of being ideologically against mining, of adopting confrontational and adversarial approaches to companies, and of being inherently opposed to collaborative relationships. The Counsellor's language also suggested that these groups *perceive* themselves as human rights defenders and *perceive* a culture of impunity for mining companies in Honduras.

Two weeks after the Counsellor released his report, a group of twenty-four Canadian NGOs, unions and churches sent a letter to Canada's Minister of International Trade calling for its retraction.[130] In their letter, these groups accused the Counsellor of making "sweeping, unsubstantiated, biased and irresponsible accusations against Canadian CSOs" which minimize the agency of entire communities, local civil society leaders and organizations in Honduras who have long expressed legitimate concerns about the extractive sector and regularly mobilized in defense of their rights and environment.[131] The civil society letter further argued that the Counsellor had misrepresented the role of Canadian NGOs in Honduras and fundamentally misunderstood the nature of international solidarity relationships between organizations. The letter also stated that the Counsellor "minimizes the danger faced by human rights defenders in Honduras" which has been widely recognized by numerous international human rights bodies. These groups charged that the Counsellor's "irresponsible assertions" may give license to certain actors in Honduras to take action against international organizations, something which has occurred in recent years.

It seems fair to say that the CSR Counsellor's 2017 country trip report resulted in a total breakdown of his relationship with a considerable cross-section of Canadian civil society. Given the nature of the statements, the report may have also directly damaged his relationship with civil society groups abroad. This result is ironic given that the Counsellor's primarily mandate was to facilitate dialogue and his goal in visiting Honduras was "constructive intervention". To date, the Minister of International Trade has not requested retraction of the report.

---

aspx?lang=eng (last accessed 1 October 2018).

[130] Above Ground et al., Letter from Canadian civil society organizations to the Honourable François-Philippe Champagne, Minister of International Trade. 28 July 2017, http://aboveground. ngo/wp-content/uploads/2017/07/CSO-letter-re-CSR-Counsellor-Honduras-Report.pdf   (last accessed 1 October 2018).

[131] Above Ground et al., Letter from Canadian civil society organizations to the Honourable François-Philippe Champagne, Minister of International Trade. 28 July 2017, http://aboveground. ngo/wp-content/uploads/2017/07/CSO-letter-re-CSR-Counsellor-Honduras-Report.pdf   (last accessed 1 October 2018).

In sum, advocates critiqued the efficacy and even the legitimacy of the 2014 CSR policy in three ways. First, by critically analysing the NCP's response to complaints against Canadian resource companies submitted after 2014. Second, by evaluating the CSR policy against the norms articulated in the UN *Guiding Principles*. And third, by rallying together to publically challenge the CSR Counsellor's judgment and capacity to facilitate constructive dialogue. Together, these strategies combined empirical study, normative analysis and political critique. The next section will examine how advocates took their dissatisfaction with the Canadian CSR policy status quo to international fora.

5 Building Strong Consensus with International Human Rights Bodies (2002–2017)

Previous sections of this chapter have referred to numerous civil society reports that documented the human rights concerns of communities affected by the Canadian extractive industry abroad and further argued that Canada's existing CSR policies are inadequate. In conjunction with these strategies, civil society organizations persistently brought this evidence before international human rights bodies, asking them to evaluate Canada's approach to its international extractive sector in light of its international human rights obligations. In the United Nations (UN) system, advocates brought their concerns to treaty bodies, Special Rapporteurs and Working Groups, all tasked with interpreting core UN human rights treaties and reviewing state signatories' compliance. In the Organization of American States (OAS), advocates made submissions to the Inter-American Commission on Human Rights (IACHR) at thematic hearings addressing Canada's human rights obligations in the area of extractive industries abroad.

This international legal and advocacy work generated a significant body of commentary. Over a period of 15 years, human rights bodies in both systems pronounced on the human rights and environmental impacts of Canadian resource extraction abroad and the concomitant responsibilities of the Canadian state. In total, between 2002 and 2017, seven UN bodies issued at least ten separate statements to Canada on these issues: the UN Special Rapporteur on Toxic Waste,[132] the Committee on the

---

[132] UN Economic and Social Council, Adverse effects of the illicit movement and dumping of toxic and dangerous products and wastes on the enjoyment of human rights, Mission to Canada, UN Doc E/CN.4/2003/56/Add.2, 14 January 2003, para 126.

Elimination of Racial Discrimination,[133] the Committee on the Rights of the Child,[134] the Human Rights Committee,[135] the Committee on Economic, Social and Cultural Rights,[136] the Committee on the Elimination of Discrimination Against Women,[137] and most recently, the UN Working Group on Business and Human Rights.[138]

In 2013, 2014 and again in 2017, the IACHR dedicated three thematic hearings specifically to the topic of Canadian resource companies in Latin America and the Canadian government's associated policies, laws and responsibility.[139] It also received submissions on this issue in 2015 from the Human Rights Research and Education Centre at the University of Ottawa[140] and from the Counsel of Latin

---

[133] UN Committee on the Elimination of Racial Discrimination, Concluding observations of the Committee on the Elimination of Racial Discrimination: Canada, UN Doc CERD/C/CAN/CO/18, 25 March 2007, para 17; UN Committee on the Elimination of Racial Discrimination, Concluding observations of the Committee on the Elimination of Racial Discrimination: Canada, UN Doc CERD/C/CAN/CO/19-20, 4 April 2012, para 14; UN Committee on the Elimination of Racial Discrimination, Early Warning and Urgent Action Procedure Letter to the Permanent Representative of Canada to the United Nations, UN Doc CERD/89th/EWUAP/GH/MJA/ks, 27 May 2016; UN Committee on the Elimination of Racial Discrimination, Concluding observations on the combined twenty-first to twenty-third periodic report of Canada, UN Doc CERD/C/CAN/CO/21-23, 13 September 2017, para 21.

[134] UN Committee on the Rights of the Child, Concluding observations on the combined third and fourth periodic report of Canada, adopted by the Committee at its sixty-first session (17 September–5 October 2012), UN Doc CRC/C/CAN/CO/3-4., 6 December 2012, para 28.

[135] UN Human Rights Committee, Concluding observations on the sixth periodic report of Canada, UN Doc CCPR/C/CAN/CO/6, 13 August 2015, para 6.

[136] UN Economic and Social Council, Committee on Economic, Social and Cultural Rights, Concluding observations on the sixth periodic report of Canada, UN Doc E/C.12/CAN/CO/6, 23 March 2016, para 15.

[137] UN Committee on the Elimination of Discrimination against Women, Concluding observations on the combined eighth and ninth periodic reports of Canada, UN Doc CEDAW/C/CAN/CO/8-9, 25 November 2016, para. 18.

[138] UN Office of the High Commissioner of Human Rights, Statement at the end of Visit to Canada by the United Nations Working Group on Business and Human Rights, 1 June 2017, http://www.ohchr.org/EN/NewsEvents/Pages/DisplayNews.aspx?NewsID=21680&LangID=E (last accessed 1 October 2018).

[139] Canadian Network for Corporate Accountability & Justice & Corporate Accountability Project, Human Rights, Indigenous Rights and Canada's Extraterritorial Obligations. Inter-American Commission on Human Rights, Thematic Hearing for 153rd Period of Sessions. 28 October 2014, http://cnca-rcrce.ca/wp-content/uploads/2016/05/canada_mining_cidh_oct_28_2014_final.pdf (last accessed 1 October 2018); Working Group on Mining and Human Rights in Latin America, The impact of Canadian Mining in Latin America and Canada's Responsibility: Executive Summary of the Report submitted to the Inter-American Commission on Human Rights. 2013, http://www.dplf.org/sites/default/files/report_canadian_mining_executive_summary.pdf   (last accessed 1 October 2018); Inter-American Commission on Human Rights, Measures to prevent human rights violations by Canadian extractive industries that operate in Latin America, Schedule of Public Hearings, 166th Sess. 7 December 2017, p. 2, http://www.oas.org/en/iachr/sessions/docs/Calendario-166-audiencias-en.pdf (last accessed 1 October 2018).

[140] Human Rights Research and Education Centre, Extraterritoriality and Responsibility of Home States in the Protection of Human Rights for the Activities of Extractive Industries in Latin America, IACHR Thematic Hearing on Corporations, Human Rights and Prior Consultation in the

American Catholic Bishops[141] at hearings of a more general nature. On this basis, the IACHR has commented on two separate occasions on Canada's obligations with respect to these issues.[142] Taking the statements from UN and OAS bodies in combination, in total eight international human rights bodies made at least twelve relevant statements to Canada between 2002 and 2017.

The timing of these statements in relation to the development of Canada's CSR policies is important. The first two UN statements on these issues occurred in 2002 and 2007, before Canada had announced its 2009 CSR policy. In the 5 years that the 2009 policy was in place, advocates obtained two more statements from UN human rights bodies and participated in two IAHRC hearings. However, the majority of the above-cited statements from international human rights bodies occurred in a short 3-year period after Canada updated its CSR policy in late 2014.

One possible explanation for this distribution is that the 2014 policy change did little if anything to remedy concerns with the 2009 policy, making Canada appear increasingly intransigent in its commitment to a voluntary approach. In this context, advocates intensified their efforts to frame their concerns in terms of Canada's international human rights commitments. Another important factor is that advocates began to accumulate a breadth and depth of research establishing problems with company conduct, state conduct and state policies. International human rights bodies clearly found this research compelling and they responded accordingly with strong statements to Canada.

Taken together, these statements contain three main themes. First, human rights bodies commonly expressed concern in response to numerous reports and findings that Canadian resource companies are causing environmental harm and contributing to human rights violations in the developing countries where they operate. Second, all of the bodies in question called on the Canadian government to establish effective legislative and administrative law measures to oversee companies and to prevent human rights violations abroad. In this respect, several statements recommended that Canada monitor the human rights impacts of Canadian companies' overseas

---

Americas. 18 March 2015, https://cdp-hrc.uottawa.ca/sites/cdp-hrc.uottawa.ca/files/hrrec-_oral_presentation_iachr-_march_17_2015.pdf (last accessed 1 October 2018).

[141] Departamento de justicia y solidaridad del Consejo Episcopal Latinoamericano (CELAM) et al., Posición de la Iglesia católica ante vulneración y abusos contra los derechos humanos de las poblaciones afectadas por las industrias extractivas en América Latina, Audiencia pública ante la Comisión Interamericana de Derechos Humanos, 154th Sess. 19 March 2015, https://justiceprojectdotorg1.files.wordpress.com/2017/08/informe-final-celam-repam-2015.pdf (last accessed 1 October 2018), p. 12; Due Process of Law Foundation, Comunicado: Iglesia Católica ante CIDH sobre DDHH e industrias extractivas en América Latina. 18 March 2015, http://www.dplf.org/es/news/comunicado-iglesia-catolica-ante-cidh-sobre-ddhh-e-industrias-extractivas-en-america-latina (last accessed 1 October 2018); Obispos denuncian peligros de la minería en Latinoamérica. El Observador: De la Actualidad. 23 March 2015, http://elobservadorenlinea.com/2015/03/obispos-denuncian-peligros-de-la-mineria-en-latinoamerica/ (last accessed 1 October 2018).

[142] Organization of American States, IACHR Wraps Up its 153rd Session, Press Release, 7 November 2014, http://www.oas.org/en/iachr/media_center/PReleases/2014/131.asp (last accessed 1 October 2018); Inter-American Commission on Human Rights (2015) paras 20, 23, 78-9, 136-8, 141.

operations and require companies to undertake human rights impact assessments of proposed projects.

Third, a considerable majority of these bodies made recommendations about access to justice in Canada. This included recommendations that Canada establish an effective state-based non-judicial system of independent investigation of allegations against Canadian companies, including accountability mechanisms and possible sanctions such as the withdrawal of state support.[143] This line of recommendations also included reforms to ensure access to judicial remedies in Canada. In sum, numerous international human rights bodies sent a strong, unified and consistent message over a period of 15 years that Canada's CSR policies were inadequate from the perspective of its international obligations.

6 Creating and Advocating for Concrete Law Reform Proposals (2009–2016)

In addition to the strategies mentioned above, Canadian advocates focused their efforts on developing law and policy proposals in Canada that aimed to address, at least in some way, the human rights impact of Canadian extractive companies abroad.[144] Most of these efforts focused on the creation of an effective home-state non-judicial grievance mechanism. The first set of proposals in this regarded emerged from the recommendations of two government commissioned reports (described in Sect. 2): the 2005 report of the Parliamentary Sub-committee on Human Rights and International Development, and the 2007 report of the Advisory Committee for the National Roundtables on Corporate Social Responsibility and the Extractive Industry in Developing Countries.[145]

Unsatisfied with the 2009 CSR Policy response to these reports, civil society groups in Canada worked hard to support Bill C-300, *An Act respecting corporate*

---

[143] More research is needed to identify the significance of this consensus. As far back as 2011, Seck argued that Canadian efforts to regulate could serve as evidence of state practice supporting the emergence of customary international rules with consequences for the international community as a whole. Seck observed that customary international law rules could support the position that home state jurisdiction to regulate and adjudicate to prevent and remedy environmental and human rights harms is either permissible or mandatory: see Seck (2011), p. 113.

[144] For a detailed analysis of the standards, scope of application, sanctions and enforcement mechanisms contemplated in these proposals, see: Kamphuis (2012).

[145] See House of Commons Standing Committee on Foreign Affairs and International Trade, Mining in Developing Countries: Corporate Social Responsibility. 38th Parl, 1st Sess, 14th Rep. 2005, http://www.ourcommons.ca/DocumentViewer/en/38-1/FAAE/report-14 (last accessed 1 October 2018); Advisory Group Report, National Roundtables on Corporate Social Responsibility (CSR) and the Canadian Extractive Industry in Developing Countries. 1 May 2007, http://www.pdac.ca/docs/default-source/priorities/public-affairs/csr-national-roundtables-background.pdf?sfvrsn=720e9e50_12 (last accessed 1 October 2018).

accountability for the activities of mining, oil or gas in developing countries,[146] proposed by an opposition Member of Parliament. The Bill would have required certain Canadian companies to comply with international human rights standards in their overseas operations and would have obligated the Ministers of Foreign Affairs and International Trade to receive complaints about these companies. If either Minister determined that a company had not met the standards specified, the Bill would have required the withdrawal of Export Development Canada loans, Canada Pension Plan equity holdings, as well as diplomatic support. The Bill would have also made the provision of these forms of financial support conditional on companies' compliance with the standards specified. With a minority Conservative government in power, Bill C-300 passed first and second reading in the Canadian Parliament before it was narrowly defeated in 2010 in its third and final reading.[147]

Following the defeat of Bill C-300, opposition Members of Parliament introduced two related bills between 2010 and 2013. The first, Bill C-571, *An Act respecting corporate practices relating to the purchase of minerals from the Great Lakes Region of Africa*[148] would have required certain companies to undertake due diligence, and the second, Bill C-323, *An Act to amend the Federal Courts Act (international promotion and protection of human rights)*[149] would have given the Canadian federal courts universal jurisdiction over claims of violations of international human rights law. Neither Bill moved beyond initial stages.

6.1 Draft Legislation: The Business & Human Rights Act (2016)

The concept of an independent Canadian ombudsperson with the power to receive complaints about the human rights impacts of the Canadian extractive industry abroad first appeared as draft legislation in 2014 with Bill C-584—*An Act respecting the corporate social responsibility inherent in the activities of Canadian*

---

[146] Bill C-300, An Act respecting Corporate Accountability for the Activities of Mining, Oil or Gas in Developing Countries, 2nd Sess, 40th Parl. 2009, http://www.ourcommons.ca/Content/ Bills/402/Private/C-300/C-300_1/C-300_1.PDF (last accessed 1 October 2018), section 3.

[147] Those who voted against Bill C-300 cited concerns that it would "negatively impact Canada's competitiveness as a world leader in mining": Dagenais P, Canadian Mining Industry Wins with Bill C-300's Defeat. Canadian Mining Journal, 1 December 2010, http://www.canadianmining-journal.com/features/canadian-mining-industry-wins-with-bill-c-300-s-defeat/ (last accessed 1 October 2018). Advocates for the Bill reported that industry launched an intense lobby and misinformation campaign against the Bill: Seck (2011); Coumans (2012), p. 673.

[148] Bill C-571, Trade in Conflict Minerals Act: An Act respecting corporate practices relating to the purchase of minerals from the Great Lakes Region of Africa, 3rd Sess, 40th Parl. 2010, https:// openparliament.ca/bills/40-3/C-571/ (last accessed 1 October 2018).

[149] Bill C-323, An Act to amend the Federal Courts Act (international promotion and protection of human rights), 2nd Sess, 41st Parl. 2013, https://openparliament.ca/bills/41-2/C-323/ (last accessed 1 October 2018).

extractive corporations in developing countries.[150] Like those before it, this Bill, proposed by an opposition Member of Parliament, was defeated at a preliminary stage. However, after nearly a decade in power, the federal Conservative government fell the next year in 2015. The Liberal Party came to power on an election platform that included a commitment to implementing an ombudsperson for the Canadian extractive sector abroad.[151]

With the apparent opportunity for legislative change at hand, the CNCA intensified its work on model legislation, unveiling *The Global Leadership in Business and Human Rights Act: An Act to Create an Independent Human Rights Ombudsperson for the International Extractive Sector*[152] in late 2016. This proposal was considerably more sophisticated and comprehensive than previous proposals. It likely drew some inspiration from a similar concept developed by two Canadian law professors in a book published 2 years prior.[153] Also, unlike previous proposals, the CNCA did not bring the *Business & Human Rights Act* forward in the Parliamentary process. Rather, they presented it to government representatives in countless private meetings. This section will describe the proposed Act's main features in the following categories: administrative body, regulatory objectives and jurisdiction; standards; investigatory powers and recommendations; and potential sanctions.

6.2 Administrative Body, Regulatory Objectives and Jurisdiction

The draft *Business and Human Rights Act* aimed to address the harms suffered by individuals and the natural environment in foreign states in connection with Canadian extractive industries.[154] In relation to these harms, the Act's objectives

---

[150] Bill C-584, An Act respecting the Corporate Social Responsibility Inherent in the Activities of Canadian Extractive Corporations in Developing Countries, 2nd Sess, 41st Parl. 2014, https://www.parl.ca/LegisInfo/BillDetails.aspx?Language=E&billId=6489787&View=0 (last accessed 1 October 2018).

[151] Cumming J, What the Liberals, Greens and NDP Have to Say on Mining in Canada. Huffington Post, 5 October 2015, http://www.huffingtonpost.ca/john-cumming/mining-canada-federal-election_b_8235824.html (last accessed 1 October 2018).

[152] Canadian Network on Corporate Accountability, The Global Leadership in Business and Human Rights Act: An Act to Create an Independent Human Rights Ombudsperson for the International Extractive Sector, Draft Model Legislation. 2 November 2016, http://cnca-rcrce.ca/wp-content/uploads/2016/03/The-Global-Leadership-in-Business-and-Human-Rights-Act-An-act-to-create-an-independent-human-rights-ombudsperson-for-the-international-extractive-sector-11022016.pdf (last accessed 1 October 2018).

[153] Simons and Macklin (2014). There are however important differences between the CSR agency that Simons and Macklin propose and the CNCA legislative proposal. The focus of the former was on government due diligence prior to offering companies' public supports, while the latter focused on dispute resolution.

[154] Canadian Network on Corporate Accountability, The Global Leadership in Business and Human Rights Act: An Act to Create an Independent Human Rights Ombudsperson for the International

were: to promote avoidance of harms; to promote meaningful participation of individuals, groups and local communities in decisions that affect them; to investigate and report on harms; and to promote the resolution, remedy and full reparation of harm.[155] It also aimed to increase accountability and transparency with respect to harms.[156]

In order to meet these objectives, the proposed legislation would have created an oversight body called the Office of the Extractive Industries Human Rights Ombudsperson, appointed by a majority vote of the members of the House of Commons and the Senate as a public servant and an Officer of Parliament, independent from the Government.[157] Anyone employed, on the board of directors or otherwise closely associated with Canadian extractive companies in the previous 5 years would not have been eligible for the appointment.[158]

The proposed Act required a prospective Ombudsperson to have qualifications in three main arenas: (1) expertise and experience in the investigation and documentation of human rights infringements; (2) knowledge of international best practice in gender-sensitive investigation and analysis; and (3) experience in at least one of the

---

Extractive Sector, Draft Model Legislation. 2 November 2016, http://cnca-rcrce.ca/wp-content/uploads/2016/03/The-Global-Leadership-in-Business-and-Human-Rights-Act-An-act-to-create-an-independent-human-rights-ombudsperson-for-the-international-extractive-sector-11022016.pdf (last accessed 1 October 2018), section 3.20.

[155] Canadian Network on Corporate Accountability, The Global Leadership in Business and Human Rights Act: An Act to Create an Independent Human Rights Ombudsperson for the International Extractive Sector, Draft Model Legislation. 2 November 2016, http://cnca-rcrce.ca/wp-content/uploads/2016/03/The-Global-Leadership-in-Business-and-Human-Rights-Act-An-act-to-create-an-independent-human-rights-ombudsperson-for-the-international-extractive-sector-11022016.pdf (last accessed 1 October 2018), section 3.20. Throughout the proposed Act, the Ombudsperson is required to undertake their duties with gender sensitivity.

[156] Canadian Network on Corporate Accountability, The Global Leadership in Business and Human Rights Act: An Act to Create an Independent Human Rights Ombudsperson for the International Extractive Sector, Draft Model Legislation. 2 November 2016, http://cnca-rcrce.ca/wp-content/uploads/2016/03/The-Global-Leadership-in-Business-and-Human-Rights-Act-An-act-to-create-an-independent-human-rights-ombudsperson-for-the-international-extractive-sector-11022016.pdf (last accessed 1 October 2018), section 3.21.

[157] Canadian Network on Corporate Accountability, The Global Leadership in Business and Human Rights Act: An Act to Create an Independent Human Rights Ombudsperson for the International Extractive Sector, Draft Model Legislation. 2 November 2016, http://cnca-rcrce.ca/wp-content/uploads/2016/03/The-Global-Leadership-in-Business-and-Human-Rights-Act-An-act-to-create-an-independent-human-rights-ombudsperson-for-the-international-extractive-sector-11022016.pdf (last accessed 1 October 2018), sections 3.1, 3.2, 3.8.

[158] Canadian Network on Corporate Accountability, The Global Leadership in Business and Human Rights Act: An Act to Create an Independent Human Rights Ombudsperson for the International Extractive Sector, Draft Model Legislation. 2 November 2016, http://cnca-rcrce.ca/wp-content/uploads/2016/03/The-Global-Leadership-in-Business-and-Human-Rights-Act-An-act-to-create-an-independent-human-rights-ombudsperson-for-the-international-extractive-sector-11022016.pdf (last accessed 1 October 2018), section 3.8. The proposed Act includes other provisions to avoid the existence of a conflict of interest between the Ombudsperson and the Canadian companies that would be subjected to the Act. The Office of the Ombudsperson would also include one or more assistants and other staff: sections 3.11–3.16.

following areas: international best practice in the investigation of sexual violence, extractive industries, Indigenous rights and human rights and environmental impact assessment and auditing.[159]

Another important feature of the CNCA's draft legislation was the intended scope of its application to any corporation, with a Canadian nexus, engaged in the commercial development of oil, gas or minerals in a foreign state.[160] A Canadian nexus existed if a company: (1) was listed on a Canadian stock exchange; (2) incorporated anywhere in Canada; (3) had a principal place of business in Canada; or (4) was receiving or had received support, subsidy, promotion, partnership or protection from the Canadian government or a government agency.[161] The proposed Act also captured any affiliate of, including a subsidiary or a company controlled by, a Canadian corporation, also engaged in the commercial development of oil, gas or minerals.[162] Accordingly, the Ombudsperson's jurisdiction to investigate would have been established if there was a nexus between the subject of the complaint and

---

[159] Canadian Network on Corporate Accountability, The Global Leadership in Business and Human Rights Act: An Act to Create an Independent Human Rights Ombudsperson for the International Extractive Sector, Draft Model Legislation. 2 November 2016, http://cnca-rcrce.ca/wp-content/uploads/2016/03/The-Global-Leadership-in-Business-and-Human-Rights-Act-An-act-to-create-an-independent-human-rights-ombudsperson-for-the-international-extractive-sector-11022016.pdf (last accessed 1 October 2018), section 3.10.

[160] Canadian Network on Corporate Accountability, The Global Leadership in Business and Human Rights Act: An Act to Create an Independent Human Rights Ombudsperson for the International Extractive Sector, Draft Model Legislation. 2 November 2016, http://cnca-rcrce.ca/wp-content/uploads/2016/03/The-Global-Leadership-in-Business-and-Human-Rights-Act-An-act-to-create-an-independent-human-rights-ombudsperson-for-the-international-extractive-sector-11022016.pdf (last accessed 1 October 2018), sections 2.3, 6.1, 6.2.

[161] Canadian Network on Corporate Accountability, The Global Leadership in Business and Human Rights Act: An Act to Create an Independent Human Rights Ombudsperson for the International Extractive Sector, Draft Model Legislation. 2 November 2016, http://cnca-rcrce.ca/wp-content/uploads/2016/03/The-Global-Leadership-in-Business-and-Human-Rights-Act-An-act-to-create-an-independent-human-rights-ombudsperson-for-the-international-extractive-sector-11022016.pdf (last accessed 1 October 2018), section 5.1.

[162] Canadian Network on Corporate Accountability, The Global Leadership in Business and Human Rights Act: An Act to Create an Independent Human Rights Ombudsperson for the International Extractive Sector, Draft Model Legislation. 2 November 2016, http://cnca-rcrce.ca/wp-content/uploads/2016/03/The-Global-Leadership-in-Business-and-Human-Rights-Act-An-act-to-create-an-independent-human-rights-ombudsperson-for-the-international-extractive-sector-11022016.pdf (last accessed 1 October 2018), sections 2.1, 2.2, 2.3, 2.9, 5.1. Control is defined as owning 20% or more of the voting interests in another company, controlling 30% of the Board of Directors, control over management and policies, or control over salary levels for executives or employees at another company: s 2.2.

Canada.[163] Notably, the scope of the Ombudsperson's proposed jurisdiction paral lels that set out in existing Canadian legislation with extra-territorial reach.[164]

6.3 Standards

Under the draft *Business & Human Rights Act*, the Ombudsperson had a duty to initiate an investigation where a complaint named a company with a Canadian nexus and alleged a specified harm.[165] The proposed Act defined harm[166] as an infringement of any of the human rights referred to in numerous instruments of international law: nine core UN human rights treaties,[167] two UN Declarations,[168] nine core ILO

---

[163] Canadian Network on Corporate Accountability, The Global Leadership in Business and Human Rights Act: An Act to Create an Independent Human Rights Ombudsperson for the International Extractive Sector, Draft Model Legislation. 2 November 2016, http://cnca-rcrce.ca/wp-content/uploads/2016/03/The-Global-Leadership-in-Business-and-Human-Rights-Act-An-act-to-create-an-independent-human-rights-ombudsperson-for-the-international-extractive-sector-11022016.pdf (last accessed 1 October 2018), section 6.2(i).

[164] The Extractive Sector Transparency Measures Act applies to any company engaged in, or that controls another company engaged in, the commercial development of oil, gas or minerals in Canada or abroad. This Act captures companies listed on Canadian stock exchanges that have a place of business in Canada, that do business in Canada or have assets in Canada. It requires companies to report payments of a certain size made to any government or governmental body in Canada or in a foreign state: S.C. 2014, c. 39, section 376, sections 2, 8, 9.

[165] Canadian Network on Corporate Accountability, The Global Leadership in Business and Human Rights Act: An Act to Create an Independent Human Rights Ombudsperson for the International Extractive Sector, Draft Model Legislation. 2 November 2016, http://cnca-rcrce.ca/wp-content/uploads/2016/03/The-Global-Leadership-in-Business-and-Human-Rights-Act-An-act-to-create-an-independent-human-rights-ombudsperson-for-the-international-extractive-sector-11022016.pdf (last accessed 1 October 2018), sections 6.1, 6.2.

[166] Canadian Network on Corporate Accountability, The Global Leadership in Business and Human Rights Act: An Act to Create an Independent Human Rights Ombudsperson for the International Extractive Sector, Draft Model Legislation, 2 November 2016, http://cnca-rcrce.ca/wp-content/uploads/2016/03/The-Global-Leadership-in-Business-and-Human-Rights-Act-An-act-to-create-an-independent-human-rights-ombudsperson-for-the-international-extractive-sector-11022016.pdf (last accessed 1 October 2018), section 2.5.

[167] International Covenant on Civil and Political Rights (ICCPR); International Covenant on Economic, Social and Cultural Rights (ICESCR); International Convention on the Elimination of All Forms of Racial Discrimination (ICERD); Convention on the Elimination of All Forms of Discrimination Against Women (CEDAW); Convention against Torture and Other Cruel, Inhuman or Degrading Treatment or Punishment (UNCAT); Convention on the Rights of the Child (CRC); Convention on the Protection of the Rights of All Migrant Workers and Members of Their Families (CMW); Convention on the Rights of Persons With Disabilities (CRPD); International Convention for the Protection of All Persons from Enforced Disappearance (CED).

[168] UN Declaration on the Rights of Indigenous Peoples (UNDRIP); UN Declaration on the Right and Responsibility of Individuals, Groups and Organs of Society to Promote and Protect Universally Recognized Human Rights and Fundamental Freedoms.

Conventions,[169] the Geneva Conventions and one OECD Convention.[170] Together, these sources of international human rights law would have established the formal standards for evaluating Canadian companies. When determining whether or not specified standards had been infringed, the draft Act required the Ombudsperson to consider: the practice of competent international bodies, certain international environmental standards[171] and the UN *Guiding Principles*.[172] The CNCA's Ombudsperson would also have had the discretion to consider international CSR norms, including state-based, multi-stakeholder and norms emanating from international financial institutions.[173]

In relation to these standards, a complaint could allege that a Canadian company had, by act or omission, caused or contributed to a specified harm in a foreign state.[174] An investigation would have similarly been triggered by allegations of a significant risk that such harm could occur. The same thresholds would have applied

---

[169] Indigenous and Tribal Peoples Convention, 1989 (No. 169); Freedom of Association and Protection of the Right to Organise Convention, 1948 (No. 87); Right to Organise and Collective Bargaining Convention, 1949 (No. 98); Forced Labour Convention, 1930 (No. 29); Abolition of Forced Labour Convention, 1957 (No. 105); Minimum Age Convention, 1973 (No. 138); Worst Forms of Child Labour Convention, 1999 (No. 182); Equal Remuneration Convention, 1951 (No. 100); Discrimination (Employment and Occupation) Convention, 1958 (No. 111).

[170] OECD Convention on Combating Bribery of Foreign Public Officials in International Business Transactions.

[171] Rio Declaration on Environment and Development; UN Human Rights Council, Report of the Independent Expert on the issue of human rights obligations relating to the enjoyment of a safe, clean, healthy and sustainable environment, John H. Knox. Mapping report, Un Doc. A/HRC/25/53, 30 December 2013.

[172] Canadian Network on Corporate Accountability, The Global Leadership in Business and Human Rights Act: An Act to Create an Independent Human Rights Ombudsperson for the International Extractive Sector, Draft Model Legislation. 2 November 2016, http://cnca-rcrce.ca/wp-content/uploads/2016/03/The-Global-Leadership-in-Business-and-Human-Rights-Act-An-act-to-create-an-independent-human-rights-ombudsperson-for-the-international-extractive-sector-11022016.pdf (last accessed 1 October 2018), section 13.2.

[173] OECD Guidelines on Multinational Enterprises; OECD Due Diligence Guidance for Responsible Supply Chains of Minerals from Conflict-Affected and High Risk Areas; OECD Due Diligence Guidance for Meaningful Stakeholder Engagement in the Extractive Sector; IFC Performance Standards on Environmental and Social Sustainability; Guidance Notes to those standards; the World Bank Group's Environmental, Health and Safety General Guidelines; Voluntary Principles on Security and Human Rights; Sustainability reporting guidelines of the Global Reporting Initiative; and any international Codes of Conduct, or Corporate Codes of Conduct, which the company in question has signed on to or adopted.

[174] Canadian Network on Corporate Accountability, The Global Leadership in Business and Human Rights Act: An Act to Create an Independent Human Rights Ombudsperson for the International Extractive Sector, Draft Model Legislation. 2 November 2016, http://cnca-rcrce.ca/wp-content/uploads/2016/03/The-Global-Leadership-in-Business-and-Human-Rights-Act-An-act-to-create-an-independent-human-rights-ombudsperson-for-the-international-extractive-sector-11022016.pdf (last accessed 1 October 2018), sections 6.1, 6.2. The proposed Act would not subject complaints to a limitation period and would extend a certain level of protection to complainants from civil suit in respect of their complaint: sections 4.4, 4.7.

to third parties in a material contractual relationship with a Canadian company.[175] The proposed Ombudsperson would also have had the discretion to initiate an investigation without a complaint where they suspected that such harm had occurred.[176] However, if the alleged harms were trivial or the complaint was frivolous, vexatious or not made in good faith, the Ombudsperson retained the discretion to decline to investigate.[177]

6.4 Investigatory Powers and Recommendations

In terms of the investigation itself, the CNCA proposal obliged the Ombudsperson to take into account the personal circumstances of complainants, including by designing specialized procedural rules to this end.[178] In order to collect evidence in the course of an investigation, the Ombudsperson could have received submissions and requested documents and evidence from the parties.[179] The Ombudsperson

---

[175] Canadian Network on Corporate Accountability, The Global Leadership in Business and Human Rights Act: An Act to Create an Independent Human Rights Ombudsperson for the International Extractive Sector, Draft Model Legislation. 2 November 2016, http://cnca-rcrce.ca/wp-content/uploads/2016/03/The-Global-Leadership-in-Business-and-Human-Rights-Act-An-act-to-create-an-independent-human-rights-ombudsperson-for-the-international-extractive-sector-11022016.pdf (last accessed 1 October 2018), section 6.2.

[176] Canadian Network on Corporate Accountability, The Global Leadership in Business and Human Rights Act: An Act to Create an Independent Human Rights Ombudsperson for the International Extractive Sector, Draft Model Legislation. 2 November 2016, http://cnca-rcrce.ca/wp-content/uploads/2016/03/The-Global-Leadership-in-Business-and-Human-Rights-Act-An-act-to-create-an-independent-human-rights-ombudsperson-for-the-international-extractive-sector-11022016.pdf (last accessed 1 October 2018), section 6.3.

[177] Canadian Network on Corporate Accountability, The Global Leadership in Business and Human Rights Act: An Act to Create an Independent Human Rights Ombudsperson for the International Extractive Sector, Draft Model Legislation. 2 November 2016, http://cnca-rcrce.ca/wp-content/uploads/2016/03/The-Global-Leadership-in-Business-and-Human-Rights-Act-An-act-to-create-an-independent-human-rights-ombudsperson-for-the-international-extractive-sector-11022016.pdf (last accessed 1 October 2018), section 6.4.

[178] Canadian Network on Corporate Accountability, The Global Leadership in Business and Human Rights Act: An Act to Create an Independent Human Rights Ombudsperson for the International Extractive Sector, Draft Model Legislation. 2 November 2016, http://cnca-rcrce.ca/wp-content/uploads/2016/03/The-Global-Leadership-in-Business-and-Human-Rights-Act-An-act-to-create-an-independent-human-rights-ombudsperson-for-the-international-extractive-sector-11022016.pdf (last accessed 1 October 2018), section 8.1. In particular the Ombudsperson would be required to consider the age, gender and health of the complainant, as well as the nature of the violence alleged, including sexual violence.

[179] Canadian Network on Corporate Accountability, The Global Leadership in Business and Human Rights Act: An Act to Create an Independent Human Rights Ombudsperson for the International Extractive Sector, Draft Model Legislation. 2 November 2016, http://cnca-rcrce.ca/wp-content/uploads/2016/03/The-Global-Leadership-in-Business-and-Human-Rights-Act-An-act-to-create-an-independent-human-rights-ombudsperson-for-the-international-extractive-sector-11022016.pdf (last accessed 1 October 2018), sections 8.2, 8.4, 8.5.

could also have resorted to the courts to request a warrant to search a location and/ or an order to produce documents, including the examination, under oath or not, of the person named in the order.[180] Finally, the draft legislation established terms for coordinating between the Ombudsperson's investigation and other Canadian legal procedures[181] and it would have allowed the Ombudsperson to gather evidence in a foreign state with permission.[182] In short, the Ombudsperson contemplated in the proposed Act was imbued with extensive investigatory powers, which in some cases could be enforced and supervised by a Canadian court.

The CNCA proposal provided that an investigation could be discontinued for one of three reasons. First, the investigation would end if the Ombudsperson was of the opinion that there was no harm, or risk of harm, and that there were no compelling reasons to continue the investigation.[183] Second, an investigation would discontinue

---

[180] Canadian Network on Corporate Accountability, The Global Leadership in Business and Human Rights Act: An Act to Create an Independent Human Rights Ombudsperson for the International Extractive Sector, Draft Model Legislation. 2 November 2016, http://cnca-rcrce.ca/wp-content/ uploads/2016/03/The-Global-Leadership-in-Business-and-Human-Rights-Act-An-act-to-create-an-independent-human-rights-ombudsperson-for-the-international-extractive-sector-11022016. pdf (last accessed 1 October 2018), sections 8.9, 8.10. The Act required reasonable grounds to believe that the location contained evidence that would assist in the investigation. Upon obtaining a warrant, the Ombudsperson would have been authorized to search the location and was required to report back to the justice who had issued the warrant. The ombudsperson could have also requested a court order for an investigative interview in order to gather more information, provided that reasonable attempts have been made to obtain the information by other means: section 8.11.

[181] First, it would give the Ombudsperson the power to suspend an investigation if the matter is already before a Canadian or foreign court. If the matter is in a foreign court, the Ombudsperson must be satisfied that the proceedings are independent, impartial, and not subject to delay: Canadian Network on Corporate Accountability, The Global Leadership in Business and Human Rights Act: An Act to Create an Independent Human Rights Ombudsperson for the International Extractive Sector, Draft Model Legislation. 2 November 2016, http://cnca-rcrce.ca/wp-content/ uploads/2016/03/The-Global-Leadership-in-Business-and-Human-Rights-Act-An-act-to-create-an-independent-human-rights-ombudsperson-for-the-international-extractive-sector-11022016. pdf (last accessed 1 October 2018), sections 7.1, 7.3. Second, if during an investigation the Ombudsperson believes that there is evidence of the commission of an offence against the laws of Canada or a foreign jurisdiction, they may disclose this evidence to the appropriate officials. Notably this is not required: sections 8.7, 8.8. Third, none of the information obtained in an investigative interview conducted by court order can be used in any criminal proceedings against the witness, with the exception of criminal prosecution for perjury: sections 8.14, 8.15. Fourth, upon concluding the investigation, the Ombudsperson can recommend further investigations by a separate authority: section 13.4(iv).

[182] Canadian Network on Corporate Accountability, The Global Leadership in Business and Human Rights Act: An Act to Create an Independent Human Rights Ombudsperson for the International Extractive Sector, Draft Model Legislation. 2 November 2016, http://cnca-rcrce.ca/wp-content/ uploads/2016/03/The-Global-Leadership-in-Business-and-Human-Rights-Act-An-act-to-create-an-independent-human-rights-ombudsperson-for-the-international-extractive-sector-11022016. pdf (last accessed 1 October 2018), section 9. The Ombudsperson would be required to inform the foreign government of the planned activities and would to endeavour to enter into a mutual assistance agreement with the local authorities in the foreign state.

[183] Canadian Network on Corporate Accountability, The Global Leadership in Business and Human Rights Act: An Act to Create an Independent Human Rights Ombudsperson for the International

if the parties entered into a settlement agreement in accordance with certain requirements.[184] In this respect, the draft Act would have permitted mediation, provided
that: the Ombudsperson believed the matter was appropriate for mediation; the
complainant had given informed consent to mediation; and the relevant facts were
known.[185] The Ombudsperson would have had the discretion to approve (or not) a
mediated settlement agreement, having regard to the Act's objectives.[186] Final agreements would have been binding on the parties and enforceable in a Canadian
court.[187]

The third basis upon which an investigation could conclude was if the proposed
Ombudsperson were to find that a Canadian company, or a third party with whom it
is in a material contractual relationship, had failed to respect applicable human
rights. This was defined as a situation where the entity in question had, by act or
omission, caused or contributed to harm in a foreign state, or there was a significant
risk that it would do so.[188] Upon making such a finding, the proposed Ombudsperson

---

Extractive Sector, Draft Model Legislation. 2 November 2016, http://cnca-rcrce.ca/wp-content/
uploads/2016/03/The-Global-Leadership-in-Business-and-Human-Rights-Act-An-act-to-create-
an-independent-human-rights-ombudsperson-for-the-international-extractive-sector-11022016.
pdf (last accessed 1 October 2018), section 12.1(iii).

[184] Canadian Network on Corporate Accountability, The Global Leadership in Business and Human
Rights Act: An Act to Create an Independent Human Rights Ombudsperson for the International
Extractive Sector, Draft Model Legislation. 2 November 2016, http://cnca-rcrce.ca/wp-content/
uploads/2016/03/The-Global-Leadership-in-Business-and-Human-Rights-Act-An-act-to-create-
an-independent-human-rights-ombudsperson-for-the-international-extractive-sector-11022016.
pdf (last accessed 1 October 2018), section 12.1(i).

[185] Canadian Network on Corporate Accountability, The Global Leadership in Business and Human
Rights Act: An Act to Create an Independent Human Rights Ombudsperson for the International
Extractive Sector, Draft Model Legislation. 2 November 2016, http://cnca-rcrce.ca/wp-content/
uploads/2016/03/The-Global-Leadership-in-Business-and-Human-Rights-Act-An-act-to-create-
an-independent-human-rights-ombudsperson-for-the-international-extractive-sector-11022016.
pdf (last accessed 1 October 2018), sections 11.1, 11.2. The Ombudsperson may decide to pay for
the legal expenses of the complainant(s) participating in mediation: section 11.5.

[186] Canadian Network on Corporate Accountability, The Global Leadership in Business and Human
Rights Act: An Act to Create an Independent Human Rights Ombudsperson for the International
Extractive Sector, Draft Model Legislation. 2 November 2016, http://cnca-rcrce.ca/wp-content/
uploads/2016/03/The-Global-Leadership-in-Business-and-Human-Rights-Act-An-act-to-create-
an-independent-human-rights-ombudsperson-for-the-international-extractive-sector-11022016.
pdf (last accessed 1 October 2018), section 11.7.

[187] Canadian Network on Corporate Accountability, The Global Leadership in Business and Human
Rights Act: An Act to Create an Independent Human Rights Ombudsperson for the International
Extractive Sector, Draft Model Legislation. 2 November 2016, http://cnca-rcrce.ca/wp-content/
uploads/2016/03/The-Global-Leadership-in-Business-and-Human-Rights-Act-An-act-to-create-
an-independent-human-rights-ombudsperson-for-the-international-extractive-sector-11022016.
pdf (last accessed 1 October 2018), section 11.6.

[188] Canadian Network on Corporate Accountability, The Global Leadership in Business and Human
Rights Act: An Act to Create an Independent Human Rights Ombudsperson for the International
Extractive Sector, Draft Model Legislation. 2 November 2016, http://cnca-rcrce.ca/wp-content/
uploads/2016/03/The-Global-Leadership-in-Business-and-Human-Rights-Act-An-act-to-create-
an-independent-human-rights-ombudsperson-for-the-international-extractive-sector-11022016.

was required to give any affected party reasonable notice and an opportunity to respond.[189]

Following an adverse finding, the Ombudsperson was further required to issue a public report with an opinion, reasons and appropriate recommendations "of any kind, to any person, or any agency and body of the Government of Canada".[190] With respect to the company, recommendations might have included: to remedy and repair harm done; to prevent further harm with respect to the specific complaint; or to avoid future harm in all of its operations. Recommendations could also have been directed at consultation with affected communities at the project level or at a company's consultation policies and practices more generally. The proposed Ombudsperson could have also made recommendations to the complainant, the company or a third party regarding steps to avoid conflict arising from a project. Finally, with respect to the Government of Canada, the Ombudsperson had the discretion to make recommendations, "regarding any acts or omissions in the case under investigation" or any related practice, law or policy or the need for any practice.[191]

Building on this rubric of potential recommendations following an adverse finding, the draft Act contemplated significant follow up provisions. The proposed Ombudsperson's recommendations would have included specific timeframes and the addressees of a recommendation were required to provide written notice of their progress. Moreover, complainants retained a right to offer their perspective on the implementation of recommendations and the Ombudsperson was required to issue a follow-up report.[192]

---

pdf (last accessed 1 October 2018), section 13.1.

[189] Canadian Network on Corporate Accountability, The Global Leadership in Business and Human Rights Act: An Act to Create an Independent Human Rights Ombudsperson for the International Extractive Sector, Draft Model Legislation. 2 November 2016, http://cnca-rcrce.ca/wp-content/uploads/2016/03/The-Global-Leadership-in-Business-and-Human-Rights-Act-An-act-to-create-an-independent-human-rights-ombudsperson-for-the-international-extractive-sector-11022016.pdf (last accessed 1 October 2018), section 13.12.

[190] Canadian Network on Corporate Accountability, The Global Leadership in Business and Human Rights Act: An Act to Create an Independent Human Rights Ombudsperson for the International Extractive Sector, Draft Model Legislation. 2 November 2016, http://cnca-rcrce.ca/wp-content/uploads/2016/03/The-Global-Leadership-in-Business-and-Human-Rights-Act-An-act-to-create-an-independent-human-rights-ombudsperson-for-the-international-extractive-sector-11022016.pdf (last accessed 1 October 2018), section 13.4.

[191] Canadian Network on Corporate Accountability, The Global Leadership in Business and Human Rights Act: An Act to Create an Independent Human Rights Ombudsperson for the International Extractive Sector, Draft Model Legislation. 2 November 2016, http://cnca-rcrce.ca/wp-content/uploads/2016/03/The-Global-Leadership-in-Business-and-Human-Rights-Act-An-act-to-create-an-independent-human-rights-ombudsperson-for-the-international-extractive-sector-11022016.pdf (last accessed 1 October 2018), section 13.4.

[192] Canadian Network on Corporate Accountability, The Global Leadership in Business and Human Rights Act: An Act to Create an Independent Human Rights Ombudsperson for the International Extractive Sector, Draft Model Legislation. 2 November 2016, http://cnca-rcrce.ca/wp-content/uploads/2016/03/The-Global-Leadership-in-Business-and-Human-Rights-Act-An-act-to-create-an-independent-human-rights-ombudsperson-for-the-international-extractive-sector-11022016.pdf (last accessed 1 October 2018), sections 13.5–13.7.

In this connection, it is important to acknowledge the provisions of the CNCA's proposed Act that aimed to ensure transparency throughout the grievance process: in the decision to investigate, in the investigation itself, and in the outcome. First, the investigation would have begun with notice to the subjects of the investigation, which would also be posted publically.[193] Alternatively, if the Ombudsperson decided not to investigate, the complainant would be informed in writing with reasons.[194] Where the parties agreed to a settlement, the Ombudsperson was required to issue a public report on the settlement at the conclusion of the investigation, or, in lieu of this report, the parties could agree to publically disclose a written summary of the complaint, investigation and the settlement. Notably, this joint disclosure had to be approved by the Ombudsperson in light of the draft Act's mandate to improve transparency and accountability.[195]

Finally, following the conclusion of an investigation, reports and follow-up reports would have been made public and shared with relevant international bodies as well as the federal Parliament.[196] When issuing these reports, the Ombudsperson would have had the discretion to deem sources, information or evidence obtained in the investigation confidential for reasons of privacy, commercial sensitivity, privi-

---

[193] Canadian Network on Corporate Accountability, The Global Leadership in Business and Human Rights Act: An Act to Create an Independent Human Rights Ombudsperson for the International Extractive Sector, Draft Model Legislation. 2 November 2016, http://cnca-rcrce.ca/wp-content/uploads/2016/03/The-Global-Leadership-in-Business-and-Human-Rights-Act-An-act-to-create-an-independent-human-rights-ombudsperson-for-the-international-extractive-sector-11022016.pdf (last accessed 1 October 2018), sections 6.8–6.10.

[194] Canadian Network on Corporate Accountability, The Global Leadership in Business and Human Rights Act: An Act to Create an Independent Human Rights Ombudsperson for the International Extractive Sector, Draft Model Legislation. 2 November 2016, http://cnca-rcrce.ca/wp-content/uploads/2016/03/The-Global-Leadership-in-Business-and-Human-Rights-Act-An-act-to-create-an-independent-human-rights-ombudsperson-for-the-international-extractive-sector-11022016.pdf (last accessed 1 October 2018), section 6.5. A complainant can also ask for reconsideration for the refusal to investigate. The Ombudsperson would also have extensive provisions directing the Ombudsperson's exercise of discretion to suspend an investigation where the human rights concerns have also been brought to a Canadian or foreign court: section 7.

[195] Canadian Network on Corporate Accountability, The Global Leadership in Business and Human Rights Act: An Act to Create an Independent Human Rights Ombudsperson for the International Extractive Sector, Draft Model Legislation. 2 November 2016, http://cnca-rcrce.ca/wp-content/uploads/2016/03/The-Global-Leadership-in-Business-and-Human-Rights-Act-An-act-to-create-an-independent-human-rights-ombudsperson-for-the-international-extractive-sector-11022016.pdf (last accessed 1 October 2018), section 11.8.

[196] Canadian Network on Corporate Accountability, The Global Leadership in Business and Human Rights Act: An Act to Create an Independent Human Rights Ombudsperson for the International Extractive Sector, Draft Model Legislation. 2 November 2016, http://cnca-rcrce.ca/wp-content/uploads/2016/03/The-Global-Leadership-in-Business-and-Human-Rights-Act-An-act-to-create-an-independent-human-rights-ombudsperson-for-the-international-extractive-sector-11022016.pdf (last accessed 1 October 2018), sections 13.9–13.12.

lege or safety.[197] However, the Ombudsperson would also have had the discretion to weigh these confidentiality concerns against the public interest in disclosure.[198]

6.5 Potential Sanctions

Finally, the draft *Business and Human Rights Act* would have equipped the Ombudsperson with the power to recommend a limited set of sanctions. This power would have been triggered where the proposed Ombudsperson was not satisfied that the company had taken, or was undertaking, all reasonable steps to comply with either the terms of a settlement or any recommendations. In these circumstances, the Ombudsperson could have recommended to any and all government agencies or departments that they withdraw any existing support or subsidy and terminate any promotion or protection of the company or the project for a stipulated period, or until specific conditions were met.[199] If the company was not currently receiving any such support, the Ombudsperson could have recommended that it be deemed ineligible for future support. In limited circumstances, the draft Act would have allowed the Ombudsperson to recommend sanctions of this nature before giving the company a chance to comply with recommended remedies. This route would only have been available where the Ombudsperson had found harms of such a serious nature that it would be inappropriate for the Government of Canada to provide the company with support.

Finally, the proposed legislation included a limited enforcement mechanism in relation to these narrow sanctions. If the Ombudsperson believed that the government has failed to implement the recommended sanction within the stipulated time-

---

[197] Canadian Network on Corporate Accountability, The Global Leadership in Business and Human Rights Act: An Act to Create an Independent Human Rights Ombudsperson for the International Extractive Sector, Draft Model Legislation. 2 November 2016, http://cnca-rcrce.ca/wp-content/uploads/2016/03/The-Global-Leadership-in-Business-and-Human-Rights-Act-An-act-to-create-an-independent-human-rights-ombudsperson-for-the-international-extractive-sector-11022016.pdf (last accessed 1 October 2018), section 10.

[198] Canadian Network on Corporate Accountability, The Global Leadership in Business and Human Rights Act: An Act to Create an Independent Human Rights Ombudsperson for the International Extractive Sector, Draft Model Legislation. 2 November 2016, http://cnca-rcrce.ca/wp-content/uploads/2016/03/The-Global-Leadership-in-Business-and-Human-Rights-Act-An-act-to-create-an-independent-human-rights-ombudsperson-for-the-international-extractive-sector-11022016.pdf (last accessed 1 October 2018), section 10.6. A person who might be affected by the Ombudsperson's decision to disclose otherwise confidential information in the public interest may apply to Federal Court for judicial review.

[199] Canadian Network on Corporate Accountability, The Global Leadership in Business and Human Rights Act: An Act to Create an Independent Human Rights Ombudsperson for the International Extractive Sector, Draft Model Legislation. 2 November 2016, http://cnca-rcrce.ca/wp-content/uploads/2016/03/The-Global-Leadership-in-Business-and-Human-Rights-Act-An-act-to-create-an-independent-human-rights-ombudsperson-for-the-international-extractive-sector-11022016.pdf (last accessed 1 October 2018), section 14.2.

frame, they could serve the government body in question with a notice of non-compliance, requiring it either to establish that it had complied, or to provide reasons for its actions or inactions.[200] Upon receipt of a government response, the Ombudsperson could have then applied to Federal Court for judicial review of the reasonableness of the response. Complainants would have had the opportunity to appear as a party to the review with funding for their reasonable legal expenses.[201] In sum, the proposed legislation allowed for potential enforcement (judicial review) only with respect to a decision on the part of the Canadian government *not* to withdraw support and protection from a company that had violated human rights abroad.[202]

6.6   *Analysis of the Draft* Business & Human Rights Act

The CNCA's International Extractive Industry Ombudsperson draft legislation emerged as an important innovation and strategic manoeuvre in the debate over home state non-judicial grievance mechanisms in Canada. Among its strengths, three stand out. First, its standards drew directly from a large number of international human rights instruments. Second, it envisioned relatively strong investigation, participation and public reporting features. Third, it contemplated a strong prerogative for the Ombudsperson to issue, on the basis of case-specific findings, a potentially wide range of recommendations to the Canadian government, the complainant and the company in question with respect to remedies, policies and practices.

These strengths are countered by the draft Act's relative weakness in the area of enforcement. The proposed Ombudsperson had no power to enforce its recommendations with respect to its company-specific findings, including any recommended remedies. Its only recourse vis-à-vis a non-compliant company was to attempt to leverage the withdrawal of Canadian government support in order to pressure the company to comply with applicable recommendations. If the government were to refuse to comply with this effort, such leverage would only have been available if

---

[200] Canadian Network on Corporate Accountability, The Global Leadership in Business and Human Rights Act: An Act to Create an Independent Human Rights Ombudsperson for the International Extractive Sector, Draft Model Legislation. 2 November 2016, http://cnca-rcrce.ca/wp-content/uploads/2016/03/The-Global-Leadership-in-Business-and-Human-Rights-Act-An-act-to-create-an-independent-human-rights-ombudsperson-for-the-international-extractive-sector-11022016.pdf (last accessed 1 October 2018), section 14.4.

[201] Canadian Network on Corporate Accountability, The Global Leadership in Business and Human Rights Act: An Act to Create an Independent Human Rights Ombudsperson for the International Extractive Sector, Draft Model Legislation. 2 November 2016, http://cnca-rcrce.ca/wp-content/uploads/2016/03/The-Global-Leadership-in-Business-and-Human-Rights-Act-An-act-to-create-an-independent-human-rights-ombudsperson-for-the-international-extractive-sector-11022016.pdf (last accessed 1 October 2018), section 14.5.

[202] Further research is required to identify how Canadian administrative law principles might apply to the government's response to the Ombudsperson's recommendations more generally.

the Ombudsperson could convince a Canadian court that the government's refusal was unreasonable, under administrative law principles.

The CNCA's proposed Ombudsperson regime appeared to be organized around a calculated trade-off between strong independent investigations, public transparency and broad scope for recommendations on one hand; and on the other, very limited enforcement power, including no enforcement of recommended remedies and tenuous enforcement of recommended withdrawals of government support. Access to remedy under this regime would have depended entirely on the capacity of the Ombudsperson's findings and recommendations to generate public (including governmental) pressure on companies. The proposed legislation's (albeit weak) sanction feature could not directly result in remedies. Rather, it was solely directed at the public conscience, in the sense that, if successfully activated, it could eliminate state support for an offending company. The actual impact of such a sanction on any given company would likely depend significantly on the circumstances of the company, and perhaps even more significantly, on the nature of the withdrawal of state support. Recall that the concept of state supports articulated in the draft Act was very broad. At any rate, for companies that do not receive dedicated diplomatic or financial state support, the available sanction under the proposed regime would have been greatly limited.

7   The Canadian Ombudsperson for Responsible Enterprise (January 2018)

At first it seemed that the CNCA's strategic trade-offs in its model legislation had failed to render the desired results. This chapter began with a short description of a 2017 activist protest demanding government action on the CNCA's proposal. The protestors' frustration stemmed in part from the governing Liberal Party's representations during the 2015 election campaign. At that time, Liberal Party documents professed to share "Canadians' concerns about the actions of some Canadian mining companies operating overseas" and claimed it had "long been fighting for transparency, accountability and sustainability in the mining sector."[203] The Liberals promised to ensure that corporations engaged in resource extraction with government support respect international environmental standards and human rights, including by setting up an independent Ombudsperson office to consider complaints made against Canadian companies and to investigate those complaints where warranted.[204]

---

[203] Cumming J, What the Liberals, Greens and NDP Have to Say on Mining in Canada. Huffington Post, 5 October 2015, http://www.huffingtonpost.ca/john-cumming/mining-canada-federal-election_b_8235824.html (last accessed 1 October 2018).

[204] Cumming J, What the Liberals, Greens and NDP Have to Say on Mining in Canada. Huffington Post, 5 October 2015, http://www.huffingtonpost.ca/john-cumming/mining-canada-federal-election_b_8235824.html (last accessed 1 October 2018); Canadian Network on Corporate

During the first 2 years of their 4-year mandate, the Liberals failed to make good on these promises in two consecutive budgets.[205] After the 2015 election, key federal Ministers declined to say that change was needed and refused to publicly reiterate their Party's pre-election commitments.[206] Then, in Fall 2017, the government took an unexpectedly active interest in the issues when the federal Parliamentary Subcommittee on International Human Rights decided to convene hearings on human rights and resources extraction in Latin America.

However, after several weeks of hearings, the CNCA sent an urgent letter to the subcommittee, raising serious concerns that the hearings were skewed.[207] In addition to calling very few civil society representatives, the committee ultimately declined to call any witnesses representing: Indigenous peoples and affected communities in Latin America, experts on Canada's international human rights obligations, and the proponents and legal experts behind the CNCA draft legislation.[208] The 2017 hearings were a marked departure from the 2005 SCFAIT hearings, which had invited a relatively wide range of perspectives including from human rights experts, a spectrum of civil society representatives and affected communities.[209]

As the subcommittee hearings wrapped up, advocates argued that they had been "designed to justify the do-nothing status quo" and that the process had precluded any critical examination of Canada's current policy.[210] Then, unexpectedly, this dismal assessment of the political moment was abruptly cast into doubt. In the final weeks of 2017, government officials told Canadian media that plans were underway

---

Accountability, Parliamentary Report Card, http://cnca-rcrce.ca/wp-content/uploads/2016/03/Parliamentary-Report-Card-Corporate-Accountability-for-Canadas-mining-oil-and-gas-sectors-sept-20151.pdf (last accessed 1 October 2018), p. 2.

[205] Canadian Network on Corporate Accountability, Canadian Network Expresses Concern that Federal Budget does not Mention Human Rights Ombudsperson, Press Release. 22 March 2017, http://cnca-rcrce.ca/recent-works/press-release-canadian-network-expresses-concern-that-federal-budget-does-not-mention-human-rights-ombudsperson/ (last accessed 1 October 2018).

[206] Mazereeuw P, Liberals "Seriously" Considering Mining Ombudsperson, says Federal Corporate Social Responsibility Adviser. The Hill Times, 9 November 2016, https://www.hilltimes.com/2016/11/09/feds-seriously-considering-mining-ombudsman-says-canadas-corporate-social-responsibility-envoy/86691 (last accessed 1 October 2018).

[207] Letter from Canadian Network on Corporate Accountability to the Members of the Canadian Parliamentary Subcommittee on International Human Rights, 19 October 2017 (on file with author).

[208] House of Commons, Subcommittee on International Human Rights, Human Rights Surrounding Natural Resource Extraction within Latin America. 2017 https://www.ourcommons.ca/Committees/en/SDIR/StudyActivity?studyActivityId=9618050 (last accessed 1 October 2018).

[209] House of Commons Standing Committee on Foreign Affairs and International Trade, Mining in Developing Countries: Corporate Social Responsibility. 38th Parl, 1st Sess, 14th Rep. 2005, http://www.ourcommons.ca/DocumentViewer/en/38-1/FAAE/report-14 (last accessed 1 October 2018), Appendix A.

[210] Moore J, House subcommittee hearings on mining in Latin America a public disservice: The committee hasn't heard from people most directly affected by Canadian mining operations in the region. The Hill Times, Opinion, 18 October 2017, https://www.hilltimes.com/2017/10/18/house-subcommittee-hearings-mining-latin-america-public-disservice/122327 (last accessed 1 October 2018).

to announce a change to Canada's CSR policies in the area of extractive industries abroad.[211] On January 17, 2018, the Minister of International Trade made good on this promise and announced his intention to create the Canadian Ombudsperson for Responsible Enterprise (CORE) as part of the government's "progressive trade" agenda.[212]

While the announcement involved only a few specific details, it is clear that the government's CORE mechanism will adopt many of the features proposed in the CNCA's *Business & Human Rights Act*.[213] For example, the forthcoming Ombudsperson will be mandated to independently investigate allegations of human rights abuses abroad against Canadian companies operating in the mining, oil and gas, or garment industries. The Ombudsperson will be empowered to compel documents, report independently, recommend remedy and monitor implementation. This includes recommendations for compensation, corporate policy changes and apologies, where appropriate. The Ombudsperson will also have the power to recommend changes to government policy and/or the withdrawal of trade advocacy support and Export Development Canada financial support. To support the development of the Ombudsperson's mandate and operating procedures, a Multi-Stakeholder Advisory Body (MSAB) of experts from business and civil society will be put in place. The MSAB will counsel the government on the further development of its laws, policies and practices with respect to business and human rights.

8 Conclusion and Future Research

There are many details to work out following the Canadian government's early 2018 announcement of its intention to create a Canadian Ombudsperson for Responsible Enterprise (CORE). However, there can be no doubt that this new home-state non-judicial grievance mechanism will be globally unprecedented and signals a sea change in Canadian law and policy. It is also absolutely clear that this turn of events is a direct result of nearly two decades of Canadian activism, in collaboration with partner organizations, affected communities and human rights defenders around the world. The Minister of International Trade actually acknowledged and celebrated Canadian advocates in his public address announcing the CORE.

[211] McSheffrey E, Trudeau government may dig up the truth about Canadian mines. National Observer, 6 December 2017, https://www.nationalobserver.com/2017/12/06/news/raids-incarceration-and-decimated-indigenous-land-stains-canadas-reputation (last accessed 1 October 2018).

[212] Global Affairs Canada, The Government of Canada brings leadership to responsible business conduct abroad, News Release. 17 January 2018, https://www.canada.ca/en/global-affairs/news/2018/01/the_government_ofcanadabringsleadershiptoresponsiblebusinesscond.html (last accessed 1 October 2018).

[213] Global Affairs Canada, Responsible business conduct abroad – Questions and answers. 2018, http://www.international.gc.ca/trade-agreements-accords-commerciaux/topics-domaines/other-autre/faq.aspx?lang=eng (last accessed 1 October 2018).

This chapter has examined how Canadian advocates employed law and politics to address concerns with global economic injustice in the Canadian resource sector. Four main strategies emerge from this account. First, advocates worked with affected communities abroad to document harms allegedly connected to Canadian extractive projects. In doing so, they compiled detailed case studies of social, economic and environmental harm, as well as studies based on aggregate data on infringements of civil liberties. Some case studies led to litigation in Canada, which in turn helped establish the credibility of advocates' allegations of harms. In developing their account of the nature of the problem, advocates also tracked the practices and policies employed by the Canadian state to support Canadian companies abroad. In this area, they identified insufficient government transparency, accountability, and even practices that appeared to exacerbate harm or the risk of harm.

Second, advocates engaged with Canada's voluntary CSR mechanisms, including by assisting affected communities to bring complaints. This generated the data necessary to critically examine these mechanisms' performance and outcomes. Advocates also critically analyzed the government's CSR policy normatively, against criteria for effectiveness, as well as politically, in relation to the CSR Counsellor's judgment and capacity to facilitate dialogue with civil society.

Third, advocates presented their concerns with respect to Canadian companies' conduct and Canadian state practices and policies to a wide range of international human rights bodies. These bodies in turn sought representations from the Canadian state and in some cases industry representatives or companies themselves. In their statements, international bodies were unified and categorical in their conclusion that Canada was falling short of its international law obligations in this area and that reform was necessary.

Advocates appealed to this body of data, reports and normative statements in order to pursue a fourth strategy, building a compelling case for law reform in Canada. To do so, they developed and advanced concrete reform proposals through a number of formal channels: parliamentary committee hearings, multi-stakeholder roundtables, legislation proposals to Parliament from opposition members, and finally through draft legislation proposed directly to the Liberal majority government. In the process, advocates consistently refined their law reform proposals, ultimately trading strong transparency and investigatory powers for weak or no enforcement powers.

Importantly, advocates also used political methods to advocate for their proposals. References to many of these tactics appear throughout this chapter: coalition building, speaking tours, documentary films, opinion editorials, open letters to high ranking officials, rallies, sit-ins and petitions. The main objective was to convince law makers, and the broader Canadian public, that Canada needs an effective non-judicial grievance mechanism and laws to condition state support for resource companies on compliance with human rights standards.

Running through all of these strategies is advocates' larger strategic decision to coalesce their efforts around calls for an effective home-state non-judicial grievance mechanism. From one perspective, this kind of mechanism is attractive because, relative to judicial mechanisms, it is a potentially less expensive, more accessible avenue for seeking mediated solutions and remedies in the jurisdiction that has the strongest institutions and the most power vis-à-vis companies. From a critical legal studies perspective, perhaps the most interesting feature of the mechanism now emerging in Canada is its potential capacity to expose the political, economic and legal relationship between a capital-exporting country and its transnational corporations. One important feature of the Canadian debate has been a consistent focus on state supports for companies and the legal frameworks that govern these supports.

However, at this critical point of transition and on the eve of a new status quo, there are unsurprisingly many unanswered questions. Two of these are worth mentioning here. First, it is uncertain that the emerging Canadian non-judicial grievance mechanism will actually be effective. As already observed, it represents a clear trade-off between strong investigatory and disclosure powers and zero power to enforce recommendations or remedies that benefit communities. It remains to be seen whether or not transparent and independent investigations, based on a full record of evidence, will on their own be able to improve the situation of affected communities or secure remedies in practice. While the government has now conceded that a purely voluntary approach is not effective, the question of what constitutes an effective home-state non-judicial mechanism is far from settled. In fact, with the government's announcement of a forthcoming Ombudsperson, this debate is really only beginning in Canada. As before, empirical evaluations of the mechanism's performance will be important. Another important future area of research will be to develop a clear normative framework for evaluating the effectiveness of home-state non-judicial grievance mechanisms, based on accepted principles of international law as well as on experience with their implementation.[214]

The Canadian government's announcement also neatly skirts a second line of questioning, one that has been lurking in the background for some time now. The Canadian debate on the terms and conditions that should govern the state's political, legal and economic support for companies is also only just beginning. The Ombudsperson discussion to date has focused on investigating company misconduct and withdrawing existing political and economic supports or denying future supports. However, advocates' research to date has indicated that there are serious issues with state due diligence at the outset, before support is provided. There are also unanswered questions about the norms that should govern state support and

---

[214] A starting point for the development of such a framework would be the Guiding Principles, UN Office of the High Commissioner of Human Rights, Guiding Principles on Business and Human Rights: Implementing the United Nations "Protect, Respect and Remedy" Framework, UN Doc HR/PUB/11/04, 2011; and the Maastricht Principles, External obligations (ETOS) for human rights beyond borders, Maastricht principles on extraterritorial obligations of states in the area of economic, social and cultural rights. 2013, http://www.etoconsortium.org/en/main-navigation/library/maastricht-principles/ (last accessed 1 October 2018). The Guiding Principles have been widely endorsed by states while the Maastricht Principles are preferred by many human rights organizations. Further analysis on the substantive convergences and differences between these documents on the topic of non-judicial grievance mechanisms would be useful. For a first step toward this kind of anlaysis see Kamphuis and Gardner (2019).

how the Canadian public can satisfy itself that public officials and agents are abiding by these norms.

Moreover, to date the Canadian debate has focused primarily on diplomatic and financial support (loans) for companies. However, this focus must not distract from the many ways in which the Canadian government facilitates and enables global markets and the resources extraction industry in particular.[215] There are many other legal regimes that constitute and support companies and more research is needed to identify how state supports could be addressed in these other areas. At stake is the nature of the relationship between the state and the transnational corporation, as well as the state's obligations to further the public interest, social justice and the protection of human rights.[216]

For the moment though, the commitment, creativity and tenacity of Canadian advocates must be celebrated. After nearly 20 years of sustained advocacy they have accomplished an incredible feat in moving Canadian policy from voluntary mediation to a mandatory investigation approach to alleged human rights violations abroad. Undoubtedly, the Canadian experience offers a wealth of materials for advocates around the world who seek to pressure their home states to regulate the human rights impacts of their companies' overseas operations. At the same time, it is difficult to identify a single lesson or strategy that was most important in the Canada debate. The most plausible answer is that they were all important and perhaps even essential.

This being said, the account put forward in this chapter does reveal that three important factors converged in the 2 years prior to the government's decision to change its long standing voluntary CSR policy: the publication of the 2016 JCAP report aggregating data on violence in Latin America over a 15 year period; the 2016 launch of the CNCA's draft *Business & Human Rights Act*; and the proliferation of strong statements from numerous international human rights bodies between 2016 and 2017. While the election of a new government was important, the Liberal Party's delay and clear reluctance to make good on its campaign promises indicates that a new government alone was certainly not sufficient. In the end, perhaps two things are certain: that the experiment with law's capacity to create a more just global economy is only just beginning, and that partnership between legal researchers and social justice advocates is a critical part of the journey.

Acknowledgements This chapter was supported in part by the work of the Justice & Corporate Accountability Project (JCAP). Thank you to Lavinia Floarea and Heather Hall for research assistance and to the organizers of the 2017 Thompson Rivers University (TRU) Arts Colloquium (Canada) and the 2016 Human Rights in the Extractive Industries conference at Goethe-University (Germany) for the opportunity to discuss some of the materials presented here. This paper also benefited from conversations with Shin Imai, Ruth Buchanan and Robert Wai. Any errors are my own.

---

[215] Simons and Macklin (2014) and Kamphuis (2012).

[216] Drache (2001), Augenstein and Kinley (2015) and Spiro (2013).

References

Augenstein D, Kinley D (2015) Beyond the 100 acre wood: in which international human rights law finds new ways to tame global corporate power. Int J Hum Rights 19(6):828–848

Barton BJ (1993) Canadian law of mining. Canadian Institute of Resource Law, Calgary

Brown S (ed) (2012) Struggling for effectiveness: CIDA and Canadian foreign aid. McGill-Queen's University Press, Montreal

Coumans C (2012) Mining and access to justice: from sanction and remedy to weak non-judicial grievance mechanisms. UBC Law Rev 45(3):651–690

Daniel C, Wilde-Ramsing J, Genovese K, Sandjojo V (2015) Remedy remains rare. An analysis of 15 years of NCP cases and their contribution to improve access to remedy for victims of corporate misconduct. OECD Watch, Amsterdam

Deneault A (2015) Canada: a new tax haven (trans: Browne C). TalonBooks, Vancouver

Drache D (ed) (2001) The market or the public domain: global governance & the asymmetry of power. Routledge, London

Global Witness (2016) On dangerous ground: the killing and criminalization of land and environmental defenders worldwide. Global Witness, London

Gordon T, Webber JR (2016) Blood of extraction: Canadian imperialism in Latin America. Fernwood Publishing, Nova Scotia

Hughes EL, Kwasniak AJ, Lucas AR (2016) Public lands and resources law in Canada. Irwin Law, Toronto

Imai S, Mehranvar L, Sander J (2007) Breaching indigenous law: Canadian mining in Guatemala. Indigenous Law J 6(1):101–139

Inter-American Commission on Human Rights (2015) Indigenous peoples. Afro-descendent communities, and natural resources: human rights protection in the context of extraction, exploitation, and development activities. OAS, Washington, D.C.

Kamphuis C (2012) Canadian mining companies & domestic law reform: a critical legal account. German Law J 13(9):1456–1486

Kamphuis C, Gardner L (2019) Effectiveness framework for home-state non-judicial grievance mechanisms. In: Manirabona A, Vega Cardenas Y (eds) Extractive industries and human rights in an era of global justice. Lexis Nexis, Toronto, pp 75–100

McGee B (2009) The community referendum: participatory democracy and the right to free, prior and informed consent to development. Berkeley J Int Law 27(2):570–635

Organisation for Economic Co-operation and Development (2011) OECD guiding principles for multinational enterprises 2011 edition. OECD Publishing, Paris

Seck SL (2011) Canadian mining internationally and the UN guiding principles on business and human rights. Can Yearb Int Law 49:51–116

Seck SL (2012) Home state regulation of environmental human rights harms as transnational private regulatory governance. German Law J 13(12):1363–1385

Simons P (2015) Canada's enhanced CSR strategy: human rights due diligence and access to justice for victims of extraterritorial corporate human rights abuses. Can Bus Law J 56(2):167–207

Simons P, Macklin A (2014) The governance gap: extractive industries, human rights, and the home state advantage. Routledge, New York

Spiro PJ (2013) Constraining global corporate power: a short introduction. Vanderbilt J Transnatl Law 46(4):1101–1118

Walter M, Martinez-Alier J (2010) How to be heard when nobody wants to listen: community action against mining in Argentina. Can J Dev Stud 30(1):281–301

Charis Kamphuis is assistant professor at Thompson Rivers University Faculty of Law and a PhD candidate at Osgoode Hall Law School. After clerking at the Federal Court of Appeal of Canada, she was called to the Bar of Ontario in 2009. She holds a degree in international development studies from the University of Toronto and law degrees from the University of Saskatchewan and Osgoode Hall Law School. Her research crosses multiple areas of law in relation to transnational resource extraction, corporate accountability, home-state extra-territorial responsibilities and Indigenous rights.

Transnational Human Rights and Environmental Litigation: A Study of Case Law Relating to Shell in Nigeria

Liesbeth F. H. Enneking

Contents

1   Introduction   512
2   Background   514
    2.1   The Environmental Impact of Oil Extraction Activities in the Niger Delta   514
    2.2   Corporate Accountability for Human Rights and Environmental Violations
        Abroad   516
3   Transnational Human Rights Litigation Relating to Shell Operations in Nigeria   519
    3.1   The *Wiwa*-Case (US)   519
    3.2   The *Kiobel*-Case (US)   522
    3.3   The *Kiobel II*-Case (Netherlands)   525
4   Transnational Environmental Litigation Relating to Shell Operations in Nigeria   527
    4.1   The *Akpan*-Case (Netherlands)   527
    4.2   The *Bodo*-Case (UK)   530
    4.3   The *Okpabi*-Case (UK)   531
5   Discussion   534
    5.1   Jurisdiction   535
       5.1.1   Personal Jurisdiction in Foreign Direct Liability Cases Before EU Member
            State Courts   535
       5.1.2   Personal Jurisdiction in Foreign Direct Liability Cases Before US Courts   538
    5.2   Applicable Law   540
    5.3   Legal Basis for Corporate Liability   542
    5.4   Procedural Rules and Practices   546
6   Conclusion   549
References   550

L. F. H. Enneking (✉)
Erasmus School of Law, Erasmus University Rotterdam, Rotterdam, The Netherlands
e-mail: enneking@law.eur.nl

© Springer Nature Switzerland AG 2019   511
I. Feichtner et al. (eds.), *Human Rights in the Extractive Industries*,
Interdisciplinary Studies in Human Rights 3,
https://doi.org/10.1007/978-3-030-11382-7_17

1   Introduction

In June 2017, four widows of Nigerian environmental activists initiated a civil law-suit against Royal Dutch Shell and its Nigerian subsidiary Shell Petroleum and Development Company before the Hague District Court in the Netherlands.[1] The lawsuit relates to events that took place in the Ogoniland region of the Niger delta in the mid-1990s, as residents were protesting against the environmental degrada-tion caused by oil exploration and production activities in the area while also demanding a share in oil revenues and greater political autonomy. In November 1995, government troops arrested nine leaders of the resistance movement (who later became known as the 'Ogoni Nine'), including the Nigerian author Ken Saro-Wiwa and Dr. Barinem Kiobel, and sentenced them to death after a military trial that was widely perceived as violating international standards.[2]

These events resulted not only in international outrage, but also in the pursuit of legal action by the victims' next of kin against oil multinational Shell, which was the main oil producer in the region. They accused Shell companies of having aided and abetted the Nigerian government in committing human rights abuses by, *inter alia*, providing the Nigerian military forces with logistical support, weapons, food and monetary compensation. Between 1996 and 2004, two different lawsuits were brought before US federal courts against Shell companies by two groups of Nigerian plaintiffs, who sought damages and other forms of relief for the harm they had suf-fered in relation to these events.[3] In June 2009, Shell agreed to an out-of-court set-tlement with respect to the claims filed by one of these groups, led by the son of Ken Saro-Wiwa.[4] However, this settlement did not pertain to the claims brought by the Kiobel group of plaintiffs, led by the widow of Barinem Kiobel. Litigation on these claims continued until April 2013, when the US Supreme Court affirmed a 2010 judgment by the Court of Appeals for the Second Circuit in which the case had been dismissed for lack of subject matter jurisdiction.[5]

---

[1] Prakken d'Oliveira, Shell summoned to court for involvement in unlawful executions in Nigeria. Human Rights Lawyers, 29 June 2017, http://www.prakkendoliveira.nl/en/news/shell-summoned-to-court-for-involvement-in-unlawful-executions-in-nigeria/ (last accessed 1 October 2018).

[2] Amnesty International, In the dock – Shell's complicity in the arbitrary execution of the Ogoni Nine. Amnesty International Ltd. 2017, https://www.amnestyusa.org/wp-content/uploads/2017/06/FINAL-KIOBEL-BRIEFING.pdf (last accessed 1 October 2018).

[3] See for an overview: Business & Human rights Resource Centre, Shell lawsuit (re Nigeria - Kiobel & Wiwa). https://business-humanrights.org/en/shell-lawsuit-re-nigeria-kiobel-wiwa (last accessed 21 August 2018); Center for constitutional rights, Wiwa et al v. Royal Dutch Petroleum et al. https://ccrjustice.org/home/what-we-do/our-cases/wiwa-et-al-v-royal-dutch-petroleum-et-al (last accessed 1 October 2018).

[4] See for an overview: Center for constitutional rights, Factsheet: The Case Against Shell. 24 March 2009,   https://ccrjustice.org/home/get-involved/tools-resources/fact-sheets-and-faqs/factsheet-case-against-shell (last accessed 1 October 2018).

[5] Supreme Court of the United States, Case No. 10-1491, *Kiobel v. Royal Dutch Petroleum Co.*, 133 S.Ct. 1659 (2013).

It is in the wake of these events that Esther Kiobel and three of the other widows decided to bring their case before the District Court of The Hague, where Shell has its corporate headquarters. Their claim is not the first to have been pursued before the Dutch courts against Shell in relation to the harmful impacts of its oil extraction activities in Nigeria. In 2008 and 2009, farmers from three Nigerian villages initiated claims against Shell before the Hague District Court in relation to various oil spill incidents from Shell-operated pipelines in the Niger Delta.[6] Meanwhile, other Niger Delta communities have pursued two similar cases relating to the environmental impacts of Shell's oil exploration and production activities before courts in the UK.[7]

It is sometimes suggested that in the absence of an international framework to regulate the transnational activities of multinational enterprises, litigation before domestic courts presents a much-needed strategy to hold these corporate actors accountable for the adverse human rights and environmental impacts of their activities.[8] Although courts in some host countries, including Nigeria, have been confronted with quite a number of cases in this context,[9] it is home country courts in the global north in particular that have witnessed a sharp increase over the past two decades of corporate accountability lawsuits relating to human rights violations and environmental damage in host countries.[10] Reasons for victims and NGOs in these cases to bring their claims before home country rather than host country courts often involve inadequate options for redress in the host country, for instance due to a lack of independence of the local judiciary, fear of discrimination or persecution, a local legal system that is ill-equipped to deal effectively with complex legal claims, or difficulties in getting local court verdicts enforced. At the same time, the pursuit of litigation before home country courts may be preferred because it opens up the possibility of addressing, not only before a court of law but also before the courts of public opinion in the home country, the role that the parent companies of the multinational enterprises involved should play in preventing the activities of their foreign subsidiaries or supply chain partners from having a detrimental impact on human rights and the environment in host countries.[11]

---

[6] See for an overview: Milieudefensie, Timeline: the course of the lawsuit. Friends of the Earth Netherlands https://en.milieudefensie.nl/shell-in-nigeria/timeline-the-course-of-the-lawsuit (last accessed 1 October 2018).

[7] See for an overview: Leigh Day, Nigeria - oil spills. https://www.leighday.co.uk/International/Corporate-accountability-by-issue/Environmental-damage/Nigeria (last accessed 1 October 2018) and Leigh Day, The Bodo Community v. Shell claim. https://www.leighday.co.uk/International/Further-insights/Detailed-case-studies/The-Bodo-claim (last accessed 21 August 2018).

[8] Schrempf-Stirling and Wettstein (2017); Enneking (2012a); Zerk (2006), pp. 198–240; Frynas (2004).

[9] Frynas (2004), pp. 371–373; Frynas (1999).

[10] Christensen and Hausman (2016), with respect to ATS-based litigation before US federal courts; Enneking (2017a), pp. 40–42; Enneking et al. (2016), with respect to claims brought before courts in six European countries.

[11] Enneking (2017a), p. 48; Enneking et al. (2016), p. 81; Enneking (2012a), pp. 107–117.

However, as will also be exemplified by this case law study, litigation is by no means a panacea, not even in home countries that in theory offer ample opportunities for adequate redress and public impact through litigation. This chapter will analyse and compare the aforementioned six cases against Shell (i.e., two in the US and one in the Netherlands dealing with human rights-related harm, and one in the Netherlands and two in the UK dealing with environmental harm), to highlight the opportunities and thresholds this type of litigation presents for host country citizens seeking to hold multinational enterprises accountable for the detrimental human rights and environmental impacts of their activities. It will start out with some background information on the impact of oil extraction activities in the Niger Delta, on the international debate on socially responsible business conduct, and on the issue of corporate accountability in this context (Sect. 2). It will then analyze the main legal issues at stake in the three transnational human rights cases (Sect. 3) and the three transnational environmental cases (Sect. 4) against Shell. This will be followed by a discussion of the insights that the combined study of these cases offers us (Sect. 5), and a brief conclusion (Sect. 6).

2 Background

2.1 The Environmental Impact of Oil Extraction Activities in the Niger Delta

Large-scale oil exploration and production activities in the Nigerian Niger Delta started out in the 1950s. They were handled by a joint venture operated by Shell Petroleum Development Company of Nigeria (SPDC). SPDC was at that time a (sub-)subsidiary of the Dutch Koninklijke Nederlandse Petroleum Maatschappij N.V. and the British Shell Transport and Trading Company plc, which in 2005 merged to form the Anglo-Dutch holding company Royal Dutch Shell plc (RDS).

While the oil and gas sector has played a significant role in the Nigerian economy over the past decades and continues to do so, the Nigerian government has faced significant challenges in managing the sector and in adequately governing the country's natural resources.[12] One of the main issues is that oil exploration and production activities in Nigeria have had a devastating impact on the local environment, in particular the fragile ecosystem of the Niger Delta.[13] Over the years, countless oil spill incidents have occurred in the area, partly due to sabotage and partly due to poor maintenance of the pipelines.[14]

---

[12] See in more detail: Nigeria Extractive Industries Transparency Initiative, https://eiti.org/nigeria (last accessed 1 October 2018). See also, for instance: Yakubu (2017), pp. 8–9.

[13] Yakubu (2017) and Ite et al. (2016).

[14] See in more detail, with a focus on the Ogoniland region of the Niger Delta: United Nations Environment Programme, Environmental assessment of Ogoniland. 2011, https://postconflict. unep.ch/publications/OEA/UNEP_OEA.pdf (last accessed 1 October 2018).

Especially in the Ogoniland region, strong local resistance developed throughout the late 1980s and early 1990s against the environmental consequences of local oil production activities. Local activists criticized the Nigerian government's oil policy as well as the oil companies involved, and demanded a share in oil revenues and greater political autonomy. Their protests led to violent conflict in the region, which attracted international attention and resulted in the cessation of oil exploration and production activities in the Ogoniland region in 1993. The social upheaval did not abate, however, and in November 1995 resulted in the military trial and hanging of the resistance movement's nine leaders.[15]

Meanwhile, oil spill incidents continued to occur throughout the Niger Delta, also in the Ogoniland region. In 2011, the United Nations Environment Programme (UNEP) released an extensive environmental assessment of Ogoniland, in which it strongly criticized the local oil industry for the environmental impact of their operations on the region, and the Nigerian authorities for their failure to adequately regulate those operations.[16] The report included recommendations to the Nigerian government to, *inter alia*, comprehensively review the existing legislation on contaminated site clean-up, and set up an Environmental Restoration Fund for Ogoniland, funded jointly by the government and the oil industry, with a view to conducting a major clean-up operation to restore the local environment in the Niger Delta. It also included recommendations to SPDC to, *inter alia*, review its procedures for oil spill clean-up and remediation, and improve its contracting and supervision.[17]

Still, many of the spill sites identified in the UNEP report remain contaminated to this day, as the implementation of the report has faced considerable delay.[18] At the same time, new oil spills keep occurring on a regular basis.[19] According to Shell's own reporting, in 2016 there were around 50 spill incidents from Shell-operated pipelines in Nigeria, with a total volume of around 800 tonnes of oil spilt.[20] The

---

[15] United Nations Environment Programme, Environmental assessment of Ogoniland. 2011, https://postconflict.unep.ch/publications/OEA/UNEP_OEA.pdf (last accessed 1 October 2018), p. 25; Yakubu (2017), pp. 2–5.

[16] United Nations Environment Programme, Environmental assessment of Ogoniland. 2011, https://postconflict.unep.ch/publications/OEA/UNEP_OEA.pdf (last accessed 1 October 2018), pp. 138–151.

[17] United Nations Environment Programme, Environmental assessment of Ogoniland. 2011, https://postconflict.unep.ch/publications/OEA/UNEP_OEA.pdf (last accessed 1 October 2018), pp. 205–206, 228.

[18] Ezeamalu B, 10 months after Nigerian govt's launch of Ogoni clean-up, "not a drop of oil cleaned". Premium Times, 5 April 2017, https://www.premiumtimesng.com/regional/south-south-regional/227980-10-months-nigerian-govts-launch-ogoni-clean-not-drop-oil-cleaned-group.html (last accessed 1 October 2018); Yakubu (2017).

[19] Vidal J, Niger delta oil spill clean-up launched – but could take a quarter of a century. The Guardian, 2 June 2016, https://www.theguardian.com/global-development/2016/jun/02/niger-delta-oil-spill-clean-up-launched-ogoniland-communities-1bn (last accessed 1 October 2018).

[20] Shell Sustainability Report 2016, Environmental Data, http://reports.shell.com/sustainability-report/2016/data-and-reporting/environmental-data.html (last accessed 1 October 2018).

company indicates that the far majority (90%) of the larger oil spills in that year resulted from theft and sabotage, which remains a major issue in the area.[21]

At the same time, there are some major socio-legal issues that remain unresolved. A fundamental point of contention is whether the Nigerian federal government, which has full ownership over the country's oil and gas resources, affords the Niger Delta communities where oil is produced a fair and equitable share of the revenues. On the other hand, the question arises whether it does enough to ensure that the negative impacts of oil production activities on those same communities are minimized and/or compensated. Although the oil and gas sector in Nigeria is subject to different laws and regulations, Nigerian regulatory agencies lack the capacity, resources and/or political will to enforce them.[22]

As a result, it is up to the local victims of oil pollution themselves to seek redress from the oil companies involved through negotiated settlements or local court actions. This is however problematic for several reasons, including their limited resources, long delays in the judicial process, issues of representativeness (who is entitled to bring an action with a view to protecting a public interest such as the environment), and the strict requirements of proof that are associated with the available legal bases for civil liability claims under Nigerian law. Depending on the circumstances of the case, a particular issue may arise from the fact that the plaintiffs, who typically have less technical knowledge and more limited access to relevant evidence than their corporate opponents, may need to prove that the oil spill was the result of a cause other than sabotage or vandalism in order to be able to claim compensation. Even where they are able to overcome these thresholds, they are often faced with local courts' reluctance to grant injunctions (*i.e.*, court orders compelling the corporate defendants to carry out or refrain from specific acts), low compensation awards, and—in some cases—defendants' unwillingness to abide by local court decisions.[23]

2.2 Corporate Accountability for Human Rights and Environmental Violations Abroad

The 2011 UNEP report fed into an ongoing international debate on the responsibilities of multinational enterprises for the detrimental human rights and environmental impacts of their transnational business activities. This debate has over the past two

---

[21] Shell Sustainability Report 2016, Spill prevention and response, http://reports.shell.com/sustainability-report/2016/managing-operations/our-activities-in-nigeria/spill-prevention-and-response.html (last accessed 1 October 2018).

[22] Ekhator (2016); Emeseh (2011), pp. 63–66.

[23] Emeseh (2011), pp. 64–66; Amnesty International, Nigeria: petroleum, pollution and poverty in the Niger Delta. Amnesty International Publications 2009, https://www.amnestyusa.org/reports/nigeria-petroleum-pollution-and-poverty-in-the-niger-delta-report/ (last accessed 1 October 2018), pp. 70–78.

decades resulted in growing pressure on multinational enterprises, especially those based in the global north, to prevent and where necessary remedy harm caused to people and the environment as a result of their operations—or those of their (foreign) business partners, subsidiaries and/or sub-contractors—in host countries.[24] It gained extra momentum with the publication, also in 2011, of the UN Guiding Principles on Business and Human Rights (UNGPs),[25] which set out an international policy framework relating to the duties and responsibilities of states and corporate actors in preventing and remedying corporate human rights abuse.[26]

The UNGPs have proven highly authoritative and have, despite the fact that they do not create any binding legal standards, profoundly impacted the debate on international corporate social responsibility, which encompasses human rights but also environmental, labour and health & safety issues. This has resulted in the introduction over the past few years of a variety of legislative initiatives, especially in European states, aimed at creating transparency and/or accountability as regards the detrimental human rights and environmental impacts that result from the activities of multinational enterprises. Examples include the UK Modern Slavery Act 2015 (introducing a reporting obligation with respect to labour exploitation in the production chain), the Swiss *Loi fédérale sur les prestations de sécurité privées fournies à l'étranger* (introducing an obligation for private military and security companies to prevent participation in armed conflicts abroad), and the French *Loi relative au devoir de vigilance des sociétés mères et des entreprises donneuses d'ordre* (introducing an obligation to implement a due diligence plan to prevent adverse human rights and environmental impacts, also by subsidiaries and sub-contractors).

Closely connected to these developments with respect to corporate responsibility for the detrimental human rights and environmental impacts of transnational business activities, are the transnational corporate accountability lawsuits that are the subject of this chapter. Multinational enterprises have over the past two decades increasingly been confronted with liability lawsuits brought before courts in the global north in relation to the detrimental impacts of their activities on human rights and the environment in the global south.[27] The trend towards this type of litigation started out in the mid-1990s in the US, where the majority of these 'foreign direct liability claims' have so far been pursued. It was triggered, among other things, by

---

[24] Bernaz (2017); Enneking (2012a), pp. 9–44; McBarnet et al. (2007).

[25] UN Human Rights Council, Report of the Special Representative of the Secretary General on the issue of human rights and transnational corporations and other business enterprises, John Ruggie, Guiding Principles on Business and Human Rights: Implementing the United Nations "Protect, Respect and Remedy" Framework, UN Doc. A/HRC/17/31, 21 March 2011. The United Nations Guiding Principles on Business and Human Rights, which were endorsed by the UN Human Rights Council in June 2011, UN Doc. A/HRC/RES/17/4, 16 June 2011, provide an operationalization of the 2008 "Protect, Respect and Remedy" UN policy framework for Business and Human Rights, UN Doc. A/HRC/8/5, 7 April 2008.

[26] Bernaz (2017) and Černič and Van Ho (2015).

[27] See in more detail: Enneking (2017b), pp. 989–990; Enneking (2017a), pp. 39–43; Enneking (2012a, 2014a).

the increasing use from the mid-1980s onwards of the Alien Tort Statute (ATS)[28]—a US federal statute that had been enacted in 1789 but lain dormant ever since—as a basis for subject matter jurisdiction of US federal courts over civil liability claims relating to international human rights violations committed anywhere in the world.[29] In combination with lenient rules on personal jurisdiction and a plaintiff-friendly litigation culture, this combination of factors has so far resulted in more than 150 claims before US federal courts against both US and non-US multinationals that have allegedly contributed to human rights abuses in host countries.[30]

Similar claims have been pursued against multinational enterprises before domestic courts in countries such as Australia, Canada, the UK, Sweden, the Netherlands, Germany and Italy. In the absence of an ATS equivalent outside the US federal system, most of these claims have been based on general rules of tort law. This means that most of these cases have been framed as violations of written and unwritten norms pertaining to due care with respect to the human rights, health and safety, labour circumstances and/or the natural environment of host country individuals, employees, neighbours and communities.[31] In countries like France and Switzerland, where the possibilities to push for the initiation of criminal investigations and to join criminal procedures with civil claims are relatively broad, foreign direct liability claims have mostly taken the form of criminal liability cases. In a 2015 study on corporate duties of care in the context of international corporate social responsibility, we estimated that around 40 civil and criminal liability lawsuits dealing with these issues have been initiated in the Netherlands, Belgium, Germany, France, the UK and Switzerland between 1990 and 2015.[32]

Although companies from a wide variety of industries have been confronted with these 'foreign direct liability claims', multinational enterprises in the extractive industries seem to be particularly vulnerable to this type of litigation.[33] One reason is that resource extraction has a strong impact on the lives and the living environment of individuals, neighbours, employees and communities. It presents particular challenges for fragile states and developing countries and is often seen as a key factor in triggering, escalating or sustaining violent conflict.[34] Another reason is that the host countries where resource extraction takes place often feature weak

---

[28] 28 United States Code, Paragraph 1350.

[29] Christensen and Hausman (2016); Young (2015); Enneking (2012a), pp. 77–85.

[30] See for estimates: Christensen and Hausman (2016), pp. 796–797; Drimmer and Lamoree (2011), p. 465.

[31] Enneking (2017a), pp. 40–43; Enneking (2014a); Enneking (2012a), pp. 87–91.

[32] Enneking et al. (2016), pp. 643–648, as reproduced (in English) in Enneking (2017a), p. 42.

[33] Of the around 150 lawsuits that are featured on the website of the Business & Human Rights Resource Centre, more than one-third are aimed against companies in the oil, gas & coal industry (24) and in the mining industry (28), https://business-humanrights.org/en/corporate-legal-account-ability/case-profiles/industry/natural-resources (last accessed 1 October 2018).

[34] See, in more detail: The United Nations Interagency Framework Team for Preventive Action, Toolkit and guidance for preventing land and natural resources conflict – Extractive industries and conflict. 2012, http://www.un.org/en/land-natural-resources-conflict/pdfs/GN_Extractive.pdf (last accessed 1 October 2018).

governance structures, meaning that legal standards aimed at protecting local populations from the adverse impacts of extraction are not very strict.[35] At the same time, the chances for victims of obtaining remedies before local courts in these countries may be limited due to corruption and/or favoritism, as was mentioned before, especially so if the host country government is itself involved in or stands to benefit greatly from the activities at issue, which is often the case in the extractive industries and in particular in the petroleum industry.[36] This particular combination of factors creates a strong incentive for victims to turn to courts in the home counties of the multinationals involved, usually with the help of NGOs, in search of a more adequate protection of local populations' rights and interests.

Over the past two decades, foreign direct liability claims have been pursued against a range of multinational enterprises involved in resource extraction activities in relation to the alleged human rights and environmental impacts of their operations in various host countries. These include cases against Chevron, ENI and Shell relating to the detrimental impacts of their oil exploration and production activities in the Niger Delta.[37] Shell, in addition to the aforementioned human rights-related actions before US and Dutch courts, has also faced various actions before English and Dutch courts in relation to the environmental damage caused by oil spills from pipelines in the Niger Delta.[38] These cases, and the case law that they have generated, will be the focus of the next sections.

3 Transnational Human Rights Litigation Relating to Shell Operations in Nigeria

3.1 The Wiwa-Case (US)

The claims in the *Wiwa*-case were initiated before the US District Court for the Southern District of New York in November 1996 on the basis of the Alien Tort Statute.[39] The plaintiffs sought to hold two Shell holding companies (the

---

[35] Simons (2014), pp. 16–17.

[36] Natural Resource Governance Institute, State participation and state-owned enterprises – Roles, benefits and challenges. NRGI Reader March 2015, https://resourcegovernance.org/sites/default/files/nrgi_State-Participation-and-SOEs.pdf (last accessed 1 October 2018). Extractive Industries Transparency Initiative, Role of state-owned enterprises, https://eiti.org/role-of-stateowned-enterprises (last accessed 1 October 2018).

[37] See, for an overview of cases: Business & Human Rights Resource Centre, https://business-humanrights.org/en/corporate-legal-accountability/case-profiles/industry/natural-resources (last accessed 1 October 2018). See also, for example: Simons and Macklin (2014).

[38] Business & Human Rights Resource Centre, https://business-humanrights.org/en/corporate-legal-accountability/case-profiles/company/s (last accessed 1 October 2018).

[39] See for the full timeline: Center for constitutional rights, Wiwa et al. v. Royal Dutch Petroleum et al., https://ccrjustice.org/home/what-we-do/our-cases/wiwa-et-al-v-royal-dutch-petroleum-et-al (last accessed 1 October 2018).

Netherlands-based Royal Dutch Petroleum Company and the UK-based Shell Transport and Trading Company) liable for complicity in the human rights abuses perpetrated by the Nigerian military junta against two of the environmental activists who had been executed in November 1995.[40] They claimed that the executions were part of a pattern of collaboration and/or conspiracy between the two Shell companies and the Nigerian military junta, aimed at suppressing opposition to the exploitation by Shell of oil and gas resources in the Ogoniland region and the Niger Delta more generally. As a result, the plaintiffs argued, the companies had become responsible for the violations of international human rights norms—including, *inter alia*, extrajudicial killing, torture, arbitrary detention, and crimes against humanity—by the military regime.[41]

In response to these claims, the defendant companies submitted a variety of grounds for dismissal of the case. One of the main points of contention was whether the US court seized of the matter could exercise personal jurisdiction over the defendant holding companies, which were based in England and the Netherlands. The District Court decided in 1998 that it could exercise personal jurisdiction over the defendants. The court held that the holding companies could be said to be 'doing business' in New York, as they were listed on the New York stock exchange and had an investor relations office there. It however granted the defendants' motion to dismiss the case on the basis of *forum non conveniens*, holding that England was an adequate alternative forum in which to conduct the litigation and that this would be preferable, considering the fact that the case had only few connections to the US legal order or the New York forum.[42]

The District Court's decision was reversed in 2000 by the Court of Appeals for the Second Circuit, which agreed with the lower court's finding of personal jurisdiction but disagreed with its dismissal of the case on the basis of *forum non conveniens*. The appellate court held that in balancing the different interests at stake, the District Court had given insufficient weight to the choice of the New York forum by the plaintiffs, two of whom were lawful US residents. Another factor that it considered to be relevant was the expense and inconvenience that dismissal of the case in favour of a British (or Dutch) forum would impose on the impecunious plaintiffs, as weighed against the minimal inconvenience to the defendants—also given their vast financial resources—of retaining the case in the New York forum.[43] The court also found that in particular with respect to violations of the international prohibition on torture, which was one of the international human rights violations in dispute, the

---

[40] Center for constitutional rights, Wiwa et al. Royal Dutch Petroleum et al., https://ccrjustice.org/home/what-we-do/our-cases/wiwa-et-al-v-royal-dutch-petroleum-et-al (last accessed 1 October 2018).

[41] Earthrights international, Wiwa v. Royal Dutch Shell, https://earthrights.org/wp-content/uploads/legal/Wiwa-Original-Complaint_0.pdf (last accessed 1 October 2018).

[42] United States District Court for the Southern District of New York, 25 Sept 1998, *Wiwa et al. v. Royal Dutch Petroleum and Shell Transport and Trading Company*, 96 Civ. 8386.

[43] United States Court of Appeals for the second circuit, Docket Nos. 99-7223[L], 99-7245[XAP], *Wiwa et al. v. Royal Dutch Petroleum and Shell Transport and Trading Company* (hereinafter: Wiwa v. Shell), CA 2nd Cir. 14 September 2000, 226 F.3d 88.

United States had a policy interest in providing a forum for the adjudication of claims relating to such violations, and that the District Court had failed to take account of this policy interest.[44]

An additional lawsuit was filed in 2001 against Brian Anderson, managing director of Shell's Nigerian subsidiary SPDC at the time of the incidents. In 2002, the District Court denied the defendants' further motions for dismissal with respect to the majority of the claims in both cases.[45] The lawsuits against the holding companies and Brian Anderson were joined by seven additional plaintiffs in 2003, and in 2004 a new complaint was filed against SPDC itself. The main points of contention were the question whether the court could exercise personal jurisdiction over SPDC, and the question whether the human rights violations at issue fell within the scope of the federal court's subject matter jurisdiction on the basis of the ATS. This latter question followed from a 2004 decision by the US Supreme Court on the scope and interpretation of the ATS in an unrelated ATS-based case, the *Sosa*-case. In this case, the Court had held that federal courts could only assume subject matter jurisdiction under the ATS over claims relating to violations of modern-day norms of customary international law that were universally accepted, sufficiently specific, and of an obligatory nature.[46]

With respect to the first issue, the District Court determined in 2008 that SPDC did not have the necessary 'continuous and systematic business contacts with the United States' for the court to assume personal jurisdiction over SPDC.[47] This decision was vacated and remanded, however, by summary order of the Court of Appeals in early June 2009, as the court considered that the plaintiffs had not had sufficient opportunities for discovery of evidence relevant to the issue.[48] With respect to the second issue, the District Court determined in April 2009 that all but one of the customary international law norms at stake in the cases against the holding

---

[44] United States Court of Appeals for the second circuit, Docket Nos. 99-7223[L], 99-7245[XAP], *Wiwa et al. v. Royal Dutch Petroleum and Shell Transport and Trading Company* (hereinafter: Wiwa v. Shell), CA 2nd Cir. 14 September 2000, 226 F.3d 88, paras. 56–66, where the court explains that in passing the Torture Victim Prevention Act (28 U.S.C. § 1350) in 1991, which resembles the 1789 Alien Tort Statute but has both a narrower focus (torture under colour of law of a foreign nation) and a broader legal scope, the US Congress expressed a policy of U.S. law favouring the adjudication in U.S. courts of suits related to torture in violation of international law.

[45] Earthrights international, United States District Court for the Southern District of New York, 2002 U.S. Dist. LEXIS 3293, *Wiwa et al. v. Royal Dutch Petroleum and Shell Transport and Trading Company, Wiwa et al. v Brian Anderson*, 22 February 2002, https://earthrights.org/wp-content/uploads/legal/Wiwa-district-court-opinion-Feb-2002.pdf (last accessed 1 October 2018).

[46] United States Supreme Court, No. 03–339, *Sosa v. Alvarez-Machain*, 542 U.S. 692 (2004).

[47] United States District Court Southern District of New York, Case 1:04-cv-02665-KMW-HBP, Document 31, *Wiwa et al. v. Royal Dutch Petroleum and Shell Transport and Trading Company, Wiwa et al. v Shell Petroleum Development Company of Nigeria*, 4 March 2008, https://ccrjustice.org/sites/default/files/assets/3.4.08%20Order%20and%20Opinion%20%2331.pdf (last accessed 1 October 2018).

[48] United States Court of Appeals for the second circuit, Case 1:01-cv-01909-KMW-HBP, Document 112, *Wiwa et al. v. Shell Petroleum Development Company of Nigeria*, CA 2nd Cir. 29 June 2009, 08-1803 Cv.

companies and Brian Anderson were sufficiently universal, specific and obligatory to meet the *Sosa*-standard and thus to confer subject matter jurisdiction upon it under the ATS. This meant that these cases were allowed to move forward to trial on the merits.[49]

On 8 June 2009, on the eve of trial of the cases against the holding companies and Brian Anderson and less than a week after the Court of Appeals' decision to remand the case against SPDC, the parties came to an out-of-court settlement. Although it was stipulated in the agreement that the defendants in these three cases denied any wrongdoing or liability, the defendants agreed to settle with the plaintiffs in view of the uncertainties, burden and expense that a continuation of the litigation would present. The settlement sum of $15.5 million was meant to provide the plaintiffs involved with compensation and to cover a portion of their legal costs; in addition, a trust was established for the benefit of the Ogoni people.[50] As part of the settlement, the claims brought against the Shell holding companies, Brian Anderson and SPDC were dismissed.

3.2   The **Kiobel**-*Case (US)*[51]

In 2002, a very similar set of claims had been filed against Shell before the same New York District Court by Esther Kiobel, the wife of one of the other activists who had been killed, and a number of other Nigerians from the Ogoni region.[52] In this case, the defendant holding companies focused their defense on the issue whether the claims fell within the subject matter jurisdiction of the federal court under the ATS. In September 2006, the District Court partly granted and partly denied a motion to dismiss all claims brought by the defendants, holding that only those claims relating to Shell's alleged involvement in torture, arbitrary arrest and detention, and crimes against humanity by the Nigerian military, were actionable under the ATS.[53] It did so with reference to the aforementioned *Sosa*-case, in which the

---

[49] United States District Court Southern District of New York, *Wiwa et al. v. Royal Dutch Petroleum, Wiwa et al. v Brian Anderson*, 23 April 2009, https://ccrjustice.org/sites/default/files/assets/04.23.09%20Judge%20Wood%20Order%20regarding%20SMJ.pdf (last accessed 1 October 2018).

[50] United States District Court Southern District of New York, *Wiwa et al. v. Royal Dutch Petroleum, Wiwa et al. v Brian Anderson*, Settlement Agreement and Mutual Release, https://ccrjustice.org/sites/default/files/assets/Wiwa_v_Shell_SETTLEMENT_AGREEMENT.Signed-1.pdf (last accessed 1 October 2018).

[51] This section is partly based on Enneking (2012b).

[52] See for the full timeline: Center for constitutional rights, Kiobel v. Royal Dutch Petroleum Co. (Amicus), https://ccrjustice.org/home/what-we-do/our-cases/kiobel-v-royal-dutch-petroleum-co-amicus (last accessed 1 October 2018).

[53] United States District Court Southern District of New York, 02 Civ. 7618, *Kiobel et al. v. Royal Dutch Petroleum Company and Shell Transport and Trading Company*, 29 September 2006, https://ccrjustice.org/sites/default/files/assets/2006.09.29_Order_re_interloctory_appeal.pdf (last

Supreme Court had set out that only violations of contemporary norms of customary international law with the same definite content and acceptance among civilized nations as "the historical paradigms familiar when [the ATS] was enacted", could be the subject of ATS-claims.[54]

However, while providing some clarification with respect to the interpretation and scope of application of the Alien Tort Statute, the *Sosa*-judgment had left many issues unresolved. One unresolved question was whether claims against corporate rather than individual defendants were actionable under the Alien Tort Statute. This question, which had not been dealt with in the District Court's judgment and also had not been briefed or argued on appeal,[55] became the focal point of a summary judgment rendered by the Court of Appeals for the Second Circuit in 2010, in which the case was dismissed altogether.[56]

In a majority opinion, the court held that civil claims against corporate actors do not fall within the scope of the subject-matter jurisdiction granted by the ATS, meaning that corporate actors cannot be held liable at all under this statute for their involvement in international human rights violations. It considered, first of all, that the scope of liability under the ATS is governed by standards of customary international law rather than by (the more lenient) standards of domestic federal law. It then considered that there are no specific, universal and obligatory norms of customary international law that hold corporations liable for violations of the law of nations, including international human rights violations. This led to the conclusion that "[...] *corporate liability has not attained a discernible, much less universal, acceptance among nations of the world in their relations inter se, and it cannot, as a result, form the basis of a suit under the ATS*".[57]

The Appeals Court's decision, which effectively closed the door to all ATS-based claims against corporate defendants (at least in the Second Circuit), gave rise to much controversy. The decision itself was not unanimous, with one of the three judges concurring only in the dismissal of the complaint, but not in the opinion itself.[58] Appeals Courts in a number of other circuits clearly indicated in subsequent rulings in ATS-based foreign direct liability cases that they rejected the Second Circuit's reading of corporate liability under the ATS.[59] Still, the decision delivered

---

accessed 1 October 2018).

[54] United States Supreme Court, No. 03–339, *Sosa v. Alvarez-Machain*, 542 U.S. 692 (2004).

[55] See the information in the timeline at Center for constitutional rights, Kiobel v. Royal Dutch Petroleum Co. (Amicus), https://ccrjustice.org/home/what-we-do/our-cases/kiobel-v-royal-dutch-petroleum-co-amicus (last accessed 1 October 2018).

[56] United States Court of Appeals for the second circuit, 621 F3d 111, *Kiobel et al. v. Royal Dutch Petroleum Company and Shell Transport and Trading Company*, 17 September 2010.

[57] United States Court of Appeals for the second circuit, 621 F3d 111, *Kiobel et al. v. Royal Dutch Petroleum Company and Shell Transport and Trading Company*, 17 September 2010, pp. 148–149.

[58] United States Court of Appeals for the second circuit, 621 F3d 111, *Kiobel et al. v. Royal Dutch Petroleum Company and Shell Transport and Trading Company*, 17 September 2010, pp. 149–188.

[59] Enneking (2012a), p. 124.

a painful blow to those propagating ATS-based civil litigation as a way to hold corporate actors accountable before US federal courts for their involvement in international human rights violations perpetrated abroad, and led commentators to query whether the ruling meant the end of ATS-claims against corporate defendants.[60]

The plaintiffs petitioned the US Supreme Court, which in October 2011 agreed to hear their appeal on the issue of corporate liability under the ATS. In a somewhat unusual turn of events, however, the Supreme Court in March 2012, following oral arguments on the issue, asked to be briefed by the parties on a different, broader issue. The question raised by the Court was whether the ATS did in fact allow US federal courts to hear lawsuits in relation to alleged international human rights violations that had occurred outside of the territory of the United States. This question relating to the extraterritorial scope of the ATS had not yet been dealt with specifically in any of the ATS-cases. It was particularly pertinent in the *Kiobel*-case, however, because of the fact that it involved foreign plaintiffs, foreign defendants and conduct occurring outside the US. The question of extraterritorial scope had not come up previously as an issue of personal jurisdiction or *forum non conveniens* in the *Kiobel*-case, since the defendant holding companies, perhaps in view of the Court of Appeals' 2000 decision in the *Wiwa*-case, had not filed for dismissal on that basis.

In April 2013, the US Supreme Court issued a judgment in which it affirmed the dismissal of the *Kiobel*-case by the Court of Appeals for the Second Circuit, albeit on the basis of its interpretation of the extraterritorial scope of the ATS rather than on the basis of the issue of corporate liability under the ATS that had been raised by the Court of Appeals.[61] The majority opinion relied on the 'presumption against extraterritorial application', a canon of statutory interpretation according to which a US statute does not apply extraterritorially unless it clearly indicates otherwise. The majority argued that since the drafters of the ATS in 1789 had not explicitly provided that the statute's reach should extend beyond US territory, it must be assumed that the statute only applies to norm violations perpetrated within the US (or on the high seas). The opinion was largely motivated by concerns regarding the potential foreign policy consequences of allowing ATS-based claims with limited connections to the US legal order to be dealt with by US courts. According to the majority, "[…] *there is no indication that the ATS was passed to make the United States a uniquely hospitable forum for the enforcement of international norms*".[62]

Still, the Supreme Court's majority opinion in the Kiobel-case has left some room for maneuver, as it suggested that the presumption against extraterritorial

---

[60] Keitner CI, Keitner on Kiobel and the future of the Alien Tort Statute. Conflict of Laws weblog 21 September 2010, http://conflictoflaws.net/2010/keitner-on-kiobel-and-the-future-of-the-alien-tort-statute (last accessed 1 October 2018); Childress T, Is it the end of the Alien Tort Statute?. Conflict of Laws weblog 17 September 2010, http://conflictoflaws.net/2010/is-it-the-end-of-the-alien-tort-statute (last accessed 1 October 2018).

[61] United States Supreme Court, No. 10–1491, *Kiobel v. Royal Dutch Petroleum*, 133 S.Ct. 1659 (2013).

[62] United States Supreme Court, No. 10–1491, *Kiobel v. Royal Dutch Petroleum*, 133 S.Ct. 1659 (2013), p. 1668.

application may be displaced in cases that "[...] *touch and concern the territory of the United States* [...] *with sufficient force*".[63] It should be noted, however, that in a more recent decision the Supreme Court has put further restrictions on the role that US federal courts may play in providing judicial remedies for (corporate) human rights violations in a transnational context on the basis of the ATS (see Sect. 5.3).[64]

3.3 The Kiobel II-*Case (Netherlands)*

As it turns out, the 2013 decision by the US Supreme Court in the *Kiobel*-case, 11 years after the case was initiated and 17 years after the events that it sought to address had taken place, did not put to an end the legal dispute between Esther Kiobel and Shell. Since the case was dismissed in the US on jurisdictional grounds (i.e., the scope of the ATS) and not on the merits (i.e., the issue of liability), Esther Kiobel and three other widows of the deceased Nigerian activists were able to file the case anew before the District Court in The Hague (without raising any issues relating to the recognition of foreign judgments).

The widows submitted a claim based on domestic Nigerian human rights law seeking a declaratory judgment by the Dutch court that RDS (as well as its predecessors Shell Petroleum Company and Shell Transport and Trading Company) and SPDC are liable for complicity in the human rights violations that were perpetrated by the Nigerian military government against the Ogoni Nine in 1995. In addition, they demanded a public apology by Shell, compensatory damages (for material and immaterial harm), and exemplary damages (a form of damages aimed not at compensating the harm suffered by the victims but rather at punishing the perpetrator for its misconduct and deterring similar misconduct in the future).[65]

At the time of writing, this case is still at a preliminary stage and has thus not yet generated any case law in the Netherlands. It has, however, led to an interesting decision by a US federal court due to the fact that the plaintiffs, in preparation for this lawsuit, filed a petition in a New York District Court seeking access to documents relating to the human rights cases against Shell that had been litigated in the US. Basis for the petition was the US Foreign Legal Assistance Statute (28 U.S.C. § 1782), which allows for judicial assistance by US federal courts to plaintiffs in international litigation, also with the aim of encouraging foreign courts to provide similar assistance in cases brought before US courts. As discovery in the different but related US actions against Shell had been shared, the documents concerned also included those that were produced in the course of the extensive discovery taken in the *Wiwa*-cases.

---

[63] United States Supreme Court, No. 10–1491, *Kiobel v. Royal Dutch Petroleum*, 133 S.Ct. 1659 (2013), p. 1669.

[64] United States Supreme Court, No. 16–499, *Joseph Jesner et al. v. Arab Bank*, PLC, 548 U.S. (2018).

[65] Statement of claim, on file with the author, pp. 43–46, 113–115.

In January 2017, the US District Court for the Southern District of New York ordered the law firm that had represented Shell in the US actions, Cravath, Swaine & Moore, LLP, to hand over the requested documents for use in the proceedings against Shell before the Hague District Court, subject to a confidentiality agreement between the parties.[66] The judge considered, among other things, that absent judicial assistance by the US court the Dutch action possibly could not proceed, since Dutch procedural law requires sufficient evidence to be presented at the outset of the proceedings and since Shell had argued in a related case (the *Akpan*-case)[67] that it was no longer in possession of many of the requested documents. Furthermore, the judge was not convinced by the defendants' argument that Dutch courts would be unreceptive to such assistance—despite the fact that the Dutch government had, in an *amicus brief* in relation to the *Kiobel*-case,[68] expressed concern over "plaintiff-favoring" US rules of civil procedure like those relating to discovery. The mere fact that the Dutch legal system has more limited rules of discovery would, according to the judge, not necessarily mean that Dutch courts would object to judicial assistance by a US court on this matter.[69]

In February 2017, Cravath, Swaine & Moore filed an appeal and applied for a stay of the court order pending the appeal; that stay was granted in March 2017.[70] In July 2018, the US Court of Appeals for the Second Circuit reversed the District Court's order that the law firm should hand over the requested documents for use in the Dutch *Kiobel*-case.[71] It held that although the District Court had jurisdiction over Kiobel's petition, granting it was an abuse of discretion. Circumstances that the court deemed relevant were the fact that the real party from whom documents were sought—*i.e.* Shell—was itself a participant in the proceedings in the Netherlands, thus diminishing the need for legal assistance by US courts, and the fact that the petition appeared to be an attempt to circumvent the more restrictive discovery practices in the Netherlands. Further reasons for the Appeals Court to reverse the order involved the fact that the documents had been made available in the prior proceedings

---

[66] In repetition by Esther Kiobel […], United States District Court Southern District of New York, No. 1:2016cv07992, Document 21, *Kiobel v. Cravath, Swaine & Moore, LLP*, 24 January 2017, http://law.justia.com/cases/federal/district-courts/new-york/nysdce/1:2016cv07992/463897/21/ (last accessed 1 October 2018).

[67] See Sect. 4.1 for a more detailed discussion of this case.

[68] See, with further references, Enneking (2012b), p. 399.

[69] In repetition by Esther Kiobel […], United States District Court Southern District of New York, No. 1:2016cv07992, Document 21, *Kiobel v. Cravath, Swaine & Moore, LLP*, 24 January 2017, http://law.justia.com/cases/federal/district-courts/new-york/nysdce/1:2016cv07992/463897/21/ (last accessed 1 October 2018).

[70] In repetition by Esther Kiobel […], United States District Court Southern District of New York, Case 1:16-cv-07992-AKH, Document 29, *Kiobel v. Cravath, Swaine & Moore, LLP*, 2 March 2017, http://royaldutchshellplc.com/wp-content/uploads/2017/03/Kiobeldoc29.pdf (last accessed 1 October 2018).

[71] United States Court of Appeals for the Second circuit, No. 17-424-cv, *Esther Kiobel v. Cravath, Swaine & Moore LLP*, 10 July 2018, https://cases.justia.com/federal/appellate-courts/ca2/17-424/17-424-2018-07-10.pdf (last accessed 1 October 2018).

before US courts subject to a confidentiality order that expressly barred Kiobel from using the documents in any other litigation, and concerns for the impact that a grant of the petition in this case might have on lawyer-client relations also in other cases.[72]

4 Transnational Environmental Litigation Relating to Shell Operations in Nigeria

4.1 The Akpan-Case (Netherlands)[73]

In 2008 and 2009, a number of civil liability claims were filed before the Hague District Court against RDS and SPDC by four Nigerian farmers and the Dutch NGO Milieudefensie, in relation to various oil spill incidents from SPDC-operated pipelines in the Niger Delta. The farmers claimed that the oil spills had caused damage to their lands and fishponds and had compromised their livelihoods, and that the defendant companies were liable for this damage on the basis of the tort of negligence under Nigerian law.

The core allegation against the Nigerian subsidiary was that it had not exercised due care in preventing the oil spills from occurring, by failing to take adequate measures to prevent the spills and/or to mitigate their consequences, and by failing to properly clean up the contaminated sites afterwards. The core allegation against the parent company was that it had failed to exercise due care by not using its influence over the group's environmental policies to ensure that the local oil extraction activities engaged in by its Nigerian subsidiary were undertaken with due care for the local population and the local environment. On the basis of these allegations, the plaintiffs asked the court for a declaratory judgment that the defendant companies were jointly and severally liable, as well as for court orders compelling the defendants to carry out overdue maintenance on the pipelines, to complete the clean-up of the affected lands and fishponds, and to draw up contingency plans for future oil spills.[74]

The defendant companies contested plaintiffs' claims on a number of grounds. Among the main points of contention were the questions whether the Dutch court could assume jurisdiction over the claims against the Nigerian subsidiary, whether the oil spills had been caused by faulty maintenance (as claimed by the plaintiffs) or by sabotage (as claimed by the defendants), and whether under Nigerian law a

---

[72] United States Court of Appeals for the Second circuit, No. 17-424-cv, *Esther Kiobel v. Cravath, Swaine & Moore LLP*, 10 July 2018, https://cases.justia.com/federal/appellate-courts/ca2/17-424/17-424-2018-07-10.pdf (last accessed 1 October 2018).

[73] This section is partly based on Enneking (2014a).

[74] See the court documents at Milieudefensie, Shell courtcase: Motion to produce documents Goi, https://milieudefensie.nl/actueel/defense-in-843a-motion-oruma.pdf (last accessed 1 October 2018).

parent company owes a duty of care towards third parties that may suffer harm as a result of activities carried out by its (sub-)subsidiary.

In December 2009 and February 2010, the District Court determined that it had jurisdiction to hear not only the claims against the parent company, but also those against the Nigeria-based subsidiary. The court's jurisdiction over the claims against the parent company was a given under the EU's Brussels I Regulation,[75] which deals with the jurisdiction of EU Member State courts in civil and commercial matters. Pursuant to the Regulation's general rule, Dutch courts have jurisdiction over claims against corporate defendants that are domiciled (*i.e.* have their statutory seat, central administration and/or principal place of business) in the Netherlands, which was the case for RDS as it is headquartered in the Netherlands.[76]

By contrast, the court's jurisdiction over the claims against the foreign subsidiary was by no means self-evident, since these fell outside the scope of the Brussels I regime (with the defendant not being domiciled in the Netherlands nor in any other EU Member State) and had only limited connections with the Dutch legal order. Nonetheless, the court assumed jurisdiction also over the claims against the subsidiary on the basis of a Dutch domestic rule on international jurisdiction that allows Dutch courts to exercise jurisdiction over claims against co-defendants in proceedings in which they have jurisdiction with respect to one of the defendants.[77] The District Court decided that the causes of action against the two defendants in this case were connected in such a way as to justify a joint consideration for reasons of efficiency. It rejected the defendants' argument that the claims against the parent company constituted an abuse of procedural rights as they were 'evidently without merit' and 'merely serve(d) as an anchor' to create jurisdiction over the claims against the subsidiary.[78]

In another interlocutory ruling in September 2011, the court determined, among other things, that the applicable law on the basis of which the claims were to be adjudicated was Nigerian tort law, and dismissed a request made by the plaintiffs for Shell to provide exhibits of certain key evidentiary documents.[79]

In its final ruling in January 2013, the court, on the basis of the evidence presented to it, came to the conclusion that the oil spills were the result of sabotage, and not the result of faulty maintenance as had been argued by the plaintiffs. This, in

---

[75] Council Regulation (EC) No 44/2001 of 22 December 2000 on jurisdiction and the recognition and enforcement of judgments in civil and commercial matters, OJ 2001 L 12/1 (16 January 2001) (hereinafter: Brussels I Regulation), which has been replaced for proceedings instituted on or after 10 January 2015 by the Regulation (EU) No. 1215/2012 of the European Parliament and of the Council of 12 December 2012 on jurisdiction and the recognition and enforcement of judgments in civil and commercial matters (recast), OJ 2012 L 351/1 (hereinafter: Brussels I Regulation (recast)).

[76] Articles 2 and 60 Brussels I Regulation (now Articles 4 and 63 Brussels I Regulation (recast)).

[77] Article 7(1) Dutch Code of Civil Procedure.

[78] The Hague District Court, 24 February 2010, *Akpan et al. v Royal Dutch Shell and Shell Petroleum Development Company of Nigeria*, ECLI:NL:RBSGR:2010:BM1469, paras. 3.1–3.8.

[79] The Hague District Court, 24 February 2010, *Akpan et al. v. Royal Dutch Shell and Shell Petroleum Development Company of Nigeria*, ECLI:NL:RBSGR:2010:BM1469.

combination with the fact that under Nigerian law the operator of an oil pipeline is not liable, in principle, for harm resulting from oil spills caused by sabotage, led the court to dismiss the claims against the Nigerian Shell subsidiary SPDC in two out of the three proceedings.[80] The court also dismissed all of the claims against the parent company RDS, holding that under Nigerian tort law a parent company does not in principle have a legal obligation to prevent its subsidiaries from causing harm to third parties except under special circumstances, which the court did not find to exist.[81]

Still, the court did not send the plaintiffs home empty-handed, as it did grant the claims against SPDC in one of the proceedings that related to two oil spills in 2006 and 2007 from an abandoned wellhead near the village of Ikot Ada Udo (the *Akpan*-case). It ordered SPDC to pay compensation for the resulting loss. Although starting, also here, from the assumption that the immediate cause of the oil spills had been sabotage, the court in this specific case decided that SPDC had been negligent in leaving behind the wellhead without adequately securing it, thus making it easy for saboteurs to unscrew its valves. This led the court to conclude that in failing to take sufficient precautions against the risk of sabotage, SPDC had violated the duty of care it owed to the neighbouring farmers.[82]

In December 2015, the Hague Court of Appeal confirmed the District Court's findings that jurisdiction existed not only with respect to the claims against the parent company but also those against the subsidiary, and that the claims against the parent company were not evidently without merit.[83] Although the decision was an interlocutory judgment on a number of preliminary issues and as such did not address the question of liability, the court did indicate that it considered parent company liability to be a possible scenario in this type of litigation and also in the case at hand.[84] It denied a request by the defendant companies for an interlocutory appeal, which means that they will have to wait until the Court has rendered its final judgment on the merits of the case before they may file an appeal to the Dutch Supreme Court.[85] However, the proceedings in the case have stalled after this December 2015

---

[80] The Hague District Court, 30 January 2013, *Dooh et al. v Royal Dutch Shell and Shell Petroleum Development Company of Nigeria*, ECLI:NL:RBDHA:2013:BY9845, paras. 4.43–4.58; The Hague District Court, 30 January 2013, *Oguru et al. v Royal Dutch Shell and Shell Petroleum Development Company of Nigeria*, ECLI:NL:RBDHA:2013:BY9850, paras. 4.45–4.60.

[81] The Hague District Court, 30 January 2013, *Akpan et al. v. Royal Dutch Shell and Shell Petroleum Development Company of Nigeria*, ECLI:NL:RBDHA:2013:BY9854, paras. 4.26–4.34.

[82] The Hague District Court, 30 January 2013, *Akpan et al. v. Royal Dutch Shell and Shell Petroleum Development Company of Nigeria*, ECLI:NL:RBDHA:2013:BY9854, paras. 4.38–4.46.

[83] The Hague Court of Appeal, 18 December 2015, *Akpan et al. v. Royal Dutch Shell and Shell Petroleum and Development Company of Nigeria*, ECLI:NL:GHDHA:22015:3587.

[84] See, for a translation of relevant quotes: Enneking (2017b).

[85] The Hague Court of Appeal, 18 December 2015, *Akpan et al. v. Royal Dutch Shell and Shell Petroleum and Development Company of Nigeria*, ECLI:NL:GHDHA:22015:3587, para. 2.2. See, in more detail: Enneking (2017b).

decision pending the results of an expert study on the causes of the oil spills, meaning that the court has yet to reach a verdict on the merits of the case.[86]

4.2   The Bodo-Case (UK)

In March 2012, a large group of Nigerian farmers and fishermen filed a civil liability
suit before the London High Court against RDS and SPDC in relation to two oil
spill incidents in 2008 and 2009, close to the Bodo village in the Niger Delta. The
plaintiffs sought to hold the two defendant companies liable for the damage caused
by these spills to their health, lands and livelihoods, claiming that the spills were a
result of the old age and poor maintenance of the Shell-operated pipelines in question and that Shell had been too slow in responding to the incidents. They demanded
compensation of the damage they had suffered as a result of the oil spills as well as
a court order obliging Shell to adequately clean up the affected areas.[87]

In July 2011, following a statement by the plaintiff's lawyers that they were
intending to file a lawsuit on this matter, SPDC admitted liability for the two oil
spills. A formal agreement was subsequently concluded between RDS and the
plaintiffs holding that SPDC would accept liability under Nigerian law and that it
would accept the jurisdiction of the English courts, on the condition that no further
claims would be pursued on the matter against the parent company RDS.[88] However,
in subsequent negotiations the parties were not able to come to an agreement, which
resulted in the submission of the matter to the English High Court. Subsequent
negotiations also failed, as the parties were unable to agree on the amount of oil spilt
and the extent of the damage caused by the oil spills.[89]

In June 2014, a first judgment was rendered on a number of preliminary issues
relating to the interpretation of the Nigerian legal framework applicable to the
case.[90] Two of the key issues at stake were whether Nigerian statutory law governed
the claims to the exclusion of other potential legal bases (like the common law torts
of negligence and/or public nuisance), and whether under Nigerian statutory law

---

[86] See milieudefensie, Shell in Nigeria, Tijdlijn: verloop van de rechtszaak tegen Shell, https://
milieudefensie.nl/shell-in-nigeria/tijdlijn-rechtszaak-shell (last accessed 1 October 2018), where it
is mentioned that the experts have been appointed only in March 2018.

[87] See, in more detail and with further references: Business & Human Rights Resource Centre,
Shell, http://business-humanrights.org/en/shell-lawsuit-oil-spills-bodo-community-in-nigeria (last
accessed 1 October 2018).

[88] Compare: The United Kingdom High Court of Justice, 2017 EWHC 89 (TCC), *His Royal
Highness Emere Godwin Bebe Okpabi and Others v. Royal Dutch Shell Plc and Shell Petroleum
Development Company of Nigeria Ltd*, paras. 40–43.

[89] Leigh Day, History of the Bodo litigation, https://www.leighday.co.uk/International/Further-
insights/Detailed-case-studies/The-Bodo-claim/History-of-the-Bodo-litigation (last accessed 1
October 2018).

[90] The United Kingdom High Court of Justice, [2014] EWHC 1973 (TCC), *The Bodo Community
and others v The Shell Petroleum Development Company of Nigeria Ltd*.

SPDC could be held liable for damage caused by oil spills from its pipelines if those originated in sabotage rather than faulty maintenance.[91] The presiding judge, Justice Akenhead, decided on the basis of an assessment of relevant Nigerian statutory provisions and case law that the plaintiffs could only claim compensation on the basis of statutory provisions in this case.[92] He further decided that under the relevant provisions, damage caused by breakage or leakage from pipelines as a result of third party malicious acts was in principle excluded and thus not recoverable, although there remained a theoretical possibility of liability for neglect in the protection of the pipeline.[93]

In January 2015, just a few months before the High Court was set to proceed to a further examination of the merits of the case on the basis of the evidence produced, the parties reached an out-of-court settlement. As part of this settlement, SPDC agreed to pay £ 35 million to the individual plaintiffs and another £ 20 million to the Bodo community as a whole. In addition, the company promised to start with the clean-up of the oil damage in the affected area. According to the plaintiffs' lawyers, the judgment resulted in one of the largest payouts to a community following environmental damage.[94]

4.3 The Okpabi-Case (UK)

In late 2015 and early 2016, two sets of damages claims were filed against RDS and SPDC on behalf of over 40,000 Nigerian plaintiffs in relation to pollution and environmental damage caused by oil spills from Shell-operated pipelines in and around the Ogale and Bille communities. The plaintiffs brought their claims, in which they applied for both damages and injunctive relief, before the London High Court, which however dismissed the case in January 2017.[95] In its judgment, the court dealt with a number of preliminary issues, including first and foremost the question

---

[91] The United Kingdom High Court of Justice, [2014] EWHC 1973 (TCC), *The Bodo Community and others v The Shell Petroleum Development Company of Nigeria Ltd*, para. 9.

[92] The United Kingdom High Court of Justice, [2014] EWHC 1973 (TCC), *The Bodo Community and others v The Shell Petroleum Development Company of Nigeria Ltd*, paras. 21–69.

[93] The United Kingdom High Court of Justice, [2014] EWHC 1973 (TCC), *The Bodo Community and others v The Shell Petroleum Development Company of Nigeria Ltd*, paras. 70–93.

[94] LeighDay, Shell agrees £55m compensation deal for Niger Delta community, https://www.leigh-day.co.uk/News/2015/January-2015/Shell-agrees-55m-compensation-deal-for-Nigeria-Del (last accessed 1 October 2018).

[95] The United Kingdom High Court of Justice, 2017 EWHC 89 (TCC), *His Royal Highness Emere Godwin Bebe Okpabi and Others v. Royal Dutch Shell Plc and Shell Petroleum Development Company of Nigeria Ltd*.

whether there was a real issue to be tried between the plaintiffs and parent company RDS[96]—or, in other words, whether those claims had any merit.[97]

The presiding judge, Justice Fraser, concluded that under English law, which he equated with Nigerian law for the purpose of deciding the preliminary issues at hand,[98] there was no duty of care on the part of RDS to the plaintiffs. He considered, *inter alia*, two cases in which the England and Wales Court of Appeal had dealt with the question whether a parent company may under certain circumstances owe a duty of care towards employees of subsidiaries who have suffered asbestos-related injuries as a result of working for the subsidiary.[99] He found that under the precedents set out in these cases, read in conjunction with the more general case law on the common law duty of care for acts and/or omissions that cause harm to another,[100] the plaintiffs would not be able to demonstrate the required relationship of proximity between the parent company and the Nigerian plaintiffs, nor that it would be fair, just and reasonable for the court to impose such a duty on the parent company. According to Justice Fraser, at least two of the relevant factors that had been identified in the aforementioned cases were absent in the case before him: there was not such a measure of control, direction and/or supervision by RDS over SPDC's operations as to give rise to a duty of care for the parent company in relation to those who might be affected by its subsidiary's activities, nor did a situation exist of reliance by SPDC on any specialist knowledge by RDS that might give rise to such a duty.[101]

Justice Fraser's decision that there was no arguable case under English and/or Nigerian law that parent company RDS owed the plaintiffs a duty of care was also decisive for the viability of the claims against the subsidiary. The latter were brought before the English High Court on the basis of the assertion that the subsidiary was a necessary and proper party to the claims against the parent company, over whom jurisdiction existed under the Brussels I regime since RDS is incorporated in the UK.[102] However, as the plaintiffs were unable to convince the court that there was a

---

[96] The United Kingdom High Court of Justice, 2017 EWHC 89 (TCC), *His Royal Highness Emere Godwin Bebe Okpabi and Others v. Royal Dutch Shell Plc and Shell Petroleum Development Company of Nigeria Ltd*, compare para. 3.1(3) of Practice Direction 6B – Service out of the Jurisdiction.

[97] The United Kingdom High Court of Justice, 2017 EWHC 89 (TCC), *His Royal Highness Emere Godwin Bebe Okpabi and Others v. Royal Dutch Shell Plc and Shell Petroleum Development Company of Nigeria Ltd*, paras. 62, 69.

[98] The United Kingdom High Court of Justice, 2017 EWHC 89 (TCC), *His Royal Highness Emere Godwin Bebe Okpabi and Others v. Royal Dutch Shell Plc and Shell Petroleum Development Company of Nigeria Ltd*, paras. 50–61.

[99] The United Kingdom Court of Appeal, [2012] EWCA Civ 525, *Chandler v. Cape Plc* and The United Kingdom Court of Appeal, [2014] EWCA Civ 635, *Thompson v. The Renwick Group Plc*.

[100] The United Kingdom House of Lords, [1990] 2 AC 605, *Caparo Industries plc v. Dickman*.

[101] The United Kingdom High Court of Justice, 2017 EWHC 89 (TCC), *His Royal Highness Emere Godwin Bebe Okpabi and Others v. Royal Dutch Shell Plc and Shell Petroleum Development Company of Nigeria Ltd*, paras. 107–117.

[102] The United Kingdom High Court of Justice, 2017 EWHC 89 (TCC), *His Royal Highness Emere Godwin Bebe Okpabi and Others v. Royal Dutch Shell Plc and Shell Petroleum Development Company of Nigeria Ltd*, paras. 11–21, 118–119. See also Articles 4 and 63 Brussels I Regulation

real issue to be tried between them and parent company RDS (the anchor defendant), they failed to meet one of the threshold requirements for such an anchoring construction. Thus, there existed no jurisdictional basis for the claims against subsidiary SPDC before the English courts. Justice Fraser also considered that access to justice would not be denied to the plaintiffs even if the proceedings were not to continue in London, as plaintiffs would be able to pursue their claims before the courts in Nigeria.[103]

The plaintiffs filed an appeal of the High Court's decision, but to no avail; in February 2018 the England and Wales Court of Appeal dismissed the appeal. Lord Justice Simon, writing for the court and joined by Lord Chancellor Vos, held that the plaintiffs were not able to prove that they had a properly arguable case that parent company RDS (the anchor defendant) owed them a duty of care, although he reached this conclusion on different grounds than those put forward by the High Court and also on the basis of partly different evidentiary material (as some new evidence had emerged over the course of the appeal).[104] According to Lord Justice Simon, the plaintiffs had not proven and would not be able to prove that RDS exercised control over those aspects of SPDC's local operations related to controlling the risk of oil spills. He held that the fact that there were concerns at the level of the parent company about oil spills, security issues and environmental damage (and related reputational concerns), that there was a desire at the level of the parent company to ensure that proper systems were put in place to deal with these issues, and that the parent company had put in place an overall system to ensure best uniform practices throughout the group, was not sufficient to demonstrate control by RDS over SPDC's operations, nor direct responsibility by RDS for the local practices and failures at issue.[105]

Lord Justice Sales disagreed with this decision, however, and in a separate opinion expressed the view that the evidence deployed by the plaintiffs at the jurisdictional stage of the proceedings was sufficient to show that the plaintiffs had a good arguable case against RDS that ought to be tried.[106] The case has not been definitively

---

(recast).

[103] The United Kingdom High Court of Justice, 2017 EWHC 89 (TCC), *His Royal Highness Emere Godwin Bebe Okpabi and Others v. Royal Dutch Shell Plc and Shell Petroleum Development Company of Nigeria Ltd*, paras. 118–122.

[104] The United Kingdom Court of Appeal, [2018] EWCA Civ 191, *His Royal Highness Emere Godwin Bebe Okpabi and Others v. Royal Dutch Shell Plc and Shell Petroleum Development Company of Nigeria Ltd*, paras. 1–133 (opinion by Lord Justice Simon) and paras. 174–209 (opinion by Lord Chancellor Vos).

[105] The United Kingdom Court of Appeal, [2018] EWCA Civ 191, *His Royal Highness Emere Godwin Bebe Okpabi and Others v. Royal Dutch Shell Plc and Shell Petroleum Development Company of Nigeria Ltd*, paras. 118–127. See also, with a slightly different approach, Lord Chancellor Vos at The United Kingdom Court of Appeal, [2018] EWCA Civ 191, *His Royal Highness Emere Godwin Bebe Okpabi and Others v. Royal Dutch Shell Plc and Shell Petroleum Development Company of Nigeria Ltd*, paras. 191–206.

[106] The United Kingdom Court of Appeal, [2018] EWCA Civ 191, *His Royal Highness Emere Godwin Bebe Okpabi and Others v. Royal Dutch Shell Plc and Shell Petroleum Development Company of Nigeria Ltd*, paras. 134–173 (opinion by Lord Justice Sales).

concluded yet, as the plaintiffs have filed for leave to appeal to the UK Supreme Court.[107]

5 Discussion

In all six cases discussed here what is at issue is the liability of Shell companies for harm caused to local populations and/or the environment in connection with Shell's oil exploration and production operations in Nigeria. Taking a step back from the specifics of each case, it becomes apparent that there are more commonalities and that all of these cases—not just the three human rights-related ones—are in fact interrelated. In this section, I derive from the study of these cases some more general observations relating to the opportunities and thresholds faced by host country citizens seeking to bring this type of litigation against multinational enterprises before home country courts.

The outcome of foreign direct liability cases such as the ones described here is determined by four main factors. Firstly, does the court seized of the matter have jurisdiction to hear the claim? Secondly, which national system of tort law will the court apply in determining the merits of the claim? Thirdly, on which legal bases can claims be brought and what are the conditions for liability connected to these legal bases? Fourthly, what are the relevant procedural rules and practices in the forum country and to what extent are they conducive to the pursuit of this type of litigation?[108]

It should be noted that unless otherwise specified, the inferences drawn in this discussion are not based on the *Kiobel II*-case, as this case is still at such an early stage of the proceedings that there are only limited legal data to draw from. Furthermore, the primary focus when discussing the relevant legal framework will be on the rules that apply in cases brought before EU Member State courts, since the US Supreme Court's decision in the *Kiobel*-case suggests (and subsequent developments confirm[109]) that this is where the future lies for foreign direct liability cases against EU-based corporate defendants like Shell.

---

[107] Owen C and Bristow A, Okpabi v. Shell appeal highlights important points regarding parent company liability. Simmons & Simmons elexica, 26 February 2018, http://www.elexica.com/en/legal-topics/dispute-resolution-commercial/260218-okpabi-v-shell (last accessed 1 October 2018); Roorda L, Okpabi v. Shell on appeal: foreign direct liability in troubled waters. Rights as Usual, 23 February 2018, http://www.rightsasusual.com/?p=1194 (last accessed 1 October 2018).

[108] Enneking (2012a), pp. 129–203. See also, more specifically on the applicable law factor and the procedural rules and practices factor: Enneking (2017a).

[109] Supreme Court of the United States, No. 10-1491, *Kiobel v. Royal Dutch Petroleum Co. et al.*, para. 5.3 with respect to the recent decision of the Supreme Court of the United States, No. 16-499, *Jesner v. Arab Bank*.

5.1 Jurisdiction

In the cases discussed here, the question whether the home country courts seized have jurisdiction to hear the claims brought before them features prominently. This is not surprising considering the transnational nature of foreign direct liability cases; host country victims sue multinational enterprises before home country courts in relation to harm caused in the host country as a result of activities that are often largely situated in the host country where the local business operations take place. At the same time, those activities may also be linked to corporate activities in the home country, where relevant policies are designed and decisions are taken at head-quarters' level.

It is important to make a distinction between the jurisdictional challenges at issue in the *Kiobel*-case (US) and those at issue in the other cases. In the *Kiobel*-case (US), the legal debate focused on a matter of subject-matter jurisdiction, as it essentially concerned (like the debate in many ATS-based cases) questions relating to the delimitation of regulatory powers between the US state legal systems and the US federal legal system with respect to the subject matter in dispute. In the other cases, the legal debate focused on the matter of personal jurisdiction, in particular the authority of domestic courts to entertain suits relating to disputes that involve a 'foreign' element, like a party domiciled in another country or activities that have taken place abroad.

5.1.1 Personal Jurisdiction in Foreign Direct Liability Cases Before EU Member State Courts

Whether a court may exercise personal jurisdiction in cases involving foreign parties and/or harmful activities abroad is generally determined by the forum country's domestic rules on personal jurisdiction. In the EU, the rules on personal jurisdiction in civil matters have been partly unified by the Brussels I regime.[110] Under this regime, corporate defendants that are domiciled (*i.e.*, have their statutory seat, their central administration or their principal place of business) in one or more EU Member States, can be sued before the courts in those Member States (and, under

---

[110] For claims relating to civil and commercial matters filed before EU Member State courts on or after 10 January 2015, the relevant instrument is the Brussels I Regulation recast (Regulation (EU) No. 1215/2012 of the European Parliament and of the Council of 12 December 2012 on jurisdiction and the recognition and enforcement of judgments in civil and commercial matters (recast), OJ 2012 L351/1 (20 December 2012)). Its predecessor, the Brussels I Regulation (Council Regulation (EC) No. 44/2001 of 22 December 2000 on jurisdiction and the recognition and enforcement of judgments in civil and commercial matters, OJ 2001 L12/1 (16 January 2001)), applied to claims filed between 1 March 2002 and 9 January 2015. For claims filed before 1 March 2002, the relevant instrument was the Brussels Convention (Convention of 27 September 1968 on Jurisdiction and the Enforcement of Judgments in Civil and Commercial Matters, OJ 1998 C 27/1 (26 January 1998)).

certain circumstances, also before the courts in other EU Member States).[111] Claims against corporate defendants that are not domiciled in an EU Member State fall outside the scope of the Brussels I regime, meaning that personal jurisdiction over those claims can only be established if there is a basis for doing so in the relevant domestic provisions of the EU Member State where the case is brought.[112]

Accordingly, in foreign direct liability cases before EU Member State courts, jurisdictional issues will typically arise not with respect to the claims against EU-based corporate defendants, but with respect to those against non-EU-based corporate defendants. In all Member States alike, the possibilities for establishing jurisdiction over the latter are limited, with the main opportunities being: (a) domestic provisions on connected claims/multiple defendants, and (b) domestic provisions on *forum necessitatis*.[113]

(a) Connected Claims

Domestic provisions on connected claims/multiple defendants open up the opportunity—subject to varying requirements—to in effect 'extend' the jurisdiction of an EU Member State court regarding a foreign direct liability claim against a parent company domiciled there (the 'anchor defendant') to a closely connected claim against a non-EU-based subsidiary. They play a role in three out of the four foreign direct liability cases discussed here: the *Akpan*-case and the *Kiobel II*-case in the Netherlands and the *Okpabi*-case in the UK. In the *Bodo*-case, the court did not have to decide on the issue of jurisdiction because of the formal agreement between the parties that SPDC would accept jurisdiction of the English courts.

The Dutch courts in the *Akpan*-case and the English courts in the *Okpabi*-case apply different standards and come to different conclusions with respect to the anchoring construction. There are two main reasons for this difference. First of all, the English rule of procedural law on service out of the jurisdiction, which formed the basis of the anchoring construction in the *Okpabi*-case, requires that there is between the plaintiffs and the anchor defendant "[...] *a real issue which it is reasonable for the court to try*".[114] Accordingly, the plaintiffs need to prove, at an early stage in the proceedings when they have had limited chances to get access to relevant evidence that is in the hands of the corporate defendants, that they have a good arguable case (*i.e.*, a case with a real prospect of success) against the anchor defendant—in this case: the parent company.[115]

---

[111] Art. 4(1) jo. 63(1) Brussels I Regulation (recast).

[112] Augenstein and Jägers (2017); Enneking et al. (2016), pp. 142–151; Enneking (2012a), pp. 205–214.

[113] Augenstein and Jägers (2017), pp. 27–34; Enneking et al. (2016), pp. 142–151, 274–277, 319–322, 376–381, 435–440, 489–492.

[114] Practice Direction 6B – Service out of the jurisdiction, para. 3.1 (3)(a), https://www.justice.gov.uk/courts/procedure-rules/civil/rules/part06/pd_part06b#3.1 (last accessed 1 October 2018).

[115] See also, on the relevant standard, The United Kingdom Court of Appeal, [2018] EWCA Civ 191, *His Royal Highness Emere Godwin Bebe Okpabi and Others v. Royal Dutch Shell Plc and Shell Petroleum Development Company of Nigeria Ltd*, paras. 27–33.

By contrast, under the Dutch domestic provision on connected claims, which formed the basis for jurisdiction over the claims against the subsidiary in the Dutch *Akpan*-case, the test is different.[116] Here the burden of proof as regards the (lack of) merits of the claim at the jurisdictional stage of the proceedings is on the defendants, who will have to raise this issue as part of an abuse of (procedural) law defence. The Dutch courts' decisions on this issue in the *Akpan*-case, both at first instance and on appeal, show that the threshold for allowing such a defence is high. According to the Hague Court of Appeal,

> If it is clear in advance that the claims against RDS (the so-called 'anchor claims') are obviously bound to fail and for that reason cannot possibly be allowed, it is hard to imagine that reasons of efficiency nonetheless justify a joint hearing. There is no question of a claim that is 'certain to fail', however, now that it cannot be ruled out in advance that a parent company may, in certain circumstances, be liable for damages resulting from acts or omissions of a (sub)subsidiary.[117]

This is a very different approach than that of the English courts in the *Okpabi*-case, where already at the jurisdictional stage of the proceedings the plaintiffs were required to show, on the basis of the available evidence, that they had a good arguable case against parent company RDS.

The second reason for the difference in outcomes of the English and the Dutch courts' assessments of the anchoring construction is that the courts reached different conclusions as regards the potential existence of a duty of care on the part of the parent company viz-à-viz the plaintiffs, as discussed further in Sect. 5.3.

(b) Forum Necessitatis

In order for an EU Member State court to assume personal jurisdiction over a foreign direct liability case on the basis of *forum necessitatis*, the plaintiffs need to be able to show that it would be impossible or unreasonably burdensome for them to pursue their claims in the host country. The High Court decision in the *Okpabi*-case shows that this requirement may pose a threshold even in the north-south context of foreign direct liability cases. Justice Fraser notes that "[t]*he evidence before the court is that access to justice in Nigeria would not be denied to the claimants if these proceedings were not to continue in London*".[118] He notes as a relevant factor that according to Nigerian law, the plaintiffs may rely on Conditional Fee Agreements (a legal funding arrangement where the costs of legal representation will only have to be paid if the case is won and compensation is awarded) in order to fund a claim

---

[116]Art. 7(1) Dutch Code of Civil Procedure. See, in more detail: Enneking et al. (2016), pp. 142–151.

[117]The Hague Court of Appeal, 18 December 2015, *Dooh et al. v. Royal Dutch Shell and Shell Petroleum and Development Company of Nigeria*, ECLI:NL:GHDHA:2015:3586, para. 3.2.

[118]The United Kingdom High Court of Justice, 2017 EWHC 89 (TCC), *His Royal Highness Emere Godwin Bebe Okpabi and Others v. Royal Dutch Shell Plc and Shell Petroleum Development Company of Nigeria Ltd*, paras. 120–121.

before the Nigerian courts. Moreover, he is not convinced by the plaintiffs' assertions about the delays in legal proceedings in Nigeria.[119]

Another requirement that in most domestic European legal systems will need to be fulfilled for successful reliance on *forum necessitatis* as a basis for jurisdiction, is the existence of a sufficient connection between the case and the forum state. In a recent French foreign direct liability case relating to unlawful dismissals of Gabonese railroad workers, this connection was found in the fact that at the time the procedure in France was initiated, 63% of the shares of the Gabonese company that had dismissed the railroad workers were held by a French parent company.[120] The parent-subsidiary connection may thus not only play a role in foreign direct liability claims brought against non-EU-based corporate defendants on the basis of connected claims/multiple defendants provisions, but also in those brought on the basis of *forum necessitatis* provisions. This is important, as it is likely that a restrictive approach towards anchoring constructions in cases where jurisdiction is based on connected claims/multiple defendants, like in the *Okpabi*-case, may increase the focus on *forum necessitatis* as a basis for jurisdiction in future cases.

5.1.2 Personal Jurisdiction in Foreign Direct Liability Cases Before US Courts

The rules on personal jurisdiction that will be applied in foreign direct liability cases brought before US courts tend to be more liberal than those in cases before EU Member State courts.[121] An example is the exercise of personal jurisdiction by the US courts over the non-US-based Shell holding companies in the *Wiwa*-case on the basis of the presence of an investor relations office (with activities unrelated to the dispute). The underlying doctrine is that of 'general jurisdiction', pursuant to which—according to the interpretation at the time of the relevant decisions in the *Wiwa*-case—a defendant with 'continuous and systematic contacts' in a certain US state may be sued there even for claims that were unrelated to the defendants' actual activities in that state. This doctrine has generally been considered highly controversial ('exorbitant') outside the US and has no real equivalent either under the Brussels I regime or under the domestic provisions on personal jurisdiction of the EU Member States.[122] EU Member State courts would in principle not exercise personal jurisdiction under similar circumstances, which may also affect their willingness to

---

[119] The United Kingdom High Court of Justice, 2017 EWHC 89 (TCC), *His Royal Highness Emere Godwin Bebe Okpabi and Others v. Royal Dutch Shell Plc and Shell Petroleum Development Company of Nigeria Ltd*, paras. 120–121.

[120] Cour d'Appel de Paris, Nos. S 11/05955 and S11/05959 (on file with the author), 10 September 2015, p. 14.

[121] See, for a general comparison between the European and US approaches to jurisdiction: O'Brian (2003), pp. 493–498. See also Enneking (2012a), pp. 140–152.

[122] Bonacorsi (2014); O'Brian (2003), pp. 495–496, 499. See also for example: s. 1139(2) of the UK Companies Act 2006, which in combination with Civil Procedure Rules part 6.9 does permit a form of 'doing business' jurisdiction before English courts, Bonacorsi (2014), p. 1841.

recognize and enforce a decision by a US court in which it has assumed personal jurisdiction on this basis.[123]

It has to be noted, however, that the difference between the relevant US and EU approaches to personal jurisdiction has been mitigated in practice by prudential doctrines like *forum non conveniens* (on the basis of which a case may be dismissed if the court deems that it could more conveniently be tried in a foreign forum), as well as by more restrictive interpretations of the relevant US rules on personal jurisdiction in recent years.[124] At the same time, the effects of broad exercises of personal jurisdiction in ATS-based cases like the *Wiwa*-case have become mitigated by the restrictions with respect to the extraterritorial application of the ATS that the US Supreme Court has introduced in the *Kiobel*-case—restrictions that essentially relate to the scope of the subject matter jurisdiction that US federal courts may exercise under the ATS. In the more recent case of *Jesner v. Arab Bank*, which was brought by non-US victims of terrorist attacks in the Middle East against Arab Bank—headquartered in Jordan but with offices in New York—for allegedly having facilitated the attacks by paying the relatives of the terrorist operatives who conducted them, the Supreme Court has adopted an even more restrictive approach on the matter.[125] The result is that it is not possible anymore to use the ATS as a basis for claims against non-US corporations, even if the case has a nexus to the US legal order.[126]

---

[123] Although a further discussion of this issue would go outside the scope of this article, it is questionable whether a decision by an US court that would have sustained the claims and granted compensation to the *Wiwa*-plaintiffs would have been enforceable in the Netherlands, due to the fact that the legal basis on which personal jurisdiction was assumed in that case by the US courts would probably have been considered 'exorbitant' (here in the sense of 'not internationally accepted') by a Dutch court. See also Enneking (2014b), p. 57.

[124] See *inter alia*: Supreme Court of the United States, No. 10-76, *Goodyear Dunlop Tires Operations, S. A., et al. v. Brown*, 564 U.S. 915; Supreme Court of the United States, No. 11-965, *Daimler AG v. Bauman*, 134 S. Ct. 746.

[125] Supreme Court of the United States, No. 16-499, *Jesner et al. v. Arab Bank PLC*, 548 U.S. (2018), https://www.supremecourt.gov/opinions/17pdf/16-499_1a7d.pdf (last accessed 1 October 2018).

[126] Anderson SR, Cutting federal common law off at the stem in Jesner v. Arab Bank. American Constitution Society, weblog, 2 May 2018, https://www.acslaw.org/acsblog/cutting-federal-common-law-off-at-the-stem-in-jesner-v-arab-bank (last accessed 1 October 2018); Dodge WS, Jesner v. Arab Bank: The Supreme Court preserves the possibility of human rights suits against U.S. corporations. Just Security, weblog, 26 April 2018, https://www.justsecurity.org/55404/jesner-v-arab-bank-supreme-court-preserves-possibility-human-rights-suits-u-s-corporations/ (last accessed 1 October 2018); Howe A, Opinion analysis: Court bars lawsuits against foreign corporations under Alien Tort Statute. Howe on the Court, weblog, 24 April 2018, http://amylhowe.com/2018/04/24/court-bars-lawsuits-foreign-corporations-alien-tort-statute/ (last accessed 1 October 2018).

5.2 Applicable Law

Another question that arises from the transnational nature of foreign direct liability cases, is which country's provisions on civil liability are to be applied by the court in deciding the issue of liability. These may be the provisions on civil liability of the host country, where the harm has been caused, or those of the home country, where actions and decisions at headquarters' level can be situated that may be said to constitute (part of) the harmful activities.[127] The applicable law issue may be crucial in cases where liability standards, rules relating to the burden of proof or prescription of claims, available remedies and/or damages levels differ in the legal systems involved. It is also often considered relevant by civil society organizations seeking to 'mobilize' home country-based policymakers, investors, consumers and corporate actors through strategic litigation aimed at addressing and preventing corporate involvement in human rights and environmental violations abroad. From their perspective, a decision by a home country court on parent company liability may be more interesting, in its contribution to the development of a body of precedent and/or in its expected impact on home state policies and corporate behaviour, when it is based on home country rather than host country provisions of civil liability.[128]

When looking at the issue of applicable law, there is a significant difference between ATS-based cases like the *Wiwa*-case and the *Kiobel*-case, on the one hand, and the cases brought before EU Member State courts on the basis of general rules of tort law, on the other. Due to the focus in ATS-based cases on (alleged violations of) international rules of conduct and on the scope and interpretation of the ATS itself, the issue of potential conflict between home country and host country standards of liability has played only a subordinate role. This is different in the non-ATS-based cases against Shell discussed here,[129] where the courts do conduct a classic choice-of-law analysis in order to determine which law to apply. The result of this analysis in *Akpan*, *Bodo*, and *Okpabi* is that the issue of liability is determined on the basis of Nigerian tort law, on the basis of the general rule on applicable

---

[127] Enneking (2017a), pp. 43–49.

[128] See, in more detail on the use of strategic litigation (also sometimes referred to as public interest litigation or impact litigation) in the business and human rights context, for instance: Terwindt C and Schliemann C, Transnational strategic litigation: an emerging part of civil society's repertoire for corporate accountability. State of civil society report 2017 – Guest essays civil society and the private sector, 2017, https://www.civicus.org/documents/reports-and-publications/SOCS/2017/essays/transnational-strategic-litigation-an-emerging-part-of-civil-society's-repertoire-for-corporate-accountability.pdf (last accessed 1 October 2018); Enneking (2017a), pp. 61–64; Backer LC et al., Democratizing the global business and human rights project by catalyzing strategic litigation from the bottom up. Working Papers Coalition for Peace and Ethics No. 12/1, 2014, https://doi.org/10.2139/ssrn.2325994 (last accessed 1 October 2018); Enneking (2012a).

[129] This is also different in the foreign direct liability cases that have been brought before United State courts on the basis of the tort of negligence, but a further discussion of the different conflict-of-laws provisions that would apply to these cases depending on the state in which they are brought, would go beyond the scope of this article.

law in tort-based cases that the law to be applied is that of the country where the harm occurs.[130]

Interestingly, the courts reach different conclusions as to the Nigerian legal standards that should be applied, and as to the correct interpretation of those standards in light of the facts and circumstances of the cases at hand—which are very similar in all three cases. One issue that the courts do agree on is that in order to determine whether the Shell group's parent company can be said to owe a duty of care to local Nigerian communities affected by oil spills from Shell-operated pipelines, it is possible to rely on relevant precedents in English tort law (due to the historic connection between the Nigerian tort system and the English one). This is important, since under Nigerian tort law there is no relevant precedent on the issue of parent company liability, whereas such precedent does exist under English tort law (see Sect. 5.3).

Another point worth mentioning here is that the EU's Rome II Regulation on the law applicable to non-contractual obligations, which applies to harmful events that have occurred on or after 11 January 2009, will govern the applicable law question in future foreign direct liability cases before EU Member State courts. The regime's main rule is that the law applicable in civil liability cases is that of the country where the harm has occurred, i.e. host country tort law in foreign direct liability cases. However, Art. 7 Rome II introduces a special rule for cases relating to environmental harm. If in such cases the conduct that has given rise to the damage has taken place in another country than that where the damage has arisen, the victims may choose applicability of the law of the former country rather than that of the latter.[131]

In its original proposal for the Regulation, the Commission makes clear that the point of this special rule on environmental damage was

> [...] to establish a legislative policy that contributes to raising the general level of environmental protection, especially as the author of the environmental damage, unlike other torts or delicts, generally derives an economic benefit from his harmful activity.[132]

The Commission refers to victims in low-protection countries that absent this rule "[...] *would not enjoy the higher level of protection available in neighbouring countries*" and to operators that have "[...] *an incentive to establish* [their] *facilities at the border so as to discharge toxic substances into a river and enjoy the benefit of the neighbouring country's laxer rules*". However, the same reasoning seems to apply to situations of non-neighbouring host and home countries. And indeed, in the *Okpabi*-case, which partly relates to oil spills that have occurred after 11 January 2009, the plaintiffs seek to invoke Art. 7 Rome II in order to have English rather

---

[130] Compare Article 4(1) Regulation (EC) No. 864/2007 of the European Parliament and of the Council of 11 July 2007 on the law applicable to non-contractual obligations (Rome II).

[131] Enneking (2017a), pp. 52–57.

[132] Explanatory Memorandum Regulation (EC) No. 864/2007 of the European Parliament and of the Council of 11 July 2007 on the law applicable to non-contractual obligations (Rome II), COM(2003) 427, p. 19.

than Nigerian tort law applied to their case. The issue is not pursued in depth by Justice Fraser, however, who holds that:

> [i]n practice, given the substantial similarity between English and Nigerian common law, the difference is immaterial for the purposes of these jurisdictional challenges.[133]

This reference to Art. 7 Rome II raises the question, however, whether the provision's exclusive focus on harmful events resulting in environmental damage is justified in light of the growing trend towards foreign direct liability cases, also before courts in the EU Member States. After all, the issue of double standards that forms the basis of these cases is not limited to environmental standards, but also relates to human rights standards, labour standards and health & safety standards. Yet, under the current wording of Article 7, the plaintiffs in a case like *Okpabi* could be allowed to choose applicability of home country rather than host country tort law, whereas the plaintiffs in for instance the *Kiobel II*-case would not, due to the case's focus on human rights harm rather than environmental harm. Especially with respect to the cases discussed here, which may be framed as human rights matters but may also be framed as environmental matters, while sharing a common background in the environmental degradation caused by oil exploration and production activities in the Niger Delta, this distinction causes a discrepancy that may be considered unjustified. It has therefore been argued that an extension of the rule's scope to human rights-related damage (as well as, possibly, health and safety related damage) should seriously be considered.[134]

5.3 Legal Basis for Corporate Liability

One of the key issues in all of the cases discussed here is what requirements need to be met in order for a court to hold the corporate defendants accountable for human rights and environmental violations abroad. Those requirements depend on the particular legal basis of the plaintiffs' claims. The *Wiwa*-case and the *Kiobel*-case stand out from the other cases discussed here due to the fact that they are based on the ATS and not on general rules of tort law, like the other cases (with the exception of the *Kiobel II*-case, as will be discussed below).

In the end, there have only been very few cases in which US federal courts in foreign direct liability cases on the basis of the ATS have actually come to a decision on the issue of corporate liability for complicity in international human rights violations.[135] A 2009 overview by Simpson (updated in March 2013 after the Supreme Court's decision in the *Kiobel*-case) indicates that there has only been one successful

---

[133] The United Kingdom High Court of Justice, 2017 EWHC 89 (TCC), *His Royal Highness Emere Godwin Bebe Okpabi and Others v. Royal Dutch Shell Plc and Shell Petroleum Development Company of Nigeria Ltd*, para. 55.

[134] Enneking (2017a), pp. 65, 75–76.

[135] Christensen and Hausman (2016), pp. 796–797.

ATS-based claim against a corporation, although it also shows that out-of-court settlements were reached in about a dozen corporate ATS-cases (including the *Wiwa*-case).[136]

At the same time, the requirements for ATS-based foreign direct liability cases have become increasingly strict over the past two decades.[137] The decision by the Court of Appeals for the Second Circuit in the *Kiobel*-case that corporate actors could not be held liable for complicity in international human rights violations under the ATS, signalled a turning point in the discussion on corporate accountability for human rights and environmental violations abroad, as it threatened to close the door to ATS-based foreign direct liability cases. Since on appeal the Supreme Court chose to engage with the issue of extraterritoriality (*i.e.*, whether international human rights violations that have taken place outside of the US can lead to liability under the ATS) rather than with the issue of corporate liability, it neither confirmed nor reversed the judgment by the Court of Appeals.

The question whether the ATS extends to civil claims against corporate actors in relation to (complicity in) international human rights violations was raised again before the US Supreme Court in the case of *Jesner v. Arab Bank*. However, the Court's decision with respect to the issue of corporate liability under the ATS was so fractured in this case that the issue as of yet remains unresolved.[138] As a result, the *Jesner*-decision leaves open the possibility, in theory at least, of ATS-based claims against US corporations for international human rights violations committed outside of the US. It has been noted, however, that in practice the decision is likely to restrict the role that US federal courts may play in the future in providing judicial remedies for corporate human rights violations in a transnational context, also with respect to this remaining category of cases.[139]

As a result of these developments, the focus is shifting away from the possibilities of bringing foreign direct liability cases before US federal courts on the basis of the ATS, to the possibilities of bringing this type of litigation before US state courts and before courts in the EU Member States. Whether this means that US state courts will soon see an increase in this type of litigation remains to be seen, although it appears that there are no structural barriers and may even be some relative advantages (when compared to ATS-based litigation before US federal courts) to the pursuit of foreign direct liability cases there.[140] At the same time, there seems to be a relatively steady increase in cases relating to corporate accountability for human

---

[136] Simpson S, Alien Tort Statute cases resulting in plaintiff victories. The view from LL2 weblog, 11 November 2009, https://viewfromll2.com/2009/11/11/alien-tort-statute-cases-resulting-in-plaintiff-victories/ (last accessed 1 October 2018).

[137] Childress (2012).

[138] Supreme Court of the United States, No. 16-499, *Jesner et al. v. Arab Bank PLC*, 548 U.S. (2018), https://www.supremecourt.gov/opinions/17pdf/16-499_1a7d.pdf (last accessed 1 October 2018).

[139] Anderson SR, Cutting federal common law off at the stem in Jesner v. Arab Bank. American Constitution Society, weblog, 2 May 2018, https://www.acslaw.org/acsblog/cutting-federal-common-law-off-at-the-stem-in-jesner-v-arab-bank (last accessed 1 October 2018).

[140] Davis and Whytock (2017).

rights and environmental abuses abroad that are being pursued before EU Member State courts, with numbers increasing more rapidly in recent years.[141]

As mentioned, these cases are often pursued on the basis of general rules of tort law, and the tort of negligence more particularly, as is exemplified by the *Akpan*, *Bodo*, and *Okpabi* cases discussed here. The *Kiobel II*-case is an exception, in that the plaintiffs in this case seek to base their claims on a specific cause of action under Nigerian law relating to complicity in human rights violations.[142] According to the statement of claim, there are a great many Nigerian cases in which such liability has been accepted, often in relation to incidents involving the procurement, provocation or even encouragement by private actors, including legal persons, of unlawful arrest and/or unlawful detention by the authorities.[143] It remains to be seen whether the gap created by the US Supreme Court's *Kiobel*-judgment with respect to litigation concerning international human rights violations committed outside the US can partly be filled by these types of human rights-related causes of action that may be available in the law of some host countries, like Nigeria but also for instance South Africa.[144]

In the tort-based cases, one of the main substantive issues has been that of parent company liability. It played a pivotal role in the *Akpan* and *Okpabi*-cases. The only court in these cases to have addressed the issue at the merits stage was the Hague District Court in the *Akpan*-case, which, as mentioned before, dismissed the claims against the parent company. The issue was addressed at the jurisdiction stage by the Hague Court of Appeal in the *Akpan*-case and by the London High Court and the Court of Appeal in the *Okpabi*-case, in the course of their respective assessments of whether the claims against RDS could act as an anchor for jurisdiction over the claims against SPDC. It should be noted in this respect that although the arguments and case law relating to the issue of parent company liability and to the anchoring construction that were relied on by the parties before the different courts in these two cases were largely the same, they were assessed by the courts in different ways.

Of the four courts involved, the Hague Court of Appeal seemed most open to the possibility of parent company liability—at least so far, as it has not reached a decision on the merits of the case. In its December 2015 interim judgment the court stated, *inter alia*:

> Considering the foreseeable serious consequences of oil spills to the local environment from a potential spill source, it cannot be ruled out from the outset that the parent company may be expected in such a case to take an interest in preventing spills (or in other words, that there is a duty of care [...]), the more so if it has made the prevention of environmental

---

[141] Enneking et al. (2016).

[142] Nigerian Human Rights Enforcement Rules, 2009, http://www.refworld.org/pdfid/54f97e064.pdf (last accessed 1 October 2018). See in more detail the statement of claim, on file with the author.

[143] Statement of claim, on file with the author, paras. 148–154.

[144] See in detail with respect to the South African context: Verdonck L, The international legal framework on business and human rights and its domestic operationalisation – Strategic litigation on mining and a healthy environment in South Africa. Dissertation, Ghent University 2017 (on file with the author).

damage by the activities of group companies a spearhead and is, to a certain degree, actively involved in and managing the business operations of such companies, which is not to say that without this attention and involvement a violation of the duty of care is unthinkable and that culpable negligence with regard to the said interests can never result in liability.[145]

With this statement, it may have set the stage for a more lenient approach at the merits stage than that of the Hague District Court, which held in this respect, among other things:

[...] the general fact that RDS made the prevention of environmental damage caused by operations of its (sub) subsidiaries the main focus of its policy and that to some extent, RDS is involved in SPDC's policy constitutes insufficient reason to rule that under Nigerian law, RDS assumed a duty of care in respect of the people living in the vicinity of the oil pipelines and oil facilities of SPDC.[146]

Also according to the leading opinion by Lord Justice Simon in the *Okpabi*-case, who was joined by Lord Chancellor Vos, the plaintiffs were required to demonstrate the existence of control by the parent company over its subsidiary and/or of active involvement by the parent company in the operations by the subsidiary.[147] In contrast to the Hague District Court's approach to the matter, however, the plaintiffs in the *Okpabi*-case were required to do so already at the jurisdictional stage. In addition, Lord Justice Simon drew a sharp distinction between mandatory group policies on the one hand, and actual control over the material operations of the subsidiary, on the other:

It is [...] important to distinguish between a parent company which controls, or shares control of, the material operations on the one hand, and a parent company which issues mandatory policies and standards which are intended to apply throughout a group of companies in order to ensure conformity with particular standards. The issuing of mandatory policies plainly cannot mean that a parent has taken control of the operations of a subsidiary (and, necessarily, every subsidiary) such as to give rise to a duty of care in favour of any person or class of persons affected by the policies.[148]

Upon evaluation of the available evidence, this led him to conclude that while the plaintiffs' evidence did show that there were mandatory group policies in place on

---

[145] The Hague Court of Appeal, 18 December 2015, *Dooh et al. v. Royal Dutch Shell and Shell Petroleum and Development Company of Nigeria*, ECLI:NL:GHDHA:2015:3586, para. 3.2.

[146] The Hague District Court, 30 January 2013, *Akpan et al. v. Royal Dutch Shell and Shell Petroleum Development Company of Nigeria*, ECLI:NL:RBDHA:2013:BY9854, para. 4.33. English translation available at http://www.elaw.org/system/files/final-judgment-shell-oil-spill-ikot-ada-udo.pdf.

[147] The United Kingdom Court of Appeal, [2018] EWCA Civ 191, *His Royal Highness Emere Godwin Bebe Okpabi and Others v. Royal Dutch Shell Plc and Shell Petroleum Development Company of Nigeria Ltd*, paras. 118–127 (opinion by Lord Justice Simon). See for a more detailed analysis of this judgment: Owen C and Bristow A, Okpabi v. Shell appeal highlights important points regarding parent company liability. Simmons & Simmons Elexica, weblog, 26 February 2018, http://www.elexica.com/en/legal-topics/dispute-resolution-commercial/260218-okpabi-v-shell (last accessed 1 October 2018).

[148] The United Kingdom Court of Appeal, [2018] EWCA Civ 191, *His Royal Highness Emere Godwin Bebe Okpabi and Others v. Royal Dutch Shell Plc and Shell Petroleum Development Company of Nigeria Ltd*, para. 89.

relevant issues, it did not show actual control over the material operations of the subsidiary:

> It is plain that there were concerns about the security of SPDC's operations in Nigeria and that this concern was expressed at a high level. This is hardly surprising since it affected both Shell's general reputation and the output of an important source of oil. However, the concern was to ensure that there were proper controls and not to exercise control.[149]

Lord Justice Sales, who disagreed with the majority's opinion, took a less restrictive approach, as he felt that it was well arguable that RDS had given directions to SPDC regarding important aspects of the management of the pipeline and facilities, specifically in relation to controlling the risk of oil spills and had also sought to monitor and enforce those directions. It could in his opinion be argued that by doing so, RDS had involved itself in the management of the operation and security of the pipeline and facilities in a direct and substantial way, thus exercising a degree of real control in relation to those matters that went significantly beyond the mere setting of group-wide standards.[150]

5.4   Procedural Rules and Practices

Procedural rules and practices tend to play a pivotal role in foreign direct liability cases due to the inequality of arms that typically exists between the host country plaintiffs and the corporate defendants as regards financial means, access to relevant information, degree of organization, and availability of legal expertise. As already mentioned, the rediscovery of the ATS is only part of the reason for the rise of this type of litigation in the US since the mid-1990s, as the plaintiff-friendly US civil litigation culture has also played a major role in this respect. This plaintiff-friendliness is grounded in, *inter alia*: the possibility of contingency fee arrangements with legal representatives (on the basis of which the lawyer's remuneration consists of an agreed percentage of the final sum, which also means that the lawyer gets no remuneration at all if the suit is lost); the availability of class actions (which allow the combination of multiple claims, and/or multiple defendants, in one procedure); a liberal regime on access to evidence (involving a procedural duty that a party must in principle present all documents the other party requests and considers relevant for the case); and the fact that in principle, each party bears its own litigation costs regardless of the outcome (which gives claimants a greater incentive to pursue even risky cases).[151]

---

[149] The United Kingdom Court of Appeal, [2018] EWCA Civ 191, *His Royal Highness Emere Godwin Bebe Okpabi and Others v. Royal Dutch Shell Plc and Shell Petroleum Development Company of Nigeria Ltd*, para. 125.

[150] The United Kingdom Court of Appeal, [2018] EWCA Civ 191, *His Royal Highness Emere Godwin Bebe Okpabi and Others v. Royal Dutch Shell Plc and Shell Petroleum Development Company of Nigeria Ltd*, paras. 141, 172.

[151] Magnus (2010), pp. 109–118.

The civil litigation culture in the EU Member States tends to be much less conducive to the pursuit of foreign direct liability cases.[152] Yet, the four cases under discussion here that have been pursued before English and Dutch courts rather than in the US show that it is by no means impossible to bring this type of litigation outside the US. It should be noted that, overall, relevant rules of civil procedure in cases before English courts tend to be more favourable for (would-be) plaintiffs than they are in the Netherlands, which likely explains why the overall number of foreign direct liability cases brought before English courts is much higher than the overall number of these cases that have been brought before Dutch courts.[153] Relevant factors include the fact that, like in the US, claimants before English courts can enter into contingency fee arrangements (or arrangements with a similar purport) with legal representatives, make use of collective redress mechanisms in cases involving large groups of claimants, and request the disclosure by their corporate opponents of relevant evidence.[154] Furthermore, as more foreign direct liability cases are being pursued in the UK, English law firms (in particular the London-based firm Leigh Day, which represented the plaintiffs in both the *Bodo*-case and the *Okpabi*-case) and courts are getting more and more expertise in dealing with both the organizational and the legal aspects of these lawsuits.[155]

In the Netherlands, by contrast, conditional fee agreements are not available in principle, the possibilities for collective redress are more limited than in cases before English courts (although broader than in other European countries like Belgium, Germany, France and Switzerland), and the statutory regime on access to evidence (more specifically: the production of exhibits) in civil procedures is relatively strict. This latter factor has played a pivotal role in the *Akpan*-case, as the restrictive interpretation of the Dutch rule on document disclosure that was adopted by the Hague District Court in this case seriously hampered the plaintiffs' prospects for proving crucial elements of their claim, including their assertion that the oil spills in dispute were caused by faulty maintenance rather than sabotage (as claimed by Shell) and their assertions with respect to the involvement by RDS in SPDC's policies and local activities. The fact that the Hague Court of Appeal has been more liberal in granting the plaintiffs access to relevant evidence is likely to enhance the plaintiffs' chances of proving their claims, both those against the Nigerian subsidiary and those against the parent company, on appeal.[156] Still, the inherently strict Dutch statutory regime on access to evidence is likely to remain a potential stumbling block also for plaintiffs in future foreign direct liability cases before Dutch courts, especially since the *Kiobel II* case suggests that the possibilities to circumvent

---

[152] Enneking et al. (2016), Enneking (2012a), pp. 187–202.

[153] Compare Enneking et al. (2016), pp. 196–217, 455–459, 643–648.

[154] Enneking et al. (2016), pp. 455–459; Meeran (2013); Hodges (2008).

[155] Enneking et al. (2016), chapter 3.

[156] Enneking et al. (2016), pp. 214–217; Enneking (2013).

this regime by relying on documents produced in the course of relevant proceedings abroad, may be limited.[157]

Together with the issue of personal jurisdiction, procedural rules and practices are crucial in determining whether or not it is feasible for host country victims of human rights violations and environmental damage by internationally operating business enterprises, to pursue corporate accountability lawsuits in relation to these issues before home country courts. This is recognized also in the UNGPs, which include an obligation for states to

> [...] take appropriate steps to ensure the effectiveness of domestic judicial mechanisms when addressing business-related human rights abuses, including considering ways to reduce legal, practical and other relevant barriers that could lead to a denial of access to remedies.[158]

According to the UNGPs, an example of a legal barrier is the situation that

> [...] claimants face a denial of justice in a host State and cannot access home State courts regardless of the merits of the claim.[159]

In addition, they specifically mention issues relating to the costs of bringing claims, difficulties in securing legal representation and limited options for collective redress as examples of practical and procedural barriers to accessing judicial remedies.[160]

The access to justice issue came to the fore in the *Okpabi*-case, where the plaintiffs pointed to the way experts are paid in Nigeria and to delays in legal proceedings in Nigeria.[161] Justice Fraser, however, was not convinced by their arguments. He noted further that in Nigeria conditional fee agreements were permitted and in use for cases such as the one at hand. He thus considered the case to be "[...] *a world away*" from foreign direct liability cases originating in host countries where impecunious plaintiffs would "[...] *simply have no ability to bring legal proceedings at all* [...] *given the way that such litigation is funded (or, more accurately, not funded)*".[162] The access to justice issue has also been raised in the *Kiobel II*-case, where plaintiffs have argued that they would not receive a fair trial before a Nigerian court, since the justices that served on the military tribunal that convicted their husbands were still part of the Nigerian court system. Since this case is still at a prelimi-

---

[157] Compare United States Court of Appeals for the Second circuit, No. 17-424-cv, *Esther Kiobel v. Cravath, Swaine & Moore LLP*, 10 July 2018, https://cases.justia.com/federal/appellate-courts/ca2/17-424/17-424-2018-07-10.pdf (last accessed 1 October 2018) and Verkerk (2013).

[158] Principle 26 UN Guiding Principles on Business and Human Rights (UNGPs).

[159] Commentary to Principle 26 UN Guiding Principles on Business and Human Rights (UNGPs).

[160] Commentary to Principle 26 UN Guiding Principles on Business and Human Rights (UNGPs).

[161] The United Kingdom High Court of Justice, 2017 EWHC 89 (TCC), *His Royal Highness Emere Godwin Bebe Okpabi and Others v. Royal Dutch Shell Plc and Shell Petroleum Development Company of Nigeria Ltd*, paras. 118–122.

[162] The United Kingdom High Court of Justice, 2017 EWHC 89 (TCC), *His Royal Highness Emere Godwin Bebe Okpabi and Others v. Royal Dutch Shell Plc and Shell Petroleum Development Company of Nigeria Ltd*, para. 120.

nary stage, however, it remains to be seen whether and how the Hague District Court will deal with this issue.

6 Conclusion

This chapter analyzed and compared six transnational civil liability cases brought before courts in the US, the UK and the Netherlands against Shell. Although the procedural routes taken in each of these six cases are very different, as are their outcomes, they share a common background in that they all seek to address the detrimental impacts of oil exploration and production activities by multinational enterprises (here: Shell) on local populations and/or the environment in host states (here: Nigeria). The question central to all of these cases is whether and to what extent a multinational enterprise can be held accountable for such detrimental impacts, and, crucially, whether it is not just the local subsidiary but also the home country-based parent company that has a legal responsibility to try to prevent them.

It precisely this question of parent company liability that has over the past two decades become more and more prominent not only in legal debates surrounding similar cases, but also in socio-political debates pertaining to responsible business conduct in global value chains and business & human rights. Unfortunately, not only for the plaintiffs involved but also for those participating in these socio-political debates, these six cases have rendered few definitive answers to this central question. Despite the fact that, taken together, these cases represent 41 years of litigation, only one of them so far has yielded a final court judgment dealing with the issue of corporate accountability, a judgment that is now under appeal.

Still, this does not mean that the other cases and the judgments rendered in those cases have been meritless. Overall, they present a clear picture of the opportunities that exist for those seeking access to remedies before home state courts in relation to corporate violations of human rights and the environment in host countries. At the same time, they also show that despite the emphasis in the UNGPs on adequate access to judicial remedies, also before home state courts where necessary, plaintiffs in these cases are still confronted with serious thresholds on their way to a court judgment on the merits and, potentially, redress for the harm done. In fact, recent decisions like that of the US Supreme Court in the *Kiobel*-case and that of the England and Wales Court of Appeal in the *Okpabi*-case seem to suggest that rather than being reduced, legal barriers to the pursuit of this type of litigation may actually be on the increase.

At the same time, these cases make visible the human and environmental costs for people in countries in the global south, like Nigeria, that seem to be inextricably connected to oil exploration and production activities that generate wealth for companies and people in countries in the global north, like the US, the UK and the Netherlands. They also provide an insight into the complex issues faced by companies operating in countries with weak governance structures where legal standards aimed at protecting local populations from the adverse impacts of those activities are not very strict. In the end, foreign direct liability cases have the potential of creating clarity on the level of care that is expected of multinational enterprises operating in such countries, of raising awareness among home country policymakers, investors and consumers on the potentially detrimental impacts of those operations, and of allowing those detrimentally affected to seek redress. Analysing these cases jointly rather than separately is key to a better understanding of the extent to which this potential is indeed being realized in practice.

References

Augenstein D, Jägers N (2017) Judicial remedies – the issue of jurisdiction. In: Álvarez-Rubio JJ, Yiannibas K (eds) Human rights in business – removal of barriers to access to justice in the European Union. Routledge, London, pp 7–37

Bernaz N (2017) Business and human rights: history, law and policy – bridging the accountability gap. Routledge, Abingdon

Bonacorsi K (2014) Not at home with "at-home" jurisdiction. Fordham Int Law J 37(6):1821–1858

Černič JL, Van Ho TL (2015) Human rights and business: direct corporate accountability for human rights. Wolf Legal Publishers, Oisterwijk

Childress DE III (2012) The Alien Tort statute, federalism and the next wave of international law litigation. Georgetown Law J 100(3):709–757

Christensen D, Hausman DK (2016) Measuring the economic effect of Alien Tort Statute liability. J Law Econ Organ 32(4):794–815

Davis S, Whytock CA (2017) State remedies for human rights. Boston Univ Law Rev 98:397–484

Drimmer JC, Lamoree SR (2011) Think globally, sue locally: trends and out-of-court tactics in transitional tort actions. Berkeley J Int Law 29(2):456–527

Ekhator EO (2016) Public regulation of the oil and gas industry in Nigeria: an evaluation. Annu Surv Int Comp Law 21(1):43. Article 6

Emeseh E (2011) The Niger Delta crisis and the question of access to justice. In: Obi C, Rustad SA (eds) Oil and insurgency in the Niger Delta – managing the complex politics of petro-violence. Zed Books, London, pp 55–70

Enneking LFH (2012a) Foreign direct liability and beyond? – Exploring the role of tort law in promoting international corporate social responsibility. Eleven International Publishing, The Hague

Enneking LFH (2012b) Multinational corporations, human rights violations and a 1789 US statute: a brief exploration of the case of Kiobel v. Shell. Nederlands Internationaal Privaatrecht 30(3):396–400

Enneking LFH (2013) Multinationals and transparency in foreign direct liability cases. Dovenschmidt Q 1(3):134–147

Enneking LFH (2014a) The future of foreign direct liability? Utrecht Law Rev 10(1):44–54

Enneking LFH (2014b) Civiele aansprakelijkheid voor (dreigende) milieuschade in een internationale context. In: Teesing N (ed) Duurzame handel in juridisch perspectief. Boom Juridische Uitgevers, The Hague, pp 33–65

Enneking LFH (2017a) Judicial remedies: the issue of applicable law. In: Álvarez-Rubio JJ, Yiannibas K (eds) Human rights in business – removal of barriers to access to justice in the European Union. Routledge, London, pp 38–77

Enneking LFH (2017b) Paying the price for socially irresponsible business practices? – Corporate liability for violations of human rights and the environment abroad. Aktuelle Juristische Praxis 26(8):988–997

Enneking L, Kristen F, Pijl K, Waterbolk T, Emaus J, Hiel M, Schaap A, Giesen I (2016) Zorgplichten van Nederlandse ondernemingen inzake internationaal maatschappelijk verantwoord ondernemen. Boomjuridisch, Den Haag

Frynas JG (1999) Legal change in Africa: evidence from oil-related litigation in Nigeria. J Afr Law 43:121–150

Frynas JG (2004) Social and environmental litigation against transnational firms in Africa. J Mod Afr Stud 42(3):363–388

Hodges CJS (2008) The reform of class and representative actions in European legal systems: a new framework for collective redress in Europe. Hart, Oxford

Ite A, Ufot U, Ite M, Isaac I, Ibok U (2016) Petroleum industry in Nigeria: environmental issues, National environmental legislation and implementation of international environmental law. Am J Environ Prot 4(1):21–37

Magnus U (2010) Why is US tort law so different? J Eur Tort Law 1(1):102–124

McBarnet D, Voiculescu A, Campbell T (2007) The new corporate accountability – corporate social responsibility and the law. Cambridge University Press, Cambridge

Meeran R (2013) Access to remedy: the United Kingdom experience of MNC tort litigation for human rights violations. In: Deva S, Bilchitz D (eds) Human rights obligations of business – beyond the corporate responsibility to respect? Cambridge University Press, Cambridge, pp 378–402

O'Brian WE Jr (2003) The Hague Convention on jurisdiction and judgments: the way forward. Modern Law Rev 66(4):491–509

Schrempf-Stirling J, Wettstein F (2017) Beyond guilty verdicts: human rights litigation and its impact on corporations' human rights policies. J Bus Ethics 145(3):545–562

Simons P (2014) Introduction. In: Simons P, Macklin A (eds) The governance gap – extractive industries, human rights, and the home state advantage. Routledge, London, pp 1–21

Simons P, Macklin A (2014) The governance gap – extractive industries, human rights, and the home state advantage. Routledge, London

Verkerk RR (2013) Multinational corporations and human rights – civil procedure as a means of obtaining transparency. Dovenschmidt Q 1(3):148–151

Yakubu OH (2017) Addressing environmental health problems in Ogoniland through implementation of United Nations Environment Program recommendations: environmental management strategies. Environments 4(2):28. Article No. 18

Young EA (2015) Universal jurisdiction, the Alien Tort Statute, and transnational public law-litigation after Kiobel. Duke Law J 64(6):1023–1128

Zerk JA (2006) Multinationals and corporate social responsibility – limitations and opportunities in international law. Cambridge University Press, Cambridge

Liesbeth F. H. Enneking   is Endowed Professor on the Legal Aspects of International Corporate Social Responsibility at Erasmus School of Law in Rotterdam. She has a PhD from Utrecht University and, during the 2015–2016 academic year, she held a rotating professorship position at the University of Leuven's Department of Law. Enneking is actively involved in legal and socio-political debates on corporate social responsibility, fair trade, and business & human rights.

CPSIA information can be obtained
at www.ICGtesting.com
Printed in the USA
LVHW082136190619
621795LV00001B/9/P